D1272850

PLATO

X

LAWS I

PLATO

IN TWELVE VOLUMES

X

LAWS
VOLUME I, BOOKS I-VI

WITH AN ENGLISH TRANSLATION BY

R. G. BURY, Litt.D.
FORMERLY SCHOLAR OF TRINITY COLLEGE ,CAMBRIDGE

CAMBRIDGE, MASSACHUSETTS
HARVARD UNIVERSITY PRESS
LONDON
WILLIAM HEINEMANN LTD
MCMLXVII

First printed 1926
Reprinted 1942, 1952, 1961, 1967

Printed in Great Britain

CONTENTS

INTRODUCTION

ACCORDING to tradition, Plato was born in 427 B.C. and died in 347 B.C., leaving behind him as his last work the *Laws*. We may, therefore, suppose that the last decade of his life was mainly occupied with its composition. The internal evidence of the work itself sufficiently confirms tradition. Not only does it lack the charm and vigour of the earlier dialogues, but it is marked also by much uncouthness of style, and by a tendency to pedantry, tautology and discursive garrulity which seems to point to the failing powers of the author. Moreover, the author himself indicates his own advanced age by the artistic device of representing the three interlocutors in the dialogue as old men, and by the stress he repeatedly lays upon the fact of their age, as well as upon the reverence due from the young to the old.

The scene is laid in Crete, and it is during a walk from Cnosus to the grotto of Zeus on Mount Ida, on a long midsummer day, that the conversation here related is supposed to have taken place. Of the three old men, one is an Athenian, one (Clinias) a Cretan, one (Megillus) a Spartan. The protagonist is the Athenian, and nearly all the talking is done by him. His companions are little more than listeners, rather dull of wit, and incapable of adding

vii

anything original to the discussion. The choice of their nationality, however, is significant, since the main body of the laws framed for the Model City is derived from the codes actually in force in Athens, Sparta and Crete.

Voluminous and discursive as the *Laws* is, and framed, apparently, on no artistic plan, it is difficult for a reader to find his way through the maze and to see what connexion exists between the various parts and the relevance of each part to the argument as a whole. To help towards an understanding it may be well to give a brief analysis of the argument, book by book.

Book I.—Divine though their lawgivers were, the laws of Sparta and Crete are deficient, inasmuch as they aim solely at Courage, which is but one fraction of Virtue. A more important virtue is Temperance, or the right attitude towards pleasure and pain. For the promotion of temperance we need tests, and drinking-parties form admirable tests, although their educational value in this connexion has not hitherto been recognised.

Book II.—Another use of strong drink is to inspire age with something of the fire of youth, so that the old may take an active part in Music and may direct the musical training of the young on the right lines. A discussion of music and dancing leads up to the conclusion that we must form a " Dionysiac Chorus " of old men to act as an Academy of Music and to maintain a correct standard of taste in all that concerns Drama and the Arts.

Book III.—Beginning with primitive man, the survivors of the Flood, an historical survey is made of the origin and development of civic communities and their laws. The Dorian Confederacy, the Persian Empire, and the Athenian Democracy are examined in turn, and the seeds of political decay in each of them are pointed out. It is shown, from these examples, how the extremes of liberty and of tyranny are alike disastrous.

Book IV.—Clinias, it appears, has been appointed a joint-founder of a new Magnesian Colony. This gives a practical turn to the discussion, and henceforth the question is—how is such a colony to be rightly shaped? The conditions of the colony, as described by Clinias, suggest to the Athenian observations on the danger of a seaboard and foreign trade, and on the advantages of a heterogeneous population. If a "true polity" is to be successfully established, chance must aid skill, and a wise despot must co-operate with a divine lawgiver; for a "true polity" is one wherein Law reigns with undisputed sway, and where all the laws are framed in the interests of the community *as a whole*. To the Law, as also to God and to all superior powers, man is bound to render duty and service in all humility. In order to inculcate this attitude of voluntary and intelligent obedience, laws must be provided with preambles or preludes of an explanatory and hortatory description.

Book V.—As an example of such a hortatory prelude, the duty of paying due honour to the Soul, as the most divine part of man, is expounded at length. Then follow a number of detailed regulations regarding the selection of citizens, the number of households in the State, allotments and their arrangements, and property-holdings.

Book VI.—The State officials to be appointed

are enumerated, and the methods of their appointment prescribed—Law-wardens, Military Officers,—Council,—Religious Officials,—Stewards for Market, City and Country,—Presidents of Music and Gymnastics (chief of whom is the Superintendent of Education),—Judges. Then comes legislation dealing with the organisation of the households in tribes, —festivals and social functions,—marriage (which is a civic duty) and the ceremonies which attend it,—slaves and their treatment,—public and private buildings,—the regulation of private life and domestic affairs (discussing how far these should be legally controlled),—the time-limits proper for marriage, and for military service and the holding of public office.

Book VII.—Regulations for the education of the young. Up to the age of three continual movement is to be prescribed for children; from three to six, regulated play; after six, regular instruction in music and gymnastic, combined with play. Emphasis is laid on the need of left-hand training, and the value of ambidexterity. Then follows a discussion on the subjects of right selection in regard to dance and song, and the relation of Art and Religion to the ultimate aim of human life. It is laid down that the education of females must be identical with that of males, and that the supreme task for all is self-perfection. But the Lawgiver's work in regulating education is rendered specially difficult owing to the natural intractability of the child. Rules are given respecting instruction in reading, writing and lyre-playing, together with supplementary observations on gymnastic and dancing. A discourse on "mathematical necessity" serves as a preface to advice concerning arithmetic and geometry; and this is followed by regulations for field-sports.

Book VIII.—Regulations for military exercises and sham-fights, with a disquisition on the defects in the characters of States, such as the commercial spirit, which hinder due military training; and further observations regarding details of military training. Next to be dealt with are—the sex-instinct, with advice for its regulation,—the production and distribution of food,—laws for the control of agriculture,—artisans,—foreign trade,—the distribution of home and foreign produce,—markets.

Book IX.—Legal actions and penalties for the crimes of sacrilege and high treason, followed by a digression dealing with the art of legislation, the motives of crime, and the use of the terms "voluntary" and "involuntary" as applied to criminal actions. Cases of "Crimes against the person"— murder, wounding and assault.

Book X.—A discussion of atheism and irreligion, and how they are caused and promulgated, is followed by a threefold argument directed against three types of misbelievers, viz. (a) those who deny the existence of gods; (b) those who assert that the gods take no interest in men or their affairs (whereas it is a duty incumbent on all to believe firmly in a supreme Providence); (c) those who hold that the gods are corruptible by bribes. Laws are enacted to suppress these various forms of impiety, and also to prohibit private cults.

Book XI.—Regulations and observations concerning property-rights,—buying and selling,—commercial honesty,—retail-trade and inn-keeping,—breaches of contract,—military rewards,—last wills and testaments,—orphans,—family disputes,—divorce,—the honour due to age,—injuries by means of drugs and witchcraft,—thefts and acts of violence,—insanity,— abusive language,—public ridicule,—mendicancy,— the responsibility of masters for the acts of their slaves,—witnesses in courts of law,—the employment of professional advocates.

Book XII.—Regulations and observations concerning the duties of ambassadors,—the wickedness of theft, especially of State property,—the benefit to the State of habits of discipline in the citizens,— hence military service, with carefully adjudged rewards and penalties, must be universally compulsory—the Court of Examiners, their appointment and their duties,—oaths forbidden in the law-courts, —promptness in executing sentences,—foreign travel by the citizens, when permissible, and in what respect beneficial to the State. Various minor regulations are added respecting stolen goods, rights of search, property-holdings, etc. Then follows a review of the judicial arrangements, including appeals, with further observations on the importance of the study of Law, and on executions. After some supplementary rules have been given concerning funerals and tombs, we come to a description of the Nocturnal Synod, its function and constitution, and the training of its members; and with this the work concludes.

It will be clear from this analysis that the title of *Laws* is a very insufficient—not to say misleading—description of its contents. Barely one-third of the work consists of " laws " in the literal sense of the term; the rest is a far-ranging discussion of all

that concerns the life of man as a "political animal."
Human nature in general is the main theme of the
latter part of Book I, Book II, and large sections of
Books V and VII ; while the earlier part of Book I,
Book III, and Book IV have for their main theme
human nature in its social and civic aspect. In the
other books, moreover, which do actually deal with
"laws" Plato is enabled to introduce much that
would otherwise be excluded by means of his novel
theory of the twofold nature of law. Laws, he
argues, ought not only to coerce but also to persuade ;
therefore to every law there should be prefixed a
preamble or prelude, explaining and justifying the
law. This legal prelude he compares (by a play on
the double sense of νόμος—"law" and musical
"chant") with the proem or prologue of an ode or
drama. The whole of Book X, which purports to be
a special prelude to the law against impiety, is in
reality a general prelude, discussing the existence of
the gods, and the nature of the soul, in fact, a
disquisition *de rerum natura*. And in Book VII,
again, we have what is more of a general than of a
special prelude dealing with the subject of the sex-
instinct and its indulgence.

In his view of the State Plato relaxes the rigidity
of the communistic principles he had advocated in
the *Republic* : he allows the individual citizen to
possess a wife and family of his own and a certain
amount of private property. None the less, he
constantly insists on the entire subordination of the
individual to the State, on the principle (which holds
throughout the universe) that no *part* is independent,
but every part exists for the sake of its *whole*. Consequently the State he pictures—the Model City of

the Magnesians—although confessedly inferior to the
Ideal Republic, is one in which the life of every man
and woman, from the cradle to the grave, is strictly
regulated by legal prescriptions. At all costs
anarchy must be suppressed, discipline maintained.

The authority thus claimed for the State is justified
by means of the deification of Law. The supreme
Divinity is Reason (νοῦς), the Ruler of the Heavens,
and Law (νόμος) is nothing else than the dispensation
of Reason (νοῦ διανομή). Hence our State is, in fact,
a Theocracy; and all the sanctions of religion can be
invoked in support of its constitution and its laws.
He that offendeth against the law, or its officers,
offendeth against God.

The aim of Reason is always the Good, and this,
therefore, is the objective of the State and its
laws. They aim at the cultivation and conservation
of virtue, or civic excellence (ἀρετή). But of Virtue
as a whole there are two species which receive
special attention in the *Laws*, namely, Temperance
or Self-control (σωφροσύνη), and Wisdom (φρόνησις or
νοῦς). The promotion of temperance is the main
subject of Book I, and the elaborate regulations for
the education of the young are all directed to foster
this virtue. The main requisite for the bulk of the
citizens is a self-controlled and law-abiding disposition : the key-notes of their lives should be reverence
(αἰδώς) and "moderation" (μετριότης)—a "sweet
reasonableness" which yields willing obedience to the
higher powers. But for a select body of the highest
officials (as for the "Guardian" class of the *Republic*)
a higher type of education is required, calculated to
promote the superior virtue of wisdom. The
"Nocturnal Synod" described in Book XII is

designed to be the special repository of Wisdom in the Model City; and since it alone contains any element of divine Reason, it alone can be trusted to supplement or amend the divine ordinances handed down by the original Lawgiver.

But the main duty of the Nocturnal Synod—as, indeed, of all the State officials—is that of conservation (σωτηρία), the maintenance of the *status quo*. In the higher spheres of religion and science this duty devolves upon the Synod, in the sphere of Art it devolves upon the Dionysiac Chorus. Both these bodies are composed mostly of old men: the natural conservatism of the old will make them the best " saviours " (σωτῆρες) of the State, because the most stubborn opponents of every kind of innovation.

The concentration of all the political power in the hands of the old is, in truth, one of the most characteristic features of the *Laws*, and another sign of its author's age. The Model City would be only too likely, one thinks, to strike the youth of to-day as a Paradise for the old but a Purgatory for the young.

Since most of the power is thus given to a limited class, it is fair to describe the State of the *Laws* as a moderate oligarchy; although the historical survey in Book III, with its discussion of political types, might lead one to expect a rather different, and more liberal, combination of monarchy with democracy— the principle of order with the principle of freedom. As it is, the average citizen is given but little freedom, except the freedom to obey. And, though the State here pictured has been not unfitly described as " a mixture of Athenian constitutional forms and Athenian freedom with Spartan training and Spartan order, a practical *via media* between the two extremes of contemporary Greece," [1] yet it must be confessed that there is much more of the Spartan element in the mixture than of the Athenian, much less of democracy than of aristocracy. The " Athenian Stranger " of the *Laws* is no less of an anti-democrat than the " Socrates " of the *Republic*; and his conviction of the natural perversity and stupidity of the average man has increased with the passing of the years. The saying *vox populi, vox dei* is, for Plato, the supreme lie.

Politics and Ethics are, naturally, the subjects with which the *Laws* is mainly concerned; but in the Tenth Book we get something also of psychological and metaphysical doctrine. In his vindication of Religion in that Book—to which reference has been made above—Plato elaborates that view of Soul as the principle of self-movement which he had indicated, much earlier, in the *Phaedrus*. His discussion of the relation of Soul to Motion, on the one hand, and to Reason, on the other, together with his new classification of the kinds of motion, and his distinction between primary and secondary motions, form the most valuable additions to Platonic philosophy which the *Laws* contains.

In conclusion, be it said that besides much that is tedious in matter and ungraceful in style, the *Laws* also contains (to quote Jowett) " a few passages which are very grand and noble " ; and " no other writing of Plato shows so profound an insight into the world and into human nature as the *Laws*." In it the philosopher-statesman has garnered the last

---

[1] E. Barker, *Political Thought of Plato and Aristotle*, p. 202.

fruits of many years of experience and of reflection; and, as he himself would have us believe, the principles it enunciates are valid for all time.

The only English commentary on the *Laws* is that by E. B. England, a work of fine scholarship and most valuable, the text being based on Burnet's. Schanz's text contains only the first six books. Of other recent contributions to the study of the work, those of C. Ritter (1896) and O. Apelt (1916) are the most important. The text here printed is based on that of the Zurich edition of Baiter, Orelli, and Winckelmann (1839), the chief deviations from which are indicated in the foot-notes.

LIST OF PLATO'S WORKS

SHOWING THEIR DIVISION INTO VOLUMES
IN THIS EDITION AND THEIR PLACE IN
THE EDITION OF
H. STEPHANUS (VOLS. I.–III., PARIS, 1578).

LIST OF PLATO'S WORKS

LAWS

ΝΟΜΟΙ

ΤΑ ΤΟΥ ΔΙΑΛΟΓΟΥ ΠΡΟΣΩΠΑ

ΑΘΗΝΑΙΟΣ ΞΕΝΟΣ, ΚΛΕΙΝΙΑΣ ΚΡΗΣ,
ΜΕΓΙΛΛΟΣ ΛΑΚΕΔΑΙΜΟΝΙΟΣ

Α

ΑΘ. Θεὸς ἤ τις ἀνθρώπων ὑμῖν, ὦ ξένοι, εἴληφε
τὴν αἰτίαν τῆς τῶν νόμων διαθέσεως ;

ΚΛ. Θεός, ὦ ξένε, θεός, ὥς γε τὸ δικαιότατον
εἰπεῖν· παρὰ μὲν ἡμῖν Ζεύς, παρὰ δὲ Λακεδαιμονίοις, ὅθεν ὅδ' ἐστίν, οἶμαι φάναι τούτους
Ἀπόλλωνα. ἦ γάρ ;

ΜΕ. Ναί.

ΑΘ. Μῶν οὖν καθ' Ὅμηρον λέγεις, ὡς τοῦ
Β Μίνω φοιτῶντος πρὸς τὴν τοῦ πατρὸς ἑκάστοτε
συνουσίαν δι' ἐνάτου ἔτους καὶ κατὰ τὰς παρ'
ἐκείνου φήμας ταῖς πόλεσιν ὑμῖν θέντος τοὺς
νόμους ;

ΚΛ. Λέγεται γὰρ οὕτω παρ' ἡμῖν· καὶ δὴ καὶ
τὸν ἀδελφόν γε αὐτοῦ Ῥαδάμανθυν, ἀκούετε γὰρ
τὸ ὄνομα, δικαιότατον γεγονέναι. τοῦτον οὖν
625 φαῖμεν ἂν ἡμεῖς γε οἱ Κρῆτες ἐκ τοῦ τότε διανέμειν τὰ περὶ τὰς δίκας ὀρθῶς τοῦτον τὸν ἔπαινον
αὐτὸν εἰληφέναι.

---

[1] Cp. Hom. Od. 19. 178 f.

2

LAWS

[OR ON LEGISLATION, POLITICAL]

CHARACTERS

AN ATHENIAN STRANGER, CLINIAS OF CRETE,
MEGILLUS OF LACEDAEMON

BOOK I

ATH. To whom do you ascribe the authorship
of your legal arrangements, Strangers? To a god
or to some man?

CLIN. To a god, Stranger, most rightfully to a
god. We Cretans call Zeus our lawgiver; while in
Lacedaemon, where our friend here has his home,
I believe they claim Apollo as theirs. Is not that
so, Megillus?

MEG. Yes.

ATH. Do you then, like Homer,[1] say that Minos
used to go every ninth year to hold converse with
his father Zeus, and that he was guided by his
divine oracles in laying down the laws for your
cities?

CLIN. So our people say. And they say also
that his brother Rhadamanthys,—no doubt you have
heard the name,—was exceedingly just. And certainly we Cretans would maintain that he won this
title owing to his righteous administration of justice
in those days.

3

625 ΑΘ. Καὶ καλόν γε τὸ κλέος υἱεῖ τε Διὸς μάλα πρέπον. ἐπειδὴ δὲ ἐν τοιούτοις ἤθεσι τέθραφθε νομικοῖς σύ τε καὶ ὅδε, προσδοκῶ οὐκ ἂν ἀηδῶς ἡμᾶς [1] περί τε πολιτείας τὰ νῦν καὶ νόμων τὴν διατριβὴν λέγοντάς τε καὶ ἀκούοντας ἅμα κατὰ τὴν πορείαν ποιήσασθαι.[2] πάντως δ' ἥ γε ἐκ
B Κνωσοῦ ὁδὸς εἰς τὸ τοῦ Διὸς ἄντρον καὶ ἱερόν, ὡς ἀκούομεν, ἱκανή, καὶ ἀνάπαυλαι κατὰ τὴν ὁδόν, ὡς εἰκός, πνίγους ὄντος τὰ νῦν ἐν τοῖς ὑψηλοῖς δένδρεσίν εἰσι σκιαραί, καὶ ταῖς ἡλικίαις πρέπον ἂν ἡμῶν εἴη τὸ διαναπαύεσθαι πυκνὰ ἐν αὐταῖς, λόγοις τε ἀλλήλους παραμυθουμένους τὴν ὁδὸν ἅπασαν οὕτω μετὰ ῥᾳστώνης διαπερᾶναι.

ΚΛ. Καὶ μὴν ἔστι γε, ὦ ξένε, προϊόντι κυπαρίττων τε ἐν τοῖς ἄλσεσιν ὕψη καὶ κάλλη
C θαυμάσια, καὶ λειμῶνες ἐν οἷσιν ἀναπαυόμενοι διατρίβοιμεν ἄν.

ΑΘ. Ὀρθῶς λέγεις.

ΚΛ. Πάνυ μὲν οὖν· ἰδόντες δὲ μᾶλλον φήσομεν. ἀλλ' ἴωμεν ἀγαθῇ τύχῃ.

ΑΘ. Ταῦτ' εἴη. καί μοι λέγε, κατὰ τί τὰ ξυσσίτιά τε ὑμῖν συντέταχεν ὁ νόμος καὶ τὰ γυμνάσια καὶ τὴν τῶν ὅπλων ἕξιν;

ΚΛ. Οἶμαι μέν, ὦ ξένε, καὶ παντὶ ῥᾴδιον ὑπολαβεῖν εἶναι τά γε ἡμέτερα. τὴν γὰρ τῆς χώρας
D πάσης Κρήτης φύσιν ὁρᾶτε, ὡς οὐκ ἔστι, καθάπερ ἡ τῶν Θετταλῶν, πεδιάς. διὸ δὴ καὶ τοῖς μὲν ἵπποις ἐκεῖνοι χρῶνται μᾶλλον, δρόμοισι δὲ ἡμεῖς· ἥδε γὰρ ἀνώμαλος αὖ καὶ πρὸς τὴν τῶν

---

[1] ἡμᾶς wanting in Paris MS.

4

LAWS, BOOK I

ATH. Yes, his renown is indeed glorious and well befitting a son of Zeus. And, since you and our friend Megillus were both brought up in legal institutions of so noble a kind, you would, I imagine, have no aversion to our occupying ourselves as we go along in discussion on the subject of government and laws. Certainly, as I am told, the road from Cnosus to the cave[1] and temple of Zeus is a long one, and we are sure to find, in this sultry weather, shady resting-places among the high trees along the road: in them we can rest ofttimes, as befits our age, beguiling the time with discourse, and thus complete our journey in comfort.

CLIN. True, Stranger; and as one proceeds further one finds in the groves cypress-trees of wonderful height and beauty, and meadows too, where we may rest ourselves and talk.

ATH. You say well.

CLIN. Yes, indeed: and when we set eyes on them we shall say so still more emphatically. So let us be going, and good luck attend us!

ATH. Amen! And tell me now, for what reason did your law ordain the common meals you have, and your gymnastic schools and military equipment?

CLIN. Our Cretan customs, Stranger, are, as I think, such as anyone may grasp easily. As you may notice, Crete, as a whole, is not a level country, like Thessaly: consequently, whereas the Thessalians mostly go on horseback, we Cretans are runners, since this land of ours is rugged and more suitable

---

[1] The grotto of Dicte on Mt. Ida.

[2] ποιήσασθαι Schanz : ποιήσεσθαι MSS.

625 πεζῇ δρόμων ἄσκησιν μᾶλλον σύμμετρος. ἐλα-
φρὰ δὴ τὰ ὅπλα ἀναγκαῖον ἐν τῷ τοιούτῳ
κεκτῆσθαι καὶ μὴ βάρος ἔχοντα θεῖν· τῶν δὴ
τόξων καὶ τοξευμάτων ἡ κουφότης ἁρμόττειν
δοκεῖ. ταῦτ᾿ οὖν πρὸς τὸν πόλεμον ἡμῖν ἅπαντα
E ἐξήρτυται, καὶ πάνθ᾿ ὁ νομοθέτης, ὥς γ᾿ ἐμοὶ
φαίνεται, πρὸς τοῦτο βλέπων συνετάττετο, ἐπεὶ
καὶ τὰ ξυσσίτια κινδυνεύει ξυναγαγεῖν ὁρῶν ὡς
πάντες, ὁπόταν στρατεύωνται, τόθ᾿ ὑπ᾿ αὐτοῦ
τοῦ πράγματος ἀναγκάζονται φυλακῆς αὑτῶν
ἕνεκα ξυσσιτεῖν τοῦτον τὸν χρόνον· ἄνοιαν δή
μοι δοκεῖ καταγνῶναι τῶν πολλῶν ὡς οὐ μαν-
θανόντων ὅτι πόλεμος ἀεὶ πᾶσι διὰ βίου ξυνεχής
ἐστι πρὸς ἁπάσας τὰς πόλεις· εἰ δὴ πολέμου
γε ὄντος φυλακῆς ἕνεκα δεῖ ξυσσιτεῖν καί τινας
ἄρχοντας καὶ ἀρχομένους διακεκοσμημένους εἶναι
626 φύλακας αὑτῶν, τοῦτο καὶ ἐν εἰρήνῃ δραστέον.
ἣν γὰρ καλοῦσιν οἱ πλεῖστοι τῶν ἀνθρώπων
εἰρήνην, τοῦτ᾿ εἶναι μόνον ὄνομα, τῷ δ᾿ ἔργῳ
πάσαις πρὸς πάσας τὰς πόλεις ἀεὶ πόλεμον
ἀκήρυκτον κατὰ φύσιν εἶναι. καὶ σχεδὸν ἀνευ-
ρήσεις οὕτω σκοπῶν τὸν Κρητῶν νομοθέτην, ὡς
εἰς τὸν πόλεμον ἅπαντα δημοσίᾳ καὶ ἰδίᾳ τὰ
νόμιμα ἡμῖν ἀποβλέπων συνετάξατο, καὶ κατὰ
ταῦτα οὕτω φυλάττειν παρέδωκε τοὺς νόμους,
B ὡς τῶν ἄλλων οὐδενὸς οὐδὲν ὄφελος ὄν, οὔτε
κτημάτων οὔτ᾿ ἐπιτηδευμάτων, ἂν μὴ τῷ πολέμῳ
ἄρα κρατῇ τις· πάντα δὲ τὰ τῶν νικωμένων
ἀγαθὰ τῶν νικώντων γίγνεσθαι.

ΑΘ. Καλῶς γε, ὦ ξένε, φαίνει μοι γεγυμνάσθαι

for the practice of foot-running. Under these conditions we are obliged to have light armour for running and to avoid heavy equipment; so bows and arrows are adopted as suitable because of their lightness. Thus all these customs of ours are adapted for war, and, in my opinion, this was the object which the lawgiver had in view when he ordained them all. Probably this was his reason also for instituting common meals: he saw how soldiers, all the time they are on campaign, are obliged by force of circumstances to mess in common, for the sake of their own security. And herein, as I think, he condemned the stupidity of the mass of men in failing to perceive that all are involved ceaselessly in a lifelong war against all States. If, then, these practices are necessary in war,—namely, messing in common for safety's sake, and the appointment of relays of officers and privates to act as guards,—they must be carried out equally in time of peace. For (as he would say) "peace," as the term is commonly employed, is nothing more than a name, the truth being that every State is, by a law of nature, engaged perpetually in an informal war with every other State. And if you look at the matter from this point of view you will find it practically true that our Cretan lawgiver ordained all our legal usages, both public and private, with an eye to war, and that he therefore charged us with the task of guarding our laws safely, in the conviction that without victory in war nothing else, whether possession or institution, is of the least value, but all the goods of the vanquished fall into the hands of the victors.

ATH. Your training, Stranger, has certainly, as it

626 πρὸς τὸ διειδέναι τὰ Κρητῶν νόμιμα. τόδε δέ
μοι φράζε ἔτι σαφέστερον· ὃν γὰρ ὅρον ἔθου
C τῆς εὖ πολιτευομένης πόλεως, δοκεῖς μοι λέγειν
οὕτω κεκοσμημένην οἰκεῖν δεῖν ὥστε πολέμῳ νικᾶν
τὰς ἄλλας πόλεις. ἢ γάρ;

ΚΛ. Πάνυ μὲν οὖν· οἶμαι δὲ καὶ τῷδε οὕτω
ξυνδοκεῖν.

ΜΕ. Πῶς γὰρ ἂν ἄλλως ἀποκρίναιτο, ὦ θεῖε,
Λακεδαιμονίων γε ὁστισοῦν;

ΑΘ. Πότερ' οὖν δὴ πόλεσι μὲν πρὸς πόλεις
ὀρθὸν τοῦτ' ἐστί, κώμῃ δὲ πρὸς κώμην ἕτερον;

ΚΛ. Οὐδαμῶς.

ΑΘ. Ἀλλὰ ταὐτόν;

ΚΛ. Ναί.

ΑΘ. Τί δέ; πρὸς οἰκίαν οἰκία τῶν ἐν τῇ
κώμῃ, καὶ πρὸς ἄνδρα ἀνδρὶ ἑνὶ πρὸς ἕνα,
ταὐτὸν ἔτι;

ΚΛ. Ταὐτόν.

D ΑΘ. Αὐτῷ δὲ πρὸς αὑτὸν πότερον ὡς πολεμίῳ
πρὸς πολέμιον διανοητέον, ἢ πῶς ἔτι λέγομεν;

ΚΛ. Ὦ ξένε Ἀθηναῖε—οὐ γάρ σε Ἀττικὸν
ἐθέλοιμ' ἂν προσαγορεύειν. δοκεῖς γάρ μοι τῆς
θεοῦ ἐπωνυμίας ἄξιος εἶναι μᾶλλον ἐπονομάζε-
σθαι· τὸν γὰρ λόγον ἐπ' ἀρχὴν ὀρθῶς ἀν-
αγαγὼν σαφέστερον ἐποίησας, ὥστε ῥᾷον ἀνευρή-
σεις ὅτι νῦν δὴ ὑφ' ἡμῶν ὀρθῶς ἐρρήθη τὸ
πολεμίους εἶναι πάντας πᾶσι δημοσίᾳ τε καὶ ἰδίᾳ
<καὶ>[1] ἑκάστους αὐτοὺς σφίσιν αὐτοῖς.

E ΑΘ. Πῶς εἴρηκας, ὦ θαυμάσιε;

ΚΛ. Κἀνταῦθα, ὦ ξένε, τὸ νικᾶν αὐτὸν αὑτὸν

---

[1] < καὶ > added by Ast, Schanz.

LAWS, BOOK I

seems to me, given you an excellent understanding of the legal practices of Crete. But tell me this more clearly still : by the definition you have given of the well-constituted State you appear to me to imply that it ought to be organised in such a way as to be victorious in war over all other States. Is that so ?

CLIN. Certainly it is ; and I think that our friend here shares my opinion.

MEG. No Lacedaemonian, my good sir, could possibly say otherwise.

ATH. If this, then, is the right attitude for a State to adopt towards a State, is the right attitude for village towards village different ?

CLIN. By no means.

ATH. It is the same, you say ?

CLIN. Yes.

ATH. Well then, is the same attitude right also for one house in the village towards another, and for each man towards every other ?

CLIN. It is.

ATH. And must each individual man regard himself as his own enemy ? Or what do we say when we come to this point ?

CLIN. O Stranger of Athens,—for I should be loth to call you a man of Attica, since methinks you deserve rather to be named after the goddess Athena, seeing that you have made the argument more clear by taking it back again to its starting-point ; whereby you will the more easily discover the justice of our recent statement that, in the mass, all men are both publicly and privately the enemies of all, and individually also each man is his own enemy.

ATH. What is your meaning, my admirable sir ?

CLIN. It is just in this war, my friend, that the

626 πασῶν νικῶν πρώτη τε καὶ ἀρίστη, τὸ δὲ ἡττᾶσθαι
αὐτὸν ὑφ᾽ ἑαυτοῦ πάντων αἴσχιστόν τε ἅμα καὶ
κάκιστον. ταῦτα γὰρ ὡς πολέμου ἐν ἑκάστοις
ἡμῶν ὄντος πρὸς ἡμᾶς αὐτοὺς σημαίνει.

ΑΘ. Πάλιν τοίνυν τὸν λόγον ἀναστρέψωμεν.
ἐπειδὴ γὰρ εἷς ἕκαστος ἡμῶν ὁ μὲν κρείττων
627 αὑτοῦ, ὁ δὲ ἥττων ἐστί, πότερα φῶμεν οἰκίαν
τε καὶ κώμην καὶ πόλιν ἔχειν ταὐτὸν τοῦτο ἐν
αὑταῖς ἢ μὴ φῶμεν;

ΚΛ. Τὸ κρεῖττω τε αὑτῆς εἶναι λέγεις τινά, τὴν
δ᾽ ἥττω;

ΑΘ. Ναί.

ΚΛ. Καὶ τοῦτο ὀρθῶς ἤρου· πάνυ γὰρ ἔστι
καὶ σφόδρα τὸ τοιοῦτον, οὐχ ἥκιστα ἐν ταῖς
πόλεσιν· ἐν ὁπόσαις μὲν γὰρ οἱ ἀμείνονες νικῶσι
τὸ πλῆθος καὶ τοὺς χείρους, ὀρθῶς ἂν αὕτη
κρείττων τε αὑτῆς λέγοιθ᾽ ἡ πόλις ἐπαινοῖτό τε
ἂν δικαιότατα τῇ τοιαύτῃ νίκῃ· τοὐναντίον δέ,
ὅπου τἀναντία.

B ΑΘ. Τὸ μὲν τοίνυν εἴ ποτ᾽ ἐστί που τὸ χεῖρον
κρεῖττον τοῦ ἀμείνονος ἐάσωμεν· μακροτέρου γὰρ
λόγου· τὸ δὲ ὑπὸ σοῦ λεγόμενον μανθάνω νῦν, ὡς
ποτε πολῖται ξυγγενεῖς καὶ τῆς αὐτῆς πόλεως
γεγονότες ἄδικοι καὶ πολλοὶ ξυνελθόντες δικαίους
ἐλάττους ὄντας βιάσονται δουλούμενοι, καὶ ὅταν
μὲν κρατήσωσιν, ἥττων ἡ πόλις αὑτῆς ὀρθῶς
αὕτη λέγοιτ᾽ ἂν ἅμα καὶ κακή, ὅπου δ᾽ ἂν
ἡττῶνται, κρείττων τε καὶ ἀγαθή.

C ΚΛ. Καὶ μάλα ἄτοπον, ὦ ξένε, τὸ νῦν λεγό-
μενον· ὅμως δ᾽ ὁμολογεῖν οὕτως ἀναγκαιότατον.

---

[1] Cp. *Rep.* 430 E ff. : *Proverbs* xvi. 32.

victory over self is of all victories the first and best
while self-defeat is of all defeats at once the worst
and the most shameful. For these phrases signify
that a war against self exists within each of us.[1]

ATH. Now let us take the argument back in the
reverse direction. Seeing that individually each of
us is partly superior to himself and partly inferior,
are we to affirm that the same condition of things
exists in house and village and State, or are we to
deny it?

CLIN. Do you mean the condition of being partly
self-superior and partly self-inferior?

ATH. Yes.

CLIN. That, too, is a proper question; for such a
condition does most certainly exist, and in States
above all. Every State in which the better class
is victorious over the populace and the lower classes
would rightly be termed "self-superior," and would
be praised most justly for a victory of this kind;
and conversely, when the reverse is the case.

ATH. Well then, leaving aside the question as to
whether the worse element is ever superior to the
better (a question which would demand a more
lengthy discussion), what you assert, as I now perceive, is this,—that sometimes citizens of one stock
and of one State who are unjust and numerous may
combine together and try to enslave by force those
who are just but fewer in number, and wherever
they prevail such a State would rightly be termed
"self-inferior" and bad, but "self-superior" and
good wherever they are worsted.

CLIN. This statement is indeed most extraordi-
nary, Stranger; none the less we cannot possibly
reject it.

627 ΑΘ. Εχε δή· καὶ τόδε πάλιν ἐπισκεψώμεθα.
πολλοὶ ἀδελφοί που γένοιντ᾽ ἂν ἑνὸς ἀνδρός τε
καὶ μιᾶς υἱεῖς, καὶ δὴ καὶ θαυματτὸν οὐδὲν τοὺς
πλείους μὲν ἀδίκους αὐτῶν γίγνεσθαι, τοὺς δὲ
ἐλάττους δικαίους.

ΚΛ. Οὐ γὰρ οὖν.

ΑΘ. Καὶ οὐκ ἂν εἴη γε πρέπον ἐμοί τε καὶ
ὑμῖν τοῦτο θηρεύειν, ὅτι νικώντων μὲν τῶν πονηρῶν ἥ τε οἰκία καὶ ἡ ξυγγένεια αὕτη πᾶσα ἥττων
D αὑτῆς λέγοιτ᾽ ἄν, κρείττων δὲ ἡττωμένων· οὐ γὰρ
εὐσχημοσύνης τε καὶ ἀσχημοσύνης ῥημάτων ἕνεκα
τὰ νῦν σκοπούμεθα πρὸς τὸν τῶν πολλῶν λόγον,
ἀλλ᾽ ὀρθότητός τε καὶ ἁμαρτίας πέρι νόμων, ἥτις
ποτέ ἐστι φύσει.

ΚΛ. Ἀληθέστατα, ὦ ξένε, λέγεις.

ΜΕ. Καλῶς μὲν οὖν, ὥς γε ἐμοὶ ξυνδοκεῖν τό γε
τοσοῦτον τὰ νῦν.

ΑΘ. Ἴδωμεν δὴ καὶ τόδε· τούτοις τοῖς ἄρτι
λεγομένοις ἀδελφοῖς γένοιτ᾽ ἄν πού τις δικαστής;

ΚΛ. Πάνυ γε.

ΑΘ. Πότερος οὖν ἀμείνων; ὅστις τοὺς μὲν
E ἀπολέσειεν αὐτῶν ὅσοι κακοί, τοὺς δὲ βελτίους
ἄρχειν αὐτοὺς αὐτῶν προστάξειεν, ἢ ὅδε ὃς ἂν
τοὺς μὲν χρηστοὺς ἄρχειν, τοὺς χείρους δ᾽ ἐάσας
ζῆν ἄρχεσθαι ἑκόντας ποιήσειε; τρίτον δέ που
δικαστὴν πρὸς ἀρετὴν εἴπωμεν, εἴ τις εἴη τοιοῦτος,
628 ὅστις παραλαβὼν ξυγγένειαν μίαν διαφερομένην
μήτε ἀπολέσειε μηδένα, διαλλάξας δὲ εἰς τὸν
ἐπίλοιπον χρόνον νόμους αὐτοῖς θεὶς πρὸς ἀλλήλους παραφυλάττειν δύναιτο ὥστε εἶναι φίλους.

ATH. Stay a moment : here too is a case we must further consider. Suppose there were a number of brothers, all sons of the same parents, it would not be at all surprising if most of them were unjust and but few just.

CLIN. It would not.

ATH. And, moreover, it would ill beseem you and me to go a-chasing after this form of expression, that if the bad ones conquered the whole of this family and house should be called " self-inferior," but " self-superior " if they were defeated ; for our present reference to the usage of ordinary speech is not concerned with the propriety or impropriety of verbal phrases but with the essential rightness or wrongness of laws.

CLIN. Very true, Stranger.

MEG. And finely spoken, too, up to this point, as I agree.

ATH. Let us also look at this point : the brothers we have just described would have, I suppose, a judge?

CLIN. Certainly.

ATH. Which of the two would be the better—a judge who destroyed all the wicked among them and charged the good to govern themselves, or one who made the good members govern and, while allowing the bad to live, made them submit willingly to be governed? And there is a third judge we must mention (third and best in point of merit),— if indeed such a judge can be found,—who in dealing with a single divided family will destroy none of them but reconcile them and succeed, by enacting laws for them, in securing amongst them thenceforward permanent friendliness.

628 ΚΛ. Μακρῷ ἀμείνων γίγνοιτ᾽ ἂν ὁ τοιοῦτος δικαστής τε καὶ νομοθέτης.

ΑΘ. Καὶ μὴν τοὐναντίον γε ἢ πρὸς πόλεμον ἂν βλέπων αὐτοῖς τοὺς νόμους διανομοθετοῖ.

ΚΛ. Τοῦτο μὲν ἀληθές.

ΑΘ. Τί δ᾽ ὁ τὴν πόλιν ξυναρμόττων; πρὸς πόλεμον αὐτῆς ἂν τὸν ἔξωθεν βλέπων τὸν βίον Β κοσμοῖ μᾶλλον, ἢ πρὸς πόλεμον τὸν ἐν αὐτῇ γιγνόμενον ἑκάστοτε, ἣ δὴ καλεῖται στάσις; ὃν μάλιστα μὲν ἅπας ἂν βούλοιτο μήτε γενέσθαι ποτὲ ἐν ἑαυτοῦ πόλει γενόμενόν τε ὡς τάχιστα ἀπαλλάττεσθαι.

ΚΛ. Δῆλον ὅτι πρὸς τοῦτον.

ΑΘ. Πότερα δ᾽ ἀπολομένων αὖ τῶν ἑτέρων εἰρήνην τῆς στάσεως γενέσθαι, νικησάντων δὲ ποτέρων, δέξαιτ᾽ ἄν τις μᾶλλον ἢ φιλίας τε καὶ εἰρήνης ὑπὸ διαλλαγῶν γενομένης, <καὶ>[1] οὕτω C τοῖς ἔξωθεν πολεμίοις προσέχειν ἀνάγκην εἶναι τὸν νοῦν;

ΚΛ. Οὕτω πᾶς ἂν ἐθέλοι πρότερον ἢ 'κείνως περὶ τὴν αὑτοῦ γίγνεσθαι πόλιν.

ΑΘ. Οὐκοῦν καὶ νομοθέτης ὡσαύτως;

ΚΛ. Τί μήν;

ΑΘ. Ἆρ᾽ οὖν οὐ τοῦ ἀρίστου ἕνεκα πάντα ἂν τὰ νόμιμα τιθείη πᾶς;

ΚΛ. Πῶς δ᾽ οὔ;

ΑΘ. Τό γε μὴν ἄριστον οὔτε ὁ πόλεμος οὔτε ἡ στάσις, ἀπευκτὸν δὲ τὸ δεηθῆναι τούτων, εἰρήνη δὲ πρὸς ἀλλήλους ἅμα καὶ φιλοφροσύνη. καὶ δή

---

[1] <καὶ> I insert (Schanz brackets εἰρήνην . . . γενέσθαι and ἀνάγκην εἶναι).

CLIN. A judge and lawgiver of that kind would be by far the best.

ATH. But mark this: his aim, in the laws he enacted for them, would be the opposite of war.

CLIN. That is true.

ATH. And what of him who brings the State into harmony? In ordering its life would he have regard to external warfare rather than to the internal war, whenever it occurs, which goes by the name of "civil" strife? For this is a war as to which it would be the desire of every man that, if possible, it should never occur in his own State, and that, if it did occur, it should come to as speedy an end as possible.

CLIN. Evidently he would have regard to civil war.

ATH. And would anyone prefer that the citizens should be obliged to devote their attention to external enemies after internal concord had been secured by the destruction of one section and the victory of their opponents rather than after the establishment of friendship and peace by terms of conciliation?

CLIN. Everyone would prefer the latter alternative for his own State rather than the former.

ATH. And would not the lawgiver do the same?

CLIN. Of course.

ATH. Would not every lawgiver in all his legislation aim at the highest good?

CLIN. Assuredly.

ATH. The highest good, however, is neither war nor civil strife—which things we should pray rather to be saved from—but peace one with another and friendly feeling. Moreover, it would seem that the

628D καὶ τὸ νικᾶν, ὡς ἔοικεν, αὐτὴν αὑτὴν πόλιν οὐκ ἦν
τῶν ἀρίστων ἀλλὰ τῶν ἀναγκαίων· ὅμοιον ὡς εἰ
κάμνον σῶμα ἰατρικῆς καθάρσεως τυχὸν ἡγοῖτό τις
ἄριστα πράττειν τότε, τῷ δὲ μηδὲ τὸ παράπαν
δεηθέντι σώματι μηδὲ προσέχοι τὸν νοῦν, ὡσαύτως δὲ καὶ πρὸς πόλεως εὐδαιμονίαν ἢ καὶ ἰδιώτου
διανοούμενος οὕτω τις οὔτ᾽ ἄν ποτε πολιτικὸς
γένοιτο ὀρθῶς, πρὸς τὰ ἔξωθεν πολεμικὰ ἀποβλέπων μόνον καὶ πρῶτον, οὔτ᾽ ἂν νομοθέτης
ἀκριβής, εἰ μὴ χάριν εἰρήνης τὰ πολέμου νομο-
E θετοίη μᾶλλον ἢ τῶν πολεμικῶν ἕνεκα τὰ τῆς
εἰρήνης.

ΚΛ. Φαίνεται μέν πως ὁ λόγος οὗτος, ὦ ξένε,
ὀρθῶς εἰρῆσθαι· θαυμάζω γε μὴν εἰ τά τε παρ᾽
ἡμῖν νόμιμα καὶ ἔτι τὰ περὶ Λακεδαίμονα μὴ
πᾶσαν τὴν σπουδὴν τούτων ἕνεκα πεποίηται.

ΑΘ. Τάχ᾽ ἂν ἴσως· δεῖ δ᾽ οὐδὲν σκληρῶς ἡμᾶς
629 αὐτοῖς διαμάχεσθαι τὰ νῦν, ἀλλ᾽ ἠρέμα ἀνερωτᾶν,
ὡς μάλιστα περὶ ταῦτα ἡμῶν τε καὶ ἐκείνων
σπουδαζόντων. καί μοι τῷ λόγῳ ξυνακολου-
θήσατε. προστησώμεθα γοῦν Τύρταιον, τὸν
φύσει μὲν Ἀθηναῖον, τῶνδε δὲ πολίτην γενόμενον,
ὃς δὴ μάλιστα ἀνθρώπων περὶ ταῦτα ἐσπούδακεν,
εἰπὼν ὅτι

οὔτ᾽ ἂν μνησαίμην οὔτ᾽ ἐν λόγῳ ἄνδρα τιθείμην

B οὔτ᾽ εἴ τις πλουσιώτατος ἀνθρώπων εἴη, φησίν,
οὔτ᾽ εἰ πολλὰ ἀγαθὰ κεκτημένος, εἰπὼν σχεδὸν
ἅπαντα, ὃς μὴ περὶ τὸν πόλεμον ἄριστος γίγνοιτ᾽
ἀεί. ταῦτα γὰρ ἀκήκοάς που καὶ σὺ τὰ ποιήματα·
ὅδε μὲν γάρ, οἶμαι, διακορὴς αὐτῶν ἐστί.

victory we mentioned of a State over itself is not one of the best things but one of those which are necessary. For imagine a man supposing that a human body was best off when it was sick and purged with physic, while never giving a thought to the case of the body that needs no physic at all! Similarly, with regard to the well-being of a State or an individual, that man will never make a genuine statesman who pays attention primarily and solely to the needs of foreign warfare, nor will he make a finished lawgiver unless he designs his war legislation for peace rather than his peace legislation for war.

CLIN. This statement, Stranger, is apparently true; yet, unless I am much mistaken, our legal usages in Crete, and in Lacedaemon too, are wholly directed towards war.

ATH. Very possibly; but we must not now attack them violently, but mildly interrogate them, since both we and your legislators are earnestly interested in these matters. Pray follow the argument closely. Let us take the opinion of Tyrtaeus (an Athenian by birth and afterwards a citizen of Lacedaemon), who, above all men, was keenly interested in our subject. This is what he says:[1] "Though a man were the richest of men, though a man possessed goods in plenty (and he specifies nearly every good there is), if he failed to prove himself at all times most valiant in war, no mention should I make of him, nor take account of him at all." No doubt you also have heard these poems; while our friend Megillus is, I imagine, surfeited with them.

---

[1] Tyrtaeus, xii. (Bergk). Tyrtaeus wrote war-songs at Sparta about 680 B.C.

629　ΜΓ.　Πάνυ μὲν οὖν.

ΚΛ.　Καὶ μὴν καὶ παρ᾽ ἡμᾶς ἐλήλυθε κομισθέντα
ἐκ Λακεδαίμονος.

ΑΘ.　Ἴθι νυν[1] ἀνερώμεθα κοινῇ τουτονὶ τὸν
C ποιητὴν οὑτωσί πως, Ὦ Τύρταιε, ποιητὰ θειότατε·
δοκεῖς γὰρ δὴ σοφὸς ἡμῖν εἶναι καὶ ἀλαθός, ὅτι
τοὺς μὲν ἐν τῷ πολέμῳ διαφέροντας διαφερόντως
ἐγκεκωμίακας· ἤδη οὖν τυγχάνομεν ἐγώ τε καὶ
ὅδε καὶ Κλεινίας ὁ Κνώσιος οὑτοσὶ ξυμφερόμενοί
σοι περὶ τούτου σφόδρα, ὡς δοκοῦμεν· εἰ δὲ περὶ
τῶν αὐτῶν λέγομεν ἀνδρῶν ἢ μή, βουλόμεθα
σαφῶς εἰδέναι. λέγε οὖν ἡμῖν, ἆρα εἴδη δύο πολέμου, καθάπερ ἡμεῖς, ἡγεῖ καὶ σὺ σαφῶς; ἢ πῶς;
Πρὸς ταῦτα, οἶμαι, κἂν πολὺ φαυλότερος εἴποι
D Τυρταίου τις τἀληθές, ὅτι δύο, τὸ μὲν ὃ καλοῦμεν
ἅπαντες στάσιν, ὃς δὴ πάντων πολέμων χαλε-
πώτατος, ὡς ἔφαμεν ἡμεῖς νῦν δή· τὸ δ᾽ ἄλλο
πολέμου θήσομεν, οἶμαι, γένος ἅπαντες, ᾧ πρὸς
τοὺς ἐκτός τε καὶ ἀλλοφύλους χρώμεθα διαφε-
ρόμενοι, πολὺ πραότερον ἐκείνου.

ΚΛ.　Πῶς γὰρ οὔ;

ΑΘ.　Φέρε δή, ποτέρους καὶ πρὸς πότερον
ἐπαινῶν τοῖν πολέμοιν[2] οὕτως ὑπερεπήνεσας, τοὺς
δ᾽ ἔψεξας τῶν ἀνδρῶν; ἔοικας μὲν γὰρ πρὸς τὸν[3]
E ἐκτός· εἴρηκας γοῦν ὧδε ἐν τοῖς ποιήμασιν, ὡς
οὐδαμῶς τοὺς τοιούτους ἀνεχόμενος, Οἳ μὴ τολ-
μήσωσι μὲν

　　　　ὁρᾶν φόνον αἱματόεντα,
καὶ δῃῶν ὀρέγοιντ᾽ ἐγγύθεν ἱστάμενοι.

Οὐκοῦν τὰ μετὰ ταῦτα εἴποιμεν ἂν ἡμεῖς ὅτι Σὺ

---

[1] νυν Schanz: νῦν δὴ Zur.: νῦν Paris MS.
[2] τοῖν πολέμοιν, C. Post: τὸν πόλεμον, MSS., edd.

MEG. I certainly am.

CLIN. And I can assure you they have reached Crete also, shipped over from Lacedaemon.

ATH. Come now, let us jointly interrogate this poet somehow on this wise: "O Tyrtaeus, most inspired of poets (for assuredly you seem to us both wise and good in that you have eulogised excellently those who excel in war), concerning this matter we three—Megillus, Clinias of Cnosus and myself—are already in entire accord with you, as we suppose; but we wish to be assured that both we and you are alluding to the same persons. Tell us then: do you clearly recognise, as we do, two distinct kinds of war?" In reply to this I suppose that even a much less able man than Tyrtaeus would state the truth, that there are two kinds, the one being that which we all call "civil," which is of all wars the most bitter, as we said just now, while the other kind, as I suppose we shall all agree, is that which we engage in when we quarrel with foreigners and aliens—a kind much milder than the former.

CLIN. Certainly.

ATH. "Come, then, which kind of warriors, fighting in which kind of war, did you praise so highly, while blaming others? Warriors, apparently, who fight in war abroad. At any rate, in your poems you have said that you cannot abide men who dare not

‘ face the gory fray and smite the foe in close combat.’ ”

Then we should proceed to say, "It appears, O

---

³ τὸν Baiter, Schanz : τοὺς MSS.

629 μὲν ἐπαινεῖς, ὡς ἔοικας, ὦ Τύρταιε, μάλιστα τοὺς
πρὸς τὸν ὀθνεῖόν τε καὶ ἔξωθεν πόλεμον γιγνομένους ἐπιφανεῖς. Φαίη ταῦτ᾽ ἄν που καὶ ὁμολογοῖ ;

630 ΚΛ. Τί μήν ;

ΑΘ. Ἡμεῖς δέ γε ἀγαθῶν ὄντων τούτων ἔτι
φαμὲν ἀμείνους εἶναι καὶ πολὺ τοὺς ἐν τῷ μεγίστῳ
πολέμῳ γιγνομένους ἀρίστους διαφανῶς. ποιητὴν
δὲ καὶ ἡμεῖς μάρτυρα ἔχομεν, Θέογνιν, πολίτην
τῶν ἐν Σικελίᾳ Μεγαρέων, ὅς φησι

πιστὸς ἀνὴρ χρυσοῦ τε καὶ ἀργύρου
ἀντερύσασθαι
ἄξιος ἐν χαλεπῇ, Κύρνε, διχοστασίῃ.

τοῦτον δὴ φαμεν ἐν πολέμῳ χαλεπωτέρῳ ἀμείνονα
ἐκείνου πάμπολυ γίγνεσθαι, σχεδὸν ὅσον ἀμείνων
δικαιοσύνη καὶ σωφροσύνη καὶ φρόνησις εἰς ταὐτὸν
B ἐλθοῦσαι[1] μετ᾽ ἀνδρίας <αὐτῆς μόνης ἀνδρίας>.[2]
πιστὸς μὲν γὰρ καὶ ὑγιὴς ἐν στάσεσιν οὐκ ἄν
ποτε γένοιτο ἄνευ ξυμπάσης ἀρετῆς· διαβάντες δ᾽
εὖ καὶ μαχόμενοι ἐθέλοντες ἀποθνήσκειν ἔν γ᾽ ᾧ[3]
πολέμῳ φράξει Τύρταιος, τῶν μισθοφόρων εἰσὶ πάμ-
πολλοι, ὧν οἱ πλεῖστοι γίγνονται θρασεῖς καὶ ἄδικοι
καὶ ὑβρισταὶ καὶ ἀφρονέστατοι σχεδὸν ἁπάντων,
ἐκτὸς δή τινων μάλα ὀλίγων. ποῖ δὴ τελευτᾷ
νῦν ἡμῖν οὗτος ὁ λόγος, καὶ τί φανερόν ποτε
ποιῆσαι βουληθεὶς λέγει ταῦτα ; δῆλον ὅτι τόδε,
ὡς παντὸς μᾶλλον καὶ ὁ τῇδε παρὰ Διὸς νομοθέτης,
C πᾶς τε οὖ καὶ σμικρὸν ὄφελος, οὐκ ἄλλοσε[4] ἢ

[1] ἐλθοῦσαι Eusebius and Proclus : ἐλθοῦσα MSS.
[2] < αὐτῆς . . . ἀνδρίας > added by Euseb., Procl.
[3] ἔν γ᾽ ᾧ : ἐν τῷ MSS. : ἐν ᾧ Euseb. : ἐν τῷ πολέμῳ, ᾧ
φράζει Winckelmann.

Tyrtaeus, that you are chiefly praising those who achieve distinction in foreign and external warfare." To this, I presume, he would agree, and say " Yes " ?

CLIN. Of course.

ATH. Yet, brave though these men are, we still maintain that they are far surpassed in bravery by those who are conspicuously brave in the greatest of wars ; and we also have a poet for witness,—Theognis (a citizen of Sicilian Megara), who says :[1]

" In the day of grievous feud, O Cyrnus, the loyal warrior is worth his weight in silver and gold."

Such a man, in a war much more grievous, is, we say, ever so much better than the other—nearly as much better, in fact, as the union of justice, prudence and wisdom with courage is better than courage by itself alone. For a man would never prove himself loyal and sound in civil war if devoid of goodness in its entirety ; whereas in the war of which Tyrtaeus speaks there are vast numbers of mercenaries ready to die fighting [2] "with well-planted feet apart," of whom the majority, with but few exceptions, prove themselves reckless, unjust, violent, and pre-eminently foolish. What, then, is the conclusion to which our present discourse is tending, and what point is it trying to make clear by these statements ? Plainly it is this : both the Heaven-taught legislator of Crete and every legislator who is worth his salt will most assuredly legislate always with a single eye to

[1] Theognis, v. 77–8 (Bergk). He wrote sententious poetry about 550 B.C.

[2] Tyrt. xi. 21.

---

[4] ἄλλοσε Heindorf : ἄλλο MSS.

630 πρὸς τὴν μεγίστην ἀρετὴν μάλιστα βλέπων ἀεὶ
θήσει τοὺς νόμους· ἔστι δέ, ὥς φησι Θέογνις, αὕτη
πιστότης ἐν τοῖς δεινοῖς, ἥν τις δικαιοσύνην ἂν
τελέαν ὀνομάσειεν. ἣν δ' αὖ Τύρταιος ἐπήνεσε
D μάλιστα, καλὴ μὲν καὶ κατὰ καιρὸν κεκοσμημένη
τῷ ποιητῇ, τετάρτη μέντοι ὅμως ἀριθμῷ τε καὶ
δυνάμει τοῦ τιμία εἶναι λέγοιτ' ἂν ὀρθότατα.

ΚΛ. Ὦ ξένε, τὸν νομοθέτην ἡμῶν ἀποβάλλομεν
εἰς τοὺς πόρρω νομοθεσίας ;[1]

ΑΘ. Οὐχ ἡμεῖς γε, ὦ ἄριστε, ἀλλ' ἡμᾶς
αὐτούς, ὅταν οἰώμεθα πάντα τά τ' ἐν Λακεδαίμονι
καὶ τὰ τῇδε πρὸς τὸν πόλεμον μάλιστα βλέποντας
Λυκοῦργόν τε καὶ Μίνω τίθεσθαι τὰ νόμιμα.

ΚΛ. Τὸ δὲ πῶς χρὴν ἡμᾶς λέγειν ;

ΑΘ. Ὥσπερ τό τε ἀληθές, οἶμαι, καὶ τὸ δίκαιον
E ὑπέρ γε θείου ἀνδρὸς[2] διαλεγομένους λέγειν, οὐχ
ὡς πρὸς ἀρετῆς τι μόριον, καὶ ταῦτα τὸ φαυλότα-
τον, ἐτίθη βλέπων, ἀλλὰ πρὸς πᾶσαν ἀρετήν, καὶ
κατ' εἴδη ζητεῖν αὐτοὺς[3] τοὺς νόμους, οὐδ' ἅπερ
οἱ τῶν νῦν εἴδη προτιθέμενοι ζητοῦσιν· οὗ γὰρ
ἂν ἕκαστος ἐν χρείᾳ γίγνηται, τοῦτο ζητεῖ νῦν
παραθέμενος, ὁ μὲν τὰ περὶ τῶν κλήρων καὶ
ἐπικλήρων, ὁ δὲ τῆς αἰκίας πέρι, ἄλλοι δὲ ἄλλα
631 ἄττα μυρία τοιαῦτα· ἡμεῖς δέ φαμεν εἶναι τὸ περὶ
νόμους ζήτημα τῶν εὖ ζητούντων, ὥσπερ νῦν
ἡμεῖς ἠρξάμεθα. καὶ σοῦ τὴν μὲν ἐπιχείρησιν τῆς
ἐξηγήσεως περὶ τοὺς νόμους παντάπασιν ἄγαμαι·
τὸ γὰρ ἀπ' ἀρετῆς ἄρχεσθαι, λέγοντα ὡς ἐτίθη
ταύτης ἕνεκα τοὺς νόμους, ὀρθόν· ὅτι δὲ πάντα εἰς

---

[1] νομοθεσίας Ritter, Apelt : νομοθέτας MSS.
[2] θείου ἀνδρὸς Badham : θείας MSS.
[3] αὐτοὺς : αὐτῶν MSS.

the highest goodness and to that alone; and this
(to quote Theognis) consists in "loyalty in danger,"
and one might term it "complete righteousness."
But that goodness which Tyrtaeus specially praised,
fair though it be and fitly glorified by the poet,
deserves nevertheless to be placed no higher than
fourth in order and estimation.[1]

CLIN. We are degrading our own lawgiver,
Stranger, to a very low level!

ATH. Nay, my good Sir, it is ourselves we are
degrading, in so far as we imagine that it was with a
special view to war that Lycurgus and Minos laid
down all the legal usages here and in Lacedaemon.

CLIN. How, then, ought we to have stated the
matter?

ATH. In the way that is, as I think, true and
proper when talking of a divine hero. That is to
say, we should state that he enacted laws with an
eye not to some one fraction, and that the most
paltry, of goodness, but to goodness as a whole, and
that he devised the laws themselves according to
classes, though not the classes which the present
devisers propound. For everyone now brings forward and devises just the class which he needs: one
man deals with inheritances and heiresses, another
with cases of battery, and so on in endless variety.
But what we assert is that the devising of laws,
when rightly conducted, follows the procedure
which we have now commenced. Indeed, I greatly
admire the way you opened your exposition of the
laws; for to make a start with goodness and say that
that was the aim of the lawgiver is the right way.
But in your further statement that he legislated

[1] *i.e.* courage comes after wisdom, prudence and justice.

23

631 μόριον ἀρετῆς, καὶ ταῦτα τὸ σμικρότατον, ἐπανα-
φέροντα ἔφησθα αὐτὸν νομοθετεῖν, οὔτε ὀρθῶς ἔτι
μοι κατεφάνης λέγων τόν τε ὕστερον νῦν λόγον
τοῦτον πάντα εἴρηκα διὰ ταῦτα. πῇ δὴ οὖν σε
ἔτ᾽ ἂν ἐβουλόμην διελόμενον λέγειν αὐτός τε
B ἀκούειν ; βούλει σοι φράζω ;

ΚΛ. Πάνυ μὲν οὖν.

ΑΘ. ᾿Ω ξένε, ἐχρῆν εἰπεῖν, οἱ Κρητῶν νόμοι οὐκ
εἰσὶ μάτην διαφερόντως ἐν πᾶσιν εὐδόκιμοι τοῖς
Ἕλλησιν· ἔχουσι γὰρ ὀρθῶς τοὺς αὐτοῖς χρωμένους εὐδαίμονας ἀποτελοῦντες· πάντα γὰρ τὰ ἀγαθὰ
πορίζουσι. διπλᾶ δὲ ἀγαθά ἐστι, τὰ μὲν ἀνθρώπινα, τὰ δὲ θεῖα· ἤρτηται δ᾽ ἐκ τῶν θείων θάτερα·
καὶ ἐὰν μὲν δέχηταί τις τὰ μείζονα, παρίσταται [1]
καὶ τὰ ἐλάττονα, εἰ δὲ μή, στέρεται ἀμφοῖν·
C ἔστι δὲ τὰ μὲν ἐλάττονα ὧν ἡγεῖται μὲν ὑγίεια,
κάλλος δὲ δεύτερον, τὸ δὲ τρίτον ἰσχὺς εἴς τε
δρόμον καὶ εἰς τὰς ἄλλας πάσας κινήσεις τῷ
σώματι, τέταρτον δὲ δὴ πλοῦτος, οὐ τυφλός, ἀλλ᾽
ὀξὺ βλέπων, ἄνπερ ἅμ᾽ ἔπηται φρονήσει. ὃ δὴ
πρῶτον αὖ τῶν θείων ἡγεμονοῦν ἐστὶν ἀγαθῶν, ἡ
φρόνησις, δεύτερον δὲ μετὰ νοῦ σώφρων ψυχῆς
ἕξις· ἐκ δὲ τούτων μετ᾽ ἀνδρίας κραθέντων τρίτον
D ἂν εἴη δικαιοσύνη, τέταρτον δὲ ἀνδρία. ταῦτα δὲ
πάντα ἐκείνων ἔμπροσθεν τέτακται φύσει, καὶ δὴ
καὶ τῷ νομοθέτῃ τακτέον οὕτω. μετὰ δὲ ταῦτα
τὰς ἄλλας προστάξεις τοῖς πολίταις εἰς ταῦτα
βλεπούσας αὐτοῖς εἶναι διακελευστέον, τούτων δὲ
τὰ μὲν ἀνθρώπινα εἰς τὰ θεῖα, τὰ δὲ θεῖα εἰς τὸν
ἡγεμόνα νοῦν ξύμπαντα βλέπειν. περί τε γάμους
ἀλλήλοις ἐπικοινουμένους, μετά τε ταῦτα ἐν

[1] παρίσταται Badham, Schanz : πόλις, κτᾶται MSS.

wholly with reference to a fraction of goodness, and that the smallest fraction, you seemed to me to be in error, and all this latter part of my discourse was because of that. What then is the manner of exposition I should have liked to have heard from you? Shall I tell you?

CLIN. Yes, by all means.

ATH. "O Stranger" (thus you ought to have said), "it is not for nothing that the laws of the Cretans are held in superlatively high repute among all the Hellenes. For they are true laws inasmuch as they effect the well-being of those who use them by supplying all things that are good. Now goods are of two kinds, human and divine; and the human goods are dependent on the divine, and he who receives the greater acquires also the less, or else he is bereft of both. The lesser goods are those of which health ranks first, beauty second; the third is strength, in running and all other bodily exercises; and the fourth is wealth—no blind god Plutus, but keen of sight, provided that he has wisdom for companion. And wisdom, in turn, has first place among the goods that are divine, and rational temperance of soul comes second; from these two, when united with courage, there issues justice, as the third; and the fourth is courage. Now all these are by nature ranked before the human goods, and verily the lawgiver also must so rank them. Next, it must be proclaimed to the citizens that all the other instructions they receive have these in view; and that, of these goods themselves, the human look up to the divine, and the divine to reason as their chief. And in regard to their marriage connexions, and to their

631 ταῖς τῶν παίδων γεννήσεσι καὶ τροφαῖς, ὅσοι τε
ἄρρενες καὶ ὅσαι θήλειαι, νέων τε ὄντων καὶ ἐπὶ
E τὸ πρεσβύτερον ἰόντων μέχρι γήρως, τιμῶντα
ὀρθῶς ἐπιμελεῖσθαι δεῖ καὶ ἀτιμάζοντα, ἐν πάσαις
ταῖς τούτων ὁμιλίαις τάς τε λύπας αὐτῶν καὶ
τὰς ἡδονὰς καὶ τὰς ἐπιθυμίας ξυμπάντων τε
632 ἐρώτων τὰς σπουδὰς ἐπεσκεμμένον καὶ παραπεφυ-
λαχότα ψέγειν τε ὀρθῶς καὶ ἐπαινεῖν δι' αὐτῶν
τῶν νόμων. ἐν ὀργαῖς τε αὖ καὶ ἐν φόβοις, ὅσαι
τε διὰ δυστυχίαν ταραχαὶ ταῖς ψυχαῖς γίγνονται
καὶ ὅσαι ἐν εὐτυχίαις τῶν τοιούτων ἀποφυγαί,
ὅσα τε κατὰ νόσους ἢ κατὰ πολέμους ἢ πενίας ἢ
τὰ τούτοις ἐναντία γιγνόμενα προσπίπτει τοῖς
B ἀνθρώποις παθήματα, ἐν πᾶσι τοῖς τοιούτοις τῆς
ἑκάστων διαθέσεως διδακτέον καὶ ὁριστέον τό τε
καλὸν καὶ μή. μετὰ δὲ ταῦτα ἀνάγκη τὸν νομοθέτην τὰς κτήσεις τῶν πολιτῶν καὶ τὰ ἀναλώ-
ματα φυλάττειν, ὅντινα ἂν γίγνηται τρόπον,
καὶ τὰς πρὸς ἀλλήλους πᾶσι τούτοις κοινωνίας
καὶ διαλύσεις ἑκούσί τε καὶ ἄκουσι, καθ' ὁποῖον
ἂν ἕκαστον πράττωσι τῶν τοιούτων πρὸς ἀλλήλους, ἐπισκοπεῖν τό τε δίκαιον καὶ μή, ἐν οἷς ἐστί
τε καὶ ἐν οἷς ἐλλείπει, καὶ τοῖς μὲν εὐπειθέσι
τῷ νόμῳ[1] τιμὰς ἀπονέμειν, τοῖς δὲ δυσπειθέσι
C δίκας τακτὰς ἐπιτιθέναι, μέχριπερ ἂν πρὸς τέλος
ἁπάσης πολιτείας ἐπεξελθὼν ἴδῃ τῶν τελευτησάντων τίνα δεῖ τρόπον ἑκάστοις γίγνεσθαι τὰς
ταφὰς καὶ τιμὰς ἅστινας αὐτοῖς ἀπονέμειν δεῖ.
κατιδὼν δὲ ὁ θεὶς τοὺς νόμους ἅπασι τούτοις
φύλακας ἐπιστήσει, τοὺς μὲν διὰ φρονήσεως, τοὺς

---

1 τῷ νόμῳ Stephens : τῶν νόμων MSS.

subsequent breeding and rearing of children, male and female, both during youth and in later life up to old age, the lawgiver must supervise the citizens, duly apportioning honour and dishonour; and in regard to all their forms of intercourse he must observe and watch their pains and pleasures and desires and all intense passions, and distribute praise and blame correctly by the means of the laws themselves. Moreover, in the matter of anger and of fear, and of all the disturbances which befall souls owing to misfortune, and of all the avoidances thereof which occur in good-fortune, and of all the experiences which confront men through disease or war or penury or their opposites,—in regard to all these definite instruction must be given as to what is the right and what the wrong disposition in each case. It is necessary, in the next place, for the lawgiver to keep a watch on the methods employed by the citizens in gaining and spending money, and to supervise the associations they form with one another, and the dissolutions thereof, whether they be voluntary or under compulsion; he must observe the manner in which they conduct each of these mutual transactions, and note where justice obtains and where it is lacking. To those that are obedient he must assign honours by law, but on the disobedient he must impose duly appointed penalties. Then finally, when he arrives at the completion of the whole constitution, he has to consider in what manner in each case the burial of the dead should be carried out, and what honours should be assigned to them. This being settled, the framer of the laws will hand over all his statutes to the charge of Wardens—guided some by wisdom, others by true

PLATO

632 δὲ δι' ἀληθοῦς δόξης ἰόντας, ὅπως πάντα ταῦτα
ξυνδήσας ὁ νοῦς ἑπόμενα σωφροσύνῃ καὶ δικαιο-
σύνῃ ἀποφήνῃ, ἀλλὰ μὴ πλούτῳ μηδὲ φιλοτιμίᾳ.

D οὕτως, ὦ ξένοι, ἔγωγε ἤθελον ἂν ὑμᾶς, καὶ ἔτι νῦν
βούλομαι, διεξελθεῖν πῶς ἐν τοῖς τοῦ Διὸς λεγομένοις νόμοις τοῖς τε τοῦ Πυθίου Ἀπόλλωνος, οὓς
Μίνως τε καὶ Λυκοῦργος ἐθέτην, ἔνεστί τε πάντα
ταῦτα, καὶ ὅπη τάξιν τινὰ εἰληφότα διάδηλά ἐστι
τῷ περὶ νόμων ἐμπείρῳ τέχνῃ εἴτε καί τισιν ἔθεσι,
τοῖς δὲ ἄλλοις ἡμῖν οὐδαμῶς ἐστὶ καταφανῆ.

ΚΛ. Πῶς οὖν, ὦ ξένε, λέγειν χρὴ τὰ μετὰ
ταῦτα ;

ΑΘ. Ἐξ ἀρχῆς πάλιν ἔμοιγε δοκεῖ χρῆναι δι-
E εξελθεῖν, καθάπερ ἠρξάμεθα, τὰ τῆς ἀνδρίας πρῶτον ἐπιτηδεύματα· ἔπειτα ἕτερον καὶ αὖθις ἕτερον
εἶδος τῆς ἀρετῆς διέξιμεν, ἐὰν βούλησθε· ὅπως δ'
ἂν τὸ πρῶτον διεξέλθωμεν, πειρασόμεθα αὐτὸ
παράδειγμα θέμενοι καὶ τἆλλα οὕτω διαμυθολο-
γοῦντες παραμύθια ποιήσασθαι τῆς ὁδοῦ· ὕστερον
δὲ ἀρετῆς πάσης, ἅ γε νῦν δὴ διήλθομεν, ἐκεῖσε
βλέποντα ἀποφανοῦμεν, ἂν θεὸς ἐθέλῃ.

633 ΜΕ. Καλῶς λέγεις, καὶ πειρῶ πρῶτον κρίνειν
τὸν τοῦ Διὸς ἐπαινέτην τόνδε ἡμῖν.

ΑΘ. Πειράσομαι καὶ σέ τε καὶ ἐμαυτόν· κοινὸς
γὰρ ὁ λόγος· λέγετε οὖν· τὰ ξυσσίτιά φαμεν καὶ
τὰ γυμνάσια πρὸς τὸν πόλεμον ἐξευρῆσθαι τῷ
νομοθέτῃ ;

28

LAWS, BOOK I

opinion—to the end that Reason, having bound all
into one single system, may declare them to be
ancillary neither to wealth nor ambition, but to
temperance and justice.'' In this manner, Strangers,
I could have wished (and I wish it still) that you had
fully explained how all these regulations are inherent
in the reputed laws of Zeus and in those of the
Pythian Apollo which were ordained by Minos and
Lycurgus, and how their systematic arrangement is
quite evident to him who, whether by art or practice,
is an expert in law, although it is by no means
obvious to the rest of us.

CLIN. What then, Stranger, should be the next
step in our argument?

ATH. We ought, as I think, to do as we did at
first—start from the beginning to explain first
the institutions which have to do with courage;
and after that we shall, if you wish, deal with a
second and a third form of goodness. And as soon
as we have completed our treatment of the first
theme, we shall take that as our model and by a
discussion of the rest on similar lines beguile the
way; and at the end of our treatment of goodness
in all its forms we shall make it clear, if God will,
that the rules we discussed just now had goodness
for their aim.

MEG. A good suggestion! And begin with our
friend here, the panegyrist of Zeus—try first to put
him to the test.

ATH. Try I will, and to test you too and myself;
for the argument concerns us all alike. Tell me
then: do we assert that the common meals and the
gymnasia were devised by the lawgiver with a view
to war?

633 ΜΕ. Ναί.

ΑΘ. Καὶ τρίτον ἢ τέταρτον; ἴσως γὰρ ἂν
οὕτω χρείη διαριθμήσασθαι καὶ περὶ τῶν τῆς
ἄλλης ἀρετῆς εἴτε μερῶν εἴτε ἄττ' αὐτὰ καλεῖν
χρεών ἐστι, δηλοῦντα μόνον ἃ λέγει.

Β ΜΕ. Τρίτον τοίνυν, ἔγωγε εἴποιμ' ἂν καὶ Λακεδαιμονίων ὁστισοῦν, τὴν θήραν εὗρε.

ΑΘ. Τέταρτον δὲ ἢ πέμπτον εἰ δυναίμεθα
λέγειν πειρώμεθα.

ΜΕ. Ἔτι τοίνυν καὶ τὸ τέταρτον ἔγωγε πειρώ-
μην ἂν λέγειν τὸ περὶ τὰς καρτερήσεις τῶν ἀλγηδόνων πολὺ παρ' ἡμῖν γιγνόμενον ἔν τε ταῖς πρὸς
ἀλλήλους ταῖς χερσὶ μάχαις καὶ ἐν ἁρπαγαῖς τισὶ
διὰ πολλῶν πληγῶν ἑκάστοτε γιγνομέναις·[1] ἔτι
δὲ καὶ κρυπτεία τις ὀνομάζεται θαυμαστῶς πολύ-
C πονος πρὸς τὰς καρτερήσεις, χειμώνων τε ἀνυπο-
δησίαι καὶ ἀστρωσίαι καὶ ἄνευ θεραπόντων αὐτοῖς
ἑαυτῶν διακονήσεις, νύκτωρ τε πλανωμένων διὰ
πάσης τῆς χώρας καὶ μεθ' ἡμέραν. ἔτι δὲ κἂν
ταῖς γυμνοπαιδιαῖς δειναὶ καρτερήσεις παρ' ἡμῖν
γίγνονται τῇ τοῦ πνίγους ῥώμῃ διαμαχομένων,
καὶ πάμπολλα ἕτερα, σχεδὸν ὅσα οὐκ ἂν παύ-
σαιτό τις ἑκάστοτε διεξιών.

ΑΘ. Εὖ γε, ὦ Λακεδαιμόνιε ξένε, λέγεις. τὴν
ἀνδρίαν δέ, φέρε, τί θῶμεν; πότερον ἁπλῶς
οὕτως εἶναι πρὸς φόβους καὶ λύπας διαμάχην
D μόνον, ἢ καὶ πρὸς πόθους τε καὶ ἡδονὰς καί τινας
δεινὰς θωπείας κολακικάς, αἳ καὶ τῶν σεμνῶν

---

[1] γιγνομέναις Ast, Schanz: γιγνομένων MSS.

LAWS, BOOK I

MEG. Yes.

ATH. And is there a third institution of the kind, and a fourth? For probably one ought to employ this method of enumeration also in dealing with the subdivisions (or whatever we ought to call them) of the other forms of goodness, if only one makes one's meaning clear.

MEG. The third thing he devised was hunting: so I and every Lacedaemonian would say.

ATH. Let us attempt also to state what comes fourth,—and fifth too, if possible.

MEG. The fourth also I may attempt to state: it is the training, widely prevalent amongst us, in hardy endurance of pain, by means both of manual contests and of robberies carried out every time at the risk of a sound drubbing; moreover, the "Crypteia," [1] as it is called, affords a wonderfully severe training in hardihood, as the men go bare-foot in winter and sleep without coverlets and have no attendants, but wait on themselves and rove through the whole countryside both by night and by day. Moreover in our games,[2] we have severe tests of endurance, when men unclad do battle with the violence of the heat,—and there are other instances so numerous that the recital of them would be well-nigh endless.

ATH. Splendid, O Stranger of Lacedaemon! But come now, as to courage, how shall we define it? Shall we define it quite simply as battling against fears and pains only, or as against desires also and pleasures, with their dangerous enticements and

[1] Or "Secret Service." Young Spartans policed the country to suppress risings among the Helots.
[2] The "Naked Games," held about midsummer.

633 οἰομένων εἶναι τοὺς θυμοὺς [μαλάττουσαι]¹
κηρίνους ποιοῦσιν;

ΜΕ. Οἶμαι μὲν οὕτω, πρὸς ταῦτα ξύμπαντα.

ΑΘ. Εἰ γοῦν μεμνήμεθα τοὺς ἔμπροσθεν λόγους,
ἥττω τινὰ ὅδε καὶ πόλιν ἔλεγεν αὐτὴν αὑτῆς καὶ
ἄνδρα. ἢ γάρ, ὦ ξένε Κνώσιε;

ΚΛ. Καὶ πάνυ γε.

Ε ΑΘ. Νῦν οὖν πότερα λέγομεν τὸν τῶν λυπῶν
ἥττω κακὸν ἢ καὶ τὸν τῶν ἡδονῶν;

ΚΛ. Μᾶλλον, ἔμοιγε δοκεῖ, τὸν τῶν ἡδονῶν· καὶ
πάντες που μᾶλλον λέγομεν τὸν ὑπὸ τῶν ἡδονῶν
κρατούμενον τοῦτον τὸν ἐπονειδίστως ἥττονα
ἑαυτοῦ πρότερον ἢ τὸν ὑπὸ τῶν λυπῶν.

634 ΑΘ. Ὁ Διὸς οὖν δὴ καὶ ὁ Πυθικὸς νομοθέτης
οὐ δή που χωλὴν τὴν ἀνδρίαν νενομοθετήκατον,
πρὸς τὰ ἀριστερὰ μόνον δυναμένην ἀντιβαίνειν,
πρὸς δὲ τὰ δεξιὰ καὶ κομψὰ καὶ θωπευτικὰ
ἀδυνατοῦσαν; ἢ πρὸς ἀμφότερα;

ΚΛ. Πρὸς ἀμφότερα ἔγωγε ἀξιῶ.

ΑΘ. Λέγωμεν τοίνυν πάλιν, ἐπιτηδεύματα ποῖα
ἔσθ' ὑμῖν ἀμφοτέραις ταῖς πόλεσιν, ἃ γεύοντα
τῶν ἡδονῶν καὶ οὐ φεύγοντα αὐτάς, καθάπερ τὰς
λύπας οὐκ ἔφευγεν ἀλλ' ἄγοντα εἰς μέσας ἠνάγ-
Β καζε καὶ ἔπειθε τιμαῖς ὥστε κρατεῖν αὐτῶν· ποῦ
δὴ τοῦτ' ἔστι ταὐτὸν περὶ τὰς ἡδονὰς συντεταγ-
μένον ἐν τοῖς νόμοις; λεγέσθω, τί τοῦτ' ἐστὶν ὃ
καὶ ἀπεργάζεται ὑμῖν ὁμοίως πρός τε ἀλγηδόνας
καὶ πρὸς ἡδονὰς τοὺς αὐτοὺς ἀνδρείους νικῶντάς

---

¹ [μαλάττουσαι] omitted by best MSS.

flatteries, which melt men's hearts like wax—even men most reverenced in their own conceit.

MEG. The latter definition is, I think, the right one : courage is battling against them all.

ATH. Earlier in our discourse (if I am not mistaken) Clinias here used the expression " self-inferior " of a State or an individual : did you not do so, O Stranger of Cnosus ?

CLIN. Most certainly.

ATH. At present do we apply the term "bad " to the man who is inferior to pains, or to him also who is inferior to pleasures ?

CLIN. To the man who is inferior to pleasures more than to the other, in my opinion. All of us, indeed, when we speak of a man who is shamefully self-inferior, mean one who is mastered by pleasures rather than one who is mastered by pains.

ATH. Then surely the lawgiver of Zeus and he of Apollo did not enact by law a lame kind of courage, able only to defend itself on the left and unable to resist attractions and allurements on the right, but rather one able to resist on both sides ?

CLIN. On both sides, as I would maintain.

ATH. Let us, then, mention once more the State institutions in both your countries which give men a taste of pleasures instead of shunning them,—just as they did not shun pains but plunged their citizens into the midst of them and so compelled them, or induced them by rewards, to master them. Where, pray, in your laws is the same policy adopted in regard to pleasures ? Let us declare what regulation of yours there is which causes the same men to be courageous toward pains and pleasures alike,

634 τε ἃ δεῖ νικᾶν καὶ οὐδαμῶς ἥττους πολεμίων τῶν
ἐγγύτατα ἑαυτῶν καὶ χαλεπωτάτων.

ΜΕ. Οὕτω μὲν τοίνυν, ὦ ξένε, καθάπερ πρὸς
τὰς ἀλγηδόνας εἶχον νόμους ἀντιτεταγμένους
πολλοὺς εἰπεῖν, οὐκ ἂν ἴσως εὐποροίην κατὰ
μεγάλα μέρη καὶ διαφανῆ λέγων περὶ τῶν ἡδονῶν·
C κατὰ δὲ σμικρὰ ἴσως εὐποροίην ἄν.

ΚΛ. Οὐ μὴν οὐδ' ἂν αὐτός ἔγωγε ἐν τοῖς κατὰ
Κρήτην νόμοις ἔχοιμι ἐμφανὲς ὁμοίως ποιεῖν τὸ
τοιοῦτον.

ΑΘ. Ὦ ἄριστοι ξένων, καὶ οὐδέν γε θαυμαστόν.
ἀλλ' ἂν ἄρα τις ἡμῶν περὶ τοὺς ἑκάστων οἴκοι
νόμους ψέξῃ τι, βουλόμενος ἰδεῖν τό τε ἀληθὲς
ἅμα καὶ τὸ βέλτιστον, μὴ χαλεπῶς ἀλλὰ πράως
ἀποδεχώμεθα ἀλλήλων.

D ΚΛ. Ὀρθῶς, ὦ ξένε Ἀθηναῖε, εἴρηκας, καὶ
πειστέον.

ΑΘ. Οὐ γὰρ ἄν, ὦ Κλεινία, τηλικοῖσδε ἀνδράσι
πρέποι τὸ τοιοῦτον.

ΚΛ. Οὐ γὰρ οὖν.

ΑΘ. Εἰ μὲν τοίνυν ὀρθῶς ἢ μή τις ἐπιτιμᾷ τῇ
τε Λακωνικῇ καὶ τῇ Κρητικῇ πολιτείᾳ, [ὁ] λόγος
ἂν ἕτερος εἴη· τὰ δ' οὖν λεγόμενα πρὸς τῶν
πολλῶν ἴσως ἐγὼ μᾶλλον ἔχοιμ' ἂν ὑμῶν ἀμφοτέρων λέγειν. ὑμῖν μὲν γάρ, εἴπερ καὶ μετρίως
κατεσκεύασται τὰ τῶν νόμων, εἷς τῶν καλλίστων
ἂν εἴη νόμων μὴ ζητεῖν τῶν νέων μηδένα ἐᾶν ποῖα
E καλῶς αὐτῶν ἢ μὴ καλῶς ἔχει, μιᾷ δὲ φωνῇ καὶ
ἐξ ἑνὸς στόματος πάντας συμφωνεῖν ὡς πάντα
καλῶς κεῖται θέντων θεῶν, καὶ ἐάν τις ἄλλως
λέγῃ, μὴ ἀνέχεσθαι τὸ παράπαν ἀκούοντας·
γέρων δὲ εἴ τίς τι ξυννοεῖ τῶν παρ' ὑμῖν, πρὸς

conquering where they ought to conquer and in no wise worsted by their nearest and most dangerous enemies.

MEG. Although, Stranger, I was able to mention a number of laws that dealt with mastery over pains, in the case of pleasures I may not find it equally easy to produce important and conspicuous examples; but I might perhaps furnish some minor instances.

CLIN. Neither could I in like manner give myself clear examples from the Cretan laws.

ATH. And no wonder, my most excellent friends. If then, in his desire to discover what is true and superlatively good, any one of us should find fault with any domestic law of his neighbours, let us take one another's remarks in good part and without resentment.

CLIN. You are right, Stranger: that is what we must do.

ATH. Yes, for resentment would ill become men of our years.

CLIN. Ill indeed.

ATH. Whether men are right or wrong in their censures of the Laconian polity and the Cretan— that is another story; anyhow, what is actually said by most men I, probably, am in a better position to state than either of you. For in your case (your laws being wisely framed) one of the best of your laws will be that which enjoins that none of the youth shall inquire which laws are wrong and which right, but all shall declare in unison, with one mouth and one voice, that all are rightly established by divine enactment, and shall turn a deaf ear to anyone who says otherwise; and further, that if any old man has any stricture to pass on any of your

634 ἄρχοντά τε καὶ πρὸς ἡλικιώτην μηδενὸς ἐναντίον
νέου ποιεῖσθαι τοὺς τοιούτους λόγους.

ΚΛ. Ὀρθότατά γε, ὦ ξένε, λέγεις, καὶ καθάπερ
635 μάντις ἀπὼν τῆς τότε διανοίας τοῦ τιθέντος αὐτὰ
νῦν ἐπιεικῶς μοι δοκεῖς ἐστοχάσθαι καὶ σφόδρα
ἀληθῆ λέγειν.

ΑΘ. Οὐκοῦν ἡμῖν τὰ νῦν ἐρημία μὲν νέων,
αὐτοὶ δ' ἕνεκα γήρως ἀφείμεθ' ὑπὸ τοῦ νομοθέτου
διαλεγόμενοι περὶ αὐτῶν τούτων μόνοι πρὸς
μόνους μηδὲν ἂν πλημμελεῖν ;

ΚΛ. Ἔστι ταῦτα· οὕτως[εἰς ἃ]¹ καὶ μηδέν γε
ἀνῇς ἐπιτιμῶν τοῖς νόμοις ἡμῶν· οὐ γὰρ τό γε
γνῶναί τι τῶν μὴ καλῶν ἄτιμον, ἀλλὰ ἴασιν ἐξ
αὐτοῦ συμβαίνει γίγνεσθαι τῷ μὴ φθόνῳ τὰ λεγό-
B μενα ἀλλ' εὐνοίᾳ δεχομένῳ.

ΑΘ. Καλῶς. οὐ μὴν ἐπιτιμῶν γε ἐρῶ τοῖς
νόμοις πω πρὶν βεβαίως εἰς δύναμιν διασκέψασθαι,
μᾶλλον δὲ ἀπορῶν. ὑμῖν γὰρ ὁ νομοθέτης μόνοις
Ἑλλήνων καὶ βαρβάρων, ὧν ἡμεῖς πυνθανόμεθα,
τῶν μεγίστων ἡδονῶν καὶ παιδιῶν ἐπέταξεν
ἀπέχεσθαι καὶ μὴ γεύεσθαι, τὸ δὲ τῶν λυπῶν καὶ
φόβων, ὅπερ ἄρτι διεληλύθαμεν, ἡγήσατο εἴ τις
ἐκ παίδων φευξεῖται διὰ τέλους, ὁπόταν εἰς
C ἀναγκαίους ἔλθῃ πόνους καὶ φόβους καὶ λύπας,
φευξεῖσθαι τοὺς ἐν ἐκείνοις γεγυμνασμένους καὶ
δουλεύσειν αὐτοῖς. ταὐτὸν δὴ τοῦτ', οἶμαι, καὶ πρὸς
τὰς ἡδονὰς ἔδει διανοεῖσθαι τὸν αὐτὸν νομοθέτην,
λέγοντα αὐτὸν πρὸς ἑαυτὸν ὡς ἡμῖν ἐκ νέων εἰ
ἄπειροι τῶν μεγίστων ἡδονῶν οἱ πολῖται γενή-

---

¹ [εἰς ἃ] bracketed by England.

36

laws, he must not utter such views in the presence
of any young man, but before a magistrate or one
of his own age.

CLIN. A very sound observation, Stranger; and
just like a diviner, far away though you are from
the original lawgiver, you have fairly spotted, as I
think, his intention, and described it with perfect
truth.

ATH. Well, there are no young people with us
now; so we may be permitted by the lawgiver, old
as we are, to discuss these matters among ourselves
privately without offence.

CLIN. That is so. Do you, then, have no scruple
in censuring our laws; for there is nothing discreditable in being told of some flaw; rather it is
just this which leads to a remedy, if the criticism be
accepted not peevishly but in a friendly spirit.

ATH. Good! But until I have investigated your
laws as carefully as I can I shall not censure them
but rather express the doubts I feel. You alone of
Greeks and barbarians, so far as I can discover,
possess a lawgiver who charged you to abstain from
the greatest of pleasures and amusements and taste
them not; but concerning pains and fears, as we
said before, he held the view that anyone who shuns
them continuously from childhood onward, when
confronted with unavoidable hardships and fears and
pains, will be put to flight by the men who are
trained in such things, and will become their slave.
Now I presume that this same lawgiver should have
held the same view about pleasures as well, and
should have argued with himself that, if our citizens
grow up from their youth unpractised in the greatest
pleasures, the consequence must be that, when they

37

635 σονται, [καὶ]¹ ἀμελέτητοι γιγνόμενοι ἐν ταῖς
ἡδοναῖς καρτερεῖν καὶ μηδὲν τῶν αἰσχρῶν ἀναγ-
D κάζεσθαι ποιεῖν ἕνεκα τῆς γλυκυθυμίας τῆς πρὸς
τὰς ἡδονάς, ταὐτὸν πείσονται τοῖς ἡττωμένοις τῶν
φόβων· δουλεύσουσι τρόπον ἕτερον καὶ ἔτ᾽ αἰσχίω
τοῖς γε δυναμένοις καρτερεῖν ἐν ταῖς ἡδοναῖς καὶ
τοῖς κεκτημένοις τὰ περὶ τὰς ἡδονάς, ἀνθρώποις
ἐνίοτε παντάπασι κακοῖς, καὶ τὴν ψυχὴν τῇ μὲν
δούλην τῇ δὲ ἐλευθέραν ἕξουσι, καὶ οὐκ ἄξιοι
ἁπλῶς ἀνδρεῖοι καὶ ἐλευθέριοι ἔσονται προσαγο-
ρεύεσθαι. σκοπεῖτε οὖν εἴ τι τῶν νῦν λεγομένων
ὑμῖν κατὰ τρόπον δοκεῖ λέγεσθαι.
E ΚΛ. Δοκεῖ μὲν ἡμῖν γέ πως λεγομένου τοῦ
λόγου, περὶ δὲ τηλικούτων εὐθὺς πεπιστευκέναι
ῥᾳδίως μὴ νέων τε ᾖ μᾶλλον καὶ ἀνοήτων.
ΑΘ. Ἀλλ᾽ εἰ τὸ μετὰ ταῦτα διεξίοιμεν ὧν
προὐθέμεθα, ὦ Κλεινία τε καὶ Λακεδαιμόνιε ξένε,
—μετ᾽ ἀνδρίαν γὰρ δὴ σωφροσύνης πέρι λέγωμεν,
—μῶν τι² διαφέρον ἐν ταύταις ταῖς πολιτείαις
ἢ 'ν ταῖς τῶν εἰκῇ πολιτευομένων ἀνευρήσομεν,
636 ὥσπερ τὰ περὶ τὸν πόλεμον νῦν δή ;
ΜΕ. Σχεδὸν οὐ ῥᾴδιον· ἀλλ᾽ ἔοικε γὰρ τά τε
ξυσσίτια καὶ τὰ γυμνάσια καλῶς εὑρῆσθαι πρὸς
ἀμφοτέρας.
ΑΘ. Ἔοικε δῆτα, ὦ ξένοι, χαλεπὸν εἶναι τὸ
περὶ τὰς πολιτείας ἀναμφισβητήτως ὁμοίως ἔργῳ
καὶ λόγῳ γίγνεσθαι. κινδυνεύει γάρ, καθάπερ
ἐν τοῖς σώμασιν, οὐ δυνατὸν εἶναι προστάξαι τι
πρὸς ἓν σῶμα ἓν ἐπιτήδευμα, ἐν ᾧ οὐκ ἂν φανείη

¹ [καὶ] bracketed by W.-Möllendorff.
² μῶν τι Badham : τί MSS. (after ἢ I insert 'ν).

find themselves amongst pleasures without being trained in the duty of resisting them and of refusing to commit any disgraceful act, because of the natural attraction of pleasures, they will suffer the same fate as those who are worsted by fears : they will, that is to say, in another and still more shameful fashion be enslaved by those who are able to hold out amidst pleasures and those who are versed in the art of pleasure,—people who are sometimes wholly vicious : thus their condition of soul will be partly enslaved and partly free, and they will not deserve to be called, without qualification, free men and men of courage. Consider, then, whether you at all approve these remarks of mine.

CLIN. On the face of them, we are inclined to approve ; but to yield quick and easy credence in matters of such importance would, I fear, be rash and thoughtless.

ATH. Well then, O Clinias, and thou, Stranger of Lacedaemon, suppose we discuss the second of the subjects we proposed, and take temperance next after courage : shall we discover any point in which these polities are superior to those framed at random, as we found just now in regard to their military organisation ?

MEG. Hardly an easy matter ! Yet probably the common meals and the gymnasia are well devised to foster both these virtues.

ATH. In truth, Strangers, it seems a difficult thing for State institutions to be equally beyond criticism both in theory and in practice. Their case resembles that of the human body, where it seems impossible to prescribe any given treatment for each case without finding that this same prescription is

636 ταὐτὸν τοῦτο τὰ μὲν βλάπτον τὰ ἡμῶν σώματα,
B τὰ δὲ καὶ ὠφελοῦν· ἐπεὶ καὶ τὰ γυμνάσια ταῦτα
καὶ τὰ ξυσσίτια πολλὰ μὲν ἄλλα νῦν ὠφελεῖ τὰς
πόλεις, πρὸς δὲ τὰς στάσεις χαλεπά· δηλοῦσι δὲ
Μιλησίων καὶ Βοιωτῶν καὶ Θουρίων παῖδες. καὶ
δὴ καὶ πάλαι ὂν νόμιμον[1] δοκεῖ τοῦτο τὸ ἐπιτήδευμα καὶ <τὰς>[2] κατὰ φύσιν [τὰς] περὶ τὰ
ἀφροδίσια ἡδονὰς οὐ μόνον ἀνθρώπων ἀλλὰ καὶ
θηρίων διεφθαρκέναι. καὶ τούτων τὰς ὑμετέρας
πόλεις πρώτας ἄν τις αἰτιῷτο καὶ ὅσαι τῶν
C ἄλλων μάλιστα ἅπτονται τῶν γυμνασίων· καὶ
εἴτε παίζοντα εἴτε σπουδάζοντα ἐννοεῖν δεῖ τὰ
τοιαῦτα, ἐννοητέον ὅτι τῇ θηλείᾳ καὶ τῇ τῶν
ἀρρένων φύσει εἰς κοινωνίαν ἰούσῃ τῆς γεννήσεως
ἡ περὶ ταῦτα ἡδονὴ κατὰ φύσιν ἀποδεδόσθαι
δοκεῖ, ἀρρένων δὲ πρὸς ἄρρενας ἢ θηλειῶν πρὸς
θηλείας παρὰ φύσιν καὶ τῶν πρώτων τὸ τόλμημα
εἶναι δι' ἀκράτειαν ἡδονῆς. πάντες δὲ δὴ Κρητῶν
τὸν περὶ τὸν Γανυμήδη μῦθον κατηγοροῦμεν, ὡς
D λογοποιησάντων τούτων· ἐπειδὴ παρὰ Διὸς αὐτοῖς
οἱ νόμοι πεπιστευμένοι ἦσαν γεγονέναι, τοῦτον τὸν
μῦθον προστεθεικέναι κατὰ τοῦ Διός, ἵνα ἑπόμενοι
δὴ τῷ θεῷ καρπῶνται καὶ ταύτην τὴν ἡδονήν. τὸ
μὲν οὖν τοῦ μύθου χαιρέτω, νόμων δὲ πέρι δια-
σκοπουμένων ἀνθρώπων ὀλίγου πᾶσά ἐστιν ἡ
σκέψις περί τε τὰς ἡδονὰς καὶ τὰς λύπας ἔν τε
πόλεσι καὶ ἐν ἰδίοις ἤθεσι· δύο γὰρ αὗται πηγαὶ
μεθεῖνται φύσει ῥεῖν, ὧν ὁ μὲν ἀρυτόμενος ὅθεν
τε δεῖ καὶ ὁπότε καὶ ὁπόσον εὐδαιμονεῖ, καὶ πόλις

---

[1] πάλαι ὂν νόμιμον Boeckh : παλαιὸν νόμον MSS.
[2] <τὰς> added by Boeckh, bracketing the next [τὰς].

partly beneficial and partly injurious to the body. So these common meals, for example, and these gymnasia, while they are at present beneficial to the States in many other respects, yet in the event of civil strife they prove dangerous (as is shown by the case of the youth of Miletus, Bocotia and Thurii); [1] and, moreover, this institution, when of old standing, is thought to have corrupted the pleasures of love which are natural not to men only but also natural to beasts. For this your States are held primarily responsible, and along with them all others that especially encourage the use of gymnasia. And whether one makes the observation in earnest or in jest, one certainly should not fail to observe that when male unites with female for procreation the pleasure experienced is held to be due to nature, but contrary to nature when male mates with male or female with female, and that those first guilty of such enormities were impelled by their slavery to pleasure. And we all accuse the Cretans of concocting the story about Ganymede. Because it was the belief that they derived their laws from Zeus, they added on this story about Zeus in order that they might be following his example in enjoying this pleasure as well. Now with the story itself we have no more concern; but when men are investigating the subject of laws their investigation deals almost entirely with pleasures and pains, whether in States or in individuals. These are the two fountains which gush out by nature's impulse; and whoever draws from them a due supply at the due place and

---

[1] Plato here ascribes the revolutions which occurred in these places to the intensive military training of the youth. Thurii was a Greek town in S. Italy, an off-shoot of Sybaris.

636E ὁμοίως καὶ ἰδιώτης καὶ ζῶον ἅπαν, ὁ δ᾽ ἀνεπι-
στημόνως ἅμα καὶ ἐκτὸς τῶν καιρῶν τἀναντία
ἂν ἐκείνῳ ζῴη.

ΜΕ. Λέγεται μὲν ταῦτα, ὦ ξένε, καλῶς πως, οὐ
μὴν ἀλλ᾽ ἀφασία γ᾽ ἡμᾶς λαμβάνει τί ποτε χρὴ
λέγειν πρὸς ταῦτα. ὅμως δ᾽ ἔμοιγε ὀρθῶς δοκεῖ
τὸ τὰς ἡδονὰς φεύγειν διακελεύεσθαι τόν γε ἐν
Λακεδαίμονι νομοθέτην· περὶ δὲ τῶν ἐν Κνωσῷ
637 νόμων ὅδε, ἂν ἐθέλῃ, βοηθήσει. τὰ δ᾽ ἐν Σπάρτῃ
κάλλιστ᾽ ἀνθρώπων δοκεῖ μοι κεῖσθαι τὰ περὶ
τὰς ἡδονάς· οὗ γὰρ μάλιστ᾽ ἄνθρωποι καὶ
μεγίσταις προσπίπτουσιν ἡδοναῖς καὶ ὕβρεσι καὶ
ἀνοίᾳ πάσῃ, τοῦτ᾽ ἐξέβαλεν ὁ νόμος ἡμῶν ἐκ τῆς
χώρας ξυμπάσης, καὶ οὔτ᾽ ἂν ἐπ᾽ ἀγρῶν ἴδοις
οὔτ᾽ ἐν ἄστεσιν ὅσων Σπαρτιάταις μέλει συμπόσια
οὐδ᾽ ὁπόσα τούτοις ξυνεπόμενα πάσας ἡδονὰς
κινεῖ κατὰ δύναμιν, οὐδ᾽ ἔστιν ὅστις ἂν ἀπαντῶν
κωμάζοντί τινι μετὰ μέθης οὐκ ἂν τὴν μεγίστην
Β δίκην εὐθὺς ἐπιθείη, καὶ οὐδ᾽ ἂν Διονύσια
πρόφασιν ἔχοντ᾽ αὐτὸν ῥύσαιτο,[1] ὥσπερ ἐν
ἁμάξαις εἶδόν ποτε παρ᾽ ὑμῖν ἐγώ. καὶ ἐν
Τάραντι δὲ παρὰ τοῖς ἡμετέροις ἀποίκοις πᾶσαν
ἐθεασάμην τὴν πόλιν περὶ τὰ Διονύσια μεθύου-
σαν· παρ᾽ ἡμῖν δ᾽ οὐκ ἔστ᾽ οὐδὲν τοιοῦτον.

ΑΘ. Ὦ Λακεδαιμόνιε ξένε, ἐπαινετὰ μὲν πάντ᾽
ἐστὶ τὰ τοιαῦτα, ὅπου τινὲς ἔνεισι καρτερήσεις,
C ὅπου δ᾽ ἀνεῖνται, βλακικώτερα· ταχὺ γάρ σου

---

[1] ῥύσαιτο Athenaeus, England : λύσαιτο MSS.

time is blessed—be it a State or an individual or
any kind of creature; but whosoever does so without understanding and out of due season will fare
contrariwise.

MEG. What you say, Stranger, is excellent, I
suppose; none the less I am at a loss to know what
reply I should make to it. Still, in my opinion, the
Lacedaemonian lawgiver was right in ordaining the
avoidance of pleasures, while as to the laws of
Cnosus—our friend Clinias, if he thinks fit, will
defend them. The rules about pleasures at Sparta
seem to me the best in the world. For our law
banished entirely from the land that institution
which gives the most occasion for men to fall into
excessive pleasures and riotings and follies of every
description; neither in the country nor in the cities
controlled by Spartiates is a drinking-club to be seen
nor any of the practices which belong to such and
foster to the utmost all kinds of pleasure. Indeed
there is not a man who would not punish at once
and most severely any drunken reveller he chanced
to meet with, nor would even the feast of Dionysus
serve as an excuse to save him—a revel such as I
once upon a time witnessed "on the waggons"[1] in
your country; and at our colony of Tarentum, too,
I saw the whole city drunk at the Dionysia. But
with us no such thing is possible.

ATH. O Stranger of Lacedaemon, all such indul-
gences are praiseworthy where there exists a strain
of firm moral fibre, but where this is relaxed they
are quite stupid. An Athenian in self-defence

[1] At the Feast of Dionysus in Athens it was customary for
revellers mounted on waggons to indulge in scurrilous
language during the processions.

637 λάβοιτ' ἄν τις τῶν παρ' ἡμῶν ἀμυνόμενος, δεικνὺς
τὴν τῶν γυναικῶν παρ' ὑμῖν ἄνεσιν. ἅπασι δὴ
τοῖς τοιούτοις, καὶ ἐν Τάραντι καὶ παρ' ἡμῖν καὶ
παρ' ὑμῖν δέ, μία ἀπόκρισις ἀπολύεσθαι δοκεῖ
τοῦ μὴ κακῶς ἔχειν ἀλλ' ὀρθῶς· πᾶς γὰρ ἀποκρι-
νόμενος ἐρεῖ θαυμάζοντι ξένῳ, τὴν παρ' αὐτοῖς
ἀήθειαν ὁρῶντι, Μὴ θαύμαζε, ὦ ξένε· νόμος ἔσθ'
ἡμῖν οὗτος, ἴσως δ' ὑμῖν περὶ αὐτῶν τούτων
D ἕτερος. ἡμῖν δ' ἐστὶ νῦν, ὦ φίλοι ἄνδρες, οὐ περὶ
τῶν ἀνθρώπων τῶν ἄλλων ὁ λόγος, ἀλλὰ περὶ
τῶν νομοθετῶν αὐτῶν κακίας τε καὶ ἀρετῆς. ἔτι
γὰρ οὖν εἴπωμεν πλείω περὶ ἁπάσης μέθης· οὐ
γὰρ σμικρόν ἐστι τὸ ἐπιτήδευμα οὐδὲ φαύλου
διαγνῶναι νομοθέτου. λέγω δ' οὐκ οἴνου περὶ
πόσεως τὸ παράπαν ἢ μή, μέθης δὲ αὐτῆς πέρι,
πότερον ὥσπερ Σκύθαι χρῶνται καὶ Πέρσαι
χρηστέον, καὶ ἔτι Καρχηδόνιοι καὶ Κελτοὶ καὶ
E Ἴβηρες καὶ Θρᾷκες, πολεμικὰ ξύμπαντα ὄντα
ταῦτα γένη, ἢ καθάπερ ὑμεῖς· ὑμεῖς μὲν γάρ,
ὅπερ λέγεις, τὸ παράπαν ἀπέχεσθε, Σκύθαι δὲ
καὶ Θρᾷκες ἀκράτῳ παντάπασι χρώμενοι, γυναῖκές
τε καὶ αὐτοί, καὶ κατὰ τῶν ἱματίων καταχεόμενοι
καλὸν καὶ εὔδαιμον ἐπιτήδευμα ἐπιτηδεύειν νενο-
μίκασι. Πέρσαι δὲ σφόδρα μὲν χρῶνται καὶ ταῖς
ἄλλαις τρυφαῖς, ἃς ὑμεῖς ἀποβάλλετε, ἐν τάξει
δὲ μᾶλλον τούτων.

638 ΜΕ. Ὦ λῷστε, διώκομεν δέ γε ἡμεῖς πάντας
τούτους ὅταν ὅπλα εἰς τὰς χεῖρας λάβωμεν.

ΑΘ. Ὦ ἄριστε, μὴ λέγε ταῦτα· πολλαὶ γὰρ δὴ
φυγαὶ καὶ διώξεις ἀτέκμαρτοι γεγόνασί τε καὶ
ἔσονται, διὸ φανερὸν ὅρον τοῦτον οὐκ ἄν ποτε

might at once retaliate by pointing to the looseness of the women in your country. Regarding all such practices, whether in Tarentum, Athens or Sparta, there is one answer that is held to vindicate their propriety. The universal answer to the stranger who is surprised at seeing in a State some unwonted practice is this: "Be not surprised, O Stranger: such is the custom with us: with you, perhaps, the custom in these matters is different." But, my dear Sirs, our argument now is not concerned with the rest of mankind but with the goodness or badness of the lawgivers themselves. So let us deal more fully with the subject of drunkenness in general; for it is a practice of no slight importance, and it requires no mean legislator to understand it. I am now referring not to the drinking or non-drinking of wine generally, but to drunkenness pure and simple, and the question is—ought we to deal with it as the Scythians and Persians do and the Carthaginians also, and Celts, Iberians and Thracians, who are all warlike races, or as you Spartans do; for you, as you say, abstain from it altogether, whereas the Scythians and Thracians, both men and women, take their wine neat and let it pour down over their clothes, and regard this practice of theirs as a noble and splendid practice; and the Persians indulge greatly in these and other luxurious habits which you reject, albeit in a more orderly fashion than the others.

MEG. But we, my good Sir, when we take arms in our hands, put all these people to rout.

ATH. Say not so, my dear Sir; for there have been, in fact, in the past and there will be in the future many a flight and many a pursuit which are past explaining, so that victory or defeat in battle

638 λέγοιμεν ἀλλ᾽ ἀμφισβητήσιμον περὶ καλῶν
ἐπιτηδευμάτων καὶ μή, νίκην τε καὶ ἧτταν
λέγοντες μάχης. ἐπεὶ δὴ[1] γὰρ αἱ μείζους τὰς
ἐλάττους πόλεις νικῶσι μαχόμεναι καὶ κατα-
B δουλοῦνται, Συρακόσιοι μὲν Λοκρούς, οἳ δὴ
δοκοῦσιν εὐνομώτατοι τῶν περὶ ἐκεῖνον τὸν τόπον
γεγονέναι, Κείους δὲ Ἀθηναῖοι· μυρία δ᾽ ἄλλα
τοιαῦτ᾽ ἂν εὕροιμεν. ἀλλὰ περὶ αὐτοῦ ἑκάστου
ἐπιτηδεύματος πειρώμεθα λέγοντες πείθειν ἡμᾶς
αὐτούς, νίκας δὲ καὶ ἥττας ἐκτὸς λόγου τὰ νῦν
θῶμεν, λέγωμεν δ᾽ ὡς τὸ μὲν τοιόνδε ἐστὶ καλόν,
τὸ δὲ τοιόνδε οὐ καλόν. πρῶτον δ᾽ ἀκούσατέ τί
μου περὶ αὐτῶν τούτων ὡς δεῖ τό τε χρηστὸν καὶ
τὸ μὴ σκοπεῖν.

C ΜΕ. Πῶς οὖν δὴ λέγεις ;

ΑΘ. Δοκοῦσί μοι πάντες οἱ λόγῳ τι λαβόντες
ἐπιτήδευμα καὶ προθέμενοι ψέγειν αὐτὸ ἢ ἐπαινεῖν
εὐθὺς ῥηθὲν οὐδαμῶς δρᾶν κατὰ τρόπον, ἀλλὰ
ταὐτὸν ποιεῖν οἷον εἰ δή τις ἐπαινέσαντός τινος
τυρόν,[2] βρῶμα ὡς ἀγαθόν, εὐθὺς ψέγοι, μὴ
διαπυθόμενος αὐτοῦ μήτε τὴν ἐργασίαν μήτε τὴν
προσφοράν, ὅντινα τρόπον καὶ οἷστισι καὶ μεθ᾽
ὧν καὶ ὅπως ἔχοντα καὶ ὅπως [προσφέρειν][3]
D ἔχουσι· νῦν δὴ ταὐτόν μοι δοκοῦμεν ἡμεῖς ἐν τοῖς
λόγοις ποιεῖν· περὶ μέθης γὰρ ἀκούσαντες τοσοῦτον μόνον εὐθὺς οἱ μὲν ψέγειν αὐτό, οἱ δ᾽
ἐπαινεῖν, καὶ μάλα ἀτόπως. μάρτυσι γὰρ καὶ
ἐγγυηταῖς[4] χρώμενοι ἐπαινοῦμεν ἑκάτεροι, καὶ

---

[1] ἐπεὶ δὴ England : ἐπειδὴ MSS.
[2] τυρόν : τυρούς Cornarius : πυρούς MSS.
[3] [προσφέρειν] bracketed by Madvig, Schanz.
[4] ἐγγυηταῖς C. J. Post : ἐπαινέταις MSS., edd.

could never be called a decisive, but rather a questionable, test of the goodness or badness of an institution. Larger States, for example, are victorious in battle over smaller States, and we find the Syracusans subjugating the Locrians, who are reputed to have been the best-governed of the peoples in that part of the world: and the Athenians the Ceians,—and we could find countless other instances of the same kind. So let us leave victories and defeats out of account for the present, and discuss each several institution on its own merits in the endeavour to convince ourselves, and explain in what way one kind is good and another bad. And to begin with, listen to my account of the right method of inquiring into the merits and demerits of institutions.

MEG. What is your account of it?

ATH. In my opinion all those who take up an institution for discussion and propose, at its first mention, to censure it or commend it, are proceeding in quite the wrong way. Their action is like that of a man who, when he hears somebody praising cheese as a good food, at once starts to disparage it, without having learnt either its effects or its mode of administration—in what form it should be administered and by whom and with what accompaniments, and in what condition and to people in what condition. This, as it seems to me, is exactly what we are now doing in our discourse. At the first mention of the mere name of drunkenness, straightway we fall, some of us to blaming it, others to praising it; which is most absurd. Each party relies on the aid of witnesses, and while the one

638 οἱ μέν, ὅτι πολλοὺς παρεχόμεθα, ἀξιοῦμέν τι
λέγειν κύριον, οἱ δέ, ὅτι τοὺς μὴ χρωμένους αὐτῷ
ὁρῶμεν νικῶντας μαχομένους· ἀμφισβητεῖται δ᾽
αὖ καὶ τοῦθ᾽ ἡμῖν. εἰ μὲν δὴ καὶ περὶ ἑκάστων
οὕτω καὶ τῶν ἄλλων νομίμων διέξιμεν, οὐκ ἂν
Ε ἔμοιγε κατὰ νοῦν εἴη. τρόπον δὲ ἄλλον ὃν ἐμοὶ
φαίνεται δεῖν ἐθέλω λέγειν περὶ αὐτοῦ τούτου,
τῆς μέθης, πειρώμενος ἂν ἄρα δύνωμαι τὴν περὶ
ἁπάντων τῶν τοιούτων ὀρθὴν μέθοδον ἡμῖν δηλοῦν,
ἐπειδὴ καὶ μυρία ἐπὶ μυρίοις ἔθνη περὶ αὐτῶν
ἀμφισβητοῦντα ὑμῖν πόλεσι δυεῖν τῷ λόγῳ
διαμάχοιτ᾽ ἄν.

ΜΕ. Καὶ μὴν εἴ τινα ἔχομεν ὀρθὴν σκέψιν τῶν
639 τοιούτων, οὐκ ἀποκνητέον ἀκούειν.

ΑΘ. Σκεψώμεθα δή πῃ τῇδε· φέρε, εἴ τις αἰγῶν
τροφὴν καὶ τὸ ζῷον αὐτό, κτῆμα ὡς ἔστι καλόν,
ἐπαινοίη, ἄλλος δέ τις ἑωρακὼς αἶγας χωρὶς
νεμομένας αἰπόλου ἐν ἐργασίμοις χωρίοις δρώσας
κακὰ διαψέγοι, καὶ πᾶν θρέμμα ἄναρχον ἢ μετὰ
[τῶν] κακῶν ἀρχόντων ἰδὼν οὕτω μέμφοιτο, τὸν
τοῦ τοιούτου ψόγον ἡγούμεθα ὑγιὲς ἄν ποτε ψέξαι
καὶ ὁτιοῦν;

ΜΕ. Καὶ πῶς;

Β ΑΘ. Χρηστὸς δὲ ἄρχων ἔσθ᾽ ἡμῖν ἐν πλοίοις
πότερον ἐὰν τὴν ναυτικὴν ἔχῃ ἐπιστήμην μόνον,
ἄν τ᾽ οὖν ναυτιᾷ ἄν τε μή; ἢ πῶς ἂν λέγοιμεν;

ΜΕ. Οὐδαμῶς, ἄν γε πρὸς τῇ τέχνῃ ἔχῃ καὶ
τοῦτο τὸ πάθος ὃ λέγεις.

ΑΘ. Τί δ᾽ ἄρχων στρατοπέδων; ἆρ᾽ ἐὰν τὴν

48

party claims that its statement is convincing on the ground of the large number of witnesses produced, the other does so on the ground that those who abstain from wine are seen to be victorious in battle; and then this point also gives rise to a dispute. Now it would not be at all to my taste to go through all the rest of the legal arrangements in this fashion; and about our present subject, drunkenness, I desire to speak in quite another fashion (in my opinion, the right fashion), and I shall endeavour, if possible, to exhibit the correct method for dealing with all such subjects; for indeed the view of them adopted by your two States would be assailed and controverted by thousands upon thousands of nations.

MEG. Assuredly, if we know of a right method of investigating these matters, we are bound to give it a ready hearing.

ATH. Let us adopt some such method as this. Suppose that a man were to praise the rearing of goats, and the goat itself as a fine thing to own, and suppose also that another man, who had seen goats grazing without a herd and doing damage on cultivated land, were to run them down, and find fault equally with every animal he saw that was without a master or under a bad master,—would such a man's censure, about any object whatsoever, be of the smallest value?

MEG. Certainly not.

ATH. Do we call the man who possesses only nautical science, whether or not he suffers from sea-sickness, a good commander on a ship—or what?

MEG. By no means good, if along with his skill he suffers in the way you say.

ATH. And how about the army-commander? Is a

49

639 πολεμικὴν ἔχῃ ἐπιστήμην, ἱκανὸς ἄρχειν, κἂν
δειλὸς ὢν ἐν τοῖς δεινοῖς ὑπὸ μέθης του [1] φόβου
ναυτιᾷ;

ΜΕ. Καὶ πῶς;

ΑΘ. Ἂν δὲ αὖ μήτ' ἔχῃ τὴν τέχνην δειλός
τ' ᾖ;

ΜΕ. Παντάπασί τινα πονηρὸν λέγεις, καὶ
οὐδαμῶς ἀνδρῶν ἄρχοντα, ἀλλά τινων σφόδρα
γυναικῶν.

C ΑΘ. Τί δ' ἐπαινέτην ἢ ψέκτην κοινωνίας ἡστιν-
οσοῦν, ἢ πέφυκέ τε ἄρχων εἶναι μετ' ἐκείνου τε
ὠφέλιμός ἐστιν· ὁ δὲ μήθ' ἑωρακὼς εἴη ποτ' ὀρθῶς
αὐτὴν αὐτῇ κοινωνοῦσαν μετ' ἄρχοντος, ἀεὶ δὲ
ἄναρχον ἢ μετὰ κακῶν ἀρχόντων ξυνοῦσαν·
οἰώμεθα δή ποτε τοὺς τοιούτους θεωροὺς τῶν
τοιούτων κοινωνιῶν χρηστόν τι ψέξειν ἢ ἐπαινέ-
σεσθαι;

ΜΕ. Πῶς δ' ἄν; μηδέποτέ γε ἰδόντας μηδὲ
ξυγγενομένους ὀρθῶς γενομένῳ μηδενὶ τῶν τοιούτων
D κοινωνημάτων;

ΑΘ. Ἔχε δή· τῶν πολλῶν κοινωνιῶν ξυμπότας
καὶ ξυμπόσια θεῖμεν ἂν μίαν τινὰ ξυνουσίαν
εἶναι;

ΜΕ. Καὶ σφόδρα γε.

ΑΘ. Ταύτην οὖν μῶν ὀρθῶς γιγνομένην ἤδη τις
πώποτε ἐθεάσατο; καὶ σφῷν μὲν ἀποκρίνασθαι
ῥάδιον ὡς οὐδεπώποτε τὸ παράπαν· οὐ γὰρ
ἐπιχώριον ὑμῖν τοῦτο οὐδὲ νόμιμον· ἐγὼ δ' ἐντε-
τύχηκά τε πολλαῖς καὶ πολλαχοῦ, καὶ προσέτι
πάσας ὡς ἔπος εἰπεῖν διηρώτηκα, καὶ σχεδὸν
E ὅλην μὲν οὐδεμίαν ὀρθῶς γιγνομένην ἑώρακα οὐδ'

[1] του: τοῦ MSS., edd.

man fit for command, provided that he has military
science, even though he be a coward and sea-sick
with a kind of tipsy terror when danger comes?

MEG. Certainly not.

ATH. And suppose he has no military skill, besides
being a coward?

MEG. You are describing an utterly worthless
fellow, not a commander of men at all, but of the
most womanish of women.

ATH. Now take the case of any social institution
whatsoever which naturally has a commander and
which, under its commander, is beneficial; and
suppose that someone, who had never seen the
conduct of the institution under its commander, but
seen it only when with no commander or bad
commanders, were to commend the institution or
censure it: do we imagine that either the praise or
the blame of such an observer of such an institution
is of any value?

MEG. Certainly not, when the man has never
seen nor shared in an institution of the kind that
was properly conducted.

ATH. Now stay a moment! Shall we lay it down
that, of the numerous kinds of social institutions, that
of banqueters and banquetings forms one?

MEG. Most certainly.

ATH. Now has anyone ever yet beheld this
institution rightly conducted? Both of you can
easily make answer—"Never yet at all," for with
you this institution is neither customary nor legal;
but I have come across many modes of banqueting
in many places, and I have also inquired into nearly
all of them, and I have scarcely seen or heard of a
single one that was in all points rightly conducted;

639 ἀκήκοα, μόρια δ᾽ εἴ που σμικρὰ καὶ ὀλίγα, τὰ
πολλὰ δὲ ξύμπανθ᾽ ὡς εἰπεῖν διημαρτημένα.

ΚΛ. Πῶς δὴ ταῦτα, ὦ ξένε, λέγεις ; εἰπὲ ἔτι
σαφέστερον· ἡμεῖς μὲν γάρ, ὅπερ εἶπες, ἀπειρίᾳ
640 τῶν τοιούτων, οὐδ᾽ ἐντυγχάνοντες ἂν ἴσως εὐθύς
γε γνοῖμεν τό τε ὀρθὸν καὶ μὴ γιγνόμενον ἐν
αὑτοῖς.

ΑΘ. Εἰκὸς λέγεις· ἀλλ᾽ ἐμοῦ φράζοντος πειρῶ
μανθάνειν. τὸ μὲν γὰρ ἐν πάσαις τε ξυνόδοις
καὶ κοινωνίαις πράξεων ὡντινωνοῦν ὡς ὀρθὸν
πανταχοῦ ἑκάστοις ἄρχοντα εἶναι, μανθάνεις ;

ΚΛ. Πῶς γὰρ οὔ ;

ΑΘ. Καὶ μὴν ἐλέγομεν νῦν δή, μαχομένων ὡς
ἀνδρεῖον δεῖ τὸν ἄρχοντα εἶναι.

ΚΛ. Πῶς δ᾽ οὔ ;

ΑΘ. Ὁ μὴν ἀνδρεῖος τῶν δειλῶν ὑπὸ φόβων
ἧττον τεθορύβηται.

Β ΚΛ. Καὶ τοῦτο οὕτως.

ΑΘ. Εἰ δ᾽ ἦν τις μηχανὴ μηδὲν τὸ παράπαν
δεδιότα μηδὲ θορυβούμενον ἐπιστῆσαι στρατο-
πέδῳ στρατηγόν, ἆρ᾽ οὐ τοῦτ᾽ ἂν παντὶ τρόπῳ
ἐπράττομεν ;

ΚΛ. Σφόδρα μὲν οὖν.

ΑΘ. Νῦν δέ γε οὐ στρατοπέδου περὶ λέγομεν
ἄρχοντος ἐν ἀνδρῶν ὁμιλίαις ἐχθρῶν ἐχθροῖς μετὰ
πολέμου, φίλων δ᾽ ἐν εἰρήνῃ πρὸς φίλους κοινωνη-
σόντων φιλοφροσύνης.

ΚΛ. Ὀρθῶς.

C ΑΘ. Ἔστι δέ γε ἡ τοιαύτη συνουσία, εἴπερ
ἔσται μετὰ μέθης, οὐκ ἀθόρυβος· ἢ γάρ ;

for if any were right at all, it was only in a few
details, and most of them were almost entirely on
the wrong lines.

CLIN. What do you mean by that, Stranger?
Explain yourself more clearly; for since we are
(as you observed) without any experience of such
institutions, even if we did come across them, we
would probably fail to see at once what was right in
them and what wrong.

ATH. That is very probable. Try, however, to
learn from my description. This you understand—
that in all gatherings and associations for any
purpose whatsoever it is right that each group should
always have a commander.

CLIN. Of course.

ATH. Moreover, we have recently said that the
commander of fighting men must be courageous.

CLIN. Of course.

ATH. The courageous man is less perturbed by
alarms than the coward.

CLIN. That is true, too.

ATH. Now if there had existed any device for
putting an army in charge of a general who was
absolutely impervious to fear or perturbation, should
we not have made every effort to do so?

CLIN. Most certainly.

ATH. But what we are discussing now is not the
man who is to command an army in time of war, in
meetings of foe with foe, but the man who is to
command friends in friendly association with friends
in time of peace.

CLIN. Quite so.

ATH. Such a gathering, if accompanied by
drunkenness, is not free from disturbance, is it?

53

640 ΚΛ. Πῶς γάρ; ἀλλ᾽ οἶμαι πᾶν τοὐναντίον.

ΑΘ. Οὐκοῦν πρῶτον μὲν καὶ τούτοις ἄρχοντος δεῖ;

ΚΛ. Τί μήν; ὡς οὐδενί γε πράγματι.

ΑΘ. Πότερον οὖν ἀθόρυβον, εἰ δυνατὸν εἴη, τὸν τοιοῦτον ἄρχοντα ἐκπορίζεσθαι δεῖ;

ΚΛ. Πῶς γὰρ οὔ;

ΑΘ. Καὶ μὴν περί γε συνουσίας, ὡς ἔοικεν, αὐτὸν φρόνιμον εἶναι δεῖ. γίγνεται γὰρ φύλαξ D τῆς τε ὑπαρχούσης φιλίας αὐτοῖς, καὶ ἔτι πλείονος ἐπιμελητὴς ὅπως ἔσται διὰ τὴν τότε ξυνουσίαν.

ΚΛ. Ἀληθέστατα.

ΑΘ. Οὐκοῦν νήφοντά τε καὶ σοφὸν ἄρχοντα μεθυόντων δεῖ καθιστάναι, καὶ μὴ τοὐναντίον; μεθυόντων γὰρ μεθύων καὶ νέος ἄρχων μὴ σοφός, εἰ μὴ κακὸν ἀπεργάσαιτό τι μέγα, πολλῇ χρῷτ᾽ ἂν ἀγαθῇ τύχῃ.

ΚΛ. Παμπόλλῃ μὲν οὖν.

ΑΘ. Οὐκοῦν εἰ μὲν γιγνομένων ὡς δυνατὸν ὀρθότατα τούτων ἐν ταῖς πόλεσι τῶν ξυνουσιῶν E μέμφοιτό τις, ἐπικαλῶν αὐτῷ τῷ πράγματι, τάχ᾽ ἂν ὀρθῶς ἴσως μέμφοιτο· εἰ δὲ ἁμαρτανόμενον ὡς οἷόν τε μάλιστα ἐπιτήδευμά τις ὁρῶν λοιδορεῖ, πρῶτον μὲν δῆλον ὡς ἀγνοεῖ τοῦτ᾽ αὐτὸ γιγνόμενον οὐκ ὀρθῶς, εἶθ᾽ ὅτι πᾶν τούτῳ τῷ τρόπῳ φανεῖται πονηρόν, δεσπότου τε καὶ ἄρχοντος νήφοντος χωρὶς πραττόμενον. ἢ οὐ ξυννοεῖς 641 τοῦθ᾽, ὅτι μεθύων κυβερνήτης καὶ πᾶς παντὸς ἄρχων ἀνατρέπει πάντα εἴτε πλοῖα εἴτε ἅρματα εἴτε στρατόπεδον, εἴθ᾽ ὅ τί ποτ᾽ εἴη τὸ κυβερνώμενον ὑπ᾽ αὐτοῦ;

54

CLIN. Certainly not ; quite the reverse, I imagine.

ATH. So those people also need, in the first place, a commander?

CLIN. Undoubtedly—they above all.

ATH. Should we, if possible, provide them with a commander who is imperturbable?

CLIN. Certainly.

ATH. Naturally, also, he should be wise about social gatherings. For he has both to preserve the friendliness which already exists among the company and to see that the present gathering promotes it still further.

CLIN. Very true.

ATH. Then the commander we set over drunken men should be sober and wise, rather than the opposite? For a commander of drunkards who was himself drunken, young, and foolish would be very lucky if he escaped doing some serious mischief.

CLIN. Uncommonly lucky.

ATH. Suppose, then, that a man were to find fault with such institutions in States where they are managed in the best possible way, having an objection to the institution in itself, he might perhaps be right in doing so ; but if a man abuses an institution when he sees it managed in the worst way possible, it is plain that he is ignorant, first, of the fact that it is badly conducted, and secondly, that every institution will appear similarly bad when it is carried on without a sober ruler and commander. For surely you perceive that a sea-captain, and every commander of anything, if drunk, upsets everything, whether it be a ship or a chariot or an army or anything else that is under his captaincy.

641 κλ. Παντάπασι τοῦτό γε ἀληθὲς εἴρηκας, ὦ
ξένε· τοὐπὶ τῷδε δ᾽ ἡμῖν λέγε, τί ποτ᾽, ἂν γίγνηται
τοῦτο ὀρθῶς [1] τὸ περὶ τὰς πόσεις νόμιμον, ἀγαθὸν
ἂν δράσειεν ἡμᾶς; οἷον ὃ νῦν δὴ ἐλέγομεν, εἰ
στράτευμα ὀρθῆς ἡγεμονίας τυγχάνοι, νίκη πολέμου τοῖς ἑπομένοις ἂν γίγνοιτο, οὐ σμικρὸν
ἀγαθόν, καὶ τἆλλ᾽ οὕτω· συμποσίου δὲ ὀρθῶς
B παιδαγωγηθέντος τί μέγα ἰδιώταις ἢ τῇ πόλει
γίγνοιτ᾽ ἄν;

αθ. Τί δέ; παιδὸς ἑνὸς ἢ καὶ χοροῦ παιδαγωγηθέντος κατὰ τρόπον ἑνὸς τί μέγα τῇ πόλει
φαῖμεν ἂν γίγνεσθαι; ἢ τοῦτο οὕτως ἐρωτη-
θέντες εἴποιμεν ἂν ὡς ἑνὸς μὲν βραχὺ τῇ πόλει
γίγνοιτ᾽ ἂν ὄφελος, εἰ δ᾽ ὅλως ἐρωτᾷς παιδείαν
τῶν παιδευθέντων, τί μέγα τὴν πόλιν ὀνίνησιν, οὐ
χαλεπὸν εἰπεῖν ὅτι παιδευθέντες μὲν εὖ γίγνοιντ᾽
ἂν ἄνδρες ἀγαθοί, γενόμενοι δὲ τοιοῦτοι τά τ᾽
C ἄλλα πράττοιεν καλῶς, ἔτι δὲ κἂν νικῷεν τοὺς
πολεμίους μαχόμενοι. παιδεία μὲν οὖν φέρει καὶ
νίκην, νίκη δ᾽ ἐνίοτε ἀπαιδευσίαν· πολλοὶ γὰρ
ὑβριστότεροι διὰ πολέμων νίκας γενόμενοι μυρίων
ἄλλων κακῶν δι᾽ ὕβριν ἐνεπλήσθησαν, καὶ παιδεία μὲν οὐδεπώποτε γέγονε Καδμεία, νῖκαι δὲ
ἀνθρώποις πολλαὶ δὴ τοιαῦται γεγόνασί τε καὶ
ἔσονται.

κλ. Δοκεῖς ἡμῖν, ὦ φίλε, τὴν ἐν τοῖς οἴνοις
D κοινὴν διατριβὴν ὡς εἰς παιδείας μεγάλην μοῖραν
τείνουσαν λέγειν, ἂν ὀρθῶς γίγνηται.

---

[1] ὀρθῶς Schanz: ὀρθὸν MSS.

CLIN. What you say, Stranger, is perfectly true. In the next place, then, tell us this :—suppose this institution of drinking were rightly conducted, of what possible benefit would it be to us? Take the case of an army, which we mentioned just now : there, given a right leader, his men will win victory in war, which is no small benefit ; and so too with the other cases : but what solid advantage would accrue either to individuals or to a State from the right regulation of a wine-party?

ATH. Well, what great gain should we say would accrue to the State from the right control of one single child or even of one band of children? To the question thus put to us we should reply that the State would benefit but little from one ; if, however, you are putting a general question as to what solid advantage the State gains from the education of the educated, then it is quite simple to reply that well-educated men will prove good men, and being good they will conquer their foes in battle, besides acting nobly in other ways. Thus, while education brings also victory, victory sometimes brings lack of education ; for men have often grown more insolent because of victory in war, and through their insolence they have become filled with countless other vices ; and whereas education has never yet proved to be "Cadmeian,"[1] the victories which men win in war often have been, and will be, "Cadmeian."

CLIN. You are implying, my friend, as it seems to us, that the convivial gathering, when rightly conducted, is an important element in education.

[1] *i.e.* involving more loss than gain—a proverbial expression, possibly derived from the fate of the "Sparti" (sprung from the dragon's teeth sown by Cadmus, founder of Thebes) who slew one another : cp. "Pyrrhic" victory.

641 ΑΘ. Τί μήν;

ΚΛ. Ἔχοις ἂν οὖν τὸ μετὰ τοῦτ' εἰπεῖν ὡς ἔστι τὸ νῦν εἰρημένον ἀληθές;

ΑΘ. Τὸ μὲν ἀληθές, ὦ ξένε, διισχυρίζεσθαι ταῦτα οὕτως ἔχειν, πολλῶν ἀμφισβητούντων, θεοῦ· εἰ δ' ὅπῃ ἐμοὶ φαίνεται δεῖ λέγειν, οὐδεὶς φθόνος, ἐπείπερ ὡρμήκαμέν γε τοὺς λόγους περὶ νόμων καὶ πολιτείας ποιεῖσθαι τὰ νῦν.

ΚΛ. Τοῦτ' αὐτὸ δὴ πειρώμεθα τὸ σοὶ δοκοῦν
Ε περὶ τῶν νῦν ἀμφισβητουμένων καταμαθεῖν.

ΑΘ. Ἀλλὰ χρὴ ποιεῖν οὕτως, ὑμᾶς τε ἐπὶ τὸ μαθεῖν καὶ ἐμὲ ἐπὶ τὸ δηλῶσαι πειρώμενον ἁμῶς γέ πως ξυντεῖναι τὸν λόγον. πρῶτον δέ μου ἀκούσατε τὸ τοιόνδε· τὴν πόλιν ἅπαντες ἡμῶν Ἕλληνες ὑπολαμβάνουσιν ὡς φιλόλογός τέ ἐστι καὶ πολύλογος, Λακεδαίμονα δὲ καὶ Κρήτην, τὴν μὲν βραχύλογον, τὴν δὲ πολύνοιαν μᾶλλον ἢ
642 πολυλογίαν ἀσκοῦσαν. σκοπῶ δὴ μὴ δόξαν ὑμῖν παράσχωμαι περὶ σμικροῦ πολλὰ λέγειν, μέθης πέρι σμικροῦ πράγματος παμμήκη λόγον ἀνακαθαιρόμενος. τὸ δὲ ἡ κατὰ φύσιν αὐτοῦ διόρθωσις οὐκ ἂν δύναιτο ἄνευ μουσικῆς ὀρθότητός ποτε σαφὲς οὐδ' ἱκανὸν ἐν τοῖς λόγοις ἀπολαβεῖν· μουσικὴ δὲ ἄνευ παιδείας τῆς πάσης οὐκ ἂν αὖ ποτὲ δύναιτο· ταῦτα δὲ παμπόλλων ἐστὶ λόγων. ὁρᾶτε οὖν τί ποιῶμεν· εἰ ταῦτα μὲν ἐάσαιμεν ἐν
Β τῷ παρόντι, μετεκβαῖμεν δ' εἰς ἕτερόν τινα νόμων πέρι λόγον.

ΜΕ. Ὦ ξένε Ἀθηναῖε, οὐκ οἶσθ' ἴσως ὅτι τυγχάνει ἡμῶν ἡ ἑστία τῆς πόλεως οὖσα ὑμῶν πρόξενος. ἴσως μὲν οὖν καὶ πᾶσι τοῖς παισίν,

ATH. Assuredly.

CLIN. Could you then show us, in the next place, how this statement is true?

ATH. The truth of my statement, which is disputed by many, it is for God to assert; but I am quite ready to give, if required, my own opinion, now that we have, in fact, embarked on a discussion of laws and constitutions.

CLIN. Well, it is precisely your opinion about the questions now in dispute that we are trying to learn.

ATH. Thus, then, we must do,—you must brace yourself in the effort to learn the argument, and I to expound it as best I can. But, first of all, I have a preliminary observation to make: our city, Athens, is, in the general opinion of the Greeks, both fond of talk and full of talk, but Lacedaemon is scant of talk, while Crete is more witty [1] than wordy; so I am afraid of making you think that I am a great talker about a small matter, if I spin out a discourse of prodigious length about the small matter of drunkenness. But the fact is that the right ordering of this could never be treated adequately and clearly in our discourse apart from rightness in music, nor could music, apart from education as a whole; and these require lengthy discussions. Consider, then, what we are to do: suppose we leave these matters over for the present, and take up some other legal topic instead.

MEG. O Stranger of Athens, you are not, perhaps, aware that our family is, in fact, a "proxenus" [2] of your State. It is probably true of all

---

[1] A polite way of alluding to the proverbial mendacity of the Cretans (cp. Ep. *Titus* i. 12: κρῆτες ἀεὶ ψεῦσται).

[2] A "proxenus" was a native who acted as official representative of a foreign State.

642 ἐπειδὰν ἀκούσωσιν ὅτι τινός εἰσι πόλεως προ-
ξενοι, ταύτῃ τις εὔνοια ἐκ νέων εὐθὺς ἐνδύεται
ἕκαστον [ἡμῶν τῶν προξένων τῇ πόλει],¹ ὡς
δευτέρᾳ οὔσῃ πατρίδι μετὰ τὴν αὑτοῦ πόλιν· καὶ
δὴ καὶ ἐμοὶ νῦν ταὐτὸ τοῦτο ἐγγέγονεν. ἀκούων γὰρ
C τῶν παίδων εὐθύς, εἴ τι μέμφοιντο ἢ καὶ ἐπαινοῖεν
Λακεδαιμόνιοι Ἀθηναίους, ὡς ἡ πόλις ὑμῶν, ὦ
Μέγιλλε, ἔφασαν, ἡμᾶς οὐ καλῶς ἢ καλῶς ἔρρεξε,
—ταῦτα δὴ ἀκούων καὶ μαχόμενος πρὸς αὐτὰ ὑπὲρ
ὑμῶν ἀεὶ πρὸς τοὺς τὴν πόλιν εἰς ψόγον ἄγοντας
πᾶσαν εὔνοιαν ἔσχον, καί μοι νῦν ἥ τε φωνὴ
προσφιλὴς ὑμῶν, τό τε ὑπὸ πολλῶν λεγόμενον,
ὡς ὅσοι Ἀθηναίων εἰσὶν ἀγαθοὶ διαφερόντως εἰσὶ
τοιοῦτοι, δοκεῖ ἀληθέστατα λέγεσθαι· μόνοι γὰρ
D ἄνευ ἀνάγκης, αὐτοφυῶς [θείᾳ μοίρᾳ, ἀληθῶς
καὶ οὔ τι πλαστῶς]² εἰσὶν ἀγαθοί. θαρρῶν δὴ
ἐμοῦ γε ἕνεκα λέγοις ἂν τοσαῦτα ὁπόσα σοι
φίλον.

ΚΛ. Καὶ μήν, ὦ ξένε, καὶ τὸν παρ' ἐμοῦ λόγον
ἀκούσας τε καὶ ἀποδεξάμενος θαρρῶν ὁπόσα
βούλει λέγε. τῇδε γὰρ ἴσως ἀκήκοας ὡς Ἐπι-
μενίδης γέγονεν ἀνὴρ θεῖος, ὃς ἦν ἡμῖν οἰκεῖος,
ἐλθὼν δὲ πρὸ τῶν Περσικῶν δέκα ἔτεσι πρότερον
παρ' ὑμᾶς κατὰ τὴν τοῦ θεοῦ μαντείαν θυσίας
τε ἐθύσατό τινας, ἃς ὁ θεὸς ἀνεῖλε, καὶ δὴ καὶ
φοβουμένων τὸν Περσικὸν Ἀθηναίων στόλον
E εἶπεν ὅτι δέκα μὲν ἐτῶν οὐχ ἥξουσιν, ὅταν δὲ
ἔλθωσιν, ἀπαλλαγήσονται πράξαντες οὐδὲν ὧν
ἤλπιζον παθόντες τε ἢ δράσαντες πλείω κακά.

---

¹ [ἡμῶν . . . πόλει] bracketed by Badham, Schanz.
² [θείᾳ . . . πλαστῶς] bracketed by Valckenaer.

children that, when once they have been told that
they are "proxeni" of a certain State, they conceive an affection for that State even from infancy,
and each of them regards it as a second mother-
land, next after his own country. That is precisely
the feeling I now experience. For through hearing
mere children crying out—whenever they, being the
Lacedaemonians, were blaming the Athenians for
anything or praising them—"Your State, Megillus,
has done us a bad turn or a good one,"—through
hearing such remarks, I say, and constantly fighting
your battles against those who were thus decrying
your State, I acquired a deep affection for it; so that
now not only do I delight in your accent, but I
regard as absolutely true the common saying that
"good Athenians are always incomparably good,"
for they alone are good not by outward compulsion
but by inner disposition. Thus, so far as I am concerned, you may speak without fear and say all you
please.

CLIN. My story, too, Stranger, when you hear it,
will show you that you may boldly say all you wish.
You have probably heard how that inspired man
Epimenides, who was a family connexion of ours,
was born in Crete; and how ten years [1] before the
Persian War, in obedience to the oracle of the god,
he went to Athens and offered certain sacrifices
which the god had ordained; and how, moreover,
when the Athenians were alarmed at the Persians'
expeditionary force, he made this prophecy—"They
will not come for ten years, and when they do
come, they will return back again with all their
hopes frustrated, and after suffering more woes than

---

[1] Epimenides really lived about 600 B.C.

642 τότ᾽ οὖν ἐξενώθησαν ὑμῖν οἱ πρόγονοι ἡμῶν, καὶ
εὔνοιαν ἐκ τόσου ἔγωγε ὑμῖν καὶ οἱ ἡμέτεροι
643 ἔχουσι γονῆς.

ΑΘ. Τὰ μὲν τοίνυν ὑμέτερα ἀκούειν, ὡς ἔοικεν,
ἕτοιμ᾽ ἂν εἴη· τὰ δ᾽ ἐμὰ βούλεσθαι μὲν ἕτοιμα,
δύνασθαι δὲ οὐ πάνυ ῥᾴδια, ὅμως δὲ πειρατέον.
πρῶτον δὴ οὖν πρὸς τὸν λόγον ὁρισώμεθα παιδείαν τί ποτ᾽ ἐστὶ καὶ τίνα δύναμιν ἔχει· διὰ
γὰρ ταύτης φαμὲν ἰτέον εἶναι τὸν προκεχειρισ-
μένον ἐν τῷ νῦν λόγον ὑφ᾽ ἡμῶν, μέχριπερ ἂν
πρὸς τὸν θεὸν ἀφίκηται.

ΚΛ. Πάνυ μὲν οὖν δρῶμεν ταῦτα, εἴπερ σοί
γε ἡδύ.

B   ΑΘ. Λέγοντος τοίνυν ἐμοῦ τί ποτε χρὴ φάναι
παιδείαν εἶναι, σκέψασθε ἂν ἀρέσκῃ τὸ λεχθέν.

ΚΛ. Λέγοις ἄν.

ΑΘ. Λέγω δή, καί φημι τὸν ὁτιοῦν ἀγαθὸν
ἄνδρα μέλλοντα ἔσεσθαι τοῦτο αὐτὸ ἐκ παίδων
εὐθὺς μελετᾶν δεῖν παίζοντά τε καὶ σπουδάζοντα
ἐν τοῖς τοῦ πράγματος ἑκάστοις προσήκουσιν·
οἷον τὸν μέλλοντα ἀγαθὸν ἔσεσθαι γεωργὸν ἢ
C τινα οἰκοδόμον, τὸν μὲν οἰκοδομοῦντά τι τῶν
παιδείων οἰκοδομημάτων παίζειν χρή, τὸν δ᾽ αὖ
γεωργοῦντα, καὶ ὄργανα ἑκατέρῳ σμικρά, τῶν
ἀληθινῶν μιμήματα, παρασκευάζειν τὸν τρέφοντα
αὐτῶν ἑκάτερον· καὶ δὴ καὶ τῶν μαθημάτων ὅσα
ἀναγκαῖα προμεμαθηκέναι προμανθάνειν, οἷον
τέκτονα μετρεῖν ἢ σταθμᾶσθαι καὶ πολεμικὸν
ἱππεύειν παίζοντα ἤ τι τῶν τοιούτων ἄλλο
ποιεῖν,[1] καὶ πειρᾶσθαι διὰ τῶν παιδιῶν ἐκεῖσε
τρέπειν τὰς ἡδονὰς καὶ ἐπιθυμίας τῶν παίδων,

[1] ποιεῖν Boeckh, Schanz: ποιοῦντα MSS.

they inflict." Then our forefathers became guest-friends of yours, and ever since both my fathers and I myself have cherished an affection for Athens.

ATH. Evidently, then, you are both ready to play your part as listeners. But as for my part, though the will is there, to compass the task is hard: still, I must try. In the first place, then, our argument requires that we should define education and describe its effects: that is the path on which our present discourse must proceed until it finally arrives at the god of Wine.

CLIN. By all means let us do so, since it is your wish.

ATH. Then while I am stating how education ought to be defined, you must be considering whether you are satisfied with my statement.

CLIN. Proceed with your statement.

ATH. I will. What I assert is that every man who is going to be good at any pursuit must practise that special pursuit from infancy, by using all the implements of his pursuit both in his play and in his work. For example, the man who is to make a good builder must play at building toy houses, and to make a good farmer he must play at tilling land; and those who are rearing them must provide each child with toy tools modelled on real ones. Besides this, they ought to have elementary instruction in all the necessary subjects,—the carpenter, for instance, being taught in play the use of rule and measure, the soldier taught riding or some similar accomplishment. So, by means of their games, we should endeavour to turn the tastes and desires of the children in the direction of that object which

63

643 οἳ ἀφικομένους αὐτοὺς δεῖ τέλος ἔχειν. κεφάλαιοι
D δὴ παιδείας λέγομεν τὴν ὀρθὴν τροφήν, ἣ τοῦ
παίζοντος τὴν ψυχὴν εἰς ἔρωτα μάλιστα ἄξει
τούτου, ὃ δεήσει γενόμενον ἄνδρ᾽ αὐτὸν τέλειον
εἶναι τῆς τοῦ πράγματος ἀρετῆς· ὁρᾶτε οὖν εἰ
μέχρι τούτου γε, ὅπερ εἶπον, ὑμῖν ἀρέσκει τὸ
λεχθέν.

ΚΛ. Πῶς γὰρ οὔ;

ΑΘ. Μὴ τοίνυν μηδ᾽ ὃ λέγομεν εἶναι παιδείαν
ἀόριστον γένηται. νῦν γὰρ ὀνειδίζοντες ἐπαι-
νοῦντές θ᾽ ἑκάστων τὰς τροφὰς λέγομεν ὡς τὸν
E μὲν πεπαιδευμένον ἡμῶν ὄντα τινά, τὸν δὲ
ἀπαίδευτον, ἐνίοτε εἰς <τά>¹ τε καπηλείας καὶ
ναυκληρίας καὶ ἄλλων τοιούτων μάλα πεπαιδευμένον σφόδρα ἄνθρωπον·² οὐ γὰρ ταῦτα
ἡγουμένων, ὡς ἔοικεν, εἶναι παιδείαν ὁ νῦν
λόγος ἂν εἴη, τὴν δὲ πρὸς ἀρετὴν ἐκ παίδων
παιδείαν, ποιοῦσαν ἐπιθυμητήν τε καὶ ἐραστὴν
τοῦ πολίτην γενέσθαι τέλεον, ἄρχειν τε καὶ ἄρχεσθαι ἐπιστάμενον μετὰ δίκης. ταύτην τὴν
644 τροφὴν ἀφορισάμενος ὁ λόγος οὗτος, ὡς ἐμοὶ
φαίνεται, νῦν βούλοιτ᾽ ἂν μόνην παιδείαν προσαγορεύειν, τὴν δὲ εἰς χρήματα τείνουσαν ἤ τινα
πρὸς ἰσχὺν ἢ καὶ πρὸς ἄλλην τινὰ σοφίαν ἄνευ
νοῦ καὶ δίκης βάναυσόν τ᾽ εἶναι καὶ ἀνελεύθερον
καὶ οὐκ ἀξίαν τὸ παράπαν παιδείαν καλεῖσθαι.
ἡμεῖς δὴ μηδὲν ὀνόματι διαφερώμεθ᾽ αὐτοῖς, ἀλλ᾽
ὁ νῦν δὴ λόγος ἡμῖν ὁμολογηθεὶς μενέτω, ὡς οἵ γε
ὀρθῶς πεπαιδευμένοι σχεδὸν ἀγαθοὶ γίγνονται,
B καὶ δεῖ δὴ τὴν παιδείαν μηδαμοῦ ἀτιμάζειν, ὡς

¹ εἰς <τά>: εἰς MSS. (πράγματα for μάλα Ast, alii alia).

forms their ultimate goal. First and foremost, education, we say, consists in that right nurture which most strongly draws the soul of the child when at play to a love for that pursuit of which, when he becomes a man, he must possess a perfect mastery. Now consider, as I said before, whether, up to this point, you are satisfied with this statement of mine.

CLIN. Certainly we are.

ATH. But we must not allow our description of education to remain indefinite. For at present, when censuring or commending a man's upbringing, we describe one man as educated and another as uneducated, though the latter may often be uncommonly well educated in the trade of a pedlar or a skipper, or some other similar occupation. But we, naturally, in our present discourse are not taking the view that such things as these make up education : the education we speak of is training from childhood in goodness, which makes a man eagerly desirous of becoming a perfect citizen, understanding how both to rule and be ruled righteously. This is the special form of nurture to which, as I suppose, our present argument would confine the term "education"; whereas an upbringing which aims only at money-making or physical strength, or even some mental accomplishment devoid of reason and justice, it would term vulgar and illiberal and utterly unworthy of the name "education." Let us not, however, quarrel over a name, but let us abide by the statement we agreed upon just now, that those who are rightly educated become, as a rule, good, and that one should in no case disparage education, since it stands

---

² πεπαιδευμένον . . . ἄνθρωπον Cornarius : πεπαιδευμένων . . . ἀνθρώπων MSS.

644 πρῶτον τῶν καλλίστων τοῖς ἀρίστοις ἀνδράσι
παραγιγνόμενον· καὶ εἴ ποτε ἐξέρχεται, δυνατὸν
δ᾽ ἐστὶν ἐπανορθοῦσθαι, τοῦτ᾽ ἀεὶ δραστέον διὰ
βίου παντὶ κατὰ δύναμιν.

ΚΛ. Ὀρθῶς, καὶ συγχωροῦμεν ἃ λέγεις.

ΑΘ. Καὶ μὴν πάλαι γε συνεχωρήσαμεν ὡς
ἀγαθῶν μὲν ὄντων τῶν δυναμένων ἄρχειν αὑτῶν,
κακῶν δὲ τῶν μή.

ΚΛ. Λέγεις ὀρθότατα.

ΑΘ. Σαφέστερον ἔτι τοίνυν ἀναλάβωμεν τοῦτ᾽
C αὐτὸ ὅ τί ποτε λέγομεν. καί μοι δι᾽ εἰκόνος
ἀποδέξασθε ἐάν πως δυνατὸς ὑμῖν γένωμαι
δηλῶσαι τὸ τοιοῦτον.

ΚΛ. Λέγε μόνον.

ΑΘ. Οὐκοῦν ἕνα μὲν ἡμῶν ἕκαστον αὐτῶν
τιθῶμεν;

ΚΛ. Ναί.

ΑΘ. Δύο δὲ κεκτημένον ἐν αὑτῷ ξυμβούλω
ἐναντίω τε καὶ ἄφρονε, ὣ προσαγορεύομεν ἡδονὴν
καὶ λύπην;

ΚΛ. Ἔστι ταῦτα.

ΑΘ. Πρὸς δὲ τούτοιν ἀμφοῖν αὖ δόξας μελλόντων, οἷν κοινὸν μὲν ὄνομα ἐλπίς, ἴδιον δὲ
φόβος μὲν ἡ πρὸ λύπης ἐλπίς, θάρρος δὲ ἡ πρὸ
D τοῦ ἐναντίου. ἐπὶ δὲ πᾶσι τούτοις λογισμός, ὅ
τί ποτ᾽ αὐτῶν ἄμεινον ἢ χεῖρον· ὃς γενόμενος
δόγμα πόλεως κοινὸν νόμος ἐπωνόμασται.

ΚΛ. Μόγις μέν πως ἐφέπομαι, λέγε μὴν τὸ
μετὰ ταῦτα ὡς ἑπομένου.

first among the finest gifts that are given to the best men; and if ever it errs from the right path, but can be put straight again, to this task every man, so long as he lives, must address himself with all his might.

CLIN. You are right, and we agree with what you say.

ATH. Further, we agreed long ago that if men are capable of ruling themselves, they are good, but if incapable, bad.

CLIN. Quite true.

ATH. Let us, then, re-state more clearly what we meant by this. With your permission, I will make use of an illustration in the hope of explaining the matter.

CLIN. Go ahead.

ATH. May we assume that each of us by himself is a single unit?

CLIN. Yes.

ATH. And that each possesses within himself two antagonistic and foolish counsellors, whom we call by the names of pleasure and pain?

CLIN. That is so.

ATH. And that, besides these two, each man possesses opinions about the future, which go by the general name of "expectations"; and of these, that which precedes pain bears the special name of "fear," and that which precedes pleasure the special name of "confidence"; and in addition to all these there is "calculation," pronouncing which of them is good, which bad; and "calculation," when it has become the public decree of the State, is named "law."

CLIN. I have some difficulty in keeping pace with you: assume, however, that I do so, and proceed.

644 ΜΕ. Καὶ ἐν ἐμοὶ μὴν ταὐτὸ τοῦτο πάθος ἔνι.

ΑΘ. Περὶ δὴ τουτων διανοηθῶμεν οὑτωσί. θαῦμα μὲν ἕκαστον ἡμῶν ἡγησώμεθα τῶν ζώων θεῖον, εἴτε ὡς παίγνιον ἐκείνων εἴτε ὡς σπουδῇ τινι ξυνεστηκός· οὐ γὰρ δὴ τοῦτό γε γιγνώσκομεν·
Ε τόδε δὲ ἴσμεν, ὅτι ταῦτα τὰ πάθη ἐν ἡμῖν οἷον νεῦρα ἢ μήρινθοί τινες ἐνοῦσαι σπῶσί τε ἡμᾶς καὶ ἀλλήλαις ἀνθέλκουσιν ἐναντίαι οὖσαι ἐπ᾽ ἐναντίας πράξεις, οὗ δὴ διωρισμένη ἀρετὴ καὶ κακία κεῖται· μιᾷ γάρ φησιν ὁ λόγος δεῖν τῶν ἕλξεων ξυνεπόμενον ἀεὶ καὶ μηδαμῇ ἀπολειπόμενον ἐκείνης ἀνθέλκειν τοῖς ἄλλοις νεύροις ἕκα-
645 στον, ταύτην δ᾽ εἶναι τὴν τοῦ λογισμοῦ ἀγωγὴν χρυσῆν καὶ ἱεράν, τῆς πόλεως κοινὸν νόμον ἐπικαλουμένην, ἄλλας δὲ σκληρὰς καὶ σιδηρᾶς, τὴν δὲ μαλακὴν <μίαν τε>[1] ἅτε χρυσῆν οὖσαν, τὰς δὲ ἄλλας παντοδαποῖς εἴδεσιν ὁμοίας· δεῖν δὴ τῇ καλλίστῃ ἀγωγῇ τῇ τοῦ νόμου ἀεὶ ξυλλαμβάνειν ἅτε γὰρ τοῦ λογισμοῦ καλοῦ μὲν ὄντος, πράου δὲ καὶ οὐ βιαίου, δεῖσθαι ὑπηρετῶν αὐτοῦ τὴν ἀγωγήν, ὅπως ἂν <ἐν>ἡμῖν τὸ χρυσοῦν γένος νικᾷ τὰ
Β ἄλλα γένη. καὶ οὕτω δὴ περὶ θαυμάτων ὡς ὄντων ἡμῶν ὁ μῦθος ἄρ᾽ ἔτι[2] σεσωσμένος ἂν εἴη, καὶ τὸ κρείττω ἑαυτοῦ καὶ ἥττω εἶναι τρόπον τινὰ φανερὸν ἂν γίγνοιτο μᾶλλον ὃ νοεῖ, καὶ ὅτι πόλιν καὶ ἰδιώτην, τὸν μὲν λόγον ἀληθῆ λαβόντα ἐν ἑαυτῷ περὶ τῶν ἕλξεων τούτων τούτῳ ἑπόμενον δεῖ ζῆν, πόλιν δὲ ἢ παρὰ θεῶν τινὸς ἢ παρ᾽ ἀνθρώπου του[3] γνόντος ταῦτα λόγον παραλαβοῦσαν, νόμον θεμέ-

[1] <μίαν τε> I insert (Schanz marks lacuna after οὖσαν).
[2] ἄρ᾽ ἔτι Badham: ἀρετῆς MSS.

MEG. I am in exactly the same predicament.

ATH. Let us conceive of the matter in this **way.** Let us suppose that each of us living creatures is an ingenious puppet of the gods, whether contrived by way of a toy of theirs or for some serious purpose—for as to that we know nothing; but this we do know, that these inward affections of ours, like sinews or cords, drag us along and, being opposed to each other, pull one against the other to opposite actions; and herein lies the dividing line between goodness and badness. For, as our argument declares, there is one of these pulling forces which every man should always follow and nohow leave hold of, counteracting thereby the pull of the other sinews: it is the leading-string, golden and holy, of " calculation," entitled the public law of the State; and whereas the other cords are hard and steely and of every possible shape and semblance, this one is flexible and uniform, since it is of gold. With that most excellent leading-string of the law we must needs co-operate always ; for since calculation is excellent, but gentle rather than forceful, its leading-string needs helpers to ensure that the golden kind within us may vanquish the other kinds. In this way our story comparing ourselves to puppets will not fall flat, and the meaning of the terms " self-superior " and " self-inferior " will become somewhat more clear, and also how necessary it is for the individual man to grasp the true account of these inward pulling forces and to live in accordance therewith, and how necessary for the State (when it has received such an account either from a god or from a man who knows) to make this into a law for itself and be

---

³ παρ' ἀνθρώπου του : παρὰ τούτου τοῦ MSS. (παρὰ αὐτοῦ τούτου Eusebius).

645 νην, αὐτῇ τε ὁμιλεῖν καὶ ταῖς ἄλλαις πόλεσιν.
C οὕτω καὶ κακία δὴ καὶ ἀρετὴ σαφέστερον ἡμῖν
διηρθρωμένον ἂν εἴη. ἐναργεστέρου δ' αὐτοῦ
γενομένου καὶ παιδεία καὶ τἆλλα ἐπιτηδεύματα
ἴσως ἔσται μᾶλλον καταφανῆ, καὶ δὴ καὶ τὸ περὶ
τῆς ἐν τοῖς οἴνοις διατριβῆς, ὃ δοξασθείη μὲν ἂν
εἶναι φαύλου πέρι μῆκος πολὺ λόγων περιττὸν
εἰρημένον, φανείη[1] δὲ τάχ' ἂν ἴσως τοῦ μήκους
γ' αὐτῶν οὐκ ἀπάξιον.

ΚΛ. Εὖ λέγεις, καὶ περαίνωμεν ὅ τί περ ἂν
τῆς γε νῦν διατριβῆς ἄξιον γίγνηται.

D ΑΘ. Λέγε δή· προσφέροντες τῷ θαύματι τούτῳ
τὴν μέθην ποῖόν τί ποτε αὐτὸ ἀπεργαζόμεθα ;

ΚΛ. Πρὸς τί δὲ σκοπούμενος αὐτὸ ἐπανερωτᾷς ;

ΑΘ. Οὐδέν πω πρὸς ὅ τι, τοῦτο δὲ ὅλως κοινω-
νῆσαν τούτῳ ποῖόν τι ξυμπίπτει γίγνεσθαι. ἔτι
δὲ σαφέστερον ὃ βούλομαι πειράσομαι φράζειν.
ἐρωτῶ γὰρ τὸ τοιόνδε· ἆρα σφοδροτέρας τὰς
ἡδονὰς καὶ λύπας καὶ θυμοὺς καὶ ἔρωτας ἡ τῶν
οἴνων πόσις ἐπιτείνει ;

ΚΛ. Πολύ γε.

E ΑΘ. Τί δ' αὖ τὰς αἰσθήσεις καὶ μνήμας καὶ
δόξας καὶ φρονήσεις ; πότερον ὡσαύτως σφοδροτέρας, ἢ πάμπαν ἀπολείπει ταῦτα αὐτόν, ἂν
κατακορής τις τῇ μέθῃ γίγνηται ;

ΚΛ. Ναί, πάμπαν ἀπολείπει.

ΑΘ. Οὐκοῦν εἰς ταὐτὸν ἀφικνεῖται τὴν τῆς
ψυχῆς ἕξιν τῇ τότε ὅτε νέος ἦν παῖς ;

---

[1] Zur. assigns φανείη . . . ἀπάξιον to Clin., Εὖ λέγεις . . .
γίγνηται to Ath., and Λέγε δή to Clin.: I follow Hermann
and later edd.

guided thereby in its intercourse both with itself
and with all other States. Thus both badness **and**
goodness would be differentiated for us more clearly ;
and these having become more evident, probably
education also and the other institutions will appear
less obscure ; and about the institution of the wine-
party in particular it may very likely be shown that
it is by no means, as might be thought, **a** paltry
matter which it is absurd to discuss at great length
but rather a matter which fully merits prolonged
discussion.

CLIN. Quite right : let us go through with every
topic that seems important for the present discussion.

ATH. Tell me now : if we give strong drink to
this puppet of ours, what effect will it have on its
character ?

CLIN. In reference to what particular do you **ask**
this question ?

ATH. To no particular, for the moment : I am
putting the question in general terms—" when this
shares in that, what sort of thing does it become in
consequence ? " I will try to convey my meaning
still more clearly : what I ask is this—does the
drinking of wine intensify pleasures and pains and
passions and lusts ?

CLIN. Yes, greatly.

ATH. And how about sensations and recollections
and opinions and thoughts ? Does it make them
likewise more intense ? Or rather, do not these
quit a man entirely if he becomes surfeited with
drink ?

CLIN. Yes, they quit him entirely.

ATH. He then arrives at the same condition of
soul as when he was a young child ?

645   ΚΛ. Τί μήν ;

     ΑΘ. ῞Ηκιστα δὴ τότ᾿ ἂν αὐτὸς αὑτοῦ γίγνοιτο ἐγκρατής.

646   ΚΛ. ῞Ηκιστα.

     ΑΘ. ᾿Αρ᾿ οὖν πονηρότατος, φαμέν, ὁ τοιοῦτος ;

     ΚΛ. Πολύ γε.

     ΑΘ. Οὐ μόνον ἄρ᾿, ὡς ἔοικεν, ὁ γέρων δὶς παῖς γίγνοιτ᾿ ἄν, ἀλλὰ καὶ ὁ μεθυσθείς.

     ΚΛ. ῎Αριστα εἶπες, ὦ ξένε.

     ΑΘ. Τούτου δὴ τοῦ ἐπιτηδεύματος ἔσθ᾿ ὅστις λόγος ἐπιχειρήσει πείθειν ἡμᾶς ὡς χρὴ γεύεσθαι καὶ μὴ φεύγειν παντὶ σθένει κατὰ τὸ δυνατόν ;

     ΚΛ. ῎Εοικ᾿ εἶναι· σὺ γοῦν φὴς καὶ ἕτοιμος ἦσθα νῦν δὴ λέγειν.

B   ΑΘ. ᾿Αληθῆ μέντοι μνημονεύεις. καὶ νῦν γ᾿ εἰμὶ ἕτοιμος, ἐπειδήπερ σφώ γε ἐθελήσειν προθύμως ἔφατον ἀκούειν.

     ΚΛ. Πῶς δ᾿ οὐκ ἀκουσόμεθα ; κἂν εἰ μηδενὸς ἄλλου χάριν, ἀλλὰ τοῦ θαυμαστοῦ γε καὶ ἀτόπου, εἰ δεῖ ἑκόντα ποτὲ ἄνθρωπον εἰς ἅπασαν φαυλότητα ἑαυτὸν ἐμβάλλειν.

     ΑΘ. Ψυχῆς λέγεις. ἢ γάρ ;

     ΚΛ. Ναί.

     ΑΘ. Τί δὲ σώματος, ὦ ἑταῖρε, εἰς πονηρίαν, λεπτότητά τε καὶ αἶσχος καὶ ἀδυναμίαν ; θαυμάζοιμεν ἂν εἴ ποτέ τις ἑκὼν ἐπὶ τὸ τοιοῦτον

C ἀφικνεῖται ;

     ΚΛ. Πῶς γὰρ οὔ ;

     ΑΘ. Τί οὖν ; τοὺς εἰς τὰ ἰατρεῖα αὐτοὺς βαδίζοντας ἐπὶ φαρμακοποσίᾳ ἀγνοεῖν οἰόμεθα ὅτι μετ᾿ ὀλίγον ὕστερον καὶ ἐπὶ πολλὰς ἡμέρας

CLIN. He does.

ATH. So at that moment he will have very little control of himself?

CLIN. Very little.

ATH. And such a man is, we say, very bad?

CLIN. Very, indeed.

ATH. It appears, then, that not the greybeard only may be in his " second childhood," but the drunkard as well.

CLIN. An admirable observation, Stranger.

ATH. Is there any argument which will undertake to persuade us that this is a practice we ought to indulge in, instead of shunning it with all our might so far as we possibly can?

CLIN. It appears that there is: at any rate you assert this, and you were ready just now to argue it.

ATH. You are right in your reminder, and I am still ready to do so, now that you and Megillus have both expressed your willingness to listen to me.

CLIN. Of course we shall listen, if only on account of the surprising paradox that, of his own free will, a man ought to plunge into the depths of depravity.

ATH. Depravity of soul, you mean, do you not?

CLIN. Yes.

ATH. And how about plunging into a bad state of body, such as leanness or ugliness or impotence? Should we be surprised if a man of his own free will ever got into such a state?

CLIN. Of course we should.

ATH. Well then, do we suppose that persons who go of themselves to dispensaries to drink medicines are not aware that soon afterwards, and for many days to come, they will find themselves in a bodily

646 ἕξουσι τοιοῦτον τὸ σῶμα οἷον εἰ διὰ τέλους ἔχειν μέλλοιεν ζῆν οὐκ ἂν δέξαιντο; ἢ τοὺς ἐπὶ τὰ γυμνάσια καὶ πόνους ἰόντας οὐκ ἴσμεν ὡς ἀσθενεῖς εἰς τὸ παραχρῆμα γίγνονται;

ΚΛ. Πάντα ταῦτα ἴσμεν.

ΑΘ. Καὶ ὅτι τῆς μετὰ ταῦτα ὠφελείας ἕνεκα ἑκόντες πορεύονται;

D ΚΛ. Κάλλιστα.

ΑΘ. Οὐκοῦν χρὴ καὶ τῶν ἄλλων ἐπιτηδευμάτων πέρι διανοεῖσθαι τὸν αὐτὸν τρόπον;

ΚΛ. Πάνυ γε.

ΑΘ. Καὶ τῆς περὶ τὸν οἶνον ἄρα διατριβῆς ὡσαύτως διανοητέον, εἴπερ ἔνι τοῦτο ἐν τούτοις ὀρθῶς διανοηθῆναι.

ΚΛ. Πῶς δ' οὔ;

ΑΘ. Ἂν ἄρα τινὰ ἡμῖν ὠφέλειαν ἔχουσα φαίνηται μηδὲν τῆς περὶ τὸ σῶμα ἐλάττω, τῇ γε ἀρχῇ τὴν σωμασκίαν νικᾷ τῷ τὴν μὲν μετ' ἀλγηδόνων εἶναι, τὴν δὲ μή.

E ΚΛ. Ὀρθῶς λέγεις, θαυμάζοιμι δ' ἂν εἴ τι δυναίμεθα τοιοῦτον ἐν αὐτῷ καταμαθεῖν.

ΑΘ. Τοῦτ' αὐτὸ δὴ νῦν, ὡς ἔοικ', ἡμῖν ἤδη πειρατέον φράζειν. καί μοι λέγε· δύο φόβων εἴδη σχεδὸν ἐναντία δυνάμεθα κατανοῆσαι;

ΚΛ. Ποῖα δή;

ΑΘ. Τὰ τοιάδε· φοβούμεθα μέν που τὰ κακά, προσδοκῶντες γενήσεσθαι.

ΚΛ. Ναί.

ΑΘ. Φοβούμεθα δέ γε πολλάκις δόξαν, ἡγούμενοι δοξάζεσθαι κακοὶ πράττοντες ἢ λέγοντές τι 647 τῶν μὴ καλῶν· ὃν δὴ καὶ καλοῦμεν τὸν φόβον ἡμεῖς γε, οἶμαι δὲ καὶ πάντες, αἰσχύνην.

74

condition such as would make life intolerable[1] if it were to last for ever? And we know, do we not, that men who go to the gymnasia for hard training commence by becoming weaker?

CLIN. All this we know.

ATH. We know also that they go there voluntarily for the sake of the subsequent benefit?

CLIN. Quite true.

ATH. Should one not take the same view of the other institutions also?

CLIN. Certainly.

ATH. Then one must also take the same view of the practice of wine-drinking, if one can rightly class it amongst the others.

CLIN. Of course one must.

ATH. If then this practice should be shown to be quite as beneficial for us as bodily training, certainly at the outset it is superior to it, in so far as it is not, like bodily training, accompanied by pain.

CLIN. That is true; but I should be surprised if we succeeded in discovering in it any benefit.

ATH. That is precisely the point which we must at once try to make plain. Tell me now: can we discern two kinds of fear, of which the one is nearly the opposite of the other?

CLIN. What kinds do you mean?

ATH. These: when we expect evils to occur, we fear them.

CLIN. Yes.

ATH. And often we fear reputation, when we think we shall gain a bad repute for doing or saying something base; and this fear we (like everybody else, I imagine) call shame.

[1] Evidently, drastic purgatives were commonly prescribed.

647 ΚΛ. Τί δ' οὔ;

ΑΘ. Τούτους δὴ δύο ἔλεγον φόβους· ὧν ὁ
ἕτερος ἐναντίος μὲν ταῖς ἀλγηδόσι καὶ τοῖς ἄλλοις
φόβοις, ἐναντίος δ' ἐστὶ ταῖς πλείσταις καὶ
μεγίσταις ἡδοναῖς.

ΚΛ. Ὀρθότατα λέγεις.

ΑΘ. Ἆρ' οὖν οὐ καὶ[1] νομοθέτης, καὶ πᾶς οὗ
καὶ σμικρὸν ὄφελος, τοῦτον τὸν φόβον ἐν τιμῇ
μεγίστῃ σέβει καί, καλῶν αἰδῶ, τὸ τούτῳ θάρρος
ἐναντίον ἀναίδειάν τε προσαγορεύει καὶ μέγιστον
B κακὸν ἰδίᾳ τε καὶ δημοσίᾳ πᾶσι νενόμικεν;

ΚΛ. Ὀρθῶς λέγεις.

ΑΘ. Οὐκοῦν τά τ' ἄλλα πολλὰ καὶ μεγάλα ὁ
φόβος ἡμᾶς οὗτος σώζει, καὶ τὴν ἐν τῷ πολέμῳ
νίκην καὶ σωτηρίαν ἓν πρὸς ἓν οὐδὲν οὕτω σφόδρα
ἡμῖν ἀπεργάζεται. δύο γὰρ οὖν ἐστὸν τὰ τὴν
νίκην ἀπεργαζόμενα, θάρρος μὲν πολεμίων, φίλων
δὲ φόβος αἰσχύνης περὶ κάκης.[2]

ΚΛ. Ἔστι ταῦτα.

ΑΘ. Ἄφοβον ἡμῶν ἄρα δεῖ γίγνεσθαι καὶ
C φοβερὸν ἕκαστον· ὧν δ' ἑκάτερον ἕνεκα, διῃρήμεθα.

ΚΛ. Πάνυ μὲν οὖν.

ΑΘ. Καὶ μὴν ἄφοβόν γε ἕκαστον βουληθέντες
ποιεῖν φόβων πολλῶν τινων, εἰς φόβον ἄγοντες
αὐτὸν μετὰ νόμου τοιοῦτον ἀπεργαζόμεθα.

ΚΛ. Φαινόμεθα.

ΑΘ. Τί δ' ὅταν ἐπιχειρῶμέν τινα φοβερὸν

---

[1] οὐ καὶ Ast : οὐκ ἂν Zur., MSS.
[2] περὶ κάκης : πέρι κακῆς MSS., edd.

76

CLIN. Of course.

ATH. These are the two fears I was meaning; and of these the second is opposed to pains and to all other objects of fear, and opposed also to the greatest and most numerous pleasures.[1]

CLIN. Very true.

ATH. Does not, then, the lawgiver, and every man who is worth anything, hold this kind of fear in the highest honour, and name it "modesty"; and to the confidence which is opposed to it does he not give the name "immodesty," and pronounce it to be for all, both publicly and privately, a very great evil?

CLIN. Quite right.

ATH. And does not this fear, besides saving us in many other important respects, prove more effective than anything else in ensuring for us victory in war and security? For victory is, in fact, ensured by two things, of which the one is confidence towards enemies, the other, fear of the shame of cowardice in the eyes of friends.

CLIN. That is so.

ATH. Thus each one of us ought to become both fearless and fearful; and that for the several reasons we have now explained.

CLIN. Certainly.

ATH. Moreover, when we desire to make a person fearless in respect of a number of fears, it is by drawing him, with the help of the law, into fear that we make him such.

CLIN. Apparently.

ATH. And how about the opposite case, when we

---

[1] *i.e.* shame, which is fear of disgrace, induces fortitude under pain and the power of resisting vicious pleasures.

647 ποιεῖν μετὰ δίκης, ἆρ᾽ οὐκ ἀναισχυντίᾳ ξυμβάλ-
λοντας αὐτὸν καὶ προσγυμνάζοντας νικᾶν δεῖ
ποιεῖν διαμαχόμενον αὐτοῦ ταῖς ἡδοναῖς; ἢ τῇ
μὲν δειλίᾳ τῇ ἐν αὑτῷ προσμαχόμενον καὶ νικῶντα
D αὐτὴν δεῖ τέλεον οὕτω γίγνεσθαι πρὸς ἀνδρίαν,
ἄπειρος δὲ δήπου καὶ ἀγύμναστος ὢν τῶν τοιούτων
ἀγώνων ὁστισοῦν οὐδ᾽ ἂν ἥμισυς ἑαυτοῦ γένοιτο
πρὸς ἀρετήν, σώφρων δὲ ἄρα τελέως ἔσται μὴ
πολλαῖς ἡδοναῖς καὶ ἐπιθυμίαις προτρεπούσαις
ἀναισχυντεῖν καὶ ἀδικεῖν διαμεμαχημένος καὶ
νενικηκὼς μετὰ λόγου καὶ ἔργου καὶ τέχνης ἔν
τε παιδιαῖς καὶ ἐν σπουδαῖς, ἀλλ᾽ ἀπαθὴς ὢν
πάντων τῶν τοιούτων;

ΚΛ. Οὔκουν τόν γ᾽ εἰκότα λόγον ἂν ἔχοι.

E ΑΘ. Τί οὖν; φόβου φάρμακον ἔσθ᾽ ὅς τις θεὸς
ἔδωκεν ἀνθρώποις, ὥστε ὁπόσῳ πλέον ἂν ἐθέλῃ
τις πίνειν αὐτοῦ, τοσούτῳ μᾶλλον αὐτὸν νομίζειν
648 καθ᾽ ἑκάστην πόσιν δυστυχῆ γίγνεσθαι, καὶ
φοβεῖσθαι τὰ παρόντα καὶ τὰ μέλλοντα αὐτῷ
πάντα, καὶ τελευτῶντα εἰς πᾶν δέος ἰέναι τὸν
ἀνδρειότατον ἀνθρώπων, ἐκκοιμηθέντα δὲ καὶ
τοῦ πώματος ἀπαλλαγέντα πάλιν ἑκάστοτε τὸν
αὐτὸν γίγνεσθαι;

ΚΛ. Καὶ τί τοιοῦτον φαῖμεν ἄν, ὦ ξένε, ἐν
ἀνθρώποις γεγονέναι πῶμα;

ΑΘ. Οὐδέν· εἰ δ᾽ οὖν ἐγένετό ποθεν, ἔσθ᾽ ὅ τι
πρὸς ἀνδρίαν ἦν ἂν νομοθέτῃ χρήσιμον; οἷον τὸ
τοιόνδε περὶ αὐτοῦ καὶ μάλα εἴχομεν ἂν αὐτῷ
διαλέγεσθαι Φέρε, ὦ νομοθέτα, εἴτε Κρησίν, εἴθ᾽

attempt with the aid of justice to make a man fearful? Is it not by pitting him against shamelessness and exercising him against it that we must make him victorious in the fight against his own pleasures? Or shall we say that, whereas in the case of courage it is only by fighting and conquering his innate cowardice that a man can become perfect, and no one unversed and unpractised in contests of this sort can attain even half the excellence of which he is capable,—in the case of temperance, on the other hand, a man may attain perfection without a stubborn fight against hordes of pleasures and lusts which entice towards shamelessness and wrong-doing, and without conquering them by the aid of speech and act and skill, alike in play and at work,—and, in fact, without undergoing any of these experiences?

CLIN. It would not be reasonable to suppose so.

ATH. Well then: in the case of fear does there exist any specific, given by God to men, such that, the more a man likes to drink of it, the more, at every draught, he fancies himself plunged in misfortune and dreads alike things present and things to come, till finally, though he be the bravest of men, he arrives at a state of abject terror; whereas, when he has once got relieved of the potion and slept it off, he always becomes his normal self again?

CLIN. What potion of the kind can we mention, Stranger, as existing anywhere?

ATH. There is none. Supposing, however, that there had been one, would it have been of any service to the lawgiver for promoting courage? For instance, we might quite well have addressed him concerning it in this wise: "Come now, O lawgiver, —whether it be Cretans you are legislating for or

PLATO

648B οἷστισινοῦν νομοθετεῖς, πρῶτον μὲν τῶν πολιτῶν
ἆρ' ἂν δέξαιο βάσανον δυνατὸς εἶναι λαμβάνειν
ἀνδρίας τε πέρι καὶ δειλίας ;

ΚΛ. Φαίη που πᾶς ἂν δῆλον ὅτι.

ΑΘ. Τί δέ ; μετ' ἀσφαλείας καὶ ἄνευ κινδύνων
μεγάλων ἢ μετὰ τῶν ἐναντίων ;

ΚΛ. Καὶ τοῦτο <τὸ>[1] μετὰ τῆς ἀσφαλείας
ξυνομολογήσει πᾶς.

ΑΘ. Χρῷο δ' ἂν εἰς τοὺς φόβους τούτους ἄγων
καὶ ἐλέγχων ἐν τοῖς παθήμασιν, ὥστε ἀναγκάζειν
ἄφοβον γίγνεσθαι, παρακελευόμενος καὶ νουθετῶν
C καὶ τιμῶν, τὸν δὲ ἀτιμάζων, ὅστις σοι μὴ πείθοιτο
εἶναι τοιοῦτος οἷον σὺ τάττοις ἐν πᾶσι ; καὶ
γυμνασάμενον μὲν εὖ καὶ ἀνδρείως ἀζήμιον ἀπαλ-
λάττοις ἄν, κακῶς δὲ ζημίαν ἐπιτιθείς ; ἢ τὸ
παράπαν οὐκ ἂν χρῷο, μηδὲν ἄλλο ἐγκαλῶν τῷ
πώματι ;

ΚΛ. Καὶ πῶς οὐκ ἂν χρῷτο, ὦ ξένε ;

ΑΘ. Γυμνασία γοῦν, ὦ φίλε, παρὰ τὰ νῦν
θαυμαστὴ ῥᾳστώνης ἂν εἴη καθ' ἕνα καὶ κατ'
D ὀλίγους καὶ καθ' ὁπόσους τις ἀεὶ βούλοιτο· καὶ
εἴ τέ τις ἄρα μόνος ἐν ἐρημίᾳ, τὸ τῆς αἰσχύνης
ἐπίπροσθεν ποιούμενος, πρὶν εὖ σχεῖν ἡγούμενος
ὁρᾶσθαι μὴ δεῖν, οὕτω πρὸς τοὺς φόβους γυμνά-
ζοιτο, πῶμα μόνον ἀντὶ μυρίων πραγμάτων
παρασκευαζόμενος, ὀρθῶς ἄν τι πράττοι, εἴ τέ
τις ἑαυτῷ πιστεύων φύσει καὶ μελέτῃ καλῶς

---

[1] <τὸ> added by England.

anyone else,—would not your first desire be to have a test of courage and of cowardice which you might apply to your citizens?"

CLIN. Obviously everyone of them would say "Yes."

ATH. "And would you desire a test that was safe and free from serious risks, or the reverse?"

CLIN. All will agree, also, that the test must be safe.

ATH. "And would you utilise the test by bringing men into these fears and proving them while thus affected, so as to compel them to become fearless; employing exhortations, admonitions and rewards,— but degradation for all those that refused to conform wholly to the character you prescribed? And would you acquit without penalty everyone who had trained himself manfully and well, but impose a penalty on everyone who had done so badly? Or would you totally refuse to employ the potion as a test, although you have no objection to it on other grounds?"

CLIN. Of course he would employ it, Stranger.

ATH. At any rate, my friend, the training involved would be wonderfully simple, as compared with our present methods, whether it were applied to individuals singly, or to small groups, or to groups ever so large. Suppose, then, that a man, actuated by a feeling of shame and loth to show himself in public before he was in the best of condition, should remain alone by himself while undergoing this training against fears and relying on the potion alone for his solitary equipment, instead of endless exercises,—he would be acting quite rightly : so too would he who, trusting in himself that by nature and practice he is already well equipped, should have no hesitation in

648 παρεσκευάσθαι μηδὲν ὀκνοῖ μετὰ ξυμποτῶν
πλειόνων γυμναζόμενος ἐπιδείκνυσθαι τὴν ἐν τῇ
τοῦ πώματος ἀναγκαίᾳ διαφορᾷ δύναμιν ὑπερθέων
E καὶ κρατῶν, ὥστε ὑπ᾿ ἀσχημοσύνης μηδὲ ἓν
σφάλλεσθαι μέγα μηδ᾿ ἀλλοιοῦσθαι δι᾿ ἀρετήν,
πρὸς δὲ τὴν ἐσχάτην πόσιν ἀπαλλάττοιτο πρὶν
ἀφικνεῖσθαι, τὴν πάντων ἧτταν φοβούμενος
ἀνθρώπων τοῦ πώματος.

κλ. Ναί· σωφρονοίη γ᾿ ἄν,[1] ὦ ξένε, καὶ ὁ
τοιοῦτος οὕτω πράττων.

649 αθ. Πάλιν δὴ πρὸς τὸν νομοθέτην λέγωμεν
τάδε· Εἶεν, ὦ νομοθέτα, τοῦ μὲν δὴ φόβου
σχεδὸν οὔτε θεὸς ἔδωκεν ἀνθρώποις τοιοῦτον
φάρμακον οὔτε αὐτοὶ μεμηχανήμεθα· τοὺς γὰρ
γόητας οὐκ ἐν θοίνῃ λέγω· τῆς δὲ ἀφοβίας καὶ
τοῦ λίαν θαρρεῖν καὶ ἀκαίρως [ἃ μὴ χρή],[2] πότερον
ἔστι πῶμα, ἢ πῶς λέγομεν;

κλ. Ἔστι, φήσει που, τὸν οἶνον φράζων.

αθ. Ἦ καὶ τοὐναντίον ἔχει τοῦτο τῷ νῦν δὴ
λεγομένῳ; πίοντα τὸν ἄνθρωπον αὐτὸν αὑτοῦ
ποιεῖ πρῶτον ἵλεων εὐθὺς μᾶλλον ἢ πρότερον,
καὶ ὁπόσῳ ἂν πλέον αὐτοῦ γεύηται, τοσούτῳ
B πλειόνων ἐλπίδων ἀγαθῶν πληροῦσθαι[3] καὶ
δυνάμεως εἰς δόξαν; καὶ τελευτῶν δὴ πάσης ὁ
τοιοῦτος παρρησίας ὡς σοφὸς ὢν μεστοῦται καὶ
ἐλευθερίας, πάσης δὲ ἀφοβίας ὥστε εἰπεῖν τε
ἀόκνως ὁτιοῦν, ὡσαύτως δὲ καὶ πρᾶξαι; πᾶς[4]
ἡμῖν, οἶμαι, ταῦτ᾿ ἂν συγχωροῖ.

κλ. Τί μήν;

---

[1] γ᾿ ἄν conj. England : γάρ MSS. (γὰρ ἄν Stallb.)
[2] [ἃ μὴ χρή] I bracket.

training in company with a number of drinking companions and showing off how for speed and strength he is superior to the potency of the draughts he is obliged to drink, with the result that because of his excellence he neither commits any grave impropriety nor loses his head, and who, before they came to the last round, should quit the company, through fear of the defeat inflicted on all men by the wine-cup.

CLIN. Yes, Stranger, this man too would be acting temperately.

ATH. Once more let us address the lawgiver and say: "Be it so, O lawgiver, that for producing fear no such drug apparently has been given to men by God, nor have we devised such ourselves (for quacks I count not of our company); but does there exist a potion for inducing fearlessness and excessive and untimely confidence,—or what shall we say about this?"

CLIN. Presumably, he will assert that there is one, —naming wine.

ATH. And is not this exactly the opposite of the potion described just now? For, first, it makes the person who drinks it more jovial than he was before, and the more he imbibes it, the more he becomes filled with high hopes and a sense of power, till finally, puffed up with conceit, he abounds in every kind of licence of speech and action and every kind of audacity, without a scruple as to what he says or what he does. Everyone, I imagine, would agree that this is so.

CLIN. Undoubtedly.

---

[3] πληροῦσθαι MSS. : πληροῦται Zur.
[4] Zur. gives πᾶς . . . συγχωροῖ to *Clin.*, and τί μήν; to *Meg.*: I follow Cornarius, Ast, *al.*

649 ΑΘ. Ἀναμνησθῶμεν δὴ τόδε, ὅτι δύ' ἔφαμεν
ἡμῶν ἐν ταῖς ψυχαῖς δεῖν θεραπεύεσθαι, τὸ μὲν
C ὅπως ὅ τι μάλιστα θαρρήσομεν, τὸ δὲ τοὐναντίον
ὅ τι μάλιστα φοβησόμεθα.

ΚΛ. Ἃ τῆς αἰδοῦς ἔλεγες, ὡς οἰόμεθα.

ΑΘ. Καλῶς μνημονεύετε. ἐπειδὴ δὲ τήν τε
ἀνδρίαν καὶ τὴν ἀφοβίαν ἐν τοῖς φόβοις δεῖ κατα-
μελετᾶσθαι, σκεπτέον ἄρα τὸ ἐναντίον ἐν τοῖς
ἐναντίοις θεραπεύεσθαι δέον ἂν εἴη.

ΚΛ. Τό γ' οὖν εἰκός.

ΑΘ. Ἃ παθόντες ἄρα πεφύκαμεν διαφερόντως
θαρραλέοι τ' εἶναι καὶ θρασεῖς, ἐν τούτοις δέον ἄν,
ὡς ἔοικ', εἴη τὸ μελετᾶν ὡς ἥκιστα εἶναι ἀναισχύν-
D τους τε καὶ θρασύτητος γέμοντας, φοβεροὺς δὲ εἰς
τό τι τολμᾶν ἑκάστοτε λέγειν ἢ πάσχειν ἢ καὶ
δρᾶν αἰσχρὸν ὁτιοῦν.

ΚΛ. Ἔοικεν.

ΑΘ. Οὐκοῦν ταῦτά ἐστι πάντα ἐν οἷς ἐσμὲν
τοιοῦτοι, θυμός, ἔρως, ὕβρις, ἀμαθία, φιλοκέρδεια,
ἀφειδία,[1] καὶ ἔτι τοιάδε, πλοῦτος, κάλλος, ἰσχύς,
καὶ πάνθ' ὅσα δι' ἡδονῆς αὖ μεθύσκοντα παράφρο-
νας ποιεῖ· τούτων δ' εὐτελῆ τε καὶ ἀσινεστέραν
πρῶτον μὲν πρὸς τὸ λαμβάνειν πεῖραν, εἶτα εἰς τὸ
μελετᾶν, πλὴν τῆς ἐν οἴνῳ βασάνου καὶ παιδιᾶς
E τίνα ἔχομεν μηχανὴν[2] εἰπεῖν ἔμμετρον μᾶλλον, ἂν
καὶ ὁπωστιοῦν μετ' εὐλαβείας γίγνηται; σκοπῶ-
μεν γὰρ δή· δυσκόλου ψυχῆς καὶ ἀγρίας, ἐξ ἧς
ἀδικίαι μυρίαι γίγνονται, πότερον ἰόντα εἰς τὰ
ξυμβόλαια πεῖραν λαμβάνειν, κινδυνεύοντα περὶ
αὑτῷ,[3] σφαλερώτερον, ἢ ξυγγενόμενον μετὰ τῆς

---

[1] ἀφειδία: δειλία MSS. (bracketed by Ast).
[2] μηχανὴν G. G. Müller: ἡδονὴν MSS., edd.
[3] αὑτῷ Bekker, Schanz: αὑτῶν MSS.

ATH. Let us recall our previous statement that we must cultivate in our souls two things—namely, the greatest possible confidence, and its opposite, the greatest possible fear.

CLIN. Which you called, I think, the marks of modesty.

ATH. Your memory serves you well. Since courage and fearlessness ought to be practised amidst fears, we have to consider whether the opposite quality ought to be cultivated amidst conditions of the opposite kind.

CLIN. It certainly seems probable.

ATH. It appears then that we ought to be placed amongst those conditions which naturally tend to make us exceptionally confident and audacious when we are practising how to be as free as possible from shamelessness and excessive audacity, and fearful of ever daring to say or suffer or do anything shameful.

CLIN. So it appears.

ATH. And are not these the conditions in which we are of the character described,—anger, lust, insolence, ignorance, covetousness, and extravagance; and these also,—wealth, beauty, strength, and everything which intoxicates a man with pleasure and turns his head? And for the purpose, first, of providing a cheap and comparatively harmless test of these conditions, and, secondly, of affording practice in them, what more suitable device can we mention than wine, with its playful testing—provided that it is employed at all carefully? For consider: in the case of a man whose disposition is morose and savage (whence spring numberless iniquities), is it not more dangerous to test him by entering into money transactions with him, at one's own personal risk, than by associating

650 τοῦ Διονύσου θεωρίας ; ἢ πρὸς τἀφροδίσια ἡττη-
μένης τινὸς ψυχῆς βάσανον λαμβάνειν, ἐπιτρέποντα αὐτοῦ θυγατέρας τε καὶ υἱεῖς καὶ γυναῖκα,[1]
οὕτως ἐν τοῖς φιλτάτοις κινδυνεύσαντα, ἦθος
ψυχῆς θεάσασθαι ; καὶ μυρία δὴ λέγων οὐκ ἄν
τίς ποτε ἀνύσειεν, ὅσῳ διαφέρει τὸ μετὰ παιδιᾶς
τὴν ἄλλως ἄνευ μισθοῦ ζημιώδους θεωρεῖν· καὶ
δὴ καὶ τοῦτο μὲν αὐτὸ περί γε τούτων οὔτ' ἂν
B Κρῆτας οὔτ' ἄλλους ἀνθρώπους οὐδένας οἰόμεθα
ἀμφισβητῆσαι, μὴ οὐ πεῖράν τε ἀλλήλων ἐπιεικῆ
ταύτην εἶναι τό τε τῆς εὐτελείας καὶ ἀσφαλείας
καὶ τάχους διαφέρειν πρὸς τὰς ἄλλας βασάνους.

ΚΛ. Ἀληθὲς τοῦτό γε.

ΑΘ. Τοῦτο μὲν ἄρ' ἂν τῶν χρησιμωτάτων ἓν
εἴη, τὸ γνῶναι τὰς φύσεις τε καὶ ἕξεις τῶν ψυχῶν,
τῇ τέχνῃ ἐκείνῃ ἧς ἐστι ταῦτα θεραπεύειν· ἔστι
δέ που, φαμέν, ὡς οἶμαι, πολιτικῆς. ἢ γάρ ;

ΚΛ. Πάνυ μὲν οὖν.

[1] γυναῖκα Ast, Schanz : γυναῖκας MSS.

with him with the help of Dionysus and his festive insight? And when a man is a slave to the pleasures of sex, is it not a more dangerous test to entrust to him one's own daughters and sons and wife, and thus imperil one's own nearest and dearest, in order to discover the disposition of his soul? In fact, one might quote innumerable instances in a vain endeavour to show the full superiority of this playful method of inspection which is without either serious consequence or costly damage. Indeed, so far as that is concerned, neither the Cretans, I imagine, nor any other people would dispute the fact that herein we have a fair test of man by man, and that for cheapness, security and speed it is superior to all other tests.

CLIN. That certainly is true.

ATH. This then—the discovery of the natures and conditions of men's souls—will prove one of the things most useful to that art whose task it is to treat them; and that art is (as I presume we say) the art of politics: is it not so?

CLIN. Undoubtedly.

B

ΑΘ. Τὸ δὴ μετὰ τοῦτο, ὡς ἔοικε, σκεπτέον ἐκεῖνο περὶ αὐτῶν, πότερα τοῦτο μόνον ἀγαθὸν ἔχει, τὸ κατιδεῖν πῶς ἔχομεν τὰς φύσεις, ἢ καί τι μέγεθος ὠφελείας ἄξιον πολλῆς σπουδῆς ἔνεστ᾽ ἐν τῇ κατ᾽ ὀρθὸν χρείᾳ τῆς ἐν οἴνῳ συνουσίας. τί οὖν δὴ λέγομεν; ἔνεσθ᾽, ὡς ὁ λόγος ἔοικε βούλεσθαι σημαίνειν· ὅπῃ δὲ καὶ ὅπως, ἀκούωμεν προσέχοντες τὸν νοῦν, μή πῃ παραποδισθῶμεν ὑπ᾽ αὐτοῦ.

ΚΛ. Λέγ᾽ οὖν.

ΑΘ. Ἀναμνησθῆναι τοίνυν ἔγωγε πάλιν ἐπι-
653 θυμῶ τί ποτ᾽ ἐλέγομεν [1] ἡμῖν εἶναι τὴν ὀρθὴν παιδείαν. τούτου γάρ, ὥς γ᾽ ἐγὼ τοπάζω τὰ νῦν, ἔστιν ἐν τῷ ἐπιτηδεύματι τούτῳ καλῶς κατορθουμένῳ σωτηρία.

ΚΛ. Μέγα λέγεις.

ΑΘ. Λέγω τοίνυν τῶν παίδων παιδικὴν εἶναι πρώτην αἴσθησιν ἡδονὴν καὶ λύπην, καὶ ἐν οἷς ἀρετὴ ψυχῇ καὶ κακία παραγίγνεται πρῶτον, ταῦτ᾽ εἶναι· φρόνησιν δὲ καὶ ἀληθεῖς δόξας βεβαίους, εὐτυχὴς [2] ὅτῳ καὶ πρὸς τὸ γῆρας παρεγένετο· τέλεος δ᾽ οὖν ἔστ᾽ ἄνθρωπος ταῦτα καὶ τὰ
B ἐν τούτοις πάντα κεκτημένος ἀγαθά. παιδείαν δὴ λέγω τὴν παραγιγνομένην πρῶτον παισὶν ἀρετήν, ἡδονὴ δὲ καὶ φιλία καὶ λύπη καὶ μῖσος ἂν ὀρθῶς ἐν ψυχαῖς ἐγγίγνωνται μήπω δυναμένων λόγον [3]

---

[1] ποτ᾽ ἐλέγομεν Madvig, Schanz: ποτε λέγομεν MSS.
[2] εὐτυχὴς Ast: εὐτυχὲς MSS.

BOOK II

ATH. In the next place, we probably ought to enquire, regarding this subject, whether the discerning of men's natural dispositions is the only gain to be derived from the right use of wine-parties, or whether it entails benefits so great as to be worthy of serious consideration. What do we say about this? Our argument evidently tends to indicate that it does entail such benefits; so how and wherein it does so let us now hear, and that with minds attentive, lest haply we be led astray by it.

CLIN. Say on.

ATH. I want us to call to mind again our definition of right education. For the safe-keeping of this depends, as I now conjecture, upon the correct establishment of the institution mentioned.

CLIN. That is a strong statement!

ATH. What I state is this,—that in children the first childish sensations are pleasure and pain, and that it is in these first that goodness and badness come to the soul; but as to wisdom and settled true opinions, a man is lucky if they come to him even in old age; and he that is possessed of these blessings, and all that they comprise, is indeed a perfect man. I term, then, the goodness that first comes to children "education." When pleasure and love, and pain and hatred, spring up rightly in the souls of those who are unable as yet to grasp a rational

---

² λόγον Euseb., Schanz : λόγῳ MSS.

653 λαμβάνειν, λαβόντων δὲ τὸν λόγον συμφωνήσωσι τῷ
λόγῳ, ⟨τῷ⟩ [1] ὀρθῶς εἰθίσθαι ὑπὸ τῶν προσηκόντων
ἐθῶν· αὐτη ἔσθ' [2] ἡ ξυμφωνία ξύμπασα μὲν ἀρετή,
τὸ δὲ περὶ τὰς ἡδονὰς καὶ λύπας τεθραμμένον
αὐτῆς ὀρθῶς, ὥστε μισεῖν μὲν ἃ χρὴ μισεῖν εὐθὺς
C ἐξ ἀρχῆς μέχρι τέλους, στέργειν δὲ ἃ χρὴ στέργειν,
τοῦτ' αὐτὸ ἀποτεμὼν τῷ λόγῳ καὶ παιδείαν προσαγορεύων, κατά γε τὴν ἐμὴν ὀρθῶς ἂν προσ-
αγορεύοις.

ΚΛ. Καὶ γάρ, ὦ ξένε, ἡμῖν καὶ τὰ πρότερον
ὀρθῶς σοι παιδείας πέρι καὶ τὰ νῦν εἰρῆσθαι
δοκεῖ.

ΑΘ. Καλῶς τοίνυν. τούτων γὰρ δὴ τῶν ὀρθῶς
τεθραμμένων ἡδονῶν καὶ λυπῶν παιδειῶν οὐσῶν
χαλᾶται τοῖς ἀνθρώποις καὶ διαφθείρεται τὰ
D πολλὰ ἐν τῷ βίῳ, θεοὶ δὲ οἰκτείραντες τὸ τῶν
ἀνθρώπων ἐπίπονον πεφυκὸς γένος ἀναπαύλας τε
αὐτοῖς τῶν πόνων ἐτάξαντο τὰς τῶν ἑορτῶν
ἀμοιβὰς [τοῖς θεοῖς], [3] καὶ Μούσας Ἀπόλλωνά τε
μουσηγέτην καὶ Διόνυσον ξυνεορταστὰς ἔδοσαν, ἵν'
ἐπανορθῶνται τάς γε [4] τροφὰς γενόμενοι [5] ἐν
ταῖς ἑορταῖς μετὰ θεῶν. ὁρᾶν οὖν χρὴ πότερον
ἀληθὴς ἡμῖν κατὰ φύσιν ὁ λόγος ὑμνεῖται τὰ νῦν,
ἢ πῶς. φησὶ δὲ τὸ νέον ἅπαν ὡς ἔπος εἰπεῖν τοῖς
τε σώμασι καὶ ταῖς φωναῖς ἡσυχίαν ἄγειν οὐ
E δύνασθαι, κινεῖσθαι δὲ ἀεὶ ζητεῖν καὶ φθέγγεσθαι,
τὰ μὲν ἁλλόμενα καὶ σκιρτῶντα, οἷον ὀρχούμενα
μεθ' ἡδονῆς καὶ προσπαίζοντα, τὰ δὲ φθεγγόμενα
πάσας φωνάς· τὰ μὲν οὖν ἄλλα ζῷα οὐκ ἔχειν

[1] ⟨τῷ⟩ Stallbaum.
[2] αὕτη ἔσθ' Euseb.: αὐτήσθ' MSS.: αὐτῆς θ' Zur.
[3] [τοῖς θεοῖς] omitted by Schanz, after Clem. Alex.
[4] γε Hermann: τε MSS.: omitted by Zur.

account; and when, after grasping the rational account, they consent thereunto through having been
rightly trained in fitting practices:—this consent,
viewed as a whole, is goodness, while the part of it
that is rightly trained in respect of pleasures and
pains, so as to hate what ought to be hated, right
from the beginning up to the very end, and to love
what ought to be loved,—if you were to mark this
part off in your definition and call it "education,"
you would be giving it, in my opinion, its right name.

CLIN. You are quite right, Stranger, as it seems
to us, both in what you said before and in what you
say now about education.

ATH. Very good. Now these forms of child-
training, which consist in right discipline in pleasures
and pains, grow slack and weakened to a great
extent in the course of men's lives; so the gods, in
pity for the human race thus born to misery, have
ordained the feasts of thanksgiving as periods of
respite from their troubles; and they have granted
them as companions in their feasts the Muses and
Apollo the master of music, and Dionysus, that they
may at least set right again their modes of discipline
by associating in their feasts with gods. We must
consider, then, whether the account that is harped on
nowadays is true to nature? What it says is that,
almost without exception, every young creature is
incapable of keeping either its body or its tongue
quiet, and is always striving to move and to cry,
leaping and skipping and delighting in dances and
games, and uttering, also, noises of every description.
Now, whereas all other creatures are devoid of any

---

⁵ γενόμενοι Wagner, Schanz: γενομένας MSS.

653 αἴσθησιν τῶν ἐν ταῖς κινήσεσι τάξεων οὐδὲ
ἀταξιῶν, οἷς δὴ ῥυθμὸς ὄνομα καὶ ἁρμονία· ἡμῖν
δὲ οὓς εἴπομεν τοὺς θεοὺς συγχορευτὰς δεδόσθαι,
τούτους εἶναι καὶ τοὺς δεδωκότας τὴν ἔνρυθμόν τε
καὶ ἐναρμόνιον αἴσθησιν μεθ' ἡδονῆς, ᾗ δὴ κινεῖν
654 τε ἡμᾶς καὶ χορηγεῖν ἡμῶν τούτους, ᾠδαῖς τε καὶ
ὀρχήσεσιν ἀλλήλοις ξυνείροντας, χορούς τε ὠνο-
μακέναι παρὰ τῆς χαρᾶς ἔμφυτον ὄνομα. πρῶτον
δὴ τοῦτο ἀποδεξώμεθα; θῶμεν παιδείαν εἶναι
πρώτην διὰ Μουσῶν τε καὶ Ἀπόλλωνος; ἢ πῶς;

ΚΛ. Οὕτως.

ΑΘ. Οὐκοῦν ὁ μὲν ἀπαίδευτος ἀχόρευτος ἡμῖν
Β ἔσται, τὸν δὲ πεπαιδευμένον ἱκανῶς κεχορευκότα
θετέον;

ΚΛ. Τί μήν;

ΑΘ. Χορεία γε μὴν ὄρχησίς τε καὶ ᾠδὴ τὸ
ξύνολόν ἐστιν.

ΚΛ. Ἀναγκαῖον.

ΑΘ. Ὁ καλῶς ἄρα πεπαιδευμένος ᾄδειν τε καὶ
ὀρχεῖσθαι δυνατὸς ἂν εἴη καλῶς.

ΚΛ. Ἔοικεν.

ΑΘ. Ἴδωμεν δὴ τί ποτ' ἐστὶ τὸ νῦν αὖ λεγόμενον.

ΚΛ. Τὸ ποῖον δή;

ΑΘ. Καλῶς ᾄδει, φαμέν, καὶ καλῶς ὀρχεῖται·
C πότερον εἰ καὶ καλὰ ᾄδει καὶ καλὰ ὀρχεῖται
προσθῶμεν ἢ μή;

ΚΛ. Προσθῶμεν.

ΑΘ. Τί δ', ἂν τὰ καλά τε ἡγούμενος εἶναι καλὰ

perception of the various kinds of order and disorder in movement (which we term rhythm and harmony), to us men the very gods, who were given, as we said, to be our fellows in the dance, have granted the pleasurable perception of rhythm and harmony, whereby they cause us to move and lead our choirs, linking us one with another by means of songs and dances; and to the choir they have given its name from the "cheer" implanted therein.[1] Shall we accept this account to begin with, and postulate that education owes its origin to Apollo and the Muses?

CLIN. Yes.

ATH. Shall we assume that the uneducated man is without choir-training, and the educated man fully choir-trained?

CLIN. Certainly.

ATH. Choir-training, as a whole, embraces of course both dancing and song.

CLIN. Undoubtedly.

ATH. So the well-educated man will be able both to sing and dance well.

CLIN. Evidently.

ATH. Let us now consider what this last statement of ours implies.

CLIN. Which statement?

ATH. Our words are,—"he sings well and dances well": ought we, or ought we not, to add,—"provided that he sings good songs and dances good dances"?

CLIN. We ought to add this.

ATH. How then, if a man takes the good for

[1] Here χορός is fancifully derived from χαρά, "joy." For similar etymologies, see the *Cratylus, passim.*

654 καὶ τὰ αἰσχρὰ αἰσχρὰ οὕτως αὐτοῖς χρῆται·
βέλτιον ὁ τοιοῦτος πεπαιδευμένος ἡμῖν ἔσται τὴν
χορείαν τε καὶ μουσικὴν ὃς ἂν τῷ μὲν σώματι καὶ
τῇ φωνῇ τὸ διανοηθὲν εἶναι καλὸν ἱκανῶς ὑπηρετεῖν
δυνηθῇ ἑκάστοτε, χαίρῃ δὲ μὴ τοῖς καλοῖς μηδὲ
μισῇ τὰ μὴ καλά, ἢ ʼκεῖνος ὃς ἂν τῇ μὲν φωνῇ
καὶ τῷ σώματι μὴ πάνυ δυνατὸς ᾖ κατορθοῦν ἢ
D διανοεῖται,[1] τῇ δὲ ἡδονῇ καὶ λύπῃ κατορθοῖ, τὰ
μὲν ἀσπαζόμενος, ὅσα καλά, τὰ δὲ δυσχεραίνων,
ὁπόσα μὴ καλά;

ΚΛ. Πολὺ τὸ διαφέρον, ὦ ξένε, λέγεις τῆς
παιδείας.

ΑΘ. Οὐκοῦν εἰ μὲν τὸ καλὸν ᾠδῆς τε καὶ
ὀρχήσεως πέρι γιγνώσκομεν τρεῖς ὄντες, ἴσμεν
καὶ τὸν πεπαιδευμένον τε καὶ ἀπαίδευτον ὀρθῶς·
εἰ δὲ ἀγνοοῦμέν γε τοῦτο, οὐδ᾽ εἴ τις παιδείας ἐστὶ
E φυλακὴ καὶ ὅπου διαγιγνώσκειν ἄν ποτε δυναίμεθα. ἆρ᾽ οὐχ οὕτως;

ΚΛ. Οὕτω μὲν οὖν.

ΑΘ. Ταῦτ᾽ ἄρα μετὰ τοῦθ᾽ ἡμῖν αὖ, καθάπερ
κυσὶν ἰχνευούσαις, διερευνητέον, σχῆμά τε καλὸν
καὶ μέλος κατ᾽[2] ᾠδὴν καὶ ὄρχησιν. εἰ δὲ ταῦθ᾽
ἡμᾶς διαφυγόντα οἰχήσεται, μάταιος ὁ μετὰ ταῦθ᾽
ἡμῖν περὶ παιδείας ὀρθῆς εἴθ᾽ Ἑλληνικῆς εἴτε
βαρβαρικῆς λόγος ἂν εἴη.

ΚΛ. Ναί.

ΑΘ. Εἶεν· τί δὲ δὴ τὸ καλὸν χρὴ φάναι σχῆμα
ἢ μέλος εἶναί ποτε; φέρε, ἀνδρικῆς ψυχῆς ἐν
655 πόνοις ἐχομένης[3] καὶ δειλῆς ἐν τοῖς αὐτοῖς τε καὶ
ἴσοις ἆρ᾽ ὅμοια τά τε σχήματα καὶ τὰ φθέγματα
ξυμβαίνει γίγνεσθαι;

---

[1] ᾖ διανοεῖται Badham, Schanz : ᾖ διανοεῖσθαι MSS.

good and the bad for bad and treats them accordingly? Shall we regard such a man as better trained in choristry and music when he is always able both with gesture and voice to represent adequately that which he conceives to be good, though he feels neither delight in the good nor hatred of the bad,— or when, though not wholly able to represent his conception rightly by voice and gesture, he yet keeps right in his feelings of pain and pleasure, welcoming everything good and abhorring everything not good?

CLIN. There is a vast difference between the two cases, Stranger, in point of education.

ATH. If, then, we three understand what constitutes goodness in respect of dance and song, we also know who is and who is not rightly educated; but without this knowledge we shall never be able to discern whether there exists any safeguard for education or where it is to be found. Is not that so?

CLIN. It is.

ATH. What we have next to track down, like hounds on the trail, is goodness of posture and tunes in relation to song and dance; if this eludes our pursuit, it will be in vain for us to discourse further concerning right education, whether of Greeks or of barbarians.

CLIN. Yes.

ATH. Well then, however shall we define goodness of posture or of tune? Come, consider: when a manly soul is beset by troubles, and a cowardly soul by troubles identical and equal, are the postures and utterances that result in the two cases similar?

---

² κατ' Ritter, England : καὶ MSS.

³ ἐχομένης Stephens, Ast : ἐρχομένης MSS.

655 κλ. Καὶ πῶς, ὅτε γε μηδὲ τὰ χρώματα ;

αθ. Καλῶς γε, ὦ ἑταῖρε· ἀλλ' ἐν γὰρ μουσικῇ καὶ σχήματα μὲν καὶ μέλη ἔνεστι, περὶ ῥυθμὸν καὶ ἁρμονίαν οὔσης τῆς μουσικῆς, ὥστε εὔρυθμον μὲν καὶ εὐάρμοστον, εὔχρων δὲ μέλος ἢ σχῆμα οὐκ ἔστιν ἀπεικάσαντα ὥσπερ οἱ χοροδιδάσκαλοι ἀπεικάζουσιν ὀρθῶς φθέγγεσθαι· τὸ δὲ τοῦ δειλοῦ τε καὶ ἀνδρείου σχῆμα ἢ μέλος ἔστι τε καὶ ὀρθῶς
B προσαγορεύειν ἔχει τὰ μὲν τῶν ἀνδρείων καλά, τὰ τῶν δειλῶν δὲ αισχρά. καὶ ἵνα δὴ μὴ μακρολογία πολλή τις γίγνηται περὶ ταῦθ' ἡμῖν ἅπαντα, ἁπλῶς ἔστω τὰ μὲν ἀρετῆς ἐχόμενα ψυχῆς ἢ σώματος, εἴτε αὐτῆς εἴτε τινὸς εἰκόνος, ξύμπαντα σχήματά τε καὶ μέλη καλά, τὰ δὲ κακίας αὖ τοὐναντίον ἅπαν.

κλ. Ὀρθῶς τε προκαλεῖ καὶ ταῦθ' ἡμῖν οὕτως ἔχειν ἀποκεκρίσθω τὰ νῦν.

αθ. Ἔτι δὴ τόδε· πότερον ἅπαντες πάσαις
C χορείαις ὁμοίως χαίρομεν, ἢ πολλοῦ δεῖ ;

κλ. Τοῦ παντὸς μὲν οὖν.

αθ. Τί ποτ' ἂν οὖν λέγωμεν τὸ πεπλανηκὸς ἡμᾶς εἶναι ; πότερον οὐ ταὐτά ἐστι καλὰ ἡμῖν πᾶσιν, ἢ τὰ μὲν αὐτά, ἀλλ' οὐ δοκεῖ ταὐτὰ εἶναι ; οὐ γάρ που ἐρεῖ γέ τις ὥς ποτε τὰ τῆς κακίας ἢ ἀρετῆς καλλίονα χορεύματα, οὐδ' ὡς αὐτὸς μὲν χαίρει τοῖς τῆς μοχθηρίας σχήμασιν, οἱ δ' ἄλλοι ἐναντίᾳ ταύτης Μούσῃ τινί. καί τοι λέγουσί γε οἱ πλεῖστοι μουσικῆς ὀρθότητα εἶναι τὴν ἡδονὴν

---

[1] "Music" comprises both dance and song (including instrumental accompaniment), whether executed by single

CLIN. How could they be, when even their complexions differ in colour?

ATH. Well said, my friend. But in fact, while postures and tunes do exist in music,[1] which deals with rhythm and harmony, so that one can rightly speak of a tune or posture being "rhythmical" or "harmonious," one cannot rightly apply the choir-masters' metaphor "well-coloured" to tune and posture; but one can use this language about the posture and tune of the brave man and the coward, and one is right in calling those of the brave man good, and those of the coward bad. To avoid a tediously long disquisition, let us sum up the whole matter by saying that the postures and tunes which attach to goodness of soul or body, or to some image thereof, are universally good, while those which attach to badness are exactly the reverse.

CLIN. Your pronouncement is correct, and we now formally endorse it.

ATH. Another point:—do we all delight equally in choral dancing, or far from equally?

CLIN. Very far indeed.

ATH. Then what are we to suppose it is that misleads us? Is it the fact that we do not all regard as good the same things, or is it that, although they are the same, they are thought not to be the same? For surely no one will maintain that the choric performances of vice are better than those of virtue, or that he himself enjoys the postures of turpitude, while all others delight in music of the opposite kind. Most people, however, assert that the value of music consists in its power of affording pleasure

performers or by groups (χορεία). The "postures" are those of the dancer, the "tunes" those of the singer.

655D ταῖς ψυχαῖς πορίζουσαν δύναμιν· ἀλλὰ τοῦτο
μὲν οὔτε ἀνεκτὸν οὔτε ὅσιον τὸ παράπαν φθέγγεσθαι. τόδε δὲ μᾶλλον εἰκὸς πλανᾶν ἡμᾶς.

ΚΛ. Τὸ ποῖον;

ΑΘ. Ἐπειδὴ μιμήματα τρόπων ἐστὶ τὰ περὶ
τὰς χορείας, ἐν πράξεσί τε παντοδαπαῖς γιγνόμενα καὶ τύχαις, καὶ ἤθεσι καὶ μιμήσεσι[1] δι-
εξιόντων ἑκάστων, οἷς μὲν ἂν πρὸς τρόπου τὰ
ῥηθέντα ἢ μελῳδηθέντα ἢ καὶ ὁπωσοῦν χορευ-
θέντα ἢ κατὰ φύσιν ἢ κατὰ ἔθος ἢ κατ᾽ ἀμφότερα,
E τούτους μὲν καὶ τούτοις χαίρειν τε καὶ ἐπαινεῖν
αὐτὰ καὶ προσαγορεύειν καλὰ ἀναγκαῖον, οἷς δ᾽
ἂν παρὰ φύσιν ἢ τρόπον ἤ τινα ξυνήθειαν, οὔτε
χαίρειν δυνατὸν οὔτε ἐπαινεῖν αἰσχρά τε προσαγορεύειν. οἷς δ᾽ ἂν τὰ μὲν τῆς φύσεως ὀρθὰ
ξυμβαίνῃ, τὰ δὲ τῆς συνηθείας ἐναντία, ἢ τὰ μὲν
τῆς συνηθείας ὀρθά, τὰ δὲ τῆς φύσεως ἐναντία,
οὗτοι δὴ ταῖς ἡδοναῖς τοὺς ἐπαίνους ἐναντίους
656 προσαγορεύουσιν· ἡδέα γὰρ τούτων ἕκαστα εἶναί
φασι, πονηρὰ δέ, καὶ ἐναντίον ἄλλων οὓς οἴονται
φρονεῖν αἰσχύνονται μὲν κινεῖσθαι τῷ σώματι τὰ
τοιαῦτα, αἰσχύνονται δὲ ᾄδειν ὡς ἀποφαινόμενοι
καλὰ μετὰ σπουδῆς, χαίρουσι δὲ παρ᾽ αὐτοῖς.

ΚΛ. Ὀρθότατα λέγεις.

ΑΘ. Μῶν οὖν τι βλάβην ἔσθ᾽ ἥντινα φέρει τῷ
χαίροντι πονηρίας ἢ σχήμασιν ἢ μέλεσιν, ἤ τιν᾽

---

[1] μιμήσεσι some MSS. : μιμήμασι other MSS., Zur.

---

[1] *i.e.* music is commonly judged solely by the amount of
pleasure it affords, without any regard to the quality of the
pleasure. The *Athenian* proceeds to show how dangerous a

98

to the soul.[1] But such an assertion is quite intolerable, and it is blasphemy even to utter it. The fact
which misleads us is more probably the following—

CLIN. What?

ATH. Inasmuch as choric performances are representations of character, exhibited in actions and
circumstances of every kind, in which the several
performers enact their parts by habit and imitative
art, whenever the choric performances are congenial
to them in point of diction, tune or other features
(whether from natural bent or from habit, or from
both these causes combined), then these performers
invariably delight in such performances and extol
them as excellent; whereas those who find them
repugnant to their nature, disposition or habits
cannot possibly delight in them or praise them, but
call them bad. And when men are right in their
natural tastes but wrong in those acquired by
habituation, or right in the latter but wrong in the
former, then by their expressions of praise they
convey the opposite of their real sentiments; for
whereas they say of a performance that it is pleasant
but bad, and feel ashamed to indulge in such bodily
motions before men whose wisdom they respect, or
to sing such songs (as though they seriously
approved of them), they really take a delight in
them in private.

CLIN. Very true.

ATH. Does the man who delights in bad postures
and tunes suffer any damage thereby, or do those

doctrine this is : music, he maintains, should not be used
merely to pander to the low tastes of the populace, but
rather treated as an educational instrument for the
elevation of public morals.

656 ὠφέλειαν αὖ τοῖς πρὸς τἀναντία τὰς ἡδονὰς
ἀποδεχομένοις ;

ΚΛ. Εἰκός γε.

Β ΑΘ. Πότερον εἰκὸς ἢ καὶ ἀναγκαῖον ταὐτὸν
εἶναι ὅπερ ὅταν τις πονηροῖς ἤθεσι ξυνὼν κακῶν
ἀνθρώπων μὴ μισῇ, χαίρῃ δὲ ἀποδεχόμενος, ψέγῃ
δὲ ὡς ἐν παιδιᾶς μοίρᾳ, ὀνειρώττων αὐτοῦ τὴν
μοχθηρίαν ; τότε ὁμοιοῦσθαι δή που ἀνάγκη τὸν
χαίροντα, ὁποτέροις ἂν χαίρῃ, ἐὰν ἄρα καὶ ἐπαινεῖν αἰσχύνηται. καίτοι τοῦ τοιούτου τί μεῖζον
ἀγαθὸν ἢ κακὸν φαῖμεν ἂν ἡμῖν ἐκ πάσης ἀνάγκης
γίγνεσθαι ;

ΚΛ. Δοκῶ μὲν οὐδέν.

C ΑΘ. Ὅπου δὴ νόμοι καλῶς εἰσὶ κείμενοι ἢ καὶ
εἰς τὸν ἔπειτα χρόνον ἔσονται <περὶ> [1] τὴν περὶ
τὰς Μούσας παιδείαν τε καὶ παιδιάν, οἰόμεθα
ἐξέσεσθαι τοῖς ποιητικοῖς, ὅ τί περ ἂν αὐτὸν τὸν
ποιητὴν ἐν τῇ ποιήσει τέρπῃ ῥυθμοῦ ἢ μέλους ἢ
ῥήματος ἐχόμενον, τοῦτο διδάσκοντα καὶ τοὺς
τῶν εὐνόμων παῖδας καὶ νέους ἐν τοῖς χοροῖς ὅ
τι ἂν τύχῃ ἀπεργάζεσθαι πρὸς ἀρετὴν ἢ μοχθηρίαν ;

ΚΛ. Οὔ τοι δὴ τοῦτό γε λόγον ἔχει· πῶς γὰρ
ἄν ;

D ΑΘ. Νῦν δέ γε αὐτὸ ὡς ἔπος εἰπεῖν ἐν πάσαις
ταῖς πόλεσιν ἔξεστι δρᾶν, πλὴν κατ' Αἴγυπτον.

ΚΛ. Ἐν Αἰγύπτῳ δὲ δὴ πῶς τὸ τοιοῦτον φῂς
νενομοθετῆσθαι ;

ΑΘ. Θαῦμα καὶ ἀκοῦσαι. πάλαι γὰρ δή ποτε,
ὡς ἔοικεν, ἐγνώσθη παρ' αὐτοῖς οὗτος ὁ λόγος ὃν
τὰ νῦν λέγομεν ἡμεῖς, ὅτι καλὰ μὲν σχήματα,
καλὰ δὲ μέλη δεῖ μεταχειρίζεσθαι ταῖς συνηθείαις

who take pleasure in the opposite gain therefrom any benefit?

CLIN. Probably.

ATH. Is it not probable or rather inevitable that the result here will be exactly the same as what takes place when a man who is living amongst the bad habits of wicked men, though he does not really abhor but rather accepts and delights in those habits, yet censures them casually, as though dimly aware of his own turpitude? In such a case it is, to be sure, inevitable that the man thus delighted becomes assimilated to those habits, good or bad, in which he delights, even though he is ashamed to praise them. Yet what blessing could we name, or what curse, greater than that of assimilation which befalls us so inevitably?

CLIN. There is none, I believe.

ATH. Now where laws are, or will be in the future, rightly laid down regarding musical education and recreation, do we imagine that poets will be granted such licence that they may teach whatever form of rhythm or tune or words they best like themselves to the children of law-abiding citizens and the young men in the choirs, no matter what the result may be in the way of virtue or depravity?

CLIN. That would be unreasonable, most certainly.

ATH. But at present this licence is allowed in practically every State, with the exception of Egypt.

CLIN. How, then, does the law stand in Egypt?

ATH. It is marvellous, even in the telling. It appears that long ago they determined on the rule of which we are now speaking, that the youth of a State should practise in their rehearsals postures and

---

[1] $<\pi\epsilon\rho\iota>$ added by Schanz.

656 τοὺς ἐν ταῖς πόλεσι νέους. ταξάμενοι δὲ ταῦτα
ἄττα ἐστὶ καὶ ὁποῖ' ἄττα, ἀπέφηναν ἐν τοῖς ἱεροῖς,
E καὶ παρὰ ταῦτ' οὐκ ἐξῆν οὔτε ζωγράφοις οὔτ'
ἄλλοις ὅσοι σχήματα καὶ ὁμοῖ' ἄττα [1] ἀπεργάζονται καινοτομεῖν οὐδ' ἐπινοεῖν ἀλλ' ἄττα ἢ τὰ
πάτρια, οὐδὲ νῦν ἔξεστιν, οὔτ' ἐν τούτοις οὔτ' ἐν
μουσικῇ ξυμπάσῃ. σκοπῶν δ' εὑρήσεις αὐτόθι
τὰ μυριοστὸν ἔτος γεγραμμένα ἢ τετυπωμένα,
657 οὐχ ὡς ἔπος εἰπεῖν μυριοστὸν ἀλλ' ὄντως, τῶν νῦν
δεδημιουργημένων οὔτε τι καλλίονα οὔτ' αἰσχίω,
τὴν αὐτὴν δὲ τέχνην ἀπειργασμένα.

κλ. Θαυμαστὸν λέγεις.

αθ. Νομοθετικὸν μὲν οὖν καὶ πολιτικὸν ὑπερ-
βαλλόντως. ἀλλ' ἕτερα φαῦλ' ἂν εὕροις αὐτόθι·
τοῦτο δ' οὖν τὸ περὶ μουσικὴν ἀληθές τε καὶ
ἄξιον ἐννοίας, ὅτι δυνατὸν ἄρ' ἦν περὶ τῶν τοιούτων
νομοθετεῖσθαι βεβαίως θ' ἱεροῦν τὰ [2] μέλη τὰ
τὴν ὀρθότητα φύσει παρεχόμενα· τοῦτο δὲ θεοῦ ἢ
θείου τινὸς ἂν εἴη, καθάπερ ἐκεῖ φασὶ τὰ τὸν
B πολὺν τοῦτον σεσωσμένα χρόνον μέλη τῆς Ἴσιδος
ποιήματα γεγονέναι. ὥσθ', ὅπερ ἔλεγον, εἰ δύναιτό
τις ἑλεῖν αὐτῶν καὶ ὁπωσοῦν τὴν ὀρθότητα, θαρροῦντα χρὴ εἰς νόμον ἄγειν καὶ τάξιν αὐτά· ὡς ἡ
τῆς ἡδονῆς καὶ λύπης ζήτησις τοῦ καινῇ ζητεῖν
ἀεὶ μουσικῇ χρῆσθαι σχεδὸν οὐ μεγάλην τινὰ
δύναμιν ἔχει πρὸς τὸ διαφθεῖραι τὴν καθιερωθεῖ-
σαν χορείαν ἐπικαλοῦσα ἀρχαιότητα. τὴν γοῦν
ἐκεῖ οὐδαμῶς ἔοικε δυνατὴ γεγονέναι διαφθεῖραι,
πᾶν δὲ τοὐναντίον.

---

[1] ὁμοῖ' ἄττα: ὁποῖ' ἄττα MSS. : ὁμοιώματα Apelt.
[2] θ' ἱεροῦν τὰ: θαρροῦντα MSS. (καὶ βεβαίως καθιεροῦν τὰ
England).

tunes that are good : these they prescribed in detail and posted up in the temples, and outside this official list it was, and still is, forbidden to painters and all other producers of postures and representations to introduce any innovation or invention, whether in such productions or in any other branch of music, over and above the traditional forms. And if you look there, you will find that the things depicted or graven there 10,000 years ago (I mean what I say, not loosely but literally 10,000) are no whit better or worse than the productions of to-day, but wrought with the same art.

CLIN. A marvellous state of affairs !

ATH. Say rather, worthy in the highest degree of a statesman and a legislator. Still, you would find in Egypt other things that are bad. This, however, is a true and noteworthy fact, that as regards music it has proved possible for the tunes which possess a natural correctness to be enacted by law and permanently consecrated. To effect this would be the task of a god or a godlike man,—even as in Egypt they say that the tunes preserved throughout all this lapse of time are the compositions of Isis. Hence, as I said, if one could by any means succeed in grasping the principle of correctness in tune, one might then with confidence reduce them to legal form and prescription, since the tendency of pleasure and pain to indulge constantly in fresh music has, after all, no very great power to corrupt choric forms that are consecrated, by merely scoffing at them as antiquated. In Egypt, at any rate, it seems to have had no such power of corrupting,—in fact, quite the reverse.

657C κλ. Φαίνεται οὕτως ἂν ταῦτα ἔχειν ἐκ τῶν
ὑπὸ σοῦ τὰ νῦν λεχθέντων.

αθ. Ἀρ' οὖν θαρροῦντες λέγωμεν τὴν τῇ
μουσικῇ καὶ τῇ παιδιᾷ μετὰ χορείας χρείαν
ὀρθὴν εἶναι τοιῷδέ τινι τρόπῳ; χαίρομεν ὅταν
οἰώμεθα εὖ πράττειν, καὶ ὁπόταν χαίρωμεν,
οἰόμεθα εὖ πράττειν αὖ; μῶν οὐχ οὕτως;

κλ. Οὕτω μὲν οὖν.

αθ. Καὶ μὴν ἔν γε τῷ τοιούτῳ χαίροντες
ἡσυχίαν οὐ δυνάμεθα ἄγειν.

κλ. Ἔστι ταῦτα.

D αθ. Ἀρ' οὖν οὐχ ἡμῶν οἱ μὲν νέοι αὐτοὶ
χορεύειν ἕτοιμοι, τὸ δὲ τῶν πρεσβυτέρων ἡμῶν
ἐκείνους αὖ θεωροῦντες διάγειν ἡγούμεθα πρεπόντως, χαίροντες τῇ ἐκείνων παιδιᾷ τε καὶ
ἑορτάσει, ἐπειδὴ τὸ παρ' ἡμῖν ἡμᾶς ἐλαφρὸν
ἐκλείπει νῦν, ὃ ποθοῦντες καὶ ἀσπαζόμενοι τίθεμεν οὕτως ἀγῶνας τοῖς δυναμένοις ἡμᾶς ὅτι
μάλιστα εἰς τὴν νεότητα μνήμῃ ἐπεγείρειν;

κλ. Ἀληθέστατα.

αθ. Μῶν οὖν οἰώμεθα καὶ κομιδῇ μάτην τὸν
E νῦν λεγόμενον λόγον περὶ τῶν ἑορταζόντων λέγειν
τοὺς πολλούς, ὅτι τοῦτον δεῖ σοφώτατον ἡγεῖσθαι
καὶ κρίνειν νικᾶν, ὃς ἂν ἡμᾶς εὐφραίνεσθαι καὶ
χαίρειν ὅτι μάλιστα ἀπεργάζηται; δεῖ γὰρ δή,
ἐπείπερ ἀφείμεθά γε παίζειν ἐν τοῖς τοιούτοις,
τὸν πλείστους καὶ μάλιστα χαίρειν ποιοῦντα,
τοῦτον μάλιστα τιμᾶσθαί τε καί, ὅπερ εἶπον νῦν
δή, τὰ νικητήρια φέρειν. ἆρ' οὐκ ὀρθῶς λέγεταί
658 τε τοῦτο καὶ πράττοιτ' ἄν, εἰ ταύτῃ γίγνοιτο;

κλ. Τάχ' ἄν.

CLIN. Such would evidently be the case, judging from what you now say.

ATH. May we confidently describe the correct method in music and play, in connexion with choristry, in some such terms as this : we rejoice whenever we think we are prospering, and, conversely, whenever we rejoice we think we are prospering? Is not that so?

CLIN. Yes, that is so.

ATH. Moreover, when in this state of joy we are unable to keep still.

CLIN. True.

ATH. Now while our young men are fitted for actually dancing themselves, we elders regard ourselves as suitably employed in looking on at them, and enjoying their sport and merry-making, now that our former nimbleness is leaving us; and it is our yearning regret for this that causes us to propose such contests for those who can best arouse in us through recollection, the dormant emotions of youth.

CLIN. Very true.

ATH. Thus we shall not dismiss as entirely groundless the opinion now commonly expressed about merry-makers,—namely, that he who best succeeds in giving us joy and pleasure should be counted the most skilful and be awarded the prize. For, seeing that we give ourselves up on such occasions to recreation, surely the highest honour and the prize of victory, as I said just now, should be awarded to the performer who affords the greatest enjoyment to the greatest number. Is not this the right view, and the right mode of action too, supposing it were carried out ?

CLIN. Possibly.

658 ΑΘ. Ἀλλ᾽, ὦ μακάριε, μὴ ταχὺ τὸ τοιοῦτον κρίνωμεν, ἀλλὰ διαιροῦντες αὐτὸ κατὰ μέρη σκοπώμεθα τοιῷδέ τινι τρόπῳ· τί ἄν, εἴ ποτέ τις οὕτως ἁπλῶς ἀγῶνα θείη ὁντινοῦν, μηδὲν ἀφορίσας μήτε γυμνικὸν μήτε μουσικὸν μήθ᾽ ἱππικόν, ἀλλὰ πάντας συναγαγὼν τοὺς ἐν τῇ πόλει προείποι θεὶς νικητήρια τὸν βουλόμενον ἥκειν ἀγωνιούμενον ἡδονῆς πέρι μόνον, ὃς δ᾽ ἂν τέρψῃ τοὺς θεατὰς

B μάλιστα, μηδὲν ἐπιταττόμενος ᾧτινι τρόπῳ, νικήσῃ δὲ αὐτὸ τοῦτο ὅτι μάλιστα ἀπεργασάμενος καὶ κριθῇ τῶν ἀγωνισαμένων ἥδιστος γεγονέναι· τί ποτ᾽ ἂν ἡγούμεθα ἐκ ταύτης τῆς προρρήσεως ξυμβαίνειν;

ΚΛ. Τοῦ πέρι λέγεις;

ΑΘ. Εἰκός που τὸν μέν τινα ἐπιδεικνύναι, καθάπερ Ὅμηρος, ῥαψῳδίαν, ἄλλον δὲ κιθαρῳδίαν, τὸν δέ τινα τραγῳδίαν, τὸν δ᾽ αὖ κωμῳδίαν. οὐ θαυμαστὸν δὲ εἴ τις καὶ θαύματα ἐπιδεικνὺς

C μάλιστ᾽ ἂν νικᾶν ἡγοῖτο. τούτων δὴ τοιούτωι καὶ ἑτέρων ἀγωνιστῶν μυρίων ἐλθόντων ἔχομεν εἰπεῖν τίς ἂν νικῴη δικαίως;

ΚΛ. Ἄτοπον ἤρου· τίς γὰρ ἂν ἀποκρίνοιτό σοι τοῦτο ὡς γνοὺς ἄν ποτε πρὶν [ἀκοῦσαί τε][1] καὶ τῶν ἀθλητῶν ἑκάστων αὐτήκοος αὐτὸς γενέσθαι;

ΑΘ. Τί οὖν δή; βούλεσθε ἐγὼ σφῷν τὴν ἄτοπον ταύτην ἀπόκρισιν ἀποκρίνωμαι;

ΚΛ. Τί μήν;

ΑΘ. Εἰ μὲν τοίνυν τὰ πάνυ σμικρὰ κρίνοι παιδία, κρινοῦσι τὸν τὰ θαύματα ἐπιδεικνύντα. ἢ γάρ;

[1] [ἀκοῦσαί τε] bracketed by Schanz.

ATH. But, my dear sir, we must not decide this matter hastily; rather we must analyse it thoroughly and examine it in some such fashion as this: suppose a man were to organize a competition, without qualifying or limiting it to gymnastic, musical or equestrian sports; and suppose that he should assemble the whole population of the State and, proclaiming that this is purely a pleasure-contest in which anyone who chooses may compete, should offer a prize to the competitor who gives the greatest amusement to the spectators,—without any restrictions as to the methods employed,—and who excels all others just in doing this in the highest possible degree, and is adjudged the most pleasure-giving of the competitors: what do we suppose would be the effect of such a proclamation?

CLIN. In what respect do you mean?

ATH. The natural result would be that one man would, like Homer, show up a rhapsody, another a harp-song, one a tragedy and another a comedy; nor should we be surprised if someone were even to fancy that he had the best chance of winning with a puppet-show. So where such as these and thousands of others enter the competition, can we say who will deserve to win the prize?

CLIN. An absurd question; for who could possibly pretend to know the answer before he had himself actually heard each of the competitors?

ATH. Very well, then; do you wish me to supply you with the answer to this absurd question?

CLIN. By all means.

ATH. If the tiniest children are to be the judges, they will award the prize to the showman of puppets, will they not?

658D   ΚΛ.   Πῶς γὰρ οὔ;

ΑΘ.   Ἐὰν δέ γ᾽ οἱ μείζους παῖδες, τὸν τὰς
κωμῳδίας· τραγῳδίαν δὲ αἵ τε πεπαιδευμέναι τῶν
γυναικῶν καὶ τὰ νέα μειράκια καὶ σχεδὸν ἴσως
τὸ πλῆθος πάντων.

ΚΛ.   Ἴσως δῆτα.

ΑΘ.   Ῥαψῳδὸν δέ, καλῶς Ἰλιάδα καὶ Ὀδύσσειαν
ἤ τι τῶν Ἡσιοδείων διατιθέντα, τάχ᾽ ἂν ἡμεῖς οἱ
γέροντες ἥδιστα ἀκούσαντες νικᾶν ἂν φαῖμεν
πάμπολυ.   τίς οὖν ὀρθῶς ἂν νενικηκὼς εἴη, τοῦτο
μετὰ τοῦτο· ἢ γάρ;

ΚΛ.   Ναί.

E   ΑΘ.   Δῆλον ὡς ἔμοιγε καὶ ὑμῖν ἀναγκαῖόν ἐστι
φάναι τοὺς ὑπὸ τῶν ἡμετέρων ἡλικιωτῶν κριθέντας
ὀρθῶς ἂν νικᾶν.   τὸ γὰρ ἔπος [1] ἡμῖν τῶν νῦν δὴ
πάμπολυ δοκεῖ τῶν ἐν ταῖς πόλεσιν ἁπάσαις καὶ
πανταχοῦ βέλτιστον γίγνεσθαι.

ΚΛ.   Τί μήν;

ΑΘ.   Συγχωρῶ δὴ τό γε τοσοῦτον καὶ ἐγὼ τοῖς
πολλοῖς, δεῖν τὴν μουσικὴν ἡδονῇ κρίνεσθαι, μὴ
μέντοι τῶν γε ἐπιτυχόντων, ἀλλὰ σχεδὸν ἐκείνην
εἶναι Μοῦσαν καλλίστην, ἥτις τοὺς βελτίστους
659   καὶ ἱκανῶς πεπαιδευμένους τέρπει, μάλιστα δὲ
ἥτις ἕνα τὸν ἀρετῇ τε καὶ παιδείᾳ διαφέροντα.
διὰ ταῦτα δὲ ἀρετῆς φαμὲν δεῖσθαι τοὺς τούτων
κριτάς, ὅτι τῆς τε ἄλλης μετόχους αὐτοὺς εἶναι
δεῖ φρονήσεως καὶ δὴ καὶ τῆς ἀνδρίας.   οὔτε γὰρ
παρὰ θεάτρου δεῖ τόν γε ἀληθῆ κριτὴν κρίνειν
μανθάνοντα καὶ ἐκπληττόμενον ὑπὸ θορύβου τῶν
πολλῶν καὶ τῆς αὐτοῦ ἀπαιδευσίας, οὔτ᾽ αὖ γι-

---

[1] ἔπος Apelt: ἔθος MSS.

CLIN. Certainly they will.

ATH. And older lads to the exhibitor of comedies; while the educated women and the young men, and the mass of the people in general, will award it to the shower of tragedies.

CLIN. Most probably.

ATH. And we old men would very likely take most delight in listening to a rhapsode giving a fine recitation of the Iliad or the Odyssey or of a piece from Hesiod, and declare that he is easily the winner. Who then would rightly be the winner of the prize? That is the next question, is it not?

CLIN. Yes.

ATH. Evidently we three cannot avoid saying that those who are adjudged the winners by our own contemporaries would win rightly. For in our opinion epic poetry is by far the best to be found nowadays anywhere in any State in the world.

CLIN. Of course.

ATH. Thus much I myself am willing to concede to the majority of men,—that the criterion of music should be pleasure; not, however, the pleasure of any chance person; rather I should regard that music which pleases the best men and the highly educated as about the best, and as quite the best if it pleases the one man who excels all others in virtue and education. And we say that the judges of these matters need virtue for the reason that they need to possess not only wisdom in general, but especially courage. For the true judge should not take his verdicts from the dictation of the audience, nor yield weakly to the uproar of the crowd or his own lack of education; nor again, when he knows the truth, should he give his verdict carelessly

659 γνώσκοντα δι' ἀνανδρίαν καὶ δειλίαν ἐκ ταὐτοῦ
στόματος οὗπερ τοὺς θεοὺς ἐπεκαλέσατο μέλλων
B κρίνειν, ἐκ τούτου ψευδόμενον ἀποφαίνεσθαι
ῥαθύμως τὴν κρίσιν· οὐ γὰρ μαθητής, ἀλλὰ
διδάσκαλος, ὥς γε τὸ δίκαιον, θεατῶν μᾶλλον ὁ
κριτὴς καθίζει, καὶ ἐναντιωσόμενος τοῖς τὴν
ἡδονὴν μὴ προσηκόντως μηδὲ ὀρθῶς ἀποδιδοῦσι
θεαταῖς, [ἐξῆν γὰρ δὴ τῷ παλαιῷ τε καὶ Ἑλληνικῷ
νόμῳ]¹ καθάπερ ὁ Σικελικός τε καὶ Ἰταλικὸς
νόμος νῦν τῷ πλήθει τῶν θεατῶν ἐπιτρέπων καὶ
τὸν νικῶντα διακρίνων χειροτονίαις διέφθαρκε μὲν
C τοὺς ποιητὰς αὐτούς—πρὸς γὰρ τὴν τῶν κριτῶν
ἡδονὴν ποιοῦσιν οὖσαν φαύλην, ὥστε αὐτοὶ
αὐτοὺς οἱ θεαταὶ παιδεύουσι—διέφθαρκε δ' αὐτοῦ
τοῦ θεάτρου τὰς ἡδονάς· δέον γὰρ αὐτοὺς ἀεὶ
βελτίω τῶν αὐτῶν ἠθῶν ἀκούοντας βελτίω τὴν
ἡδονὴν ἴσχειν, νῦν αὐτοῖς δρῶσι πᾶν τοὐναντίον
ξυμβαίνει. τί ποτ' οὖν ἡμῖν τὰ νῦν αὖ διαπε-
ρανθέντα τῷ λόγῳ σημαίνειν βούλεται; σκοπεῖσθ'
εἰ τόδε.

ΚΛ. Τὸ ποῖον;

ΑΘ. Δοκεῖ μοι τρίτον ἢ τέταρτον ὁ λόγος εἰς
D ταὐτὸν περιφερόμενος ἥκειν, ὡς ἄρα παιδεία μέν
ἐσθ' ἡ παίδων ὁλκή τε καὶ ἀγωγὴ πρὸς τὸν ὑπὸ
τοῦ νόμου λόγον ὀρθὸν εἰρημένον καὶ τοῖς ἐπιει-
κεστάτοις καὶ πρεσβυτάτοις δι' ἐμπειρίαν ξυνδε-
δογμένον ὡς ὄντως ὀρθός ἐστιν· ἵν' οὖν ἡ ψυχὴ
τοῦ παιδὸς μὴ ἐναντία χαίρειν καὶ λυπεῖσθαι
ἐθίζηται τῷ νόμῳ καὶ τοῖς ὑπὸ τοῦ νόμου πεπεισ-
μένοις, ἀλλὰ ξυνέπηται χαίρουσά τε καὶ λυ-

¹ [ἐξῆν . . . νόμῳ] bracketed by England.

through cowardice and lack of spirit, thus swearing falsely out of the same mouth with which he invoked Heaven when he first took his seat as judge.[1]   For, rightly speaking, the judge sits not as a pupil, but rather as a teacher of the spectators, being ready to oppose those who offer them pleasure in a way that is unseemly or wrong; and that is what the present law of Sicily and Italy actually does: by entrusting the decision to the spectators, who award the prize by show of hands, not only has it corrupted the poets (since they adapt their works to the poor standard of pleasure of the judges, which means that the spectators are the teachers of the poets), but it has corrupted also the pleasures of the audience; for whereas they ought to be improving their standard of pleasure by listening to characters superior to their own, what they now do has just the opposite effect.   What, then, is the conclusion to be drawn from this survey?   Is it this, do you suppose?

CLIN.   What?

ATH.   This is, I imagine, the third or fourth time that our discourse has described a circle and come back to this same point—namely, that education is the process of drawing and guiding children towards that principle which is pronounced right by the law and confirmed as truly right by the experience of the oldest and the most just.   So in order that the soul of the child may not become habituated to having pains and pleasures in contradiction to the law and those who obey the law, but in conformity thereto, being pleased and pained at the same things

---

[1] Judges at musical and gymnastic contests, like all State-officials, took an oath to discharge their duties with fidelity.   See further, Bk. vi. 764 ff.

659 πουμένη τοῖς αὐτοῖς τούτοις οἷσπερ ὁ γέρων,
E τούτων ἕνεκα, ἃς ᾠδὰς καλοῦμεν, ὄντως μὲν
ἐπῳδαὶ ταῖς ψυχαῖς φαίνονται [1] νῦν γεγονέναι,
πρὸς τὴν τοιαύτην ἣν λέγομεν συμφωνίαν ἐσπου-
δασμέναι, διὰ δὲ τὸ σπουδὴν μὴ δύνασθαι φέρειν
τὰς τῶν νέων ψυχὰς παιδιαί τε καὶ ᾠδαὶ καλεῖσθαι καὶ πράττεσθαι, καθάπερ τοῖς κάμνουσί
τε καὶ ἀσθενῶς ἴσχουσι τὰ σώματα ἐν ἡδέσι τισὶ
660 σιτίοις καὶ πώμασι τὴν χρηστὴν πειρῶνται
τροφὴν προσφέρειν οἷς μέλει τούτων, τὴν δὲ
τῶν πονηρῶν ἐν ἀηδέσιν, ἵνα τὴν μὲν ἀσπάζωνται,
τὴν δὲ μισεῖν ὀρθῶς ἐθίζωνται· ταὐτὸν δὴ καὶ τὸν
ποιητικὸν ὁ ὀρθὸς νομοθέτης ἐν τοῖς καλοῖς ῥήμασι
καὶ ἐπαινετοῖς πείσει τε καὶ ἀναγκάσει μὴ πείθων
τὰ τῶν σωφρόνων τε καὶ ἀνδρείων καὶ πάντως
ἀγαθῶν ἀνδρῶν ἔν τε ῥυθμοῖς σχήματα καὶ ἐν
ἁρμονίαις μέλη ποιοῦντα ὀρθῶς ποιεῖν.
B ΚΛ. Νῦν οὖν οὕτω δοκοῦσί σοι, πρὸς Διός, ὦ
ξένε, ἐν ταῖς ἄλλαις πόλεσι ποιεῖν; ἐγὼ μὲν γὰρ
καθ' ὅσον αἰσθάνομαι, πλὴν παρ' ἡμῖν ἢ παρὰ
Λακεδαιμονίοις, ἃ σὺ νῦν λέγεις οὐκ οἶδα
πραττόμενα, καινὰ δὲ ἄττα ἀεὶ γιγνόμενα περί
τε τὰς ὀρχήσεις καὶ περὶ τὴν ἄλλην μουσικὴν
ξύμπασαν, οὐχ ὑπὸ νόμων μεταβαλλόμενα ἀλλ'
ὑπό τινων ἀτάκτων ἡδονῶν, πολλοῦ δεουσῶν τῶν
αὐτῶν εἶναι <ἀεὶ> [2] καὶ κατὰ ταὐτά, ὡς σὺ κατ'
Αἴγυπτον ἀφερμηνεύεις, ἀλλ' οὐδέποτε τῶν
αὐτῶν.
C ΑΘ. Ἄριστά γ', ὦ Κλεινία. εἰ δ' ἔδοξά σοι ἃ
σὺ λέγεις λέγειν ὡς νῦν γιγνόμενα, οὐκ ἂν θαυ-

---

[1] φαίνονται: αὗται MSS., edd.
[2] <ἀεὶ> I add.

as the old man,—for this reason we have what we call "chants," which evidently are in reality incantations[1] seriously designed to produce in souls that conformity and harmony of which we speak. But inasmuch as the souls of the young are unable to endure serious study, we term these "plays" and "chants," and use them as such,—just as, when people suffer from bodily ailments and infirmities, those whose office it is try to administer to them nutriment that is wholesome in meats and drinks that are pleasant, but unwholesome nutriment in the opposite, so that they may form the right habit of approving the one kind and detesting the other. Similarly in dealing with the poet, the good legislator will persuade him—or compel him—with his fine and choice language to portray by his rhythms the gestures, and by his harmonies the tunes, of men who are temperate, courageous, and good in all respects, and thereby to compose poems aright.

CLIN. In Heaven's name, Stranger, do you believe that that is the way poetry is composed nowadays in other States? So far as my own observation goes, I know of no practices such as you describe except in my own country and in Lacedaemon; but I do know that novelties are always being introduced in dancing and all other forms of music, which changes are due not to the laws, but to disorderly tastes; and these are so far from being constantly uniform and stable—like the Egyptian ones you describe—that they are never for a moment uniform.

ATH. Nobly spoken, O Clinias! If, however, I seemed to you to say that the practices you refer to

---

[1] *i.e.* charms or magic formulae, chanted over sick persons (or over snakes, *Euthyd.* 290 A): cp. 664 B.

660 μάζοιμι εἰ μὴ σαφῶς λέγων ἃ διανοοῦμαι τοῦτο
ἐποίησα καὶ ἔπαθον· ἀλλ' ἃ βούλομαι γίγνεσθαι
περὶ μουσικήν, τοιαῦτ' ἄττα εἶπον ἴσως, ὥστε
σοὶ δόξαι ταῦτα ἐμὲ λέγειν. λοιδορεῖν γὰρ
πράγματα ἀνίατα καὶ πόρρω προβεβηκότα
ἁμαρτίας οὐδαμῶς ἡδύ, ἀναγκαῖον δ' ἐνίοτ' ἐστίν.
ἐπειδὴ δὲ ταῦτα ξυνδοκεῖ καὶ σοί, φέρε φῂς παρ'
D ὑμῖν καὶ τοῖσδε μᾶλλον ἢ παρὰ τοῖς ἄλλοις
Ἕλλησι γίγνεσθαι τὰ τοιαῦτα ;

ΚΛ. Τί μήν ;

ΑΘ. Τί δ' εἰ καὶ παρὰ τοῖς ἄλλοις γίγνοιθ' οὕτω,
πότερον αὐτὰ καλλιόνως οὕτως εἶναι φαῖμεν ἂν ἢ
καθάπερ νῦν γίγνεται γιγνόμενα ;

ΚΛ. Πολύ που τὸ διαφέρον, εἰ καθάπερ παρά
τε τοῖσδε καὶ παρ' ἡμῖν, καὶ ἔτι καθάπερ εἶπες
σὺ νῦν δὴ δεῖν εἶναι, γίγνοιτο.

ΑΘ. Φέρε δή, ξυνομολογησώμεθα τὰ νῦν. ἄλλο
E τι παρ' ὑμῖν ἐν πάσῃ παιδείᾳ καὶ μουσικῇ τὰ
λεγόμενά ἐστι τάδε ; τοὺς ποιητὰς ἀναγκάζετε
λέγειν ὡς ὁ μὲν ἀγαθὸς ἀνὴρ σώφρων ὢν καὶ
δίκαιος εὐδαίμων ἐστὶ καὶ μακάριος, ἐάν τε
μέγας καὶ ἰσχυρὸς ἐάν τε σμικρὸς καὶ ἀσθενὴς
ᾖ, καὶ ἐὰν πλουτῇ καὶ μή· ἐὰν δὲ ἄρα πλουτῇ
μὲν Κινύρα τε καὶ Μίδα μᾶλλον, ᾖ δὲ ἄδικος,
ἄθλιός τ' ἐστὶ καὶ ἀνιαρῶς ζῇ· καὶ Οὔτ' ἂν
μνησαίμην, φησὶν ὑμῖν ὁ ποιητής, εἴπερ ὀρθῶς
λέγει, οὔτ' ἐν λόγῳ ἄνδρα τιθείμην, ὃς μὴ
πάντα τὰ λεγόμενα καλὰ μετὰ δικαιοσύνης
πράττοι καὶ κτῷτο, καὶ δὴ καὶ δηίων τοιοῦτος

---

[1] Tyrtaeus xii. 6 ; see Bk. i. 629. Cinyras was a fabled
king of Cyprus, son of Apollo and priest of Aphrodite.
Midas, king of Phrygia, was noted for his wealth.

are in use now, very likely your mistake arose from my own failure to express my meaning clearly; probably I stated my own desires with regard to music in such a way that you imagined me to be stating present facts. To denounce things that are beyond remedy and far gone in error is a task that is by no means pleasant; but at times it is unavoidable. And now that you hold the same opinion on this subject, come, tell me, do you assert that such practices are more general among the Cretans and the Lacedaemonians than among the other Greeks?

CLIN. Certainly.

ATH. Suppose now that they were to become general among the rest also,—should we say that the method of procedure then would be better than it is now?

CLIN. The improvement would be immense, if things were done as they are in my country and in that of our friends here, and as, moreover, you yourself said just now they ought to be done.

ATH. Come now, let us come to an understanding on this matter. In all education and music in your countries, is not this your teaching? You oblige the poets to teach that the good man, since he is temperate and just, is fortunate and happy, whether he be great or small, strong or weak, rich or poor; whereas, though he be richer even "than Cinyras or Midas," [1] if he be unjust, he is a wretched man and lives a miserable life. Your poet says—if he speaks the truth—"I would spend no word on the man, and hold him in no esteem," who without justice performs or acquires all the things accounted good; and again he describes how the just man

115

661 ὧν ὀρέγοιτο ἐγγύθεν ἱστάμενος, ἄδικος δὲ
ὢν μήτε τολμῷ ὁρῶν φόνον αἱματόεντα μήτε
νικῷ θεῶν Θρηΐκιον Βορέην, μήτε ἄλλο αὑτῷ
μηδὲν τῶν λεγομένων ἀγαθῶν γίγνοιτό ποτε· τὰ
γὰρ ὑπὸ τῶν πολλῶν λεγόμενα ἀγαθὰ οὐκ ὀρθῶς
λέγεται. λέγεται γὰρ ὡς ἄριστον μὲν ὑγιαίνειν,
δεύτερον δὲ κάλλος, τρίτον δὲ πλοῦτος. μυρία
δὲ ἄλλα ἀγαθὰ λέγεται· καὶ γὰρ ὀξὺ ὁρᾶν καὶ
B ἀκούειν καὶ πάντα ὅσα ἔχεται τῶν αἰσθήσεων
εὐαισθήτως ἔχειν, ἔτι δὲ καὶ τὸ ποιεῖν τυραννοῦντα
ὅ τι ἂν ἐπιθυμῇ, καὶ τὸ δὴ τέλος ἁπάσης μακα-
ριότητος εἶναι τὸ πάντα ταῦτα κεκτημένον ἀθάνατον εἶναι γενόμενον ὅτι τάχιστα. ὑμεῖς δὲ καὶ
ἐγώ που τάδε λέγομεν, ὡς ταῦτά ἐστι ξύμπαντα
δικαίοις μὲν καὶ ὁσίοις ἀνδράσιν ἄριστα κτήματα,
ἀδίκοις δὲ κάκιστα ξύμπαντα ἀρξάμενα ἀπὸ τῆς
ὑγιείας. καὶ δὴ καὶ τὸ ὁρᾶν καὶ τὸ ἀκούειν καὶ
C αἰσθάνεσθαι καὶ τὸ παράπαν ζῆν μέγιστον μὲν
κακὸν τὸν ξύμπαντα χρόνον ἀθάνατον ὄντα καὶ
κεκτημένον πάντα τὰ λεγόμενα ἀγαθὰ πλὴν
δικαιοσύνης τε καὶ ἀρετῆς ἁπάσης, ἔλαττον δέ,
ἂν ὡς ὀλίγιστον ὁ τοιοῦτος χρόνον ἐπιζῶν ᾖ.[1]
ταῦτα δὴ λέγειν οἶμαι τοὺς παρ' ὑμῖν ποιητάς,
ἅπερ ἐγώ, πείσετε καὶ ἀναγκάσετε, καὶ ἔτι τούτοις
ἑπομένους ῥυθμούς τε καὶ ἁρμονίας ἀποδιδόντας
παιδεύειν οὕτω τοὺς νέους ὑμῶν.[2] ἦ γάρ ; ὁρᾶτε·
D ἐγὼ μὲν γὰρ λέγω σαφῶς τὰ μὲν κακὰ λεγόμενα
ἀγαθὰ τοῖς ἀδίκοις εἶναι, τοῖς δὲ δικαίοις κακά,
τὰ δ' ἀγαθὰ τοῖς μὲν ἀγαθοῖς ὄντως ἀγαθά, τοῖς
δὲ κακοῖς κακά. ὅπερ οὖν ἠρόμην, ἆρα ξυμφωνοῦ-
μεν ἐγώ τε καὶ ὑμεῖς ; ἢ πῶς ;

[1] ἐπιζῶν ᾖ Schanz: ἐπιζῴη MSS.

" drives his spear against the foe at close quarters,"
whereas the unjust man dares not "to look upon the
face of bloody death," nor does he outpace in speed
of foot " the north wind out of Thrace," nor acquire
any other of the things called " good." For the
things which most men call good are wrongly so
described. Men say that the chief good is health,
beauty the second, wealth the third ; and they call
countless other things " goods "—such as sharpness
of sight and hearing, and quickness in perceiving all
the objects of sense ; being a king, too, and doing
exactly as you please ; and to possess the whole
of these goods and become on the spot an immortal,
that, as they say, is the crown and top of all felicity.
But what you and I say is this,—that all these
things are very good as possessions for men who are
just and holy, but for the unjust they are (one and
all, from health downwards) very bad ; and we say
too that sight and hearing and sensation and even
life itself are very great evils for the man endowed
with all the so-called goods, but lacking in justice
and all virtue, if he is immortal for ever, but a lesser
evil for such a man if he survives but a short time.
This, I imagine, is what you (like myself) will
persuade or compel your poets to teach, and compel
them also to educate your youth by furnishing them
with rhythms and harmonies in consonance with this
teaching. Am I not right ? Just consider : what I
assert is that what are called " evils " are good for
the unjust, but evil for the just, while the so-called
" goods " are really good for the good, but bad for
the bad. Are you in accord with me, then,—that
was my question,—or how stands the matter ?

---

661 ΚΛ. Τὰ μὲν ἔμοιγε φαινόμεθά πως, τὰ δ' οὐδαμῶς.

ΑΘ. Ἆρ' οὖν ὑγίειάν τε κεκτημένον καὶ πλοῦτον καὶ τυραννίδα διὰ τέλους, καὶ ἔτι προστίθημι ὑμῖν ἰσχὺν διαφέρουσαν καὶ ἀνδρίαν μετ' ἀθα-
Ε νασίας, καὶ μηδὲν ἄλλο αὐτῷ τῶν λεγομένων κακῶν εἶναι γιγνόμενον, ἀδικίαν δὲ καὶ ὕβριν ἔχοντα ἐν αὐτῷ μόνον—τὸν οὕτω ζῶντα ἴσως ὑμᾶς οὐ πείθω μὴ οὐκ ἄρα εὐδαίμονα ἀλλ' ἄθλιον γίγνεσθαι σαφῶς;

ΚΛ. Ἀληθέστατα λέγεις.

ΑΘ. Εἶεν· τί οὖν τὸ μετὰ τοῦτ' εἰπεῖν ἡμᾶς χρεών; ἀνδρεῖος γὰρ δὴ καὶ ἰσχυρὸς καὶ καλὸς καὶ πλούσιος, καὶ ποιῶν ὅ τί περ ἐπιθυμοῖ τὸν
662 βίον ἅπαντα, οὐχ ὑμῖν δοκεῖ, εἴπερ ἄδικος εἴη καὶ ὑβριστής, ἐξ ἀνάγκης αἰσχρῶς ἂν ζῆν; ἢ τοῦτο μὲν ἴσως ἂν συγχωρήσαιτε, τό γε αἰσχρῶς;

ΚΛ. Πάνυ μὲν οὖν.

ΑΘ. Τί δέ; τὸ καὶ κακῶς;

ΚΛ. Οὐκ ἂν ἔτι τοῦθ' ὁμοίως.

ΑΘ. Τί δέ; τὸ καὶ ἀηδῶς καὶ μὴ ξυμφερόντως αὐτῷ;

ΚΛ. Καὶ πῶς ἂν ταῦτά γ' ἔτι ξυγχωροῖμεν;

ΑΘ. Ὅπως; εἰ θεὸς ἡμῖν, ὡς ἔοικεν, ὦ φίλοι,
Β δοίη τις συμφωνίαν, ὡς νῦν γε σχεδὸν ἀπᾴδομεν ἀπ' ἀλλήλων. ἐμοὶ γὰρ δὴ φαίνεται ταῦτα οὕτως ἀναγκαῖα, ὡς οὐδέ, ὦ φίλε Κλεινία, Κρήτη νῆσος σαφῶς· καὶ νομοθέτης ὢν ταύτῃ πειρῴμην ἂν τοὺς

118

CLIN. We are, apparently, partly in accord, but partly quite the reverse.

ATH. Take the case of a man who has health and wealth and absolute power in perpetuity,—in addition to which I bestow on him, if you like, matchless strength and courage, together with immortality and freedom from all the other "evils" so-called,—but a man who has within him nothing but injustice and insolence : probably I fail to convince you that the man who lives such a life is obviously not happy but wretched ?

CLIN. Quite true.

ATH. Well, then, what ought I to say next? Do you not think that if a man who is courageous, strong, beautiful, and rich, and who does exactly as he likes all his life long, is really unjust and insolent, he must necessarily be living a base life? Probably you will agree at any rate to call it "base"?

CLIN. Certainly.

ATH. And also a bad life [1]?

CLIN. We would not go so far as to admit that.

ATH. Well, would you admit the epithets "unpleasant" and "unprofitable to himself"?

CLIN. How could we agree to such further descriptions?

ATH. "How?" do you ask? Only (as it seems, my friend) if some god were to grant us concord, since at present we are fairly at discord one with another. In my opinion these facts are quite indisputable—even more plainly so, my dear Clinias, than the fact that Crete is an island; and were I a legis-

---

[1] κακῶς ζῆν, "to live badly" may mean either "to live wickedly" or "to live wretchedly": Clinias takes it in this latter sense.

PLATO

662 τε ποιητὰς ἀναγκάζειν φθέγγεσθαι καὶ πάντας
τοὺς ἐν τῇ πόλει, ζημίαν τε ὀλίγου μεγίστην
ἐπιτιθείην ἄν, εἴ τις ἐν τῇ χώρᾳ φθέγξαιτο ὡς
C εἰσί τινες ἄνθρωποί ποτε πονηροὶ μέν, ἡδέως δὲ
ζῶντες, ἢ λυσιτελοῦντα μὲν ἄλλα ἐστὶ καὶ κερδα-
λέα, δικαιότερα δὲ ἄλλα, καὶ πολλὰ ἄττ' ἂν παρὰ
τὰ νῦν λεγόμενα ὑπό τε Κρητῶν καὶ Λακεδαιμονίων, ὡς ἔοικε, καὶ δή που καὶ τῶν ἄλλων ἀνθρώπων
διάφορα πείθοιμ' ἂν τοὺς πολίτας μοι φθέγγεσθαι·
φέρε γάρ, ὦ πρὸς Διός τε καὶ Ἀπόλλωνος, ὦ
ἄριστοι τῶν ἀνδρῶν, εἰ τοὺς νομοθετήσαντας ὑμῖν
αὐτοὺς τούτους ἐροίμεθα θεούς, ἆρ' ὁ δικαιότατός
D ἐστι βίος ἥδιστος, ἢ δύ' ἐστόν τινε βίω, οἷν ὁ μὲν
ἥδιστος ὢν τυγχάνει, δικαιότατος δ' ἕτερος; εἰ
δὴ δύο φαῖεν, ἐροίμεθ' ἂν ἴσως αὐτοὺς πάλιν,
εἴπερ ὀρθῶς ἐπανερωτῶμεν, ποτέρους δ' εὐδαιμο-
νεστέρους χρὴ λέγειν, τοὺς τὸν δικαιότατον ἢ τοὺς
τὸν ἥδιστον διαβιοῦντας βίον; εἰ μὲν δὴ φαῖεν
τοὺς τὸν ἥδιστον, ἄτοπος αὐτῶν ὁ λόγος ἂν
γίγνοιτο. βούλομαι δέ μοι μὴ ἐπὶ θεῶν λέγεσθαι τὸ τοιοῦτον, ἀλλ' ἐπὶ πατέρων καὶ νο-
E μοθετῶν μᾶλλον, καί μοι τὰ ἔμπροσθεν ἠρωτη-
μένα πατέρα τε καὶ νομοθέτην ἠρωτήσθω, ὁ δ'
εἰπέτω ὡς ὁ ζῶν τὸν ἥδιστον βίον ἐστὶ μακα-
ριώτατος. εἶτα μετὰ ταῦτα ἔγωγ' ἂν φαίην, Ὦ
πάτερ, οὐχ ὡς εὐδαιμονέστατά με ἐβούλου ζῆν;
ἀλλ' ἀεὶ διακελευόμενος οὐδὲν ἐπαύου ζῆν με ὡς
δικαιότατα. ταύτῃ μὲν οὖν ὁ τιθέμενος εἴτε νομοθέτης εἴτε καὶ πατὴρ ἄτοπος ἄν, οἶμαι, καὶ
ἄπορος φαίνοιτο τοῦ ξυμφωνοῦντως ἑαυτῷ λέγειν.
εἰ δ' αὖ τὸν δικαιότατον εὐδαιμονέστατον ἀπο-

lator, I should endeavour to compel the poets and all the citizens to speak in this sense; and I should impose all but the heaviest of penalties on anyone in the land who should declare that any wicked men lead pleasant lives, or that things profitable and lucrative are different from things just; and there are many other things contrary to what is now said, as it seems, by Cretans and Lacedaemonians,—and of course by the rest of mankind,—which I should persuade my citizens to proclaim. For, come now, my most excellent sirs, in the name of Zeus and Apollo, suppose we should interrogate those very gods themselves who legislated for you, and ask: " Is the most just life the most pleasant; or are there two lives, of which the one is most pleasant, the other most just?" If they replied that there were two, we might well ask them further, if we were to put the correct question: " Which of the two ought one to describe as the happier, those that live the most just or those that live the most pleasant life?" If they replied, " Those that live the most pleasant life," that would be a monstrous statement in their mouths. But I prefer not to ascribe such statements to gods, but rather to ancestors and lawgivers: imagine, then, that the questions I have put have been put to an ancestor and lawgiver, and that he has stated that the man who lives the most pleasant life is the happiest. In the next place I would say to him this: " O father, did you not desire me to live as happily as possible? Yet you never ceased bidding me constantly to live as justly as possible." And hereby, as I think, our lawgiver or ancestor would be shown up as illogical and incapable of speaking consistently with himself. But if, on the other hand, he were to

662 φαίνοιτο βίον εἶναι, ζητοῖ που πᾶς ἂν ὁ ἀκούων,
οἶμαι, τί ποτ' ἐν αὐτῷ τὸ τῆς ἡδονῆς κρεῖττον
ἀγαθόν τε καὶ καλὸν ὁ νομοθέτης [1] ἐνὸν ἐπαινεῖ;
663 τί γὰρ δὴ δικαίῳ χωριζόμενον ἡδονῆς ἀγαθὸν ἂν
γίγνοιτο; φέρε, κλέος τε καὶ ἔπαινος πρὸς
ἀνθρώπων τε καὶ θεῶν ἆρ' ἐστὶν ἀγαθὸν μὲν
καὶ καλόν, ἀηδὲς δέ, δύσκλεια δὲ τἀναντία;
ἥκιστα, ὦ φίλε νομοθέτα, φήσομεν. ἀλλὰ τὸ
μήτε τινὰ ἀδικεῖν μήτε ὑπό τινος ἀδικεῖσθαι μῶν
ἀηδὲς μέν, ἀγαθὸν δὲ ἢ καλόν, τὰ δ' ἕτερα ἡδέα
μέν, αἰσχρὰ δὲ καὶ κακά;

ΚΛ. Καὶ πῶς;

ΑΘ. Οὐκοῦν ὁ μὲν μὴ χωρίζων λόγος ἡδύ τε
καὶ δίκαιον [καὶ ἀγαθόν τε καὶ καλὸν] [2] πιθανός
Β γ', εἰ μηδὲν ἕτερον, πρὸς τό τινα ἐθέλειν ζῆν τὸν
ὅσιον καὶ δίκαιον βίον, ὥστε νομοθέτῃ γε αἴσχιστος λόγων καὶ ἐναντιώτατος ὃς ἂν μὴ φῇ ταῦτα
οὕτως ἔχειν· οὐδεὶς γὰρ ἂν ἑκὼν ἐθέλοι πείθεσθαι
πράττειν τοῦτο ὅτῳ μὴ τὸ χαίρειν τοῦ λυπεῖσθαι
πλέον ἔπεται. σκοτοδινίαν [3] δὲ τὸ πόρρωθεν
ὁρώμενον πᾶσί τε ὡς ἔπος εἰπεῖν καὶ δὴ καὶ τοῖς
παισὶ παρέχει· νομοθέτης δ' ἡμῖν δόξαν εἰς
τοὐναντίον τούτου καταστήσει τὸ σκότος ἀφελών,
C καὶ πείσει ἁμῶς γέ πως ἔθεσι καὶ ἐπαίνοις καὶ
λόγοις ὡς ἐσκιαγραφημένα τὰ δίκαιά ἐστι καὶ
ἄδικα, τὰ μὲν ἄδικα τῷ τοῦ δικαίου ἐναντίῳ [4]
φαινόμενα, ἐκ μὲν ἀδίκου καὶ κακοῦ ἑαυτοῦ θεω-

---

[1] νομοθέτης Badham, Schanz: νόμος MSS.
[2] [καὶ . . . καλὸν] bracketed by England.
[3] σκοτοδινίαν England: σκοτοδινιᾶν MSS.
[4] ἐναντίῳ Apelt: ἐναντίως MSS.

declare the most just life to be the happiest, everyone who heard him would, I suppose, enquire what
is the good and charm it contains which is superior to
pleasure, and for which the lawgiver praises it. For,
apart from pleasure, what good could accrue to a just
man? "Come, tell me, is fair fame and praise from
the mouths of men and gods a noble and good thing,
but unpleasant, while ill-fame is the opposite?" "By
no means, my dear lawgiver," we shall say. And is
it unpleasant, but noble and good, neither to injure
anyone nor be injured by anyone, while the opposite
is pleasant, but ignoble and bad?

CLIN. By no means.

ATH. So then the teaching which refuses to separate the pleasant from the just helps, if nothing else,
to induce a man to live the holy and just life, so
that any doctrine which denies this truth is, in the
eyes of the lawgiver, most shameful and most hateful;
for no one would voluntarily consent to be induced
to commit an act, unless it involves as its consequence
more pleasure than pain. Now distance has the
effect of befogging the vision of nearly everybody,
and of children especially; but our lawgiver will
reverse the appearance by removing the fog,[1] and by
one means or another—habituation, commendation,
or argument—will persuade people that their notions
of justice and injustice are illusory pictures, unjust
objects appearing pleasant and just objects most
unpleasant to him who is opposed to justice, through
being viewed from his own unjust and evil stand-

---

[1] *i.e.* the lawgiver will make justice clear and distinct by
bringing citizens close up to it: discipline in just actions
will give them a near and true view of it, and correct the
wrong impression due to distance.

PLATO

663 ρούμενα, ἡδέα, τὰ δὲ δίκαια ἀηδέστατα, ἐκ δὲ
δικαίου πάντα τἀναντία πάντη πρὸς ἀμφότερα.

ΚΛ. Φαίνεται.

ΑΘ. Τὴν δ' ἀλήθειαν τῆς κρίσεως ποτέραν
κυριωτέραν εἶναι φῶμεν ; πότερα τὴν τῆς χείρονος
ψυχῆς ἢ τὴν τῆς βελτίονος ;

ΚΛ. Ἀναγκαῖόν που τὴν τῆς ἀμείνονος.

D ΑΘ. Ἀναγκαῖον ἄρα τὸν ἄδικον βίον οὐ μόνον
αἰσχίω καὶ μοχθηρότερον, ἀλλὰ καὶ ἀηδέστερον
τῇ ἀληθείᾳ τοῦ δικαίου τε εἶναι καὶ ὁσίου βίου.

ΚΛ. Κινδυνεύει κατά γε τὸν νῦν λόγον, ὦ
φίλοι.

ΑΘ. Νομοθέτης δὲ οὗ τι καὶ σμικρὸν ὄφελος, εἰ
καὶ μὴ τοῦτο ἦν οὕτως ἔχον, ὡς καὶ νῦν αὐτὸ
ᾕρηχ' ὁ λόγος ἔχειν, εἴπερ τι καὶ ἄλλο ἐτόλμησεν
ἂν ἐπ' ἀγαθῷ ψεύδεσθαι πρὸς τοὺς νέους, ἔστιν ὅ
τι τούτου ψεῦδος λυσιτελέστερον ἂν ἐψεύσατο
ποτε καὶ δυνάμενον μᾶλλον <πείθειν>[1] ποιεῖν
E μὴ βίᾳ ἀλλ' ἑκόντας <πάντας>[2] πάντα τὰ
δίκαια ;

ΚΛ. Καλὸν μὲν ἡ ἀλήθεια, ὦ ξένε, καὶ μόνιμον·
ἔοικε μὴν οὐ ῥάδιον εἶναι πείθειν.

ΑΘ. Εἶεν· τὸ μέντοι Σιδώνιον[3] μυθολόγημα
ῥάδιον ἐγένετο πείθειν, οὕτως ἀπίθανον ὄν, καὶ
ἄλλα μυρία.

ΚΛ. Ποῖα ;

ΑΘ. Τὸ σπαρέντων ποτὲ ὀδόντων ὁπλίτας ἐξ
αὐτῶν φῦναι. καί τοι μέγα γ' ἐστὶ νομοθέτῃ
664 παράδειγμα τοῦ πείσειν ὅ τι ἂν ἐπιχειρῇ τις
πείθειν τὰς τῶν νέων ψυχάς, ὥστε οὐδὲν ἄλλο

---

[1] <πείθειν> added by Stephens, Schanz.
[2] <πάντας> added by Euseb.

124

point, but when seen from the standpoint of justice, both of them appear in all ways entirely the opposite.

CLIN. So it appears.

ATH. In point of truth, which of the two judgments shall we say is the more authoritative,—that of the worse soul or that of the better?

CLIN. That of the better, undoubtedly.

ATH. Undoubtedly, then, the unjust life is not only more base and ignoble, but also in very truth more unpleasant, than the just and holy life.

CLIN. It would seem so, my friends, from our present argument.

ATH. And even if the state of the case were different from what it has now been proved to be by our argument, could a lawgiver who was worth his salt find any more useful fiction than this (if he dared to use any fiction at all in addressing the youths for their good), or one more effective in persuading all men to act justly in all things willingly and without constraint?

CLIN. Truth is a noble thing, Stranger, and an enduring; yet to persuade men of it seems no easy matter.

ATH. Be it so; yet it proved easy to persuade men of the Sidonian fairy-tale,[1] incredible though it was, and of numberless others.

CLIN. What tales?

ATH. The tale of the teeth that were sown, and how armed men sprang out of them. Here, indeed, the lawgiver has a notable example of how one can, if he tries, persuade the souls of the young of any-

---

[1] About Cadmus; cp. *Rep.* 414 C.

[3] μέντοι Σιδώνιον England: μὲν τοῦ Σιδωνίου MSS.

664 αὐτὸν δεῖ σκοποῦντα ἀνευρίσκειν ἢ τί πείσας
μέγιστον ἀγαθὸν ἐργάσαιτο ἂν πόλιν, τούτου δὲ
πέρι πᾶσαν μηχανὴν εὑρίσκειν ὅντιν’ ἄν[1] ποτε
τρόπον ἡ τοιαύτη ξυνοικία πᾶσα περὶ τούτων ἓν
καὶ ταὐτὸν ὅτι μάλιστα φθέγγοιτ’ ἀεὶ διὰ βίου
παντὸς ἔν τε ᾠδαῖς καὶ μύθοις καὶ λόγοις. εἰ δ’
οὖν ἄλλῃ πῃ δοκεῖ ἢ ταύτῃ, πρὸς ταῦτα οὐδεὶς
φθόνος ἀμφισβητῆσαι τῷ λόγῳ.

B ΚΛ. Ἀλλ’ οὔ μοι φαίνεται πρός γε ταῦτα
δύνασθαι ἡμῶν ἀμφισβητῆσαί ποτ’ ἂν οὐδέτερος.

ΑΘ. Τὸ μετὰ τοῦτο τοίνυν ἐμὸν ἂν εἴη λέγειν.
φημὶ γὰρ ἅπαντας δεῖν ἐπᾴδειν τρεῖς ὄντας τοὺς
χοροὺς ἔτι νέαις οὔσαις ταῖς ψυχαῖς καὶ ἁπαλαῖς
τῶν παίδων, τά τε ἄλλα καλὰ λέγοντας πάντα
ὅσα διεληλύθαμέν τε καὶ ἔτι διέλθοιμεν ἄν, τὸ δὲ
κεφάλαιον αὐτῶν τοῦτο ἔστω· τὸν αὐτὸν ἥδιστόν
τε καὶ ἄριστον ὑπὸ θεῶν βίον λέγεσθαι φάσκοντες
C ἀληθέστατα ἐροῦμεν ἅμα καὶ μᾶλλον πείσομεν
οὓς δεῖ πείθειν ἢ ἐὰν ἄλλως πως φθεγγώμεθα
λέγοντες.

ΚΛ. Συγχωρητέον ἃ λέγεις.

ΑΘ. Πρῶτον μὲν τοίνυν ὁ Μουσῶν χορὸς ὁ
παιδικὸς ὀρθότατ’ ἂν εἰσίοι πρῶτος τὰ τοιαῦτα
εἰς τὸ μέσον ᾀσόμενος ἁπάσῃ σπουδῇ καὶ ὅλῃ τῇ
πόλει, δεύτερος δὲ ὁ μέχρι τριάκοντα ἐτῶν, τόν τε
Παιᾶνα ἐπικαλούμενος μάρτυρα τῶν λεγομένων
ἀληθείας πέρι καὶ τοῖς νέοις ἵλεων μετὰ πειθοῦς
D γίγνεσθαι ἐπευχόμενος. δεῖ δὲ δὴ καὶ ἔτι τρίτους

---

[1] ὅντιν’ ἄν Schanz : ὅντινα MSS.

---

[1] At Spartan festivals it was customary to have three
choirs—of boys, young men, and older men.

thing, so that the only question he has to consider
in his inventing is what would do most good to the
State, if it were believed; and then he must devise
all possible means to ensure that the whole of the
community constantly, so long as they live, use
exactly the same language, so far as possible, about
these matters, alike in their songs, their tales, and
their discourses. If you, however, think otherwise,
I have no objection to your arguing in the opposite
sense.

CLIN. Neither of us, I think, could possibly argue
against your view.

ATH. Our next subject I must handle myself. I
maintain that all the three choirs [1] must enchant the
souls of the children, while still young and tender,
by rehearsing all the noble things which we have
already recounted, or shall recount hereafter; and
let this be the sum of them: in asserting that one
and the same life is declared by the gods to be both
most pleasant and most just, we shall not only be
saying what is most true, but we shall also convince
those who need convincing more forcibly than we
could by any other assertion.

CLIN. We must assent to what you say.

ATH. First, then, the right order of procedure
will be for the Muses' choir of children to come
forward first to sing these things with the utmost
vigour and before the whole city; second will come
the choir of those under thirty, invoking Apollo
Paian [2] as witness of the truth of what is said, and
praying him of his grace to persuade the youth.
The next singers will be the third choir, of those

---

[2] *i.e.* "the Healer." Cp. the medicinal sense of ἐπᾴδειν,
"enchant," in B4 above. Music is to be a medicine of the soul.

PLATO

664 τοὺς ὑπὲρ τριάκοντα ἔτη μέχρι τῶν ἑξήκοντα
γεγονότας ᾄδειν· τοὺς δὲ μετὰ ταῦτα, οὐ γὰρ ἔτι
δυνατοὶ φέρειν ᾠδάς, μυθολόγους περὶ τῶν αὐτῶν
ἠθῶν διὰ θείας φήμης καταλελεῖφθαι.

ΚΛ. Λέγεις δέ, ὦ ξένε, τίνας τούτους τοὺς
χοροὺς τοὺς τρίτους; οὐ γὰρ πάνυ ξυνίεμεν
σαφῶς ὅ τί ποτε βούλει φράζειν αὐτῶν πέρι.

ΑΘ. Καὶ μὴν εἰσί γε οὗτοι σχεδὸν ὧν χάριν οἱ
πλεῖστοι τῶν ἔμπροσθεν ἐρρήθησαν λόγων.

Ε   ΚΛ. Οὔπω μεμαθήκαμεν, ἀλλ᾽ ἔτι σαφέστερον
πειρῶ φράζειν.

ΑΘ. Εἴπομεν, εἰ μεμνήμεθα, κατ᾽ ἀρχὰς τῶν
λόγων ὡς ἡ φύσις ἁπάντων τῶν νέων διάπυρος
οὖσα ἡσυχίαν οὐχ οἷά τε ἄγειν οὔτε κατὰ τὸ
σῶμα οὔτε κατὰ τὴν φωνὴν εἴη, φθέγγοιτο δ᾽ ἀεὶ
ἀτάκτως καὶ πηδῷη· τάξεως δ᾽ αἴσθησιν τούτων
ἀμφοτέρων τῶν ἄλλων μὲν ζῴων οὐδὲν ἐφάπτοιτο,
ἡ δὲ ἀνθρώπου φύσις ἔχοι μόνη τοῦτο· τῇ δὴ τῆς
665 κινήσεως τάξει ῥυθμὸς ὄνομα εἴη, τῇ δ᾽ αὖ τῆς
φωνῆς, τοῦ τε ὀξέος ἅμα καὶ βαρέος συγκεραννυ-
μένων, ἁρμονία ὄνομα προσαγορεύοιτο, χορεία δὲ
τὸ ξυναμφότερον κληθείη. θεοὺς δ᾽ ἔφαμεν ἐλε-
οῦντας ἡμᾶς συγχορευτάς τε καὶ χορηγοὺς ἡμῖν
δεδωκέναι τόν τε Ἀπόλλωνα καὶ Μούσας, καὶ δὴ
καὶ τρίτον ἔφαμεν, εἰ μεμνήμεθα, Διόνυσον.

ΚΛ. Πῶς δ᾽ οὐ μεμνήμεθα;

ΑΘ. Ὁ μὲν τοίνυν τοῦ Ἀπόλλωνος καὶ τῶν
Μουσῶν χορὸς εἴρηνται, τὸν δὲ τρίτον καὶ τὸν
Β λοιπὸν χορὸν ἀνάγκη τοῦ Διονύσου λέγεσθαι.

ΚΛ. Πῶς δή; λέγε· μάλα γὰρ ἄτοπος γίγνοιτ᾽

over thirty and under sixty; and lastly, there were left those who, being no longer able to uplift the song, shall handle the same moral themes in stories and by oracular speech.

CLIN. Whom do you mean, Stranger, by these third choristers? For we do not grasp very clearly what you intend to convey about them.

ATH. Yet they are in fact the very people to whom most of our previous discourse was intended to lead up.

CLIN. We are still in the dark: try to explain yourself more clearly still.

ATH. At the commencement of our discourse we said, if we recollect, that since all young creatures are by nature fiery, they are unable to keep still either body or voice, but are always crying and leaping in disorderly fashion; we said also that none of the other creatures attains a sense of order, bodily and vocal, and that this is possessed by man alone; and that the order of motion is called "rhythm," while the order of voice (in which acute and grave tones are blended together) is termed "harmony," and to the combination of these two the name "choristry" is given. We stated also that the gods, in pity for us, have granted to us as fellow-choristers and choir-leaders Apollo and the Muses,—besides whom we mentioned, if we recollect, a third, Dionysus.

CLIN. Certainly we recollect.

ATH. The choir of Apollo and that of the Muses have been described, and the third and remaining choir must necessarily be described, which is that of Dionysus.

CLIN. How so? Tell us; for at the first mention

665 ἂν ὥς γ' ἐξαίφνης ἀκούσαντι Διονύσου πρεσβυτῶν
χορός, εἰ ἄρα οἱ ὑπὲρ τριάκοντα καὶ πεντήκοντα
δὲ γεγονότες ἔτη μέχρι ἑξήκοντα αὐτῷ χορεύσουσιν.[1]

ΑΘ. Ἀληθέστατα μέντοι λέγεις. λόγου δὴ
δεῖ πρὸς ταῦτα, οἶμαι, ὅπῃ τοῦτο εὔλογον οὕτω
γιγνόμενον ἂν γίγνοιτο.

ΚΛ. Τί μήν;

ΑΘ. Ἆρ' οὖν ἡμῖν τά γε ἔμπροσθεν ὁμολο-
γεῖται;

C ΚΛ. Τοῦ πέρι;

ΑΘ. Τὸ δεῖν πάντα ἄνδρα καὶ παῖδα, ἐλεύθερον
καὶ δοῦλον, θῆλύν τε καὶ ἄρρενα, καὶ ὅλῃ τῇ πόλει
ὅλην τὴν πόλιν αὐτὴν αὑτῇ ἐπᾴδουσαν μὴ παύε-
σθαί ποτε ταῦτα ἃ διεληλύθαμεν ἁμῶς γέ πως ἀεὶ
μεταβαλλόμενα καὶ πάντως παρεχόμενα ποικι-
λίαν, ὥστε ἀπληστίαν εἶναί τινα τῶν ὕμνων τοῖς
ᾄδουσι καὶ ἡδονήν.

ΚΛ. Πῶς δ' οὐχ ὁμολογοῖτο ἂν δεῖν ταῦτα οὕτω
πράττεσθαι;

D ΑΘ. Ποῦ δὴ τοῦθ' ἡμῖν τὸ ἄριστον τῆς πόλεως,
ἡλικίαις τε καὶ ἅμα φρονήσεσι πιθανώτατον ὂν
τῶν ἐν τῇ πόλει, ᾆδον τὰ κάλλιστα μέγιστ' ἂν
ἐξεργάζοιτο ἀγαθά; ἢ τοῦτο ἀνοήτως οὕτως
ἀφήσομεν, ὃ κυριώτατον ἂν εἴη τῶν καλλίστων τε
καὶ ὠφελιμωτάτων ᾠδῶν;

ΚΛ. Ἀλλ' ἀδύνατον τὸ μεθιέναι, ὥς γε τὰ νῦν
λεγόμενα.

ΑΘ. Πῶς οὖν πρέπον ἂν εἴη τοῦτο; ὁρᾶτε εἰ
τῇδε.

ΚΛ. Πῇ δή;

ΑΘ. Πᾶς που γιγνόμενος πρεσβύτερος ὄκνου

of it, a Dionysiac choir of old men sounds mighty strange,—if you mean that men over thirty, and even men over fifty and up to sixty, are really going to dance in his honour.

ATH. That is, indeed, perfectly true. It needs argument, I fancy, to show how such a procedure would be reasonable.

CLIN. It does.

ATH. Are we agreed about our previous proposals ?

CLIN. In what respect ?

ATH. That it is the duty of every man and child —bond and free, male and female,—and the duty of the whole State, to charm themselves unceasingly with the chants we have described, constantly changing them and securing variety in every way possible, so as to inspire the singers with an insatiable appetite for the hymns and with pleasure therein.

CLIN. Assuredly we would agree as to the duty of doing this.

ATH. Then where should we put the best element in the State,—that which by age and judgment alike is the most influential it contains,—so that by singing its noblest songs it might do most good? Or shall we be so foolish as to dismiss that section which possesses the highest capacity for the noblest and most useful songs?

CLIN. We cannot possibly dismiss it, judging from what you now say.

ATH. What seemly method can we adopt about it ? Will the method be this ?

CLIN. What ?

ATH. Every man as he grows older becomes

---

¹ χορεύσουσιν MSS. : χορεύουσιν Zur.

665 πρὸς τὰς ᾠδὰς μεστός, καὶ χαίρει τε ἧττον πράττων τοῦτο καὶ ἀνάγκης γιγνομένης αἰσχύνοιτ᾽ ἂν
Ε μᾶλλον, ὅσῳ πρεσβύτερος καὶ σωφρονέστερος
γίγνεται, τόσῳ μᾶλλον. ἆρ᾽ οὐχ οὕτως ;
ΚΛ. Οὕτω μὲν οὖν.

ΑΘ. Οὐκοῦν ἐν θεάτρῳ γε καὶ παντοίοις ἀνθρώποις ᾄδειν ἑστὼς ὀρθὸς ἔτι μᾶλλον αἰσχύνοιτ᾽
ἄν. καὶ ταῦτά γ᾽ εἰ καθάπερ οἱ περὶ νίκης χοροὶ
ἀγωνιζόμενοι πεφωνασκηκότες ἰσχνοί τε καὶ
ἄσιτοι ἀναγκάζοιντο ᾄδειν οἱ τοιοῦτοι, παντάπασί
που ἀηδῶς τε καὶ αἰσχυντηλῶς ᾄδοντες ἀπροθύ-
μως ἂν τοῦτ᾽ ἐργάζοιντο.

666 ΚΛ. Ἀναγκαιότατα μέντοι λέγεις.

ΑΘ. Πῶς οὖν αὐτοὺς παραμυθησόμεθα προθύμους εἶναι πρὸς τὰς ᾠδάς ; ἆρ᾽ οὐ νομοθετήσομεν
πρῶτον μὲν τοὺς παῖδας μέχρι ἐτῶν ὀκτωκαίδεκα
τὸ παράπαν οἴνου μὴ γεύεσθαι, διδάσκοντες ὡς οὐ
χρὴ πῦρ ἐπὶ πῦρ ὀχετεύειν εἴς τε τὸ σῶμα καὶ τὴν
ψυχήν, πρὶν ἐπὶ τοὺς πόνους ἐγχειρεῖν πορεύεσθαι,
τὴν ἐμμανῆ εὐλαβούμενοι ἕξιν τῶν νέων· μετὰ δὲ
τοῦτο οἴνου μὲν δὴ γεύεσθαι τοῦ μετρίου μέχρι
Β τριάκοντα ἐτῶν, μέθης δὲ καὶ πολυοινίας τὸ
παράπαν τὸν νέον ἀπέχεσθαι· τετταράκοντα δὲ
ἐπιβαίνοντα ἐτῶν, ἐν τοῖς ξυσσιτίοις εὐωχηθέντα,
καλεῖν τούς τε ἄλλους θεοὺς καὶ δὴ καὶ Διόνυσον
παρακαλεῖν εἰς τὴν τῶν πρεσβυτῶν τελετὴν ἅμα
καὶ παιδιάν, ἣν τοῖς ἀνθρώποις ἐπίκουρον τῆς τοῦ
γήρως αὐστηρότητος ἐδωρήσατο [τὸν οἶνον]¹
φάρμακον ὥστ᾽ ἀνηβᾶν ἡμᾶς, καὶ δυσθυμίας
λήθῃ² γίγνεσθαι μαλακώτερον ἐκ σκληροτέρου
C τὸ τῆς ψυχῆς ἦθος, καθάπερ εἰς πῦρ σίδηρον

---

¹ [τὸν οἶνον] I bracket (so too England).

reluctant to sing songs, and takes less pleasure in doing so ; and when compelled to sing, the older he is and the more temperate, the more he will feel ashamed. Is it not so ?

CLIN. It is.

ATH. Surely, then, he will be more than ever ashamed to get up and sing in the theatre, before people of all sorts. Moreover, if old men like that were obliged to do as the choristers do, who go lean and fasting when training their voices for a competition, they would assuredly find singing an unpleasant and degrading task, and they would undertake it with no great readiness.

CLIN. That is beyond a doubt.

ATH. How then shall we encourage them to take readily to singing ? Shall we not pass a law that, in the first place, no children under eighteen may touch wine at all, teaching that it is wrong to pour fire upon fire either in body or in soul, before they set about tackling their real work, and thus guarding against the excitable disposition of the young ? And next, we shall rule that the young man under thirty may take wine in moderation, but that he must entirely abstain from intoxication and heavy drinking. But when a man has reached the age of forty, he may join in the convivial gatherings and invoke Dionysus, above all other gods, inviting his presence at the rite (which is also the recreation) of the elders, which he bestowed on mankind as a medicine potent against the crabbedness of old age, that thereby we men may renew our youth, and that, through forgetfulness of care, the temper of our souls may lose its hardness and become softer and more

---

² λήθῃ Burges, Burnet : λήθην MSS.

666 ἐντεθέντα τηκόμενον,[1] καὶ οὕτως εὐπλαστότερον
εἶναι; πρῶτον μὲν δὴ διατεθεὶς οὕτως ἕκαστος
ἆρ' οὐκ ἂν ἐθέλοι προθυμότερόν γε, ἧττον αἰσχυ-
νόμενος, οὐκ ἐν πολλοῖς ἀλλ' ἐν μετρίοις, καὶ οὐκ
ἐν ἀλλοτρίοις ἀλλ' ἐν οἰκείοις, ᾄδειν τε καὶ ὃ
πολλάκις εἰρήκαμεν ἐπᾴδειν;

ΚΛ. Καὶ πολύ γε.

ΑΘ. Εἰς μέν γε τὸ προάγειν τοίνυν αὐτοὺς
D μετέχειν ἡμῖν ᾠδῆς οὗτος ὁ τρόπος οὐκ ἂν παντάπασιν ἀσχήμων γίγνοιτο.

ΚΛ. Οὐδαμῶς.

ΑΘ. Ποίαν δὲ οἴσουσιν[2] οἱ ἄνδρες [φωνὴν ἢ
Μοῦσαν];[3] ἢ δῆλον ὅτι πρέπουσαν αὐτοῖς ἀεί[4]
γέ τινα.

ΚΛ. Πῶς γὰρ οὔ;

ΑΘ. Τίς ἂν οὖν πρέποι θείοις ἀνδράσιν; ἆρ' ἂν
ἡ τῶν χορῶν;

ΚΛ. Ἡμεῖς γοῦν, ὦ ξένε, καὶ οἵδε οὐκ ἄλλην ἄν
τινα δυναίμεθα ᾠδὴν ἢ ἣν ἐν τοῖς χοροῖς ἐμάθομεν
ξυνήθεις ᾄδειν γενόμενοι.

ΑΘ. Εἰκότως γε· ὄντως γὰρ οὐκ ἐπήβολοι
E γεγόνατε τῆς καλλίστης ᾠδῆς. στρατοπέδου γὰρ
πολιτείαν ἔχετε, ἀλλ' οὐκ ἐν ἄστεσι κατῳκηκότων,
ἀλλ' οἷον ἀθρόους πώλους ἐν ἀγέλῃ νεμομένους
φορβάδας τοὺς νέους κέκτησθε. λαβὼν δὲ ὑμῶν
οὐδεὶς τὸν αὑτοῦ, παρὰ τῶν ξυννόμων σπάσας
σφόδρα ἀγριαίνοντα καὶ ἀγανακτοῦντα, ἱπποκό-
μον τε ἐπέστησεν ἰδίᾳ καὶ παιδεύει ψήχων τε καὶ
ἡμερῶν καὶ πάντα προσήκοντα ἀποδιδοὺς τῇ

---

[1] τηκόμενον: γιγνόμενον MSS., edd.
[2] οἴσουσιν: αἴσουσιν MSS.: ἤσουσιν Porson, Schanz.
[3] [φωνὴν ἢ Μοῦσαν] bracketed by W.-Möllendorff.

ductile, even as iron when it has been forged in the fire. Will not this softer disposition, in the first place, render each one of them more ready and less ashamed to sing chants and "incantations" (as we have often called them), in the presence, not of a large company of strangers, but of a small number of intimate friends?

CLIN. Yes! much more ready.

ATH. So then, for the purpose of inducing them to take a share in our singing, this plan would not be altogether unseemly.

CLIN. By no means.

ATH. What manner of song will the men raise? Will it not, evidently, be one that suits their own condition in every case?

CLIN. Of course.

ATH. What song, then, would suit godlike men? Would a choric song[1]?

CLIN. At any rate, Stranger, we and our friends here would be unable to sing any other song than that which we learnt by practice in choruses.

ATH. Naturally; for in truth you never attained to the noblest singing. For your civic organisation is that of an army rather than that of city-dwellers, and you keep your young people massed together like a herd of colts at grass: none of you takes his own colt, dragging him away from his fellows, in spite of his fretting and fuming, and puts a special groom in charge of him, and trains him by rubbing him down and stroking him and using all the means

---

[1] *i.e.* a song suited for singing by a chorus at a festival or other public occasion.

---

[4] ἀεί Schanz: δεῖ MSS.

666 παιδοτροφίᾳ, ὅθεν οὐ μόνον ἀγαθὸς ἂν στρατιώ-
667 της εἴη, πόλιν δὲ καὶ ἄστη δυνάμενος διοικεῖν, ὃν
δὴ κατ' ἀρχὰς εἴπομεν τῶν Τυρταίου πολεμικῶν
εἶναι πολεμικώτερον, τέταρτον ἀρετῆς ἀλλ' οὐ
πρῶτον τὴν ἀνδρίαν κτῆμα τιμῶντα ἀεὶ καὶ πανταχοῦ ἰδιώταις τε καὶ ξυμπάσῃ πόλει.

ΚΛ. Οὐκ οἶδα ἡμῶν, ὦ ξένε, ὅπη πάλιν αὖ
τοὺς νομοθέτας φαυλίζεις.

ΑΘ. Οὐκ, ὦ 'γαθέ, προσέχων τούτῳ τὸν νοῦν
δρῶ τοῦτο, εἴπερ· ἀλλ' ὁ λόγος ὅπη φέρει, ταύτῃ
πορευώμεθα, εἰ βούλεσθε. εἰ γὰρ ἔχομεν Μοῦσαν
τῆς τῶν χορῶν καλλίω καὶ τῆς ἐν τοῖς κοινοῖς
B θεάτροις, πειρώμεθα ἀποδοῦναι τούτοις οὕς φαμεν
ἐκείνην μὲν αἰσχύνεσθαι, ζητεῖν δὲ ἥτις καλλίστη
ταύτης κοινωνεῖν.

ΚΛ. Πάνυ γε.

ΑΘ. Οὐκοῦν πρῶτον μὲν δεῖ τόδε γε ὑπάρχειν
ἅπασιν ὅσοις συμπαρέπεταί τις χάρις, ἢ τοῦτο
αὐτὸ μόνον αὐτοῦ τὸ σπουδαιότατον εἶναι ἤ τινα
ὀρθότητα ἢ τὸ τρίτον ὠφέλειαν; οἷον δὴ λέγω
ἐδωδῇ μὲν καὶ πόσει καὶ ξυμπάσῃ τροφῇ παρέ-
πεσθαι μὲν τὴν χάριν, ἣν ἡδονὴν ἂν προσείποιμεν·
C ἣν δὲ ὀρθότητά τε καὶ ὠφέλειαν, ὅπερ ὑγιεινὸν
τῶν προσφερομένων λέγομεν ἑκάστοτε, τοῦτ' αὐτὸ
εἶναι ἐν αὐτοῖς καὶ τὸ ὀρθότατον.

ΚΛ. Πάνυ μὲν οὖν.

---

[1] The following passage (down to 669 B) deals with the
considerations of which a competent judge must take account
in the sphere of music and art. He must have regard
to three things—" correctness " (the truth of the copy to
the original), moral effect or " utility," and " charm " or

LAWS, BOOK II

proper to child-nursing, that so he may turn out not only a good soldier, but able also to manage a State and cities—in short, a man who (as we said at the first) is more of a warrior than the warriors of Tyrtaeus, inasmuch as always and everywhere, both in States and in individuals, he esteems courage as the fourth in order of the virtues, not the first.

CLIN. Once again, Stranger, you are—in a sort of a way—disparaging our lawgivers.

ATH. It is not intentionally, my friend, that I do so—if I am doing it; but whither the argument leads us, thither, if you please, let us go. If we know of a music that is superior to that of the choirs or to that of the public theatres, let us try to supply it to those men who, as we said, are ashamed of the latter, yet are eager to take a part in that music which is noblest.

CLIN. Certainly.

ATH.[1] Now, in the first place, must it not be true of everything which possesses charm as its concomitant, that its most important element is either this charm in itself, or some form of correctness, or, thirdly, utility? For instance, meat and drink and nutriment in general have, as I say, for concomitant that charm which we should term pleasure; but as regards their correctness and utility, what we call the wholesomeness of each article administered is precisely the most correct element they contain.

CLIN. Certainly.

pleasure. Though this last, by itself, is no criterion of artistic excellence, it is a natural "concomitant" (in the mind of the competent judge) when the work of art in question possesses a high degree of both "utility" and "correctness."

667 ΑΘ. Καὶ μὴν καὶ τῇ μαθήσει παρακολουθεῖν μὲν τό γε τῆς χάριτος τὴν ἡδονήν, τὴν δὲ ὀρθότητα καὶ τὴν ὠφέλειαν καὶ τὸ εὖ καὶ τὸ καλῶς τὴν ἀλήθειαν εἶναι τὴν ἀποτελοῦσαν.

ΚΛ. Ἔστιν οὕτως.

D ΑΘ. Τί δέ; τῇ τῶν ὁμοίων ἐργασίᾳ, ὅσαι τέχναι εἰκαστικαί, ἆρ᾽ οὐκ, ἂν τοῦτο ἐξεργάζωνται, τὸ μὲν ἡδονὴν ἐν αὐτοῖς γίγνεσθαι, παρεπόμενον ἐὰν γίγνηται, χάριν αὐτὸ δικαιότατον ἂν εἴη προσαγορεύειν;

ΚΛ. Ναί.

ΑΘ. Τὴν δέ γε ὀρθότητά που τῶν τοιούτων ἡ ἰσότης ἄν, ὡς ἐπὶ τὸ πᾶν εἰπεῖν, ἐξεργάζοιτο τοῦ τε τοσούτου καὶ τοῦ τοιούτου πρότερον, ἀλλ᾽ οὐχ ἡδονή.

ΚΛ. Καλῶς.

ΑΘ. Οὐκοῦν ἡδονὴ κρίνοιτ᾽ ἂν μόνον ἐκεῖνο E ὀρθῶς, ὃ μήτε τινὰ ὠφέλειαν μήτε ἀλήθειαν μήτε ὁμοιότητα ἀπεργαζόμενον παρέχεται, μηδ᾽ αὖ γε βλάβην, ἀλλ᾽ αὐτοῦ τούτου μόνου ἕνεκα γίγνοιτο τοῦ ξυμπαρεπομένου τοῖς ἄλλοις, τῆς χάριτος, ἣν δὴ κάλλιστά τις ὀνομάσαι ἂν ἡδονήν, ὅταν μηδὲν αὐτῇ τούτων ἐπακολουθῇ;

ΚΛ. Ἀβλαβῆ λέγεις ἡδονὴν μόνον.

ΑΘ. Ναί, καὶ παιδιάν γε εἶναι τὴν αὐτὴν ταύτην λέγω τότε ὅταν μήτε τι βλάπτῃ μήτε ὠφελῇ σπουδῆς ἢ λόγου ἄξιον.

ΚΛ. Ἀληθέστατα λέγεις.

ΑΘ. Ἆρ᾽ οὖν οὐ πᾶσαν μίμησιν φαῖμεν ἂν ἐκ τῶν νῦν λεγομένων ἥκιστα ἡδονῇ προσήκειν κρί-
668 νεσθαι καὶ δόξῃ μὴ ἀληθεῖ, καὶ δὴ καὶ πᾶσαι ἰσότητα; οὐ γὰρ εἴ τῳ δοκεῖ ἢ [μή]¹ τις χαίρει,

138

ATH. Learning, too, is accompanied by the element of charm, which is pleasure; but that which produces its correctness and utility, its goodness and nobleness, is truth.

CLIN. Quite so.

ATH. Then how about the imitative arts which produce likenesses? If they succeed in their productions, should not any concomitant pleasure which results therefrom be most properly called "charm"?

CLIN. Yes.

ATH. But, speaking generally, the correctness of these things would be the result not, primarily, of pleasure, but of equality in respect of both quality and quantity.[1]

CLIN. Excellent!

ATH. Then we shall rightly judge by the criterion of pleasure that object only which, in its effects, produces neither utility nor truth nor similarity, nor yet harm, and which exists solely for the sake of the concomitant element of charm,—which element will best be named "pleasure" whenever it is accompanied by none of the other qualities mentioned.

CLIN. You mean only harmless pleasure.

ATH. Yes, and I say that this same pleasure is also play, whenever the harm or good it does is negligible.

CLIN. Very true.

ATH. Should we not then assert, as a corollary, that no imitation should be judged by the criterion of pleasure or of untrue opinion, nor indeed should any kind of equality be so judged? The reason

---

[1] *i.e.* a "likeness" must be "equal" to its original both in character and size.

---

[1] [μή] bracketed by Cornarius.

668 τῷ τοι¹ τό γε ἴσον ἴσον οὐδὲ τὸ σύμμετρον ἂν εἴη σύμμετρον ὅλως, ἀλλὰ τῷ ἀληθεῖ πάντων μάλιστα, ἥκιστα δὲ ὁτῳοῦν ἄλλῳ.

ΚΛ. Παντάπασι μὲν οὖν.

ΑΘ. Οὐκοῦν μουσικήν γε πᾶσάν φαμεν εἰκαστικήν τε εἶναι καὶ μιμητικήν;

ΚΛ. Τί μήν;

ΑΘ. Ἥκιστ᾽ ἄρα ὅταν τις μουσικὴν ἡδονῇ φῇ κρίνεσθαι, τοῦτον ἀποδεκτέον τὸν λόγον, καὶ ζητητέον ἥκιστα ταύτην ὡς σπουδαίαν, εἴ τις B ἄρα που καὶ γίγνοιτο, ἀλλ᾽ ἐκείνην τὴν ἔχουσαν τὴν ὁμοιότητα τῷ τοῦ καλοῦ μιμήματι.

ΚΛ. Ἀληθέστατα.

ΑΘ. Καὶ τούτοις δὴ τοῖς τὴν καλλίστην ᾠδήν τε ζητοῦσι καὶ Μοῦσαν ζητητέον, ὡς ἔοικεν, οὐχ ἥτις ἡδεῖα, ἀλλ᾽ ἥτις ὀρθή. μιμήσεως γὰρ ἦν, ὡς ἔφαμεν, ὀρθότης, εἰ τὸ μιμηθὲν ὅσον τε καὶ οἷον ἦν ἀποτελοῖτο.

ΚΛ. Πῶς γὰρ οὔ;

ΑΘ. Καὶ μὴν τοῦτό γε πᾶς ἂν ὁμολογοῖ περὶ τῆς μουσικῆς, ὅτι πάντα τὰ περὶ αὐτήν ἐστι C ποιήματα μίμησίς τε καὶ ἀπεικασία. καὶ τοῦτό γε μῶν οὐκ ἂν ξύμπαντες ὁμολογοῖεν ποιηταί τε καὶ ἀκροαταὶ καὶ ὑποκριταί;

ΚΛ. Καὶ μάλα.

ΑΘ. Δεῖ δὴ καθ᾽ ἕκαστόν γε, ὡς ἔοικε, γιγνώσκειν τῶν ποιημάτων, ὅ τί ποτέ ἐστί, τὸν μέλλοντα ἐν αὐτῷ μὴ ἁμαρτήσεσθαι. μὴ γὰρ γιγνώσκων

¹ τῷ τοι Schmidt: τῷ MSS.

why the equal is equal, or the symmetrical symmetrical, is not at all because a man so opines, or is
charmed thereby, but most of all because of truth,
and least of all for any other reason.

CLIN. Most certainly.

ATH. We assert, do we not, that all music is
representative and imitative?

CLIN. Of course.

ATH. So whenever a man states that pleasure is
the criterion of music, we shall decisively reject his
statement; and we shall regard such music as the
least important of all (if indeed any music is important) and prefer that which possesses similarity
in its imitation of the beautiful.

CLIN. Very true.

ATH. Thus those who are seeking the best singing and music must seek, as it appears, not that
which is pleasant, but that which is correct; and
the correctness of imitation consists, as we say, in
the reproduction of the original in its own proper
quantity and quality.

CLIN. Of course.

ATH. And this is certainly true of music, as
everyone would allow,—that all its productions are
imitative and representative;[1] that much, at least,
they would all admit,—poets, audience, and actors
alike,—would they not?

CLIN. They would.

ATH. Now the man who is to judge a poem[2]
unerringly must know in each particular case the
exact nature of the poem; for if he does not know

[1] Cp. 655 D, above. The music (songs and tunes) of
dramatic compositions is specially alluded to.

[2] Or musical composition.

668 τὴν οὐσίαν, τί ποτε βούλεται καὶ ὅτου ποτέ
ἐστιν εἰκὼν ὄντως, σχολῇ τήν γε ὀρθότητα τῆς
βουλήσεως ἢ καὶ ἁμαρτίαν αὐτοῦ διαγνώσεται.

ΚΛ. Σχολῇ· πῶς δ' οὔ;

D ΑΘ. Ὁ δὲ τὸ ὀρθῶς μὴ γιγνώσκων ἆρ' ἄν ποτε
τό γε εὖ καὶ τὸ κακῶς δυνατὸς εἴη διαγνῶναι;
λέγω δ' οὐ πάνυ σαφῶς, ἀλλ' ὧδε σαφέστερον
ἴσως ἂν λεχθείη.

ΚΛ. Πῶς;

ΑΘ. Εἰσὶ δή που κατὰ τὴν ὄψιν ἡμῖν ἀπεικα-
σίαι μυρίαι.

ΚΛ. Ναί.

ΑΘ. Τί οὖν; εἴ τις καὶ ἐν τούτοις ἀγνοοῖ
τῶν μεμιμημένων ὅ τί ποτέ ἐστιν ἕκαστον
τῶν σωμάτων, ἆρ' ἄν ποτε τό γε ὀρθῶς αὐτῶν
εἰργασμένον γνοίη; λέγω δὲ τὸ τοιόνδε, οἷον τοὺς
ἀριθμοὺς [τοῦ σώματος καὶ]¹ ἑκάστων τῶν μερῶν
E τὰς <τε> θέσεις ᾗ ἔχει, ὅσοι τ' εἰσὶ καὶ ὁποῖα
παρ' ὁποῖα αὐτῶν κείμενα τὴν προσήκουσαν τάξιν
ἀπείληφε, καὶ ἔτι δὴ χρώματά τε καὶ σχήματα,
ἢ πάντα ταῦτα τεταραγμένως εἴργασται. μῶν
δοκεῖ ταῦτ' ἄν ποτε διαγνῶναί τις τὸ παράπαν
ἀγνοῶν ὅ τί ποτέ ἐστι τὸ μεμιμημένον ζῷον;

ΚΛ. Καὶ πῶς;

ΑΘ. Τί δ'; εἰ γιγνώσκοιμεν ὅτι τὸ γεγραμμένον ἢ τὸ πεπλασμένον ἐστὶν ἄνθρωπος, καὶ
τὰ μέρη πάντα τὰ ἑαυτοῦ καὶ χρώματα ἅμα καὶ
669 σχήματα ἀπείληφεν ὑπὸ τῆς τέχνης, ἆρά γε
ἀναγκαῖον ἤδη τῷ ταῦτα γνόντι καὶ ἐκεῖνο ἑτοίμως γιγνώσκειν, εἴτε καλὸν εἴτε ὅπῃ ποτὲ ἐλλιπὲς
αὖ εἴη κάλλους;

¹ [τοῦ σώματος καὶ] I bracket, and add <τε> after τὰς.

its essence,—what its intention is and what the actual original which it represents,—then he will hardly be able to decide how far it succeeds or fails in fulfilling its intention.

CLIN. Hardly, to be sure.

ATH. And would a man who does not know what constitutes correctness be able to decide as to the goodness or badness of a poem? But I am not making myself quite clear: it might be clearer if I put it in this way—

CLIN. In what way?

ATH. As regards objects of sight we have, of course, thousands of representations.

CLIN. Yes.

ATH. How, then, if in this class of objects a man were to be ignorant of the nature of each of the bodies represented,—could he ever know whether it is correctly executed? What I mean is this: whether it preserves the proper dimensions and the positions of each of the bodily parts, and has caught their exact number and the proper order in which one is placed next another, and their colours and shapes as well,—or whether all these things are wrought in a confused manner. Do you suppose that anyone could possibly decide these points if he were totally ignorant as to what animal was being represented?

CLIN. How could he?

ATH. Well, suppose we should know that the object painted or moulded is a man, and know that art has endowed him with all his proper parts, colours, and shapes,—is it at once inevitable that the person who knows this can easily discern also whether the work is beautiful, or wherein it is deficient in beauty?

PLATO

669 κλ. Πάντες μεντᾶν, ὡς ἔπος εἰπεῖν, ὦ ξένε, τὰ καλὰ τῶν ζώων ἐγιγνώσκομεν.

αθ. Ὀρθότατα λέγεις. ἆρ᾽ οὖν οὐ περὶ ἑκάστην εἰκόνα καὶ ἐν γραφικῇ καὶ ἐν μουσικῇ καὶ πάντῃ τὸν μέλλοντα ἔμφρονα κριτὴν ἔσεσθαι δεῖ

B ταῦτα τρία ἔχειν, ὅ τέ ἐστι πρῶτον γιγνώσκειν, ἔπειτα ὡς ὀρθῶς, ἔπειθ᾽ ὡς εὖ, τὸ τρίτον, εἴργασται τῶν εἰκόνων ἡτισοῦν [ῥήμασί τε καὶ μέλεσι καὶ τοῖς ῥυθμοῖς];[1]

κλ. Ἔοικε γοῦν.

αθ. Μὴ τοίνυν ἀπείπωμεν λέγοντες τὸ περὶ τὴν μουσικὴν ᾗ χαλεπόν. ἐπειδὴ γὰρ ὑμνεῖται περὶ αὐτὴν διαφερόντως ἢ τὰς ἄλλας εἰκόνας, εὐλαβείας δὴ δεῖται πλείστης πασῶν εἰκόνων. ἁμαρτών τε γάρ τις μέγιστ᾽ ἂν βλάπτοιτο, ἤθη

C κακὰ φιλοφρονούμενος, χαλεπώτατόν τε αἰσθέσθαι διὰ τὸ τοὺς ποιητὰς φαυλοτέρους εἶναι ποιητὰς αὐτῶν τῶν Μουσῶν. οὐ γὰρ ἂν ἐκεῖναί γε ἐξαμάρτοιέν ποτε τοσοῦτον, ὥστε ῥήματα ἀνδρῶν ποιήσασαι τὸ σχῆμα γυναικῶν καὶ μέλος ἀποδοῦναι, καὶ μέλος ἐλευθέρων αὖ καὶ σχήματα ξυνθεῖσαι ῥυθμοὺς δούλων καὶ ἀνελευθέρων προσαρμόττειν, οὐδ᾽ αὖ ῥυθμοὺς καὶ σχῆμα ἐλευθέριον ὑποθεῖσαι μέλος ἢ λόγον ἐναντίον ἀπο-

D δοῦναι τοῖς ῥυθμοῖς· ἔτι δὲ θηρίων φωνὰς καὶ ἀνθρώπων καὶ ὀργάνων καὶ πάντας ψόφους εἰς ταὐτὸ οὐκ ἄν ποτε ξυνθεῖεν, ὡς ἕν τι μιμούμεναι.

---

[1] [ῥήμασί . . . ῥυθμοῖς] bracketed by England.

[1] In what follows, the main features censured are—*incongruity*, when the words, tunes and gestures of an acted piece of music are out of harmony; *senselessness*, when tunes and gestures are divorced from words; *barbarousness*, when

144

CLIN. If that were so, Stranger, practically all of us would know what animals are beautiful.

ATH. You are quite right. In regard, then, to every representation—whether in painting, music or any other art—must not the judicious critic possess these three requisites: first, a knowledge of the nature of the original; next, a knowledge of the correctness of the copy; and thirdly, a knowledge of the excellence with which the copy is executed?

CLIN. It would seem so, certainly.

ATH. Let us not hesitate, then, to mention the point wherein lies the difficulty of music. Just because it is more talked about than any other form of representation, it needs more caution than any. The man who blunders in this art will do himself the greatest harm, by welcoming base morals; and, moreover, his blunder is very hard to discern, inasmuch as our poets are inferior as poets to the Muses themselves.[1] For the Muses would never blunder so far as to assign a feminine tune and gesture to verses composed for men, or to fit the rhythms of captives and slaves to a tune and gestures framed for free men, or conversely, after constructing the rhythms and gestures of free men, to assign to the rhythms a tune or verses of an opposite style. Nor would the Muses ever combine in a single piece the cries of beasts and men, the clash of instruments, and noises of all kinds, by way of representing a single object;

the thing represented is paltry or uncouth (such as a duck's quack); *virtuosity*, when the performer makes a display of the control he has over his limbs and instruments, like a mountebank or "contortionist." All these are marks of *bad* music from the point of view of the educationist and statesman, since they are neither "correct" nor morally elevating.

669 ποιηταὶ δ' ἀνθρώπινοι σφόδρα τὰ τοιαῦτα ἐμ-
πλέκοντες καὶ συγκυκῶντες ἀλόγως γέλωτ' ἂν
παρασκευάζοιεν τῶν ἀνθρώπων ὅσοις[1] φησὶν
Ὀρφεὺς "λαχεῖν ὥραν τῆς τέρψιος." ταῦτά τε
γὰρ ὁρῶσι πάντα κυκώμενα καὶ εἴ τι[2] διασπῶσιν
οἱ ποιηταὶ ῥυθμὸν μὲν καὶ σχήματα μέλους
χωρίς, λόγους ψιλοὺς εἰς μέτρα τιθέντες, μέλος
Ε δ' αὖ καὶ ῥυθμὸν ἄνευ ῥημάτων, ψιλῇ κιθαρίσει
τε καὶ αὐλήσει προσχρώμενοι, ἐν οἷς δὴ παγχάλεπον ἄνευ λόγου γιγνόμενον ῥυθμόν τε καὶ ἁρμονίαν
γιγνώσκειν ὅ τί τε βούλεται καὶ ὅτῳ ἔοικε τῶν
ἀξιολόγων μιμημάτων. ἀλλ' ὑπολαβεῖν ἀναγκαῖον ὅτι τὸ τοιοῦτόν γε πολλῆς ἀγροικίας μεστὸν
πᾶν, ὁπόσον τάχους τε καὶ ἀπταισίας καὶ φωνῆς
θηριώδους σφόδρα <ἐρᾷ> [φίλον],[3] ὥστ' αὐλήσει
γε χρῆσθαι καὶ κιθαρίσει πλὴν ὅσον ὑπὸ ὄρχησίν
670 τε καὶ ᾠδήν· ψιλῷ δ' ἑκατέρῳ πᾶσά τις ἀμουσία
καὶ θαυματουργία γίγνοιτ' ἂν τῆς χρήσεως. ταῦτα μὲν ἔχει ταύτῃ λόγον· ἡμεῖς δέ γε οὐχ ὅ τι
μὴ δεῖ ταῖς Μούσαις ἡμῶν προσχρῆσθαι τοὺς
ἤδη τριακοντούτας καὶ τῶν πεντήκοντα πέραν
γεγονότας σκοπούμεθα, ἀλλ' ὅ τί ποτε δεῖ. τόδε
μὲν οὖν ἐκ τούτων ὁ λόγος ἡμῖν δοκεῖ μοι σημαίνειν ἤδη τῆς γε χορικῆς Μούσης ὅτι πεπαιδεῦσθαι δεῖ βέλτιον τοὺς πεντηκοντούτας, ὅσοις
Β περ ἂν ᾄδειν προσήκῃ. τῶν γὰρ ῥυθμῶν καὶ
τῶν ἁρμονιῶν ἀναγκαῖον αὐτοῖς ἐστιν εὐαισθήτως
ἔχειν καὶ γιγνώσκειν· ἢ πῶς τις τὴν ὀρθότητα
γνώσεται τῶν μελῶν [ᾧ προσήκεν ἢ μὴ προσῆκε
τοῦ Δωριστὶ καὶ τοῦ ῥυθμοῦ ὃν ὁ ποιητὴς αὐτῷ
προσῆψεν, ὀρθῶς ἢ μή] ;[4]

¹ ὅσοις H. Richards: ὅσους MSS., edd.

whereas human poets, by their senselessness in mixing such things and jumbling them up together, would furnish a theme for laughter to all the men who, in Orpheus' phrase, "have attained the full flower of joyousness." For they behold all these things jumbled together, and how, also, the poets rudely sunder rhythm and gesture from tune, putting tuneless words into metre, or leaving tune and rhythm without words, and using the bare sound of harp or flute, wherein it is almost impossible to understand what is intended by this wordless rhythm and harmony, or what noteworthy original it represents. Such methods, as one ought to realise, are clownish in the extreme in so far as they exhibit an excessive craving for speed, mechanical accuracy, and the imitation of animals' sounds, and consequently employ the pipe and the harp without the accompaniment of dance and song; for the use of either of these instruments by itself is the mark of the mountebank or the boor. Enough, then, of that matter: now as to ourselves. What we are considering is, not how those of us who are over thirty years old, or beyond fifty, ought not to make use of the Muses, but how they ought to do so. Our argument already indicates, I think, this result from our discussion,—that all men of over fifty that are fit to sing ought to have a training that is better than that of the choric Muse. For they must of necessity possess knowledge and a quick perception of rhythms and harmonies; else how shall a man know which tunes are correct?

---

[2] εἴ τι Badham, Schanz: ἔτι MSS.

[3] <ἐρᾷ> I add, and bracket φίλον.

[4] [ᾧ . . . μή] bracketed by England.

670 κλ. Δῆλον ὡς οὐδαμῶς.

αθ. Γελοῖος γὰρ ὅ γε πολὺς ὄχλος ἡγούμενος ἱκανῶς γιγνώσκειν τό τ' εὐάρμοστον καὶ εὔρυθμον καὶ μή, ὅσοι προσᾴδειν αὐλῷ[1] καὶ βαίνειν ἐν C ῥυθμῷ γεγόνασι διηναγκασμένοι· ὅτι δὲ δρῶσι ταῦτα ἀγνοοῦντες αὐτῶν ἕκαστα, οὐ συλλογίζονται. τὸ δέ που προσήκοντα μὲν ἔχον πᾶν μέλος ὀρθῶς ἔχει, μὴ προσήκοντα δὲ ἡμαρτημένως.

κλ. Ἀναγκαιότατα.

αθ. Τί οὖν; ὁ μηδὲ ὅ τί ποτ' ἔχει γιγνώσκων ἆρα, ὅ τί περ εἴπομεν, ὡς ὀρθῶς γε αὐτὸ ἔχει γνώσεταί ποτε ἐν ὁτῳοῦν;

κλ. Καὶ τίς μηχανή;

αθ. Τοῦτ' οὖν, ὡς ἔοικεν, ἀνευρίσκομεν αὖ τὰ νῦν, ὅτι τοῖς ᾠδοῖς ἡμῖν, οὓς νῦν παρακαλοῦμεν D καὶ ἑκόντας τινὰ τρόπον ἀναγκάζομεν ᾄδειν, μέχρι γε τοσούτου πεπαιδεῦσθαι σχεδὸν ἀναγκαῖον, μέχρι τοῦ δυνατὸν εἶναι ξυνακολουθεῖν ἕκαστον ταῖς τε βάσεσι τῶν ῥυθμῶν καὶ ταῖς χορδαῖς ταῖς τῶν μελῶν, ἵνα καθορῶντες τάς τε ἁρμονίας καὶ τοὺς ῥυθμοὺς ἐκλέγεσθαί τε τὰ προσήκοντα οἷοί τ' ὦσιν, ἃ τοῖς τηλικούτοις τε καὶ τοιούτοις ᾄδειν πρέπον, καὶ οὕτως ᾄδωσι, καὶ ᾄδοντες αὐτοί τε ἡδονὰς τὸ παραχρῆμα ἀσινεῖς ἥδωνται καὶ τοῖς νεωτέροις ἡγεμόνες ἠθῶν χρηστῶν ἀσπασμοῦ E προσήκοντος γίγνωνται. μέχρι δὲ τοσούτου παιδευθέντες ἀκριβεστέραν ἂν παιδείαν τῆς ἐπὶ τὸ

_____
[1] αὐλῷ Badham, Schanz: αὐτῶν MSS.

CLIN. Obviously he cannot know this at all.

ATH. It is absurd of the general crowd to imagine that they can fully understand what is harmonious and rhythmical, or the reverse, when they have been drilled to sing to the flute or step in time; and they fail to comprehend that, in doing each of these things, they do them in ignorance. But the fact is that every tune which has its appropriate elements is correct, but incorrect if the elements are inappropriate.

CLIN. Undoubtedly.

ATH. What then of the man who does not know in the least what the tune's elements are? Will he ever know about any tune, as we said, that it is correct?

CLIN. There is no possible means of his doing so.

ATH. We are now once more, as it appears, discovering the fact that these singers of ours (whom we are now inviting and compelling, so to say, of their own free will to sing) must almost necessarily be trained up to such a point that every one of them may be able to follow both the steps[1] of the rhythms and the chords of the tunes, so that, by observing the harmonies and rhythms, they may be able to select those of an appropriate kind, which it is seemly for men of their own age and character to sing, and may in this wise sing them, and in the singing may not only enjoy innocent pleasure themselves at the moment, but also may serve as leaders to the younger men in their seemly adoption of noble manners. If they were trained up to such a point, their training would be more thorough than

---

[1] *i.e.* dance-steps and gestures: "chords" nearly equals "notes," with which the "steps" should "keep time."

670 πλῆθος φερούσης εἶεν μετακεχειρισμένοι καὶ τῆς
περὶ τοὺς ποιητὰς αὐτούς. τὸ γὰρ τρίτον οὐδεμία ἀνάγκη ποιητῇ γιγνώσκειν, εἴτε καλὸν εἴτε
μὴ καλὸν τὸ μίμημα, τὸ δ᾽ ἁρμονίας καὶ ῥυθμοῦ
σχεδὸν ἀνάγκη· τοῖς δὲ πάντα τὰ τρία τῆς
671 ἐκλογῆς ἕνεκα τοῦ καλλίστου καὶ δευτέρου, ἢ
μηδέποτε ἱκανὸν ἐπῳδὸν γίγνεσθαι νέοις πρὸς
ἀρετήν. καὶ ὅπερ ὁ λόγος ἐν ἀρχαῖς ἐβουλήθη,
τὴν τῷ τοῦ Διονύσου χορῷ βοήθειαν ἐπιδεῖξαι
καλῶς λεγομένην, εἰς δύναμιν εἴρηκε. σκοπώμεθα
δὴ εἰ τοῦθ᾽ οὕτω γέγονε. θορυβώδης μέν που ὁ
ξύλλογος ὁ τοιοῦτος ἐξ ἀνάγκης προϊούσης τῆς
πόσεως ἐπὶ μᾶλλον ἀεὶ ξυμβαίνει γιγνόμενος,
ὅπερ ὑπεθέμεθα κατ᾽ ἀρχὰς ἀναγκαῖον εἶναι
B γίγνεσθαι περὶ τῶν νῦν συγγιγνομένων.[1]

ΚΛ. Ἀνάγκη.

ΑΘ. Πᾶς δέ γε αὐτὸς αὑτοῦ κουφότερος αἴρεται
καὶ γέγηθέ τε καὶ παρρησίας ἐμπίπλαται καὶ
ἀνηκουστίας ἐν τῷ τοιούτῳ τῶν πέλας, ἄρχων δ᾽
ἱκανὸς ἀξιοῖ ἑαυτοῦ τε καὶ τῶν ἄλλων γεγονέναι.

ΚΛ. Τί μήν;

ΑΘ. Οὐκοῦν ἔφαμεν, ὅταν γίγνηται ταῦτα,
καθάπερ τινὰ σίδηρον, τὰς ψυχὰς τῶν πινόντων
διαπύρους γιγνομένας μαλθακωτέρας γίγνεσθαι
C καὶ νεωτέρας, ὥστε εὐαγώγους ξυμβαίνειν τῷ
δυναμένῳ καὶ ἐπισταμένῳ παιδεύειν τε καὶ
πλάττειν, καθάπερ ὅτ᾽ ἦσαν νέαι; τοῦτον δ᾽

---

[1] συγγιγνομένων : γιγνομένων MSS. : λεγομένων Euseb.,
Schanz.

that of the majority, or indeed of the poets themselves. For although it is almost necessary for a
poet to have a knowledge of harmony and rhythm,
it is not necessary for him to know the third point
also—namely, whether the representation is noble
or ignoble[1]; but for our older singers a knowledge
of all these three points is necessary, to enable them
to determine what is first, what second in order of
nobility; otherwise none of them will ever succeed
in attracting the young to virtue by his incantations.
The primary intention of our argument, which was
to demonstrate that our defence of the Dionysiac
chorus was justifiable, has now been carried out to
the best of our ability. Let us consider if that
is really so. Such a gathering inevitably tends, as
the drinking proceeds, to grow ever more and more
uproarious; and in the case of the present day
gatherings that is, as we said at the outset, an
inevitable result.

CLIN. Inevitable.

ATH. Everyone is uplifted above his normal self,
and is merry and bubbles over with loquacious
audacity himself, while turning a deaf ear to his
neighbours, and regards himself as competent to
rule both himself and everyone else.

CLIN. To be sure.

ATH. And did we not say that when this takes
place, the souls of the drinkers turn softer, like iron,
through being heated, and younger too; whence
they become ductile, just as when they were young,
in the hands of the man who has the skill and
ability to train and mould them. And now, even as

---

[1] *i.e.* the composer, as such, is not concerned with the
moral (or psychological) effect of the piece.

671 εἶναι τὸν πλάστην τὸν αὐτὸν ὥσπερ τότε, τὸν
ἀγαθὸν νομοθέτην, οὗ νόμους εἶναι δεῖ συμπο-
τικούς, δυναμένους τὸν εὔελπιν καὶ θαρραλέον
ἐκεῖνον γιγνόμενον καὶ ἀναισχυντότερον τοῦ
δέοντος, καὶ οὐκ ἐθέλοντα τάξιν καὶ τὸ κατὰ μέρος
σιγῆς καὶ λόγου καὶ πόσεως καὶ μούσης ὑπο-
μένειν, ἐθέλειν ποιεῖν πάντα τούτοις τἀναντία,
D καὶ εἰσιόντι τῷ μὴ καλῷ θάρρει τὸν κάλλιστον
διαμαχούμενον¹ φόβον εἰσπέμπειν οἵους τ' εἶναι
μετὰ δίκης, ὃν αἰδῶ τε καὶ αἰσχύνην [θεῖον
φόβον]² ὠνομάκαμεν;

κλ. Ἔστι ταῦτα.

αθ. Τούτων δέ γε τῶν νόμων εἶναι νομοφύλακας καὶ συνδημιουργοὺς αὐτοῖς τοὺς ἀθορύβους
καὶ νήφοντας τῶν μὴ νηφόντων στρατηγούς, ὧν
δὴ χωρὶς μέθῃ διαμάχεσθαι δεινότερον ἢ πολεμίοις
εἶναι μὴ μετὰ ἀρχόντων ἀθορύβων, καὶ τὸν αὖ
μὴ δυνάμενον ἐθέλειν πείθεσθαι τούτοις καὶ τοῖς
E ἡγεμόσι τοῖς τοῦ Διονύσου, τοῖς ὑπὲρ ἑξήκοντα
ἔτη γεγονόσιν, ἴσην καὶ μείζω τὴν αἰσχύνην
φέρειν ἢ τὸν τοῖς τοῦ Ἄρεος ἀπειθοῦντα ἄρχουσιν.

κλ. Ὀρθῶς.

αθ. Οὐκοῦν εἴ γε εἴη τοιαύτη μὲν μέθη,
τοιαύτη δὲ παιδιά, μῶν οὐκ ὠφεληθέντες ἂν οἱ
τοιοῦτοι συμπόται καὶ μᾶλλον φίλοι ἢ πρότερον
ἀπαλλάττοιντο ἀλλήλων, ἀλλ' οὐχ ὥσπερ τὰ
νῦν ἐχθροί, κατὰ νόμους δὴ³ πᾶσαν τὴν ξυνουσίαν
672 ξυγγενόμενοι καὶ ἀκολουθήσαντες ὁπότε ἀφηγοῖντο
οἱ νήφοντες τοῖς μὴ νήφουσιν;

κλ. Ὀρθῶς, εἴ γε δὴ εἴη τοιαύτη οἵαν νῦν
λέγεις.

¹ διαμαχούμενον H. Richards: διαμαχόμενον MSS.

then, the man who is to mould them is the good legislator; he must lay down banqueting laws, able to control that banqueter who becomes confident and bold and unduly shameless, and unwilling to submit to the proper limits of silence and speech, of drinking and of music, making him consent to do in all ways the opposite,—laws able also, with the aid of justice, to fight against the entrance of such ignoble audacity, by bringing in that most noble fear which we have named "modesty" and "shame."

CLIN. That is so.

ATH. And as law-wardens of these laws and co-operators therewith, there must be sober and sedate men to act as commanders over the un-sober; for to fight drunkenness without these would be a more formidable task than to fight enemies without sedate leaders. Any man who refuses willingly to obey these men and the officers of Dionysus (who are over sixty years of age) shall incur as much disgrace as the man who disobeys the officers of Ares, and even more.

CLIN. Quite right.

ATH. If such was the character of the drinking and of the recreation, would not such fellow-drinkers be the better for it, and part from one another better friends than before, instead of enemies, as now? For they would be guided by laws in all their intercourse, and would listen to the directions given to the un-sober by the sober.

CLIN. True, if it really were of the character you describe.

---

² [θεῖον φόβον] bracketed by Badham, Schanz.
³ δὴ England: δὲ MSS.

672 ΑΘ. Μὴ τοίνυν ἐκεῖνό γ' ἔτι τῆς τοῦ Διονύσου
δωρεᾶς ψέγωμεν ἁπλῶς, ὡς ἔστι κακὴ καὶ εἰς
πόλιν οὐκ ἀξία παραδέχεσθαι. καὶ γὰρ ἔτι
πλείω τις ἂν ἐπεξέλθοι λέγων, ἐπεὶ καὶ τὸ
μέγιστον ἀγαθὸν ὃ δωρεῖται λέγειν μὲν ὄκνος
εἰς τοὺς πολλοὺς διὰ τὸ κακῶς τοὺς ἀνθρώπους
Β αὐτὸ ὑπολαβεῖν καὶ γνῶναι λεχθέν.

ΚΛ. Τὸ ποῖον δή;

ΑΘ. Λόγος τις ἅμα καὶ φήμη ὑπορρεῖ πως,
ὡς ὁ θεὸς οὗτος ὑπὸ τῆς μητρυιᾶς Ἥρας διεφο-
ρήθη τῆς ψυχῆς τὴν γνώμην, διὸ τάς τε βακχείας
καὶ πᾶσαν τὴν μανικὴν ἐμβάλλει χορείαν τιμω-
ρούμενος· ὅθεν καὶ τὸν οἶνον ἐπὶ τοῦτ' αὐτὸ
δεδώρηται. ἐγὼ δὲ τὰ μὲν τοιαῦτα τοῖς ἀσφαλὲς
ἡγουμένοις εἶναι λέγειν περὶ θεῶν ἀφίημι λέγειν,
τὸ δὲ τοσόνδε οἶδα, ὅτι πᾶν ζῷον, ὅσον αὐτῷ
C προσήκει νοῦν ἔχειν τελεωθέντι, τοῦτον καὶ
τοσοῦτον οὐδὲν ἔχον ποτὲ φύεται. ἐν τούτῳ δὴ
τῷ χρόνῳ ἐν ᾧ μήπω κέκτηται τὴν οἰκείαν
φρόνησιν, πᾶν μαίνεταί τε καὶ βοᾷ ἀτάκτως, καὶ
ὅταν ἀκταινώσῃ ἑαυτὸ τάχιστα, ἀτάκτως αὖ
πηδᾷ. ἀναμνησθῶμεν δὲ ὅτι μουσικῆς τε καὶ
γυμναστικῆς ἔφαμεν ἀρχὰς ταύτας εἶναι.

ΚΛ. Μεμνήμεθα· τί δ' οὔ;

ΑΘ. Οὐκοῦν καὶ ὅτι τὴν ῥυθμοῦ τε καὶ ἁρμονίας
D αἴσθησιν τοῖς ἀνθρώποις ἡμῖν ἐνδεδωκέναι τὴν
ἀρχὴν ταύτην ἔφαμεν, Ἀπόλλωνα δὲ καὶ Μούσας
καὶ Διόνυσον συναιτίους[1] γεγονέναι;

---

[1] συναιτίους: θεῶν αἰτίους MSS. : τούτων αἰτίους Cornarius.

---

[1] i.e. the "frenzied" motion ascribed to Dionysus is, rather

ATH. Then we must no longer, without qualification, bring that old charge against the gift of Dionysus, that it is bad and unworthy of admittance into a State. Indeed, one might enlarge considerably on this subject; for the greatest benefit that gift confers is one which one hesitates to declare to the multitude, since, when declared, it is misconceived and misunderstood.

CLIN. What is that?

ATH. There is a secret stream of story and report to the effect that the god Dionysus was robbed of his soul's judgment by his stepmother Hera, and that in vengeance therefor he brought in Bacchic rites and all the frenzied choristry, and with the same aim bestowed also the gift of wine. These matters, however, I leave to those who think it safe to say them about deities [1]; but this much I know,— that no creature is ever born in possession of that reason, or that amount of reason, which properly belongs to it when fully developed; consequently, every creature, during the period when it is still lacking in its proper intelligence, continues all in a frenzy, crying out wildly, and, as soon as it can get on its feet, leaping wildly. Let us remember how we said that in this we have the origin of music and gymnastic. [2]

CLIN. We remember that, of course.

ATH. Do we not also remember how we said that from this origin there was implanted in us men the sense of rhythm and harmony, and that the joint authors thereof were Apollo and the Muses and the god Dionysus?

a natural instinct exhibited in all child-life, and D. helps to reduce it to rhythm.　　　[2] Cp. 653 D ff.

672　ΚΛ. Πῶς γὰρ οὔ;

ΑΘ. Καὶ δὴ καὶ τὸν οἶνόν γε, ὡς ἔοικεν, ὁ τῶν ἄλλων λόγος ἵνα μανῶμεν φησὶν ἐπὶ τιμωρίᾳ τῇ τῶν ἀνθρώπων δεδόσθαι· ὁ δὲ νῦν λεγόμενος ὑφ' ἡμῶν φάρμακον ἐπὶ τοὐναντίον φησὶν αἰδοῦς μὲν ψυχῆς κτήσεως ἕνεκα δεδόσθαι, σώματος δὲ ὑγιείας τε καὶ ἰσχύος.

ΚΛ. Κάλλιστα, ὦ ξένε, τὸν λόγον ἀπεμνημόνευκας.

Ε　ΑΘ. Καὶ τὰ μὲν δὴ τῆς χορείας ἡμίσεα διαπεπεράνθω· τὰ δ' ἡμίσεα, ὅπως ἂν ἔτι δοκῇ, περανοῦμεν ἢ καὶ ἐάσομεν;

ΚΛ. Ποῖα δὴ λέγεις, καὶ πῶς ἑκάτερα διαιρῶν;

ΑΘ. Ὅλη μέν που χορεία ὅλη παίδευσις ἦν ἡμῖν, τούτου δ' αὖ τὸ μὲν ῥυθμοί τε καὶ ἁρμονίαι τὸ κατὰ τὴν φωνήν.

ΚΛ. Ναί.

ΑΘ. Τὸ δέ γε κατὰ τὴν τοῦ σώματος κίνησιν ῥυθμὸν μὲν κοινὸν τῇ τῆς φωνῆς εἶχε κινήσει, σχῆμα δὲ ἴδιον. ἐκεῖ δὲ μέλος ἡ τῆς φωνῆς
673　κίνησις.

ΚΛ. Ἀληθέστατα.

ΑΘ. Τὰ μὲν τοίνυν τῆς φωνῆς μέχρι τῆς ψυχῆς πρὸς ἀρετὴν παιδείας,[1] οὐκ οἶδ' ὅντινα τρόπον, ὠνομάσαμεν μουσικήν.

ΚΛ. Ὀρθῶς μὲν οὖν.

ΑΘ. Τὰ δέ γε τοῦ σώματος, ἃ παιζόντων ὄρχησιν εἴπομεν, ἐὰν μέχρι τῆς τοῦ σώματος ἀρετῆς ἡ τοιαύτη κίνησις γίγνηται, τὴν ἔντεχνον ἀγωγὴν ἐπὶ τὸ τοιοῦτον αὐτοῦ γυμναστικὴν προσείπωμεν.

---

[1] ἀρετὴν παιδείας Ritter : ἀρετῆς παιδείαν MSS.

CLIN. Certainly we remember.

ATH. Moreover, as to wine, the account given by other people apparently is that it was bestowed on us men as a punishment, to make us mad ; but our own account, on the contrary, declares that it is a medicine given for the purpose of securing modesty of soul and health and strength of body.

CLIN. You have recalled our account admirably, Stranger.

ATH. We may say, then, that the one half of the subject of choristry has now been disposed of. Shall we proceed at once to deal with the other half in whatever way seems best, or shall we leave it alone ?

CLIN. What halves do you mean ? How are you dividing the subject ?

ATH. In our view, choristry as a whole is identical with education as a whole ; and the part of this concerned with the voice consists of rhythms and harmonies.

CLIN. Yes.

ATH. And the part concerned with bodily motion possesses, in common with vocal motion, rhythm ; besides which it possesses gesture as its own peculiar attribute, just as tune is the peculiar attribute of vocal motion.

CLIN. Very true.

ATH. Now the vocal actions which pertain to the training of the soul in excellence we ventured somehow to name " music."

CLIN. And rightly so.

ATH. As regards the bodily actions which we called playful dancing,—if such action attains to bodily excellence, we may term the technical guidance of the body to this end " gymnastic."

673B   κλ. Ὀρθότατα.

αθ. Τὸ δὲ τῆς μουσικῆς, ὃ νῦν δὴ σχεδὸν ἥμισυ διεληλυθέναι τῆς χορείας εἴπομεν καὶ διαπεπεράνθαι, καὶ νῦν οὕτως εἰρήσθω· τὸ δὲ ἥμισυ λέγωμεν, ἢ πῶς καὶ πῇ ποιητέον ;

κλ. Ὦ ἄριστε, Κρησὶ καὶ Λακεδαιμονίοις διαλεγόμενος, μουσικῆς πέρι διελθόντων ἡμῶν, ἐλλειπόντων δὲ γυμναστικῆς, τί ποτε οἴει σοι πότερον ἡμῶν ἀποκρινεῖσθαι πρὸς ταύτην τὴν ἐρώτησιν ;

αθ. Ἀποκεκρίσθαι ἔγωγ' ἄν σε φαίην σχεδὸν
C ταῦτ' ἐρόμενον σαφῶς, καὶ μανθάνω ὡς ἐρώτησις οὖσα αὕτη τὰ νῦν ἀπόκρισίς τ' ἐστίν, ὡς εἶπον καὶ ἔτι πρόσταξις διαπεράνασθαι τὰ περὶ γυμναστικῆς.

κλ. Ἄρισθ' ὑπέλαβές τε καὶ οὕτω δὴ ποίει.

αθ. Ποιητέον· οὐδὲ γὰρ πάνυ χαλεπόν ἐστιν εἰπεῖν ὑμῖν γε ἀμφοτέροις γνώριμα. πολὺ γὰρ ἐν ταύτῃ τῇ τέχνῃ πλέον ἐμπειρίας ἢ ἐν ἐκείνῃ μετέχετε.

κλ. Σχεδὸν ἀληθῆ λέγεις.

αθ. Οὐκοῦν αὖ ταύτης ἀρχὴ μὲν τῆς παιδιᾶς
D τὸ κατὰ φύσιν πηδᾶν εἰθίσθαι πᾶν ζῷον, τὸ δ' ἀνθρώπινον, ὡς ἔφαμεν, αἴσθησιν λαβὸν τοῦ ῥυθμοῦ ἐγέννησέ τε ὄρχησιν καὶ ἔτεκε, τοῦ δὲ μέλους ὑπομιμνήσκοντος καὶ ἐγείροντος τὸν ῥυθμόν, κοινωθέντ' ἀλλήλοις χορείαν καὶ παιδιὰν ἐτεκέτην.

κλ. Ἀληθέστατα.

CLIN. Quite rightly.

ATH. As to music, which was referred to when we said a moment ago that the one half of choristry had been described and disposed of,—let us say the same of it now; but as to the other half, are we to speak about it, or what are we to do?

CLIN. My good sir, you are conversing with Cretans and Lacedaemonians, and we have discussed the subject of music; what reply, then, to your question do you suppose that either of us will make, when the subject left still untouched is gymnastic?

ATH. You have given me a pretty clear answer, I should say, in putting this question; although it is a question, I understand it to be also (as I say) an answer—or rather, an actual injunction to give a full account of gymnastic.

CLIN. You have grasped my meaning excellently: please do so.

ATH. Do it I must; and indeed it is no very hard task to speak of things well known to you both. For you are far better acquainted with this art than with the other.

CLIN. That is about true.

ATH. The origin of the play[1] we are speaking of is to be found in the habitual tendency of every living creature to leap; and the human creature, by acquiring, as we said, a sense of rhythm, generated and brought forth dancing; and since the rhythm is suggested and awakened by the tune, the union of these two brought forth choristry and play.

CLIN. Very true.

---

[1] *i.e.* playful motion, or dancing, as contrasted with "music" (or "harmony") which springs from the tendency to *cry out*.

673 ΑΘ. Καὶ τὸ μέν, φαμέν, ἤδη διεληλύθαμεν
αὐτοῦ, τὸ δὲ πειρασόμεθα ἐφεξῆς διελθεῖν.

ΚΛ. Πάνυ μὲν οὖν.

ΑΘ. Ἐπὶ τοίνυν τῇ τῆς μέθης χρείᾳ τὸν κολο-
E φῶνα πρῶτον ἐπιθῶμεν, εἰ καὶ σφῷν ξυνδοκεῖ.

ΚΛ. Ποῖον δὴ καὶ τίνα λέγεις;

ΑΘ. Εἰ μέν τις πόλις ὡς οὔσης σπουδῆς τῷ
ἐπιτηδεύματι τῷ νῦν εἰρημένῳ χρήσεται μετὰ
νόμων καὶ τάξεως, ὡς τοῦ σωφρονεῖν ἕνεκα
μελέτῃ[1] χρωμένη, καὶ τῶν ἄλλων ἡδονῶν μὴ
ἀφέξεται ὡσαύτως καὶ κατὰ τὸν αὐτὸν λόγον,
τοῦ κρατεῖν αὐτῶν ἕνεκα μηχανωμένη, τοῦτον
μὲν τὸν τρόπον ἅπασι τούτοις χρηστέον· εἰ δ'
ὡς παιδιᾷ τε, καὶ ἐξέσται τῷ βουλομένῳ, καὶ
674 ὅταν βούληται, καὶ μεθ' ὧν ἂν βούληται, πίνειν
μετ' ἐπιτηδευμάτων ὡντινωνοῦν ἄλλων, οὐκ ἂν
τιθείμην ταύτην τὴν ψῆφον, ὡς δεῖ ποτὲ μέθῃ
χρῆσθαι ταύτην τὴν πόλιν ἢ τοῦτον τὸν ἄνδρα,
ἀλλ' ἔτι μᾶλλον τῆς Κρητῶν καὶ Λακεδαιμονίων
χρείας προσθείμην ἂν τῷ τῶν Καρχηδονίων νόμῳ,
μηδέποτε μηδένα ἐπὶ στρατοπέδου γεύεσθαι τούτου τοῦ πώματος, ἀλλ' ὑδροποσίαις ξυγγίγνεσθαι
τοῦτον τὸν χρόνον ἅπαντα, καὶ κατὰ πόλιν μήτε
δοῦλον μήτε δούλην γεύεσθαι μηδέποτε, μηδὲ
B ἄρχοντας τοῦτον τὸν ἐνιαυτὸν ὃν ἂν ἄρχωσι, μηδ'
αὖ κυβερνήτας μηδὲ δικαστὰς ἐνεργοὺς ὄντας
οἴνου γεύεσθαι τὸ παράπαν, μηδ' ὅστις βουλευ-
σόμενος εἰς βουλὴν ἀξίαν τινὰ λόγου συνέρχεται,
μηδέ γε μεθ' ἡμέραν μηδένα τὸ παράπαν, εἰ μὴ
σωμασκίας ἢ νόσων ἕνεκα, μηδ' αὖ νύκτωρ, ὅταν

---

[1] μελέτῃ Euseb., Schanz: μελέτης MSS.

ATH. Of choristry we have already discussed the one part, and we shall next endeavour to discuss the other part.

CLIN. By all means.

ATH. But, if you both agree, let us first put the finishing stroke to our discourse on the use of drink.

CLIN. What, or what kind of, finish do you mean?

ATH. If a State shall make use of the institution now mentioned in a lawful and orderly manner, regarding it in a serious light and practising it with a view to temperance, and if in like manner and with a like object, aiming at the mastery of them, it shall allow indulgence in all other pleasures,—then they must all be made use of in the manner described. But if, on the other hand, this institution is regarded in the light of play, and if anyone that likes is to be allowed to drink whenever he likes and with any companions he likes, and that in conjunction with all sorts of other institutions,—then I would refuse to vote for allowing such a State or such an individual ever to indulge in drink, and I would go even beyond the practice of the Cretans and Lacedaemonians[1]; and to the Carthaginian law, which ordains that no soldier on the march should ever taste of this potion, but confine himself for the whole of the time to water-drinking only, I would add this, that in the city also no bondsman or bondsmaid should ever taste of it; and that magistrates during their year of office, and pilots and judges while on duty, should taste no wine at all; nor should any councillor, while attending any important council; nor should anyone whatever taste of it at all, except for reasons of bodily training or health, in the day-time; nor

[1] Cp. Bk. i. 637A, B.

674 ἐπινοῇ τις παῖδας ποιεῖσθαι ἀνὴρ ἢ καὶ γυνή.
καὶ ἄλλα δὲ πάμπολλα ἄν τις λέγοι, ἐν οἷς τοῖς
νοῦν τε καὶ νόμον ἔχουσιν ὀρθὸν οὐ ποτέος οἶνος·
C ὥστε κατὰ τὸν λόγον τοῦτον οὐδ᾽ ἀμπελώνων[1]
ἂν πολλῶν δέοι οὐδ᾽ ἥτινι πόλει, τακτὰ δὲ τά
τ᾽ ἄλλα ἂν εἴη γεωργήματα καὶ πᾶσα ἡ δίαιτα,
καὶ δὴ τά γε περὶ οἶνον σχεδὸν ἁπάντων ἐμμετρό-
τατα καὶ ὀλίγιστα γίγνοιτ᾽ ἄν. οὗτος, ὦ ξένοι,
ἡμῖν, εἰ ξυνδοκεῖ, κολοφὼν ἐπὶ τῷ περὶ οἴνου
λόγῳ ῥηθέντι εἰρήσθω.

   ΚΛ. Καλῶς, καὶ ξυνδοκεῖ.

---

[1] ἀμπελώνων Euseb. : ἀμπέλων MSS.

should anyone do so by night—be he man or woman —when proposing to procreate children. Many other occasions, also, might be mentioned when wine should not be drunk by men who are swayed by right reason and law. Hence, according to this argument, there would be no need for any State to have a large number of vineyards; and while all the other agricultural products, and all the foodstuffs, would be controlled, the production of wine especially would be kept within the smallest and most modest dimensions. Let this, then, Strangers, if you agree, be the finishing stroke which we put to our discourse concerning wine.

CLIN. Very good; we quite agree.

676   ΑΘ.   Ταῦτα μὲν οὖν δὴ ταύτη· πολιτείας δ᾽
ἀρχὴν τίνα ποτὲ φῶμεν γεγονέναι ; μῶν οὐκ
ἐνθένδε τις ἂν αὐτὴν ῥᾷστά τε καὶ κάλλιστα
κατίδοι ;

ΚΛ.   Πόθεν ;

ΑΘ.   ῞Οθεν περ καὶ τὴν τῶν πόλεων ἐπίδοσιν
εἰς ἀρετὴν μεταβαινουσῶν [1] ἅμα καὶ κακίαν ἑκάστοτε θεατέον.

ΚΛ.   Λέγεις δὲ πόθεν ;

ΑΘ.   Οἶμαι μὲν ἀπὸ χρόνου μήκους τε καὶ
Β ἀπειρίας καὶ τῶν μεταβολῶν ἐν τῷ τοιούτῳ.

ΚΛ.   Πῶς λέγεις ;

ΑΘ.   Φέρε, ἀφ᾽ οὗ πόλεις τ᾽ εἰσὶ καὶ ἄνθρωποι
πολιτευόμενοι, δοκεῖς ἄν ποτε κατανοῆσαι χρόνου
πλῆθος ὅσον γέγονεν ;

ΚΛ.   Οὔκουν ῥᾴδιόν γε οὐδαμῶς.

ΑΘ.   Τὸ δέ γε, ὡς ἄπλετόν τι καὶ ἀμήχανον ἂν
εἴη.

ΚΛ.   Πάνυ μὲν οὖν τοῦτό γε.

ΑΘ.   Μῶν οὖν οὐ μυρίαι μὲν ἐπὶ μυρίαις ἡμῖν
γεγόνασι πόλεις ἐν τούτῳ τῷ χρόνῳ, κατὰ τὸν
αὐτὸν δὲ τοῦ πλήθους λόγον οὐκ ἐλάττους ἐφθαρ-
C μέναι ; πεπολιτευμέναι δ᾽ αὖ πάσας πολιτείας
πολλάκις ἑκασταχοῦ ; καὶ τοτὲ μὲν ἐξ ἐλαττόνων
μείζους, τοτὲ δὲ ἐκ μειζόνων ἐλάττους, καὶ χείρους
ἐκ βελτιόνων γεγόνασι καὶ βελτίους ἐκ χειρόνων ;

---

[1] μεταβαινουσῶν Boeckh : μεταβαίνουσαν MSS.

164

BOOK III

ATH. So much for that, then! Now, what are we to say about the origin of government? Would not the best and easiest way of discerning it be from this standpoint?

CLIN. What standpoint?

ATH. That from which one should always observe the progress of States as they move towards either goodness or badness.

CLIN. What point is that?

ATH. The observation, as I suppose, of an infinitely long period of time and of the variations therein occurring.

CLIN. Explain your meaning.

ATH. Tell me now: do you think you could ever ascertain the space of time that has passed since cities came into existence and men lived under civic rule?

CLIN. Certainly it would be no easy task.

ATH. But you can easily see that it is vast and immeasurable?

CLIN. That I most certainly can do.

ATH. During this time, have not thousands upon thousands of States come into existence, and, on a similar computation, just as many perished? And have they not in each case exhibited all kinds of constitutions over and over again? And have they not changed at one time from small to great, at another from great to small, and changed also from good to bad and from bad to good?

165

676 ΚΛ. Ἀναγκαῖον.

ΑΘ. Ταύτης δὴ πέρι λάβωμεν, εἰ δυναίμεθα, τῆς μεταβολῆς τὴν αἰτίαν· τάχα γὰρ ἂν ἴσως δείξειεν ἡμῖν τὴν πρώτην τῶν πολιτειῶν γένεσιν καὶ μετάβασιν.

ΚΛ. Εὖ λέγεις, καὶ προθυμεῖσθαι δεῖ σὲ μὲν ὃ διανοεῖ περὶ αὐτῶν ἀποφαινόμενον, ἡμᾶς δὲ ξυνεπομένους.

677 ΑΘ. Ἆρ' οὖν ὑμῖν οἱ παλαιοὶ λόγοι ἀλήθειαν ἔχειν τινὰ δοκοῦσιν ;

ΚΛ. Ποῖοι δή ;

ΑΘ. Τὸ πολλὰς ἀνθρώπων φθορὰς γεγονέναι κατακλυσμοῖς τε καὶ νόσοις καὶ ἄλλοις πολλοῖς, ἐν οἷς βραχύ τι τῶν ἀνθρώπων λείπεσθαι γένος.

ΚΛ. Πάνυ μὲν οὖν πιθανὸν τὸ τοιοῦτον πᾶν παντί.

ΑΘ. Φέρε δή, νοήσωμεν μίαν τῶν πολλῶν ταύτην τὴν τῷ κατακλυσμῷ ποτὲ γενομένην.

ΚΛ. Τὸ ποῖόν τι περὶ αὐτῆς διανοηθέντες ;

B ΑΘ. Ὡς οἱ τότε περιφυγόντες τὴν φθορὰν σχεδὸν ὄρειοί τινες ἂν εἶεν νομῆς, ἐν κορυφαῖς που σμικρὰ ζώπυρα τοῦ τῶν ἀνθρώπων διασεσωσμένα γένους.

ΚΛ. Δῆλον.

ΑΘ. Καὶ δὴ τοὺς τοιούτους γε ἀνάγκη που τῶν ἄλλων ἀπείρους εἶναι τεχνῶν καὶ τῶν ἐν τοῖς ἄστεσι πρὸς ἀλλήλους μηχανῶν εἴς τε πλεονεξίας καὶ φιλονεικίας, καὶ ὁπόσ' ἄλλα κακουργήματα πρὸς ἀλλήλους ἐπινοοῦσιν.

ΚΛ. Εἰκὸς γοῦν.

C ΑΘ. Θῶμεν δὴ τὰς ἐν τοῖς πεδίοις πόλεις καὶ

---

[1] Deucalion's Flood : cp. *Polit.* 270 C.

CLIN. Necessarily.

ATH. Of this process of change let us discover, if we can, the cause; for this, perhaps, would show us what is the primary origin of constitutions, as well as their transformation.

CLIN. You are right; and we must all exert ourselves,—you to expound your view about them, and we to keep pace with you.

ATH. Do you consider that there is any truth in the ancient tales?

CLIN. What tales?

ATH. That the world of men has often been destroyed by floods, plagues, and many other things, in such a way that only a small portion of the human race has survived.

CLIN. Everyone would regard such accounts as perfectly credible.

ATH. Come now, let us picture to ourselves one of the many catastrophes,—namely, that which occurred once upon a time through the Deluge.[1]

CLIN. And what are we to imagine about it?

ATH. That the men who then escaped destruction must have been mostly herdsmen of the hills, scanty embers of the human race preserved somewhere on the mountain-tops.

CLIN. Evidently.

ATH. Moreover, men of this kind must necessarily have been unskilled in the arts generally, and especially in such contrivances as men use against one another in cities for purposes of greed and rivalry and all the other villainies which they devise one against another.

CLIN. It is certainly probable.

ATH. Shall we assume that the cities situated in the

677 πρὸς θαλάττῃ κατοικούσας ἄρδην ἐν τῷ τότε
χρόνῳ διαφθείρεσθαι;

κλ. Θῶμεν.

αθ. Οὐκοῦν ὄργανά τε πάντα ἀπόλλυσθαι, καὶ
εἴ τι τέχνης ἦν ἐχόμενον σπουδαίως εὑρημένον ἢ
πολιτικῆς ἢ καὶ σοφίας τινὸς ἑτέρας, πάντα ἔρρειν
ταῦτα ἐν τῷ τότε χρόνῳ φήσομεν; πῶς [1] γὰρ ἄν,
ὦ ἄριστε, εἴ γε ἔμενε τάδε οὕτω τὸν πάντα χρόνον
ὡς νῦν διακεκόσμηται, καινὸν ἀνευρίσκετό ποτε
καὶ ὁτιοῦν;

D κλ. <Ἦ οὖν> τοῦτο,[2] ὅτι μὲν γὰρ μυριάκις
μύρια ἔτη διελάνθανεν ἄρα τοὺς τότε, χίλια δ᾽
ἀφ᾽ οὗ γέγονεν ἢ δὶς τοσαῦτα ἔτη τὰ μὲν Δαιδάλῳ
καταφανῆ [γέγονε],[3] τὰ δὲ Ὀρφεῖ, τὰ δὲ Παλα-
μήδει, τὰ δὲ περὶ μουσικὴν Μαρσύᾳ καὶ Ὀλύμπῳ,
περὶ λύραν δὲ Ἀμφίονι, τὰ δ᾽ ἄλλα ἄλλοις
πάμπολλα, ὡς ἔπος εἰπεῖν χθὲς καὶ πρώην γεγονότα;

αθ. Ἆρ᾽ οἶσθ᾽, ὦ Κλεινία, τὸν φίλον ὅτι
παρέλιπες, τὸν ἀτεχνῶς χθὲς γενόμενον;

κλ. Μῶν φράζεις Ἐπιμενίδην;

αθ. Ναὶ τοῦτον· πολὺ γὰρ ὑμῖν ὑπερεπήδησε
τῷ μηχανήματι τοὺς ξύμπαντας, ὦ φίλε, ὃ λόγῳ
μὲν Ἡσίοδος ἐμαντεύετο πάλαι, τῷ δ᾽ ἔργῳ ἐκεῖνος
ἀπετέλεσεν, ὡς ὑμεῖς φατέ.

E κλ. Φαμὲν γὰρ οὖν.

---

[1] With Immisch and Burnet, I assign πῶς . . . ὁτιοῦν to Ath.,
not to Clin. (as Zur., al.)

[2] <Ἦ οὖν> I add: Schanz reads ταῦτ᾽ οὔ τι, Hermann
τοῦτο οἴει: Zur. omits τοῦτο.

[3] [γέγονε] bracketed by Ast, Schanz.

---

[1] Cp. 642 D.

plains and near the sea were totally destroyed at the time?

CLIN. Let us assume it.

ATH. And shall we say that all implements were lost, and that everything in the way of important arts or inventions that they may have had,— whether concerned with politics or other sciences,— perished at that time? For, supposing that things had remained all that time ordered just as they are now, how, my good sir, could anything new have ever been invented?

CLIN. Do you mean that these things were unknown to the men of those days for thousands upon thousands of years, and that one or two thousand years ago some of them were revealed to Daedalus, some to Orpheus, some to Palamedes, musical arts to Marsyas and Olympus, lyric to Amphion, and, in short, a vast number of others to other persons—all dating, so to say, from yesterday or the day before?

ATH. Are you aware, Clinias, that you have left out your friend who was literally a man of yesterday?

CLIN. Is it Epimenides[1] you mean?

ATH. Yes, I mean him. For he far outstripped everybody you had, my friend, by that invention of his of which he was the actual producer, as you Cretans say, although Hesiod[2] had divined it and spoken of it long before.

CLIN. We do say so.

---

[2] *Op. D.* 40 f.

νήπιοι, οὐδὲ ἴσασιν ὅσῳ πλέον ἥμισυ παντός,
οὐδ' ὅσον ἐν μαλάχῃ τε καὶ ἀσφοδέλῳ μέγ' ὄνειαρ.

Hesiod's allusion to the "great virtue residing in mallow and asphodel" is supposed to have suggested to Epimenides his "invention" of a herbal concoction, or "elixir of life."

PLATO

677 ΑΘ. Οὐκοῦν οὕτω δὴ λέγωμεν ἔχειν τότε, ὅτε
ἐγένετο ἡ φθορά, τὰ περὶ τοὺς ἀνθρώπους πράγματα, μυρίαν μέν τινα φοβερὰν ἐρημίαν, γῆς δ᾽
ἀφθόνου πλῆθος πάμπολυ, ζώων δὲ τῶν ἄλλων
ἐρρόντων βουκόλι᾽ ἄττα, καὶ εἴ τί που αἰγῶν
περιλειφθὲν ἐτύγχανε γένος, σπάνια καὶ ταῦτα
678 νέμουσιν εἶναι ζῆν τό γε[1] κατ᾽ ἀρχάς.

ΚΛ. Τί μήν ;

ΑΘ. Πόλεως δὲ καὶ πολιτείας πέρι καὶ νομοθεσίας, ὧν νῦν ὁ λόγος ἡμῖν παρέστηκεν, ἆρ᾽ ὡς
ἔπος εἰπεῖν οἰόμεθα καὶ μνήμην εἶναι τὸ παράπαν ;

ΚΛ. Οὐδαμῶς.

ΑΘ. Οὐκοῦν ἐξ ἐκείνων τῶν διακειμένων οὕτω
τὰ νῦν γέγονεν ἡμῖν ξύμπαντα, πόλεις τε καὶ
πολιτεῖαι καὶ τέχναι καὶ νόμοι καὶ πολλὴ μὲν
πονηρία, πολλὴ δὲ καὶ ἀρετή ;

ΚΛ. Πῶς λέγεις ;

Β ΑΘ. Ἆρ᾽ οἰόμεθα, ὦ θαυμάσιε, τοὺς τότε ἀπείρους ὄντας πολλῶν μὲν καλῶν τῶν κατὰ τὰ ἄστη,
πολλῶν δὲ καὶ τῶν ἐναντίων, τελέους πρὸς ἀρετὴν
ἢ καὶ πρὸς κακίαν γεγονέναι ;

ΚΛ. Καλῶς εἶπες, καὶ μανθάνομεν ὃ λέγεις.

ΑΘ. Οὐκοῦν προϊόντος μὲν τοῦ χρόνου, πλη-
θύοντος δ᾽ ἡμῶν τοῦ γένους, εἰς πάντα τὰ νῦν καθε-
στηκότα προελήλυθε πάντα ;

ΚΛ. Ὀρθότατα.

ΑΘ. Οὐκ ἐξαίφνης γε, ὡς εἰκός, κατὰ σμικρὸν
δὲ ἐν παμπόλλῳ τινὶ χρόνῳ.

C ΚΛ. Καὶ μάλα πρέπει τοῦθ᾽ οὕτως.

ΑΘ. Ἐκ γὰρ τῶν ὑψηλῶν εἰς τὰ πεδία κατα-
βαίνειν, οἶμαι, πᾶσι φόβος ἔναυλος ἐγεγόνει.

[1] τό γε : τότε MSS. (τὸ England).

ATH. Shall we, then, state that, at the time when the destruction took place, human affairs were in this position: there was fearful and widespread desolation over a vast tract of land; most of the animals were destroyed, and the few herds of oxen and flocks of goats that happened to survive afforded at the first but scanty sustenance to their herdsmen?

CLIN. Yes.

ATH. And as to the matters with which our present discourse is concerned—States and state-craft and legislation,—do we think they could have retained any memory whatsoever, broadly speaking, of such matters?

CLIN. By no means.

ATH. So from those men, in that situation, there has sprung the whole of our present order—States and constitutions, arts and laws, with a great amount both of evil and of good?

CLIN. How do you mean?

ATH. Do we imagine, my good Sir, that the men of that age, who were unversed in the ways of city life—many of them noble, many ignoble,—were perfect either in virtue or in vice?

CLIN. Well said! We grasp your meaning.

ATH. As time went on and our race multiplied, all things advanced—did they not?—to the condition which now exists.

CLIN. Very true.

ATH. But, in all probability, they advanced, not all at once, but by small degrees, during an immense space of time.

CLIN. Yes, that is most likely.

ATH. For they all, I fancy, felt as it were still ringing in their ears a dread of going down from the highlands to the plains.

678　ΚΛ. Πῶς δ' οὔ;

ΑΘ. Ἀρ' οὐκ ἄσμενοι μὲν ἑαυτοὺς ἑώρων δι' ὀλιγότητα ἐν τοῖς πέριξ [1] ἐκεῖνον τὸν χρόνον, <τὰ> [2] πορεῖα δέ, ὥστ' ἐπ' ἀλλήλους τότε πορεύεσθαι κατὰ γῆν ἢ κατὰ θάλατταν, σὺν ταῖς τέχναις ὡς ἔπος εἰπεῖν πάντα σχεδὸν ἀπολώλει; ξυμμίσγειν οὖν ἀλλήλοις οὐκ ἦν, οἶμαι, σφόδρα
D δυνατόν· σίδηρος γὰρ καὶ χαλκὸς καὶ πάντα τὰ μεταλλεῖα συγκεχυμένα ἠφάνιστο, ὥστε ἀπορία πᾶσα ἦν τοῦ ἀνακαθαίρεσθαι τὰ τοιαῦτα, δρυοτομίας τε εἶχον σπάνιν. εἰ γάρ πού τι καὶ περιγεγονὸς ἦν ὄργανον ἐν ὄρεσι, ταῦτα μὲν ταχὺ κατατριβέντα ἠφάνιστο, ἄλλα δ' οὐκ ἔμελλε γενήσεσθαι πρὶν πάλιν ἡ τῶν μεταλλέων ἀφίκοιτο εἰς ἀνθρώπους τέχνη.

ΚΛ. Πῶς γὰρ ἄν;

ΑΘ. Γενεαῖς δὴ πόσαις ὕστερον οἰόμεθα τοῦθ' οὕτω γεγονέναι;

E　ΚΛ. Δῆλον ὅτι παμπόλλαις τισίν.

ΑΘ. Οὐκοῦν καὶ τέχναι ὅσαιπερ σιδήρου δέονται καὶ χαλκοῦ καὶ τῶν τοιούτων ἁπάντων, τὸν αὐτὸν χρόνον καὶ ἔτι πλείονα ἠφανισμέναι ἂν εἶεν ἐν τῷ τότε;

ΚΛ. Τί μήν;

ΑΘ. Καὶ τοίνυν στάσις ἅμα καὶ πόλεμος ἀπολώλει κατὰ τὸν τότε χρόνον πολλαχῇ.

ΚΛ. Πῶς;

ΑΘ. Πρῶτον μὲν ἠγάπων καὶ ἐφιλοφρονοῦντο ἀλλήλους δι' ἐρημίαν, ἔπειτα οὐ περιμάχητος ἦν
679 αὐτοῖς ἡ τροφή. νομῆς γὰρ οὐκ ἦν σπάνις, εἰ μή τισι κατ' ἀρχὰς ἴσως, ᾗ δὴ τὸ πλεῖστον διέζων ἐν

---

[1] πέριξ : περὶ MSS., edd.　　[2] <τὰ> added by Schanz.

CLIN. Of course.

ATH. And because there were so few of them round about in those days, were they not delighted to see one another, but for the fact that means of transport, whereby they might visit one another by sea or land, had practically all perished along with the arts? Hence intercourse, I imagine, was not very easy. For iron and bronze and all the metals in the mines had been flooded and had disappeared; so that it was extremely difficult to extract fresh metal; and there was a dearth, in consequence, of felled timber. For even if there happened to be some few tools still left somewhere on the mountains, these were soon worn out, and they could not be replaced by others until men had rediscovered the art of metal-working.

CLIN. They could not.

ATH. Now, how many generations, do we suppose, had passed before this took place?

CLIN. A great many, evidently.

ATH. And during all this period, or even longer, all the arts that require iron and bronze and all such metals must have remained in abeyance?

CLIN. Of course.

ATH. Moreover, civil strife and war also disappeared during that time, and that for many reasons.

CLIN. How so?

ATH. In the first place, owing to their desolate state, they were kindly disposed and friendly towards one another; and secondly, they had no need to quarrel about food. For they had no lack of flocks and herds (except perhaps some of them at the outset), and in that age these were what men mostly

679 τῷ τότε χρόνῳ· γάλακτος γὰρ καὶ κρεῶν οὐδαμῶς
ἐνδεεῖς ἦσαν, ἔτι δὲ θηρεύοντες οὐ φαύλην οὐδ᾽
ὀλίγην τροφὴν παρείχοντο. καὶ μὴν ἀμπεχόνης
γε καὶ στρωμνῆς καὶ οἰκήσεων καὶ σκευῶν ἐμπύ-
ρων τε καὶ ἀπύρων εὐπόρουν· αἱ πλαστικαὶ γὰρ
καὶ ὅσαι πλεκτικαὶ τῶν τεχνῶν οὐδὲ ἓν προσδέον-
B ται σιδήρου· ταῦτα δὲ πάντα τούτω τὼ τέχνα
θεὸς ἔδωκε πορίζειν τοῖς ἀνθρώποις, ἵν᾽ ὁπότε εἰς
τὴν τοιαύτην ἀπορίαν ἔλθοιεν, ἔχοι βλάστην καὶ
ἐπίδοσιν τὸ τῶν ἀνθρώπων γένος. πένητες μὲν
δὴ διὰ τὸ τοιοῦτον σφόδρα οὐκ ἦσαν, οὐδ᾽ ὑπὸ
πενίας ἀναγκαζόμενοι διάφοροι ἑαυτοῖς ἐγίγνοντο·
πλούσιοι δ᾽ οὐκ ἄν ποτ᾽ ἐγένοντο ἄχρυσοί τε καὶ
ἀνάργυροι ὄντες [ὃ τότε ἐν ἐκείνοις παρῆν].¹ ᾗ δ᾽
ἄν ποτε ξυνοικίᾳ μήτε πλοῦτος ξυνοικῇ μήτε
πενία, σχεδὸν ἐν ταύτῃ γενναιότατα ἤθη γίγνοιτ᾽
C ἄν· οὔτε γὰρ ὕβρις οὔτ᾽ ἀδικία, ζῆλοί τε αὖ καὶ
φθόνοι οὐκ ἐγγίγνονται. ἀγαθοὶ μὲν δὴ διὰ
ταῦτά τε ἦσαν καὶ διὰ τὴν λεγομένην εὐήθειαν·
ἃ γὰρ ἤκουον καλὰ καὶ αἰσχρά, εὐήθεις ὄντες
ἡγοῦντο ἀληθέστατα λέγεσθαι καὶ ἐπείθοντο.
ψεῦδος γὰρ ὑπονοεῖν οὐδεὶς ἠπίστατο διὰ σοφίαν,
ὥσπερ τὰ νῦν, ἀλλὰ περὶ θεῶν τε καὶ ἀνθρώπων
τὰ λεγόμενα ἀληθῆ νομίζοντες ἔζων κατὰ ταῦτα·
διόπερ ἦσαν τοιοῦτοι παντάπασιν οἵους αὐτοὺς
ἡμεῖς ἄρτι διεληλύθαμεν.

D ΚΛ. Ἐμοὶ γοῦν δὴ καὶ τῷδε οὕτω ταῦτα
ξυνδοκεῖ.

ΑΘ. Οὐκοῦν εἴπωμεν ὅτι γενεαὶ διαβιοῦσαι
πολλαὶ τοῦτον τὸν τρόπον τῶν πρὸ κατακλυσμοῦ
γεγονότων καὶ τῶν νῦν ἀτεχνότεροι μὲν καὶ ἀμα-

¹ [ὃ . . . παρῆν] omitted by Ficinus.

lived on: thus they were well supplied with milk and meat, and they procured further supplies of food, both excellent and plentiful, by hunting. They were also well furnished with clothing and coverlets and houses, and with vessels for cooking and other kinds; for no iron is required for the arts of moulding and weaving, which two arts God gave to men to furnish them with all these necessaries, in order that the human race might have means of sprouting and increase whenever it should fall into such a state of distress. Consequently, they were not excessively poor, nor were they constrained by stress of poverty to quarrel one with another; and, on the other hand, since they were without gold and silver, they could never have become rich. Now a community which has no communion with either poverty or wealth is generally the one in which the noblest characters will be formed; for in it there is no place for the growth of insolence and injustice, of rivalries and jealousies. So these men were good, both for these reasons and because of their simple-minded-ness, as it is called; for, being simple-minded, when they heard things called bad or good, they took what was said for gospel-truth and believed it. For none of them had the shrewdness of the modern man to suspect a falsehood; but they accepted as true the statements made about gods and men, and ordered their lives by them. Thus they were entirely of the character we have just described.

CLIN. Certainly Megillus and I quite agree with what you say.

ATH. And shall we not say that people living in this fashion for many generations were bound to be unskilled, as compared with either the antediluvians

PLATO

679 θέστεροι πρός τε τὰς ἄλλας μέλλουσιν εἶναι
τέχνας καὶ πρὸς τὰς πολεμικάς, ὅσαι τε πεζαὶ
καὶ ὅσαι κατὰ θάλατταν γίγνονται τὰ νῦν, καὶ
ὅσαι δὴ κατὰ πόλιν, ὄνομά που[1] δίκαι καὶ στάσεις
λεγόμεναι, λόγοις ἔργοις τε μεμηχανημέναι πάσας
μηχανὰς εἰς τὸ κακουργεῖν τε ἀλλήλους καὶ
Ε ἀδικεῖν, εὐηθέστεροι δὲ καὶ ἀνδρειότεροι καὶ ἅμα
σωφρονέστεροι καὶ ξύμπαντα δικαιότεροι; τὸ δὲ
τούτων αἴτιον ἤδη διεληλύθαμεν.

ΚΛ. Ὀρθῶς λέγεις.

ΑΘ. Λελέχθω δὴ ταῦτα ἡμῖν καὶ τὰ τούτοις
ξυνεπόμενα ἔτι πάντα εἰρήσθω τοῦδ᾽ ἕνεκα, ἵνα
680 νοήσωμεν τοῖς τότε νόμων τίς ποτ᾽ ἦν χρεία καὶ
τίς ἦν νομοθέτης αὐτοῖς.

ΚΛ. Καὶ καλῶς γε εἴρηκας.

ΑΘ. Ἆρ᾽ οὖν ἐκεῖνοι μὲν οὔτ᾽ ἐδέοντο νομοθετῶν
οὔτε πω ἐφίλει κατὰ τούτους τοὺς χρόνους γίγνεσθαι τὸ τοιοῦτον; οὐδὲ γὰρ γράμματά ἐστί πω
τοῖς ἐν τούτῳ τῷ μέρει τῆς περιόδου γεγονόσιν,
ἀλλ᾽ ἔθεσι καὶ τοῖς λεγομένοις πατρίοις νόμοις
ἑπόμενοι ζῶσιν.

ΚΛ. Εἰκὸς γοῦν.

ΑΘ. Πολιτείας δέ γε ἤδη καὶ τρόπος ἐστί τις
οὗτος.

ΚΛ. Τίς;

Β ΑΘ. Δοκοῦσί μοι πάντες τὴν ἐν τούτῳ τῷ
χρόνῳ πολιτείαν δυναστείαν καλεῖν, ἣ καὶ νῦν
ἔτι πολλαχοῦ καὶ ἐν Ἕλλησι καὶ κατὰ βαρβάρους ἐστί· λέγει δ᾽ αὐτήν που καὶ Ὅμηρος

---

[1] ὄνομά που: μόνον αὐτοῦ MSS. (ὀνόματι Badham)

---

[1] Cp. Arist. *Pol.* 1252ᵇ 17 ff. This " headship," which is

or the men of to-day, and ignorant of arts in general
and especially of the arts of war as now practised by
land and sea, including those warlike arts which,
disguised under the names of law-suits and factions,
are peculiar to cities, contrived as they are with
every device of word and deed to inflict mutual hurt
and injury; and that they were also more simple
and brave and temperate, and in all ways more
righteous? And the cause of this state of things we
have already explained.

CLIN. Quite true.

ATH. We must bear in mind that the whole
purpose of what we have said and of what we are
going to say next is this,—that we may understand
what possible need of laws the men of that time
had, and who their lawgiver was.

CLIN. Excellent.

ATH. Shall we suppose that those men had no
need of lawgivers, and that in those days it was not
as yet usual to have such a thing? For those born
in that age of the world's history did not as yet
possess the art of writing, but lived by following
custom and what is called " patriarchal" law.

CLIN. That is certainly probable.

ATH. But this already amounts to a kind of
government.

CLIN. What kind?

ATH. Everybody, I believe, gives the name of
"headship" to the government which then existed,
—and it still continues to exist to-day among both
Greeks and barbarians in many quarters.[1] And, of
course, Homer [2] mentions its existence in connexion

the hereditary personal authority of the father of a family
or chief of a clan, we should term "patriarchy."

[2] *Odyss.* ix. 112 ff.

PLATO

680 γεγονέναι περὶ τὴν τῶν Κυκλώπων οἴκησιν,
εἰπὼν

τοῖσιν δ᾽ οὔτ᾽ ἀγοραὶ βουληφόροι οὔτε
θέμιστες,
ἀλλ᾽ οἵ γ᾽ ὑψηλῶν ὀρέων ναίουσι κάρηνα
ἐν σπέσσι γλαφυροῖσι, θεμιστεύει δὲ ἕκαστος

Ο   παίδων ἠδ᾽ ἀλόχων, οὐδ᾽ ἀλλήλων ἀλέ-
γουσιν.

ΚΛ. Ἔοικέ γε ὁ ποιητὴς ὑμῖν οὗτος γεγονέναι
χαρίεις. καὶ γὰρ δὴ καὶ ἄλλα αὐτοῦ διεληλύθαμεν μάλ᾽ ἀστεῖα, οὐ μὴν πολλά γε· οὐ γὰρ
σφόδρα χρώμεθα οἱ Κρῆτες τοῖς ξενικοῖς ποιήμασιν.

ΜΕ. Ἡμεῖς δ᾽ αὖ χρώμεθα μέν, καὶ ἔοικέ γε
κρατεῖν τῶν τοιούτων ποιητῶν· οὐ μέντοι Λακω-
νικόν γε, ἀλλά τινα μᾶλλον Ἰωνικὸν βίον διεξέρ-
D χεται ἑκάστοτε. νῦν μὴν εὖ τῷ σῷ λόγῳ ἔοικε
μαρτυρεῖν, τὸ ἀρχαῖον αὐτῶν ἐπὶ τὴν ἀγριότητα
διὰ μυθολογίας ἐπανενεγκών.

ΑΘ. Ναί· ξυμμαρτυρεῖ γὰρ καὶ λάβωμέν γε
αὐτὸν μηνυτὴν ὅτι τοιαῦται πολιτεῖαι γίγνονταί
ποτε.

ΚΛ. Καλῶς·

ΑΘ. Μῶν οὖν οὐκ ἐκ τούτων τῶν κατὰ μίαν
οἴκησιν καὶ κατὰ γένος διεσπαρμένων ὑπὸ ἀπορίας
τῆς ἐν ταῖς φθοραῖς, ἐν οἷς τὸ πρεσβύτατον ἄρχει
διὰ τὸ τὴν ἀρχὴν αὐτοῖς ἐκ πατρὸς καὶ μητρὸς
E γεγονέναι, οἷς ἑπόμενοι καθάπερ ὄρνιθες ἀγέλην
μίαν ποιήσουσι, πατρονομούμενοι καὶ βασιλείαν
πασῶν δικαιοτάτην βασιλευόμενοι ;

with the household system of the Cyclopes, where he says—

> " No halls of council and no laws are theirs,
>   But within hollow caves on mountain heights
>   Aloft they dwell, each making his own law
>   For wife and child ; of others reck they naught."

CLIN. This poet of yours seems to have been a man of genius. We have also read other verses of his, and they were extremely fine ; though in truth we have not read much of him, since we Cretans do not indulge much in foreign poetry.

MEG. But we Spartans do, and we regard Homer as the best of them ; all the same, the mode of life he describes is always Ionian rather than Laconian. And now he appears to be confirming your statement admirably, when in his legendary account he ascribes the primitive habits of the Cyclopes to their savagery.

ATH. Yes, his testimony supports us ; so let us take him as evidence that polities of this sort do sometimes come into existence.

CLIN. Quite right.

ATH. Did they not originate with those people who lived scattered in separate clans or in single households, owing to the distress which followed after the catastrophes ; for amongst these the eldest holds rule, owing to the fact that the rule proceeds from the parents, by following whom they form a single flock, like a covey of birds, and live under a patriarchal government and a kingship which is of all kingships the most just?

PLATO

680 ΚΛ. Πάνυ μὲν οὖν.

ΑΘ. Μετὰ δὲ ταῦτά γε εἰς τὸ κοινὸν μείζους <ποιμνὰς>[1] ποιοῦντες [πόλεις] πλείους συνέρχον-ται, καὶ ἐπὶ γεωργίας τὰς ἐν ταῖς ὑπωρείαις τρέ-
681 πονται πρώτας, περιβόλους τε αἱμασιώδεις τινὰς τειχῶν <τ'>[2] ἐρύματα τῶν θηρίων ἕνεκα ποιοῦν-ται, μίαν οἰκίαν αὖ κοινὴν καὶ μεγάλην ἀποτε-λοῦντες.

ΚΛ. Τὸ γοῦν εἰκὸς ταῦθ' οὕτω γίγνεσθαι.

ΑΘ. Τί δέ; τόδε ἆρα οὐκ εἰκός;

ΚΛ. Τὸ ποῖον;

ΑΘ. Τῶν οἰκήσεων τούτων μειζόνων αὐξανο-μένων ἐκ τῶν ἐλαττόνων καὶ πρώτων, ἑκάστην τῶν σμικρῶν παρεῖναι κατὰ γένος ἔχουσαν τόν
Β τε πρεσβύτατον ἄρχοντα καὶ αὐτῆς ἔθη ἄττα ἴδια διὰ τὸ χωρὶς ἀλλήλων οἰκεῖν, ἕτερα ἀφ' ἑτέρων ὄντων τῶν γεννητόρων τε καὶ θρεψάντων ἃ εἰθίσθησαν περὶ θεούς τε καὶ ἑαυτοὺς κοσμιω-τέρων μὲν κοσμιώτερα καὶ ἀνδρικῶν ἀνδρικώτερα· καὶ κατὰ τρόπον οὕτως ἑκάστους τὰς αὑτῶν ἂν αἱρέσεις[3] εἰς τοὺς παῖδας ἀποτυπουμένους καὶ παίδων παῖδας, ὃ λέγομεν, ἥκειν ἔχοντας ἰδίους νόμους εἰς τὴν μείζονα ξυνοικίαν.

ΚΛ. Πῶς γὰρ οὔ;

C ΑΘ. Καὶ μὴν τούς γε αὑτῶν νόμους ἀρέσκειν ἑκάστοις ἀναγκαῖόν που, τοὺς δὲ τῶν ἄλλων ὑστέρους.

ΚΛ. Οὕτως.

ΑΘ. Ἀρχῇ δὴ νομοθεσίας οἷον ἐμβάντες ἐλά-θομεν, ὡς ἔοικεν.

[1] <ποιμνὰς> I add, and bracket [πόλεις].
[2] <τ'> added by W.-Möllendorff.

180

CLIN. Most certainly.

ATH. Next, they congregate together in greater numbers, and form larger droves; and first they turn to farming on the hill-sides, and make ring-fences of rubble and walls to ward off wild beasts, till finally they have constructed a single large common dwelling.

CLIN. It is certainly probable that such was the course of events.

ATH. Well, is not this also probable?

CLIN. What?

ATH. That, while these larger settlements were growing out of the original small ones, each of the small settlements continued to retain, clan by clan, both the rule of the eldest and also some customs derived from its isolated condition and peculiar to itself. As those who begot and reared them were different, so these customs of theirs, relating to the gods and to themselves, differed, being more orderly where their forefathers had been orderly, and more brave where they had been brave; and as thus the fathers of each clan in due course stamped upon their children and children's children their own cast of mind, these people came (as we say) into the larger community furnished each with their own peculiar laws.

CLIN. Of course.

ATH. And no doubt each clan was well pleased with its own laws, and less well with those of its neighbours.

CLIN. True.

ATH. Unwittingly, as it seems, we have now set foot, as it were, on the starting-point of legislation.

---

[3] ἂν αἱρέσεις Schneider, Hermann : ἀναιρέσεις MSS.

681 ΚΛ. Πάνυ μὲν οὖν.

ΑΘ. Τὸ γοῦν μετὰ ταῦτα ἀναγκαῖον αἱρεῖσθαι τοὺς συνελθόντας τούτους κοινούς τινας ἑαυτῶν, οἳ δὴ τὰ πάντων ἰδόντες νόμιμα, τά σφισιν ἀρέσκοντα αὐτῶν μάλιστα εἰς τὸ κοινὸν τοῖς ἡγεμόσι καὶ ἀγαγοῦσι τοὺς δήμους οἷον βασιλεῦσι φανερὰ
D δείξαντες ἑλέσθαι τε δόντες, αὐτοὶ μὲν νομοθέται κληθήσονται, τοὺς δὲ ἄρχοντας καταστήσαντες, ἀριστοκρατίαν τινὰ ἐκ τῶν δυναστειῶν ποιήσαντες ἢ καί τινα βασιλείαν, ἐν ταύτῃ τῇ μεταβολῇ τῆς πολιτείας οἰκήσουσιν.

ΚΛ. Ἐφεξῆς γοῦν ἂν οὕτω τε καὶ ταύτῃ γίγνοιτο.

ΑΘ. Τρίτον τοίνυν εἴπωμεν ἔτι πολιτείας σχῆμα γιγνόμενον, ἐν ᾧ δὴ πάντα εἴδη καὶ παθήματα πολιτειῶν καὶ ἅμα πόλεων ξυμπίπτει γίγνεσθαι.
E ΚΛ. Τὸ ποῖον δὴ τοῦτο;

ΑΘ. Ὁ μετὰ τὸ δεύτερον καὶ Ὅμηρος ἐπεσημήνατο, λέγων τὸ τρίτον οὕτω γεγονέναι· κτίσσε δὲ Δαρδανίην γάρ πού φησιν,

ἐπεὶ οὔπω Ἴλιος ἱρὴ
ἐν πεδίῳ πεπόλιστο, πόλις μερόπων ἀνθρώπων,
ἀλλ᾽ ἔθ᾽ ὑπωρείας ᾤκουν πολυπιδάκου Ἴδης.

682 λέγει γὰρ δὴ ταῦτα τὰ ἔπη καὶ ἐκεῖνα ἃ περὶ τῶν Κυκλώπων εἴρηκε κατὰ θεόν πως εἰρημένα καὶ κατὰ φύσιν· θεῖον γὰρ οὖν δὴ καὶ τὸ ποιητικὸν [ἐνθεαστικὸν][1] ὂν γένος ὑμνῳδοῦν πολλῶν τῶν

---

[1] [ἐνθεαστικὸν] bracketed by Boeckh, Schanz.

CLIN. We have indeed.

ATH. The next step necessary is that these people should come together and choose out some members of each clan who, after a survey of the legal usages of all the clans, shall notify publicly to the tribal leaders and chiefs (who may be termed their " kings ") which of those usages please them best, and shall recommend their adoption. These men will themselves be named "legislators," and when they have established the chiefs as " magistrates," and have framed an aristocracy, or possibly even a monarchy, from the existing plurality of " headships," they will live under the constitution thus transformed.

CLIN. The next steps would certainly be such as you describe.

ATH. Let us go on to describe the rise of a third form of constitution, in which are blended all kinds and varieties of constitutions, and of States as well.[1]

CLIN. What form is that?

ATH. The same that Homer himself mentioned next to the second, when he said that the third form arose in this way. His verses [2] run thus—

" Dardania he founded when as yet
    The holy keep of Ilium was not built
    Upon the plain, a town for mortal folk,
    But still they dwelt upon the highland slopes
    Of many-fountain'd Ida."

Indeed, these verses of his, as well as those he utters concerning the Cyclopes, are in a kind of unison with the voices of both God and Nature. For being divinely inspired in its chanting, the poetic tribe,

[1] For this "mixed" polity of the "city of the plain," cp. the description of democracy in *Rep.* 557 D ff.
[2] *Il.* xx. 216 ff.

682 κατ᾽ ἀλήθειαν γιγνομένων ξύν τισι Χάρισι καὶ Μούσαις ἐφάπτεται ἑκάστοτε.

ΚΛ. Καὶ μάλα.

ΑΘ. Εἰς δὴ τὸ πρόσθεν προέλθωμεν ἔτι τοῦ νῦν ἐπελθόντος ἡμῖν μύθου. τάχα γὰρ ἂν σημήνειέ τι τῆς ἡμετέρας πέρι βουλήσεως. οὐκοῦν χρή;

B   ΚΛ. Πάνυ μὲν οὖν.

ΑΘ. Κατῳκίσθη δή, φαμέν, ἐκ τῶν ὑψηλῶν εἰς μέγα τε καὶ καλὸν πεδίον Ἴλιον, ἐπὶ λόφον τινὰ οὐχ ὑψηλὸν καὶ ἔχοντα ποταμοὺς πολλοὺς ἄνωθεν ἐκ τῆς Ἴδης ὡρμημένους.

ΚΛ. Φασὶ γοῦν.

ΑΘ. Ἆρ᾽ οὖν οὐκ ἐν πολλοῖς τισὶ χρόνοις τοῖς μετὰ τὸν κατακλυσμὸν τοῦτο οἰόμεθα γεγονέναι;

ΚΛ. Πῶς δ᾽ οὐκ ἐν πολλοῖς;

ΑΘ. Δεινὴ γοῦν ἔοικεν αὐτοῖς λήθη τότε παρ-
C εἶναι τῆς νῦν λεγομένης φθορᾶς, ὅθ᾽ οὕτως ὑπὸ ποταμοὺς πολλοὺς καὶ ἐκ τῶν ὑψηλῶν ῥέοντας πόλιν ὑπέθεσαν, πιστεύσαντες οὐ σφόδρα ὑψηλοῖς τισὶ λόφοις.

ΚΛ. Δῆλον οὖν ὡς παντάπασί τινα μακρὸν ἀπεῖχον χρόνον τοῦ τοιούτου πάθους.

ΑΘ. Καὶ ἄλλαι γε, οἶμαι, πόλεις τότε κατῴκουν ἤδη πολλαὶ πληθυόντων τῶν ἀνθρώπων.

ΚΛ. Τί μήν;

ΑΘ. Αἵ γέ που καὶ ἐπεστρατεύσαντο αὐτῇ, καὶ κατὰ θάλατταν δὲ ἴσως, ἀφόβως ἤδη πάντων χρωμένων τῇ θαλάττῃ.

D   ΚΛ. Φαίνεται.

ΑΘ. Δέκα δ᾽ ἔτη που μείναντες Ἀχαιοὶ τὴν Τροίαν ἀνάστατον ἐποίησαν.

ΚΛ. Καὶ μάλα.

with the aid of Graces and Muses, often grasps the truth of history.

CLIN. It certainly does.

ATH. Now let us advance still further in the tale that now engages us; for possibly it may furnish some hint regarding the matter we have in view. Ought we not to do so?

CLIN. Most certainly.

ATH. Ilium was founded, we say, after moving from the highlands down to a large and noble plain, on a hill of no great height which had many rivers flowing down from Ida above.

CLIN. So they say.

ATH. And do we not suppose that this took place many ages after the Deluge?

CLIN. Many ages after, no doubt.

ATH. At any rate they seem to have been strangely forgetful of the catastrophe now mentioned, since they placed their city, as described, under a number of rivers descending from the mount, and relied for their safety upon hillocks of no great height.

CLIN. So it is evident that they were removed by quite a long interval from that calamity.

ATH. By this time, too, as mankind multiplied, many other cities had been founded.

CLIN. Of course.

ATH. And these cities also made attacks on Ilium, probably by sea too, as well as by land, since by this time all made use of the sea fearlessly.

CLIN. So it appears.

ATH. And after a stay of ten years the Achaeans sacked Troy.

CLIN. Very true.

682   ΑΘ. Οὐκοῦν ἐν τούτῳ τῷ χρόνῳ, ὄντι δεκέτει,
ὃν τὸ Ἴλιον ἐπολιορκεῖτο, τὰ τῶν πολιορκούντων
ἑκάστων οἴκοι κακὰ πολλὰ ξυνέβαινε γιγνόμενα
περὶ τὰς στάσεις τῶν νέων, οἳ καὶ ἀφικομένους
τοὺς στρατιώτας εἰς τὰς αὑτῶν πόλεις τε καὶ
Ε οἰκίας οὐ καλῶς οὐδ' ἐν δίκῃ ὑπεδέξαντο, ἀλλ'
ὥστε θανάτους τε καὶ σφαγὰς καὶ φυγὰς γενέσθαι
παμπόλλας· οἳ πάλιν ἐκπεσόντες κατῆλθον με-
ταβαλόντες ὄνομα, Δωριῆς ἀντ' Ἀχαιῶν κλη-
θέντες διὰ τὸ τὸν συλλέξαντα εἶναι τὰς τότε φυγὰς
Δωριᾶ. καὶ δὴ ταῦτά γε ἤδη πάνθ' ὑμεῖς, ὦ
Λακεδαιμόνιοι, τἀντεῦθεν μυθολογεῖτέ τε καὶ
διαπεραίνετε.

ΜΕ. Τί μήν;

ΑΘ. Ὅθεν δὴ κατ' ἀρχὰς ἐξετραπόμεθα περὶ
νόμων διαλεγόμενοι, περιπεσόντες μουσικῇ τε καὶ
ταῖς μέθαις, νῦν ἐπὶ τὰ αὐτὰ πάλιν ἀφίγμεθα
ὥσπερ κατὰ θεόν, καὶ ὁ λόγος ἡμῖν οἷον λαβὴν
ἀποδίδωσιν· ἥκει γὰρ ἐπὶ τὴν εἰς Λακεδαίμονα
683 κατοίκισιν αὐτήν, ἣν ὑμεῖς ὀρθῶς ἔφατε κατῳκίσθαι[1] καὶ Κρήτην ὡς ἀδελφοῖς νόμοις. νῦν οὖν δὴ
τοσόνδε πλεονεκτοῦμεν τῇ πλάνῃ τοῦ λόγου, διὰ
πολιτειῶν τινων καὶ κατοικισμῶν διεξελθόντες·
ἐθεασάμεθα πρώτην τε καὶ δευτέραν καὶ τρίτην
πόλιν, ἀλλήλων, ὡς οἰόμεθα, ταῖς κατοικίσεσιν

---

[1] κατῳκίσθαι Ast : κατοικεῖσθαι MSS.

---

[1] We do not hear of him elsewhere; and the account here
is so vague that it is hard to say what events (or traditions)
are alluded to. The usual story is that Dorian invaders
drove out the Achaeans from S. Greece (about 900 B.C.).
[2] Cp. 638 D.

ATH. Now during this period of ten years, while
the siege lasted, the affairs of each of the besiegers
at home suffered much owing to the seditious conduct of the young men. For when the soldiers
returned to their own cities and homes, these young
people did not receive them fittingly and justly, but
in such a way that there ensued a vast number of
cases of death, slaughter, and exile. So they, being
again driven out, migrated by sea; and because
Dorieus [1] was the man who then banded together the
exiles, they got the new name of " Dorians," instead
of " Achaeans." But as to all the events that follow
this, you Lacedaemonians relate them all fully in
your traditions.

MEG. Quite true.

ATH. And now—as it were by divine direction—
we have returned once more to the very point in
our discourse on laws where we made our digression,[2]
when we plunged into the subject of music and
drinking-parties; and we can, so to speak, get a
fresh grip upon the argument, now that it has
reached this point,—the settlement of Lacedaemon,
about which you said truly that it and Crete were
settled under kindred laws. From the wandering
course of our argument, and our excursion through
various polities and settlements, we have now gained
this much : we have discerned a first, a second and
a third State,[3] all, as we suppose, succeeding one
another in the settlements which took place during

---

[3] *i.e.* (1) the family or clan, under patriarchal "headship"; (2) the combination of clans under an aristocracy (or
monarchy); (3) the "mixed" State (or "city of the plain,"
like Troy); and (4) the confederacy, consisting, in the
example, of three States leagued together.

683 ἐχομένας ἐν χρόνου τινὸς μήκεσιν ἀπλέτοις. νῦν
δὲ δὴ τετάρτη τις ἡμῖν αὕτη πόλις, εἰ δὲ βούλεσθε,
ἔθνος ἥκει κατοικιζόμενόν τέ ποτε καὶ νῦν κατῳκισ-
B μένον. ἐξ ὧν ἀπάντων εἴ τι ξυνεῖναι δυνάμεθα
τί τε καλῶς ἢ μὴ κατῳκίσθη, καὶ ποῖοι νόμοι
σῴζουσιν αὐτῶν τὰ σῳζόμενα καὶ ποῖοι φθείρουσι
τὰ φθειρόμενα, καὶ ἀντὶ ποίων ποῖα μετατεθέντα
εὐδαίμονα πόλιν ἀπεργάζοιτ᾽ ἄν, ὦ Μέγιλλέ τε
καὶ Κλεινία, ταῦτα δὴ πάλιν οἷον ἐξ ἀρχῆς ἡμῖν
λεκτέον, εἰ μή τι τοῖς εἰρημένοις ἐγκαλοῦμεν λόγοις.

ΜΕ. Εἰ γοῦν, ὦ ξένε, τις ἡμῖν ὑπόσχοιτο θεὸς
C ὡς, ἐὰν ἐπιχειρήσωμεν τὸ δεύτερον τῇ τῆς νομοθεσίας σκέψει, τῶν νῦν εἰρημένων λόγων οὐ
χείρους οὐδ᾽ ἐλάττους ἀκουσόμεθα, μακρὰν ἂν
ἔλθοιμι ἔγωγε, καί μοι βραχεῖ ἂν δόξειεν ἡ νῦν
παροῦσα ἡμέρα γίγνεσθαι. καί τοι σχεδόν γ᾽
ἐστὶν ἡ ἐκ θερινῶν εἰς τὰ χειμερινὰ τοῦ θεοῦ
τρεπομένου.

ΑΘ. Χρὴ δὴ ταῦτα, ὡς ἔοικε, σκοπεῖν.

ΜΕ. Πάνυ μὲν οὖν.

ΑΘ. Γενώμεθα δὴ ταῖς διανοίαις ἐν τῷ τότε
χρόνῳ, ὅτε Λακεδαίμων μὲν καὶ Ἄργος καὶ Μεσ-
σήνη καὶ τὰ μετὰ τούτων ὑποχείρια τοῖς προγό-
D νοις ὑμῶν, ὦ Μέγιλλε, ἱκανῶς ἐγεγόνει· τὸ δὲ δὴ
μετὰ τοῦτο ἔδοξεν αὐτοῖς, ὥς γε λέγεται τὸ τοῦ
μύθου, τριχῇ τὸ στράτευμα διανείμαντας τρεῖς
πόλεις κατοικίζειν, Ἄργος, Μεσσήνην, Λακεδαίμονα.

ΜΕ. Πάνυ μὲν οὖν.

ΑΘ. Καὶ βασιλεὺς μὲν Ἄργους Τήμενος ἐγίγνετο, Μεσσήνης δὲ Κρεσφόντης, Λακεδαίμονος δὲ
Προκλῆς καὶ Εὐρυσθένης.

vast ages of time. And now there has emerged this
fourth State—or "nation," if you so prefer—which
was once upon a time in course of establishment and
is now established. Now, if we can gather from all
this which of these settlements was right and which
wrong, and which laws keep safe what is kept safe,
and which laws ruin what is ruined, and what
changes in what particulars would effect the happiness of the State,—then, O Megillus and Clinias,
we ought to describe these things again, making a
fresh start from the beginning,—unless we have
some fault to find with our previous statements.

MEG. I can assure you, Stranger, that if some
god were to promise us that, in making this second
attempt to investigate legislation, we shall listen to
a discourse that is no worse and no shorter than that
we have just been listening to, I for one would go a
long way to hear it; indeed, this would seem quite
a short day, although it is, as a matter of fact, close
on midsummer.

ATH. So it seems that we must proceed with our
enquiry.

MEG. Most certainly.

ATH. Let us, then, place ourselves in imagination
at that epoch when Lacedaemon, together with Argos
and Messene and the adjoining districts, had become
completely subject, Megillus, to your forefathers.
They determined next, according to the tradition,
to divide their host into three parts, and to establish
three States,—Argos, Messene and Lacedaemon.

MEG. Very true.

ATH. And Temenus became King of Argos, Cresphontes of Messene, and Procles and Eurysthenes
of Lacedaemon.

683 ΜΕ. Πῶς γὰρ οὔ ;

ΑΘ. Καὶ πάντες δὴ τούτοις ὤμοσαν οἱ τότε
Ε βοηθήσειν, ἐάν τις τὴν βασιλείαν αὐτῶν διαφθείρῃ.

ΜΕ. Τί μήν ;

ΑΘ. Βασιλεία δὲ καταλύεται, ὦ πρὸς Διός, ἢ
καί τις ἀρχὴ πώποτε κατελύθη μῶν ὑπό τινων
ἄλλων ἢ σφῶν αὐτῶν ; ἢ νῦν δὴ μὲν [ὀλίγον
ἔμπροσθεν]¹ τούτοις περιτυχόντες τοῖς λόγοις
οὕτω ταῦτ᾽ ἐτίθεμεν, νῦν δ᾽ ἐπιλελήσμεθα ;

ΜΕ. Καὶ πῶς ;

ΑΘ. Οὐκοῦν νῦν δὴ μᾶλλον βεβαιωσόμεθα τὸ
τοιοῦτον· περιτυχόντες γὰρ ἔργοις γενομένοις, ὡς
ἔοικεν, ἐπὶ τὸν αὐτὸν λόγον ἐληλύθαμεν, ὥστε οὐ
περὶ κενόν τι ζητήσομεν [τὸν αὐτὸν λόγον],² ἀλλὰ
684 περὶ γεγονός τε καὶ ἔχον ἀλήθειαν. γέγονε δὴ
τάδε· βασιλεῖαι τρεῖς βασιλευομέναις πόλεσι
τρατταῖς ὤμοσαν ἀλλήλαις ἑκάτεραι, κατὰ νόμους
οὓς ἔθεντο τοῦ τε ἄρχειν καὶ ἄρχεσθαι κοινούς,
οἱ μὲν μὴ βιαιοτέραν τὴν ἀρχὴν ποιήσεσθαι
προϊόντος τοῦ χρόνου καὶ γένους, οἱ δὲ ταῦτα
ἐμπεδούντων τῶν ἀρχόντων μήτε αὐτοὶ τὰς βασι-
λείας ποτὲ καταλύσειν μήτ᾽ ἐπιτρέψειν ἐπιχει-
ροῦσιν ἑτέροις, βοηθήσειν δὲ βασιλῆς τε βασι-
Β λεῦσιν ἀδικουμένοις καὶ δήμοις καὶ δῆμοι δήμοις
καὶ βασιλεῦσιν ἀδικουμένοις. ἆρ᾽ οὐχ οὕτως ;

ΜΕ. Οὕτω μὲν οὖν.

ΑΘ. Οὐκοῦν τό γε μέγιστον ταῖς καταστάσεσι
τῶν πολιτειῶν ὑπῆρχε ταῖς ἐν ταῖς τρισὶ πόλεσι
νομοθετουμέναις, εἴτε οἱ βασιλῆς ἐνομοθέτουν εἴτ᾽
ἄλλοι τινές ;

¹ [ὀλίγον ἔμπροσθεν] bracketed by Cobet, Schanz.
² [τὸν . . . λόγον] bracketed by Badham, Schanz.

LAWS, BOOK III

MEG. Of course.

ATH. And all the men of that time swore that they would assist these kings if anyone should try to wreck their kingdoms.

MEG. Quite so.

ATH. Is the dissolution of a kingdom, or of any government that has ever yet been dissolved, caused by any other agency than that of the rulers themselves? Or, though we made this assertion a moment ago when we happened upon this subject, have we now forgotten it?[1]

MEG. How could we possibly have forgotten?

ATH. Shall we further confirm that assertion now? For we have come to the same view now, as it appears, in dealing with facts of history; so that we shall be examining it with reference not to a mere abstraction, but to real events. Now what actually took place was this: each of the three royal houses, and the cities under their sway, swore to one another,[2] according to the laws, binding alike on ruler and subject, which they had made,—the rulers that, as time went on and the nation advanced, they would refrain from making their rule more severe, and the subjects that, so long as the rulers kept fast to their promise, they would never upset the monarchy themselves, nor would they allow others to do so; and they swore that the kings should aid both kings and peoples when wronged, and the peoples aid both peoples and kings. Was not that the way of it?

MEG. It was.

ATH. In the polities legally established—whether by the kings or others—in the three States, was not this the most important principle?

[1] Cp. 682 D, E.   [2] Cp. 692 B.

684 ΜΕ. Ποῖον;

ΑΘ. Τὸ βοηθούς γε εἶναι τὰς δύο ἐπὶ τὴν μίαν ἀεὶ πόλιν, τὴν τοῖς τεθεῖσι νόμοις ἀπειθοῦσαν.

ΜΕ. Δῆλον.

ΑΘ. Καὶ μὴν τοῦτό γε οἱ πολλοὶ προστάττουσι C τοῖς νομοθέταις, ὅπως τοιούτους θήσουσι τοὺς νόμους οὓς ἑκόντες οἱ δῆμοι καὶ τὰ πλήθη δέξονται, καθάπερ ἂν εἴ τις γυμνασταῖς ἢ ἰατροῖς προστάττοι μεθ' ἡδονῆς θεραπεύειν τε καὶ ἰᾶσθαι τὰ θεραπευόμενα σώματα.

ΜΕ. Παντάπασι μὲν οὖν.

ΑΘ. Τὸ δέ γ' ἐστὶν ἀγαπητὸν πολλάκις εἰ καί τις μετὰ λύπης μὴ μεγάλης δύναιτο εὐεκτικά τε καὶ ὑγιῆ σώματα ἀπεργάζεσθαι.

ΜΕ. Τί μήν;

D ΑΘ. Καὶ τόδε γε ἔτι τοῖς τότε ὑπῆρχεν οὐ σμικρὸν εἰς ῥαστώνην τῆς θέσεως τῶν νόμων.

ΜΕ. Τὸ ποῖον;

ΑΘ. Οὐκ ἦν τοῖς νομοθέταις ἡ μεγίστη τῶν μέμψεων, ἰσότητα αὐτοῖς τινα κατασκευάζουσι τῆς οὐσίας, ἥπερ ἐν ἄλλῃ[1] νομοθετουμέναις πόλεσι πολλαῖς γίγνεται, ἐάν τις ζητῇ γῆς τε κτῆσιν κινεῖν καὶ χρεῶν διάλυσιν, ὁρῶν ὡς οὐκ ἂν δύναιτο ἄνευ τούτων γενέσθαι ποτὲ τὸ ἴσον ἱκανῶς· ὡς ἐπιχειροῦντι δὴ νομοθέτῃ κινεῖν τῶν E τοιούτων τι πᾶς ἀπαντᾷ λέγων μὴ κινεῖν τὰ ἀκίνητα, καὶ ἐπαρᾶται γῆς τε ἀναδασμοὺς εἰσηγουμένῳ[2] καὶ χρεῶν ἀποκοπάς, ὥστ' εἰς ἀπορίαν καθίστασθαι πάντα ἄνδρα. τοῖς δὲ δὴ Δωριεῦσι

---

[1] ἄλλῃ England: ἄλλαις Zur., al.: ἀλλήλαις MSS.
[2] εἰσηγουμένῳ H. Richards, England: εἰσηγούμενον MSS.

192

MEG. What?

ATH. That the other two States should always help against the third, whenever it disobeyed the laws laid down.

MEG. Evidently.

ATH. And surely most people insist on this,— that the lawgivers shall enact laws of such a kind that the masses of the people accept them willingly ; just as one might insist that trainers or doctors should make their treatments or cures of men's bodies pleasurable.

MEG. Exactly so.

ATH. But in fact one often has to be content if one can bring a body into a sound and healthy state with no great amount of pain.

MEG. Very true.

ATH. The men of that age possessed also another advantage which helped not a little to facilitate legislation.[1]

MEG. What was that?

ATH. Their legislators, in their efforts to establish equality of property, were free from that worst of accusations which is commonly incurred in States with laws of a different kind, whenever anyone seeks to disturb the occupation of land, or to propose the abolition of debts, since he perceives that without these measures equality could never be fully secured. In such cases, if the lawgiver attempts to disturb any of these things, everyone confronts him with the cry, " Hands off," and they curse him for introducing redistributions of land and remissions of debts, with the result that every man is rendered powerless. But the Dorians had this further advan-

---

[1] Cp. 736 C.

PLATO

684 καὶ τοῦθ᾽ οὕτως ὑπῆρχε καλῶς καὶ ἀνεμεσήτως,
γῆν τε ἀναμφισβητήτως διανέμεσθαι, καὶ χρέα
μεγάλα καὶ παλαιὰ οὐκ ἦν.

ΜΕ. Ἀληθῆ.

ΑΘ. Πῇ δή ποτε οὖν, ὦ ἄριστοι, κακῶς οὕτως
αὐτοῖς ἐχώρησεν ἡ κατοίκισίς τε καὶ νομοθεσία ;

685 ΜΕ. Πῶς δή, καὶ τί μεμφόμενος αὐτῶν λέγεις ;

ΑΘ. Ὅτι τριῶν γενομένων τῶν οἰκήσεων τὰ
δύο αὐτῶν μέρη ταχὺ τήν τε πολιτείαν καὶ τοὺς
νόμους διέφθειρε, τὸ δὲ ἓν μόνον ἔμεινε, τὸ τῆς
ὑμετέρας πόλεως.

ΜΕ. Οὐ πάνυ ῥᾴδιον ἐρωτᾷς.

ΑΘ. Ἀλλὰ μὴν δεῖ γε ἡμᾶς τοῦτο ἐν τῷ νῦν
σκοποῦντας καὶ ἐξετάζοντας, περὶ νόμων παί-
ζοντας παιδιὰν πρεσβυτικὴν σώφρονα, διελθεῖν
Β τὴν ὁδὸν ἀλύπως, ὡς ἔφαμεν ἡνίκα ἠρχόμεθα
πορεύεσθαι.

ΜΕ. Τί μήν ; καὶ ποιητέον γε ὡς λέγεις.

ΑΘ. Τίν᾽ οὖν ἂν σκέψιν καλλίω ποιησαίμεθα
περὶ νόμων ἢ τούτων οἳ ταύτας διακεκοσμήκασιν ;
ἢ πόλεων περὶ τίνων εὐδοκιμωτέρων τε καὶ μειζόνων κατοικίσεων σκοποίμεθ᾽ ἄν ;

ΜΕ. Οὐ ῥᾴδιον ἀντὶ τούτων ἑτέρας λέγειν.

ΑΘ. Οὐκοῦν ὅτι μὲν διενοοῦντό γε οἱ τότε τὴν
κατασκευὴν ταύτην οὐ Πελοποννήσῳ μόνον ἔσε-
C σθαι βοηθὸν ἱκανήν, σχεδὸν δῆλον, ἀλλὰ καὶ τοῖς
Ἕλλησι πᾶσιν, εἴ τις τῶν βαρβάρων αὐτοὺς
ἀδικοῖ, καθάπερ οἱ περὶ τὸ Ἴλιον οἰκοῦντες τότε,

---

[1] i.e. the Dorian settlers, by right of conquest, were free
to do as they pleased : none of the old owners or creditors
could assert rights or claims.

tage, that they were free from all dread of giving offence, so that they could divide up their land without dispute; and they had no large debts of old standing.[1]

MEG. True.

ATH. How was it then, my good sirs, that their settlement and legislation turned out so badly?

MEG. What do you mean? What fault have you to find with it?

ATH. This, that whereas there were three States settled, two of the three[2] speedily wrecked their constitution and their laws, and one only remained stable—and that was your State, Megillus.

MEG. The question is no easy one.

ATH. Yet surely in our consideration and enquiry into this subject, indulging in an old man's sober play with laws, we ought to proceed on our journey painlessly, as we said[3] when we first started out.

MEG. Certainly, we must do as you say.

ATH. Well, what laws would offer a better subject for investigation than the laws by which those States were regulated? Or what larger or more famous States are there about whose settling we might enquire?

MEG. It would be hard to mention better instances than these.

ATH. It is fairly evident that the men of that age intended this organisation of theirs to serve as an adequate protection not only for the Peloponnesus, but for the whole of Hellas as well, in case any of the barbarians should attack them—just as the former dwellers around Ilium were emboldened

---

[2] *viz.* Argos and Messene,—the third being Laconia.
[3] Cp. 625 B.

685 πιστευοντες τῇ τῶν Ἀσσυρίων δυνάμει τῇ περὶ
Νῖνον γενομένη, θρασυνόμενοι τὸν πόλεμον ἤγει-
ραν τὸν ἐπὶ Τροίαν. ἦν γὰρ ἔτι τὸ τῆς ἀρχῆς
ἐκείνης σχῆμα τὸ σωζόμενον οὐ σμικρόν. καθάπερ νῦν τὸν μέγαν βασιλέα φοβούμεθα ἡμεῖς,
καὶ τότε ἐκείνην τὴν συσταθεῖσαν σύνταξιν ἐδέ-
δισαν οἱ τότε. μέγα γὰρ ἔγκλημα πρὸς αὐτοὺς
D ἡ τῆς Τροίας ἅλωσις τὸ δεύτερον ἐγεγόνει· τῆς
ἀρχῆς γὰρ τῆς ἐκείνων ἦν μόριον. πρὸς δὴ ταῦτ'
ἦν [1] πάντα ἡ τοῦ στρατοπέδου τοῦ τότε διανεμη-
θεῖσα εἰς τρεῖς πόλεις κατασκευὴ μία ὑπὸ βασιλέων ἀδελφῶν, παίδων Ἡρακλέους, καλῶς, ὡς [2]
ἐδόκει, ἀνευρημένη καὶ κατακεκοσμημένη καὶ
διαφερόντως τῆς ἐπὶ τὴν Τροίαν ἀφικομένης.
πρῶτον μὲν γὰρ τοὺς Ἡρακλείδας τῶν Πελο-
πιδῶν ἀμείνους ἡγοῦντο ἀρχόντων ἄρχοντας ἔχειν.
E ἔπειτ' αὖ τὸ στρατόπεδον τοῦτο τοῦ ἐπὶ Τροίαν
ἀφικομένου διαφέρειν πρὸς ἀρετήν· νενικηκέναι
γὰρ τούτους, ἡττῆσθαι [3] δ' ὑπὸ τούτων ἐκείνους,
Ἀχαιοὺς ὄντας ὑπὸ Δωριέων. ἆρ' οὐχ οὕτως
οἰόμεθα καὶ τῇ διανοίᾳ ταύτῃ κατασκευάζεσθαι
τοὺς τότε;

ΜΕ. Πάνυ μὲν οὖν.

ΑΘ. Οὐκοῦν καὶ τὸ βεβαίως οἴεσθαι ταῦθ'
ἕξειν εἰκὸς αὐτοὺς καὶ χρόνον τιν' ἂν πολὺν
686 μένειν, ἅτε κεκοινωνηκότας μὲν πολλῶν πόνων
καὶ κινδύνων ἀλλήλοις, ὑπὸ γένους δὲ ἑνὸς τῶν
βασιλέων ἀδελφῶν ὄντων διακεκοσμημένους, πρὸς

---

[1] ταῦτ' ἦν Schneider : ταύτην MSS. : ταῦτα Zur., vulg.
[2] ὡς MSS., omitted by Steph., Zur.
[3] ἡττῆσθαι Boeckh, Schanz: ἡττᾶσθαι MSS.

to embark on the Trojan War through reliance on the Assyrian power as it had been in the reign of Ninus.[1] For much of the splendour of that empire still survived; and the people of that age stood in fear of its confederate power, just as we men of to-day dread the Great King. For since Troy was a part of the Assyrian empire, the second[2] capture of Troy formed a grave charge against the Greeks. It was in view of all this that the Dorian host was at that time organised and distributed amongst three States under brother princes, the sons of Heracles;[3] and men thought it admirably devised, and in its equipment superior even to the host that had sailed to Troy. For men reckoned, first, that in the sons of Heracles they had better chiefs than the Pelopidae,[4] and further, that this army was superior in valour to the army which went to Troy, since the latter, which was Achaean, was worsted by the former, which was Dorian. Must we not suppose that it was in this way, and with this intention, that the men of that age organised themselves?

MEG. Certainly.

ATH. Is it not also probable that they would suppose this to be a stable arrangement, and likely to continue quite a long time, since they had shared together many toils and dangers, and were marshalled under leaders of a single family (their princes being brothers), and since, moreover, they had con-

---

[1] The mythical founder of the Assyrian empire, husband of Semiramis, and builder of Nineveh (dated about 2200 B.C.).

[2] The *first* "capture" was by Heracles, in the reign of Laomedon, father of Priam. Cp. *Il.* v. 640 ff.

[3] *viz.* Temenus, king of Argos, Procles and Eurysthenes of Laconia, Cresphontes of Messene.

[4] *viz.* Agamemnon and Menelaus.

686 τούτοις δ' ἔτι καὶ πολλοῖς μάντεσι κεχρημένους
εἶναι τοῖς τε ἄλλοις καὶ τῷ Δελφικῷ Ἀπόλλωνι ;

ΜΕ. Πῶς δ' οὐκ εἰκός ;

ΑΘ. Ταῦτα δὴ τὰ μεγάλα οὕτω προσδοκώμενα
διέπτατο, ὡς ἔοικε, τότε ταχύ, πλὴν ὅπερ εἴπομεν
νῦν δὴ σμικροῦ μέρους τοῦ περὶ τὸν ὑμέτερον
Β τόπον· καὶ τοῦτο δὴ πρὸς τὰ δύο μέρη πολεμοῦν
οὐ πώποτε πέπαυται μέχρι τὰ νῦν· ἐπεὶ γενομένη
γε ἡ τότε διάνοια καὶ ξυμφωνήσασα εἰς ἓν ἀν-
υπόστατον ἄν τινα δύναμιν ἔσχε κατὰ πόλεμον.

ΜΕ· Πῶς γὰρ οὔ ;

ΑΘ. Πῶς οὖν καὶ πῇ διώλετο ; ἆρ' οὐκ ἄξιον
ἐπισκοπεῖν, τηλικοῦτον καὶ τοιοῦτον σύστημα
ἥτις ποτὲ τύχη διέφθειρεν ;

ΜΕ. Σχολῇ γὰρ οὖν δή τις ἂν ἄλλοσε[1]
C σκοπῶν ἢ νόμους ἢ πολιτείας ἄλλας θεάσαιτο
σωζούσας καλὰ καὶ μεγάλα πράγματα ἢ καὶ
τοὐναντίον διαφθειρούσας τὸ παράπαν, εἰ ἀμε-
λήσειε τούτων.

ΑΘ. Τοῦτο μὲν ἄρα, ὡς ἔοικεν, εὐτυχῶς πως
ἐμβεβήκαμέν γε εἴς τινα σκέψιν ἱκανήν.

ΜΕ. Πάνυ μὲν οὖν.

ΑΘ. Ἆρ' οὖν, ὦ θαυμάσιε, λελήθαμεν ἄνθρωποι πάντες, καὶ τὰ νῦν δὴ ἡμεῖς, οἰόμενοι
μὲν ἑκάστοτέ τι καλὸν ὁρᾶν πρᾶγμα γενόμενον
καὶ θαυμαστὰ ἂν ἐργασάμενον, εἴ τις ἄρα ἠπισ-
τήθη καλῶς αὐτῷ χρῆσθαι κατά τινα τρόπον,
D τὸ δὲ νῦν γε ἡμεῖς τάχ' ἂν ἴσως περὶ τοῦτο αὐτὸ
οὔτ' ὀρθῶς διανοούμεθα[2] οὔτε κατὰ φύσιν, καὶ
δὴ καὶ περὶ τὰ ἄλλα πάντες πάντα περὶ ὧν ἂν
οὕτω διανοηθῶσιν ;

[1] ἄλλοσε Ast, Badham : ἄλλο MSS.

sulted a number of diviners and, amongst others, the Delphian Apollo?

MEG. That is certainly probable.

ATH. But it seems that these great expectations speedily vanished, except only, as we said, in regard to that small fraction, your State of Laconia; and ever since, up to the present day, this fraction has never ceased warring against the other two. For if the original intention had been realised, and if they had been in accord about their policy, it would have created a power invincible in war.

MEG. It certainly would.

ATH. How then, and by what means, was it destroyed? Is it not worth while to enquire by what stroke of fortune so grand a confederacy was wrecked?

MEG. Yes; for, if one passed over these examples, one would not be likely to find elsewhere either laws or constitutions which preserve interests thus fair and great, or, on the contrary, wreck them totally.

ATH. Thus by a piece of good luck, as it seems, we have embarked on an enquiry of some importance.

MEG. Undoubtedly.

ATH. Now, my dear sir, do not men in general, like ourselves at the present moment, unconsciously fancy that every fine object they set eyes on would produce marvellous results, if only a man understood the right way to make a fine use of it? But for us to hold such an idea in regard to the matter before us would possibly be both wrong and against nature; and the same is true of all other cases where men hold such ideas.

---

² διανοούμεθα H. Richards: διανοοίμεθα MSS.

686 ΜΕ. Λέγεις δὲ δὴ τί, καὶ περὶ τίνος σοι φῶμεν
μάλιστ' εἰρῆσθαι τοῦτον τὸν λόγον ;

ΑΘ. Ὦ 'γαθέ, καὶ αὐτὸς ἐμαυτοῦ νῦν δὴ
κατεγέλασα. ἀποβλέψας γὰρ πρὸς τοῦτον τὸν
στόλον οὗ πέρι διαλεγόμεθα, ἔδοξέ μοι πάγκαλός
τε εἶναι καὶ θαυμαστὸν ⟨ἂν⟩[1] κτῆμα παραπεσεῖν
τοῖς Ἕλλησιν, ὅπερ εἶπον, εἴ τις ἄρα αὐτῷ τότε
Ε καλῶς ἐχρήσατο.

ΜΕ. Οὐκοῦν εὖ καὶ ἐχόντως νοῦν σύ τε πάντα
εἶπες καὶ ἐπηνέσαμεν ἡμεῖς ;

ΑΘ. Ἴσως· ἐννοῶ γε μὴν ὡς πᾶς ὃς ἂν ἴδῃ τι
μέγα καὶ δύναμιν ἔχον πολλὴν καὶ ῥώμην εὐθὺς
ἔπαθε τοῦτο, ὡς εἴπερ ἐπίσταιτο ὁ κεκτημένος
αὐτῷ χρῆσθαι τοιούτῳ τε ὄντι καὶ τηλικούτῳ,
θαυμάστ' ἂν καὶ πολλὰ κατεργασάμενος εὐδαι-
μονοῖ.

687 ΜΕ. Οὐκοῦν ὀρθὸν καὶ τοῦτο ; ἢ πῶς λέγεις ;

ΑΘ. Σκόπει δὴ ποῖ βλέπων ὁ τὸν ἔπαινον
τοῦτον περὶ ἑκάστου τιθέμενος ὀρθῶς λέγει.
πρῶτον δὲ περὶ αὐτοῦ τοῦ] νῦν λεγομένου, πῶς,
εἰ κατὰ τρόπον ἠπιστήθησαν τάξαι τὸ στρατόπεδον οἱ τότε διακοσμοῦντες, τοῦ καιροῦ πῶς ἂν
ἔτυχον ; ἆρ' οὐκ εἰ ξυνέστησάν τε ἀσφαλῶς αὐτὸ
διέσωζόν τε εἰς τὸν ἀεὶ χρόνον, ὥστε αὐτούς τε
ἐλευθέρους εἶναι καὶ ἄλλων ἄρχοντας ὧν βουλη-
Β θεῖεν, καὶ ὅλως ἐν ἀνθρώποις πᾶσι καὶ Ἕλλησι
καὶ βαρβάροις πράττειν ὅ τι ἐπιθυμοῖεν αὐτοί
τε καὶ οἱ ἔκγονοι ; μῶν οὐ τούτων χάριν ἐπαινεθεῖεν[2] ἄν ;

ΜΕ. Πάνυ μὲν οὖν.

ΑΘ. Ἆρ' οὖν καὶ ὃς ἂν ἰδὼν πλοῦτον μέγαν ἢ

[1] ⟨ἂν⟩ (after κτῆμα) C. J. Taylor.
[2] ἐπαινεθεῖεν Orelli, Ritter : ἐπιθυμοῖεν MSS.

MEG. What is it you mean? And what shall we say is the special point of your remarks?

ATH. Why, my dear sir, I had a laugh at my own expense just now. For when I beheld this armament of which we are speaking, I thought it an amazingly fine thing, and that, if anyone had made a fine use of it at that time, it would have proved, as I said, a wonderful boon to the Greeks.

MEG. And was it not quite right and sensible of vou to say this, and of us to endorse it?

ATH. Possibly; I conceive, however, that everyone, when he beholds a thing that is large, powerful and strong, is instantly struck by the conviction that, if its possessor knew how to employ an instrument of that magnitude and quality, he could make himself happy by many wonderful achievements.

MEG. Is not that a right conviction? Or what is your view?

ATH. Just consider what one ought to have in view in every instance, in order to justify the bestowal of such praise. And first, with regard to the matter now under discussion,—if the men who were then marshalling the army knew how to organise it properly, how would they have achieved success? Must it not have been by consolidating it firmly and by maintaining it perpetually, so that they should be both free themselves and masters over all others whom they chose, and so that both they and their children should do in general just what they pleased throughout the world of Greeks and barbarians alike? Are not these the reasons why they would be praised?

MEG. Certainly.

ATH. And in every case where a man uses the

687 τιμὰς διαφερούσας γένους ἢ καὶ ὁτιοῦν τῶν
τοιούτων εἴπῃ ταὐτὰ ταῦτα, πρὸς τοῦτο βλέπων
εἶπεν, ὡς διὰ τοῦτ' αὐτῷ γενησόμενα ὧν ἂν
ἐπιθυμῇ πάντα ἢ τὰ πλεῖστα καὶ ὅσα ἀξιώτατα
λόγου;

ΜΕ. Ἔοικε γοῦν.

C   ΑΘ. Φέρε δή, πάντων ἀνθρώπων ἐστὶ κοινὸν
ἐπιθύμημα ἕν τι τὸ νῦν ὑπὸ τοῦ λόγου δηλούμενον
[ὡς αὐτός φησιν ὁ λόγος][1];

ΜΕ. Τὸ ποῖον;

ΑΘ. Τὸ κατὰ τὴν τῆς αὑτοῦ ψυχῆς ἐπίταξιν
τὰ γιγνόμενα γίγνεσθαι, μάλιστα μὲν ἅπαντα, εἰ
δὲ μή, τά γε ἀνθρώπινα.

ΜΕ. Τί μήν;

ΑΘ. Οὐκοῦν ἐπείπερ βουλόμεθα πάντες τὸ
τοιοῦτον ἀεὶ παῖδές τε ὄντες καὶ ἄνδρες καὶ
πρεσβῦται, τοῦτ' αὐτὸ καὶ εὐχοίμεθ' ἂν ἀναγκαίως διὰ τέλους;

ΜΕ. Πῶς δ' οὔ;

D   ΑΘ. Καὶ μὴν τοῖς γε φίλοις που ξυνευχοίμεθ'
ἂν ταῦτα ἅπερ ἐκεῖνοι ἑαυτοῖσιν.

ΜΕ. Τί μήν;

ΑΘ. Φίλος μὲν υἱὸς πατρί, παῖς ὢν ἀνδρί.

ΜΕ. Πῶς δ' οὔ;

ΑΘ. Καὶ μὴν ὧν γ' ὁ παῖς εὔχεται ἑαυτῷ
γίγνεσθαι, πολλὰ ὁ πατὴρ ἀπεύξαιτ' ἂν τοῖς
θεοῖς μηδαμῶς κατὰ τὰς τοῦ υἱέος εὐχὰς γίγνεσθαι.

ΜΕ. Ὅταν ἀνόητος ὢν καὶ ἔτι νέος εὔχηται,
λέγεις;

---

[1] [ὡς . . . λόγος] bracketed by England (after Stallb.).

language of eulogy on seeing great wealth or
eminent family distinctions or anything else of the
kind, would it not be true to say that, in using
it, he has this fact specially in mind,—that the
possessor of such things is likely, just because of
this, to realise all, or at least the most and greatest,
of his desires.

MEG. That is certainly probable.

ATH. Come now, is there one object of desire—
that now indicated by our argument—which is
common to all men?

MEG. What is that?

ATH. The desire that, if possible, everything,—
or failing that, all that is humanly possible—should
happen in accordance with the demands of one's
own heart.

MEG. To be sure.

ATH. Since this, then, is what we all wish always,
alike in childhood and manhood and old age, it is
for this, necessarily, that we should pray continually.

MEG. Of course.

ATH. Moreover, on behalf of our friends we will
join in making the same prayer which they make
on their own behalf.

MEG. To be sure.

ATH. And a son is a friend to his father, the boy
to the man.

MEG. Certainly.

ATH. Yet the father will often pray the gods
that the things which the son prays to obtain
may in no wise be granted according to the son's
prayers.

MEG. Do you mean, when the son who is praying
is still young and foolish?

687 ΑΘ. Καὶ ὅταν γε ὁ πατὴρ ὢν γέρων ᾖ καὶ
Ε σφόδρα νεανίας, μηδὲν τῶν καλῶν καὶ τῶν δικαίων
γιγνώσκων, εὔχηται μάλα προθύμως ἐν παθήμασιν ἀδελφοῖς ὢν τοῖς γενομένοις Θησεῖ πρὸς
τὸν δυστυχῶς τελευτήσαντα Ἱππόλυτον, ὁ δὲ
παῖς γιγνώσκῃ, τότε, δοκεῖς, παῖς πατρὶ συν-
εύξεται ;

ΜΕ. Μανθάνω ὃ λέγεις. λέγειν γάρ μοι δοκεῖς
ὡς οὐ τοῦτο εὐκτέον οὐδὲ ἐπεικτέον, ἕπεσθαι
πάντα τῇ ἑαυτοῦ βουλήσει, τὴν βούλησιν δὲ
μηδὲν [μᾶλλον][1] τῇ ἑαυτοῦ φρονήσει· τοῦτο δὲ
καὶ πόλιν καὶ ἕνα ἡμῶν ἕκαστον καὶ εὔχεσθαι
δεῖν καὶ σπεύδειν, ὅπως νοῦν ἕξει.

688 ΑΘ. Ναί, καὶ δὴ καὶ πολιτικόν γε ἄνδρα νομοθέτην ὡς ἀεὶ δεῖ πρὸς τοῦτο βλέποντα τιθέναι
τὰς τάξεις τῶν νόμων, αὐτός τε ἐμνήσθην καὶ
ὑμᾶς ἐπαναμιμνήσκω κατ' ἀρχάς, εἰ μεμνήμεθα,
τὰ λεχθέντα, ὅτι τὸ μὲν σφῷν ἦν παρακέλευμα
ὡς χρεὼν εἴη τὸν ἀγαθὸν νομοθέτην πάντα
πολέμου χάριν τὰ νόμιμα τιθέναι, τὸ δ' ἐμὸν
ἔλεγον ὅτι τοῦτο μὲν πρὸς μίαν ἀρετὴν οὐσῶν
τεττάρων κελεύοι τίθεσθαι τοὺς νόμους, δέοι δὲ
Β δὴ πρὸς πᾶσαν μὲν βλέπειν, μάλιστα δὲ καὶ
πρὸς πρώτην τὴν τῆς ξυμπάσης ἡγεμόνα ἀρετῆς,
φρόνησις δ' εἴη τοῦτο καὶ νοῦς καὶ δόξα μετ'
ἔρωτός τε καὶ ἐπιθυμίας τούτοις ἑπομένης. ἥκει
δὴ πάλιν ὁ λόγος εἰς ταὐτόν, καὶ ὁ λέγων ἐγὼ
νῦν λέγω πάλιν ἅπερ τότε, εἰ μὲν βούλεσθε, ὡς

---

[1] [μᾶλλον] I bracket (πολὺ μᾶλλον Schanz).

[1] Hippolytus was accused by his stepmother, Phaedra, of
attempting to dishonour her : therefore his father (Theseus)
invoked a curse upon him, and Poseidon (father of Theseus)

ATH. Yes, and also when the father, either through age or through the hot temper of youth, being devoid of all sense of right and justice, indulges in the vehement prayers of passion (like those of Theseus against Hippolytus,[1] when he met his luckless end), while the son, on the contrary, has a sense of justice,—in this case do you suppose that the son will echo his father's prayers?

MEG. I grasp your meaning. You mean, as I suppose, that what a man ought to pray and press for is not that everything should follow his own desire, while his desire in no way follows his own reason ; but it is the winning of wisdom that everyone of us, States and individuals alike, ought to pray for and strive after.

ATH. Yes. And what is more, I would recall to your recollection, as well as to my own, how it was said [2] (if you remember) at the outset that the legislator of a State, in settling his legal ordinances, must always have regard to wisdom. The injunction you gave was that the good lawgiver must frame all his laws with a view to war: I, on the other hand, maintained that, whereas by your injunction the laws would be framed with reference to one only of the four virtues, it was really essential to look to the whole of virtue, and first and above all to pay regard to the principal virtue of the four, which is wisdom and reason and opinion, together with the love and desire that accompany them. Now the argument has come back again to the same point, and I now repeat my former statement,—in

sent a bull which scared the horses of H.'s chariot so that they upset the chariot and dragged him till he was dead.
[2] 630 D ff.

688 παίζων, εἰ δ', ὡς σπουδάζων, ὅτι δή φημι εὐχῇ
χρῆσθαι σφαλερὸν εἶναι νοῦν μὴ κεκτημένον,
ἀλλὰ τἀναντία ταῖς βουλήσεσίν οἱ γίγνεσθαι.
[σπουδάζοντα δ' εἴ με τιθέναι βούλεσθε, τίθετε·][1]
C πάνυ γὰρ οὖν προσδοκῶ νῦν ὑμᾶς εὑρήσειν τῷ
λόγῳ ἑπομένους, ὃν ὀλίγον ἔμπροσθεν προὐθέμεθα, τῆς τῶν βασιλείων[2] τε φθορᾶς καὶ ὅλου
τοῦ διανοήματος οὐ δειλίαν οὖσαν τὴν αἰτίαν,
οὐδ' ὅτι τὰ περὶ τὸν πόλεμον οὐκ ἠπίσταντο
ἄρχοντές τε καὶ οὓς προσῆκεν ἄρχεσθαι, τῇ
λοιπῇ δὲ πάσῃ κακίᾳ διεφθαρμένα, καὶ μάλιστα
τῇ περὶ τὰ μέγιστα τῶν ἀνθρωπίνων πραγμάτων
ἀμαθίᾳ. ταῦτ' οὖν ὡς οὕτω γέγονε περὶ τὰ τότε
D καὶ νῦν, εἴ που, γίγνεται, καὶ ἐς τὸν ἔπειτα χρόνον
οὐκ ἄλλως συμβήσεται, ἐὰν βούλησθε, πειράσομαι
ἰὼν κατὰ τὸν ἑξῆς λόγον ἀνευρίσκειν τε καὶ ὑμῖν
δηλοῦν κατὰ δύναμιν ὡς οὖσι φίλοις.

ΚΛ. Λόγῳ μὲν τοίνυν σε, ὦ ξένε, ἐπαινεῖν
ἐπαχθέστερον, ἔργῳ δὲ σφόδρα ἐπαινεσόμεθα·
προθύμως γὰρ τοῖς λεγομένοις ἐπακολουθήσομεν,
ἐν οἷς ὅ γε ἐλευθέρως[3] ἐπαινῶν καὶ μὴ μάλιστά
ἐστι καταφανής.

ΜΕ. Ἄριστ', ὦ Κλεινία, καὶ ποιῶμεν ἃ λέγεις.
E ΚΛ. Ἔσται ταῦτα, ἐὰν θεὸς ἐθέλῃ. λέγε μόνον.

ΑΘ. Φαμὲν δή νυν, καθ' ὁδὸν ἰόντες τὴν λοιπὴν
τοῦ λόγου, τὴν μεγίστην ἀμαθίαν τότε ἐκείνην
τὴν δύναμιν ἀπολέσαι καὶ νῦν ταὐτὸν τοῦτο
πεφυκέναι ποιεῖν, ὥστε τόν γε νομοθέτην, εἰ
τοῦθ' οὕτως ἔχει, πειρατέον ταῖς πόλεσι φρόνησιν

---

[1] [σπουδάζοντα . . . τίθετε] I bracket (after England's
conj.).

jest, if you will, or else in earnest; I assert that
prayer is a perilous practice for him who is devoid
of reason, and that what he obtains is the opposite
of his desires. For I certainly expect that, as you
follow the argument recently propounded, you will
now discover that the cause of the ruin of those
kingdoms, and of their whole design, was not
cowardice or ignorance of warfare on the part
either of the rulers or of those who should have
been their subjects; but that what ruined them was
badness of all other kinds, and especially ignorance
concerning the greatest of human interests. That
this was the course of events then, and is so still,
whenever such events occur, and will be so likewise
in the future,—this, with your permission, I will
endeavour to discover in the course of the coming
argument, and to make it as clear as I can to you,
my very good friends.

CLIN. Verbal compliments are in poor taste,
Stranger; but by deed, if not by word, we shall pay
you the highest of compliments by attending eagerly
to your discourse; and that is what best shows
whether compliments are spontaneous or the reverse.

MEG. Capital, Clinias! Let us do just as you say.

CLIN. It shall be so, God willing. Only say on.

ATH. Well then, to advance further on the track
of our discourse,—we assert that it was ignorance,
in its greatest form, which at that time destroyed
the power we have described, and which naturally
produces still the same results; and if this is so, it
follows that the lawgiver must try to implant in

---

² βασιλειῶν Boeckh, Schanz: βασιλέων MSS.
³ ἐλευθέρως Ast, Schanz: ἐλεύθερος MSS.

688 μὲν ὅσην δυνατὸν ἐμποιεῖν, τὴν δ' ἄνοιαν ὅτι μάλιστα ἐξαιρεῖν.

ΚΛ. Δῆλον.

689 ΑΘ. Τίς οὖν ἡ μεγίστη δικαίως ἂν λέγοιτο ἀμαθία; σκοπεῖτε εἰ συνδόξει καὶ σφῷν λεγόμενον· ἐγὼ μὲν δὴ τὴν τοιάνδε τίθεμαι.

ΚΛ. Ποίαν;

ΑΘ. Τὴν ὅταν τῷ τι δόξαν καλὸν ἢ ἀγαθὸν εἶναι μὴ φιλῇ τοῦτο, ἀλλὰ μισῇ, τὸ δὲ πονηρὸν καὶ ἄδικον δοκοῦν εἶναι φιλῇ τε καὶ ἀσπάζηται. ταύτην τὴν διαφωνίαν λύπης τε καὶ ἡδονῆς πρὸς τὴν κατὰ λόγον δόξαν ἀμαθίαν φημὶ εἶναι τὴν ἐσχάτην, <τὴν>[1] μεγίστην δέ, ὅτι τοῦ πλήθους
B ἐστὶ τῆς ψυχῆς· τὸ γὰρ λυπούμενον καὶ ἡδόμενον αὐτῆς ὅπερ δῆμός τε καὶ πλῆθος πόλεώς ἐστιν. ὅταν οὖν ἐπιστήμαις ἢ δόξαις ἢ λόγῳ ἐναντιῶται, τοῖς φύσει ἀρχικοῖς, [ἡ ψυχή,][2] τοῦτο ἄνοιαν προσαγορεύω, πόλεώς τε, ὅταν ἄρχουσι καὶ νόμοις μὴ πείθηται τὸ πλῆθος, ταυτόν, καὶ δὴ καὶ ἑνὸς ἀνδρός, ὁπόταν καλοὶ ἐν ψυχῇ λόγοι ἐνόντες μηδὲν ποιῶσι πλέον, ἀλλὰ δὴ τούτοις πᾶν τοὐ-
C ναντίον. ταύτας πάσας ἀμαθίας τὰς πλημμελεστάτας ἔγωγ' ἂν θείην πόλεώς τε καὶ ἑνὸς ἑκάστου τῶν πολιτῶν, ἀλλ' οὐ τὰς τῶν δημιουργῶν, εἰ ἄρα μου καταμανθάνετε, ὦ ξένοι, ὃ λέγω.

---

[1] <τὴν> I add.
[2] [ἡ ψυχή,] bracketed by Badham.

---

[1] In this comparison between the Soul and the State both are regarded as consisting of two parts or elements, the ruling and the ruled, of which the former is the noblest, but the latter the "greatest" in bulk and extent. The ruling element in the Soul is Reason (νοῦς, λόγος), and in the State it is Law

States as much wisdom as possible, and to root out
folly to the utmost of his power.

CLIN. Obviously.

ATH. What kind of ignorance would deserve to
be called the "greatest"? Consider whether you
will agree with my description; I take it to be
ignorance of this kind,—

CLIN. What kind?

ATH. That which we see in the man who hates,
instead of loving, what he judges to be noble and
good, while he loves and cherishes what he judges to
be evil and unjust. That want of accord, on the
part of the feelings of pain and pleasure, with the
rational judgment is, I maintain, the extreme form
of ignorance, and also the "greatest" because it
belongs to the main mass of the soul,—for the part
of the soul that feels pain and pleasure corresponds
to the mass of the populace in the State.[1] So whenever this part opposes what are by nature the
ruling principles—knowledge, opinion, or reason,—
this condition I call folly, whether it be in a State,
when the masses disobey the rulers and the laws, or
in an individual, when the noble elements of reason
existing in the soul produce no good effect, but
quite the contrary. All these I would count as the
most discordant forms of ignorance, whether in the
State or the individual, and not the ignorance of the
artisan,—if you grasp my meaning, Strangers.

($\nu \acute{o}\mu os$) and its exponents: the subject element in the Soul
consists of sensations, emotions and desires, which (both in
bulk and in irrationality) correspond to the mass of the *volgus*
in the State. Plato's usual division of the Soul is into three
parts,—reason ($\nu o \hat{v} s$), passion ($\theta v \mu \acute{o} s$), and desire ($\dot{\epsilon} \pi \iota \theta v \mu \acute{\iota} a$):
cp. *Rep.* 435 ff.

689 κλ. Μανθάνομέν τε, ὦ φίλε, καὶ συγχωροῦμεν
ἃ λέγεις.

ΑΘ. Τοῦτο μὲν τοίνυν οὕτω κείσθω δεδογμένον
καὶ λελεγμένον,[1] ὡς τοῖς ταῦτ᾿ ἀμαθαίνουσι τῶν
πολιτῶν οὐδὲν ἐπιτρεπτέον ἀρχῆς ἐχόμενον καὶ
ὡς ἀμαθέσιν ὀνειδιστέον, ἂν καὶ πάνυ λογιστικοί
τε ὦσι καὶ πάντα τὰ κομψὰ καὶ ὅσα πρὸς τάχος
D τῆς ψυχῆς πεφυκότα διαπεπονημένοι ἅπαντα,
τοὺς δὲ τοὐναντίον ἔχοντας τούτων ὡς σοφούς
τε προσρητέον, ἂν καὶ τὸ λεγόμενον μήτε γράμ-
ματα μήτε νεῖν ἐπίστωνται, καὶ τὰς ἀρχὰς δοτέον
ὡς ἔμφροσι. πῶς γὰρ ἄν, ὦ φίλοι, ἄνευ ξυμφωνίας
γένοιτ᾿ ἂν φρονήσεως καὶ τὸ σμικρότατον εἶδος ;
οὐκ ἔστιν, ἀλλ᾿ ἡ καλλίστη καὶ μεγίστη τῶν
ξυμφωνιῶν μεγίστη δικαιότατ᾿ ἂν λέγοιτο σοφία,
ἧς ὁ μὲν κατὰ λόγον ζῶν μέτοχος, ὁ δ᾿ ἀπολει-
E πόμενος οἰκοφθόρος καὶ περὶ πόλιν οὐδαμῇ σωτὴρ ἀλλὰ πᾶν τοὐναντίον ἀμαθαίνων εἰς ταῦτα
ἑκάστοτε φανεῖται. ταῦτα μὲν οὖν, καθάπερ
εἴπομεν ἄρτι, λελεγμένα τεθήτω ταύτῃ.

κλ. Κείσθω γὰρ οὖν.

ΑΘ. Ἄρχοντας δὲ δὴ καὶ ἀρχομένους ἀναγκαῖον
ἐν ταῖς πόλεσιν εἶναί που.

κλ. Τί μήν ;

690 ΑΘ. Εἶεν· ἀξιώματα δὲ δὴ τοῦ τε ἄρχειν καὶ
ἄρχεσθαι ποῖά ἐστι καὶ πόσα, ἔν τε πόλεσι
μεγάλαις καὶ σμικραῖς ἔν τε οἰκίαις ὡσαύτως ;
ἆρ᾿ οὐχὶ ἓν μὲν τό τε πατρὸς καὶ μητρός, καὶ
ὅλως γονέας ἐκγόνων ἄρχειν ἀξίωμα ὀρθὸν
πανταχοῦ ἂν εἴη ;

[1] λελεγμένον Badham : λεγόμενον MSS. (bracketed by
Schanz).

CLIN. We do, my dear sir, and we agree with it.

ATH. Then let it be thus resolved and declared, that no control shall be entrusted to citizens thus ignorant, but that they shall be held in reproach for their ignorance, even though they be expert calculators, and trained in all accomplishments and in everything that fosters agility of soul, while those whose mental condition is the reverse of this shall be entitled "wise," even if—as the saying goes—" they spell not neither do they swim " [1]: and to these latter, as to men of sense, the government shall be entrusted. For without harmony,[2] my friends, how could even the smallest fraction of wisdom exist? It is impossible. But the greatest and best of harmonies would most properly be accounted the greatest wisdom; and therein he who lives rationally has a share, whereas he who is devoid thereof will always prove to be a home-wrecker and anything rather than a saviour of the State, because of his ignorance in these matters. So let this declaration stand, as we recently said, as one of our axioms.

CLIN. Yes, let it stand.

ATH. Our States, I presume, must have rulers and subjects.

CLIN. Of course.

ATH. Very well then: what and how many are the agreed rights or claims in the matter of ruling and being ruled, alike in States, large or small, and in households? Is not the right of father and mother one of them? And in general would not the claim of parents to rule over offspring be a claim universally just?

[1] *i.e.* are ignorant of even the most ordinary accomplishments.　　[2] Cp. *Rep.* 430 E ; 591 D.

690 ΚΛ. Καὶ μάλα.

ΑΘ. Τούτῳ δέ γε ἑπόμενον γενναίους ἀγεννῶν ἄρχειν· καὶ τρίτον ἔτι τούτοις ξυνέπεται τὸ πρεσβυτέρους μὲν ἄρχειν δεῖν, νεωτέρους δὲ ἄρχεσθαι.

ΚΛ. Τί μήν;

B ΑΘ. Τέταρτον δ' αὖ δούλους μὲν ἄρχεσθαι, δεσπότας δὲ ἄρχειν.

ΚΛ. Πῶς γὰρ οὔ;

ΑΘ. Πέμπτον γε, οἶμαι, τὸν κρείττονα μὲν ἄρχειν, τὸν ἥττω δὲ ἄρχεσθαι.

ΚΛ. Μάλα γε ἀναγκαίαν ἀρχὴν εἴρηκας.

ΑΘ. Καὶ πλείστην γε ἐν ξύμπασι τοῖς ζῴοις οὖσαν καὶ κατὰ φύσιν, ὡς ὁ Θηβαῖος ἔφη ποτὲ Πίνδαρος. τὸ δὲ μέγιστον, ὡς ἔοικεν, ἀξίωμα ἕκτον ἂν γίγνοιτο, ἕπεσθαι μὲν τὸν ἀνεπιστήμονα κελεῦον, τὸν δὲ φρονοῦντα ἡγεῖσθαί τε καὶ ἄρχειν.

C καί τοι τοῦτό γε, ὦ Πίνδαρε σοφώτατε, σχεδὸν οὐκ ἂν παρὰ φύσιν ἔγωγε φαίην γίγνεσθαι, κατὰ φύσιν δὲ τὴν τοῦ νόμου ἑκόντων ἀρχὴν ἀλλ' οὐ βίαιον πεφυκυῖαν.

ΚΛ. Ὀρθότατα λέγεις.

ΑΘ. Θεοφιλῆ δέ γε καὶ εὐτυχῆ τινα λέγοντες ἑβδόμην ἀρχὴν εἰς κλῆρόν τινα προάγομεν καὶ λαχόντα μὲν ἄρχειν, δυσκληροῦντα δὲ ἀπιόντα ἄρχεσθαι τὸ δικαιότατον εἶναί φαμεν.

ΚΛ. Ἀληθέστατα λέγεις.

D ΑΘ. Ὁρᾷς δή, φαῖμεν ἄν, ὦ νομοθέτα, πρός τινα παίζοντες τῶν ἐπὶ νόμων θέσιν ἰόντων ῥᾳδίως, ὅσα ἐστὶ περὶ[1] ἄρχοντας ἀξιώματα καὶ

---

[1] περὶ Madvig, Schanz: πρὸς MSS.

CLIN. Certainly.

ATH. And next to this, the right of the noble to rule over the ignoble; and then, following on these as a third claim, the right of older people to rule and of younger to be ruled.

CLIN. To be sure.

ATH. The fourth right is that slaves ought to be ruled, and masters ought to rule.

CLIN. Undoubtedly.

ATH. And the fifth is, I imagine, that the stronger should rule and the weaker be ruled.

CLIN. A truly compulsory form of rule!

ATH. Yes, and one that is very prevalent among all kinds of creatures, being "according to nature," as Pindar of Thebes once said.[1] The most important right is, it would seem, the sixth, which ordains that the man without understanding should follow, and the wise man lead and rule. Nevertheless, my most sapient Pindar, this is a thing that I, for one, would hardly assert to be against nature, but rather according thereto—the natural rule of law, without force, over willing subjects.

CLIN. A very just observation.

ATH. Heaven's favour and good-luck mark the seventh form of rule, where we bring a man forward for a casting of lots, and declare that if he gains the lot he will most justly be ruler, but if he fails he shall take his place among the ruled.

CLIN. Very true.

ATH. "Seest thou, O legislator,"—it is thus we might playfully address one of those who lightly start on the task of legislation—"how many are the rights pertaining to rulers, and how they are

---

[1] Cp. *Gorgias* 484 B Πίνδαρος . . . λέγει ὅτι Νόμος . . . ⟨κατὰ ῥύσιν⟩ ἄγει δικαιῶν τὸ βιαιότατον ὑπερτάτᾳ χερί.

690 ὅτι πεφυκότα πρὸς ἄλληλα ἐναντίως; νῦν γὰρ
δὴ στάσεων πηγήν τινα ἀνευρήκαμεν ἡμεῖς, ἣν
δεῖ σε θεραπεύειν. πρῶτον δὲ μεθ' ἡμῶν ἀνά-
σκεψαι πῶς τε καὶ τί παρὰ ταῦτα ἁμαρτόντες
οἱ περί τε Ἄργος καὶ Μεσσήνην βασιλῆς αὑτοὺς
ἅμα καὶ τὴν τῶν Ἑλλήνων δύναμιν οὖσαν θαυ-
Ε μαστὴν ἐν τῷ τότε χρόνῳ διέφθειραν. ἆρ' οὐκ
ἀγνοήσαντες τὸν Ἡσίοδον ὀρθότατα λέγοντα ὡς
τὸ ἥμισυ τοῦ παντὸς πολλάκις ἐστὶ πλέον;
[ὁπόταν ᾖ τὸ μὲν ὅλον λαμβάνειν ζημιῶδες, τὸ
δ' ἥμισυ μέτριον, τότε τὸ μέτριον τοῦ ἀμέτρου
πλέον ἡγήσατο, ἄμεινον ὂν χείρονος.][1]

ΚΛ. Ὀρθότατά γε.

ΑΘ. Πότερον οὖν οἰόμεθα περὶ βασιλέας τοῦτ'
ἐγγιγνόμενον ἑκάστοτε διαφθείρειν πρότερον ἢ
ἐν τοῖσι δήμοις;

691 ΚΛ. Τὸ μὲν εἰκὸς ὡς[2] τὸ πολὺ βασιλέων τοῦτο
εἶναι νόσημα ὑπερηφάνως ζώντων διὰ τρυφάς.

ΑΘ. Οὐκοῦν δῆλον ὡς πρῶτον τοῦτο οἱ τότε
βασιλῆς ἔσχον, τὸ πλεονεκτεῖν τῶν τεθέντων
νόμων, καὶ ὃ λόγῳ τε καὶ ὅρκῳ ἐπήνεσαν, οὐ
ξυνεφώνησαν αὑτοῖς, ἀλλ' ἡ διαφωνία, ὡς ἡμεῖς
φαμέν, οὖσα ἀμαθία μεγίστη, δοκοῦσα δὲ σοφία,
πάντ' ἐκεῖνα διὰ πλημμέλειαν καὶ ἀμουσίαν τὴν
πικρὰν διέφθειρεν;

ΚΛ. Ἔοικε γοῦν.

Β ΑΘ. Εἶεν· τί δὴ τὸν νομοθέτην ἔδει τότε
τιθέντα εὐλαβηθῆναι τούτου περὶ τοῦ πάθους
τῆς γενέσεως; ἆρ' ὦ πρὸς θεῶν νῦν μὲν οὐδὲν

---

[1] [ὁπόταν . . . χείρονος] bracketed by Hermann, Schanz.
[2] ὡς: καὶ MSS. : ἐπὶ Badham.

214

essentially opposed to one another? Herein we
have now discovered a source of factions, which thou
must remedy. So do thou, in the first place, join
with us in enquiring how it came to pass, and owing
to what transgression of those rights, that the kings
of Argos and Messene brought ruin alike on themselves and on the Hellenic power, splendid as it was
at that epoch. Was it not through ignorance of
that most true saying of Hesiod [1] that 'oftimes the
half is greater than the whole'?"

CLIN. Most true, indeed.

ATH. Is it our view, then, that this causes ruin
when it is found in kings rather than when found in
peoples?

CLIN. Probably this is, in the main, a disease of
kings, in whom luxury breeds pride of life.

ATH. Is it not plain that what those kings strove
for first was to get the better of the established
laws, and that they were not in accord with one
another about the pledge which they had approved
both by word and by oath; and this discord—reputed to be wisdom, but really, as we affirm, the
height of ignorance,—owing to its grating dissonance
and lack of harmony, brought the whole Greek world
to ruin?

CLIN. It would seem so, certainly.

ATH. Very well then: what precaution ought the
legislator to have taken at that time in his enactments, to guard against the growth of this disorder?
Verily, to perceive that now requires no great sagacity,

---

[1] Cp. *Op. D.* 38 ff.; *Rep.* 466 C.: the meaning is that when
"the whole" is excessive, the moderate "half" is prefer-
able; this maxim being here applied to excesses of political
power.

PLATO

691 σοφὸν γνῶναι τοῦτο οὐδ' εἰπεῖν χαλεπόν, εἰ
δὲ προϊδεῖν ἦν τότε, σοφώτερος ἂν ἦν ἡμῶν ὁ
προϊδών ;

ΜΕ. Τὸ ποῖον δὴ λέγεις ;

ΑΘ. Εἰς τὸ γεγονὸς παρ' ὑμῖν, ὦ Μέγιλλε,
ἔστι νῦν γε κατιδόντα γνῶναι, καὶ γνόντα εἰπεῖν
ῥᾴδιον, ὃ τότε ἔδει γίγνεσθαι.

ΜΕ. Σαφέστερον ἔτι λέγε.

ΑΘ. Τὸ τοίνυν σαφέστατον ἂν εἴη τὸ τοιόνδε.

ΜΕ. Τὸ ποῖον ;

C ΑΘ. Ἐάν τις μείζονα διδῷ τοῖς ἐλάττοσι
δύναμιν παρεὶς τὸ μέτριον, πλοίοις τε ἱστία καὶ
σώμασι τροφὴν καὶ ψυχαῖς ἀρχάς, ἀνατρέπεταί
που πάντα καὶ ἐξυβρίζοντα τὰ μὲν εἰς νόσους
θεῖ, τὰ δ' εἰς ἔκγονον ὕβρεως ἀδικίαν. τί οὖν
δή ποτε λέγομεν ; ἆρά γε τὸ τοιόνδε, ὡς οὐκ ἔστ',
ὦ φίλοι ἄνδρες, θνητῆς ψυχῆς φύσις ἥτις ποτὲ
δυνήσεται τὴν μεγίστην ἐν ἀνθρώποις ἀρχὴν
φέρειν νέα καὶ ἀνυπεύθυνος, ὥστε μὴ τῆς μεγίστης
D νόσου ἀνοίας πληρωθεῖσα αὑτῆς τὴν διάνοιαν
μῖσος ἔχειν πρὸς τῶν ἐγγύτατα φίλων, ὃ γενόμενον ταχὺ διέφθειρεν αὐτὴν καὶ πᾶσαν τὴν
δύναμιν ἠφάνισεν αὐτῆς ; τοῦτ' οὖν εὐλαβηθῆναι
γνόντας τὸ μέτριον μεγάλων νομοθετῶν. ὡς οὖν
δὴ <τὸ>[1] τότε γενόμενον νῦν ἔστι μετριώτατα
τοπάσαι, τόδ' ἔοικεν εἶναι.

ΜΕ. Τὸ ποῖον ;

ΑΘ. Θεὸς ἦν πρῶτον[2] κηδόμενος ὑμῶν τις, ὃς
τὰ μέλλοντα προορῶν, δίδυμον ὑμῖν φυτεύσας

---

[1] <τὸ> added by Ast.
[2] ἦν πρῶτον: εἶναι MSS. : εἴη ἂν Schanz.

216

nor is it a hard thing to declare; but the man who foresaw it in those days—if it could possibly have been foreseen—would have been a wiser man than we.

MEG. To what are you alluding?

ATH. If one looks at what has happened, Megillus, among you Lacedaemonians, it is easy to perceive, and after perceiving to state, what ought to have been done at that time.

MEG. Speak still more clearly.

ATH. The clearest statement would be this—

MEG. What?

ATH. If one neglects the rule of due measure, and gives things too great in power to things too small—sails to ships, food to bodies, offices of rule to souls—then everything is upset, and they run, through excess of insolence, some to bodily disorders, others to that offspring of insolence, injustice.[1] What, then, is our conclusion? Is it not this? There does not exist, my friends, a mortal soul whose nature, when young and irresponsible, will ever be able to stand being in the highest ruling position upon earth without getting surfeited in mind with that greatest of disorders, folly, and earning the detestation of its nearest friends; and when this occurs, it speedily ruins the soul itself and annihilates the whole of its power. To guard against this, by perceiving the due measure, is the task of the great lawgiver. So the most duly reasonable conjecture we can now frame as to what took place at that epoch appears to be this—

MEG. What?

ATH. To begin with, there was a god watching over you; and he, foreseeing the future, restricted

---

[1] Cp. Soph. *O.T.* 873 : ὕβρις φυτεύει τύραννον.

691E τὴν τῶν βασιλέων γένεσιν ἐκ μονογενοῦς, εἰς τὸ
μέτριον μᾶλλον συνέστειλε. καὶ μετὰ τοῦτο ἔτι
φύσις τις ἀνθρωπίνη μεμιγμένη θείᾳ τινὶ δυνάμει,
κατιδοῦσα ὑμῶν τὴν ἀρχὴν φλεγμαίνουσαν ἔτι,
μίγνυσι τὴν κατὰ γήρας σώφρονα δύναμιν τῇ
692 κατὰ γένος αὐθάδει ῥώμῃ, τὴν τῶν ὀκτὼ καὶ
εἴκοσι γερόντων ἰσόψηφον εἰς τὰ μέγιστα τῇ τῶν
βασιλέων ποιήσασα δυνάμει. ὁ δὲ τρίτος σωτὴρ
ὑμῖν ἔτι σπαργῶσαν καὶ θυμουμένην τὴν ἀρχὴν
ὁρῶν οἷον ψάλιον ἐνέβαλεν αὐτῇ τὴν τῶν ἐφόρων
δύναμιν, ἐγγὺς τῆς κληρωτῆς ἀγαγὼν δυνάμεως.
καὶ κατὰ δὴ τοῦτον τὸν λόγον ἡ βασιλεία παρ᾽
ὑμῖν, ἐξ ὧν ἔδει σύμμικτος γενομένη καὶ μέτρον
ἔχουσα, σωθεῖσα αὐτὴ σωτηρίας τοῖς ἄλλοις
B γέγονεν αἰτία· ἐπεὶ ἐπί γε Τημένῳ καὶ Κρεσφόντῃ
καὶ τοῖς τότε νομοθέταις, οἵτινες ἄρ᾽ ἦσαν νομο-
θετοῦντες, οὐδ᾽ ἡ Ἀριστοδήμου μερὶς ἐσώθη ποτ᾽
ἄν. οὐ γὰρ ἱκανῶς ἦσαν νομοθεσίας ἔμπειροι·
σχεδὸν γὰρ οὐκ ἄν ποτ᾽ ᾠήθησαν ⟨ἀρκεῖν⟩[1]
ὅρκοις μετριάσαι ψυχὴν νέαν λαβοῦσαν ἀρχὴν
ἐξ ἧς δυνατὸν ἦν τυραννίδα γενέσθαι. νῦν δ᾽ ὁ
θεὸς ἔδειξεν οἵαν ἔδει καὶ δεῖ δὴ τὴν μενοῦσαν
μάλιστα ἀρχὴν γίγνεσθαι. τὸ δὲ παρ᾽ ἡμῶν
C γιγνώσκεσθαι ταῦτα, ὅπερ εἶπον ἔμπροσθεν, νῦν
μὲν γενόμενον οὐδὲν σοφόν· ἐκ γὰρ παραδείγ-
ματος ὁρᾶν γεγονότος οὐδὲν χαλεπόν. εἰ δ᾽ ἦν

---

[1] ⟨ἀρκεῖν⟩ I add (μετριάσαι ἂν H. Richards).

---

[1] Lycurgus.
[2] Theopompus, king of Sparta about 750 B.C. The institution of the Ephorate is by some ascribed to him (as here),
by others to Lycurgus. Cp. Arist. Pol. 1313ᵃ 19 ff.
[3] See 683 D.

within due bounds the royal power by making your
kingly line no longer single but twofold. In the
next place, some man,[1] in whom human nature was
blended with power divine, observing your government to be still swollen with fever, blended the self-
willed force of the royal strain with the temperate
potency of age, by making the power of the eight-
and-twenty elders of equal weight with that of the
kings in the greatest matters. Then your "third
saviour,"[2] seeing your government still fretting and
fuming, curbed it, as one may say, by the power of
the ephors, which was not far removed from government by lot. Thus, in your case, according to this
account, owing to its being blended of the right
elements and possessed of due measure, the kingship
not only survived itself but ensured the survival of
all else. For if the matter had lain with Temenus
and Cresphontes[3] and the lawgivers of their day—
whosoever those lawgivers really were,—even the
portion of Aristodemus[4] could never have survived,
for they were not fully expert in the art of legislation; otherwise they could hardly have deemed it
sufficient to moderate by means of sworn pledges[5]
a youthful soul endowed with power such as might
develop into a tyranny; but now God has shown of
what kind the government ought to have been then,
and ought to be now, if it is to endure. That we
should understand this, after the occurrence, is—as
I said before[6]—no great mark of sagacity, since it
is by no means difficult to draw an inference from an
example in the past; but if, at the time, there had

---

[4] *i.e.* Lacedaemon: Aristodemus was father of Eurysthenes and Procles (cp. 683 D).
[5] Cp. 684 A.   [6] 691 B.

692 τις προορῶν τότε ταῦτα καὶ δυνάμενος μετριάσαι
τὰς ἀρχὰς καὶ μίαν ἐκ τριῶν ποιῆσαι, τά τε
νοηθέντα ἂν καλὰ τότε πάντα ἀπέσωσε καὶ οὐκ
ἄν ποτε ὁ Περσικὸς ἐπὶ τὴν Ἑλλάδα οὐδ' ἄλλος
οὐδεὶς στόλος ἂν ὥρμησε, καταφρονήσας ὡς
ὄντων ἡμῶν βραχέος ἀξίων.

ΚΛ. Ἀληθῆ λέγεις.

D   ΑΘ. Αἰσχρῶς γοῦν ἠμύναντο αὐτούς, ὦ Κλεινία. τὸ δ' αἰσχρὸν λέγω οὐχ ὡς οὐ νικῶντές γε
οἱ τότε καὶ κατὰ γῆν καὶ κατὰ θάλατταν καλὰς
νενικήκασι μάχας· ἀλλ' ὅ φημι αἰσχρὸν τότ'
εἶναι τόδε λέγω, τὸ πρῶτον μὲν ἐκείνων τῶν
πόλεων τριῶν οὐσῶν μίαν ὑπὲρ τῆς Ἑλλάδος
ἀμῦναι, τὼ δὲ δύο κακῶς οὕτως εἶναι διεφθαρμένα,
ὥστε ἡ μὲν καὶ Λακεδαίμονα διεκώλυεν ἐπαμύνειν
αὐτῇ, πολεμοῦσα αὐτῇ κατὰ κράτος, ἡ δ' αὖ
πρωτεύουσα ἐν τοῖς τότε χρόνοις τοῖς περὶ τὴν
E διανομήν,¹ ἡ περὶ τὸ Ἄργος, παρακαλουμένη ἀμύ-
νειν τὸν βάρβαρον οὔθ' ὑπήκουσεν οὔτ' ἤμυνε.
πολλὰ δὲ λέγων ἄν τις τὰ τότε γενόμενα περὶ
ἐκεῖνον τὸν πόλεμον τῆς Ἑλλάδος οὐδαμῶς εὐσχή-
μονα ἂν κατηγοροίη· οὐδ' αὖ ἀμύνασθαι τήν γε
Ἑλλάδα λέγων ὀρθῶς ἂν λέγοι, ἀλλ' εἰ μὴ τό τε
693 Ἀθηναίων καὶ τὸ Λακεδαιμονίων κοινῇ διανόημα
ἤμυνε τὴν ἐπιοῦσαν δουλείαν, σχεδὸν ἂν ἤδη
πάντ' ἦν μεμιγμένα τὰ τῶν Ἑλλήνων γένη ἐν
ἀλλήλοις καὶ βάρβαρα ἐν Ἕλλησι καὶ Ἑλληνικὰ
ἐν βαρβάροις, καθάπερ ὧν Πέρσαι τυραννοῦσι τὰ
νῦν διαπεφορημένα καὶ ξυμπεφορημένα κακῶς

---

¹ Messene.

been anyone who foresaw the result and was able to moderate the ruling powers and unify them,—such a man would have preserved all the grand designs then formed, and no Persian or other armament would ever have set out against Greece, or held us in contempt as a people of small account.

CLIN. True.

ATH. The way they repulsed the Persians, Clinias, was disgraceful. But when I say "disgraceful," I do not imply that they did not win fine victories both by land and sea in those victorious campaigns: what I call "disgraceful" is this,—that, in the first place, one only of those three States defended Greece, while the other two were so basely corrupt that one of them[1] actually prevented Lacedaemon from assisting Greece by warring against her with all its might, and Argos, the other,—which stood first of the three in the days of the Dorian settlement—when summoned to help against the barbarian, paid no heed and gave no help.[2] Many are the discreditable charges one would have to bring against Greece in relating the events of that war; indeed, it would be wrong to say that Greece defended herself, for had not the bondage that threatened her been warded off by the concerted policy of the Athenians and Lacedaemonians, practically all the Greek races would have been confused together by now, and barbarians confused with Greeks and Greeks with barbarians,—just as the races under the Persian empire to-day are either scattered abroad or jumbled together and live in a

---

[2] Cp. Hdt. vii. 148 ff. The reference is to the Persian invasion under Mardonius in 490 B.C.; but there is no other evidence for the charge here made against Messene.

693 ἐφθαρμένα¹ κατοικεῖται. ταῦτ', ὦ Κλεινία καὶ
Μέγιλλε, ἔχομεν ἐπιτιμᾶν τοῖς τε πάλαι πολι-
τικοῖς λεγομένοις καὶ νομοθέταις καὶ τοῖς νῦν,
ἵνα τὰς αἰτίας αὐτῶν ἀναζητοῦντες ἀνευρίσκωμεν
B τί παρὰ ταῦτα ἔδει πράττειν ἄλλο, οἷον δὴ καὶ τὸ
παρὸν εἴπομεν, ὡς ἄρα οὐ δεῖ μεγάλας ἀρχὰς
οὐδ' αὖ ἀμίκτους νομοθετεῖν, διανοηθέντας τὸ
τοιόνδε, ὅτι πόλιν ἐλευθέραν τε εἶναι δεῖ καὶ
ἔμφρονα καὶ ἑαυτῇ φίλην, καὶ τὸν νομοθετοῦντα
πρὸς ταῦτα βλέποντα δεῖ νομοθετεῖν. μὴ θαυ-
μάσωμεν δὲ εἰ πολλάκις ἤδη προθέμενοι ἄττα
εἰρήκαμεν ὅτι πρὸς ταῦτα δεῖ νομοθετεῖν βλέ-
C ποντα τὸν νομοθέτην, τὰ δὲ προτεθέντα οὐ ταὐτὰ
ἡμῖν φαίνεται ἑκάστοτε· ἀλλ' ἀναλογίζεσθαι χρή,
ὅταν [πρὸς τὸ σωφρονεῖν]² φῶμεν δεῖν βλέπειν
[ἢ] πρὸς φρόνησιν ἢ φιλίαν, ὡς ἔσθ' οὗτος ὁ
σκοπὸς οὐχ ἕτερος, ἀλλ' ὁ αὐτός· καὶ ἄλλα δὴ
πολλὰ ἡμᾶς τοιαῦτα ἂν γίγνηται ῥήματα, μὴ
διαταραττέτω.

ΚΛ. Πειρασόμεθα ποιεῖν οὕτως ἐπανιόντες τοὺς
λόγους· καὶ νῦν δὴ τὸ περὶ τῆς φιλίας τε καὶ
φρονήσεως καὶ ἐλευθερίας, πρὸς ὅ τι βουλόμενον³
ἔμελλες λέγειν δεῖν στοχάζεσθαι τὸν νομοθέτην,
D λέγε.

ΑΘ. Ἄκουσον δὴ νῦν. εἰσὶ πολιτειῶν οἷον
μητέρες δύο τινές, ἐξ ὧν τὰς ἄλλας γεγονέναι
λέγων ἄν τις ὀρθῶς λέγοι. καὶ τὴν μὲν προσαγορεύειν μοναρχίαν ὀρθόν, τὴν δ' αὖ δημοκρατίαν·
καὶ τῆς μὲν τὸ Περσῶν γένος ἄκρον ἔχειν, τῆς δὲ
ἡμᾶς. αἱ δ' ἄλλαι σχεδὸν ἅπασαι, καθάπερ

¹ ἐφθαρμένα: ἐσπαρμένα MSS. (bracketed by Cobet, Schanz).

miserable plight.   Such, O Megillus and Clinias, are
the charges we have to make against the so-called
statesmen and lawgivers, both of the past and of the
present, in order that, by investigating their causes,
we may discover what different course ought to have
been pursued; just as, in the case before us, we
called it a blunder to establish by law a government
that is great or unblended, our idea being that a
State ought to be free and wise and in friendship
with itself, and that the lawgiver should legislate
with a view to this.   Nor let it surprise us that,
while we have often already proposed ends which
the legislator should, as we say, aim at in his legislation, the various ends thus proposed are apparently
different.   One needs to reflect that wisdom and
friendship, when stated to be the aim in view, are
not really different aims, but identical; and, if we
meet with many other such terms, let not this fact
disturb us.

CLIN.   We shall endeavour to bear this in mind
as we traverse the arguments again.   But for the
moment, as regards friendship, wisdom and freedom,
—tell us, what was it you intended to say that the
lawgiver ought to aim at?

ATH.   Listen.   There are two mother-forms of
constitution, so to call them, from which one may truly
say all the rest are derived.   Of these the one is
properly termed monarchy, the other democracy,
the extreme case of the former being the Persian
polity, and of the latter the Athenian; the rest are

---

2 [πρὸς τὸ σωφρονεῖν] bracketed by Schanz: the following
[ἢ] is absent from the best MSS.

3 βουλόμενον: βουλόμενος MSS. (bracketed by Badham,
Schanz).

693 εἶπον, ἐκ τούτων εἰσὶ διαπεποικιλμέναι. δεῖ δὴ
οὖν καὶ ἀναγκαῖον μεταλαβεῖν ἀμφοῖν τούτοιν,
εἴπερ ἐλευθερία τ' ἔσται καὶ φιλία μετὰ φρονή-
Ε σεως· ὃ δὴ βούλεται ἡμῖν ὁ λόγος προστάττειν,
λέγων ὡς οὐκ ἄν ποτε τούτων πόλις ἄμοιρος
γενομένη πολιτευθῆναι δύναιτ' ἂν καλῶς.

ΚΛ. Πῶς γὰρ ἄν;

ΑΘ. Ἡ μὲν τοίνυν τὸ μοναρχικόν, ἡ δὲ τὸ
ἐλεύθερον ἀγαπήσασα μειζόνως ἢ ἔδει μόνον,
οὐδέτερα τὰ μέτρια κέκτηται τούτων· αἱ δὲ ὑμέ-
τεραι, ἥ τε Λακωνικὴ καὶ Κρητική, μᾶλλον.
Ἀθηναῖοι δὲ καὶ Πέρσαι τὸ μὲν πάλαι οὕτω
694 πως, τὸ νῦν δὲ ἧττον. τὰ δ' αἴτια διέλθωμεν.
ἦ γάρ;

ΚΛ. Πάντως, εἴ γέ που μέλλομεν ὃ προὐθέμεθα
περαίνειν.

ΑΘ. Ἀκούωμεν δή. Πέρσαι γὰρ ὅτε μὲν τὸ
μέτριον μᾶλλον δουλείας τε καὶ ἐλευθερίας ἦγον
ἐπὶ Κύρου, πρῶτον μὲν ἐλεύθεροι ἐγένοντο, ἔπειτα
δὲ ἄλλων πολλῶν δεσπόται. ἐλευθερίας γὰρ
ἄρχοντες, μεταδιδόντες ἀρχομένοις καὶ ἐπὶ τὸ
ἴσον ἄγοντες μᾶλλον φίλοι τε ἦσαν στρατιῶται
Β στρατηγοῖς καὶ προθύμους αὐτοὺς ἐν τοῖς κινδύ-
νοις παρείχοντο, καὶ εἴ τις αὖ φρόνιμος ἦν ἐν
αὐτοῖς καὶ βουλεύειν δυνατός, οὐ φθονεροῦ τοῦ
βασιλέως ὄντος, διδόντος δὲ παρρησίαν καὶ τι-
μῶντος τοὺς εἴς τι δυναμένους συμβουλεύειν,
κοινὴν τὴν τοῦ φρονεῖν εἰς τὸ μέσον παρείχετο
δύναμιν, καὶ πάντα δὴ τότε ἐπέδωκεν αὐτοῖς δι'
ἐλευθερίαν τε καὶ φιλίαν καὶ νοῦ κοινωνίαν.

---

¹ Cp. 756 E; Arist. Pol. 1266ᵃ 1 ff.

practically all, as I said, modifications of these two. Now it is essential for a polity to partake of both these two forms, if it is to have freedom and friendliness combined with wisdom. And that is what our argument intends to enjoin, when it declares that a State which does not partake of these can never be rightly constituted.[1]

CLIN. It could not.

ATH. Since the one embraced monarchy and the other freedom, unmixed and in excess, neither of them has either in due measure : your Laconian and Cretan States are better in this respect, as were the Athenian and Persian in old times—in contrast to their present condition. Shall we expound the reasons for this ?

CLIN. By all means—that is if we mean to complete the task we have set ourselves.

ATH. Let us attend then. When the Persians, under Cyrus, maintained the due balance between slavery and freedom, they became, first of all, free themselves, and, after that, masters of many others. For when the rulers gave a share of freedom to their subjects and advanced them to a position of equality, the soldiers were more friendly towards their officers and showed their devotion in times of danger ; and if there was any wise man amongst them, able to give counsel, since the king was not jealous but allowed free speech and respected those who could help at all by their counsel,—such a man had the opportunity of contributing to the common stock the fruit of his wisdom. Consequently, at that time all their affairs made progress, owing to their freedom, friendliness and mutual interchange of reason.

694 ΚΛ. Ἔοικέ γέ πως τὰ λεγόμενα οὕτω γεγονέναι.

C ΑΘ. Πῆ δὴ οὖν ποτὲ ἀπώλετο ἐπὶ Καμβύσου καὶ πάλιν ἐπὶ Δαρείου σχεδὸν ἐσώθη ; βούλεσθε οἷον μαντείᾳ διανοηθέντες χρώμεθα ;

ΚΛ. Φέρει γοῦν ἡμῖν σκέψιν τοῦ γ'[1] ἐφ' ὅπερ ὡρμήκαμεν.

ΑΘ. Μαντεύομαι δὴ νῦν περί γε Κύρου τὰ μὲν ἄλλ' αὐτὸν στρατηγόν τε ἀγαθὸν εἶναι καὶ φιλό-πολιν, παιδείας δὲ ὀρθῆς οὐχ ἧφθαι τὸ παράπαν οἰκονομίᾳ τε οὐδὲν τὸν νοῦν προσεσχηκέναι.

ΚΛ. Πῶς δὴ τὸ τοιοῦτον φῶμεν ;

D ΑΘ. Ἔοικεν ἐκ νέου στρατεύεσθαι διὰ βίου, ταῖς γυναιξὶ παραδοὺς τοὺς παῖδας τρέφειν, αἱ δὲ ὡς εὐδαίμονας αὐτοὺς ἐκ τῶν παίδων εὐθὺς καὶ μακαρίους ἤδη γεγονότας καὶ ἐπιδεεῖς ὄντας τού-των οὐδενὸς ἔτρεφον· κωλύουσαι δὲ ὡς οὖσιν ἱκανῶς εὐδαίμοσι μήτε αὐτοῖς ἐναντιοῦσθαι μη-δένα εἰς μηδέν, ἐπαινεῖν τε ἀναγκάζουσαι ⟨πᾶν⟩[2] πάντας τὸ λεγόμενον ἢ πραττόμενον ὑπ' αὐτῶν, ἔθρεψαν τοιούτους τινάς.

ΚΛ. Καλήν, ὡς ἔοικας, τροφὴν εἴρηκας.

E ΑΘ. Γυναικείαν μὲν οὖν βασιλίδων γυναικῶν, νεωστὶ γεγονυιῶν πλουσίων καὶ ἐν ἀνδρῶν ἐρημίᾳ, διὰ τὸ μὴ σχολάζειν ὑπὸ πολέμων καὶ πολλῶν κινδύνων, τοὺς παῖδας τρεφουσῶν.

ΚΛ. Ἔχει γὰρ λόγον.

ΑΘ. Ὁ δὲ πατήρ γε αὐτοῖς αὖ ποίμνια μὲν καὶ πρόβατα καὶ ἀγέλας ἀνδρῶν τε καὶ ἄλλων πολ-
695 λῶν πολλὰς ἐκτᾶτο, αὐτοὺς δὲ οἷς ταῦτα παρα-

---

[1] τοῦ γ': τοῦτο MSS.: τοῦ Badham, Schanz.
[2] ⟨πᾶν⟩ I add.

CLIN. Probably that is pretty much the way in which the matters you speak of took place.

ATH. How came it, then, that they were ruined in Cambyses' reign, and nearly restored again under Darius? Shall I use a kind of divination to picture this?

CLIN. Yes: that certainly will help us to gain a view of the object of our search.

ATH. What I now divine regarding Cyrus is this, —that, although otherwise a good and patriotic commander, he was entirely without a right education, and had paid no attention to household management.

CLIN. What makes us say this?

ATH. Probably he spent all his life from boyhood in soldiering, and entrusted his children to the womenfolk to rear up; and they brought them up from earliest childhood as though they had already attained to Heaven's favour and felicity, and were lacking in no celestial gift; and so by treating them as the special favourites of Heaven, and forbidding anyone to oppose them in anything, and compelling everyone to praise their every word and deed, they reared them up into what they were.

CLIN. A fine rearing, I should say!

ATH. Say rather, a womanish rearing by royal women lately grown rich, who, while the men were absent, detained by many dangers and wars, reared up the children.

CLIN. That sounds reasonable.

ATH. And their father, while gaining flocks and sheep and plenty of herds, both of men and of many other chattels, yet knew not that the children to whom he should bequeath them were without train-

PLATO

695 δώσειν ἔμελλεν ἠγνόει τὴν πατρῴαν οὐ παιδευ-
ομένους τέχνην, οὖσαν [Περσικήν, ποιμένων ὄντων
Περσῶν, τραχείας χώρας ἐκγόνων,]¹ σκληρὰν καὶ
ἱκανὴν ποιμένας ἀπεργάζεσθαι μάλα ἰσχυροὺς
καὶ δυναμένους θυραυλεῖν καὶ ἀγρυπνεῖν καί, εἰ
στρατεύεσθαι δέοι, στρατεύεσθαι. διεφθαρμένην
δὲ παιδείαν ὑπὸ τῆς λεγομένης εὐδαιμονίας [τὴν
Μηδικὴν]² περιεῖδεν ὑπὸ γυναικῶν τε καὶ εὐνού-
χων παιδευθέντας αὐτοῦ τοὺς υἱεῖς, ὅθεν ἐγένοντο
B οἵους ἦν αὐτοὺς εἰκὸς γενέσθαι, τροφῇ ἀνεπι-
πλήκτῳ τραφέντας. παραλαβόντες δ᾽ οὖν οἱ
παῖδες τελευτήσαντος Κύρου τρυφῆς μεστοὶ καὶ
ἀνεπιπληξίας, πρῶτον μὲν τὸν ἕτερον ἅτερος
ἀπέκτεινε τῷ ἴσῳ ἀγανακτῶν, μετὰ δὲ τοῦτο
αὐτὸς μαινόμενος ὑπὸ μέθης τε καὶ ἀπαιδευσίας
τὴν ἀρχὴν ἀπώλεσεν ὑπὸ Μήδων τε καὶ τοῦ λεγομένου τότε εὐνούχου, καταφρονήσαντος τῆς Καμβύσου μωρίας.

ΚΛ. Λέγεται δὴ ταῦτά γε, καὶ ἔοικε σχεδὸν
C οὕτω πως γεγονέναι.

ΑΘ. Καὶ μὴν καὶ πάλιν εἰς Πέρσας ἐλθεῖν τὴν
ἀρχὴν διὰ Δαρείου καὶ τῶν ἑπτὰ λέγεταί που.

ΚΛ. Τί μήν;

ΑΘ. Θεωρῶμεν δὴ ξυνεπόμενοι τῷ λόγῳ. Δα-
ρεῖος γὰρ βασιλέως οὐκ ἦν υἱὸς παιδείᾳ τε οὐ
διατρυφώσῃ τεθραμμένος, ἐλθὼν δ᾽ εἰς τὴν ἀρχὴν
καὶ λαβὼν αὐτὴν ἕβδομος διείλετο ἑπτὰ μέρη
τεμόμενος, ὧν καὶ νῦν ἔτι σμικρὰ ὀνείρατα λέ-

---

¹ [Περσικήν . . . ἐκγόνων] bracketed by Ast, Schanz.
² [τὴν Μηδικὴν] I bracket (cp. England).

---

¹ i.e. Cambyses killed Smerdis.

228

ing in their father's craft, which was a hard one, fit
to turn out shepherds of great strength, able to camp
out in the open and to keep watch and, if need be,
to go campaigning. He overlooked the fact that
his sons were trained by women and eunuchs and
that the indulgence shown them as "Heaven's
darlings" had ruined their training, whereby they
became such as they were likely to become when
reared with a rearing that "spared the rod." So
when, at the death of Cyrus, his sons took over the
kingdom, over-pampered and undisciplined as they
were, first, the one killed the other,[1] through annoy-
ance at his being put on an equality with himself,
and presently, being mad with drink and debauchery,
he lost his own throne at the hands of the Medes,
under the man then called the Eunuch,[2] who despised
the stupidity of Cambyses.

CLIN. That, certainly, is the story, and probably
it is near to the truth.

ATH. Further, the story tells how the kingdom
was restored to the Persians through Darius and the
Seven.

CLIN. It does.

ATH. Let us follow the story and see how things
went.[3] Darius was not a king's son, nor was he
reared luxuriously. When he came and seized the
kingdom, with his six companions, he divided it into
seven parts, of which some small vestiges remain
even to this day ; and he thought good to manage it
by enacting laws into which he introduced some

[2] *i.e.* the Magian, Gomates, who personated Smerdis and
claimed the kingdom. After seven months' reign this
usurper was slain by seven Persian nobles, of whom Darius
was one (521 B.C.).

[3] Cf. Hdt. III. 68–88.

695D λείπται, καὶ νόμους ἠξίου θέμενος οἰκεῖν ἰσότητά
τινα κοινὴν εἰσφέρων, καὶ τὸν τοῦ Κύρου δασμὸν
ὃν ὑπέσχετο Πέρσαις εἰς τὸν νόμον ἐνέδει, φιλίαν
πορίζων καὶ κοινωνίαν πᾶσι Πέρσαις, χρήμασι
καὶ δωρεαῖς τὸν Περσῶν δῆμον προσαγόμενος·
τοιγαροῦν αὐτῷ τὰ στρατεύματα μετ᾽ εὐνοίας
προσεκτήσατο χώρας οὐκ ἐλάττους ὧν κατέλιπε
Κῦρος. μετὰ δὲ Δαρεῖον ὁ τῇ βασιλικῇ καὶ τρυ-
φώσῃ πάλιν παιδευθεὶς παιδείᾳ Ξέρξης. Ὦ
Δαρεῖε, εἰπεῖν ἐστι δικαιότατον ἴσως, ὡς[1] τὸ
E Κύρου κακὸν οὐκ ἔμαθες, ἐθρέψω δὲ Ξέρξην ἐν
τοῖς αὐτοῖς ἤθεσιν ἐν οἷσπερ Κῦρος Καμβύσην.
ὁ δέ, ἅτε τῶν αὐτῶν παιδείων γενόμενος ἔκγονος,
παραπλήσια ἀπετέλεσε τοῖς Καμβύσου παθή-
μασι· καὶ σχεδὸν ἔκ γε τοσούτου βασιλεὺς ἐν
Πέρσαις οὐδείς πω μέγας ἐγγέγονεν ἀληθῶς, πλήν
γε ὀνόματι. τὸ δ᾽ αἴτιον οὐ τύχης, ὡς ὁ ἐμὸς
696 λόγος, ἀλλ᾽ ὁ κακὸς βίος ὃν οἱ τῶν διαφερόντως
πλουσίων καὶ τυράννων παῖδες τὰ πολλὰ ζῶσιν·
οὐ γὰρ μή ποτε γένηται παῖς καὶ ἀνὴρ καὶ γέρων
ἐκ ταύτης τῆς τροφῆς διαφέρων πρὸς ἀρετήν.
ἃ δή, φαμέν, τῷ νομοθέτῃ σκεπτέον, καὶ ἡμῖν δὲ
ἐν τῷ νῦν παρόντι. δίκαιον μήν, ὦ Λακεδαιμόνιοι, τοῦτό γε τῇ πόλει ὑμῶν ἀποδιδόναι, ὅτι
πενίᾳ καὶ πλούτῳ καὶ ἰδιωτείᾳ καὶ βασιλείᾳ
B διαφέρουσαν οὐδ᾽ ἡντινοῦν τιμὴν καὶ τροφὴν
νέμετε, ἃς μὴ τὸ κατ᾽ ἀρχὰς ὑμῖν θεῖον παρὰ θεοῦ
διεμαντεύσατό τινος. οὐ γὰρ δὴ δεῖ κατὰ πόλιν

---

[1] ὡς Stephens : ὃς MSS. (bracketed by Ast)

measure of political equality, and also incorporated in the law regulations about the tribute-money which Cyrus had promised the Persians, whereby he secured friendliness and fellowship amongst all classes of the Persians, and won over the populace by money and gifts; and because of this, the devotion of his armies won for him as much more land as Cyrus had originally bequeathed. After Darius came Xerxes, and he again was brought up with the luxurious rearing of a royal house : " O Darius "—for it is thus one may rightly address the father—" how is it that you have ignored the blunder of Cyrus, and have reared up Xerxes in just the same habits of life in which Cyrus reared Cambyses ? " And Xerxes, being the product of the same training, ended by repeating almost exactly the misfortunes of Cambyses. Since then there has hardly ever been a single Persian king who was really, as well as nominally, " Great." [1] And, as our argument asserts, the cause of this does not lie in luck, but in the evil life which is usually lived by the sons of excessively rich monarchs; for such an upbringing can never produce either boy or man or greybeard of surpassing goodness. To this, we say, the lawgiver must give heed, —as must we ourselves on the present occasion. It is proper, however, my Lacedaemonian friends, to give your State credit for this at least,—that you assign no different honour or training whatsoever to poverty or wealth, to the commoner or the king, beyond what your original oracle [2] declared at the bidding of some god. Nor indeed is it right that pre-eminent

---

[1] The Persian monarch was commonly styled " the Great King."

[2] The laws of Lycurgus.

696 γε εἶναι τὰς τιμὰς ὑπερεχούσας, ὅτι τίς ἐστι
πλούτῳ διαφέρων, ἐπεὶ οὐδ᾽ ὅτι ταχὺς ἢ καλὸς ἢ
ἰσχυρὸς ἄνευ τινὸς ἀρετῆς, οὐδ᾽ ἀρετῆς ἧς ἂν
σωφροσύνη ἀπῇ.

ΜΕ. Πῶς τοῦτο, ὦ ξένε, λέγεις ;

ΑΘ. Ἀνδρία που μόριον ἀρετῆς ἕν ;

ΜΕ. Πῶς γὰρ οὔ ;

ΑΘ. Δίκασον τοίνυν αὐτὸς τὸν λόγον ἀκούσας,
εἴ σοι δέξαιο ἂν σύνοικον ἢ γείτονα εἶναί τινα
σφόδρα μὲν ἀνδρεῖον, μὴ σώφρονα δὲ ἀλλ᾽
ἀκόλαστον.

C ΜΕ. Εὐφήμει.

ΑΘ. Τί δέ ; τεχνικὸν μὲν καὶ περὶ ταῦτα σο-
φόν, ἄδικον δέ ;

ΜΕ. Οὐδαμῶς.

ΑΘ. Ἀλλὰ μὴν τό γε δίκαιον οὐ φύεται χωρὶς
τοῦ σωφρονεῖν.

ΜΕ. Πῶς γὰρ ἄν ;

ΑΘ. Οὐδὲ μὴν ὅν γε σοφὸν ἡμεῖς νῦν δὴ πρού-
θέμεθα, τὸν τὰς ἡδονὰς καὶ λύπας κεκτημένον
συμφώνους τοῖς ὀρθοῖς λόγοις καὶ ἑπομένας.

ΜΕ. Οὐ γὰρ οὖν.

D ΑΘ. Ἔτι δὴ καὶ τόδε ἐπισκεψώμεθα τῶν ἐν
ταῖς πόλεσι τιμήσεων ἕνεκα, ποῖαί τε ὀρθαὶ καὶ
μὴ γίγνονται ἑκάστοτε.

ΜΕ. Τὸ ποῖον ;

ΑΘ. Σωφροσύνη ἄνευ πάσης τῆς ἄλλης ἀρετῆς
ἐν ψυχῇ τινι μεμονωμένη τίμιον ἢ ἄτιμον γίγνοιτ᾽
ἂν κατὰ δίκην ;

ΜΕ. Οὐκ ἔχω ὅπως εἴπω.

ΑΘ. Καὶ μὴν εἴρηκάς γε μετρίως· εἰπὼν γὰρ

_____
[1] Cp. 689 D.

honours in a State should be conferred on a man
because he is specially wealthy, any more than it is
right to confer them because he is swift or comely
or strong without any virtue, or with a virtue devoid
of temperance.

MEG. What do you mean by that, Stranger?

ATH. Courage is, presumably, one part of virtue.

MEG. Certainly.

ATH. Now that you have heard the argument,
judge for yourself whether you would welcome as
housemate or neighbour a man who is extremely
courageous, but licentious rather than temperate.

MEG. Don't suggest such a thing!

ATH. Well then,—a man wise in arts and crafts,
but unjust.

MEG. Certainly not.

ATH. But justice, surely, is not bred apart from
temperance.

MEG. Impossible.

ATH. Nor is he whom we recently proposed [1] as
our type of wisdom,—the man who has his feelings
of pleasure and pain in accord with the dictates of
right reason and obedient thereto.

MEG. No, indeed.

ATH. Here is a further point we must consider, in
order to judge about the conferment of honours in
States, when they are right and when wrong.

MEG. What point?

ATH. If temperance existed alone in a man's soul,
divorced from all the rest of virtue, would it justly be
held in honour or the reverse?

MEG. I cannot tell what reply to make.

ATH. Yet, in truth, you have made a reply, and a
reasonable one. For if you had declared for either

PLATO

696 δὴ ὧν ἠρόμην ὁποτερονοῦν παρὰ μέλος ἔμοιγ' ἂν
δοκεῖς φθέγξασθαι.

ΜΕ. Καλῶς τοίνυν γεγονὸς ἂν εἴη.

ΑΘ. Εἶεν· τὸ μὲν δὴ πρόσθημα, ὧν τιμαί τε
Ε καὶ ἀτιμίαι, οὐ λόγου ἀλλά τινος μᾶλλον ἀλόγου
σιγῆς ἄξιον ἂν εἴη.

ΜΕ. Σωφροσύνην μοι φαίνει λέγειν.

ΑΘ. Ναί. τὸ δέ γε τῶν ἄλλων πλεῖστα
ἡμᾶς ὠφελοῦν μετὰ τῆς προσθήκης μάλιστ' ἂν
τιμώμενον ὀρθότατα τιμῷτο, καὶ τὸ δεύτερον
δευτέρως· καὶ οὕτω δὴ κατὰ τὸν ἑξῆς λόγον τὰς
ἐφεξῆς τιμὰς λάγχανον ἕκαστον ὀρθῶς ἂν λαγ-
χάνοι.

697 ΜΕ. Ἔχει ταύτῃ.

ΑΘ. Τί οὖν; οὐ νομοθέτου καὶ ταῦτα αὖ
φήσομεν εἶναι διανέμειν;

ΜΕ. Καὶ μάλα.

ΑΘ. Βούλει δὴ τὰ μὲν ἅπαντα καὶ ἐφ' ἕκαστον
ἔργον καὶ κατὰ σμικρὰ ἐκείνῳ δῶμεν νεῖμαι, τὸ
δὲ τριχῇ διελεῖν, ἐπειδὴ νόμων ἐσμὲν καὶ αὐτοί
πως ἐπιθυμηταί, πειραθῶμεν διατεμεῖν χωρὶς τά
τε μέγιστα καὶ δεύτερα καὶ τρίτα;

ΜΕ. Πάνυ μὲν οὖν.

ΑΘ. Λέγομεν τοίνυν ὅτι πόλιν, ὡς ἔοικε, τὴν
Β μέλλουσαν σῴζεσθαί τε καὶ εὐδαιμονήσειν εἰς
δύναμιν ἀνθρωπίνην δεῖ καὶ ἀναγκαῖον τιμάς τε
καὶ ἀτιμίας διανέμειν ὀρθῶς. ἔστι δὲ ὀρθῶς ἄρα
τιμιώτατα μὲν καὶ πρῶτα τὰ περὶ τὴν ψυχὴν

---

[1] *i.e.* "temperance," regarded as merely an adjunct to civic merit, requires no further discussion at this point.

of the alternatives in my question, you would have said what is, to my mind, quite out of tune.

MEG. So it has turned out to be all right.

ATH. Very good. Accordingly, the additional element in objects deserving of honour or dishonour will be one that demands not speech so much as a kind of speechless silence.[1]

MEG. I suppose you mean temperance.

ATH. Yes. And of the rest, that which, with the addition of temperance, benefits us most would best deserve to be held in the highest honour, and the second in degree of benefit put second in order of honour; and so with each of the others in succession—to each it will be proper to assign the honour due to its rank.

MEG. Just so.

ATH. Well then, shall we not declare that the distribution of these things is the lawgiver's task?

MEG. Certainly.

ATH. Is it your wish that we should hand over the whole distribution to him, to deal with every case and all the details, while we – as legal enthusiasts ourselves also—confine ourselves to making a threefold division, and endeavour to distinguish what comes first in importance, and what second and third?[2]

MEG. By all means.

ATH. We declare, then, that a State which is to endure, and to be as happy as it is possible for man to be, must of necessity dispense honours rightly. And the right way is this: it shall be laid down that the goods of the soul are highest

---

[2] Cp. 631 B, C; 661 A ff.; 726 A ff.; Arist. *Eth. N.* 1098^b 12 ff.

697 ἀγαθὰ κεῖσθαι, σωφροσύνης ὑπαρχούσης αὐτῇ,
δεύτερα δὲ τὰ περὶ τὸ σῶμα καλὰ καὶ ἀγαθά,
καὶ τρίτα τὰ περὶ τὴν οὐσίαν καὶ χρήματα λεγόμενα. τούτων δὲ ἂν ἐκτός τις βαίνῃ νομοθέτης
ἢ πόλις, εἰς τιμὰς ἢ χρήματα προάγουσα ἤ τι
C τῶν ὑστέρων εἰς τὸ πρόσθεν τιμαῖς τάττουσα,
οὔθ' ὅσιον οὔτε πολιτικὸν ἂν δρῴη πρᾶγμα.
εἰρήσθω ταῦτα ἢ πῶς ἡμῖν;

ΜΕ. Πάνυ μὲν οὖν εἰρήσθω σαφῶς.

ΑΘ. Ταῦτα μὲν τοίνυν ἡμᾶς ἐπὶ πλέον ἐποίησεν
εἰπεῖν ἡ Περσῶν πέρι διάσκεψις τῆς πολιτείας.
ἀνευρίσκομεν δὲ [ἐπὶ][1] ἔτι χείρους αὐτοὺς γε-
γονότας· τὴν δὲ αἰτίαν φαμὲν ὅτι τὸ ἐλεύθερον
λίαν ἀφελόμενοι τοῦ δήμου, τὸ δεσποτικὸν δ'
ἐπαγαγόντες μᾶλλον τοῦ προσήκοντος, τὸ φίλον
D ἀπώλεσαν καὶ τὸ κοινὸν ἐν τῇ πόλει. τούτου δὲ
φθαρέντος οὔθ' ἡ τῶν ἀρχόντων βουλὴ ὑπὲρ
ἀρχομένων καὶ τοῦ δήμου βουλεύεται, ἀλλ' ἕνεκα
τῆς αὑτῶν ἀρχῆς, ἄν τι καὶ σμικρὸν πλέον
ἑκάστοτε ἡγῶνται ἔσεσθαι σφισιν, ἀναστάτους
μὲν πόλεις, ἀνάστατα δὲ ἔθνη φίλια πυρὶ κατα-
φθείραντες, ἐχθρῶς τε καὶ ἀνηλεῶς μισοῦντες
μισοῦνται· ὅταν τε εἰς χρείαν τοῦ μάχεσθαι περὶ
ἑαυτῶν τοὺς δήμους ἀφικνῶνται, οὐδὲν κοινὸν ἐν
E αὑτοῖς αὖ μετὰ προθυμίας τοῦ ἐθέλειν κινδυνεύειν
καὶ μάχεσθαι ἀνευρίσκουσιν, ἀλλὰ κεκτημένοι
μυριάδας ἀπεράντους λογισμῷ ἀχρήστους εἰς
πόλεμον πάσας κέκτηνται, καὶ καθάπερ ἐνδεεῖς
ἀνθρώπων μισθούμενοι, ὑπὸ μισθωτῶν καὶ ὀθνείων
ἀνθρώπων ἡγοῦνταί ποτε σωθήσεσθαι· πρὸς δὲ

---

[1] [ἐπὶ] bracketed by Stephens (ἐπὶ ἔτη Schneider).

in honour and come first, provided that the soul possesses temperance; second come the good and fair things of the body; and third the so-called goods of substance and property. And if any law-giver or State transgresses these rules, either by promoting wealth to honours, or by raising one of the lower goods to a higher rank by means of honours, he will be guilty of a breach both of religion and of statesmanship. Shall this be our declaration, or what?

MEG. By all means let us declare this plainly.

ATH. It was our investigation of the polity of the Persians that caused us to discuss these matters at greater length. We find that they grew still worse, the reason being, as we say, that by robbing the commons unduly of their liberty and introducing despotism in excess, they destroyed in the State the bonds of friendliness and fellowship. And when these are destroyed, the policy of the rulers no longer consults for the good of the subjects and the commons, but solely for the maintenance of their own power; if they think that it will profit them in the least degree, they are ready at any time to overturn States and to overturn and burn up friendly nations; and thus they both hate and are hated with a fierce and ruthless hatred. And when they come to need the commons, to fight in their support, they find in them no patriotism or readiness to endanger their lives in battle; so that, although they possess countless myriads of men, they are all useless for war, and they hire soldiers from abroad as though they were short of men, and imagine that their safety will be secured by hirelings and aliens. And besides all this, they

698 τούτοις ἀμαθαίνειν ἀναγκάζονται, λέγοντες ἔργοις ὅτι λῆρος πρὸς χρυσόν τε καὶ ἄργυρόν ἐστιν ἑκάστοτε τὰ λεγόμενα τίμια καὶ καλὰ κατὰ πόλιν.

ΜΕ. Πάνυ μὲν οὖν.

ΑΘ. Τὰ μὲν δὴ περί γε Περσῶν, ὡς οὐκ ὀρθῶς τὰ νῦν διοικεῖται διὰ τὴν σφόδρα δουλείαν τε καὶ δεσποτείαν, τέλος ἐχέτω.

ΜΕ. Πάνυ μὲν οὖν.

ΑΘ. Τὰ δὲ περὶ τὴν τῆς Ἀττικῆς αὖ πολιτείαν τὸ μετὰ τοῦτο ὡσαύτως ἡμᾶς διεξελθεῖν χρεών, ὡς ἡ παντελὴς καὶ ἀπὸ πασῶν ἀρχῶν ἐλευθερία τῆς μέτρον ἐχούσης ἀρχῆς ὑφ᾿ αἱρετῶν[1] οὐ σμικρῷ
B χείρων· ἡμῖν γὰρ κατ᾿ ἐκεῖνον τὸν χρόνον ὅτε ἡ Περσῶν ἐπίθεσις τοῖς Ἕλλησιν, ἴσως δὲ σχεδὸν ἅπασι τοῖς τὴν Εὐρώπην οἰκοῦσιν, ἐγίγνετο, πολιτεία τε ἦν παλαιὰ καὶ ἐκ τιμημάτων ἀρχαί τινες τεττάρων, καὶ δεσπότις ἐνῆν τις αἰδώς, δι᾿ ἣν δουλεύοντες τοῖς τότε νόμοις ζῆν ἠθέλομεν. καὶ πρὸς τούτοις δὴ τὸ μέγεθος τοῦ στόλου κατά τε γῆν καὶ κατὰ θάλατταν γενόμενον, φόβον ἄπορον ἐμβαλόν, δουλείαν ἔτι μείζονα ἐποίησεν
C ἡμᾶς τοῖς τε ἄρχουσι καὶ τοῖς νόμοις δουλεῦσαι. καὶ διὰ πάντα ταῦθ᾿ ἡμῖν ξυνέπεσε πρὸς ἡμᾶς αὐτοὺς σφόδρα φιλία. σχεδὸν γὰρ δέκα ἔτεσι πρὸ τῆς ἐν Σαλαμῖνι ναυμαχίας ἀφίκετο Δᾶτις Περσικὸν στόλον ἄγων πέμψαντος Δαρείου διαρρήδην ἐπί τε Ἀθηναίους καὶ Ἐρετριέας, ἐξανδραποδισάμενον ἀγαγεῖν, θάνατον αὐτῷ προειπὼν μὴ πράξαντι ταῦτα. καὶ ὁ Δᾶτις τοὺς μὲν Ἐρετριέας

---

[1] αἱρετῶν : ἑτέρων MSS., edd.

[1] That of Solon.

inevitably display their ignorance, inasmuch as by their acts they declare that the things reputed to be honourable and noble in a State are never anything but dross compared to silver and gold.

MEG. Very true.

ATH. So let this be the conclusion of our account of the Persian empire, and how its present evil administration is due to excess of slavery and of despotism.

MEG. By all means.

ATH. We ought to examine next, in like manner, the Attic polity, and show how complete liberty, unfettered by any authority, is vastly inferior to a moderate form of government under elected magistrates. At the time when the Persians made their onslaught upon the Greeks—and indeed one might say on nearly all the nations of Europe—we Athenians had an ancient constitution,[1] and magistrates based on a fourfold grading; and we had Reverence, which acted as a kind of queen, causing us to live as the willing slaves of the existing laws. Moreover, the vastness of the Persian armament that threatened us both by sea and land, by the desperate fear it inspired, bound us still more closely in the bonds of slavery to our rulers and our laws; and because of all this, our mutual friendliness and patriotism was greatly intensified. It was just about ten years before the seafight at Salamis that the Persian force arrived under Datis, whom Darius had despatched expressly against the Athenians and Eretrians, with orders to bring them back in chains, and with the warning that death would be the penalty of failure. So within a very short time Datis, with his many myriads, captured by force the

698D ἔν τινι βραχεῖ χρόνῳ παντάπασι κατὰ κράτος τε
εἷλε μυριάσι συχναῖς, καί τινα λόγον εἰς τὴν
ἡμετέραν πόλιν ἀφῆκε φοβερόν, ὡς οὐδεὶς Ἐρε-
τριέων αὐτὸν ἀποπεφευγὼς εἴη· συνάψαντες γὰρ
ἄρα τὰς χεῖρας σαγηνεύσαιεν πᾶσαν τὴν Ἐρε-
τρικὴν οἱ στρατιῶται τοῦ Δάτιδος. ὁ δὴ λόγος,
εἴτε ἀληθὴς εἴτε καὶ ὅπῃ ἀφίκετο, τούς τε ἄλλους
Ἕλληνας καὶ δὴ καὶ Ἀθηναίους ἐξέπληττε, καὶ
πρεσβευομένοις αὐτοῖς πανταχόσε βοηθεῖν οὐδεὶς
E ἤθελε πλήν γε Λακεδαιμονίων· οὗτοι δὲ ὑπό τε τοῦ
πρὸς Μεσσήνην ὄντος τότε πολέμου καὶ εἰ δή τι
διεκώλυεν ἄλλο αὐτούς, οὐ γὰρ ἴσμεν λεγόμενον,
ὕστεροι δ᾽ οὖν ἀφίκοντο τῆς ἐν Μαραθῶνι μάχης
γενομένης μιᾷ ἡμέρᾳ. μετὰ δὲ τοῦτο παρασκευαί
τε μεγάλαι λεγόμεναι καὶ ἀπειλαὶ ἐφοίτων μυρίαι
παρὰ βασιλέως. προϊόντος δὲ τοῦ χρόνου Δα-
ρεῖος μὲν τεθνάναι ἐλέχθη, νέος δὲ καὶ σφοδρὸς ὁ
υἱὸς αὐτοῦ παρειληφέναι τὴν ἀρχὴν καὶ οὐδαμῶς
699 ἀφίστασθαι τῆς ὁρμῆς. οἱ δὲ Ἀθηναῖοι πᾶν
τοῦτο ᾤοντο ἐπὶ σφᾶς αὐτοὺς παρασκευάζεσθαι
διὰ τὸ Μαραθῶνι γενόμενον, καὶ ἀκούοντες Ἄθω
τε διορυττόμενον καὶ Ἑλλήσποντον ζευγνύμενον
καὶ τὸ τῶν νεῶν πλῆθος ἡγήσαντο οὔτε κατὰ γῆν
σφίσιν εἶναι σωτηρίαν οὔτε κατὰ θάλατταν·
οὔτε γὰρ βοηθήσειν αὐτοῖς οὐδένα, μεμνημένοι ὡς
οὐδ᾽ ὅτε τὸ πρότερον ἦλθον καὶ τὰ περὶ Ἐρέτριαν
διεπράξαντο, σφίσι γε οὐδεὶς τότε ἐβοήθησεν οὐδ᾽
B ἐκινδύνευσε ξυμμαχόμενος. ταὐτὸν δὴ προσεδό-
κων καὶ τότε γενήσεσθαι τό γε κατὰ γῆν. καὶ
κατὰ θάλατταν δ᾽ αὖ πᾶσαν ἀπορίαν ἑώρων

whole of the Eretrians; and to Athens he sent on an alarming account of how not a man of the Eretrians had escaped him : the soldiers of Datis had joined hands and swept the whole of Eretria clean as with a draw-net. This account—whether true, or whatever its origin—struck terror into the Greeks generally, and especially the Athenians; but when they sent out embassies in every direction to seek aid, all refused, except the Lacedaemonians; and they were hindered by the war they were then waging against Messene, and possibly by other obstacles, about which we have no information, with the result that they arrived too late by one single day for the battle which took place at Marathon. After this, endless threats and stories of huge preparations kept arriving from the Persian king. Then, as time went on, news came that Darius was dead, and that his son, who had succeeded to the throne, was a young hothead, and still keen on the projected expedition. The Athenians imagined that all these preparations were aimed against them because of the affair at Marathon ; and when they heard of how the canal had been made through Athos, and the bridge thrown over the Hellespont, and were told of the vast number of vessels in the Persian flotilla, then they felt that there was no salvation for them by land, nor yet by sea. By land they had no hopes that anyone would come to their aid ; for they remembered how, on the first arrival of the Persians and their subjugation of Eretria, nobody helped them or ventured to join in the fight with them ; and so they expected that the same thing would happen again on this occasion. By sea, too, they saw no hope of safety, with more

PLATO

699 σωτηρίας νεῶν χιλίων καὶ ἔτι πλεόνων ἐπιφερομένων. μίαν δὴ σωτηρίαν ξυνενόουν, λεπτὴν μὲν
καὶ ἄπορον, μόνην δ᾽ οὖν, βλέψαντες πρὸς τὸ
πρότερον γενόμενον, ὡς ἐξ ἀπόρων καὶ τότε
ἐφαίνετο γενέσθαι τὸ νικῆσαι μαχομένους· ἐπὶ
δὲ τῆς ἐλπίδος ὀχούμενοι ταύτης εὕρισκον κατα-
φυγὴν αὑτοῖς εἰς αὑτοὺς μόνους εἶναι καὶ τοὺς
C θεούς. ταῦτ᾽ οὖν αὑτοῖς πάντα φιλίαν ἀλλήλων
ἐνεποίει, ὁ φόβος ὁ τότε παρὼν ὅ τε ἐκ τῶν νόμων
τῶν ἔμπροσθεν γεγονώς, ὃν δουλεύοντες τοῖς
πρόσθεν νόμοις ἐκέκτηντο, ἣν αἰδῶ πολλάκις ἐν
τοῖς ἄνω λόγοις εἴπομεν, ᾗ καὶ δουλεύειν ἔφαμεν
δεῖν τοὺς μέλλοντας ἀγαθοὺς ἔσεσθαι, ἧς ὁ δειλὸς
ἐλεύθερος καὶ ἄφοβος· ὃν εἰ τότε μὴ λεὼς [1] ἔλαβεν,
οὐκ ἄν ποτε ξυνελθὼν ἠμύνατο οὐδ᾽ ἤμυνεν ἱεροῖς
τε καὶ τάφοις καὶ πατρίδι καὶ τοῖς ἄλλοις οἰκείοις
D τε ἅμα καὶ φίλοις, ὥσπερ τότ᾽ ἐβοήθησεν, ἀλλὰ
κατὰ σμικρὰ ἂν ἐν τῷ τότε ἡμῶν ἕκαστος σκεδα-
σθεὶς ἄλλος ἄλλοσε διεσπάρη.

ΜΕ. Καὶ μάλα, ὦ ξένε, ὀρθῶς τε εἴρηκας καὶ
σαυτῷ τε καὶ τῇ πατρίδι πρεπόντως.

ΑΘ. Ἔστι ταῦτα, ὦ Μέγιλλε· πρὸς γὰρ σὲ τὰ
ἐν τῷ τότε χρόνῳ γενόμενα, κοινωνὸν τῇ τῶν
πατέρων γεγονότα φύσει, δίκαιον λέγειν. ἐπι-
σκόπει μὴν καὶ σὺ καὶ Κλεινίας εἴ τι πρὸς τὴν
E νομοθεσίαν προσήκοντα λέγομεν· οὐ γὰρ μύθων
ἕνεκα διεξέρχομαι, οὗ λέγω δ᾽ ἕνεκα· ὁρᾶτε γάρ·
ἐπειδή τινα τρόπον ταὐτὸν ἡμῖν ξυμβεβήκει

---

[1] λεὼς : δέος MSS. (δῆμος for δειλὸς Hermann)

---

[1] Cp. 646 E, 647 C, 671 D.

than a thousand war-ships bearing down against
them. One solitary hope of safety did they perceive—a slight one, it is true, and a desperate, yet
the only hope—and it they derived from the events
of the past, when victory in battle appeared to
spring out of a desperate situation ; and buoyed up
by this hope, they discovered that they must rely
for refuge on themselves only and on the gods. So
all this created in them a state of friendliness one
towards another—both the fear which then possessed
them, and that begotten of the past, which they
had acquired by their subjection to the former laws
—the fear to which, in our previous discussions,[1]
we have often given the name of "reverence,"
saying that a man must be subject to this if he
is to be good (though the coward is unfettered and
unaffrighted by it). Unless this fear had then
seized upon our people, they would never have
united in self-defence, nor would they have defended their temples and tombs and fatherland,
and their relatives and friends as well, in the way
in which they then came to the rescue ; but we
would all have been broken up at that time and
dispersed one by one in all directions.

MEG. What you say, Stranger, is perfectly true,
and worthy of your country as well as of yourself.

ATH. That is so, Megillus : it is proper to mention
the events of that period to you, since you share in
the native character of your ancestors. But both
you and Clinias must now consider whether what
we are saying is at all pertinent to our law-making ;
for my narrative is not related for its own sake, but
for the sake of the law-making I speak of. Just
reflect : seeing that we Athenians suffered practically

699 πάθος ὅπερ Πέρσαις, ἐκείνοις μὲν ἐπὶ πᾶσαν δουλείαν ἄγουσι τὸν δῆμον, ἡμῖν δ' αὖ τοὐναντίον
ἐπὶ πᾶσαν ἐλευθερίαν προτρέπουσι τὰ πλήθη,
πῶς δὴ καὶ τί λέγωμεν τοὐντεῦθεν, <εἴπερ>[1] οἱ
προγεγονότες ἡμῖν ἔμπροσθεν λόγοι τρόπον τινὰ
καλῶς εἰσὶν εἰρημένοι ;

700 ΜΕ. Λέγεις εὖ· πειρῶ δ' ἔτι σαφέστερον ἡμῖν
σημῆναι τὸ νῦν λεγόμενον.

ΑΘ. Ἔσται ταῦτα. οὐκ ἦν, ὦ φίλοι, ἡμῖν ἐπὶ
τῶν παλαιῶν νόμων ὁ δῆμός τινων κύριος, ἀλλὰ
τρόπον τινὰ ἑκὼν ἐδούλευε τοῖς νόμοις.

ΜΕ. Ποίοις δὴ λέγεις ;

ΑΘ. Τοῖς περὶ τὴν μουσικὴν πρῶτον τὴν
τότε, ἵνα ἐξ ἀρχῆς διέλθωμεν τὴν τοῦ ἐλευθέρου
λίαν ἐπίδοσιν βίου. διῃρημένη γὰρ δὴ τότε ἦν
ἡμῖν ἡ μουσικὴ κατὰ εἴδη τε ἑαυτῆς ἄττα καὶ
B σχήματα, καί τι ἦν εἶδος ᾠδῆς εὐχαὶ πρὸς θεούς,
ὄνομα δὲ ὕμνοι ἐπεκαλοῦντο· καὶ τούτῳ δὴ τὸ
ἐναντίον ἦν ᾠδῆς ἕτερον εἶδος, θρήνους δέ τις ἂν
αὐτοὺς μάλιστα ἐκάλεσε· καὶ παίωνες ἕτερον,
καὶ ἄλλο Διονύσου γ' αἴνεσες,[2] οἶμαι, διθύραμβος
λεγόμενος. νόμους τε αὐτὸ τοῦτο τοὔνομα ἐκά-
λουν, ᾠδὴν ὥς τινα ἑτέραν· ἐπέλεγον δὲ κιθαρῳ-
δικούς. τούτων δὴ διατεταγμένων καὶ ἄλλων
τινῶν οὐκ ἐξῆν ἄλλῳ εἰς ἄλλο καταχρῆσθαι μέλους
C εἶδος. τὸ δὲ κῦρος τούτων γνῶναί τε καὶ ἅμα
γνόντα δικάσαι ζημιοῦν τε αὖ τὸν μὴ πειθόμενον
οὐ σύριγξ ἦν οὐδέ τινες ἄμουσοι βοαὶ πλήθους,
καθάπερ τὰ νῦν, οὐδ' αὖ κρότοι ἐπαίνους ἀποδι

---

[1] <εἴπερ> I add (Schanz marks a lacuna).
[2] γ' αἴνεσες (so too Post) : γένεσες MSS., edd.

the same fate as the Persians—they through reducing their people to the extreme of slavery, we, on the contrary, by urging on our populace to the extreme of liberty—what are we to say was the sequel, if our earlier statements have been at all nearly correct?

MEG. Well said! Try, however, to make your meaning still more clear to us.

ATH. I will. Under the old laws, my friends, our commons had no control over anything, but were, so to say, voluntary slaves to the laws.

MEG. What laws do you mean?

ATH. Those dealing with the music of that age, in the first place,—to describe from its commencement how the life of excessive liberty grew up. Among us, at that time, music was divided into various classes and styles: one class of song was that of prayers to the gods, which bore the name of "hymns"; contrasted with this was another class, best called "dirges"; "paeans" formed another; and yet another was the "dithyramb," named, I fancy, after Dionysus. "Nomes" also were so called as being a distinct class of song; and these were further described as "citharoedic nomes."[1] So these and other kinds being classified and fixed, it was forbidden to set one kind of words to a different class of tune.[2] The authority whose duty it was to know these regulations, and, when known, to apply them in its judgments and to penalise the disobedient, was not a pipe nor, as now, the mob's unmusical shoutings, nor yet the clappings which

---

[1] *i.e.* solemn chants sung to the "cithara" or lyre. "Dithyrambs" were choral odes to Dionysus; "paeans" were mostly hymns of praise to Apollo.

[2] Cp. 657 C ff., 669 C ff.

PLATO

700 δόντες, ἀλλὰ τοῖς μὲν γεγονόσι περὶ παίδευσιν
δεδογμένον ἀκούειν ἦν αὐτοῖς μετὰ σιγῆς διὰ
τέλους, παισὶ δὲ καὶ παιδαγωγοῖς καὶ τῷ πλείστῳ
ὄχλῳ ῥάβδου κοσμούσης ἡ νουθέτησις ἐγίγνετο.

D ταῦτ' οὖν οὕτω τεταγμένως ἤθελεν ἄρχεσθαι τῶν
πολιτῶν τὸ πλῆθος, καὶ μὴ τολμᾶν κρίνειν διὰ
θορύβου· μετὰ δὲ ταῦτα προϊόντος τοῦ χρόνου
ἄρχοντες μὲν τῆς ἀμούσου παρανομίας ποιηταὶ
ἐγίγνοντο φύσει μὲν ποιητικοί, ἀγνώμονες δὲ
περὶ τὸ δίκαιον τῆς Μούσης καὶ τὸ νόμιμον,
βακχεύοντες καὶ μᾶλλον τοῦ δέοντος κατεχόμενοι
ὑφ' ἡδονῆς, κεραννύντες δὲ θρήνους τε ὕμνοις καὶ
παίωνας διθυράμβοις, καὶ αὐλῳδίας δὴ ταῖς
κιθαρῳδίαις μιμούμενοι καὶ πάντα εἰς πάντα

E ξυνάγοντες, μουσικῆς ἄκοντες ὑπ' ἀνοίας κατα-
ψευδόμενοι, ὡς ὀρθότητα μὲν οὐκ ἔχοι οὐδ'
ἡντινοῦν μουσική, ἡδονῇ δὲ τῇ τοῦ χαίροντος,
εἴτε βελτίων εἴτε χείρων ἂν εἴη τις, κρίνοιτο
ὀρθότατα. τοιαῦτα δὴ ποιοῦντες ποιήματα λόγους
τε ἐπιλέγοντες τοιούτους τοῖς πολλοῖς ἐνέθεσαν
παρανομίαν εἰς τὴν μουσικὴν καὶ τόλμαν, ὡς
ἱκανοῖς οὖσι κρίνειν. ὅθεν δὴ τὰ θέατρα ἐξ
701 ἀφώνων φωνήεντα ἐγένοντο, ὡς ἐπαΐοντα ἐν Μούσαις τό τε καλὸν καὶ μή, καὶ ἀντὶ ἀριστοκρατίας
ἐν αὐτῇ θεατροκρατία τις πονηρὰ γέγονεν. εἰ
γὰρ δὴ καὶ δημοκρατία ἐν αὐτῇ τις μόνον ἐγένετο
ἐλευθέρων ἀνδρῶν, οὐδὲν ἂν πάνυ γε δεινὸν ἦν τὸ
γεγονός. νῦν δὲ ἦρξε μὲν ἡμῖν ἐκ μουσικῆς ἡ
πάντων εἰς πάντα σοφίας δόξα καὶ παρανομία,

---

[1] Cp. *Rep.* iii. 397 A ff.
[2] *i.e.* "rule of the audience"; as we might say, the pit
and gallery sat in judgment. Cp. Arist. *Pol.* viii. 6.

mark applause : in place of this, it was a rule made
by those in control of education that they themselves
should listen throughout in silence, while the
children and their ushers and the general crowd
were kept in order by the discipline of the rod. In
the matter of music the populace willingly submitted
to orderly control and abstained from outrageously
judging by clamour; but later on, with the progress
of time, there arose as leaders of unmusical illegality
poets who, though by nature poetical, were ignorant
of what was just and lawful in music; and they,
being frenzied and unduly possessed by a spirit of
pleasure, mixed dirges with hymns and paeans with
dithyrambs, and imitated flute-tunes with harp-
tunes, and blended every kind of music with every
other; and thus, through their folly, they unwittingly bore false witness against music, as a thing
without any standard of correctness, of which the
best criterion is the pleasure of the auditor, be he a
good man or a bad.[1] By compositions of such a
character, set to similar words, they bred in the
populace a spirit of lawlessness in regard to music,
and the effrontery of supposing themselves capable
of passing judgment on it. Hence the theatre-
goers became noisy instead of silent, as though they
knew the difference between good and bad music,
and in place of an aristocracy in music there sprang
up a kind of base theatrocracy.[2] For if in music,
and music only, there had arisen a democracy of
free men, such a result would not have been so very
alarming; but as it was, the universal conceit of
universal wisdom and the contempt for law origi-
nated in the music, and on the heels of these came

701 ξυνεφέσπετο δὲ ἐλευθερία. ἄφοβοι γὰρ ἐγίγνοντο
ὡς εἰδότες, ἡ δὲ ἄδεια ἀναισχυντίαν ἐνέτεκε· τὸ
B γὰρ τὴν τοῦ βελτίονος δόξαν μὴ φοβεῖσθαι διὰ
θράσος, τοῦτ᾽ αὐτό ἐστι σχεδὸν ἡ πονηρὰ ἀναι-
σχυντία, διὰ δή τινος ἐλευθερίας λίαν ἀποτετολμη-
μένης.

ΜΕ. Ἀληθέστατα λέγεις.

ΑΘ. Ἐφεξῆς δὴ ταύτῃ τῇ ἐλευθερίᾳ ἡ τοῦ μὴ
ἐθέλειν τοῖς ἄρχουσι δουλεύειν γίγνοιτ᾽ ἄν, καὶ
ἑπομένη ταύτῃ φεύγειν πατρὸς καὶ μητρὸς καὶ
πρεσβυτέρων δουλείαν καὶ νουθέτησιν,[1] καὶ ἐγγὺς
τοῦ τέλους οὖσι νόμων ζητεῖν μὴ ὑπηκόοις εἶναι,
πρὸς αὐτῷ δὲ ἤδη τῷ τέλει ὅρκων καὶ πίστεων
καὶ τὸ παράπαν θεῶν μὴ φροντίζειν, τὴν λεγομένην [παλαιὰν][2] Τιτανικὴν φύσιν ἐπιδεικνῦσι
C καὶ μιμουμένοις· ἐπὶ τὰ αὐτὰ πάλιν ἐκεῖνα ἀφικομένους, χαλεπὸν αἰῶνα διάγοντας μὴ λῆξαί ποτε
κακῶν. τίνος δὴ καὶ ταῦθ᾽ ἡμῖν αὖ χάριν ἐλέχθη ;
δεῖν φαίνεται ἔμοιγε, οἱόνπερ ἵππον, τὸν λόγον
ἑκάστοτε ἀναλαμβάνειν, καὶ μὴ καθάπερ ἀχάλι-
D νον κεκτημένου[3] τὸ στόμα βίᾳ ὑπὸ τοῦ λόγου
φερόμενον κατὰ τὴν παροιμίαν ἀπό τινος ὄνου
πεσεῖν, ἀλλ᾽ ἐπανερωτᾶν τὸ νῦν δὴ λεχθέν, τὸ
τίνος δὴ [χάριν][4] ἕνεκα ταῦτα ἐλέχθη ;

ΜΕ. Καλῶς.

ΑΘ. Ταῦτα τοίνυν εἴρηται ἐκείνων ἕνεκα.

ΜΕ. Τίνων ;

ΑΘ. Ἐλέξαμεν ὡς τὸν νομοθέτην δεῖ τριῶν

---

[1] νουθέτησιν minor MSS.: νομοθέτησιν best MSS., Zur.
[2] [παλαιὰν] bracketed by W.-Möllendorff.
[3] κεκτημένου W.-Möllendorff: κεκτημένον MSS.
[4] [χάριν] bracketed by Hermann (ἕνεκα by Bast, Schanz).

liberty. For, thinking themselves knowing, men
became fearless; and audacity begat effrontery.
For to be fearless of the opinion of a better man,
owing to self-confidence, is nothing else than base
effrontery; and it is brought about by a liberty that
is audacious to excess.

MEG. Most true.

ATH. Next after this form of liberty would come
that which refuses to be subject to the rulers;[1] and,
following on that, the shirking of submission to
one's parents and elders and their admonitions;
then, as the penultimate stage, comes the effort to
disregard the laws; while the last stage of all is to
lose all respect for oaths or pledges or divinities,—
wherein men display and reproduce the character
of the Titans of story, who are said to have reverted
to their original state, dragging out a painful
existence with never any rest from woe. What,
again, is our object in saying all this? Evidently, I
must, every time, rein in my discourse, like a horse,
and not let it run away with me as though it had no
bridle[2] in its mouth, and so "get a toss off the
donkey"[3] (as the saying goes): consequently, I
must once more repeat my question, and ask—
"With what object has all this been said?"

MEG. Very good.

ATH. What has now been said bears on the
objects previously stated.

MEG. What were they?

ATH. We said[4] that the lawgiver must aim, in

---

[1] Cp. *Rep.* iv. 424 E.   [2] Cp. Eur. *Bacch.* 385.

[3] A play on ἀπ' ὄνου = ἀπὸ νοῦ: "to fall off the ass" was
a proverbial phrase for "to show oneself a fool": cf. Arist.
Nubes 1274: τί δῆτα ληρεῖς, ὥσπερ ἀπ' ὄνου καταπεσών.

[4] Cp. 693 B.

PLATO

701 στοχαζόμενον νομοθετεῖν, ὅπως ἡ νομοθετουμένη
πόλις ἐλευθέρα τε ἔσται καὶ φίλη ἑαυτῇ καὶ νοῦν
ἕξει. ταῦτ' ἦν. ἦ γάρ;

ΜΕ. Πάνυ μὲν οὖν.

Ε   ΑΘ. Τούτων ἕνεκα δὴ πολιτείας τήν τε δεσπο-
τικωτάτην προελόμενοι καὶ τὴν ἐλευθερικωτάτην,
ἐπισκοποῦμεν νυνὶ ποτέρα τούτων ὀρθῶς πολι-
τεύεται· λαβόντες δὲ αὐτῶν ἑκατέρας μετριότητά
τινα, τῶν μὲν τοῦ δεσπόζειν, τῶν δὲ τοῦ ἐλευθε-
ριάσαι, κατείδομεν ὅτι τότε διαφερόντως ἐν αὐταῖς
ἐγένετο εὐπραγία, ἐπὶ δὲ τὸ ἄκρον ἀγαγόντων
ἑκατέρων, τῶν μὲν δουλείας, τῶν δὲ τοὐναντίου,
οὐ συνήνεγκεν οὔτε τοῖς οὔτε τοῖς.

702   ΜΕ. Ἀληθέστατα λέγεις.

ΑΘ. Καὶ μὴν αὐτῶν γε ἕνεκα καὶ τὸ Δωρικὸν
ἐθεασάμεθα κατοικιζόμενον στρατόπεδον καὶ τὰς
τοῦ Δαρδάνου ὑπωρείας τε καὶ τὴν ἐπὶ θαλάττῃ
κατοίκισιν, καὶ τοὺς πρώτους δὴ τοὺς περιλιπεῖς
γενομένους τῆς φθορᾶς, ἔτι δὲ τοὺς ἔμπροσθεν
τούτων γενομένους ἡμῖν λόγους περὶ τε μουσικῆς
καὶ μέθης καὶ τὰ τούτων ἔτι πρότερα. ταῦτα
γὰρ πάντα εἴρηται τοῦ κατιδεῖν ἕνεκα πῶς ποτ'
Β ἂν πόλις ἄριστα οἰκοίη, καὶ ἰδίᾳ πῶς ἄν τις
βέλτιστα τὸν αὑτοῦ βίον διαγάγοι. εἰ δὲ δή τι
πεποιήκαμεν προὔργου, τίς ποτ' ἂν ἔλεγχος
γίγνοιτο ἡμῖν πρὸς ἡμᾶς αὐτοὺς λεχθείς, ὦ
Μέγιλλέ τε καὶ Κλεινία;

ΚΛ. Ἐγώ τιν', ὦ ξένε, μοι δοκῶ κατανοεῖν·
ἔοικε κατὰ τύχην τινὰ ἡμῖν τὰ τῶν λόγων τούτων
πάντων ὧν διεξήλθομεν γεγονέναι· σχεδὸν γὰρ
εἰς χρείαν αὐτῶν ἔγωγ' ἐλήλυθα τὰ νῦν, καὶ κατὰ

his legislation, at three objectives—to make the State he is legislating for free, and at unity with itself, and possessed of sense. That was so, was it not?

MEG. Certainly.

ATH. With these objects in view, we selected the most despotic of polities and the most absolutely free, and are now enquiring which of these is rightly constituted. When we took a moderate example of each—of despotic rule on the one hand, and liberty on the other,—we observed that there they enjoyed prosperity in the highest degree; but when they advanced, the one to the extreme of slavery, the other to the extreme of liberty, then there was no gain to either the one or the other.

MEG. Most true.

ATH. With the same objects in view we surveyed,[1] also, the settling of the Doric host and the homes of Dardanus at the foot of the hills and the colony by the sea and the first men who survived the Flood, together with our previous discourses [2] concerning music and revelry, as well as all that preceded these. The object of all these discourses was to discover how best a State might be managed, and how best the individual citizen might pass his life. But as to the value of our conclusions, what test can we apply in conversing among ourselves, O Megillus and Clinias?

CLIN. I think, Stranger, that I can perceive one. It is a piece of good luck for me that we have dealt with all these matters in our discourse. For I myself have now come nearly to the point when I shall need

---

[1] *i.e.* in Bk. iii. 676-693 (taken in the reverse order).
[2] *i.e.* in Books i. and ii.

702 τινα αὖ καιρὸν σύ τε παραγέγονας ἅμα καὶ
Μέγιλλος ὅδε. οὐ γὰρ ἀποκρύψομαι σφὼ τὸ
C νῦν ἐμοὶ ξυμβαῖνον, ἀλλὰ καὶ πρὸς οἰωνόν τινα
ποιοῦμαι. ἡ γὰρ πλείστη τῆς Κρήτης ἐπιχειρεῖ
τινὰ ἀποικίαν ποιήσασθαι, καὶ προστάττει τοῖς
Κνωσίοις ἐπιμεληθῆναι τοῦ πράγματος, ἡ δὲ τῶν
Κνωσίων πόλις ἐμοί τε καὶ ἄλλοις ἐννέα· ἅμα δὲ
καὶ νόμους τῶν τε αὐτόθι, εἴ τινες ἡμᾶς ἀρέσκουσι,
τίθεσθαι κελεύει, καὶ εἴ τινες ἑτέρωθεν, μηδὲν
ὑπολογιζομένους τὸ ξενικὸν αὐτῶν, ἂν βελτίους
φαίνωνται. νῦν οὖν ἐμοί τε καὶ ὑμῖν ταύτην δῶμεν
D χάριν· ἐκ τῶν εἰρημένων ἐκλέξαντες τῷ λόγῳ
συστησώμεθα πόλιν, οἷον ἐξ ἀρχῆς κατοικίζοντες,
καὶ ἅμα μὲν ἡμῖν οὗ ζητοῦμεν ἐπίσκεψις γενήσε-
ται, ἅμα δ᾽ ἐγὼ τάχ᾽ ἂν χρησαίμην εἰς τὴν
μέλλουσαν πόλιν ταύτῃ τῇ συστάσει.

ΑΘ. Οὐ πόλεμόν γε ἐπαγγέλλεις, ὦ Κλεινία·
ἀλλ᾽ εἰ μή τι Μεγίλλῳ πρόσαντες, τὰ παρ᾽ ἐμοῦ
γε ἡγοῦ σοι πάντα κατὰ νοῦν ὑπάρχειν εἰς
δύναμιν.

ΚΛ. Εὖ λέγεις.

ΜΕ. Καὶ μὴν καὶ τὰ παρ᾽ ἐμοῦ.

E ΚΛ. Κάλλιστ᾽ εἰρήκατον. ἀτὰρ πειρώμεθα
λόγῳ πρῶτον κατοικίζειν τὴν πόλιν.

them, and my meeting with you and Megillus here was quite opportune. I will make no secret to you of what has befallen me; nay, more, I count it to be a sign from Heaven. The most part of Crete is undertaking to found a colony, and it has given charge of the undertaking to the Cnosians, and the city of Cnosus has entrusted it to me and nine others. We are bidden also to frame laws, choosing such as we please either from our own local laws or from those of other countries, taking no exception to their alien character, provided only that they seem superior. Let us, then, grant this favour to me, and yourselves also; let us select from the statements we have made, and build up by arguments the framework of a State, as though we were erecting it from the foundation. In this way we shall be at once investigating our theme, and possibly I may also make use of our framework for the State that is to be formed.

ATH. Your proclamation, Clinias, is certainly not a proclamation of war! So, if Megillus has no objection, you may count on me to do all I can to gratify your wish.

CLIN. It is good to hear that.

MEG. And you can count on me too.

CLIN. Splendid of you both! But, in the first place, let us try to found the State by word.

Δ

704   ΑΘ.   Φέρε δή, τίνα δεῖ διανοηθῆναί ποτε τὴν
πόλιν ἔσεσθαι; λέγω δὲ οὔ τι τοὔνομα αὐτῆς
ἐρωτῶν ὅ τί ποτ' ἐστὶ τὰ νῦν, οὐδ' εἰς τὸν ἔπειτα
χρόνον ὅ τι δεήσει καλεῖν αὐτήν· τοῦτο μὲν γὰρ
τάχ' ἂν ἴσως καὶ ὁ κατοικισμὸς αὐτῆς ἤ τις
τόπος ἢ ποταμοῦ τινὸς ἢ κρήνης ἢ θεῶν ἐπωνυμία
τῶν ἐν τῷ τόπῳ προσθείη, τὴν αὐτῶν φήμην
B καινῇ γεννωμένῃ[1] τῇ πόλει· τόδε δὲ περὶ αὐτῆς
ἐστιν ὃ βουλόμενος μᾶλλον ἐπερωτῶ, πότερον
ἐπιθαλαττίδιος ἔσται τις ἢ χερσαία.

ΚΛ.   Σχεδόν, ὦ ξένε, ἀπέχει θαλάττης γε ἡ
πόλις ἧς πέρι τὰ νῦν δὴ λεχθέντα ἡμῖν εἰς τινας
ὀγδοήκοντα σταδίους.

ΑΘ.   Τί δέ; λιμένες ἆρ' εἰσὶ κατὰ ταῦτα αὐτῆς,
ἢ τὸ παράπαν ἀλίμενος;

ΚΛ.   Εὐλίμενος μὲν οὖν ταύτῃ γε ὡς δυνατὸν
μάλιστα, ὦ ξένε.

C   ΑΘ.   Παπαί, οἷον λέγεις· τί δέ; περὶ αὐτὴν ἡ
χώρα πότερα πάμφορος ἢ καί τινων ἐπιδεής;

ΚΛ.   Σχεδὸν οὐδενὸς ἐπιδεής.

ΑΘ.   Γείτων δὲ αὐτῆς πόλις ἆρ' ἔσται τις
πλησίον;

ΚΛ.   Οὐ πάνυ, διὸ καὶ κατοικίζεται· παλαιὰ
γάρ τις ἐξοίκησις ἐν τῷ τόπῳ γενομένη τὴν χώραν
ταύτην ἔρημον ἀπείργασται χρόνον ἀμήχανον
ὅσον.

---

[1] γεννωμένη Apelt : γενομένη MSS.

254

BOOK IV

ATH. Come now, what is this State going to be, shall we suppose? I am not asking for its present name or the name it will have to go by in the future; for this might be derived from the conditions of its settlement, or from some locality, or a river or spring or some local deity might bestow its sacred title on the new State. The point of my question about it is rather this,—is it to be an inland State, or situated on the sea-coast?

CLIN. The State which I mentioned just now, Stranger, lies about eighty stades, roughly speaking, from the sea.

ATH. Well, has it harbours on the sea-board side, or is it quite without harbours?

CLIN. It has excellent harbours on that side, Stranger, none better.

ATH. Dear me! how unfortunate![1] But what of the surrounding country? Is it productive in all respects, or deficient in some products?

CLIN. There is practically nothing that it is deficient in.

ATH. Will there be any State bordering close on it?

CLIN. None at all, and that is the reason for settling it. Owing to emigration from this district long ago, the country has lain desolate for ever so long.

---

[1] This remark is explained by what is said below, 705 A ff.

704 ΑΘ. Τί δ' αὖ; πεδίων τε καὶ ὀρῶν καὶ ὕλης
πῶς μέρος ἑκάστων ἡμῖν εἴληχεν;

D ΚΛ. Προσέοικε τῇ τῆς ἄλλης Κρήτης φύσει
ὅλη.

ΑΘ. Τραχυτέραν αὐτὴν ἢ πεδιεινοτέραν ἂν
λέγοις.

ΚΛ. Πάνυ μὲν οὖν.

ΑΘ. Οὐ τοίνυν ἀνίατός γε ἂν εἴη πρὸς ἀρετῆς
κτῆσιν. εἰ μὲν γὰρ ἐπιθαλαττία τε ἔμελλεν εἶναι
καὶ εὐλίμενος καὶ μὴ πάμφορος ἀλλ' ἐπιδεὴς
πολλῶν, μεγάλου τινὸς ἔδει σωτῆρός τε αὐτῇ
καὶ νομοθετῶν θείων τινῶν, εἰ μὴ πολλά τε
Ε ἔμελλεν ἤθη καὶ ποικίλα καὶ φαῦλα ἕξειν τοιαύτῃ
φύσει γενομένη· νῦν δὲ παραμύθιον ἔχει τὸ τῶν
ὀγδοήκοντα σταδίων. ἐγγύτερον μέν τοι τοῦ
δέοντος κεῖται τῆς θαλάττης, σχεδὸν ὅσον εὐλι-
μενωτέραν αὐτὴν φὴς εἶναι. ὅμως δὲ ἀγαπητὸν
705 καὶ τοῦτο. πρόσοικος γὰρ θάλαττα χώρα τὸ μὲν
παρ' ἑκάστην ἡμέραν ἡδύ, μάλα γε μὴν ὄντως
ἁλμυρὸν καὶ πικρὸν γειτόνημα· ἐμπορίας γὰρ
καὶ χρηματισμοῦ διὰ καπηλείας ἐμπιπλᾶσα
αὐτήν, ἤθη παλίμβολα καὶ ἄπιστα ταῖς ψυχαῖς
ἐντίκτουσα, αὐτήν τε πρὸς αὐτὴν τὴν πόλιν
ἄπιστον καὶ ἄφιλον ποιεῖ καὶ πρὸς τοὺς ἄλλους
ἀνθρώπους ὡσαύτως. παραμύθιον δὲ δὴ πρὸς
Β ταῦτα καὶ τὸ πάμφορος εἶναι κέκτηται, τραχεῖα
δὲ οὖσα δῆλον ὡς οὐκ ἂν πολύφορός τε εἴη καὶ
πάμφορος ἅμα. τοῦτο γὰρ ἔχουσα, πολλὴν
ἐξαγωγὴν ἂν παρεχομένη, νομίσματος ἀργυροῦ
καὶ χρυσοῦ πάλιν ἀντεμπίπλαιτ' ἄν, οὗ μεῖζον
κακόν, ὡς ἔπος εἰπεῖν, πόλει ἀνθ' ἑνὸς ἓν οὐδὲν

ATH. How about plains, mountains and forests? What extent of each of these does it contain?

CLIN. As a whole, it resembles in character the rest of Crete.

ATH. You would call it hilly rather than level?

CLIN. Certainly.

ATH. Then it would not be incurably unfit for the acquisition of virtue. For if the State was to be on the sea-coast, and to have fine harbours, and to be deficient in many products, instead of productive of everything,—in that case it would need a mighty saviour and divine lawgivers, if, with such a character, it was to avoid having a variety of luxurious and depraved habits.[1] As things are, however, there is consolation in the fact of that eighty stades. Still, it lies unduly near the sea, and the more so because, as you say, its harbours are good; that, however, we must make the best of. For the sea is, in very truth, "a right briny and bitter neighbour,"[2] although there is sweetness in its proximity for the uses of daily life; for by filling the markets of the city with foreign merchandise and retail trading, and breeding in men's souls knavish and tricky ways, it renders the city faithless and loveless, not to itself only, but to the rest of the world as well. But in this respect our State has compensation in the fact that it is all-productive; and since it is hilly, it cannot be highly productive as well as all-productive; if it were, and supplied many exports, it would be flooded in return with gold and silver money—the one condition of all, perhaps, that is

---

[1] Cp. Arist. *Pol.* vii. 6.
[2] Quoted from Alcman.

705 ἂν γίγνοιτο εἰς γενναίων καὶ δικαίων ἠθῶν **κτῆσιν**, ὡς ἔφαμεν, εἰ μεμνήμεθα, ἐν τοῖς πρόσθεν λόγοις.

ΚΛ. Ἀλλὰ μεμνήμεθα, καὶ συγχωροῦμεν τότε λέγειν ἡμᾶς ὀρθῶς καὶ τὰ νῦν.

C ΑΘ. Τί δὲ δή; ναυπηγησίμης ὕλης ὁ τόπος ἡμῖν τῆς χώρας πῶς ἔχει;

ΚΛ. Οὐκ ἔστιν οὔτε τις ἐλάτη λόγου ἀξία οὔτ' αὖ πεύκη, κυπάριττός τε οὐ πολλή· πίτυν τ' αὖ καὶ πλάτανον ὀλίγην ἂν εὕροι τις, οἷς δὴ πρὸς τὰ τῶν ἐντὸς τῶν πλοίων μέρη ἀναγκαῖον τοῖς ναυπηγοῖς χρῆσθαι ἑκάστοτε.

ΑΘ. Καὶ ταῦτα οὐκ ἂν κακῶς ἔχοι τῇ χώρᾳ τῆς φύσεως.

ΚΛ. Τί δή;

D ΑΘ. Μιμήσεις πονηρὰς μιμεῖσθαι τοὺς πολεμίους μὴ ῥᾳδίως δύνασθαί τινα πόλιν ἀγαθόν.

ΚΛ. Εἰς δὴ τί τῶν εἰρημένων βλέψας εἶπες ὃ λέγεις;

ΑΘ. Ὦ δαιμόνιε, φύλαττέ με εἰς τὸ κατ' ἀρχὰς εἰρημένον ἀποβλέπων, τὸ περὶ τῶν Κρητικῶν νόμων, ὡς πρὸς ἕν τι βλέποιεν· καὶ δὴ καὶ τοῦτ' ἐλεγέτην αὐτὸ εἶναι σφὼ τὸ πρὸς τὸν πόλεμον, ἐγὼ δὲ ὑπολαβὼν εἶπον ὡς ὅτι μὲν εἰς ἀρετήν ποι βλέποι τὰ τοιαῦτα νόμιμα κείμενα καλῶς ἔχοι, τὸ δ' ὅτι πρὸς μέρος ἀλλ' οὐ πρὸς πᾶσαν σχεδὸν

E οὐ πάνυ ξυνεχώρουν. νῦν οὖν ὑμεῖς μοι τῆς παρούσης νομοθεσίας ἀντιφυλάξατε ἑπόμενοι ἐὰν ἄρα τι μὴ πρὸς ἀρετὴν τεῖνον ἢ πρὸς ἀρετῆς μόριον νομοθετῶ. τοῦτον γὰρ δὴ τίθεσθαι τὸν νόμον ὀρθῶς ὑποτίθεμαι μόνον, ὃς ἂν δίκην τοξότου ἑκάστοτε στοχάζηται τούτου ὅτῳ ἂν συνεχῶς

most fatal, in a State, to the acquisition of noble
and just habits of life,—as we said, if you remember,
in our previous discourse.[1]

CLIN. We remember, and we endorse what you
said both then and now.

ATH. Well, then, how is our district off for timber
for ship-building?

CLIN. There is no fir to speak of, nor pine, and
but little cypress; nor could one find much larch or
plane, which shipwrights are always obliged to use
for the interior fittings of ships.

ATH. Those, too, are natural features which
would not be bad for the country.

CLIN. Why so?

ATH. That a State should not find it easy to copy
its enemies in bad habits is a good thing.

CLIN. To which of our statements does this
observation allude?

ATH. My dear Sir, keep a watch on me, with an
eye cast back on our opening[2] statement about the
Cretan laws. It asserted that those laws aimed at
one single object; and whereas you declared that
this object was military strength, I made the
rejoinder that, while it was right that such enactments
should have virtue for their aim, I did not at all
approve of that aim being restricted to a part,
instead of applying to the whole. So do you now,
in turn, keep a watch on my present law-making, as
you follow it, in case I should enact any law either
not tending to virtue at all, or tending only to a part
of it. For I lay it down as an axiom that no law is
rightly enacted which does not aim always, like an
archer, at that object, and that alone, which is

---

[1] Cp. 679 B.   [2] Cp. 625 D, 629 E ff.

706 [τούτων] τῶν¹ ἀεὶ καλῶν τι ξυνέπηται μόνον, τὰ δὲ
ἄλλα ξύμπαντα παραλείπῃ, ἐάν τέ τις πλοῦτος
ἐάν τε ἄρα τι τῶν ἄλλων τῶν τοιούτων ὂν τυγχάνῃ
ἄνευ τῶν προειρημένων.   τὴν δὲ δὴ μίμησιν
ἔλεγον τὴν τῶν πολεμίων τὴν κακὴν τοιάνδε
γίγνεσθαι, ὅταν οἰκῇ μέν τις πρὸς θαλάττῃ,
λυπῆται δ' ὑπὸ πολεμίων, οἷον—φράσω γὰρ οὔ τι
μνησικακεῖν βουλόμενος ὑμῖν.   Μίνως γὰρ δή
ποτε τοὺς οἰκοῦντας τὴν Ἀττικὴν παρεστήσατο
B εἰς χαλεπήν τινα φορὰν δασμοῦ, δύναμιν πολλὴν
κατὰ θάλατταν κεκτημένος.   οἱ δ' οὔτε πω πλοῖα
ἐκέκτηντο, καθάπερ νῦν, πολεμικά, οὔτ' αὖ τὴν
χώραν πλήρη ναυπηγησίμων ξύλων, ὥστ' εὐμαρῶς
ναυτικὴν παρασχέσθαι δύναμιν· οὔκουν οἷοί τ'
ἐγένοντο διὰ μιμήσεως ναυτικῆς αὐτοὶ ναῦται
γενόμενοι εὐθὺς τότε τοὺς πολεμίους ἀμύνασθαι.
ἔτι γὰρ ἂν πλεονάκις ἑπτὰ ἀπολέσαι παῖδας αὐ-
C τοῖς συνήνεγκε, πρὶν ἀντὶ πεζῶν ὁπλιτῶν μονίμων
ναυτικοὺς γενομένους ἐθισθῆναι πυκνὰ ἀποπηδῶν-
τας δρομικῶς εἰς τὰς ναῦς ταχὺ πάλιν ἀποχωρεῖν,
καὶ δοκεῖν μηδὲν αἰσχρὸν ποιεῖν μὴ τολμῶντας ἀποθνήσκειν μένοντας ἐπιφερομένων πολεμίων, ἀλλ'
εἰκυίας αὐτοῖς γίγνεσθαι προφάσεις καὶ σφόδρα
ἑτοίμας ὅπλα τε ἀπολλῦσι καὶ φεύγουσι δή τινας
οὐκ αἰσχράς, ὥς φασι, φυγάς.   ταῦτα γὰρ ἐκ
ναυτικῆς ὁπλιτείας ἔργματα² φιλεῖ ξυμβαίνειν,
οὐκ ἄξια ἐπαίνων πολλάκις μυρίων, ἀλλὰ τοὐναν-
D τίον· ἔθη γὰρ πονηρὰ οὐδέποτε ἐθίζειν δεῖ, καὶ
ταῦτα τὸ τῶν πολιτῶν βέλτιστον μέρος.   ἦν δέ
που τοῦτό γε καὶ παρ' Ὁμήρου λαβεῖν, ὅτι τὸ

---

¹ [τούτων] τῶν : τούτων (or τοῦ τῶν) MSS.

constantly accompanied by something ever-beautiful,
—passing over every other object, be it wealth or
anything else of the kind that is devoid of beauty.
To illustrate how the evil imitation of enemies,
which I spoke of, comes about, when people dwell
by the sea and are vexed by enemies, I will give
you an example (though with no wish, of course, to
recall to you painful memories). When Minos, once
upon a time, reduced the people of Attica to a
grievous payment of tribute, he was very powerful
by sea, whereas they possessed no warships at that
time such as they have now, nor was their country
so rich in timber that they could easily supply
themselves with a naval force. Hence they were
unable quickly to copy the naval methods of their
enemies and drive them off by becoming sailors
themselves. And indeed it would have profited
them to lose seventy times seven children rather
than to become marines instead of staunch foot-
soldiers; for marines are habituated to jumping
ashore frequently and running back at full speed to
their ships, and they think no shame of not dying
boldly at their posts when the enemy attack; and
excuses are readily made for them, as a matter of
course, when they fling away their arms and betake
themselves to what they describe as "no dis-
honourable flight." These "exploits" are the usual
result of employing naval soldiery, and they merit,
not "infinite praise," but precisely the opposite; for
one ought never to habituate men to base habits, and
least of all the noblest section of the citizens. That
such an institution is not a noble one might have been

---

² ἔργματα : ῥήματα MSS. (bracketed by Schanz)

PLATO

706 ἐπιτήδευμα ἦν τὸ τοιοῦτον οὐ καλόν. Ὀδυσσεὺς
γὰρ αὐτῷ λοιδορεῖ τὸν Ἀγαμέμνονα, τῶν Ἀχαιῶν
τότε ὑπὸ τῶν Τρώων κατεχομένων τῇ μάχῃ,
κελεύοντα τὰς ναῦς εἰς τὴν θάλατταν καθέλκειν,
ὁ δὲ χαλεπαίνει τε αὐτῷ καὶ λέγει

E

ὃς κέλεαι πολέμοιο συνεσταότος καὶ ἀϋτῆς
νῆας ἐϋσσέλμους ἅλαδ' ἕλκειν, ὄφρ' ἔτι
μᾶλλον
Τρωσὶ μὲν εὐκτὰ γένηται ἐελδομένοισί περ
ἔμπης,
ἡμῖν δ' αἰπὺς ὄλεθρος ἐπιρρέπῃ· οὐ γὰρ
Ἀχαιοὶ
σχήσουσιν πολέμου νηῶν ἅλαδ' ἑλκομενάων,
ἀλλ' ἀποπαπτανέουσιν, ἐρωήσουσι δὲ χάρμης.

707

ἔνθα κε σὴ βουλὴ δηλήσεται, οἷ' ἀγορεύεις.

ταῦτ' οὖν ἐγίγνωσκε καὶ ἐκεῖνος, ὅτι κακὸν ἐν
θαλάττῃ τριήρεις ὁπλίταις παρεστώσαι μαχο-
μένοις· καὶ λέοντες ἂν ἐλάφους ἐθισθεῖεν φεύγειν
τοιούτοις ἔθεσι χρώμενοι· πρὸς δὲ τούτοις αἱ διὰ
τὰ ναυτικὰ πόλεων δυνάμεις ἅμα σωτηρίας[1] τιμὰς
οὐ τῷ καλλίστῳ τῶν πολεμικῶν ἀποδιδόασι. διὰ
κυβερνητικῆς γὰρ καὶ πεντηκονταρχίας καὶ ἐρε-
B τικῆς καὶ παντοδαπῶν καὶ οὐ πάνυ σπουδαίων
ἀνθρώπων γιγνομένης τὰς τιμὰς ἑκάστοις οὐκ ἂν
δύναιτο ὀρθῶς ἀποδιδόναι τις. καί τοι πῶς ἂν
ἔτι πολιτεία γίγνοιτο ὀρθὴ τούτου στερομένη ;

ΚΛ. Σχεδὸν ἀδύνατον. ἀλλὰ μήν, ὦ ξένε, τήν
γε περὶ Σαλαμῖνα ναυμαχίαν τῶν Ἑλλήνων πρὸς
τοὺς βαρβάρους γενομένην ἡμεῖς γε οἱ Κρῆτες
τὴν Ἑλλάδα φαμὲν σῶσαι.

---

[1] σωτηρίας Badham, Schanz: σωτηρίᾳ MSS.

learnt even from Homer. For he makes Odysseus abuse Agamemnon for ordering the Achaeans to haul down their ships to the sea, when they were being pressed in fight by the Trojans; and in his wrath he speaks thus [1] :—

" Dost bid our people hale their fair-benched ships
    Seaward, when war and shouting close us round?
So shall the Trojans see their prayers fulfilled,
    And so on us shall sheer destruction fall!
For, when the ships are seaward drawn, no more
    Will our Achaeans hold the battle up,
But, backward glancing, they will quit the fray:
    Thus baneful counsel such as thine will prove."

So Homer, too, was aware of the fact that triremes lined up in the sea alongside of infantry fighting on land are a bad thing: why, even lions, if they had habits such as these, would grow used to running away from does! Moreover, States dependent upon navies for their power give honours, as rewards for their safety, to a section of their forces that is not the finest; for they owe their safety to the arts of the pilot, the captain and the rower—men of all kinds and not too respectable,—so that it would be impossible to assign the honours to each of them rightly. Yet, without rectitude in this, how can it still be right with a State? [2]

CLIN. It is well-nigh impossible. None the less, Stranger, it was the sea-fight at Salamis, fought by the Greeks against the barbarians, which, as we Cretans at least affirm, saved Greece.

---

[1] *Il.* xiv. 96 ff.
[2] Cp. 697 B, 757 A f.

707 ΑΘ. Καὶ γὰρ οἱ πολλοὶ τῶν Ἑλλήνων τε καὶ
C βαρβάρων λέγουσι ταῦτα. ἡμεῖς δέ, ὦ φίλε, ἐγώ
τε καὶ ὅδε, Μέγιλλος, φαμὲν τὴν πεζὴν μάχην
τὴν ἐν Μαραθῶνι γενομένην καὶ ἐν Πλαταιαῖς τὴν
μὲν ἄρξαι τῆς σωτηρίας τοῖς Ἕλλησι, τὴν δὲ τέλος
ἐπιθεῖναι, καὶ τὰς μὲν βελτίους τοὺς Ἕλληνας
ποιῆσαι, τὰς δὲ οὐ βελτίους, ἵν᾽ οὕτω λέγωμεν
περὶ τῶν τότε ξυσσωσασῶν ἡμᾶς μαχῶν· πρὸς
γὰρ τῇ περὶ Σαλαμῖνα τὴν περὶ τὸ Ἀρτεμίσιόν
σοι προσθήσω κατὰ θάλατταν μάχην. ἀλλὰ
D γὰρ ἀποβλέποντες νῦν πρὸς πολιτείας ἀρετὴν καὶ
χώρας φύσιν σκοπούμεθα καὶ νόμων τάξιν, οὐ τὸ
σώζεσθαί τε καὶ εἶναι μόνον ἀνθρώποις τιμιώ-
τατον ἡγούμενοι, καθάπερ οἱ πολλοί, τὸ δ᾽ ὡς
βελτίστους γίγνεσθαί τε καὶ εἶναι τοσοῦτον
χρόνον ὅσον ἂν ὦσιν. εἴρηται δ᾽ ἡμῖν, οἶμαι, καὶ
τοῦτο ἐν τοῖς πρόσθεν.

ΚΛ. Τί μήν;

ΑΘ. Τοῦτο τοίνυν σκοπώμεθα μόνον, εἰ κατὰ
τὴν αὐτὴν ὁδὸν ἐρχόμεθα βελτίστην οὖσαν πόλεσι
κατοικίσεων πέρι καὶ νομοθεσιῶν.

E ΚΛ. Καὶ πολύ γε.

ΑΘ. Λέγε δὴ τοίνυν τὸ τούτοις ἑξῆς, τίς ὁ
κατοικιζόμενος ὑμῖν λεὼς ἔσται; πότερον ἐξ
ἁπάσης Κρήτης ὁ ἐθέλων, ὡς ὄχλου τινὸς ἐν
ταῖς πόλεσιν ἑκάσταις γεγενημένου πλείονος
ἢ κατὰ τὴν ἐκ τῆς γῆς τροφήν; οὐ γάρ που
τὸν βουλόμενόν γε Ἑλλήνων συνάγετε. καί
τοί τινας ὑμῖν ἔκ τε Ἄργους ὁρῶ καὶ Αἰγίνης καὶ
708 ἄλλοθεν τῶν Ἑλλήνων εἰς τὴν χώραν κατῳκισ-

---

[1] Cp. 637 C ff.

ATH. Yes, that is what is said by most of the Greeks and barbarians. But we—that is, I myself and our friend Megillus—affirm that it was the land-battle of Marathon which began the salvation of Greece, and that of Plataea which completed it; and we affirm also that, whereas these battles made the Greeks better, the sea-fights made them worse, —if one may use such an expression about battles that helped at that time to save us (for I will let you count Artemisium also as a sea-fight, as well as Salamis). Since, however, our present object is political excellence, it is the natural character of a country and its legal arrangements that we are considering; so that we differ from most people in not regarding mere safety and existence as the most precious thing men can possess, but rather the gaining of all possible goodness and the keeping of it throughout life. This too, I believe, was stated by us before.[1]

CLIN. It was.

ATH. Then let us consider only this,—whether we are travelling by the same road which we took then, as being the best for States in the matter of settlements and modes of legislation.

CLIN. The best by far.

ATH. In the next place tell me this: who are the people that are to be settled? Will they comprise all that wish to go from any part of Crete, supposing that there has grown up in every city a surplus population too great for the country's food supply? For you are not, I presume, collecting all who wish to go from Greece; although I do, indeed, see in your country settlers from Argos, Aegina, and other parts of Greece. So tell us now from what

708 μένους· τὸ δὲ δὴ παρὸν ἡμῖν λέγε πόθεν ἔσεσθαι
φῂς στρατόπεδον τῶν πολιτῶν τὰ νῦν;

ΚΛ. Ἔκ τε Κρήτης ξυμπάσης ἔοικε γενήσεσθαι,
καὶ τῶν ἄλλων δὲ Ἑλλήνων μάλιστά μοι φαίνονται τοὺς ἀπὸ Πελοποννήσου προσδέξεσθαι ξυνοί-
κους. καὶ γάρ, ὃ νῦν δὴ λέγεις, ἀληθὲς φράζεις,
ὡς ἐξ Ἄργους εἰσί, καὶ τό γε μάλιστ' εὐδοκιμοῦν
τὰ νῦν ἐνθάδε γένος, τὸ Γορτυνικόν. ἐκ Γόρτυνος
γὰρ τυγχάνει ἀπῳκηκὸς ταύτῃ[1] τῆς Πελοποννη-
σιακῆς.

B ΑΘ. Οὐ τοίνυν εὔκολος ὁμοίως γίγνοιτ' ἂν ὁ
κατοικισμὸς ταῖς πόλεσιν, ὅταν μὴ τὸν τῶν ἐσμῶν
γίγνηται τρόπον, ἓν γένος ἀπὸ μιᾶς ἰὸν χώρας
οἰκίζηται, φίλον παρὰ φίλων, στενοχωρίᾳ τινὶ
πολιορκηθὲν γῆς ἤ τισιν ἄλλοις τοιούτοις παθήμασιν ἀναγκασθέν. ἔστι δ' ὅτε καὶ στάσεσι
βιαζόμενον ἀναγκάζοιτ' ἂν ἑτέρωσε ἀποξενοῦσθαι
πόλεώς τι μόριον· ἤδη δέ ποτε καὶ ξυνάπασα
πόλις τινῶν ἔφυγεν, ἄρδην κρείττονι κρατηθεῖσα
C πολέμῳ. ταῦτ' οὖν πάντ' ἐστὶ τῇ μὲν ῥᾴω
κατοικίζεσθαί τε καὶ νομοθετεῖσθαι, τῇ δὲ χαλε-
πώτερα. τὸ μὲν γὰρ ἕν τι εἶναι γένος ὁμόφωνον
καὶ ὁμόνομον ἔχει τινὰ φιλίαν, κοινωνὸν ἱερῶν ὂν
καὶ τῶν τοιούτων πάντων, νόμους δ' ἑτέρους καὶ
πολιτείας ἄλλας τῶν οἴκοθεν οὐκ εὐπετῶς ἀν-
έχεται, τὸ δ' ἐνίοτε πονηρίᾳ νόμων ἐστασιακὸς καὶ
διὰ συνήθειαν ζητοῦν ἔτι χρῆσθαι τοῖς αὐτοῖς
ἤθεσι, δι' ἃ καὶ πρότερον ἐφθάρη, χαλεπὸν τῷ
κατοικίζοντι καὶ νομοθετοῦντι καὶ δυσπειθὲς
D γίγνεται· τὸ δ' αὖ παντοδαπὸν ἐς ταὐτὸ ξυνερ-

---

[1] ταύτῃ : ταύτης MSS., edd.

quarters the present expedition of citizens is likely to be drawn.

CLIN. It will probably be from the whole of Crete; and of the rest of the Greeks, they seem most ready to admit people from the Peloponnese as fellow-settlers. For it is quite true, as you said just now, that we have some here from Argos, amongst them being the most famous of our clans, the Gortynian, which is a colony from Gortys, in the Peloponnese.

ATH. It would not be equally easy for States to conduct settlements in other cases as in those when, like a swarm of bees, a single clan goes out from a single country and settles, as a friend coming from friends, being either squeezed out by lack of room or forced by some other such pressing need. At times, too, the violence of civil strife might compel a whole section of a State to emigrate; and on one occasion an entire State went into exile, when it was totally crushed by an overpowering attack. All such cases are in one way easier to manage, as regards settling and legislation, but in another way harder. In the case where the race is one, with the same language and laws, this unity makes for friendliness, since it shares also in sacred rites and all matters of religion; but such a body does not easily tolerate laws or polities which differ from those of its homeland. Again, where such a body has seceded owing to civil strife due to the badness of the laws, but still strives to retain, owing to long habit, the very customs which caused its former ruin, then, because of this, it proves a difficult and intractable subject for the person who has control of its settlement and its laws. On the other hand, the clan that is formed by fusion of

708 ῥυηκὸς γένος ὑπακοῦσαι μέν τινων νόμων
καινῶν τάχα ἂν ἐθελήσειε μᾶλλον, τὸ δὲ συμ-
πνεῦσαι καὶ καθάπερ ἵππων ζεῦγος καθ᾽ ἓν ἀεὶ [1]
ταὐτόν, τὸ λεγόμενον, ξυμφυσῆσαι χρόνου πολλοῦ
καὶ παγχάλεπον. ἀλλ᾽ ὄντως ἐστὶ νομοθεσία καὶ
πόλεων οἰκισμοὶ πάντων τελεωτάτων [2] πρὸς
ἀρετὴν ἀνδρῶν.

ΚΛ. Εἰκός· ὅπῃ δ᾽ αὖ βλέπων τοῦτ᾽ εἴρηκας,
φράζ᾽ ἔτι σαφέστερον.

Ε ΑΘ. Ὦ ᾽γαθέ, ἔοικα περὶ νομοθετῶν ἐπανιὼν
καὶ σκοπῶν ἅμα ἐρεῖν τι καὶ φαῦλον· ἀλλ᾽ ἐὰν
πρὸς καιρόν τινα λέγωμεν, πρᾶγμα οὐδὲν γίγνοιτ᾽
ἂν ἔτι. καίτοι τί ποτε δυσχεραίνω ; σχεδὸν γάρ
τοι πάντα οὕτως ἔοικ᾽ ἔχειν τἀνθρώπινα.

ΚΛ. Τοῦ δὴ πέρι λέγεις ;

ΑΘ. Ἔμελλον λέγειν ὡς οὐδείς ποτε ἀνθρώπων
709 οὐδὲν νομοθετεῖ, τύχαι δὲ καὶ ξυμφοραὶ παντοῖαι
πίπτουσαι παντοίως νομοθετοῦσι τὰ πάντα ἡμῖν.
ἢ γὰρ πόλεμός τις βιασάμενος ἀνέτρεψε πολιτείας
καὶ μετέβαλε νόμους, ἢ πενίας χαλεπῆς ἀπορία·
πολλὰ δὲ καὶ νόσοι ἀναγκάζουσι καινοτομεῖν
λοιμῶν τε ἐμπιπτόντων, καὶ χρόνον ἐπὶ πολὺν
ἐνιαυτῶν πολλῶν πολλάκις ἀκαιρίας. [3] ταῦτα δὴ
πάντα προϊδών τις ἀξιώσειεν [4] ἂν εἰπεῖν ὅπερ ἐγὼ
νῦν δή, τὸ θνητὸν μὲν μηδένα νομοθετεῖν μηδέν,
Β τύχας δ᾽ εἶναι σχεδὸν ἅπαντα τὰ ἀνθρώπινα
πράγματα. τὸ δ᾽ ἔστι περί τε ναυτιλίαν καὶ
κυβερνητικὴν καὶ ἰατρικὴν καὶ στρατηγικὴν πάντα
ταῦτ᾽ εἰπόντα δοκεῖν εὖ λέγειν· ἀλλὰ γὰρ ὁμοίως

---

[1] ἓν ἀεὶ : ἕνα εἰς MSS. : ἓν εἰς Stallb., Schanz.
[2] τελεωτάτων Badham, Schanz : τελεώτατον MSS.

various elements would perhaps be more ready to submit to new laws, but to cause it to share in one spirit and pant (as they say) in unison like a team of horses would be a lengthy task and most difficult. But in truth legislation and the settlement of States are tasks that require men perfect above all other men in goodness.

CLIN. Very probably; but tell us still more clearly the purport of these observations.

ATH. My good Sir, in returning to the subject of lawgivers in our investigation, I may probably have to cast a slur on them; but if what I say is to the point, then there will be no harm in it. Yet why should I vex myself? For practically all human affairs seem to be in this same plight.

CLIN. What is it you refer to?

ATH. I was on the point of saying that no man ever makes laws, but chances and accidents of all kinds, occurring in all sorts of ways, make all our laws for us. For either it is a war that violently upsets polities and changes laws, or it is the distress due to grievous poverty. Diseases, too, often force on revolutions, owing to the inroads of pestilences and recurring bad seasons prolonged over many years. Foreseeing all this, one might deem it proper to say—as I said just now—that no mortal man frames any law, but human affairs are nearly all matters of pure chance. But the fact is that, although one may appear to be quite right in saying this about sea-faring and the arts of the pilot, the physician, and the general, yet there really is some-

---

[3] ἀκαιρίας Stallb. : ἀκαιρία Zur. (ἀκαιρίαι MSS. *al.*)
[4] ἀξιώσειεν Heindorf : ἄξειεν MSS.

709 αὖ καὶ τόδε ἔστι λέγοντα εὖ λέγειν ἐν τοῖς αὐτοῖς
τούτοις.

ΚΛ. Τὸ ποῖον ;

ΑΘ. Ὡς θεὸς μὲν πάντα καὶ μετὰ θεοῦ τύχη
καὶ καιρὸς τἀνθρώπινα διακυβερνῶσι ξύμπαντα.
ἡμερώτερον μὴν τρίτον ξυγχωρῆσαι τούτοις δεῖν
ἔπεσθαι τέχνην· καιρῷ γὰρ [χειμῶνος]¹ ξυλλα-
C βέσθαι κυβερνητικὴν ἢ μὴν² μέγα πλεονέκτημα
ἔγωγ' ἂν θείην. ἢ πῶς ;

ΚΛ. Οὕτως.

ΑΘ. Οὐκοῦν καὶ τοῖς ἄλλοις ὡσαύτως κατὰ
τὸν αὐτὸν ἂν ἔχοι λόγον ; καὶ δὴ καὶ νομοθεσία
ταὐτὸν τοῦτο δοτέον· τῶν ἄλλων ξυμπιπτόντων
ὅσα δεῖ χώρᾳ ξυντυχεῖν, εἰ μέλλοι ποτὲ εὐδαι-
μόνως οἰκήσειν, τὸν νομοθέτην ἀληθείας ἐχόμενον
τῇ τοιαύτῃ παραπεσεῖν ἑκάστοτε πόλει δεῖν.

ΚΛ. Ἀληθέστατα λέγεις.

D ΑΘ. Οὐκοῦν ὅ γε πρὸς ἕκαστόν τι τῶν εἰρημένων ἔχων τὴν τέχνην κἂν εὔξασθαί που δύναιτο
ὀρθῶς τι, <ὅ τι>³ παρὸν αὐτῷ διὰ τύχης τῆς
τέχνης ἂν μόνον ἐπιδέοι ;

ΚΛ. Πάνυ μὲν οὖν.

ΑΘ. Οἵ τε ἄλλοι γε δὴ πάντες οἱ νῦν δὴ
ῥηθέντες κελευόμενοι τὴν αὐτῶν εὐχὴν εἰπεῖν
εἴποιεν ἄν. ἢ γάρ ;

ΚΛ. Τί μήν ;

ΑΘ. Ταὐτὸν δὴ κἂν⁴ νομοθέτης, οἶμαι, δράσειεν.

ΚΛ. Ἔγωγ' οἶμαι.

---

¹ [χειμῶνος] bracketed by Badham, Schanz.
² ἢ μὴν : ἢ μή, MSS. (bracketed by Schanz)
³ τι, <ὅ τι> : τί MSS. : τι, ὃ Stephens.
⁴ κἂν : καὶ MSS. (ἂν for δὴ Schanz)

thing else that we may say with equal truth about these same things.

CLIN. What is that?

ATH. That God controls all that is, and that Chance and Occasion co-operate with God in the control of all human affairs. It is, however, less harsh to admit that these two must be accompanied by a third factor, which is Art. For that the pilots' art should co-operate with Occasion—verily I, for one, should esteem that a great advantage. Is it not so?

CLIN. It is.

ATH. Then we must grant that this is equally true in the other cases also, by parity of reasoning, including the case of legislation. When all the other conditions are present which a country needs to possess in the way of fortune if it is ever to be happily settled, then every such State needs to meet with a lawgiver who holds fast to truth.

CLIN. Very true.

ATH. Would not, then, the man who possessed art in regard to each of the crafts mentioned be able to pray aright for that condition which, if it were given by Chance, would need only the supplement of his own art?

CLIN. Certainly.

ATH. And if all the other craftsmen mentioned just now were bidden to state the object of their prayers, they could do so, could they not?

CLIN. Of course.

ATH. And the lawgiver, I suppose, could do likewise?

CLIN. I suppose so.

709 ΑΘ. Φέρε δή, νομοθέτα, πρὸς αὐτὸν φῶμεν, τί σοι καὶ πῶς πόλιν ἔχουσαν δῶμεν, ὃ λαβὼν ἕξεις ὥστ᾽ ἐκ τῶν λοιπῶν αὐτὸς τὴν πόλιν ἱκανῶς διοικῆσαι ;[1]

Ε ΚΛ. Τί μετὰ τοῦτ᾽ εἰπεῖν ὀρθῶς ἔστιν ἄρα ;

ΑΘ. Τοῦ νομοθέτου φράζωμεν τοῦτο, ἢ γάρ ;

ΚΛ. Ναί.

ΑΘ. Τόδε· τυραννουμένην μοι δότε τὴν πόλιν, φήσει· τύραννος δ᾽ ἔστω νέος καὶ μνήμων καὶ εὐμαθὴς καὶ ἀνδρεῖος καὶ μεγαλοπρεπὴς φύσει. ὃ δὲ καὶ ἐν τοῖς πρόσθεν ἐλέγομεν δεῖν ἕπεσθαι ξύμπασι τοῖς τῆς ἀρετῆς μέρεσι, καὶ νῦν τῇ
710 τυράννου ἡμῖν[2] ψυχῇ τοῦτο ξυνεπέσθω, ἐὰν μέλλῃ τῶν ἄλλων ὑπαρχόντων ὄφελος εἶναί τι.

ΚΛ. Σωφροσύνην μοι δοκεῖ φράζειν, ὦ Μέγιλλε, δεῖν εἶναι τὴν ξυνεπομένην ὁ ξένος. ἢ γάρ ;

ΑΘ. Τὴν δημώδη γε, ὦ Κλεινία, καὶ οὐχ ἥν τις σεμνύνων ἂν λέγοι, φρόνησιν προσαναγκάζων εἶναι τὸ σωφρονεῖν, ἀλλ᾽ ὅπερ εὐθὺς παισὶ καὶ θηρίοις, τοῖς μὲν <μὴ>[3] ἀκρατῶς ἔχειν πρὸς τὰς ἡδονάς, ξύμφυτον ἐπανθεῖ, τοῖς δὲ ἐγκρατῶς· ὃ
Β καὶ μονούμενον ἔφαμεν τῶν πολλῶν ἀγαθῶν λεγομένων οὐκ ἄξιον εἶναι λόγου. ἔχετε γὰρ ὃ λέγω που.

ΚΛ. Πάνυ μὲν οὖν.

---

[1] I follow here the arrangement of Ritter and Burnet.
[2] τυράννου ἡμῖν : τυραννουμένῃ MSS. (τυράννου England)
[3] <μὴ> I add.

---

[1] Cp. *Rep.* 473 C ff., 486 A ff.   [2] 696 D.
[3] 698 A ; *Phaedo* 82 A. The "academic" (or philosophic) identification of "virtue" with "wisdom" was a main feature in the Ethics of Socrates ; cp. *Rep.* 430 D ff.

ATH. " Come now, O lawgiver," let us say to him, " what are we to give you, and what condition of State, to enable you, when you receive it, thenceforward to manage the State by yourself satisfactorily ? "

CLIN. What is the next thing that can rightly be said ?

ATH. You mean, do you not, on the side of the lawgiver ?

CLIN. Yes.

ATH. This is what he will say: " Give me the State under a monarchy;[1] and let the monarch be young, and possessed by nature of a good memory, quick intelligence, courage and nobility of manner; and let that quality, which we formerly mentioned[2] as the necessary accompaniment of all the parts of virtue, attend now also on our monarch's soul, if the rest of his qualities are to be of any value."

CLIN. Temperance, as I think, Megillus, is what the Stranger indicates as the necessary accompaniment. Is it not ?

ATH. Yes, Clinias; temperance, that is, of the ordinary kind[3]; not the kind men mean when they use academic language and identify temperance with wisdom, but that kind which by natural instinct springs up at birth in children and animals, so that some are not incontinent, others continent, in respect of pleasures; and of this we said[4] that, when isolated from the numerous so-called " goods," it was of no account. You understand, of course, what I mean.

CLIN. Certainly.

[4] 696 D.

710   ΑΘ.   Ταύτην τοίνυν ἡμῖν ὁ τύραννος τὴν φύσιν
ἐχέτω πρὸς ἐκείναις ταῖς φύσεσιν, εἰ μέλλει πόλις
ὡς δυνατόν ἐστι τάχιστα καὶ ἄριστα σχήσειν
πολιτείαν ἣν λαβοῦσα εὐδαιμονέστατα διάξει.
θάττων γὰρ ταύτης καὶ ἀμείνων πολιτείας διάθε-
σις οὔτ᾽ ἔστιν οὔτ᾽ ἄν ποτε γένοιτο.

C   ΚΛ.   Πῶς δὴ καὶ τίνι λόγῳ τοῦτο, ὦ ξένε,
λέγων ἄν τις ὀρθῶς λέγειν αὐτὸν πείθοι;

ΑΘ.   Ῥᾴδιόν που τοῦτό γ᾽ νοεῖν ἔστ᾽, ὦ Κλεινία,
κατὰ φύσιν ὡς ἔστι τοῦθ᾽ οὕτως.

ΚΛ.   Πῶς λέγεις; εἰ τύραννος γένοιτο, φῄς,
νέος, σώφρων, εὐμαθής, μνήμων, ἀνδρεῖος, μεγα-
λοπρεπής;

ΑΘ.   Εὐτυχής, πρόσθες, μὴ κατ᾽ ἄλλο, ἀλλὰ
τὸ γενέσθαι τε ἐπ᾽ αὐτοῦ νομοθέτην ἄξιον ἐπαίνου
D καί τινα τύχην εἰς ταὐτὸν ἀγαγεῖν αὐτῷ. γενομένου γὰρ τούτου πάντα σχεδὸν ἀπείργασται τῷ
θεῷ, ἅπερ ὅταν βουληθῇ διαφερόντως εὖ πρᾶξαί
τινα πόλιν. δεύτερον δέ, ἐάν ποτέ τινες δύο
ἄρχοντες γίγνωνται τοιοῦτοι, τρίτον δ᾽ αὖ καὶ
κατὰ λόγον ὡσαύτως χαλεπώτερον, ὅσῳ πλείους·
ὅσῳ δ᾽ ἐναντίον, ἐναντίως.

ΚΛ.   Ἐκ τυραννίδος ἀρίστην φῂς γενέσθαι
πόλιν ἄν, ὡς φαίνει, μετὰ νομοθέτου γε ἄκρου
καὶ τυράννου κοσμίου, καὶ ῥᾷστά τε καὶ τάχιστ᾽
ἄν μεταβαλεῖν εἰς τοῦτο ἐκ τοῦ τοιούτου, δεύτερον
E δὲ ἐξ ὀλιγαρχίας. ἢ πῶς λέγεις; [καὶ τὸ τρίτον
ἐκ δημοκρατίας.][1]

----

[1] [καὶ . . . δημοκρατίας] bracketed by Hermann.

ATH. Let our monarch, then, possess this natural quality in addition to the other qualities mentioned, if the State is to acquire in the quickest and best way possible the constitution it needs for the happiest kind of life. For there does not exist, nor could there ever arise, a quicker and better form of constitution than this.

CLIN. How and by what argument, Stranger, could one convince oneself that to say this is to speak the truth?

ATH. It is quite easy to perceive at least this, Clinias, that the facts stand by nature's ordinance in the way described.

CLIN. In what way do you mean? On condition, do you say, that there should be a monarch who was young, temperate, quick at learning, with a good memory, brave and of a noble manner?

ATH. Add also "fortunate,"—not in other respects, but only in this, that in his time there should arise a praiseworthy lawgiver, and that, by a piece of good fortune, the two of them should meet; for if this were so, then God would have done nearly everything that he does when he desires that a State should be eminently prosperous. The second best condition is that there should arise two such rulers; then comes the third best, with three rulers; and so on, the difficulty increasing in proportion as the number becomes greater, and *vice versa*.

CLIN. You mean, apparently, that the best State would arise from a monarchy, when it has a first-rate lawgiver and a virtuous monarch, and these are the conditions under which the change into such a State could be effected most easily and quickly; and, next to this, from an oligarchy—or what is it you mean?

PLATO

710　ΑΘ.　Οὐδαμῶς, ἀλλ' ἐκ τυραννίδος μὲν πρῶτον,
δεύτερον δὲ ἐκ βασιλικῆς πολιτείας, τρίτον δὲ ἔκ
τινος δημοκρατίας· τὸ δὲ τέταρτον, ὀλιγαρχία
τὴν τοῦ τοιούτου γένεσιν χαλεπώτατα δύναιτ' ἂν
προσδέξασθαι· πλεῖστοι γὰρ ἐν αὐτῇ δυνάσται
γίγνονται. λέγομεν δὴ ταῦτα γίγνεσθαι τότε
ὅταν ἀληθὴς μὲν νομοθέτης γένηται φύσει, κοινὴ
δὲ αὐτῷ τις ξυμβῇ γνώμη[1] πρὸς τοὺς ἐν τῇ πόλει
711　μέγιστον δυναμένους. οὗ δ' ἂν τοῦτο ἀριθμῷ μὲν
βραχύτατον, ἰσχυρότατον δέ, καθάπερ ἐν τυ-
ραννίδι, γένηται, ταύτῃ καὶ τότε τάχος καὶ
ῥᾳστώνη τῆς μεταβολῆς γίγνεσθαι φιλεῖ.

ΚΛ.　Πῶς; οὐ γὰρ μανθάνομεν.

ΑΘ.　Καὶ μὴν εἴρηταί γ' ἡμῖν οὐχ ἅπαξ ἀλλ',
οἶμαι, πολλάκις. ὑμεῖς δὲ τάχα οὐδὲ τεθέασθε
τυραννουμένην πόλιν.

ΚΛ.　Οὐδέ γε ἐπιθυμητὴς ἔγωγ' εἰμὶ τοῦ θεά-
ματος.

B　ΑΘ.　Καὶ μὴν τοῦτό γ' ἂν ἴδοις ἐν αὐτῇ τὸ νῦν
δὴ λεγόμενον.

ΚΛ.　Τὸ ποῖον;

ΑΘ.　Οὐδὲν δεῖ πόνων οὐδέ τινος παμπόλλου
χρόνου τῷ τυράννῳ μεταβαλεῖν βουληθέντι πόλεως ἤθη, πορεύεσθαι δὲ αὐτὸν δεῖ πρῶτον ταύτῃ
ὅπῃπερ ἂν ἐθελήσῃ, ἐάν τε πρὸς ἀρετῆς ἐπιτηδεύματα προτρέπεσθαι τοὺς πολίτας ἐάν τε ἐπὶ
τοὐναντίον, αὐτὸν πρῶτον πάντα ὑπογράφοντα
τῷ πράττειν, τὰ μὲν ἐπαινοῦντα καὶ τιμῶντα, τὰ
C　δ' αὖ πρὸς ψόγον ἄγοντα, καὶ τὸν μὴ πειθόμενον
ἀτιμάζοντα καθ' ἑκάστας τῶν πράξεων.

ΚΛ.　Καί πως οἰώμεθα ταχὺ ξυνακολουθήσειν

---

[1] γνώμη Badham : ῥώμη MSS.

276

ATH. Not at all: the easiest step is from a monarchy, the next easiest from a constitutional monarchy, the third from some form of democracy. An oligarchy, which comes fourth in order, would admit of the growth of the best State only with the greatest difficulty, since it has the largest number of rulers. What I say is that the change takes place when nature supplies a true lawgiver, and when it happens that his policy is shared by the most powerful persons in the State; and wherever the State authorities are at once strongest and fewest in number, then and there the changes are usually carried out with speed and facility.

CLIN. How so? We do not understand.

ATH. Yet surely it has been stated not once, I imagine, but many times over. But you, very likely, have never so much as set eyes on a monarchical State.

CLIN. No, nor have I any craving for such a sight.

ATH. You would, however, see in it an illustration of what we spoke of just now.

CLIN. What was that?

ATH. The fact that a monarch, when he decides to change the moral habits of a State, needs no great efforts nor a vast length of time, but what he does need is to lead the way himself first along the desired path, whether it be to urge the citizens towards virtue's practices or the contrary; by his personal example he should first trace out the right lines, giving praise and honour to these things, blame to those, and degrading the disobedient according to their several deeds.

CLIN. Yes, we may perhaps suppose that the rest

711 τοὺς ἄλλους πολίτας τῷ τὴν τοιαύτην πειθὼ καὶ
ἅμα βίαν εἰληφότι ;

ΑΘ. Μηδεὶς ἡμᾶς πειθέτω, ὦ φίλοι, ἄλλῃ
θᾶττον καὶ ῥᾷον μεταβάλλειν ἄν ποτε πόλιν τοὺς
νόμους ἢ τῇ τῶν δυναστευόντων ἡγεμονίᾳ, μηδὲ
νῦν γε ἄλλῃ γίγνεσθαι μηδ' αὖθίς ποτε γενήσεσθαι. καὶ γὰρ οὖν ἡμῖν οὐ τοῦτ' ἐστὶν ἀδύνατον
D οὐδὲ χαλεπῶς ἂν γενόμενον, ἀλλὰ τόδ' ἐστὶ τὸ
χαλεπὸν γενέσθαι, καὶ ὀλίγον δὴ τὸ γεγονὸς ἐν
τῷ πολλῷ χρόνῳ· ὅταν δὲ ξυμβῇ, μυρία καὶ
πάντ' ἐν πόλει ἀγαθὰ ἀπεργάζεται, ἐν ᾗ ποτ' ἂν
ἐγγένηται.

ΚΛ. Τὸ ποῖον δὴ λέγεις ;

ΑΘ. Ὅταν ἔρως θεῖος τῶν σωφρόνων τε καὶ
δικαίων ἐπιτηδευμάτων ἐγγένηται μεγάλαις τισὶ
δυναστείαις, ἢ κατὰ μοναρχίαν δυναστευούσαις ἢ
E κατὰ πλούτων ὑπεροχὰς διαφερούσαις ἢ γενῶν· ἢ
τὴν Νέστορος ἐάν ποτέ τις ἐπανενέγκῃ φύσιν, ὃν
τῇ τοῦ λέγειν ῥώμῃ φασὶ πάντων διενεγκόντα
ἀνθρώπων πλέον ἔτι τῷ σωφρονεῖν διαφέρειν.
τοῦτ' οὖν ἐπὶ μὲν Τροίας, ὥς φασι, γέγονεν, ἐφ'
ἡμῶν δὲ οὐδαμῶς· εἰ δ' οὖν γέγονεν ἢ καὶ γενήσε-
ται τοιοῦτος ἢ νῦν ἡμῶν ἐστί τις, μακαρίως μὲν
αὐτὸς ζῇ, μακάριοι δὲ οἱ ξυνήκοοι τῶν ἐκ τοῦ
σωφρονοῦντος στόματος ἰόντων λόγων. ὡσαύτως
δὲ καὶ ξυμπάσης δυνάμεως ὁ αὐτὸς πέρι λόγος,
712 ὡς ὅταν εἰς ταὐτὸν τῷ φρονεῖν τε καὶ σωφρονεῖν
ἡ μεγίστη δύναμις ἐν ἀνθρώπῳ ξυμπέσῃ, τότε
πολιτείας τῆς ἀρίστης καὶ νόμων τῶν τοιούτων
φύεται γένεσις, ἄλλως δὲ οὐ μή ποτε γένηται.
ταῦτα μὲν οὖν καθαπερεὶ μῦθός τις λεχθεὶς
κεχρησμῳδήσθω, καὶ ἐπιδεδείχθω τῇ μὲν χαλεπὸν

of the citizens will quickly follow the ruler who adopts such a combination of persuasion and force.

ATH. Let none, my friends, persuade us that a State could ever change its laws more quickly or more easily by any other way than by the personal guidance of the rulers: no such thing could ever occur, either now or hereafter. Indeed, that is not the result which we find it difficult or impossible to bring about; what is difficult to bring about is rather that result which has taken place but rarely throughout long ages, and which, whenever it does take place in a State, produces in that State countless blessings of every kind.

CLIN. What result do you mean?

ATH. Whenever a heaven-sent desire for temperate and just institutions arises in those who hold high positions,—whether as monarchs, or because of conspicuous eminence of wealth or birth, or, haply, as displaying the character of Nestor, of whom it is said that, while he surpassed all men in the force of his eloquence, still more did he surpass them in temperance. That was, as they say, in the Trojan age, certainly not in our time; still, if any such man existed, or shall exist, or exists among us now, blessed is the life he leads, and blessed are they who join in listening to the words of temperance that proceed out of his mouth. So likewise of power in general, the same rule holds good: whenever the greatest power coincides in man with wisdom and temperance, then the germ of the best polity and of the best laws is planted;[1] but in no other way will it ever come about. Regard this as a myth oracularly uttered, and let us take it as proved that the rise of a well-governed State is in

[1] Cp. *Rep.* 473 D.

712 ὂν τὸ πόλιν εὔνομον γίγνεσθαι, τῇ δ᾽, εἴπερ
γένοιτο ὃ λέγομεν, πάντων τάχιστόν τε καὶ ῥᾷστον
μακρῷ.

ΚΛ. Ἴσως.[1]

B ΑΘ. Πειρώμεθα προσαρμόττοντες τῇ πόλει
σοι, καθάπερ παῖδες [2] πρεσβῦται, πλάττειν τῷ
λόγῳ τοὺς νόμους.

ΚΛ. Ἴωμεν δὴ καὶ μὴ μέλλωμεν ἔτι.

ΑΘ. Θεὸν δὴ πρὸς τὴν τῆς πόλεως κατασκευὴν
ἐπικαλώμεθα· ὁ δὲ ἀκούσειέ τε καὶ ἀκούσας ἵλεως
εὐμενής τε ἡμῖν ἔλθοι συνδιακοσμήσων τήν τε
πόλιν καὶ τοὺς νόμους.

ΚΛ. Ἔλθοι γὰρ οὖν.

ΑΘ. Ἀλλὰ τίνα δή ποτε πολιτείαν ἔχομεν ἐν
C νῷ τῇ πόλει προστάττειν ;

ΚΛ. Οἷον δὴ τί λέγεις βουληθείς ; φράζ᾽ ἔτι
σαφέστερον· οἷον δημοκρατίαν τινὰ ἢ ὀλιγαρχίαν
ἢ ἀριστοκρατίαν ἢ βασιλικήν. οὐ γὰρ δὴ τυραννίδα γέ που λέγοις ἄν, ὥς γ᾽ ἡμεῖς ἂν οἰηθείη-
μεν.

ΑΘ. Φέρε δὴ τοίνυν, πότερος ὑμῶν ἀποκρίνασθαι πρότερος ἂν ἐθέλοι τὴν οἴκοι πολιτείαν
εἰπών, τίς τούτων ἐστίν ;

ΜΕ. Μῶν οὖν τὸν πρεσβύτερον ἐμὲ δικαιότερον
εἰπεῖν πρότερον ;

D ΚΛ. Ἴσως.

ΜΕ. Καὶ μὴν ξυννοῶν γε, ὦ ξένε, τὴν ἐν Λακεδαίμονι πολιτείαν οὐκ ἔχω σοι φράζειν οὕτως
ἥντινα προσαγορεύειν αὐτὴν δεῖ. καὶ γὰρ τυ-
ραννίδι δοκεῖ μοι προσεοικέναι· τὸ γὰρ τῶν

---

[1] Ἴσως.: Πῶς ; MSS. (καλῶς Susemihl)

one way difficult, but in another way—given, that is, the condition we mention—it is easier by far and quicker than anything else.

CLIN. No doubt.

ATH. Let us apply the oracle to your State, and so try, like greybeard boys, to model its laws by our discourse.[1]

CLIN. Yes, let us proceed, and delay no longer.

ATH. Let us invoke the presence of the God at the establishment of the State; and may he hearken, and hearkening may he come, propitious and kindly to us-ward, to help us in the fashioning of the State and its laws.

CLIN. Yes, may he come!

ATH. Well, what form of polity is it that we intend to impose upon the State?

CLIN. What, in particular, do you refer to? Explain still more clearly. I mean, is it a democracy, an oligarchy, an aristocracy, or a monarchy? For certainly you cannot mean a tyranny: that we can never suppose.

ATH. Come now, which of you two would like to answer me first and tell me to which of these kinds his own polity at home belongs?

MEG. Is it not proper that I, as the elder, should answer first?

CLIN. No doubt.

MEG. In truth, Stranger, when I reflect on the Lacedaemonian polity, I am at a loss to tell you by what name one should describe it. It seems to me to resemble a tyranny, since the board of ephors it

---

[1] Cp. 746 A.

---

[2] παῖδες Paris MS. : παῖδα al. MSS., Zur.

712 ἐφόρων θαυμαστῶς [1] ὡς τυραννικὸν ἐν αὐτῇ
γέγονε. καί τοι ἐνίοτέ μοι φαίνεται πασῶν τῶν
πόλεων δημοκρατουμένη μάλιστ' ἐοικέναι. τὸ δ'
αὖ μὴ φάναι ἀριστοκρατίαν αὐτὴν εἶναι παντά-
Ε πασιν ἄτοπον. καὶ μὴν δὴ βασιλεία γε διὰ βίου
τ' ἐστὶν ἐν αὐτῇ καὶ ἀρχαιοτάτη πασῶν καὶ πρὸς
πάντων ἀνθρώπων καὶ ἡμῶν αὐτῶν λεγομένη.
ἐγὼ δὲ οὕτω νῦν ἐξαίφνης ἀνερωτηθεὶς [2] ὄντως,
ὅπερ εἶπον, οὐκ ἔχω διορισάμενος εἰπεῖν τίς τούτων
ἐστὶ τῶν πολιτειῶν.

ΚΛ. Ταὐτόν σοι πάθος, ὦ Μέγιλλε, κατα-
φαίνομαι πεπονθέναι· πάνυ γὰρ ἀπορῶ τὴν ἐν
Κνωσῷ πολιτείαν τούτων τινὰ διισχυριζόμενος
εἰπεῖν.

ΑΘ. Ὄντως γάρ, ὦ ἄριστοι, πολιτειῶν μετέ-
χετε· ἃς δὲ ὠνομάκαμεν νῦν, οὐκ εἰσὶ πολιτεῖαι,
πόλεων δὲ οἰκήσεις δεσποζομένων τε καὶ δου-
713 λευουσῶν μέρεσιν ἑαυτῶν τισί, τὸ τοῦ δεσπότου
δὲ ἑκάστη προσαγορεύεται κράτος. χρῆν δ' εἴπερ
τοῦ [3] τοιούτου τὴν πόλιν ἔδει ἐπονομάζεσθαι, τὸ
τοῦ ἀληθῶς τῶν τὸν νοῦν ἐχόντων δεσπόζοντος
θεοῦ ὄνομα λέγεσθαι.

ΚΛ. Τίς δ' ὁ θεός;

ΑΘ. Ἆρ' οὖν μύθῳ σμικρά γ' ἔτι προσχρησ-
τέον, εἰ μέλλομεν ἐμμελῶς πως δηλῶσαι τὸ νῦν
ἐρωτώμενον;

ΚΛ.[4] Οὐκοῦν χρὴ ταύτῃ δρᾶν;

ΑΘ. Πάνυ μὲν οὖν. τῶν γὰρ δὴ πόλεων ὧν
Β ἔμπροσθεν τὰς ξυνοικήσεις διήλθομεν, ἔτι προ-
τέρα τούτων πάμπολυ λέγεταί τις ἀρχή τε καὶ
οἴκησις γεγονέναι ἐπὶ Κρόνου μάλ' εὐδαίμων, ἧς

contains is a marvellously tyrannical feature; yet
sometimes it strikes me as, of all States, the nearest
to a democracy. Still, it would be totally absurd to
deny that it is an aristocracy; while it includes,
moreover, a life monarchy, and that the most ancient
of monarchies, as is affirmed, not only by ourselves,
but by all the world. But now that I am questioned
thus suddenly, I am really, as I said, at a loss to say
definitely to which of these polities it belongs.

CLIN. And I, Megillus, find myself equally per-
plexed; for I find it very difficult to affirm that our
Cnosian polity is any one of these.

ATH. Yes, my good Sirs; for you do, in fact, partake in a number of polities. But those we named
just now are not polities, but arrangements of States
which rule or serve parts of themselves, and each is
named after the ruling power. But if the State
ought to be named after any such thing, the name it
should have borne is that of the God who is the true
ruler of rational men.

CLIN. Who is that God?

ATH. May we, then, do a little more story-telling,
if we are to answer this question suitably?

CLIN. Should we not do so?

ATH. We should. Long ages before even those
cities existed whose formation we have described
above, there existed in the time of Cronos, it is
said, a most prosperous government and settlement,

---

[1] θαυμαστῶς Schanz : θαυμαστὸν MSS.

[2] ἀνερωτηθείς Madvig : ἂν ἐρωτηθείς MSS.

[3] του Burnet: τὸ Paris MSS., Zur. (al. τοῦ)

[4] MSS. and Zur. give οὐκοῦν . . . δρᾶν to *Ath.* and Πάνυ μὲν
οὖν to *Clin.*: I follow Schneider, Schanz, *al.*

713 μίμημα ἔχουσά ἐστιν ἥτις τῶν νῦν ἄριστα οἰκεῖται.

ΚΛ. Σφόδρ' ἄν, ὡς ἔοικ', εἴη περὶ αὐτῆς δέον ἀκουειν.

ΑΘ. Ἐμοὶ γοῦν φαίνεται· διὸ καὶ παρήγαγον αὐτὴν εἰς τὸ μέσον τοῖς λόγοις.

ΜΕ. Ὀρθότατά γε δρῶν· καὶ τόν γε ἑξῆς C περαίνων ἂν μῦθον, εἴπερ προσήκων ἐστί, μάλ' ὀρθῶς ἂν ποιοίης.

ΑΘ. Δραστέον ὡς λέγετε. φήμην τοίνυν παραδεδέγμεθα τῆς τῶν τότε μακαρίας ζωῆς, ὡς ἄφθονά τε καὶ αὐτόματα πάντα εἶχεν. ἡ δὲ τούτων αἰτία λέγεται τοιάδε τις· γιγνώσκων ὁ Κρόνος ἄρα, καθάπερ ἡμεῖς διεληλύθαμεν, ὡς ἀνθρωπεία φύσις οὐδεμία ἱκανὴ τὰ ἀνθρώπινα διοικοῦσα αὐτοκράτωρ πάντα μὴ οὐχ ὕβρεώς τε καὶ ἀδικίας μεστοῦσθαι, ταῦτ' οὖν διανοούμενος D ἐφίστη βασιλέας τε καὶ ἄρχοντας ταῖς πόλεσιν ἡμῶν οὐκ ἀνθρώπους, ἀλλὰ γένους θειοτέρου τε καὶ ἀμείνονος, δαίμονας· οἷον νῦν ἡμεῖς δρῶμεν τοῖς ποιμνίοισι καὶ ὅσων ἥμεροί εἰσιν ἀγέλαι· οὐ βοῦς βοῶν οὐδὲ αἶγας αἰγῶν ἄρχοντας ποιοῦμεν αὐτοῖσί τινας, ἀλλ' ἡμεῖς αὐτῶν δεσπόζομεν, ἄμεινον ἐκείνων γένος. ταὐτὸν δὴ καὶ ὁ θεὸς ἄρα ὡς[1] φιλάνθρωπος ὢν τότε[2] γένος ἄμεινον ἡμῶν ἐφίστη τὸ τῶν δαιμόνων, ὃ διὰ πολλῆς μὲν αὐτοῖς ῥαστώνης, πολλῆς δ' ἡμῖν ἐπιμελούμενον ἡμῶν, E εἰρήνην τε καὶ αἰδῶ καὶ εὐνομίαν καὶ ἀφθονίαν δίκης παρεχόμενον, ἀστασίαστα καὶ εὐδαίμονα τὰ τῶν ἀνθρώπων ἀπειργάζετο γένη. λέγει δὴ καὶ

---

[1] ὡς: καὶ MSS. (Schanz brackets ἄρα καὶ)

284

on which the best of the States now existing is modelled.[1]

CLIN. Evidently it is most important to hear about it.

ATH. I, for one, think so; and that is why I have introduced the mention of it.

MEG. You were perfectly right to do so; and, since your story is pertinent, you will be quite right in going on with it to the end.

ATH. I must do as you say. Well, then, tradition tells us how blissful was the life of men in that age, furnished with everything in abundance, and of spontaneous growth. And the cause thereof is said to have been this: Cronos was aware of the fact that no human being (as we have explained[2]) is capable of having irresponsible control of all human affairs without becoming filled with pride and injustice; so, pondering this fact, he then appointed as kings and rulers for our cities, not men, but beings of a race that was nobler and more divine, namely, daemons. He acted just as we now do in the case of sheep and herds of tame animals: we do not set oxen as rulers over oxen, or goats over goats, but we, who are of a nobler race, ourselves rule over them. In like manner the God, in his love for humanity, set over us at that time the nobler race of daemons who, with much comfort to themselves and much to us, took charge of us and furnished peace and modesty and orderliness and justice without stint, and thus made the tribes of men free from feud and happy.

---

[1] Cp. *Politic.* 271.　　　　[2] 691 C, D.

---

[2] τότε Hermann: τὸ MSS. (bracketed by Stallb.)

713 νῦν οὗτος ὁ λόγος ἀληθείᾳ χρώμενος, ὡς ὅσων
ἂν πόλεων μὴ θεὸς ἀλλά τις ἄρχῃ θνητός, οὐκ
ἔστι κακῶν αὐτοῖς οὐδὲ πόνων ἀνάφυξις· ἀλλὰ
μιμεῖσθαι δεῖν ἡμᾶς οἴεται πάσῃ μηχανῇ τὸν ἐπὶ
τοῦ Κρόνου λεγόμενον βίον, καὶ ὅσον ἐν ἡμῖν
ἀθανασίας ἔνεστι, τούτῳ πειθομένους δημοσίᾳ καὶ
714 ἰδίᾳ τάς τ' οἰκήσεις καὶ τὰς πόλεις διοικεῖν, τὴν
τοῦ νοῦ διανομὴν ἐπονομάζοντας νόμον. εἰ δ'
ἄνθρωπος εἷς ἢ ὀλιγαρχία τις ἢ καὶ δημοκρατία
ψυχὴν ἔχουσα ἡδονῶν καὶ ἐπιθυμιῶν ὀρεγομένην
καὶ πληροῦσθαι τούτων δεομένην, στέγουσαν δὲ
οὐδὲν ἀλλ' ἀνηνύτῳ καὶ ἀπλήστῳ κακῶν [1] νοσήματι ξυνεχομένην, ἄρξει δὴ πόλεως ἤ τινος ἰδιώτου
καταπατήσας ὁ τοιοῦτος τοὺς νόμους, ὃ νῦν δὴ
B ἐλέγομεν, οὐκ ἔστι σωτηρίας μηχανή. σκοπεῖν
δὴ δεῖ τοῦτον τὸν λόγον ἡμᾶς, ὦ Κλεινία, πότερον
αὐτῷ πεισόμεθα ἢ πῶς δράσομεν.

ΚΛ. Ἀνάγκη δή που πείθεσθαι.

ΑΘ. Ἐννοεῖς οὖν ὅτι νόμων εἴδη τινές φασιν
εἶναι τοσαῦτα ὅσαπερ πολιτειῶν ; πολιτειῶν δὲ
ἄρτι διεληλύθαμεν ὅσα λέγουσιν οἱ πολλοί. μὴ
δὴ φαύλου πέρι νομίσῃς εἶναι τὴν νῦν ἀμφισβήτησιν, περὶ δὲ τοῦ μεγίστου· τὸ γὰρ δίκαιον καὶ
τὸ ἄδικον οἷ χρὴ βλέπειν, πάλιν ἡμῖν ἀμφισβη-
τούμενον ἐλήλυθεν. οὔτε γὰρ πρὸς τὸν πόλεμον
C οὔτε πρὸς ἀρετὴν ὅλην βλέπειν δεῖ φασὶ τοὺς
νόμους, ἀλλ' ἥτις ἂν καθεστηκυῖα ᾖ πολιτεία,

---

[1] κακῶν Heindorf : κακῷ MSS. (Hermann and Schanz bracket
νοσήματι)

---

[1] A double word-play : νοῦς = νόμος, and διανομάς =
δαίμονας. Laws, being "the dispensations of reason," take
the place of the "daemons" of the age of Cronos : the divine

And even to-day this tale has a truth to tell, namely, that wherever a State has a mortal, and no god, for ruler, there the people have no rest from ills and toils; and it deems that we ought by every means to imitate the life of the age of Cronos, as tradition paints it, and order both our homes and our States in obedience to the immortal element within us, giving to reason's ordering the name of "law." [1] But if an individual man or an oligarchy or a democracy, possessed of a soul which strives after pleasures and lusts and seeks to surfeit itself therewith, having no continence and being the victim of a plague that is endless and insatiate of evil,— if such an one shall rule over a State or an individual by trampling on the laws, then there is (as I said just now) no means of salvation. This, then, is the statement, Clinias, which we have to examine, to see whether we believe it, or what we are to do.

CLIN. We must, of course, believe it.

ATH. Are you aware that, according to some, there are as many kinds of laws as there are kinds of constitutions? And how many constitutions are commonly recognized we have recently recounted.[2] Please do not suppose that the problem now raised is one of small importance; rather it is of the highest importance. For we are again [3] faced with the problem as to what ought to be the aim of justice and injustice. The assertion of the people I refer to is this,—that the laws ought not to aim either at war or at goodness in general, but ought to have regard to the benefit of the established

element in man (τὸ δαιμόνιον), which claims obedience, is reason (νοῦς).

[2] 712 C ff.   [3] Cp. 630 B, 690 B, C.

714 ταύτῃ δεῖν <ἰδεῖν>[1] τὸ ξυμφέρον, ὅπως ἄρξει τε
ἀεὶ καὶ μὴ καταλυθήσεται, καὶ τὸν φύσει ὅρον τοῦ
δικαίου λέγεσθαι κάλλισθ᾽ οὕτως.

ΚΛ. Πῶς;

ΑΘ. Ὅτι τὸ τοῦ κρείττονος ξυμφέρον ἐστί.

ΚΛ. Λέγ᾽ ἔτι σαφέστερον.

ΑΘ. Ὧδε. τίθεται δή που, φασί, τοὺς νόμους
ἐν τῇ πόλει ἑκάστοτε τὸ κρατοῦν. ἦ γάρ;

ΚΛ. Ἀληθῆ λέγεις.

ΑΘ. Ἆρ᾽ οὖν οἴει, φασί, ποτὲ δῆμον νικήσαντα
D ἤ τινα πολιτείαν ἄλλην ἢ καὶ τύραννον θήσεσθαι
ἑκόντα πρὸς ἄλλο τι πρῶτον νόμους ἢ τὸ συμφέροι
ἑαυτῷ τῆς ἀρχῆς τοῦ μένειν;

ΚΛ. Πῶς γὰρ ἄν;

ΑΘ. Οὐκοῦν καὶ ὃς ἂν ταῦτα τὰ τεθέντα παρα-
βαίνῃ, κολάσει ὁ θέμενος ὡς ἀδικοῦντα, δίκαια
εἶναι ταῦτ᾽ ἐπονομάζων;

ΚΛ. Ἔοικε γοῦν.

ΑΘ. Ταῦτ᾽ ἄρ᾽ ἀεὶ καὶ οὕτω καὶ ταύτῃ τὸ
δίκαιον ἂν ἔχοι.

ΚΛ. Φησὶ γοῦν οὗτος ὁ λόγος.

E ΑΘ. Ἔστι γὰρ τοῦτο ἓν ἐκείνων τῶν ἀξιωμάτων[2]
ἀρχῆς πέρι.

ΚΛ. Ποίων δή;

ΑΘ. Τῶν ἃ τότε ἐπεσκοποῦμεν, τίνας τίνων
ἄρχειν δεῖ. καὶ ἐφάνη δὴ γονέας μὲν ἐκγόνων,
νεωτέρων δὲ πρεσβυτέρους, γενναίους δὲ ἀγεννῶν·
καὶ συχνὰ ἄττα ἦν ἄλλ᾽, εἰ μεμνήμεθα, καὶ

---

[1] <ἰδεῖν> I add (ἰδεῖν for δεῖν Schneider).
[2] ἀξιωμάτων Schulthess: δικαιωμάτων Zur.: ἀδικημάτων
MSS.

288

polity, whatever it may be, so that it may keep in power for ever and never be dissolved ; and that the natural definition of justice is best stated in this way.

CLIN. In what way?

ATH. That justice is "what benefits the stronger." [1]

CLIN. Explain yourself more clearly.

ATH. This is how it is :—the laws (they say) in a State are always enacted by the stronger power? Is it not so?

CLIN. That is quite true.

ATH. Do you suppose, then (so they argue), that a democracy or any other government—even a tyrant—if it has gained the mastery, will of its own accord set up laws with any other primary aim than that of securing the permanence of its own authority?

CLIN. Certainly not.

ATH. Then the lawgiver will style these enactments "justice," and will punish every transgressor as guilty of injustice.

CLIN. That is certainly probable.

ATH. So these enactments will thus and herein always constitute justice.

CLIN. That is, at any rate, what the argument asserts.

ATH. Yes, for this is one of those "agreed claims" concerning government.[2]

CLIN. What "claims"?

ATH. Those which we dealt with before,—claims as to who should govern whom. It was shown that parents should govern children, the older the younger, the high-born the low-born, and (if you remember) there were many other claims, some of

---

[1] Cp. *Rep.* i. 338, ii. 367.   [2] Cp. 690 B.

PLATO

714 ἐμπόδια ἕτερα ἑτέροισι. καὶ δὴ καὶ ἓν ἦν αὐτῶν
τοῦτο, καὶ ἔφαμέν που κατὰ φύσιν τὸν νόμον
715 ἄγειν δικαιοῦντα τὸ βιαιότατον, ὡς φάναι <τὸν
Πίνδαρον>.[1]

ΚΛ. Ναί, ταῦτ᾽ ἦν ἃ τότε ἐλέχθη.

ΑΘ. Σκόπει δὴ ποτέροις τισὶν ἡ πόλις ἡμῖν
ἐστὶ παραδοτέα. γέγονε γὰρ δὴ μυριάκις ἤδη
τὸ τοιοῦτον ἔν τισι πόλεσιν.

ΚΛ. Τὸ ποῖον;

ΑΘ. Ἀρχῶν περιμαχήτων γενομένων οἱ νική-
σαντες τά τε πράγματα κατὰ τὴν πόλιν οὕτως
ἐσφετέρισαν σφόδρα, ὥστε ἀρχῆς μηδ᾽ ὁτιοῦν
μεταδιδόναι τοῖς ἡττηθεῖσι, μήτε αὐτοῖς μήτε
ἐκγόνοις, παραφυλάττοντες δὲ ἀλλήλους ζῶσιν,
B ὅπως μή ποτέ τις εἰς ἀρχὴν ἀφικόμενος ἐπαναστῇ
μεμνημένος τῶν ἔμπροσθεν γεγονότων κακῶν.
ταύτας δή πού φαμεν ἡμεῖς νῦν οὔτ᾽ εἶναι πολιτείας,
οὔτ᾽ ὀρθοὺς νόμους ὅσοι μὴ ξυμπάσης τῆς πόλεως
ἕνεκα τοῦ κοινοῦ ἐτέθησαν· οἳ δ᾽ ἕνεκα τινῶν,
στασιωτείας ἀλλ᾽ οὐ πολιτείας τούτους φαμέν,
καὶ τὰ τούτων δίκαια ἅ φασιν εἶναι, μάτην
εἰρῆσθαι. λέγεται δὲ τοῦδ᾽ ἕνεκα ταῦθ᾽ ἡμῖν,
ὡς ἡμεῖς τῇ σῇ πόλει ἀρχὰς οὔθ᾽ ὅτι πλούσιός
C ἐστί τις δώσομεν, οὔθ᾽ ὅτι τῶν τοιούτων ἄλλο
οὐδὲν κεκτημένος, ἰσχὺν ἢ μέγεθος ἤ τι γένος·
ὃς δ᾽ ἂν τοῖς τεθεῖσι νόμοις εὐπειθέστατός τ᾽ ἦ
καὶ νικᾷ ταύτην τὴν νίκην ἐν τῇ πόλει, τούτῳ

---

[1] νόμον Badham (adding τὸν Πίνδαρον after φάναι): Πίνδαρον
MSS., edd.

---

[1] Cp. 690 B, with the footnote.

which were conflicting. The claim before us is one of these, and we said that[1]—to quote Pindar—" the law marches with nature when it justifies the right of might."

CLIN. Yes, that is what was said then.

ATH. Consider now, to which class of men should we entrust our State. For the condition referred to is one that has already occurred in States thousands of times.

CLIN. What condition?

ATH. Where offices of rule are open to contest, the victors in the contest monopolise power in the State so completely that they offer not the smallest share in office to the vanquished party or their descendants; and each party keeps a watchful eye on the other, lest anyone should come into office and, in revenge for the former troubles, cause a rising against them. Such polities we, of course, deny to be polities, just as we deny that laws are true laws unless they are enacted in the interest of the common weal of the whole State. But where the laws are enacted in the interest of a section, we call them " feudalities "[2] rather than " polities "; and the " justice " they ascribe to such laws is, we say, an empty name. Our reason for saying this is that in your State we shall assign office to a man, not because he is wealthy, nor because he possesses any other quality of the kind—such as strength or size or birth; but the ministration of the laws must be assigned, as we assert, to that man who is most obedient to the laws and wins the victory for

---

[2] A word coined (like the Greek) to suggest a constitution based on "feuds" or party-divisions.

715 φαμὲν καὶ τὴν τῶν τεθέντων[1] ὑπηρεσίαν δοτέον
εἶναι τὴν μεγίστην τῷ πρώτῳ, καὶ δευτέραν τῷ
τὰ δεύτερα κρατοῦντι, καὶ κατὰ λόγον οὕτω τοῖς
ἐφεξῆς τὰ μετὰ ταῦθ' ἕκαστα ἀποδοτέον εἶναι.
τοὺς δ' ἄρχοντας λεγομένους νῦν ὑπηρέτας τοῖς
νόμοις ἐκάλεσα οὔ τι καινοτομίας ὀνομάτων ἕνεκα,
D ἀλλ' ἡγοῦμαι παντὸς μᾶλλον εἶναι παρὰ τοῦτο
σωτηρίαν τε πόλει καὶ τοὐναντίον. ἐν ᾗ μὲν γὰρ
ἂν ἀρχόμενος ᾖ καὶ ἄκυρος νόμος, φθορὰν ὁρῶ
τῇ τοιαύτῃ ἑτοίμην οὖσαν· ἐν ᾗ δὲ ἂν δεσπότης
τῶν ἀρχόντων, οἱ δὲ ἄρχοντες δοῦλοι τοῦ νόμου,
σωτηρίαν καὶ πάνθ' ὅσα θεοὶ πόλεσιν ἔδοσαν
ἀγαθὰ γιγνόμενα καθορῶ.

ΚΛ.   Ναὶ μὰ Δί', ὦ ξένε· καθ' ἡλικίαν γὰρ ὀξὺ
βλέπεις.

ΑΘ.   Νέος μὲν γὰρ ὢν πᾶς ἄνθρωπος τὰ τοιαῦτα
E ἀμβλύτατα αὐτὸς αὑτοῦ ὁρᾷ, γέρων δὲ ὀξύτατα.

ΚΛ.   Ἀληθέστατα.

ΑΘ.   Τί δὴ τὸ μετὰ ταῦτα; ἆρ' οὐχ ἥκοντας
μὲν καὶ παρόντας θῶμεν τοὺς ἐποίκους, τὸν δ'
ἑξῆς αὐτοῖς διαπεραντέον ἂν εἴη λόγον;

ΚΛ.   Πῶς γὰρ οὔ;

ΑΘ.   Ἄνδρες τοίνυν φῶμεν πρὸς αὐτούς, ὁ μὲν
δὴ θεός, ὥσπερ καὶ ὁ παλαιὸς λόγος, ἀρχήν τε
καὶ τελευτὴν καὶ μέσα τῶν ὄντων ἁπάντων ἔχων,
716 εὐθείᾳ περαίνει κατὰ φύσιν περιπορευόμενος· τῷ
δ' ἀεὶ ξυνέπεται Δίκη τῶν ἀπολειπομένων τοῦ
θείου νόμου τιμωρός, ἧς ὁ μὲν εὐδαιμονήσειν

---

[1] τεθέντων my conj. (also Apelt, independently): θεῶν
MSS.

---

[1] " Magistrates " = rulers ; " ministers " = subjects, or
servants.

obedience in the State,—the highest office to the first, the next to him that shows the second degree of mastery, and the rest must similarly be assigned, each in succession, to those that come next in order. And those who are termed "magistrates" I have now called "ministers"[1] of the laws, not for the sake of coining a new phrase, but in the belief that salvation, or ruin, for a State hangs upon nothing so much as this. For wherever in a State the law is subservient and impotent, over that State I see ruin impending; but wherever the law is lord over the magistrates, and the magistrates are servants to the law, there I descry salvation and all the blessings that the gods bestow on States.

CLIN. Aye, by Heaven, Stranger; for, as befits your age, you have keen sight.

ATH. Yes; for a man's vision of such objects is at its dullest when he is young, but at its keenest when he is old.

CLIN. Very true.

ATH. What, then, is to be our next step? May we not assume that our immigrants have arrived and are in the country, and should we not proceed with our address to them?

CLIN. Of course.

ATH. Let us, then, speak to them thus :—" O men, that God who, as old tradition[2] tells, holdeth the beginning, the end, and the centre of all things that exist, completeth his circuit by nature's ordinance in straight, unswerving course. With him followeth Justice always, as avenger of them that fall short of the divine law; and she, again, is followed by

---

[2] Probably Orphic, quoted thus by the Scholiast: Ζεὺς ἀρχή, Ζεὺς μέσσα, Διὸς δ᾽ ἐκ πάντα τέτυκται.

716 μέλλων ἐχόμενος ξυνέπεται ταπεινὸς καὶ κεκοσ-
μημένος, ὃ δέ τις ἐξαρθεὶς ὑπὸ μεγαλαυχίας ἢ
χρήμασιν ἐπαιρόμενος ἢ τιμαῖς ἢ καὶ σώματος
εὐμορφίᾳ, ἅμα νεότητι καὶ ἀνοίᾳ, φλέγεται τὴν
ψυχὴν μεθ' ὕβρεως, ὡς οὔτ' ἄρχοντος οὔτε τινὸς
ἡγεμόνος δεόμενος, ἀλλὰ καὶ ἄλλοις ἱκανὸς ὢν
B ἡγεῖσθαι, καταλείπεται ἔρημος θεοῦ, καταλειφθεὶς
δὲ καὶ ἔτι ἄλλους τοιούτους προσλαβὼν σκιρτᾷ
ταράττων πάνθ' ἅμα, καὶ πολλοῖς τισὶν ἔδοξεν
εἶναί τις, μετὰ δὲ χρόνον οὐ πολὺν ὑποσχὼν
τιμωρίαν οὐ μεμπτὴν τῇ δίκῃ ἑαυτόν τε καὶ
οἶκον καὶ πόλιν ἄρδην ἀνάστατον ἐποίησε. πρὸς
ταῦτ' οὖν οὕτω διατεταγμένα τί χρὴ δρᾶν ἢ
διανοεῖσθαι, καὶ τί μή, τὸν ἔμφρονα;

ΚΛ. Δῆλον δὴ τοῦτό γε, ὡς τῶν ξυνακολου-
θησόντων ἐσόμενον τῷ θεῷ δεῖ διανοηθῆναι πάντα
ἄνδρα.

C ΑΘ. Τίς οὖν δὴ πρᾶξις φίλη καὶ ἀκόλουθος
θεῷ; μία, καὶ ἕνα λόγον ἔχουσα ἀρχαῖον, ὅτι
τῷ μὲν ὁμοίῳ τὸ ὅμοιον ὄντι μετρίῳ φίλον ἂν
εἴη, τὰ δ' ἄμετρα οὔτ' ἀλλήλοις οὔτε τοῖς ἐμ-
μέτροις. ὁ δὴ θεὸς ἡμῖν πάντων χρημάτων
μέτρον ἂν εἴη μάλιστα, καὶ πολὺ μᾶλλον ἤ πού
τις, ὥς φασιν, ἄνθρωπος. τὸν οὖν τῷ τοιούτῳ
προσφιλῆ γενησόμενον εἰς δύναμιν ὅτι μάλιστα
καὶ αὐτὸν τοιοῦτον ἀναγκαῖον γίγνεσθαι. καὶ
κατὰ τοῦτον δὴ τὸν λόγον ὁ μὲν σώφρων ἡμῶν

---

[1] Cp. Hom. *Od.* xvii. 218: ὡς αἰεὶ τὸν ὅμοιον ἄγει θεὸς ὡς
τὸν ὅμοῖον. The expression "like to like" became proverbial,
like our "Birds of a feather," etc. Usually it was applied
more to the bad than to the good (or "moderate") to which
Plato here restricts it.

every man who would fain be happy, cleaving to her with lowly and orderly behaviour; but whoso is uplifted by vainglory, or prideth himself on his riches or his honours or his comeliness of body, and through this pride joined to youth and folly, is inflamed in soul with insolence, dreaming that he has no need of ruler or guide, but rather is competent himself to guide others,—such an one is abandoned and left behind by the God, and when left behind he taketh to him others of like nature, and by his mad prancings throweth all into confusion: to many, indeed, he seemeth to be some great one, but after no long time he payeth the penalty, not unmerited, to Justice, when he bringeth to total ruin himself, his house, and his country. Looking at these things, thus ordained, what ought the prudent man to do, or to devise, or to refrain from doing?"

CLIN. The answer is plain: Every man ought so to devise as to be of the number of those who follow in the steps of the God.

ATH. What conduct, then, is dear to God and in his steps? One kind of conduct, expressed in one ancient phrase,[1] namely, that "like is dear to like" when it is moderate, whereas immoderate things are dear neither to one another nor to things moderate. In our eyes God will be "the measure of all things" in the highest degree—a degree much higher than is any "man" they talk of.[2] He, then, that is to become dear to such an one must needs become, so far as he possibly can, of a like character; and, according to the present argument, he amongst us

[2] An allusion to the dictum of the sophist Protagoras— "Man is the measure of all things," cp. *Cratyl.* 386 A ff.; *Theaet.* 152 A.

716D θεῷ φίλος, ὅμοιος γάρ, ὁ δὲ μὴ σώφρων ἀνόμοιός
τε καὶ διάφορος καὶ <ὁ> [1] ἄδικος· καὶ τἆλλα
οὕτω κατὰ τὸν αὐτὸν λόγον ἔχει. νοήσωμεν δὴ
τούτοις ἑπόμενον εἶναι τὸν τοιόνδε λόγον, ἁπάντων
κάλλιστον καὶ ἀληθέστατον, οἶμαι, λόγων, ὡς τῷ
μὲν ἀγαθῷ θύειν καὶ προσομιλεῖν ἀεὶ [2] τοῖς θεοῖς
εὐχαῖς καὶ ἀναθήμασι καὶ ξυμπάσῃ θεραπείᾳ
θεῶν κάλλιστον καὶ ἄριστον καὶ ἀνυσιμώτατον
πρὸς τὸν εὐδαίμονα βίον καὶ δὴ καὶ διαφερόντως
E πρέπον, τῷ δὲ κακῷ τούτων τἀναντία πέφυκεν.
ἀκάθαρτος γὰρ τὴν ψυχὴν ὅ γε κακός, καθαρὸς
δὲ ὁ ἐναντίος· παρὰ δὲ μιαροῦ δῶρα οὔτ᾽ ἄνδρ᾽
ἀγαθὸν οὔτε θεὸν ἔστι ποτὲ τό γε ὀρθὸν δέχεσθαι·
717 μάτην οὖν περὶ θεοὺς ὁ πολύς ἐστι πόνος τοῖς
ἀνοσίοις, τοῖσι δὲ ὁσίοις ἐγκαιρότατος ἅπασι.
σκοπὸς μὲν οὖν ἡμῖν οὗτος οὗ δεῖ στοχάζεσθαι·
βέλη δὲ αὐτοῦ καὶ οἷον ἡ τοῖς βέλεσιν ἔφεσις,
τὰ ποῖ᾽ ἂν γιγνόμενα [3] ὀρθότατα φέροιτ᾽ ἄν;
πρῶτον μέν, φαμέν, τιμὰς τὰς μετ᾽ Ὀλυμπίους
τε καὶ τοὺς τὴν πόλιν ἔχοντας θεοὺς τοῖς χθονίοις
ἄν τις θεοῖς ἄρτια [καὶ δεύτερα] [4] καὶ ἀριστερὰ
νέμων ὀρθότατα τοῦ τῆς εὐσεβείας σκοποῦ τυγ-
B χάνοι, τοῖς δὲ τούτων ἄνωθεν [τὰ περιττὰ] [5] καὶ
ἀντίφωνα τοῖς ἔμπροσθεν ῥηθεῖσι νῦν δή. μετὰ
θεοὺς δὲ τούσδε καὶ τοῖς δαίμοσιν ὅ γ᾽ ἔμφρων

---

[1] <ὁ> added by Ritter (Schanz brackets καὶ ἄδικος).
[2] ἀεὶ Burges, Schanz : δεῖ MSS. : δὴ Zur., al.
[3] γιγνόμενα H. Richards : λεγόμενα MSS.
[4] [καὶ δεύτερα] bracketed by England.
[5] [τὰ περιττὰ] bracketed by Burnet.

---

[1] This account of the ritual proper to the worship of the
various deities is obscure. Plainly, however, it is based on
the Pythagorean doctrine of "Opposites," in which the Odd

that is temperate is dear to God, since he is like
him, while he that is not temperate is unlike and at
enmity,—as is also he who is unjust, and so likewise
with the rest, by parity of reasoning. On this there
follows, let us observe, this further rule,—and of all
rules it is the noblest and truest,—that to engage
in sacrifice and communion with the gods continually,
by prayers and offerings and devotions of every kind,
is a thing most noble and good and helpful towards
the happy life, and superlatively fitting also, for the
good man; but for the wicked, the very opposite.
For the wicked man is unclean of soul, whereas the
good man is clean; and from him that is defiled no
good man, nor god, can ever rightly receive gifts.
Therefore all the great labour that impious men
spend upon the gods is in vain, but that of the
pious is most profitable to them all. Here, then, is
the mark at which we must aim; but as to the shafts
we should shoot, and (so to speak) the flight of
them,—what kind of shafts, think you, would fly
most straight to the mark? First of all, we say,
if—after the honours paid to the Olympians and
the gods who keep the State—we should assign the
Even and the Left as their honours to the gods of
the under-world, we would be aiming most straight
at the mark of piety—as also in assigning to the
former gods the things superior, the opposites of
these.[1] Next after these gods the wise man will

(number) is "superior" to the Even, and the "Right" (side)
to the "Left" (as also the "Male" to the "Female"). It
is here laid down that "honours" (or worship) of the
"superior" grade are to be offered only to the deities of
Olympus, or of the State, and inferior honours only to the
deities of the underworld. In Greek augury, also, the *left*
was the side of ill omen (*sinister*), whereas in Roman
augury the *right* is so.

717 ὀργιάζοιτ' ἄν, ἥρωσι δὲ μετὰ τούτους. ἐπακο-
λουθεῖ δ' αὐτοῖς ἱδρύματα ἴδια πατρῴων θεῶν
κατὰ νόμον ὀργιαζόμενα· γονέων δὲ μετὰ ταῦτα
τιμαὶ ζώντων, οἷς[1] θέμις ὀφείλοντα ἀποτίνειν τὰ
πρῶτά τε καὶ μέγιστα ὀφειλήματα, χρεῶν πάντων
πρεσβύτατα· νομίζειν δέ, ἃ κέκτηται καὶ ἔχει,
πάντα εἶναι τῶν γεννησάντων καὶ θρεψαμένων
C πρὸς τὸ παρέχειν αὐτὰ εἰς ὑπηρεσίαν ἐκείνοις
κατὰ δύναμιν πᾶσαν, ἀρχόμενον ἀπὸ τῆς οὐσίας,
δεύτερα τὰ τοῦ σώματος, τρίτα τὰ τῆς ψυχῆς,
ἀποτίνοντα δανείσματα ἐπιμελείας τε καὶ ὑπερπο-
νούντων ὠδῖνας παλαιὰς ἐπὶ νέοις δανεισθείσας,
ἀποδιδόντα δὲ παλαιοῖς ἐν τῷ γήρᾳ σφόδρα κεχρη-
μένοις. παρὰ δὲ πάντα τὸν βίον ἔχειν τε καὶ
ἐσχηκέναι χρὴ πρὸς αὑτοῦ γονέας εὐφημίαν
D διαφερόντως, διότι κούφων καὶ πτηνῶν λόγων
βαρυτάτη ζημία· πᾶσι γὰρ ἐπίσκοπος τοῖς περὶ
τὰ τοιαῦτα ἐτάχθη Δίκης Νέμεσις ἄγγελος. θυ-
μουμένοις τε οὖν ὑπείκειν δεῖ καὶ ἀποπιμπλᾶσι
τὸν θυμόν, ἐάν τ' ἐν λόγοις ἐάν τ' ἐν ἔργοις δρῶσι
τὸ τοιοῦτον, ξυγγιγνώσκοντα ὡς εἰκότως μάλιστα
πατὴρ υἱεῖ δοξάζων ἀδικεῖσθαι θυμοῖτ' ἂν διαφερόντως. τελευτησάντων δὲ γονέων ταφῇ μὲν
ἡ σωφρονεστάτη καλλίστη, μήθ' ὑπεραίροντα
τῶν εἰθισμένων ὄγκων μήτ' ἐλλείποντα ὧν οἱ
E προπάτορες τοῖς ἑαυτῶν γεννηταῖς[2] ἐτίθεσαν, τάς
τε αὖ κατ' ἐνιαυτὸν τῶν ἤδη τέλος ἐχόντων
ὡσαύτως ἐπιμελείας τὰς κόσμον φερούσας ἀπο-

---

[1] οἷς Hermann, after Ficinus: ὡς MSS.
[2] τοῖς . . . γεννηταῖς Badham, Schanz: τοὺς . . . γεννητὰς
MSS.

offer worship to the daemons, and after the daemons to the heroes. After these will come private shrines legally dedicated to ancestral deities; and next, honours paid to living parents. For to these duty enjoins that the debtor should pay back the first and greatest of debts, the most primary of all dues, and that he should acknowledge that all that he owns and has belongs to those who begot and reared him, so that he ought to give them service to the utmost of his power—with substance, with body, and with soul, all three,—thus making returns for the loans of care and pain spent on the children by those who suffered on their behalf in bygone years, and recompensing the old in their old age, when they need help most. And throughout all his life he must diligently observe reverence of speech towards his parents above all things, seeing that for light and winged words there is a most heavy penalty,—for over all such matters Nemesis, messenger of Justice, is appointed to keep watch;[1] wherefore the son must yield to his parents when they are wroth, and when they give rein to their wrath either by word or deed, he must pardon them, seeing that it is most natural for a father to be especially wroth when he deems that he is wronged by his own son. When parents die, the most modest funeral rites are the best, whereby the son neither exceeds the accustomed pomp, nor falls short of what his forefathers paid to their sires; and in like manner he should duly bestow the yearly attentions, which ensure honour, on the rites already com-

---

[1] Cp. S. Matth. xii. 36: "Every idle word that men shall speak, they shall give account thereof in the day of judgment."

PLATO

717 διδόναι· τῷ δὲ μὴ παραλείπειν μνήμην ἐνδελεχῆ
718 παρεχόμενον, τούτῳ μάλιστ᾽ ἀεὶ πρεσβεύειν, δα-
πάνης τε τῆς διδομένης ὑπὸ τύχης τὸ μέτριον τοῖς
κεκμηκόσι νέμοντα. ταῦτ᾽ ἂν ποιοῦντες καὶ κατὰ
ταῦτα ζῶντες ἑκάστοτε ἕκαστοι τὴν ἀξίαν ἂν
παρὰ θεῶν καὶ ὅσοι κρείττονες ἡμῶν κομιζοίμεθα,
ἐν ἐλπίσιν ἀγαθαῖς διάγοντες τὸ πλεῖστον τοῦ
βίου. ἃ δὲ πρὸς ἐκγόνους καὶ ξυγγενεῖς καὶ
φίλους καὶ πολίτας ὅσα τε ξενικὰ πρὸς θεῶν
θεραπεύματα καὶ ὁμιλίας ξυμπάντων τούτων
ἀποτελοῦντα τὸν ἑαυτοῦ βίον φαιδρυνάμενον κατὰ
B νόμον κοσμεῖν δεῖ, τῶν νόμων αὐτῶν ἡ διέξοδος,
τὰ μὲν πείθουσα, τὰ δὲ μὴ ὑπείκοντα πειθοῖ τῶν
ἠθῶν βίᾳ καὶ δίκῃ κολάζουσα, τὴν πόλιν ἡμῖν
ξυμβουληθέντων θεῶν μακαρίαν τε καὶ εὐδαίμονα
ἀποτελεῖ. ἃ δὲ χρὴ μὲν αὖ καὶ ἀναγκαῖον εἰπεῖν
νομοθέτην ὅστις ἅπερ ἐγὼ διανοεῖται, ἐν δὲ σχήματι νόμου ἀναρμοστεῖ λεγόμενα, τούτων πέρι
δοκεῖ μοι <δεῖν>¹ δεῖγμα προενεγκόντα αὐτῷ τε
C καὶ ἐκείνοις οἷς νομοθετήσει, τὰ λοιπὰ πάντα εἰς
δύναμιν διεξελθόντα, τὸ μετὰ τοῦτο ἄρχεσθαι τῆς
θέσεως τῶν νόμων.

ΚΛ.² Ἔστι δὲ δὴ τὰ τοιαῦτα ἐν τίνι μάλιστα
σχήματι κείμενα ;

ΑΘ. Οὐ πάνυ ῥᾴδιον ἐν ἑνὶ περιλαβόντα εἰπεῖν
αὐτὰ οἷόν τινι τύπῳ, ἀλλ᾽ οὑτωσί τινα τρόπον
λάβωμεν, ἄν τι δυνώμεθα περὶ αὐτῶν βεβαιώ-
σασθαι.

ΚΛ. Λέγε τὸ ποῖον.

---

¹ <δεῖν> added by Apelt.
² Here I follow Ast's arrangement ; Zur. and most edd.
give ἔστι . . . κείμενα, with the rest, to *Ath.*

300

pleted. He should always venerate them, by never failing to provide a continual memorial, and assigning to the deceased a due share of the means which fortune provides for expenditure. Every one of us, if we acted thus and observed these rules of life, would win always a due reward from the gods and from all that are mightier than ourselves, and would pass the greatest part of our lives in the enjoyment of hopes of happiness. As regards duties to children, relations, friends and citizens, and those of service done to strangers for Heaven's sake, and of social intercourse with all those classes,—by fulfilling which a man should brighten his own life and order it as the law enjoins,—the sequel of the laws themselves, partly by persuasion and partly (when men's habits defy persuasion) by forcible and just chastisement, will render our State, with the concurrence of the gods, a blessed State and a prosperous. There are also matters which a lawgiver, if he shares my view, must necessarily regulate, though they are ill-suited for statement in the form of a law; in dealing with these he ought, in my opinion, to produce a sample for his own use and that of those for whom he is legislating, and, after expounding all other matters as best he can, pass on next to commencing the task of legislation.

CLIN. What is the special form in which such matters are laid down?

ATH. It is by no means easy to embrace them all in a single model of statement (so to speak); but let us conceive of them in some such way as this, in case we may succeed in affirming something definite about them.

CLIN. Tell us what that "something" is.

718　ΑΘ. Βουλοίμην ἂν αὐτοὺς ὡς εὐπειθεστάτους
πρὸς ἀρετὴν εἶναι, καὶ δῆλον ὅτι πειράσεται τοῦτο
ὁ νομοθέτης ἐν ἁπάσῃ ποιεῖν τῇ νομοθεσίᾳ.

D　ΚΛ. Πῶς γὰρ οὔ;

ΑΘ. Τὰ τοίνυν δὴ λεχθέντα ἔδοξέ τί μοι
προὔργου δρᾶν εἰς τὸ περὶ ὧν ἂν παραινῇ μὴ
παντάπασιν ὠμαῖς ψυχαῖς[1] [λαβόμενα], μᾶλλον
δ᾽ ἡμερώτερόν τε ἂν ἀκούειν καὶ εὐμενέστερον·
ὥστε εἰ καὶ μὴ μέγα τι, σμικρὸν δὲ τὸν ἀκούοντα,
ὅπερ φημί,[2] εὐμενέστερον γιγνόμενον εὐμαθέστερον
ἀπεργάσεται, πάνυ[3] ἀγαπητόν. οὐ γὰρ πολλή
τις εὐπέτεια οὐδὲ ἀφθονία τῶν προθυμουμένων
ὡς ἀρίστων ὅτι μάλιστα καὶ ὡς τάχιστα
E　γίγνεσθαι, τὸν δὲ Ἡσίοδον οἱ πολλοὶ σοφὸν
ἀποφαίνουσι λέγοντα ὡς ἡ μὲν ἐπὶ τὴν κακότητα
ὁδὸς λεία καὶ ἀνιδιτὶ παρέχει πορεύεσθαι, μάλα
βραχεῖα οὖσα,

τῆς δ᾽ ἀρετῆς, φησίν, ἱδρῶτα θεοὶ προπάροιθεν
ἔθηκαν
ἀθάνατοι, μακρὸς δὲ καὶ ὄρθιος οἶμος ἐς αὐτήν,
719　καὶ τρηχὺς τὸ πρῶτον· ἐπὴν δ᾽ εἰς ἄκρον ἵκηαι,
ῥηϊδίη δὴ ᾽πειτα φέρει,[4] χαλεπή περ ἐοῦσα.

ΚΛ. Καὶ καλῶς γ᾽ ἔοικε λέγοντι.

ΑΘ. Πάνυ μὲν οὖν. ὁ δὲ προάγων λόγος ὅ
γέ μοι ἀπείργασται, βούλομαι ὑμῖν εἰς τὸ μέσον
αὐτὸ θεῖναι.

ΚΛ. Τίθει δή.

ΑΘ. Λέγωμεν δὴ τῷ νομοθέτῃ διαλεγόμενοι

---

[1] ὠμαῖς ψυχαῖς : ὠμῆς ψυχῆς MSS. λαβόμενα (in marg. of
MSS.) bracketed by Madvig, Schanz.
[2] φημί Vermehren : φησίν MSS.

ATH. I should desire the people to be as docile as possible in the matter of virtue ; and this evidently is what the legislator will endeavour to effect in all his legislation.

CLIN. Assuredly.

ATH. I thought the address we have made might prove of some help in making them listen to its monitions with souls not utterly savage, but in a more civil and less hostile mood. So that we may be well content if, as I say, it renders the hearer even but a little more docile, because a little less hostile. For there is no great plenty or abundance of persons anxious to become with all speed as good as possible ; the majority, indeed, serve to show how wise Hesiod was when he said,[1] " smooth is the way that leadeth unto wickedness," and that " no sweat is needed to traverse it," since it is " passing short," but (he says)—

" In front of goodness the immortal gods
   Have set the sweat of toil, and thereunto
Long is the road and steep, and rough withal
   The first ascent ; but when the crest is won,
   'Tis easy travelling, albeit 'twas hard."

CLIN. The poet speaks nobly, I should say.

ATH. He certainly does. Now I wish to put before you what I take to be the result of the foregoing argument.

CLIN. Do so.

ATH. Let us address the lawgiver and say:

[1] *Op. D.* 287 ff.

---

[3] πάνυ Badham : πᾶν MSS.
[4] φέρει : φέρειν MSS. : πέλει Zur. (after Hesiod).

719 τόδε, Εἰπὲ ἡμῖν, ὦ νομοθέτα· εἴπερ ὅ τι χρὴ
B πράττειν ἡμᾶς καὶ λέγειν εἰδείης, ἆρ' οὐ δῆλον
ὅτι καὶ ἂν εἴποις ;

ΚΛ. Ἀναγκαῖον.

ΑΘ. Σμικρῷ δὴ πρόσθεν ἄρα οὐκ ἠκούσαμέν
σου λέγοντος ὡς τὸν νομοθέτην οὐ δεῖ τοῖς
ποιηταῖς ἐπιτρέπειν ποιεῖν ὃ ἂν αὐτοῖς ᾖ φίλον ;
οὐ γὰρ δὴ[1] εἰδεῖεν τί ποτ' ἐναντίον τοῖς νόμοις
ἂν λέγοντες βλάπτοιεν τὴν πόλιν.

ΚΛ. Ἀληθῆ μέντοι λέγεις.

ΑΘ. Ὑπὲρ δὴ τῶν ποιητῶν εἰ τάδε λέγοιμεν
πρὸς αὐτόν, ἆρ' ἂν τὰ λεχθέντα εἴη μέτρια ;

ΚΛ. Ποῖα ;

C ΑΘ. Τάδε· Παλαιὸς μῦθος, ὦ νομοθέτα, ὑπο
τε αὐτῶν ἡμῶν ἀεὶ λεγόμενός ἐστι καὶ τοῖς ἄλλοις
πᾶσι ξυνδεδογμένος, ὅτι ποιητής, ὁπόταν ἐν τῷ
τρίποδι τῆς Μούσης καθίζηται, τότε οὐκ ἔμφρων
ἐστίν, οἷον δὲ κρήνη τις τὸ ἐπιὸν ῥεῖν ἑτοίμως ἐᾷ,
καὶ τῆς τέχνης οὔσης μιμήσεως ἀναγκάζεται
ἐναντίως ἀλλήλοις ἀνθρώπους ποιῶν διατιθε-
μένους ἐναντία λέγειν αὑτῷ πολλάκις, οἶδε δὲ
οὔτ' εἰ ταῦτα οὔτ' εἰ θάτερα ἀληθῆ τῶν λεγομένων. τῷ δὲ νομοθέτῃ τοῦτο οὐκ ἔστι ποιεῖν ἐν
D τῷ νόμῳ, δύο περὶ ἑνός, ἀλλὰ ἕνα περὶ ἑνὸς ἀεὶ δεῖ
λόγον ἀποφαίνεσθαι. σκέψαι δ' ἐξ αὐτῶν τῶν
ὑπὸ σοῦ νῦν δὴ λεχθέντων. οὔσης γὰρ ταφῆς
τῆς μὲν ὑπερβεβλημένης, τῆς δὲ ἐλλειπούσης,
τῆς δὲ μετρίας, τὴν μίαν ἑλόμενος σύ, τὴν μέσην,
ταύτην προστάττεις καὶ ἐπῄνεσας ἁπλῶς. ἐγὼ
δέ, εἰ μὲν γυνή μοι διαφέρουσα εἴη πλούτῳ καὶ

───────────

[1] δὴ : ἂν MSS. (bracketed by Ast, Schanz)

304

LAWS, BOOK IV

"Tell us, O lawgiver: if you knew what we ought to do and say, is it not obvious that you would state it?"

CLIN. Inevitably.

ATH. "Now did not we hear you saying a little while ago[1] that the lawgiver should not permit the poets to compose just as they please? For they would not be likely to know what saying of theirs might be contrary to the laws and injurious to the State."

CLIN. That is quite true.

ATH. Would our address be reasonable, if we were to address him on behalf of the poets[2] in these terms?—

CLIN. What terms?

ATH. These:—"There is, O lawgiver, an ancient saying—constantly repeated by ourselves and endorsed by everyone else—that whenever a poet is seated on the Muses' tripod, he is not in his senses, but resembles a fountain, which gives free course to the upward rush of water; and, since his art consists in imitation, he is compelled often to contradict himself, when he creates characters of contradictory moods; and he knows not which of these contradictory utterances is true. But it is not possible for the lawgiver in his law thus to compose two statements about a single matter; but he must always publish one single statement about one matter. Take an example from one of your own recent statements.[3] A funeral may be either excessive or defective or moderate: of these three alternatives you chose one, the moderate, and this you prescribe, after praising it unconditionally. I, on the other hand, if (in my poem) I had a wife of sur-

[1] 656 ff.   Cp. 719 D.   [3] Cp. 717 E.

719 θάπτειν αὐτὴν διακελεύοιτο ἐν τῷ ποιήματι, τὸν
E ὑπερβάλλοντα ἂν τάφον ἐπαινοίην, φειδωλὸς δ᾽
αὖ τις καὶ πένης ἀνὴρ τὸν καταδεᾶ, μέτρον δὲ
οὐσίας κεκτημένος καὶ μέτριος αὐτὸς ὢν τὸν
αὐτὸν ἂν ἐπαινέσειέ σοι.[1] σοὶ δ᾽ οὐχ οὕτω
ῥητέον ὡς νῦν εἶπες μέτριον εἰπών, ἀλλὰ τί τὸ
μέτριον καὶ ὁπόσον ῥητέον, ἢ τὸν τοιοῦτον λόγον
μήπω σοι διανοοῦ γίγνεσθαι νόμον.

ΚΛ. Ἀληθέστατα λέγεις.

ΑΘ. Πότερον οὖν ἡμῖν ὁ τεταγμένος ἐπὶ τοῖς
νόμοις μηδὲν τοιοῦτον προαγορεύῃ ἐν ἀρχῇ τῶν
720 νόμων, ἀλλ᾽ εὐθὺς ὃ δεῖ ποιεῖν καὶ μὴ φράζῃ τε
καὶ ἐπαπειλήσας τὴν ζημίαν ἐπ᾽ ἄλλον τρέπηται
νόμον, παραμυθίας δὲ καὶ πειθοῦς τοῖς νομο-
θετουμένοις μηδὲ ἓν προσδιδῷ; καθάπερ ἰατρὸς
δέ τις ὁ μὲν οὕτως, ὁ δ᾽ ἐκείνως ἡμᾶς εἴωθεν
ἑκάστοτε θεραπεύειν,—ἀναμιμνησκώμεθα δὲ τὸν
τρόπον ἑκάτερον, ἵνα τοῦ νομοθέτου δεώμεθα,
καθάπερ ἰατροῦ δέοιντο ἂν παῖδες τὸν πρᾳότατον
αὐτὸν θεραπεύειν τρόπον ἑαυτούς. οἷον δὴ τί
λέγομεν; εἰσί πού τινες ἰατροί, φαμέν, καί τινες
ὑπηρέται τῶν ἰατρῶν, ἰατροὺς δὲ καλοῦμεν δή
που καὶ τούτους.

B ΚΛ. Πάνυ μὲν οὖν.

ΑΘ. Ἐάν τέ γ᾽ ἐλεύθεροι ὦσιν ἐάν τε δοῦλοι,
κατ᾽ ἐπίταξιν δὲ τῶν δεσποτῶν καὶ θεωρίαν καὶ
κα-᾽ ἐμπειρίαν τὴν τέχνην κτῶνται, κατὰ φύσιν
δὲ μή, καθάπερ οἱ ἐλεύθεροι αὐτοί τε μεμαθήκασιν

---

[1] ἐπαινέσειέ σοι : ἐπαινέσοι MSS. (ἐπαινοίη σοι Badham).

passing wealth, and she were to bid me bury her, would extol the tomb of excessive grandeur ; while a poor and stingy man would praise the defective tomb, and the person of moderate means, if a moderate man himself, would praise the same one as you. But you should not merely speak of a thing as ' moderate,' in the way you have now done, but you should explain what ' the moderate ' is, and what is its size ; otherwise it is too soon for you to propose that such a statement should be made law."

CLIN. Exceedingly true.

ATH. Should, then, our appointed president of the laws commence his laws with no such prefatory statement, but declare at once what must be done and what not, and state the penalty which threatens disobedience, and so turn off to another law, without adding to his statutes a single word of encouragement and persuasion ? Just as is the way with doctors, one treats us in this fashion, and another in that : they have two different methods, which we may recall, in order that, like children who beg the doctor to treat them by the mildest method, so we may make a like request of the lawgiver. Shall I give an illustration of what I mean ? There are men that are doctors, we say, and others that are doctors' assistants ; but we call the latter also, to be sure, by the name of " doctors."

CLIN. We do.

ATH. These, whether they be free-born or slaves, acquire their art under the direction of their masters, by observation and practice and not by the study of nature—which is the way in which the free-born doctors have learnt the art themselves and in which

307

PLATO

720 οὕτω τούς τε αὐτῶν διδάσκουσι παῖδας. θείης
ἂν ταῦτα δύο γένη τῶν καλουμένων ἰατρῶν;

ΚΛ. Πῶς γὰρ οὔ;

ΑΘ. Ἆρ' οὖν καὶ ξυννοεῖς ὅτι δούλων καὶ
C ἐλευθέρων ὄντων τῶν καμνόντων ἐν ταῖς πόλεσι
τοὺς μὲν δούλους σχεδόν τι οἱ δοῦλοι τὰ πολλὰ
ἰατρεύουσι περιτρέχοντες καὶ ἐν τοῖς ἰατρείοις
περιμένοντες, καὶ οὔτε τινὰ λόγον ἑκάστου πέρι
νοσήματος ἑκάστου τῶν οἰκετῶν οὐδεὶς τῶν τοιούτων ἰατρῶν δίδωσιν οὐδ' ἀποδέχεται, προστάξας
δ' αὐτῷ τὰ δόξαντα ἐξ ἐμπειρίας ὡς ἀκριβῶς
εἰδώς, καθάπερ τύραννος, αὐθαδῶς οἴχεται ἀπο-
πηδήσας πρὸς ἄλλον κάμνοντα οἰκέτην, καὶ
ῥᾳστώνην οὕτω τῷ δεσπότῃ παρασκευάζει τῶν
D καμνόντων τῆς ἐπιμελείας; ὁ δὲ ἐλεύθερος ὡς
ἐπὶ τὸ πλεῖστον τὰ τῶν ἐλευθέρων νοσήματα
θεραπεύει τε καὶ ἐπισκοπεῖ, καὶ ταῦτα ἐξετάζων
ἀπ' ἀρχῆς καὶ κατὰ φύσιν, τῷ κάμνοντι κοινού-
μενος αὐτῷ τε καὶ τοῖς φίλοις, ἅμα μὲν αὐτὸς
μανθάνει τι παρὰ τῶν νοσούντων, ἅμα δέ, καθ'
ὅσον οἷός τ' ἐστί, διδάσκει τὸν ἀσθενοῦντα αὐτόν,
καὶ οὐ πρότερον ἐπέταξε πρὶν ἄν πῃ ξυμπείσῃ,
τότε δὲ μετὰ πειθοῦς ἡμερούμενον ἀεὶ παρασκευ-
E άζων τὸν κάμνοντα, εἰς τὴν ὑγίειαν ἄγων, ἀποτελεῖν πειρᾶται. πότερον οὕτως ἢ ἐκείνως ἰατρός
τε ἰώμενος ἀμείνων καὶ γυμναστὴς γυμνάζων;
διχῇ τὴν μίαν ἀποτελῶν δύναμιν, ἢ μοναχῇ καὶ
κατὰ τὸ χεῖρον τοῖν δυοῖν καὶ ἀγριώτερον ἀπεργαζόμενος;

ΚΛ. Πολύ που διαφέρον, ὦ ξένε, τὸ διπλῇ.

---

[1] Cp. 634 D, E; 722 B, C; 857 E.

they instruct their own disciples. Would you assert that we have here two classes of what are called "doctors"?

CLIN. Certainly.

ATH. You are also aware that, as the sick folk in the cities comprise both slaves and free men, the slaves are usually doctored by slaves, who either run round the town or wait in their surgeries; and not one of these doctors either gives or receives any account of the several ailments of the various domestics, but prescribes for each what he deems right from experience, just as though he had exact knowledge, and with the assurance of an autocrat; then up he jumps and off he rushes to another sick domestic, and thus he relieves his master in his attendance on the sick. But the free-born doctor is mainly engaged in visiting and treating the ailments of free men, and he does so by investigating them from the commencement and according to the course of nature; he talks with the patient himself and with his friends, and thus both learns himself from the sufferers and imparts instruction to them, so far as possible; and he gives no prescription until he has gained the patient's consent, and only then, while securing the patient's continued docility by means of persuasion, does he attempt to complete the task of restoring him to health. Which of these two methods of doctoring shows the better doctor, or of training, the better trainer? Should the doctor perform one and the same function in two ways, or do it in one way only [1] and that the worse way of the two and the less humane?

CLIN. The double method, Stranger, is by far the better.

720 ΑΘ. Βούλει δὴ καὶ θεασώμεθα τὸ διπλοῦν τοῦτο καὶ ἁπλοῦν ἐν ταῖς νομοθεσίαις αὐταῖς γιγνόμενον ;

ΚΛ. Πῶς γὰρ οὐ βούλομαι ;

ΑΘ. Φέρε δὴ πρὸς θεῶν, τίν' ἄρα πρῶτον νόμον θεῖτ' ἂν ὁ νομοθέτης ; ἆρ' οὐ κατὰ φύσιν τὴν περὶ γενέσεως ἀρχὴν πρώτην πόλεων πέρι

721 κατακοσμήσει ταῖς τάξεσιν ;

ΚΛ. Τί μήν ;

ΑΘ. Ἀρχὴ δ' ἐστὶ τῶν γενέσεων πάσαις πόλεσιν ἆρ' οὐχ ἡ τῶν γάμων σύμμιξις καὶ κοινωνία ;

ΚΛ. Πῶς γὰρ οὔ ;

ΑΘ. Γαμικοὶ δὴ νόμοι πρῶτοι κινδυνεύουσι τιθέμενοι καλῶς ἂν τίθεσθαι πρὸς ὀρθότητα πάσῃ πόλει.

ΚΛ. Παντάπασι μὲν οὖν.

ΑΘ. Λέγωμεν δὴ πρῶτον τὸν ἁπλοῦν. ἔχοι δ' ἂν πῶς ; [1] ἴσως ὧδε· γαμεῖν δέ, ἐπειδὰν ἐτῶν ᾖ τις

B τριάκοντα, μέχρι ἐτῶν πέντε καὶ τριάκοντα· εἰ δὲ μή, ζημιοῦσθαι χρήμασί τε καὶ ἀτιμίᾳ, χρήμασι μὲν τόσοις καὶ τόσοις, τῇ καὶ τῇ δὲ ἀτιμίᾳ. ὁ μὲν ἁπλοῦς ἔστω τις τοιοῦτος περὶ γάμων, ὁ δὲ διπλοῦς ὅδε. γαμεῖν δέ, ἐπειδὰν ἐτῶν ᾖ τις τριάκοντα, μέχρι τῶν πέντε καὶ τριάκοντα, διανοηθέντα ὡς ἔστιν ᾗ τὸ ἀνθρώπινον γένος φύσει τινὶ μετείληφεν ἀθανασίας, οὗ καὶ πέφυκεν ἐπιθυμίαν ἴσχειν πᾶς

C πᾶσαν· τὸ γὰρ γενέσθαι κλεινὸν καὶ μὴ ἀνώνυμον κεῖσθαι τετελευτηκότα τοῦ τοιούτου ἐστὶν ἐπι-

---

[1] πῶς ; Badham, Schanz : πως MSS.

---

[1] Cp. 631 D,E.

ATH. Do you wish us to examine the double method and the single as applied also to actual legislation?

CLIN. Most certainly I wish it.

ATH. Come, tell me then, in Heaven's name,— what would be the first law to be laid down by the lawgiver? Will he not follow the order of nature, and in his ordinances regulate first the starting-point of generation in States?

CLIN. Of course.

ATH. Does not the starting-point of generation in all States lie in the union and partnership of marriage?[1]

CLIN. Certainly.

ATH. So it seems that, if the marriage laws were the first to be enacted, that would be the right course in every State.

CLIN. Most assuredly.

ATH. Let us state the law in its simple form first: how will it run? Probably like this:—"A man shall marry when he is thirty years old and under five and thirty;[2] if he fails to do so, he shall be punished both by a fine in money and by degradation, the fine being of such and such an amount, and the degradation of such and such a kind." Such shall be the simple form of marriage law. The double form shall be this,—"A man shall marry when he is thirty years old and under thirty-five, bearing in mind that this is the way by which the human race, by nature's ordinance, shares in immortality, a thing for which nature has implanted in everyone a keen desire. The desire to win glory, instead of lying in a name-

---

[2] But cp. 772 D. Cp. also Ar. *Pol.* 1252ᵃ 28.

721 θυμία. γένος οὖν ἀνθρώπων ἐστί τι ξυμφυὲς τοῦ
παντὸς χρόνου, ὃ διὰ τέλους αὐτῷ ξυνέπεται
καὶ συνέψεται, τούτῳ τῷ τρόπῳ ἀθάνατον ὄν,
τῷ παῖδας παίδων καταλειπόμενον ταὐτὸν καὶ ἓν
ὂν ἀεὶ γενέσει τῆς ἀθανασίας μετειληφέναι. τούτου δὴ ἀποστερεῖν ἑκόντα ἑαυτὸν οὐδέποτε ὅσιον,
ἐκ προνοίας δ᾽ ἀποστερεῖ ὃς ἂν παίδων καὶ
D γυναικὸς ἀμελῇ. πειθόμενος μὲν οὖν τῷ νόμῳ
ἀζήμιος ἀπαλλάττοιτο ἄν, μὴ πειθόμενος δὲ αὖ
μηδὲ γαμῶν ἔτη τριάκοντα γεγονὼς καὶ πέντε
ζημιούσθω μὲν κατ᾽ ἐνιαυτὸν τόσῳ καὶ τόσῳ, ἵνα
μὴ δοκῇ τὴν μοναυλίαν οἱ κέρδος καὶ ῥαστώνην
φέρειν, μὴ μετεχέτω δὲ τιμῶν ὧν ἂν οἱ νεώτεροι
ἐν τῇ πόλει τοὺς πρεσβυτέρους αὐτῶν τιμῶσιν
ἑκάστοτε. τοῦτον δὴ παρ᾽ ἐκεῖνον τὸν νόμον
ἀκούσαντα ἔξεστι περὶ ἑνὸς ἑκάστου διανοηθῆναι,
E πότερον αὐτοὺς διπλοῦς οὕτω δεῖ γίγνεσθαι τῷ
μήκει τὸ σμικρότατον, διὰ τὸ πείθειν τε ἅμα καὶ
ἀπειλεῖν, ἢ τῷ ἀπειλεῖν μόνον χρωμένους ἁπλοῦς
γίγνεσθαι τοῖς μήκεσιν.

ΜΕ. Πρὸς μὲν τοῦ Λακωνικοῦ τρόπου, ὦ
ξένε, τὸ τὰ βραχύτερα ἀεὶ προτιμᾶν· τούτων
μὴν τῶν γραμμάτων εἴ τις κριτὴν ἐμὲ κελεύοι
γίγνεσθαι πότερα βουλοίμην ἂν ἐν τῇ πόλει μοι
γεγραμμένα τεθῆναι, τὰ μακρότερ᾽ ἂν ἑλοίμην,
722 καὶ δὴ καὶ περὶ παντὸς νόμου κατὰ τοῦτο τὸ
παράδειγμα, εἰ γίγνοιτο ἑκάτερα, ταὐτὸν τοῦτ᾽
ἂν αἱροίμην. οὐ μὴν ἀλλά που καὶ Κλεινίᾳ τῷδ᾽
ἀρέσκειν δεῖ τὰ νῦν νομοθετούμενα· τούτου γὰρ
ἡ πόλις ἡ νῦν τοῖς τοιούτοις [νόμοις]¹ χρῆσθαι
διανοουμένη.

¹ [νόμοις] bracketed by England.

less grave, aims at a like object. Thus mankind is
by nature coeval with the whole of time, in that it
accompanies it continually both now and in the
future; and the means by which it is immortal is
this:—by leaving behind it children's children and
continuing ever one and the same, it thus by reproduction shares in immortality. That a man should
deprive himself thereof voluntarily is never an act
of holiness; and he who denies himself wife and
children is guilty of such intentional deprivation.
He who obeys the law may be dismissed without
penalty, but he that disobeys and does not marry
when thirty-five years old shall pay a yearly fine of
such and such an amount,—lest he imagine that single
life brings him gain and ease,—and he shall have no
share in the honours which are paid from time to
time by the younger men in the State to their
seniors." When one hears and compares this law
with the former one, it is possible to judge in each
particular case whether the laws ought to be at
least double in length, through combining threats
with persuasion, or only single in length, through
employing threats alone.

MEG. Our Laconian way, Stranger, is to prefer
brevity always. But were I bidden to choose which
of these two statutes I should desire to have enacted
in writing in my State, I should choose the longer;
and what is more, I should make the same choice in
the case of every law in which, as in the example
before us, these two alternatives were offered. It is
necessary, however, that the laws we are now enacting should have the approval of our friend Clinias
also; for it is his State which is now proposing to
make use of such things.

722 ΚΛ. Καλῶς γ', ὦ Μέγιλλε, εἶπες.

ΑΘ. Τὸ μὲν οὖν περὶ πολλῶν ἢ ὀλίγων γραμμάτων ποιήσασθαι τὸν λόγον λίαν εὔηθες· τὰ
γάρ, οἶμαι, βέλτιστα ἀλλ' οὐ τὰ βραχύτατα
B οὐδὲ τὰ μήκη τιμητέον· τὰ δ' ἐν τοῖς νῦν δὴ
νόμοις ῥηθεῖσιν οὐ διπλῷ θάτερα τῶν ἑτέρων
διάφορα μόνον εἰς ἀρετὴν τῆς χρείας, ἀλλ' ὅπερ
ἐρρήθη νῦν δή, τὸ τῶν διττῶν ἰατρῶν γένος
ὀρθότατα παρετέθη. πρὸς τοῦτο δὲ οὐδεὶς ἔοικε
διανοηθῆναι πώποτε τῶν νομοθετῶν ὡς ἐξὸν δυοῖν
χρῆσθαι πρὸς τὰς νομοθεσίας, πειθοῖ καὶ βίᾳ,
καθ' ὅσον οἷόν τε ἐπὶ τὸν ἄπειρον παιδείας ὄχλον
τῷ ἑτέρῳ χρῶνται μόνον· οὐ γὰρ πειθοῖ κεραν-
C νύντες τὴν ἀνάγκην[1] νομοθετοῦσιν, ἀλλ' ἀκράτῳ
μόνον τῇ βίᾳ. ἐγὼ δέ, ὦ μακάριοι, καὶ τρίτον
ἔτι περὶ τοὺς νόμους ὁρῶ γίγνεσθαι δέον οὐδαμῇ
τὰ νῦν γιγνόμενον.

ΚΛ. Τὸ ποῖον δὴ λέγεις;

ΑΘ. Ἐξ αὐτῶν ὧν νῦν διειλέγμεθα ἡμεῖς κατὰ
θεόν τινα γεγονός. σχεδὸν γὰρ ἐξ ὅσου περὶ τῶν
νόμων ἠργμεθα λέγειν ἐξ ἑωθινοῦ μεσημβρία τε
γέγονε καὶ ἐν ταύτῃ παγκάλῃ ἀναπαύλῃ τινὶ
γεγόναμεν, οὐδὲν ἄλλ' ἢ περὶ νόμων διαλεγόμενοι,
D νόμους δὲ ἄρτι μοι δοκοῦμεν λέγειν ἄρχεσθαι, τὰ
δ' ἔμπροσθεν ἦν πάντα ἡμῖν προοίμια νόμων. τί
δὲ ταῦτ' εἴρηκα; τόδ' εἰπεῖν βουληθείς, ὅτι λόγων
πάντων καὶ ὅσων φωνὴ κεκοινώνηκε προοίμιά τ'
ἐστὶ καὶ σχεδὸν οἷόν τινες ἀνακινήσεις, ἔχουσαί

---

[1] ἀνάγκην Ast: μάχην MSS. : ἀρχὴν Badham, Hermann.

---

[1] Cp. 720 C ff.

CLIN. I highly approve of all you have said,
Megillus.

ATH. Still, it is extremely foolish to argue about
the length or brevity of writings, for what we should
value, I suppose, is not their extreme brevity or
prolixity, but their excellence; and in the case of
the laws mentioned just now, not only does the one
form possess double the value of the other in respect
of practical excellence, but the example of the two
kinds of doctors, recently mentioned,[1] presents a very
exact analogy. But as regards this, it appears that
no legislator has ever yet observed that, while it
is in their power to make use in their law-making
of two methods,—namely, persuasion and force,—
in so far as that is feasible in dealing with the un-
cultured populace, they actually employ one method
only : in their legislation they do not temper compulsion with persuasion, but use untempered force
alone. And I, my dear sirs, perceive still a third
requisite which ought to be found in laws, but which
is nowhere to be found at present.

CLIN. What is it you allude to?

ATH. A matter which, by a kind of divine direction, has sprung out of the subjects we have now
been discussing. It was little more than dawn when
we began talking about laws, and now it is high
noon, and here we are in this entrancing resting-
place ; all the time we have been talking of nothing
but laws, yet it is only recently that we have begun,
as it seems, to utter laws, and what went before was
all simply preludes to laws. What is my object in
saying this? It is to explain that all utterances and
vocal expressions have preludes and tunings-up (as
one might call them), which provide a kind of artistic

315

722 τινα ἔντεχνον ἐπιχείρησιν χρήσιμον πρὸς τὸ μέλ-
λον περαίνεσθαι. καὶ δή που κιθαρῳδικῆς ᾠδῆς
λεγομένων νόμων καὶ πάσης Μούσης προοίμια
E θαυμαστῶς ἐσπουδασμένα πρόκειται. τῶν δὲ ὄντως
νόμων ὄντων, οὓς δὴ πολιτικοὺς εἶναί φαμεν, οὐδεὶς πώποτε οὔτ᾽ εἶπέ τι προοίμιον οὔτε ξυνθέτης
γενόμενος ἐξήνεγκεν εἰς τὸ φῶς, ὡς οὐκ ὄντος
φύσει. ἡμῖν δὲ ἡ νῦν διατριβὴ γεγονυῖα, ὡς ἐμοὶ
δοκεῖ, σημαίνει ὡς ὄντος, οἵ τέ γε δὴ διπλοῖ
ἔδοξαν νῦν δή μοι λεχθέντες νόμοι, οὐκ εἶναι
ἁπλῶς οὕτω πως διπλοῖ, ἀλλὰ δύο μέν τινε,
νόμος τε καὶ προοίμιον τοῦ νόμου· ὃ δὴ τυραννικὸν
723 ἐπίταγμα ἀπεικασθὲν ἐρρήθη τοῖς ἐπιτάγμασι τοῖς
τῶν ἰατρῶν οὓς εἴπομεν ἀνελευθέρους, τοῦτ᾽ εἶναι
νόμος ἄκρατος, τὸ δὲ πρὸ τούτου ῥηθέν, πειστικὸν
λεχθὲν ὑπὲρ¹ τοῦδε, ὄντως μὲν εἶναι πειστικόν,
προοιμίου μὴν τοῦ περὶ λόγους δύναμιν ἔχειν.
ἵνα γὰρ εὐμενῶς καὶ διὰ τὴν εὐμένειαν εὐμαθέστερον τὴν ἐπίταξιν, ὃ δή ἐστιν ὁ νόμος, δέξηται
ᾧ τὸν νόμον ὁ νομοθέτης λέγει, τούτου χάριν
εἰρῆσθαί μοι κατεφάνη πᾶς ὁ λόγος οὗτος, ὃν
πείθων εἶπεν ὁ λέγων. διὸ δὴ κατά γε τὸν ἐμὸν
B λόγον τοῦτ᾽ αὐτό, προοίμιον, ἀλλ᾽ οὐ λόγος ἂν
ὀρθῶς προσαγορεύοιτο εἶναι τοῦ νόμου. ταῦτ᾽
οὖν εἰπὼν τί τὸ μετὰ τοῦτο ἄν μοι βουληθείην
εἰρῆσθαι; τόδε, ὡς τὸν νομοθέτην πρὸ πάντων
τε ἀεὶ τῶν νόμων χρεών ἐστι μὴ ἀμοίρους αὐτοὺς

---

¹ ὑπὲρ: ὑπὸ MSS., edd.

preparation which assists towards the further development of the subject. Indeed, we have examples
before us of preludes, admirably elaborated, in those
prefixed to that class of lyric ode called the "nome," [1]
and to musical compositions of every description. But
for the "nomes" (*i.e.* laws) which are real "nomes"
—and which we designate "political"—no one has
ever yet uttered a prelude, or composed or published
one, just as though there were no such thing. But
our present conversation proves, in my opinion, that
there is such a thing; and it struck me just now
that the laws we were then stating are something
more than simply double, and consist of these two
things combined—law, and prelude to law. The
part which we called the "despotic prescription"—
comparing it to the prescriptions of the slave-doctors
we mentioned—is unblended law; but the part
which preceded this, and which was uttered as per-
suasive thereof, while it actually is "persuasion,"
yet serves also the same purpose as the prelude to
an oration.[2] To ensure that the person to whom
the lawgiver addresses the law should accept the
prescription quietly—and, because quietly, in a
docile spirit,—that, as I supposed, was the evident
object with which the speaker uttered all his per-
suasive discourse.[3] Hence, according to my argument, the right term for it would be, not legal
"statement," but "prelude," and no other word.
Having said this, what is the next statement I would
desire to make? It is this: that the lawgiver must
never omit to furnish preludes, as prefaces both to
the laws as a whole and to each individual statute,

---

[1] Cp. 700 B.   [2] Cp. 718 C f.
[3] Cp. 715 E ff.

PLATO

723 προοιμίων ποιεῖν καὶ καθ' ἕκαστον, ᾗ διοίσουσιν
ἑαυτῶν ὅσον νῦν δὴ τὼ λεχθέντε διηνεγκάτην.

ΚΛ. Τό γ' ἐμὸν οὐκ ἂν ἄλλως νομοθετεῖν διακελεύοιτο ἡμῖν τὸν τούτων ἐπιστήμονα.

C   ΑΘ. Καλῶς μὲν τοίνυν, ὦ Κλεινία, δοκεῖς μοι
τό γε τοσοῦτον λέγειν, ὅτι πᾶσί γε νόμοις ἐστὶ
προοίμια καὶ ὅτι πάσης ἀρχόμενον νομοθεσίας χρὴ
προτιθέναι παντός του[1] λόγου τὸ πεφυκὸς προοίμιον ἑκάστοις· οὐ γὰρ σμικρὸν τὸ μετὰ τοῦτ'
ἐστὶ ῥηθησόμενον, οὐδ' ὀλίγον διαφέρον ἢ σαφῶς
ἢ μὴ σαφῶς αὐτὰ μνημονεύεσθαι· τὸ μέντοι
μεγάλων πέρι λεγομένων νόμων καὶ σμικρῶν εἰ
ὁμοίως προοιμιάζεσθαι προστάττοιμεν, οὐκ ἂν
D ὀρθῶς λέγοιμεν. οὐδὲ γὰρ ᾄσματος οὐδὲ λόγου
παντὸς δεῖ τὸ τοιοῦτον δρᾶν, καί τοι πέφυκέ γε
εἶναι πᾶσιν, ἀλλ' οὐ χρηστέον ἅπασιν· αὐτῷ δὲ
τῷ τε ῥήτορι καὶ τῷ μελῳδῷ καὶ τῷ νομοθέτῃ τὸ
τοιοῦτον ἑκάστοτε ἐπιτρεπτέον.

ΚΛ. Ἀληθέστατα δοκεῖς μοι λέγειν. ἀλλὰ δὴ
μηκέτ', ὦ ξένε, διατριβὴν πλείω τῆς μελλήσεως
ποιώμεθα, ἐπὶ δὲ τὸν λόγον ἐπανέλθωμεν καὶ ἀπ'
ἐκείνων ἀρχώμεθα, εἴ σοι φίλον, ὧν οὐχ ὡς
E προοιμιαζόμενος εἶπες τότε. πάλιν οὖν, οἷόν
φασιν οἱ παίζοντες, ἀμεινόνων ἐξ ἀρχῆς δευτέρων
ἐπαναπολήσωμεν, ὡς προοίμιον ἀλλ' οὐ τὸν
τυχόντα λόγον περαίνοντες, καθάπερ ἄρτι. λάβωμεν δ' αὐτῶν ἀρχὴν ὁμολογοῦντες προοιμιάζεσθαι. καὶ τὰ μὲν περὶ θεῶν τιμῆς προγόνων
τε θεραπείας καὶ τὰ νῦν δὴ λεχθέντα ἱκανά· τὰ

---

[1] του: τοῦ MSS., edd.

[1] Cp. 716 B ff.

whereby they shall surpass their original form by as
much as the "double" examples recently given
surpassed the "single."

CLIN. I, for my part, would charge the expert in
these matters to legislate thus, and not otherwise.

ATH. You are right, I believe, Clinias, in asserting
at least thus much,—that all laws have preludes,
and that, in commencing each piece of legislation,
one ought to preface each enactment with the
prelude that naturally belongs to it—for the statement that is to follow the prelude is one of no small
importance, and it makes a vast difference whether
these statements are distinctly or indistinctly remembered; still, we should be wrong if we prescribed
that all statutes, great and small, should be equally
provided with preludes. For neither ought that to
be done in the case of songs and speeches of every
kind; for they all naturally have preludes, but we
cannot employ them always; that is a thing which
must be left in each case to the judgment of the
actual orator or singer or legislator.

CLIN. What you say is, I believe, very true. But
let us not spend more time, Stranger, in delay, but
return to our main subject, and start afresh (if you
agree) from the statements you made above—and
made not by way of prelude. Let us, then, repeat
from the start the "second thoughts" that are
"best" (to quote the players' proverb), treating
them throughout as a prelude, and not, as before, as a
chance discourse; and let us handle the opening part
as being confessedly a prelude. As to the worship of
the gods and the attention to be paid to ancestors, our
previous statement [1] is quite sufficient; it is what
comes next to these that you must try to state, until

723 δ' ἑξῆς πειρώμεθα λέγειν, μέχριπερ ἄν σοι πᾶν τὸ
προοίμιον ἱκανῶς εἰρῆσθαι δοκῇ. μετὰ δὲ τοῦτο
ἤδη τοὺς νόμους αὐτοὺς διέξει λέγων.

724 ΑΘ. Οὐκοῦν περὶ θεῶν μὲν καὶ τῶν μετὰ θεοὺς
καὶ γονέων ζώντων τε πέρι καὶ τελευτησάντων
τότε ἱκανῶς προοιμιασάμεθα, ὡς νῦν λέγομεν· τὸ
δ' ἀπολειπόμενον ἔτι τοῦ τοιούτου φαίνει μοι σὺ
διακελεύεσθαι τὰ νῦν οἷον πρὸς τὸ φῶς ἐπαν-
άγειν.

ΚΛ. Παντάπασι μὲν οὖν.

ΑΘ. Ἀλλὰ μὴν μετά γε τὰ τοιαῦτα ὡς χρὴ τὰ
περὶ τὰς ἑαυτῶν ψυχὰς καὶ τὰ σώματα καὶ τὰς
οὐσίας σπουδῆς τε πέρι καὶ ἀνέσεως ἴσχειν,
B προσῆκόν τ' ἐστὶ καὶ κοινότατον ἀναπεμπαζο-
μένους τόν τε λέγοντα καὶ τοὺς ἀκούοντας παιδείας γίγνεσθαι κατὰ δύναμιν ἐπηβόλους. ταῦτ'
οὖν ἡμῖν αὐτὰ μετ' ἐκεῖνα ὄντως ἐστὶ ῥητέα τε
καὶ ἀκουστέα.

ΚΛ. Ὀρθότατα λέγεις.

the whole of the prelude has been, in our opinion, adequately set forth by you. After that you will proceed with your statement of the actual laws.

ATH. So then the prelude we previously composed concerning the gods and those next to the gods, and concerning parents, living and dead, was, as we now declare, sufficient; and you are now bidding me, I understand, to bring up, as it were, to the light of day the residue of this same subject.

CLIN. Most certainly.

ATH. Well, surely it is both fitting and of the greatest mutual advantage that, next to the matters mentioned, the speaker and his hearers should deal with the question of the degree of zeal or slackness which men ought to use in respect of their souls, their bodies, and their goods, and should ponder thereon, and thus get a grasp of education as far as possible. Precisely this, then, is the statement which we must actually make and listen to next.

CLIN. Perfectly right.

726   ΑΘ.   Ἀκούοι δὴ πᾶς ὅσπερ νῦν δὴ τὰ περὶ θεῶν
τε ἤκουε καὶ τῶν φίλων προπατόρων· πάντων γὰρ
τῶν αὐτοῦ κτημάτων [μετὰ θεοὺς] [1] ψυχὴ θειότατον, οἰκειότατον ὄν.   τὰ δ' αὐτοῦ διττὰ πάντ' ἐστὶ
πᾶσι·   τὰ μὲν οὖν κρείττω καὶ ἀμείνω δεσπό-
ζοντα, τὰ δ' ἥττω καὶ χείρω δοῦλα.   τῶν οὖν
αὐτοῦ τὰ δεπόζοντα ἀεὶ προτιμητέον τῶν δουλευ-
727 όντων.   οὕτω δὴ τὴν αὐτοῦ ψυχὴν μετὰ θεοὺς
ὄντας δεσπότας καὶ τοὺς τούτοις ἑπομένους τιμᾶν
δεῖν λέγων δευτέραν ὀρθῶς παρακελεύομαι.   τιμᾷ
δ' ὡς ἔπος εἰπεῖν ἡμῶν οὐδεὶς ὀρθῶς, δοκεῖ δέ·
θείου [2] γὰρ ἀγαθόν που τιμή, τῶν δὲ κακῶν οὐδὲν
τίμιον, ὁ δ' ἡγούμενος ἤ τισι λόγοις ἤ δώροις
αὐτὴν αὔξειν ἤ τισιν ὑπείξεσι, μηδὲν βελτίω δὲ ἐκ
χείρονος αὐτὴν ἀπεργαζόμενος τιμᾶν μὲν δοκεῖ,
δρᾷ δὲ τοῦτο οὐδαμῶς.   αὐτίκα παῖς εὐθὺς γενόμενος ἄνθρωπος πᾶς ἡγεῖται πάντα ἱκανὸς εἶναι
γιγνώσκειν, καὶ τιμᾶν οἴεται ἐπαινῶν τὴν αὐτοῦ
Β ψυχήν, καὶ προθυμούμενος ἐπιτρέπει πράττειν ὅ
τι ἂν ἐθέλῃ· τὸ δὲ νῦν λεγόμενόν ἐστιν ὡς δρῶν
ταῦτα βλάπτει καὶ οὐ τιμᾷ· δεῖ δέ, ὥς φαμεν,
μετά γε θεοὺς δευτέραν.   οὐδέ γε ὅταν ἄνθρωπος
τῶν αὐτοῦ ἑκάστοτε ἁμαρτημάτων μὴ ἑαυτὸν αἴτιον

---

[1] [μετὰ θεοὺς] bracketed by England.
[2] θείου: θεῖον MSS.

BOOK V

ATH. LET everyone who has just heard the ordinances concerning gods and dear forefathers now give ear.

Of all a man's own belongings, the most divine is his soul, since it is most his own. A man's own belongings are invariably twofold: the stronger and better are the ruling elements, the weaker and worse those that serve; wherefore of one's own belongings one must honour those that rule above those that serve. Thus it is that in charging men to honour their own souls next after the gods who rule and the secondary divinities, I am giving a right injunction. But there is hardly a man of us all who pays honour rightly, although he fancies he does so; for honour paid to a thing divine is beneficent, whereas nothing that is maleficent confers honour; and he that thinks to magnify his soul by words or gifts or obeisances, while he is improving it no whit in goodness, fancies indeed that he is paying it honour, but in fact does not do so. Every boy, for example, as soon as he has grown to manhood, deems himself capable of learning all things, and supposes that by lauding his soul he honours it, and by eagerly permitting it to do whatsoever it pleases. But by acting thus, as we now declare, he is not honouring his soul, but injuring it; whereas, we affirm, he ought to pay honour to it next after the gods. Again, when a man counts not himself but others responsible always for his

727 ἡγῆται καὶ τῶν πλείστων κακῶν καὶ μεγίστων,
ἀλλ' ἄλλους, ἑαυτὸν δὲ ἀεὶ ἀναίτιον ἐξαιρῇ τιμῶν
τὴν αὑτοῦ ψυχήν, ὡς δὴ δοκεῖ· ὁ δὲ πολλοῦ δεῖ
C δρᾶν τοῦτο· βλάπτει γάρ. οὐδ' ὁπόταν ἡδοναῖς
παρὰ λόγον τὸν τοῦ νομοθέτου καὶ ἔπαινον
χαρίζηται, τότε οὐδαμῶς τιμᾷ, ἀτιμάζει δὲ
κακῶν καὶ μεταμελείας ἐμπιπλὰς αὐτήν. οὐδέ
γε ὁπόταν αὖ τἀναντία τοὺς ἐπαινουμένους πόνους
καὶ φόβους καὶ ἀλγηδόνας καὶ λύπας μὴ διαπονῇ
καρτερῶν, ἀλλ' ὑπείκῃ. τότε οὐ τιμᾷ ὑπείκων·
ἄτιμον γὰρ αὐτὴν ἀπεργάζεται δρῶν τὰ τοιαῦτα
ξύμπαντα. οὐδ' ὁπόταν ἡγῆται τὸ ζῆν πάντως
D ἀγαθὸν εἶναι, τιμᾷ, ἀτιμάζει δ' αὐτὴν καὶ τότε· τὰ
γὰρ ἐν Ἅιδου πράγματα πάντα κακὰ ἡγουμένης
τῆς ψυχῆς εἶναι ὑπείκει καὶ οὐκ ἀντιτείνει, διδά-
σκων τε καὶ ἐλέγχων ὡς οὐκ οἶδεν οὐδ' εἰ τἀναντία
πέφυκε μέγιστα εἶναι πάντων ἀγαθῶν ἡμῖν τὰ
περὶ τοὺς θεοὺς τοὺς ἐκεῖ. οὐδὲ μὴν πρὸ ἀρετῆς
ὁπόταν αὖ προτιμᾷ τις κάλλος, τοῦτ' ἔστιν οὐχ
ἕτερον ἢ ἡ τῆς ψυχῆς ὄντως καὶ πάντως ἀτιμία.
ψυχῆς γὰρ σῶμα ἐντιμότερον οὗτος ὁ λόγος
E φησὶν εἶναι ψευδόμενος· οὐδὲν γὰρ γηγενὲς
Ὀλυμπίων ἐντιμότερον, ἀλλ' ὁ περὶ ψυχῆς
ἄλλως δοξάζων ἀγνοεῖ ὡς θαυμαστοῦ τούτου
κτήματος ἀμελεῖ. οὐδέ γε ὁπόταν χρήματά τις
ἐρᾷ κτᾶσθαι μὴ καλῶς ἢ μὴ δυσχερῶς φέρῃ
728 κτώμενος, δώροις ἄρα τιμᾷ τότε τὴν ἑαυτοῦ
ψυχήν· παντὸς μὲν οὖν λείπει· τὸ γὰρ αὐτῆς
τίμιον ἅμα καὶ καλὸν ἀποδίδοται σμικροῦ χρυσίου·

own sins and for the most and greatest evils, and
exempts himself always from blame, thereby honouring, as he fancies, his own soul,—then he is far
indeed from honouring it, since he is doing it injury.
Again, when a man gives way to pleasures contrary
to the counsel and commendation of the lawgiver,
he is by no means conferring honour on his soul,
but rather dishonour, by loading it with woes and
remorse. Again, in the opposite case, when toils,
fears, hardships and pains are commended, and a
man flinches from them, instead of stoutly enduring
them,—then by his flinching he confers no honour
on his soul; for by all such actions he renders it
dishonoured. Again, when a man deems life at any
price to be a good thing, then also he does not
honour, but dishonour, to his soul; for he yields to
the imagination of his soul that the conditions in
Hades are altogether evil, instead of opposing it,
by teaching and convincing his soul that, for all it
knows, we may find, on the contrary, our greatest
blessings in the realm of the gods below. Again,
when a man honours beauty above goodness, this is
nothing else than a literal and total dishonouring of
the soul; for such a statement asserts that the body
is more honourable than the soul,—but falsely, since
nothing earth-born is more honourable than the
things of heaven, and he that surmises otherwise
concerning the soul knows not that in it he possesses,
and neglects, a thing most admirable. Again, when
a man craves to acquire wealth ignobly, or feels no
qualm in so acquiring it, he does not then by his
gifts pay honour to his soul,—far from it, in sooth!—
for what is honourable therein and noble he is
bartering away for a handful of gold; yet all the

728 πᾶς γὰρ ὅ τ᾽ ἐπὶ γῆς καὶ ὑπὸ γῆς χρυσὸς ἀρετῆς
οὐκ ἀντάξιος. ὡς δὲ εἰπεῖν ξυλλήβδην, ὃς ἅπερ
ἂν νομοθέτης αἰσχρὰ εἶναι καὶ κακὰ διαριθμού-
μενος τάττῃ καὶ τοὐναντίον ἀγαθὰ καὶ καλά, τῶν
μὲν ἀπέχεσθαι μὴ ἐθέλει[1] πάσῃ μηχανῇ, τὰ δὲ
ἐπιτηδεύειν ξύμπασαν κατὰ δύναμιν, οὐκ οἶδεν ἐν
B τούτοις πᾶσι πᾶς ἄνθρωπος ψυχὴν θειότατον ὂν
ἀτιμότατα καὶ κακοσχημονέστατα διατιθείς. τὴν
γὰρ λεγομένην δίκην τῆς κακουργίας τὴν μεγίστην
οὐδεὶς ὡς ἔπος εἰπεῖν λογίζεται, ἔστι δ᾽ ἡ μεγίστη
τὸ ὁμοιοῦσθαι τοῖς οὖσι κακοῖς ἀνδράσιν, ὁμοιού-
μενον δὲ τοὺς μὲν ἀγαθοὺς φεύγειν ἄνδρας καὶ
λόγους καὶ ἀποσχίζεσθαι, τοῖς δὲ προσκολλᾶσθαι
διώκοντα κατὰ τὰς ξυνουσίας· προσπεφυκότα δὲ
τοῖς τοιούτοις ἀνάγκη ποιεῖν καὶ πάσχειν ἃ πεφύ-
κασιν ἀλλήλους οἱ τοιοῦτοι ποιεῖν [καὶ][2] λέγειν.
C τοῦτο οὖν δὴ τὸ πάθος δίκη μὲν οὐκ ἔστι, καλὸν
γὰρ τό γε δίκαιον καὶ ἡ δίκη, τιμωρία δέ, ἀδικίας
ἀκόλουθος πάθη, ἧς ὅ τε τυχὼν καὶ μὴ τυγχάνων
ἄθλιος, ὁ μὲν οὐκ ἰατρευόμενος, ὁ δέ, ἵνα ἕτεροι
πολλοὶ σώζωνται, ἀπολλύμενος.

Τιμὴ δ᾽ ἐστὶν ἡμῖν, ὡς τὸ ὅλον εἰπεῖν, τοῖς μὲν
ἀμείνοσιν ἕπεσθαι, τὰ δὲ χείρονα γενέσθαι δὲ
βελτίω δυνατὰ τοῦτ᾽ αὐτὸ ὡς ἄριστα ἀποτελεῖν.
ψυχῆς οὖν ἀνθρώπῳ κτῆμα οὐκ ἔστιν εὐφυέστερον
D εἰς τὸ φυγεῖν μὲν τὸ κακόν, ἰχνεῦσαι δὲ καὶ ἑλεῖν
τὸ πάντων ἄριστον, καὶ ἑλόντα αὖ κοινῇ ξυνοικεῖν

---

[1] ἐθέλει Peipers, Schanz: ἐθέλῃ MSS.
[2] [καὶ] omitted by Paris MS. (Schanz brackets καὶ λέγειν).

---

[1] Cp. 716 C, D.

gold on earth, or under it, does not equal the price
of goodness. To speak shortly:—in respect of the
things which the lawgiver enumerates and describes
as either, on the one hand, base and evil, or, on the
other hand, noble and good, if any man refuses to
avoid by every means the one kind, and with all his
power to practise the other kind,—such a man knows
not that everyone who acts thus is treating most
dishonourably and most disgracefully that most divine
of things, his soul. Hardly anyone takes account
of the greatest "judgment" (as men call it) upon
evil-doing; that greatest judgment is this,—to grow
like unto men that are wicked, and, in so growing,
to shun good men and good counsels and cut oneself off from them,[1] but to cleave to the company
of the wicked and follow after them; and he that
is joined to such men inevitably acts and is acted
upon in the way that such men bid one another to
act. Now such a resultant condition is not a "judgment" (for justice and judgment are things honourable), but a punishment, an infliction that follows
on injustice; both he that undergoes this and he
that undergoes it not are alike wretched,—the one
in that he remains uncured, the other in that he is
destroyed in order to secure the salvation of many
others.[2]

Thus we declare that honour, speaking generally,
consists in following the better, and in doing our
utmost to effect the betterment of the worse, when it
admits of being bettered. Man has no possession
better fitted by nature than the soul for the avoidance
of evil and the tracking and taking of what is best of
all, and living in fellowship therewith, when he has

[2] Cp. 731 C, 854 C ff., 957 B ff.

PLATO

728 τὸν ἐπίλοιπον βίον· διὸ δεύτερον ἐτάχθη τιμῇ.
τὸ δὲ τρίτον, πᾶς ἂν τοῦτό γε νοήσειε, τὴν τοῦ
σώματος εἶναι κατὰ φύσιν τιμήν. τὰς δ' αὖ
τιμὰς δεῖ σκοπεῖν, καὶ τούτων τίνες ἀληθεῖς καὶ
ὅσαι κίβδηλοι· τοῦτο δὲ νομοθέτου. μηνύειν δή
μοι φαίνεται τάσδε καὶ τοιάσδε τινὰς αὐτὰς εἶναι,
τίμιον εἶναι σῶμα οὐ τὸ καλὸν οὐδὲ ἰσχυρὸν οὐδὲ
E τάχος ἔχον οὐδὲ μέγα, οὐδέ γε τὸ ὑγιεινόν—καί τοι
πολλοῖς ἂν τοῦτό γε δοκοῖ—, καὶ μὴν οὐδὲ τὰ
τούτων γ' ἐναντία, τὰ δ' ἐν τῷ μέσῳ ἁπάσης ταύτης τῆς ἕξεως ἐφαπτόμενα σωφρονέστατα ἅμα τε
ἀσφαλέστατα εἶναι μακρῷ· τὰ μὲν γὰρ χαύνους
τὰς ψυχὰς καὶ θρασείας ποιεῖ, τὰ δὲ ταπεινάς τε
καὶ ἀνελευθέρους· ὡς δ' αὕτως ἡ τῶν χρημάτων
καὶ κτημάτων κτῆσις καὶ τιμήσεως κατὰ τὸν
αὐτὸν ῥυθμὸν ἔχει. τὰ μὲν ὑπέρογκα γὰρ ἑκάσ-
729 των τούτων ἔχθρας καὶ στάσεις ἀπεργάζεται ταῖς
πόλεσι καὶ ἰδίᾳ, τὰ δ' ἐλλείποντα δουλείας ὡς τὸ
πολύ. μὴ δή τις φιλοχρημονείτω παίδων γ'
ἕνεκα, ἵνα ὅτι πλουσιωτάτους καταλίπῃ· οὔτε
γὰρ ἐκείνοις οὔτ' αὖ τῇ πόλει ἄμεινον. ἡ γὰρ
τῶν νέων ἀκολάκευτος οὐσία, τῶν δ' ἀναγκαίων
μὴ ἐνδεής, αὕτη πασῶν μουσικωτάτη τε καὶ
ἀρίστη· ξυμφωνοῦσα γὰρ ἡμῖν καὶ ξυναρμότ-
τουσα εἰς ἅπαντα ἄλυπον τὸν βίον ἀπεργάζεται.
B παισὶ δὲ αἰδῶ χρὴ πολλήν, οὐ χρυσὸν κατα-
λείπειν. οἰόμεθα δ' ἐπιπλήττοντες τοῖς νέοις
ἀναισχυντοῦσι τοῦτο καταλείψειν· τὸ δ' ἔστιν

---

[1] The first place belongs to the gods (*i.e.* to Divine
Reason).

taken it, for all his life thereafter. Wherefore the soul is put second [1] in order of honour; as for the third, everyone would conceive that this place naturally belongs to the honour due to the body. But here again one has to investigate the various forms of honour,—which of them are genuine, which spurious; and this is the lawgiver's task. Now he, as I suppose, declares that the honours are these and of these kinds:— the honourable body is not the fair body nor the strong nor the swift nor the large, nor yet the body that is sound in health,—although this is what many believe; neither is it a body of the opposite kind to any of these; rather those bodies which hold the mean position between all these opposite extremes are by far the most temperate and stable; for while the one extreme makes the souls puffed up and proud, the other makes them lowly and spiritless. The same holds good of the possession of goods and chattels, and they are to be valued on a similar scale. In each case, when they are in excess, they produce enmities and feuds both in States and privately, while if they are deficient they produce, as a rule, serfdom. And let no man love riches for the sake of his children, in order that he may leave them as wealthy as possible; for that is good neither for them nor for the State. For the young the means that attracts no flatterers, yet is not lacking in things necessary, is the most harmonious of all and the best; for it is in tune with us and in accord, and thus it renders our life in all respects painless. To his children it behoves a man to bequeath modesty, not money, in abundance. We imagine that chiding the young for their irreverence is the way to bequeath this; but no such

729 οὐκ ἐκ τοῦ νῦν παρακελεύματος τοῖς νέοις γιγνόμενον, ὃ παρακελεύονται λέγοντες ὡς δεῖ πάντα
αἰσχύνεσθαι τὸν νέον. ὁ δὲ ἔμφρων νομοθέτης
τοῖς πρεσβυτέροις ἂν μᾶλλον παρακελεύοιτο
αἰσχύνεσθαι τοὺς νέους, καὶ πάντων μάλιστα
εὐλαβεῖσθαι μή ποτέ τις αὐτὸν ἴδῃ τῶν νέων ἢ
καὶ ἐπακούσῃ δρῶντα ἢ λέγοντά τι τῶν αἰσχρῶν,
C ὡς ὅπου ἀναισχυντοῦσι γέροντες, ἀνάγκη καὶ
νέους ἐνταῦθα εἶναι ἀναιδεστάτους· παιδεία γὰρ
νέων διαφέρουσά ἐστιν ἅμα καὶ αὐτῶν οὐ τὸ
νουθετεῖν, ἀλλ' ἅπερ ἂν ἄλλον νουθετῶν εἴποι τις,
φαίνεσθαι ταῦτα αὐτὸν δρῶντα διὰ βίου. ξυγγένειαν δὲ καὶ ὁμογνίων θεῶν κοινωνίαν ἅπασαν
ταὐτοῦ φύσιν αἵματος ἔχουσαν τιμῶν τις καὶ
σεβόμενος εὔνους ἂν γενεθλίους θεοὺς εἰς παίδων
αὐτοῦ σπορὰν ἴσχοι κατὰ λόγον. καὶ μὴν τό γε
D φίλων καὶ ἑταίρων πρὸς τὰς ἐν βίῳ ὁμιλίας
εὐμενὲς ἄν τις κτῷτο μείζους μὲν καὶ σεμνοτέρας
τὰς ἐκείνων ὑπηρεσίας εἰς αὐτὸν ἡγούμενος ἢ
'κεῖνοι, ἐλάττους δ' αὖ τὰς αὐτοῦ διανοούμενος εἰς
τοὺς φίλους χάριτας αὐτῶν τῶν φίλων τε καὶ
ἑταίρων. εἰς μὴν πόλιν καὶ πολίτας μακρῷ
ἄριστος ὅστις πρὸ τοῦ Ὀλυμπίασι καὶ ἁπάντων
ἀγώνων πολεμικῶν τε καὶ εἰρηνικῶν νικᾶν δέξαιτ'
ἂν δόξῃ ὑπηρεσίας τῶν οἴκοι νόμων, ὡς ὑπηρετη-
κὼς πάντων κάλλιστ' ἀνθρώπων αὐτοῖς ἐν τῷ
E βίῳ. πρὸς δ' αὖ τοὺς ξένους διανοητέον ὡς
ἁγιώτατα ξυμβόλαια ὄντα· σχεδὸν γὰρ πάντ'
ἐστὶ τὰ τῶν ξένων [καὶ εἰς τοὺς ξένους] [1] ἁμαρτή-

---

[1] [καὶ ... ξένους] bracketed by England (after F. H.
Dale).

result follows from the admonition commonly given nowadays to the young, when people tell them that "youth must reverence everyone." Rather will the prudent lawgiver admonish the older folk to reverence the young, and above all to beware lest any of them be ever seen or heard by any of the young either doing or saying anything shameful; for where the old are shameless, there inevitably will also the young be very impudent. The most effective way of training the young—as well as the older people themselves—is not by admonition, but by plainly practising throughout one's own life the admonitions which one gives to others. By paying honour and reverence to his kinsfolk, and all who share in the worship of the tribal gods and are sprung from the same blood, a man will, in proportion to his piety, secure the good-will of the gods of Birth to bless his own begetting of children. Moreover, a man will find his friends and companions kindly disposed, in regard to life's intercourse, if he sets higher than they do the value and importance of the services he receives from them, while counting the favours he confers on them as of less value than they are deemed by his companions and friends themselves. In relation to his State and fellow-citizens that man is by far the best who, in preference to a victory at Olympia or in any other contest of war or peace, would choose to have a victorious reputation for service to his native laws, as being the one man above all others who has served them with distinction throughout his life. Further, a man should regard contracts made with strangers as specially sacred; for practically all the sins against Strangers are—as compared with those

331

729 ματα παρὰ τὰ τῶν πολιτῶν εἰς θεὸν ἀνηρτημένα
τιμωρὸν μᾶλλον· ἔρημος γὰρ ὢν ὁ ξένος ἑταίρων
τε καὶ ξυγγενῶν ἐλεεινότερος ἀνθρώποις καὶ θεοῖς.
ὁ δυνάμενος οὖν τιμωρεῖν μᾶλλον βοηθεῖ προθυ-
μότερον· δύναται δὲ διαφερόντως ὁ ξένιος ἑκάστων
730 δαίμων καὶ θεὸς τῷ ξενίῳ συνεπόμενοι Διΐ· πολλῆς
οὖν εὐλαβείας, ᾧ καὶ σμικρὸν προμηθείας ἔνι,
μηδὲν ἁμάρτημα περὶ ξένους ἁμαρτόντα ἐν τῷ βίῳ
πρὸς τὸ τέλος αὐτοῦ πορευθῆναι. ξενικῶν δ' αὖ
καὶ ἐπιχωρίων ἁμαρτημάτων τὸ περὶ τοὺς ἱκέτας
μέγιστον γίγνεται ἁμάρτημα ἑκάστοις. μεθ' οὗ
γὰρ ἱκετεύσας μάρτυρος ὁ ἱκέτης θεοῦ ἀπέτυχεν[1]
ὁμολογιῶν, φύλαξ διαφέρων οὗτος τοῦ παθόντος
γίγνεται, ὥστ' οὐκ ἄν ποτε ἀτιμώρητος πάθοι [ὁ
τυχών][2] ὧν ἔπαθε.

B   Τὰ μὲν οὖν περὶ γονέας τε καὶ ἑαυτὸν καὶ τὰ
ἑαυτοῦ, περὶ πόλιν τε καὶ φίλους καὶ ξυγγένειαν
ξενικά τε καὶ ἐπιχώρια, διεληλύθαμεν σχεδὸν
ὁμιλήματα. τὸ δὲ ποῖός τις ὢν αὐτὸς ἂν κάλλιστα
διαγάγοι τὸν βίον, ἑπόμενον τούτῳ διεξελθεῖν· ὅσα
μὴν οὐ[3] νόμος ἀλλ' ἔπαινος παιδεύων καὶ ψόγος
ἑκάστους εὐηνίους μᾶλλον καὶ εὐμενεῖς τοῖς τεθή-
σεσθαι μέλλουσι νόμοις ἀπεργάζεται,[4] ταῦτ' ἐστὶ
μετὰ τοῦτο ἡμῖν ῥητέον. ἀλήθεια δὴ πάντων μὲν
C   ἀγαθῶν θεοῖς ἡγεῖται, πάντων δὲ ἀνθρώποις· ἧς
ὁ γενήσεσθαι μέλλων μακάριός τε καὶ εὐδαίμων
ἐξ ἀρχῆς εὐθὺς μέτοχος εἴη, ἵνα ὡς πλεῖστον

---

[1] ἀπέτυχεν Badham, Schanz: ἔτυχεν MSS.
[2] [ὁ τυχών] I bracket.
[3] ὅσα μὴν οὐ W.-Möllendorff: ὅσ' ἂν μὴ MSS. (ὅσα μὴ Schanz)
[4] ἀπεργάζεται MSS.: ἀπεργάζηται Ast, Zur.

against citizens—connected more closely with an avenging deity. For the stranger, inasmuch as he is without companions or kinsfolk, is the more to be pitied by men and gods; wherefore he that is most able to avenge succours them most readily, and the most able of all, in every case, is the Strangers' daemon and god, and these follow in the train of Zeus Xenios.[1] Whoso, then, is possessed of but a particle of forethought will take the utmost care to go through life to the very end without committing any offence in respect of Strangers. Of offences against either Strangers or natives, that which touches suppliants is in every case the most grave; for when a suppliant, after invoking a god as witness, is cheated of his compact, that god becomes the special guardian of him who is wronged, so that he will never be wronged without vengeance being taken for his wrongs.

As concerns a man's social relations towards his parents, himself and his own belongings, towards the State also and friends and kindred,—whether foreign relations or domestic,—our exposition is now fairly complete. It remains to expound next the character which is most conducive to nobility of life; and after that we shall have to state all the matters which are subject, not to law, but rather to praise or blame,— as the instruments whereby the citizens are educated individually and rendered more tractable and well-inclined towards the laws which are to be imposed on them. Of all the goods, for gods and men alike, truth stands first. Thereof let every man partake from his earliest days, if he purposes to become blessed and happy, that so he may live his life as a

---

[1] The supreme Guardian of the rights of hospitality.

730 χρόνον ἀληθὴς ὢν διαβιοίη. πιστὸς γάρ· ὁ δὲ
ἄπιστος, ᾧ φίλον ψεῦδος ἑκούσιον· ὅτῳ δὲ ἀκούσιον, ἄνους. ὧν οὐδέτερον ζηλωτόν· ἄφιλος γὰρ
δὴ πᾶς ὅ τε[1] ἄπιστος καὶ <ὁ>[2] ἀμαθής, χρόνου
δὲ προϊόντος γνωσθεὶς εἰς τὸ χαλεπὸν γῆρας ἐρημίαν αὑτῷ πᾶσαν κατεσκευάσατο ἐπὶ τέλει τοῦ
D βίου, ὥστε ζώντων καὶ μὴ ἑταίρων καὶ παίδων
σχεδὸν ὁμοίως ὀρφανὸν αὑτῷ γενέσθαι τὸν βίον.
τίμιος μὲν δὴ καὶ ὁ μηδὲν ἀδικῶν· ὁ δὲ μηδ᾽ ἐπιτρέπων τοῖς ἀδικοῦσιν ἀδικεῖν πλέον ἢ διπλασίας
τιμῆς ἄξιος ἐκείνου· ὁ μὲν γὰρ ἑνός, ὁ δὲ πολλῶν
ἀντάξιος ἑτέρων, μηνύων τὴν τῶν ἄλλων τοῖς
ἄρχουσιν ἀδικίαν. ὁ δὲ καὶ ξυγκολάζων εἰς δύναμιν τοῖς ἄρχουσιν, ὁ μέγας ἀνὴρ ἐν πόλει καὶ
τέλειος οὗτος ἀναγορευέσθω νικηφόρος ἀρετῇ.

E Τὸν αὐτὸν δὴ τοῦτον ἔπαινον καὶ περὶ σωφροσύνης χρὴ λέγειν καὶ περὶ φρονήσεως, καὶ ὅσα ἄλλα
ἀγαθά τις κέκτηται δυνατὰ μὴ μόνον αὐτὸν ἔχειν,
ἀλλὰ καὶ ἄλλοις μεταδιδόναι· καὶ τὸν μὲν μεταδι-
δόντα ὡς ἀκρότατον χρὴ τιμᾶν, τὸν δ᾽ αὖ μὴ
δυνάμενον ἐθέλοντα δὲ ἐᾶν δεύτερον, τὸν δὲ φθο-
νοῦντα καὶ ἑκόντα μηδενὶ κοινωνὸν διὰ φιλίας
731 γιγνόμενον ἀγαθῶν τινῶν αὐτὸν μὲν ψέγειν, τὸ δὲ
κτῆμα μηδὲν μᾶλλον διὰ τὸν κεκτημένον ἀτιμάζειν,
ἀλλὰ κτᾶσθαι κατὰ δύναμιν. φιλονεικείτω δὲ
ἡμῖν πᾶς πρὸς ἀρετὴν ἀφθόνως. ὁ μὲν γὰρ τοιοῦ-

---

[1] τε Hermann : γε MSS.　　　[2] ⟨ὁ⟩ I add.

---

[1] Cp. 663 A, 829 A.

334

true man so long as possible. He is a trusty man;
but untrustworthy is the man who loves the voluntary lie; and senseless is the man who loves the
involuntary lie; and neither of these two is to be
envied. For everyone that is either faithless or
foolish is friendless; and since, as time goes on, he
is found out, he is making for himself, in his woeful
old-age, at life's close, a complete solitude, wherein
his life becomes almost equally desolate whether his
companions and children are living or dead. He that
does no wrong is indeed a man worthy of honour;
but worthy of twice as much honour as he, and more,
is the man who, in addition, consents not to wrong-
doers when they do wrong;[1] for while the former
counts as one man, the latter counts as many, in that
he informs the magistrates of the wrongdoing of the
rest. And he that assists the magistrates in punishing, to the best of his power,—let him be publicly
proclaimed to be the Great Man of the State and
perfect, the winner of the prize for excellence.

Upon temperance and upon wisdom one should
bestow the same praise, and upon all the other
goods which he who possesses them can not only
keep himself, but can share also with others. He
that thus shares these should be honoured as highest
in merit; and he that would fain share them but
cannot, as second in merit; while if a man is jealous
and unwilling to share any good things with anyone
in a friendly spirit, then the man himself must be
blamed, but his possession must not be disesteemed
any the more because of its possessor,—rather one
should strive to gain it with all one's might. Let
every one of us be ambitious to gain excellence, but
without jealousy. For a man of this character en-

731 τος τὰς πόλεις αὔξει, ἁμιλλώμενος μὲν αὐτός, τοὺς
ἄλλους δὲ οὐ κολούων διαβολαῖς· ὁ δὲ φθονερὸς
τῇ τῶν ἄλλων διαβολῇ δεῖν οἰόμενος ὑπερέχειν
αὐτός τε ἧττον συντείνει πρὸς ἀρετὴν τὴν ἀληθῆ,
τούς τε ἀνθαμιλλωμένους εἰς ἀθυμίαν καθίστησι
τῷ ἀδίκως ψέγεσθαι, καὶ διὰ ταῦτα ἀγύμναστον
B τὴν πόλιν ὅλην εἰς ἅμιλλαν ἀρετῆς ποιῶν σμικρο-
τέραν αὐτὴν πρὸς εὐδοξίαν τὸ ἑαυτοῦ μέρος ἀπεργάζεται. θυμοειδῆ μὲν δὴ χρὴ πάντα ἄνδρα
εἶναι, πρᾶον δὲ ὡς ὅτι μάλιστα. τὰ γὰρ τῶν
ἄλλων χαλεπὰ καὶ δυσίατα ἢ καὶ τὸ παράπαν
ἀνίατα ἀδικήματα οὐκ ἔστιν ἄλλως ἐκφυγεῖν ἢ
μαχόμενον καὶ ἀμυνόμενον νικῶντα καὶ τῷ μηδὲν
ἀνιέναι κολάζοντα, τοῦτο δὲ ἄνευ θυμοῦ γενναίου
C ψυχὴ πᾶσα ἀδύνατος δρᾶν. τὰ δ' αὖ τῶν ὅσοι
ἀδικοῦσι μέν, ἰατὰ δέ, γιγνώσκειν χρὴ πρῶτον
μὲν ὅτι πᾶς ὁ ἄδικος οὐχ ἑκὼν ἄδικος. τῶν γὰρ
μεγίστων κακῶν οὐδεὶς οὐδαμοῦ οὐδὲν ἑκὼν κε-
κτῇτο ἄν ποτε, πολὺ δ' ἥκιστα ἐν τοῖς τῶν ἑαυτοῦ
τιμιωτάτοις· ψυχὴ δ', ὡς εἴπομεν, ἀληθείᾳ γ' ἐστὶ
πᾶσι τιμιώτατον· ἐν οὖν τῷ τιμιωτάτῳ τὸ μέγιστον κακὸν οὐδεὶς ἑκὼν μή ποτε λάβῃ καὶ ζῇ διὰ
D βίου κεκτημένος αὐτό. ἀλλὰ ἐλεεινὸς μὲν πάντως
ὅ γε ἄδικος καὶ ὁ τὰ κακὰ ἔχων, ἐλεεῖν δὲ τὸν μὲν
ἰάσιμα ἔχοντα ἐγχωρεῖ καὶ ἀνείργοντα τὸν θυμὸν
πραΰνειν καὶ μὴ ἀκραχολοῦντα γυναικείως πικραι-
νόμενον διατελεῖν, τῷ δ' ἀκράτως καὶ ἀπαραμυθή-
τως πλημμελεῖ καὶ κακῷ ἐφιέναι δεῖ τὴν ὀργήν·

---

[1] Cp. *Rep.* 375 B ff., 410 C ff.

larges a State, since he strives hard himself and does
not thwart the others by calumny; but the jealous
man, thinking that calumny of others is the best
way to secure his own superiority, makes less effort
himself to win true excellence, and disheartens his
rivals by getting them unjustly blamed; whereby he
causes the whole State to be ill-trained for com-
peting in excellence, and renders it, for his part,
less large in fair repute. Every man ought to be at
once passionate and gentle in the highest degree.[1]
For, on the one hand, it is impossible to escape from
other men's wrongdoings, when they are cruel and
hard to remedy, or even wholly irremediable, otherwise than by victorious fighting and self-defence,
and by punishing most rigorously; and this no soul
can achieve without noble passion. But, on the
other hand, when men commit wrongs which are
remediable, one should, in the first place, recognize
that every wrongdoer is a wrongdoer involuntarily;[2]
for no one anywhere would ever voluntarily acquire
any of the greatest evils, least of all in his own most
precious possessions. And most precious in very
truth to every man is, as we have said, the soul. No
one, therefore, will voluntarily admit into this most
precious thing the greatest evil and live possessing
it all his life long. Now while in general the wrongdoer and he that has these evils are to be pitied, it
is permissible to show pity to the man that has evils
that are remediable, and to abate one's passion and
treat him gently, and not to keep on raging like a
scolding wife; but in dealing with the man who is
totally and obstinately perverse and wicked one must
give free course to wrath. Wherefore we affirm

[2] Cp. 860 C ff.; 863 B ff.; *Protag.* 345 D; *Tim.* 86 D.

731 διὸ δὴ θυμοειδῆ πρέπειν καὶ πρᾶόν φαμεν ἑκάστοτε [εἶναι δεῖν] ¹ τὸν ἀγαθόν.

Πάντων δὲ μέγιστον κακῶν ἀνθρώποις τοῖς
πολλοῖς ἔμφυτον ἐν ταῖς ψυχαῖς ἐστίν, οὗ πᾶς
ἑαυτῷ συγγνώμην ἔχων ἀποφυγὴν οὐδεμίαν μηχα-
E νᾶται· τοῦτο δ' ἔστιν ὃ λέγουσιν ὡς φίλος αὑτῷ
πᾶς ἄνθρωπος φύσει τ' ἐστὶ καὶ ὀρθῶς ἔχει τὸ
δεῖν εἶναι τοιοῦτον. τὸ δὲ ἀληθείᾳ γε πάντων
ἁμαρτημάτων διὰ τὴν σφόδρα ἑαυτοῦ φιλίαν
αἴτιον ἑκάστῳ γίγνεται ἑκάστοτε· τυφλοῦται
γὰρ περὶ τὸ φιλούμενον ὁ φιλῶν, ὥστε τὰ δίκαια
καὶ τὰ ἀγαθὰ καὶ τὰ καλὰ κακῶς κρίνει, τὸ αὑτοῦ
732 πρὸ τοῦ ἀληθοῦς ἀεὶ τιμᾶν δεῖν ἡγούμενος· οὔτε
γὰρ ἑαυτὸν οὔτε τὰ ἑαυτοῦ χρὴ τόν γε μέγαν
ἄνδρα ἐσόμενον στέργειν, ἀλλὰ τὰ δίκαια, ἐάν
τε παρ' αὑτῷ ἐάν τε παρ' ἄλλῳ μᾶλλον πραττόμενα τυγχάνῃ. ἐκ ταὐτοῦ δὲ ἁμαρτήματος τούτου
καὶ τὸ τὴν ἀμαθίαν τὴν παρ' αὑτῷ δοκεῖν σοφίαν
εἶναι γέγονε πᾶσιν· ὅθεν οὐκ εἰδότες, ὡς ἔπος
εἰπεῖν, οὐδὲν οἰόμεθα τὰ πάντα εἰδέναι, οὐκ ἐπι-
τρέποντες δὲ ἄλλοις ἃ μὴ ἐπιστάμεθα πράττειν,
B ἀναγκαζόμεθα ἁμαρτάνειν αὐτοὶ πράττοντες. διὸ
πάντα ἄνθρωπον χρὴ φεύγειν τὸ σφόδρα φιλεῖν
αὑτόν, τὸν δ' ἑαυτοῦ βελτίω διώκειν ἀεί,² μηδεμίαν
αἰσχύνην ἐπὶ τῷ τοιούτῳ πρόσθεν ποιούμενον.

Ἃ δὲ σμικρότερα μὲν τούτων καὶ λεγόμενα πολ-

¹ [εἶναι δεῖν] I bracket (J. B. Mayor bracketed εἶναι,
Stephens δεῖν).
² ἀεί Stobaeus : δεῖ MSS.

that it behoves the good man to be always at once passionate and gentle.

There is an evil, great above all others, which most men have, implanted in their souls, and which each one of them excuses in himself and makes no effort to avoid. It is the evil indicated in the saying that every man is by nature a lover of self, and that it is right that he should be such.[1] But the truth is that the cause of all sins in every case lies in the person's excessive love of self. For the lover is blind in his view of the object loved, so that he is a bad judge[2] of things just and good and noble, in that he deems himself bound always to value what is his own more than what is true; for the man who is to attain the title of "Great" must be devoted neither to himself nor to his own belongings, but to things just, whether they happen to be actions of his own or rather those of another man. And it is from this same sin that every man has derived the further notion that his own folly is wisdom; whence it comes about that though we know practically nothing, we fancy that we know everything; and since we will not entrust to others the doing of things we do not understand, we necessarily go wrong in doing them ourselves. Wherefore every man must shun excessive self-love, and ever follow after him that is better than himself, allowing no shame to prevent him from so doing.

Precepts that are less important than these and

---

[1] Cp. Eur. *Frag.* 460:

ἐκεῖνο γὰρ πέπονθ' ὅπερ πάντες βροτοί·
φιλῶν μάλιστ' ἐμαυτὸν οὐκ αἰσχύνομαι.

Ar. *Rhet.* 1371[b] 19; *Pol.* 1263[b] 2.

[2] Cp. *Rep.* 474 D, E.

732 λάκις ἐστί, χρήσιμα δὲ τούτων οὐχ ἧττον, χρὴ
λέγειν ἑαυτὸν ἀναμιμνήσκοντα· ὥσπερ γάρ τινος
ἀπορρέοντος ἀεὶ δεῖ τοὐναντίον ἐπιρρεῖν, ἀνάμνη-
σις δ᾽ ἐστὶν ἐπιρροὴ φρονήσεως ἀπολειπούσης.
C διὸ δὴ γελώτων τε εἴργεσθαι χρὴ τῶν ἐξαισίωι
καὶ δακρύων, παραγγέλλειν δὲ παντὶ πάντ᾽ ἄνδρα
καὶ ὅλην ⟨πόλιν⟩[1] περιχάρειαν πᾶσαν ἀπο-
κρυπτόμενον καὶ περιωδυνίαν εὐσχημονεῖν πειρᾶσθαι, κατά τε εὐπραγίας ἱσταμένου τοῦ δαίμονος
ἑκάστου καὶ κατ᾽ ἀτυχίας[2] [οἷον πρὸς ὑψηλὰ καὶ
ἀνάντη δαιμόνων ἀνθισταμένων τισὶ πράξεσιν],[3]
ἐλπίζειν δ᾽ ἀεὶ τοῖς γ᾽ ἀγαθοῖσι τὸν θεὸν ἃ
δωρεῖται, πόνων μὲν ἐπιπιπτόντων ἀντὶ μειζόνων
D ἐλάττους ποιήσειν τῶν τ᾽ αὖ νῦν παρόντων ἐπὶ τὸ
βέλτιον μεταβολάς, περὶ δὲ τὰ ἀγαθὰ τὰ ἐναντία
τούτων ἀεὶ πάντ᾽ αὐτοῖς παραγενήσεσθαι μετ᾽
ἀγαθῆς τύχης. ταύταις δὴ ταῖς ἐλπίσιν ἕκαστον
χρὴ ζῆν καὶ ταῖς ὑπομνήσεσι πάντων τῶν τοιούτων, μηδὲν φειδόμενον, ἀλλ᾽ ἀεὶ κατά τε παιδιὰς
καὶ σπουδὰς ἀναμιμνήσκοντα ἕτερόν τε καὶ ἑαυτὸν
σαφῶς.
Νῦν οὖν δὴ περὶ μὲν ἐπιτηδευμάτων, οἷα χρὴ
E ἐπιτηδεύειν, καὶ περὶ αὐτοῦ ἑκάστου, ποῖόν τινα
χρεὼν εἶναι, λέλεκται σχεδὸν ὅσα θεῖά ἐστι. τὰ
δ᾽ ἀνθρώπινα νῦν ἡμῖν οὐκ εἴρηται, δεῖ δέ· ἀνθρώποις γὰρ διαλεγόμεθα, ἀλλ᾽ οὐ θεοῖς. ἔστι
δὴ φύσει ἀνθρώπειον μάλιστα ἡδοναὶ καὶ λῦπαι
καὶ ἐπιθυμίαι, ἐξ ὧν ἀνάγκη τὸ θνητὸν πᾶν ζῷον

[1] ⟨πόλιν⟩ added by Badham.
[2] κατ᾽ ἀτυχίας Badham, Schanz: κατὰ τύχας MSS.
[3] [οἷον . . . πράξεσιν] bracketed by Schanz, after Zeller.
The clause is awkward both in sense and in construction

oftentimes repeated—but no less profitable—a man should repeat to himself by way of reminder; for where there is a constant efflux, there must also be a corresponding influx, and when wisdom flows away, the proper influx consists in recollection;[1] wherefore men must be restrained from untimely laughter and tears,[2] and every individual, as well as the whole State, must charge every man to try to conceal all show of extreme joy or sorrow, and to behave himself seemly, alike in good fortune and in evil, according as each man's Genius[3] ranges itself,—hoping always that God will diminish the troubles that fall upon them by the blessings which he bestows, and will change for the better the present evils; and as to their blessings, hoping that they, contrariwise, will, with the help of good fortune, be increased. In these hopes, and in the recollections of all these truths, it behoves every man to live, sparing no pains, but constantly recalling them clearly to the recollection both of himself and of his neighbour, alike when at work and when at play.

Thus, as regards the right character of institutions and the right character of individuals, we have now laid down practically all the rules that are of divine sanction. Those that are of human origin we have not stated as yet, but state them we must; for our converse is with men, not gods. Pleasures, pains and desires are by nature especially human; and from these, of necessity, every mortal creature is, so to

---

[1] Cp. *Phileb.* 33 E ff.
[2] Cp. *Rep.* 388 E f., 606 C f.
[3] *i.e.* divine controlling force, or destiny.

("when daemons oppose certain actions as though facing things high and steep").

732 ἀτεχνῶς οἷον ἐξηρτῆσθαί τε καὶ ἐκκρεμάμενον εἶναι
σπουδαῖς ταῖς μεγίσταις. δεῖ δὴ τὸν κάλλιστον
βίον ἐπαινεῖν, μὴ μόνον ὅτι τῷ σχήματι κρατεῖ
733 πρὸς εὐδοξίαν, ἀλλὰ καὶ ὡς, ἄν τις ἐθέλῃ γεύεσθαι
καὶ μὴ νέος ὢν φυγὰς ἀπ' αὐτοῦ γένηται, κρατεῖ
καὶ τούτῳ ὃ πάντες ζητοῦμεν, τῷ χαίρειν πλείω,
ἐλάττω δὲ λυπεῖσθαι παρὰ τὸν βίον ἅπαντα. ὡς
δὲ ἔσται τοῦτο σαφές, ἂν γεύηταί τις ὀρθῶς, ἑτοίμως καὶ σφόδρα φανήσεται. ἡ δὲ ὀρθότης τίς ;
τοῦτο ἤδη παρὰ τοῦ λόγου χρὴ λαμβάνοντα
σκοπεῖν· εἴτε οὕτως ἡμῖν κατὰ φύσιν πέφυκεν εἴτε
ἄλλως παρὰ φύσιν, βίον χρὴ παρὰ βίον ἡδίω
καὶ λυπηρότερον ὧδε σκοπεῖν. ἡδονὴν βουλόμεθα
B ἡμῖν εἶναι, λύπην δὲ οὔθ' αἱρούμεθα οὔτε βουλόμεθα, τὸ δὲ μηδέτερον ἀντὶ μὲν ἡδονῆς οὐ βουλόμεθα, λύπης δὲ ἀλλάττεσθαι βουλόμεθα· λύπην
δὲ ἐλάττω μετὰ μείζονος ἡδονῆς βουλόμεθα,
ἡδονὴν δὲ ἐλάττω μετὰ μείζονος λύπης οὐ βουλόμεθα, ἴσα δ' ἀντὶ ἴσων ἑκάτερα τούτων οὐχ ὡς
βουλόμεθα ἔχοιμεν ἂν διασαφεῖν. ταῦτα δὲ
πάντα ἐστὶ πλήθει καὶ μεγέθει καὶ σφοδρότησιν
ἰσότησί τε καὶ ὅσα ἐναντία ἐστὶ πᾶσι τοῖς
τοιούτοις, πρὸς βούλησιν διαφέροντά τε καὶ μηδὲν
C διαφέροντα πρὸς αἵρεσιν ἑκάστων. οὕτω δὴ
τούτων ἐξ ἀνάγκης διακεκοσμημένων, ἐν ᾧ μὲν
βίῳ ἔνεστι πολλὰ ἑκάτερα καὶ μεγάλα καὶ σφο-
δρά, ὑπερβάλλει δὲ τὰ τῶν ἡδονῶν, βουλόμεθα,
ἐν ᾧ δὲ τὰ ἐναντία, οὐ βουλόμεθα· καὶ αὖ ἐν ᾧ
ὀλίγα ἑκάτερα καὶ σμικρὰ καὶ ἠρεμαῖα, ὑπερβάλλει δὲ τὰ λυπηρά, οὐ βουλόμεθα, ἐν ᾧ δὲ
τἀναντία, βουλόμεθα· ἐν ᾧ δ' αὖ βίῳ ἰσορ-

say, suspended and dependent by the strongest cords of influence. Thus one should commend the noblest life, not merely because it is of superior fashion in respect of fair repute, but also because, if a man consents to taste it and not shun it in his youth, it is superior likewise in that which all men covet,—an excess, namely, of joy and a deficiency of pain throughout the whole of life. That this will clearly be the result, if a man tastes of it rightly, will at once be fully evident. But wherein does this "rightness" consist? That is the question which we must now, under the instruction of our Argument, consider; comparing the more pleasant life with the more painful, we must in this wise consider whether this mode is natural to us, and that other mode unnatural. We desire that pleasure should be ours, but pain we neither choose nor desire; and the neutral state we do not desire in place of pleasure, but we do desire it in exchange for pain; and we desire less pain with more pleasure, but we do not desire less pleasure with more pain; and when the two are evenly balanced, we are unable to state any clear preference. Now all these states—in their number, quantity, intensity, equality, and in the opposites thereof—have, or have not, influence on desire, to govern its choice of each. So these things being thus ordered of necessity, we desire that mode of life in which the feelings are many, great, and intense, with those of pleasure predominating, but we do not desire the life in which the feelings of pain predominate; and contrariwise, we do not desire the life in which the feelings are few, small, and gentle, if the painful predominate, but if the pleasurable predominate, we do desire it. Further,

733 ῥοπεῖ, καθάπερ ἐν τοῖς πρόσθεν, δεῖ διανοεῖ-
σθαι· τὸν ἰσόρροπον βίον, ὡς τῶν μὲν ὑπερβάλ-
D λοντα [1] τῷ φίλῳ ἡμῖν βουλόμεθα, τῶν δ' αὖ τοῖς
ἐχθροῖς οὐ βουλόμεθα. πάντας δὴ δεῖ διανοεῖσθαι τοὺς βίους ἡμῶν ὡς ἐν τούτοις ἐνδεδεμένοι
πεφύκασι, καὶ δεῖ διαιρεῖσθαι [2] ποίους φύσει
βουλόμεθα· εἰ δέ τι παρὰ ταῦτα ἄρα φαμὲν
βούλεσθαι, διά τινα ἄγνοιαν καὶ ἀπειρίαν τῶν
ὄντων βίων αὐτὰ λέγομεν.

Τίνες δὴ καὶ πόσοι εἰσὶ βίοι, ὧν πέρι δεῖ
προελόμενον τὸ βουλητόν τε καὶ ἑκούσιον ἀβουλήτου τε καὶ ἀκουσίου,[3] ἴδιόν τ' ἀεὶ [4] νόμον ἑαυτῷ
E ταξάμενον, τὸ φίλον ἅμα καὶ ἡδὺ καὶ ἄριστόν τε
καὶ κάλλιστον ἑλόμενον ζῆν ὡς οἷόν τ' ἐστὶν
ἄνθρωπον μακαριώτατα· λέγωμεν δὴ σώφρονα
βίον ἕνα εἶναι καὶ φρόνιμον ἕνα καὶ ἕνα τὸν
ἀνδρεῖον, καὶ τὸν ὑγιεινὸν βίον ἕνα ταξώμεθα·
καὶ τούτοις οὖσι τέτταρσιν ἐναντίους ἄλλους
τέτταρας, ἄφρονα, δειλόν, ἀκόλαστον, νοσώδη.
σώφρονα μὲν οὖν βίον ὁ γιγνώσκων θήσει πρᾶον
734 ἐπὶ πάντα καὶ ἠρεμαίας μὲν λύπας, ἠρεμαίας δὲ
ἡδονάς, μαλακὰς δὲ ἐπιθυμίας καὶ ἔρωτας οὐκ
ἐμμανεῖς παρεχόμενον· ἀκόλαστον δὲ ὀξὺν ἐπὶ
πάντα καὶ σφοδρὰς μὲν λύπας, σφοδρὰς δὲ ἡδονάς,
συντόνους δὲ καὶ οἰστρώδεις ἐπιθυμίας [τε] [5] καὶ
ἔρωτας ὡς οἷόν τ' ἐμμανεστάτους παρεχόμενον·
ὑπερβαλλούσας δὲ ἐν μὲν τῷ σώφρονι βίῳ τὰς
ἡδονὰς τῶν ἀχθηδόνων, ἐν δὲ τῷ ἀκολάστῳ τὰς

---

[1] ὑπερβάλλοντα Ritter: ὑπερβαλλόντων MSS.
[2] διαιρεῖσθαι England: διανοεῖσθαι MSS.
[3] ἀβουλήτου . . . ἀκουσίου: ἀβούλητον . . . ἀκούσιον MSS.
[4] ἴδιόν τ' ἀεὶ: ἰδόντα εἰς MSS.: ἴδιόν τιν' εἰς Badham.

we must regard the life in which there is an equal balance of pleasure and pain as we previously regarded the neutral state : we desire the balanced life in so far as it exceeds the painful life in point of what we like, but we do not desire it in so far as it exceeds the pleasant lives in point of the things we dislike. The lives of us men must all be regarded as naturally bound up in these feelings, and what kinds of lives we naturally desire is what we must distinguish ; but if we assert that we desire anything else, we only say so through ignorance and inexperience of the lives as they really are.

What, then, and how many are the lives in which a man—when he has chosen the desirable and voluntary in preference to the undesirable and the involuntary, and has made it into a private law for himself, by choosing what is at once both congenial and pleasant and most good and noble—may live as happily as man can ? Let us pronounce that one of them is the temperate life, one the wise, one the brave, and let us class t!ie healthy life as one ; and to these let us oppose four others—the foolish, the cowardly, the licentious, and the diseased. He that knows the temperate life will set it down as gentle in all respects, affording mild pleasures and mild pains, moderate appetites and desires void of frenzy ; but the licentious life he will set down as violent in all directions, affording both pains and pleasures that are extreme, appetites that are intense and maddening, and desires the most frenzied possible ; and whereas in the temperate life the pleasures outweigh the pains, in the licentious

---

⁵ [τε] bracketed by England.

734 λύπας τῶν ἡδονῶν μεγέθει καὶ πλήθει καὶ πυκνό-
τησιν. ὅθεν ὁ μὲν ἡδίων ἡμῖν τῶν βίων, ὁ δὲ
λυπηρότερος ἐξ ἀνάγκης συμβαίνει κατὰ φύσιν
B γίγνεσθαι, καὶ τόν γε βουλόμενον ἡδέως ζῆν οὐκέτι
παρείκει ἑκόντα γε ἀκολάστως ζῆν, ἀλλ' ἤδη
δῆλον ὡς, εἰ τὸ νῦν λεγόμενον ὀρθόν, πᾶς ἐξ
ἀνάγκης ἄκων ἐστὶν ἀκόλαστος· ἢ γὰρ δι' ἀμαθίαν ἢ δι' ἀκράτειαν ἢ δι' ἀμφότερα τοῦ σωφρονεῖν ἐνδεὴς ὢν ζῇ ὁ πᾶς ἀνθρώπινος ὄχλος. ταὐτὰ
δὲ περὶ νοσώδους τε καὶ ὑγιεινοῦ βίου διανοητέον,
ὡς ἔχουσι μὲν ἡδονὰς καὶ λύπας, ὑπερβάλλουσι
C δὲ ἡδοναὶ μὲν λύπας ἐν ὑγιείᾳ, λῦπαι δὲ ἡδονὰς ἐν
νόσοις. ἡμῖν δὲ ἡ βούλησις τῆς αἱρέσεως τῶν
βίων οὐχ ἵνα τὸ λυπηρὸν ὑπερβάλλῃ· ὅπου δ'
ὑπερβάλλεται, τοῦτον τὸν βίον ἡδίω κεκρίκαμεν.
ὁ δὴ σώφρων τοῦ ἀκολάστου καὶ ὁ φρόνιμος τοῦ
ἄφρονος, φαῖμεν ἄν, καὶ ὁ τῆς ἀνδρίας τοῦ τῆς
δειλίας ἐλάττονα καὶ σμικρότερα καὶ μανότερα
ἔχων ἀμφότερα, τῇ τῶν ἡδονῶν ἑκάτερος ἑκάτερον
ὑπερβάλλων, τῇ τῆς λύπης ἐκείνων ὑπερβαλλόν-
D των αὐτούς, ὁ μὲν ἀνδρεῖος τὸν δειλόν, ὁ δὲ
φρόνιμος τὸν ἄφρονα, νικῶσιν, ὥστε ἡδίους εἶναι
τοὺς βίους τῶν βίων, σώφρονα καὶ ἀνδρεῖον καὶ
φρόνιμον καὶ ὑγιεινὸν δειλοῦ καὶ ἄφρονος καὶ
ἀκολάστου καὶ νοσώδους, καὶ ξυλλήβδην τὸν
ἀρετῆς ἐχόμενον κατὰ σῶμα ἢ καὶ κατὰ ψυχὴν
τοῦ τῆς μοχθηρίας ἐχομένου βίου ἡδίω τε εἶναι
καὶ τοῖς ἄλλοις ὑπερέχειν ἐκ περιττοῦ κάλλει καὶ
ὀρθότητι καὶ ἀρετῇ καὶ εὐδοξίᾳ, ὥστε τὸν ἔχοντα
αὐτὸν ζῆν εὐδαιμονέστερον ἀπεργάζεσθαι τοῦ
E ἐναντίου τῷ παντὶ καὶ ὅλῳ.

Καὶ τὸ μὲν προοίμιον τῶν νόμων ἐνταυθοῖ

life the pains exceed the pleasures in extent, number, and frequency. Whence it necessarily results that the one life must be naturally more pleasant, the other more painful to us; and it is no longer possible for the man who desires a pleasant life voluntarily to live a licentious life, but it is clear by now (if our argument is right) that no man can possibly be licentious voluntarily: it is owing to ignorance or incontinence, or both, that the great bulk of mankind live lives lacking in temperance. Similarly with regard to the diseased life and the healthy life, one must observe that while both have pleasures and pains, the pleasures exceed the pains in health, but the pains the pleasures in disease. Our desire in the choice of lives is not that pain should be in excess, but the life we have judged the more pleasant is that in which pain is exceeded by pleasure. We will assert, then, that since the temperate life has its feelings smaller, fewer and lighter than the licentious life, and the wise life than the foolish, and the brave than the cowardly, and since the one life is superior to the other in pleasure, but inferior in pain, the brave life is victorious over the cowardly and the wise over the foolish; consequently the one set of lives ranks as more pleasant than the other: the temperate, brave, wise, and healthy lives are more pleasant than the cowardly, foolish, licentious and diseased. To sum up, the life of bodily and spiritual virtue, as compared with that of vice, is not only more pleasant, but also exceeds greatly in nobility, rectitude, virtue and good fame, so that it causes the man who lives it to live ever so much more happily than he who lives the opposite life.

Thus far we have stated the prelude of our laws,

734 λεχθὲν τῶν λόγων τέλος ἐχέτω, μετὰ δὲ τὸ
προοίμιον ἀναγκαῖόν που νόμον ἔπεσθαι, μᾶλλον
δὲ τό γε ἀληθὲς [νόμους] [1] πολιτείας ὑπογραφήν.[2]
καθάπερ οὖν δή τινα ξυνυφὴν ἢ καὶ πλέγμ᾽ ἄλλ᾽
ὁτιοῦν, οὐκ ἐκ τῶν αὐτῶν οἷόν τ᾽ ἐστὶ τήν τε
ἐφυφὴν καὶ τὸν στήμονα ἀπεργάζεσθαι, διαφέρειν
δ᾽ ἀναγκαῖον τὸ τῶν στημόνων πρὸς ἀρετὴν γένος·
ἰσχυρόν τε γὰρ καὶ τινα βεβαιότητα ἐν τοῖς
735 τρόποις εἰληφός, τὸ δὲ μαλακώτερον καὶ ἐπιεικείᾳ
τινὶ δικαίᾳ χρώμενον· ὅθεν δὴ τοὺς μεγάλας
ἀρχὰς ἐν ταῖς πόλεσιν ἄρξοντας δεῖ διακρίνεσθαί
τινα τρόπον ταύτῃ καὶ τοὺς σμικρὰς [3] παιδείᾳ
βασανισθέντας ἑκάστοτε κατὰ λόγον· ἔστον γὰρ
δὴ δύο πολιτείας εἴδη, τὸ μὲν ἀρχῶν καταστάσεις
ἑκάστοις, τὸ δὲ νόμοι ταῖς ἀρχαῖς ἀποδοθέντες.

Τὸ δὲ πρὸ τούτων ἁπάντων δεῖ διανοεῖσθαι
B τὰ τοιάδε. πᾶσαν ἀγέλην ποιμὴν καὶ βουκόλος
τροφεύς τε ἵππων, καὶ ὅσα ἄλλα τοιαῦτα, παραλαβὼν οὐκ ἄλλως μή ποτε ἐπιχειρήσῃ θεραπεύειν ἢ πρῶτον μὲν τὸν ἑκάστῃ προσήκοντα
καθαρμὸν καθάρῃ τῇ ξυνοικήσει, διαλέξας δὲ τά τε
ὑγιῆ καὶ τὰ μὴ καὶ τὰ γενναῖα καὶ ἀγεννῆ τὰ μὲν
ἀποπέμψῃ πρὸς ἄλλας τινὰς ἀγέλας, τὰ δὲ θερα-
πεύσῃ, διανοούμενος ὡς μάταιος ἂν ὁ πόνος εἴη
καὶ ἀνήνυτος περί τε σῶμα καὶ ψυχάς, ἃς φύσις
C καὶ πονηρὰ τροφὴ διεφθαρκυῖα προσαπόλλυσι τὸ

---

[1] [νόμους] bracketed by W.-Möllendorff.
[2] ὑπογραφήν W.-Möllendorff: ὑπογράφειν MSS.
[3] σμικρὰς Bücheler, Schanz: σμικρᾷ MSS.

---

[1] A play on the double sense of νόμος—" law " and musical
"nome" or "tune."

and here let that statement end : after the prelude must necessarily follow the tune,[1]—or rather, to be strictly accurate, a sketch of the State-organisation. Now, just as in the case of a piece of webbing, or any other woven article, it is not possible to make both warp and woof of the same materials, but the stuff of the warp must be of better quality—for it is strong and is made firm by its twistings, whereas the woof is softer and shows a due degree of flexibility [2]— from this we may see that in some such way we must mark out those who are to hold high offices in the State and those who are to hold low offices,[3] after applying in each case an adequate educational test. For of State-organisation there are two divisions, of which the one is the appointment of individuals to office, the other the assignment of laws to the offices.

But, in truth, before we deal with all these matters we must observe the following. In dealing with a flock of any kind, the shepherd or cowherd, or the keeper of horses or any such animals, will never attempt to look after it until he has first applied to each group of animals the appropriate purge—which is to separate the sound from the unsound, and the well-bred from the ill-bred,[4] and to send off the latter to other herds, while keeping the former under his own care ; for he reckons that his labour would be fruitless and unending if it were spent on bodies and souls which nature and ill-nurture have combined to ruin, and which themselves bring ruin on a stock

---

[2] In weaving the ancients used an upright loom, in which the fixed, vertical threads of the "warp" were of coarser fibre than the transverse threads of the "woof."

[3] Cp. **Ar.** *Pol.* 1265[b] 18 ff.   [4] Cp. *Rep.* 410 A.

735 τῶν ὑγιῶν καὶ ἀκηράτων ἠθῶν τε καὶ σωμάτων
γένος ἐν ἑκάστοις τῶν κτημάτων, ἄν τις τὰ
ὑπάρχοντα μὴ διακαθαίρηται. τὰ μὲν δὴ τῶν
ἄλλων ζώων ἐλάττων τε σπουδῇ καὶ παραδείγ-
ματος ἕνεκα μόνον ἄξια παραθέσθαι τῷ λόγῳ,
τὰ δὲ τῶν ἀνθρώπων σπουδῆς τῆς μεγίστης τῷ τε
νομοθέτῃ διερευνᾶσθαι καὶ φράζειν τὸ προσῆκον
ἑκάστοις καθαρμοῦ τε πέρι καὶ ξυμπασῶν τῶν
ἄλλων πράξεων. αὐτίκα γὰρ τὸ περὶ καθαρ-
D μοὺς πόλεως ὧδ' ἔχον ἂν εἴη· πολλῶν οὐσῶν τῶν
διακαθάρσεων αἱ μὲν ῥᾴους εἰσίν, αἱ δὲ χαλε-
πώτεραι, καὶ τὰς μὲν τύραννος μὲν ὢν καὶ νομοθέτης ὁ αὐτός, ὅσαι χαλεπαί τ' εἰσὶ καὶ ἄρισται,
δύναιτ' ἂν καθῆραι· νομοθέτης δὲ ἄνευ τυραννίδος
καθιστὰς πολιτείαν καινὴν καὶ νόμους, εἰ καὶ
τὸν πρᾴότατον τῶν καθαρμῶν καθήρειεν, ἀγαπη-
τῶς ἂν καὶ τὸ τοιοῦτον δράσειεν. ἔστι δ' ὁ μὲν
ἄριστος ἀλγεινός, καθάπερ ὅσα τῶν φαρμάκων
E τοιουτότροπα, ὁ τῇ δίκῃ μετὰ τιμωρίας εἰς τὸ
κολάζειν ἄγων, θάνατον ἢ φυγὴν τῇ τιμωρίᾳ τὸ
τέλος ἐπιτιθείς· τοὺς γὰρ μέγιστα ἐξημαρτηκότας,
ἀνιάτους δὲ ὄντας, μεγίστην δὲ οὖσαν βλάβην
πόλεως, ἀπαλλάττειν εἴωθεν. ὁ δὲ πρᾳότερός ἐστι
τῶν καθαρμῶν ὁ τοιόσδε ἡμῖν· ὅσοι διὰ τὴν τῆς
τροφῆς ἀπορίαν τοῖς ἡγεμόσιν ἐπὶ τὰ τῶν ἐχόντων μὴ ἔχοντες ἑτοίμους αὐτοὺς ἐνδείκνυνται
736 παρεσκευακότες ἔπεσθαι, τούτοις ὡς νοσήματι
πόλεως ἐμπεφυκότι δι' εὐφημίας ἀπαλλαγῆς[1]
ὄνομα ἀποικίαν τιθέμενος, εὐμενῶς ὅτι μάλιστα
ἐξεπέμψατο. παντὶ μὲν οὖν νομοθετοῦντι τοῦτο
ἁμῶς γέ πως κατ' ἀρχὰς δραστέον, ἡμῖν μὴν ἔτι

---

[1] ἀπαλλαγῆς Stephens : ἀπαλλαγὴν MSS.

that is sound and clean both in habit and in body,—
whatever the class of beast,—unless a thorough
purge be made in the existing herd. This is a
matter of minor importance in the case of other
animals, and deserves mention only by way of illustration; but in the case of man it is of the highest
importance for the lawgiver to search out and to
declare what is proper for each class both as regards
purging out and all other modes of treatment. For
instance, in respect of civic purgings, this would be
the way of it. Of the many possible modes of
purging, some are milder, some more severe; those
that are severest and best a lawgiver who was also a
despot [1] might be able to effect, but a lawgiver without despotic power might be well content if, in
establishing a new polity and laws, he could effect
even the mildest of purgations. The best purge is
painful, like all medicines of a drastic nature,—the
purge which hales to punishments by means of justice
linked with vengeance, crowning the vengeance
with exile or death: it, as a rule, clears out the
greatest criminals when they are incurable and
cause serious damage to the State. A milder form
of purge is one of the following kind:—when,
owing to scarcity of food, people are in want, and
display a readiness to follow their leaders in an
attack on the property of the wealthy,—then the
lawgiver, regarding all such as a plague inherent in
the body politic, ships them abroad as gently as
possible, giving the euphemistic title of "emigration"
to their evacuation. By some means or other this
must be done by every legislator at the beginning,

[1] Cp. 709 E ff.

736 τούτων ἀπονώτερα [1] τὰ περὶ ταῦτ' ἐστὶ συμβε-
βηκότα νῦν· οὔτε γὰρ ἀποικίαν οὔτ' ἐκλογήν τινα
καθάρσεως δεῖ μηχανᾶσθαι πρὸς τὸ παρόν, οἷον
B δέ τινων ξυρρεόντων ἐκ πολλῶν τὰ μὲν πηγῶν
τὰ δὲ χειμάρρων εἰς μίαν λίμνην ἀναγκαῖον
προσέχοντας τὸν νοῦν φυλάττειν ὅπως ὅτι κα-
θαρώτατον ἔσται τὸ συρρέον ὕδωρ, τὰ μὲν
ἐξαντλοῦντας, τὰ δ' ἀποχετεύοντας καὶ παρα-
τρέποντας. πόνος δ', ὡς ἔοικε, καὶ κίνδυνός ἐστιν
ἐν πάσῃ κατασκευῇ πολιτικῇ· τὰ δ' ἐπείπερ
λόγῳ γ' ἐστὶ τὰ νῦν ἀλλ' οὐκ ἔργῳ πραττόμενα,
πεπεράνθω τε ἡμῖν ἡ ξυλλογὴ καὶ κατὰ νοῦν
ἡ καθαρότης αὐτῆς ἔστω ξυμβεβηκυῖα· τοὺς γὰρ
C κακοὺς τῶν ἐπιχειρούντων εἰς τὴν νῦν πόλιν ὡς
πολιτευσομένους ξυνιέναι, πειρᾷ [2] πάσῃ καὶ ἱκανῷ
χρόνῳ διαβασανίσαντες, διακωλύσωμεν ἀφικνεῖσθαι, τοὺς δ' ἀγαθοὺς εἰς δύναμιν εὐμενεῖς ἵλεώς τε
προσαγώμεθα.

Τόδε δὲ μὴ λανθανέτω γιγνόμενον ἡμᾶς εὐ-
τύχημα, ὅτι καθάπερ εἴπομεν τὴν τῶν Ἡρα-
κλειδῶν ἀποικίαν εὐτυχεῖν, ὡς γῆς καὶ χρεῶν
ἀποκοπῆς καὶ νομῆς πέρι δεινὴν καὶ ἐπικίνδυνον
ἔριν ἐξέφυγεν, ἣν νομοθετεῖσθαι ἀναγκασθείσῃ
D πόλει τῶν ἀρχαίων οὔτε ἐᾶν οἷόν τε ἀκίνητον
[οὐδὲν] [3] οὔτ' αὖ κινεῖν δυνατόν ἐστί τινα τρόπον,
εὐχὴ δὲ μόνον ὡς ἔπος εἰπεῖν λείπεται καὶ σμικρὰ
μετάβασις εὐλαβὴς ἐν πολλῷ χρόνῳ σμικρὸν

---

[1] ἀπονώτερα : ἀτοπώτερα MSS. (ἀκοπώτερα Ritter)
[2] πειρᾷ Badham, Schanz : πειθοῖ MSS.
[3] [οὐδὲν] wanting in MSS.

---

[1] The citizens who are to form the new Magnesian colony
are to be drawn from various quarters, and they must be

but in our case the task is now even more simple ; for we have no need to contrive for the present either a form of emigration or any other purgative selection ; but just as when there is a confluence of floods from many sources—some from springs, some from torrents—into a single pool, we have to take diligent precautions to ensure that the water may be of the utmost possible purity, by drawing it off in some cases, and in others by making channels to divert its course.[1] Yet toil and risk, it would appear, are involved in every exercise of statecraft. Since, however, our present efforts are verbal rather than actual, let us assume that our collection of citizens is now completed, and its purity secured to our satisfaction ; for we shall test thoroughly by every kind of test and by length of time the vicious among those who attempt to enter our present State as citizens, and so prevent their arrival, whereas we shall welcome the virtuous with all possible graciousness and goodwill.

And let us not omit to notice this piece of good luck—that, just as we said [2] that the colony of the Heraclidae was fortunate in avoiding fierce and dangerous strife concerning the distribution of land and money and the cancelling of debts (so we are similarly lucky) ; for when a State is obliged to settle such strife by law, it can neither leave vested interests unaltered nor yet can it in any wise alter them, and no way is left save what one might term that of " pious aspiration " and cautious change, little by little, extended over a long period, and that way

carefully tested (like streams flowing into a reservoir) before being admitted.
[2] 684 E.

736 μεταβιβάζουσιν, ἥδε·[1] τῶν κινούντων ἀεὶ κεκτη-
μένων μὲν αὐτῶν γῆν ἄφθονον ὑπάρχειν, κεκτη-
μένων δὲ καὶ ὀφειλέτας αὐτοῖς πολλούς, ἐθελόντων
τε τούτων πῃ τοῖς ἀπορουμένοις δι' ἐπιείκειαν
E κοινωνεῖν τὰ μὲν ἀφιέντας, τὰ δὲ νεμομένους,
ἀμῇ γέ πῃ τῆς μετριότητος ἐχομένους καὶ πενίαν
ἡγουμένους εἶναι μὴ τὸ τὴν οὐσίαν ἐλάττω ποιεῖν
ἀλλὰ τὸ τὴν ἀπληστίαν πλείω. σωτηρίας τε
γὰρ ἀρχὴ μεγίστη πόλεως αὕτη γίγνεται, καὶ
ἐπὶ ταύτης οἷον κρηπῖδος μονίμου ἐποικοδομεῖν
δυνατὸν ὄντινα ἂν ὕστερον ἐποικοδομῇ τις κόσμον
πολιτικὸν προσήκοντα τῇ τοιαύτῃ καταστάσει·
737 ταύτης δὲ σαθρᾶς οὔσης [τῆς μεταβάσεως][2] οὐκ
εὔπορος ἡ μετὰ ταῦτα πολιτικὴ πρᾶξις οὐδεμιᾷ
γίγνοιτ' ἂν πόλει. ἣν ἡμεῖς μέν, ὥς φαμεν,
ἐκφεύγομεν· ὅμως δὲ εἰρῆσθαί γε ὀρθότερον, εἰ
καὶ μὴ ἐξεφεύγομεν, ὅπῃ ποτ' ἂν ἐποιούμεθα
αὐτῆς τὴν φυγήν. εἰρήσθω δὴ νῦν ὅτι διὰ τοῦ
μὴ φιλοχρηματεῖν μετὰ δίκης, ἄλλη δ' οὐκ ἔστιν
οὔτ' εὐρεῖα οὔτε στενὴ τῆς τοιαύτης μηχανῆς
διαφυγή. καὶ τοῦτο μὲν οἷον ἕρμα πόλεως ἡμῖν
κείσθω τὰ νῦν· ἀνεγκλήτους γὰρ δεῖ τὰς οὐσίας
πρὸς ἀλλήλους κατασκευάζεσθαι ἀμῶς γέ πως,
B ἢ μὴ προϊέναι πρότερον εἰς τοὔμπροσθεν ἑκόντας[3]
εἶναι τῆς ἄλλης κατασκευῆς, οἷς ᾖ παλαιὰ
ἐγκλήματα πρὸς ἀλλήλους, [καὶ][4] ὅσοις νοῦ καὶ
σμικρὸν μετῇ. οἷς δέ, ὡς ἡμῖν νῦν, θεὸς ἔδωκε
καινήν τε πόλιν οἰκίζειν καὶ μή τινας ἔχθρας
εἶναί πω πρὸς ἀλλήλους, τούτους ἔχθρας αὑτοῖς

---

[1] ἥδε Bekker, Burnet: ἡ δὲ MSS., Zur.
[2] [τῆς μεταβάσεως] bracketed by England.
[3] ἑκόντας Ast: ἑκόντα MSS.
[4] [καὶ] bracketed by Stallb.

is this:—there must already exist a supply of men to effect the change, who themselves, on each occasion, possess abundance of land and have many persons in their debt, and who are kind enough to wish to give a share of these things to those of them who are in want, partly by remissions and partly by distributions, making a kind of rule of moderation and believing that poverty consists, not in decreasing one's substance, but in increasing one's greed. For this is the main foundation of the security of a State, and on this as on a firm keel it is possible to build whatever kind of civic organisation may be subsequently built suitable for the arrangement described; but if the foundation be rotten, the subsequent political operations will prove by no means easy for any State. This difficulty, as we say, we avoid; it is better, however, that we should explain the means by which, if we had not actually avoided it, we might have found a way of escape. Be it explained, then, that that means consists in renouncing avarice by the aid of justice, and that there is no way of escape, broad or narrow, other than this device. So let this stand fixed for us now as a kind of pillar of the State. The properties of the citizens must be established somehow or other on a basis that is secure from intestine disputes; otherwise, for people who have ancient disputes with one another, men will not of their own free will proceed any further with political construction, if they have a grain of sense.[1] But as for those to whom—as to us now—God has given a new State to found, and one free as yet from internal feuds,—that those founders should excite

---

[1] There may be an allusion here to Solon; the *first* step in his political reforms was a measure for the abolition of debts ("Seisachtheia").

737 αἰτίους γενέσθαι διὰ τὴν διανομὴν τῆς γῆς τε
καὶ οἰκήσεων οὐκ ἀνθρώπινος ἂν εἴη μετὰ κάκης
πάσης ἀμαθία.

C   Τίς οὖν δὴ τρόπος ἂν εἴη τῆς ὀρθῆς διανομῆς;
πρῶτον μὲν τὸν αὐτῶν ὄγκον τοῦ ἀριθμοῦ δεῖ
τάξασθαι, πόσον εἶναι χρεών. μετὰ δὲ τοῦτο
τὴν διανομὴν τῶν πολιτῶν, καθ᾽ ὁπόσα μέρη
πλήθει καὶ ὁπηλίκα διαιρετέον αὐτούς, ἀνομο-
λογητέον· ἐπὶ δὲ ταῦτα τήν τε γῆν καὶ τὰς
οἰκήσεις ὅτι μάλιστα ἴσας ἐπινεμητέον. ὄγκος
δὴ πλήθους ἱκανὸς οὐκ ἄλλως ὀρθῶς γίγνοιτ᾽ ἂν
λεχθεὶς ἢ πρὸς τὴν γῆν καὶ τὰς τῶν πλησιοχώρων
D πόλεις, γῆς μέν, ὁπόση ποσοὺς [1] σώφρονας ὄντας
ἱκανὴ τρέφειν, πλείονος δ᾽ οὐδὲν προσδεῖ, πλήθους
δέ, ὁπόσοι τοὺς προσχώρους ἀδικοῦντάς τε αὐτοὺς
ἀμύνασθαι δυνατοὶ καὶ γείτοσιν ἑαυτῶν ἀδικουμένοις βοηθῆσαι μὴ παντάπασιν ἀπόρως δύναιντ᾽
ἄν. ταῦτα δ᾽ ἰδόντες τὴν χώραν καὶ τοὺς γείτονας
ὁριούμεθα ἔργῳ καὶ λόγοις· νῦν δὲ σχήματος
ἕνεκα καὶ ὑπογραφῆς, ἵνα περαίνηται, πρὸς τὴν
νομοθεσίαν ὁ λόγος ἴτω.

E   Πεντάκις μὲν χίλιοι ἔστωσαν καὶ τετταράκοντα,
ἀριθμοῦ τινος ἕνεκα προσήκοντος, γεωμόροι τε καὶ
ἀμυνοῦντες τῇ νομῇ· γῇ δὲ καὶ οἰκήσεις ὡσαύτως τὰ
αὐτὰ μέρη διανεμηθήτων, γενόμενα ἀνὴρ καὶ κλῆρος
ξυννομή. δύο μὲν δὴ μέρη τοῦ παντὸς ἀριθμοῦ
τὸ πρῶτον νεμηθήτω, μετὰ δὲ ταῦτα τρία τοῦ [2]
αὐτοῦ· πέφυκε γὰρ καὶ τέτταρα καὶ πέντε καὶ
μέχρι τῶν δέκα ἐφεξῆς. δεῖ δὴ περὶ ἀριθμῶν τό

---

[1] ποσοὺς England: πόσους MSS.
[2] τοῦ αὐτοῦ Stephens, Schanz: τὸν αὐτὸν MSS.

enmity against themselves because of the distribution of land and houses would be a piece of folly combined with utter depravity of which no man could be capable.

What then would be the plan of a right distribution? First, we must fix at the right total the number of citizens ; next, we must agree about the distribution of them,—into how many sections, and each of what size, they are to be divided ; and among these sections we must distribute, as equally as we can, both the land and the houses. An adequate figure for the population could not be given without reference to the territory and to the neighbouring States. Of land we need as much as is capable of supporting so many inhabitants of temperate habits, and we need no more ; and as to population, we need a number such that they will be able to defend themselves against injury from adjoining peoples, and capable also of lending some aid to their neighbours when injured. These matters we shall determine, both verbally and actually, when we have inspected the territory and its neighbours; but for the present it is only a sketch in outline of our legislation that our argument will now proceed to complete.

Let us assume that there are—as a suitable number —5,040 men, to be land-holders and to defend their plots ;[1] and let the land and houses be likewise divided into the same number of parts—the man and his allotment forming together one division. First, let the whole number be divided into two; next into three; then follow in natural order four and five, and so on up to ten. Regarding numbers,

[1] Cp. Ar. *Pol.* 1265ᵃ 30 ff.

737 γε τοσοῦτον πάντα ἄνδρα νομοθετοῦντα νενοη-
738 κέναι, τίς ἀριθμὸς καὶ ποῖος πάσαις πόλεσι
χρησιμώτατος ἂν εἴη. λέγωμεν δὴ τὸν πλείστας
καὶ ἐφεξῆς μάλιστα διανομὰς ἐν αὑτῷ κεκτημένον·
οὐ μὲν δὴ πᾶς εἰς πάντα πάσας τομὰς εἴληχεν·
ὁ δὲ τῶν τετταράκοντα καὶ πεντακισχιλίων εἴς
τε πόλεμον καὶ ὅσα κατ᾽ εἰρήνην [πρὸς ἅπαντα
τὰ ξυμβόλαια καὶ κοινωνήματα],[1] εἰσφορῶν τε
πέρι καὶ διανομῶν, οὐ πλείους μιᾶς δεουσῶν
B ἑξήκοντα δύναιτ᾽ ἂν τέμνεσθαι τομῶν, ξυνεχεῖς
δὲ ἀπὸ μιᾶς μέχρι τῶν δέκα.

Ταῦτα μὲν οὖν δὴ καὶ κατὰ σχολὴν δεῖ βεβαίως
λαβεῖν, οἷς ἂν ὁ νόμος προστάττῃ λαμβάνειν· ἔχει
γὰρ οὖν οὐκ ἄλλως ἢ ταύτῃ, δεῖ δὲ αὐτὰ ῥηθῆναι
τῶνδ᾽ ἕνεκα κατοικίζοντι πόλιν. οὔτ᾽ ἂν καινὴν ἐξ
ἀρχῆς τις ποιῇ οὔτ᾽ ἂν παλαιὰν διεφθαρμένην ἐπι-
σκευάζηται, περὶ θεῶν γε καὶ ἱερῶν, ἅττα τε ἐν τῇ
πόλει ἑκάστοις ἱδρῦσθαι δεῖ καὶ ὧντινων ἐπονομάζεσθαι θεῶν ἢ δαιμόνων, οὐδεὶς ἐπιχειρήσει κινεῖν
C νοῦν ἔχων ὅσα ἐκ Δελφῶν ἢ Δωδώνης ἢ παρ᾽ Ἄμ-
μωνος ἤ τινες ἔπεισαν παλαιοὶ λόγοι ὁπῃδή
τινας πείσαντες, φασμάτων γενομένων ἢ ἐπιπνοίας
λεχθείσης θεῶν, πεισθέντες[2] δὲ θυσίας τελε-
ταῖς συμμίκτους κατεστήσαντο εἴτε αὐτόθεν
ἐπιχωρίους εἴτ᾽ οὖν Τυρρηνικὰς εἴτε Κυπρίας
εἴτ᾽ ἄλλοθεν ὁθενοῦν, καθιέρωσαν δὲ τοῖς
τοιούτοις λόγοις φήμας τε καὶ ἀγάλματα καὶ
βωμοὺς καὶ ναούς, τεμένη τε τούτων ἑκάστοις
ἐτεμένισαν· τούτων νομοθέτῃ τὸ σμικρότατον

---

[1] [πρὸς . . . κοινωνήματα] bracketed by England.
[2] πεισθέντες W.–Möllendorff: πείσαντες MSS.

every man who is making laws must understand at least
thus much,—what number and what kind of number
will be most useful for all States. Let us choose that
which contains the most numerous and most consecutive sub-divisions. Number as a whole comprises every division for all purposes; whereas the
number 5,040, for purposes of war, and in peace for
all purposes connected with contributions and distributions, will admit of division into no more than
59 sections, these being consecutive from one up to
ten.[1]

These facts about numbers must be grasped firmly
and with deliberate attention by those who are
appointed by law to grasp them: they are exactly
as we have stated them, and the reason for stating
them when founding a State is this:—in respect of
gods, and shrines, and the temples which have to
be set up for the various gods in the State, and the
gods and daemons they are to be named after, no
man of sense,—whether he be framing a new State
or re-forming an old one that has been corrupted,—
will attempt to alter the advice from Delphi or
Dodona or Ammon, or that of ancient sayings, whatever form they take—whether derived from visions
or from some reported inspiration from heaven. By
this advice they instituted sacrifices combined with
rites, either of native origin or imported from
Tuscany or Cyprus or elsewhere; and by means
of such sayings they sanctified oracles and statues
and altars and temples, and marked off for each of
them sacred glebes. Nothing of all these should

[1] The number 5,040 is here chosen because, for a number
of moderate size, it has the greatest possible number of
divisors (59), including all the digits from 1 to 10.

738D ἀπάντων οὐδὲν κινητέον, τοῖς δὲ μέρεσιν ἑκάστοις
θεὸν ἢ δαίμονα ἢ καί τινα ἥρωα ἀποδοτέον, ἐν
δὲ τῇ τῆς γῆς διανομῇ πρώτοις ἐξαίρετα τεμένη
τε καὶ πάντα τὰ προσήκοντα ἀποδοτέον, ὅπως
ἂν ξύλλογοι ἑκάστων τῶν μερῶν κατὰ χρόνους
γιγνόμενοι τοὺς προσταχθέντας εἴς τε τὰς χρείας
ἑκάστας εὐμάρειαν παρασκευάζωσι καὶ φιλοφρον-
ῶνταί τε ἀλλήλους μετὰ θυσιῶν καὶ οἰκειῶνται
Ε καὶ γνωρίζωσιν, οὗ μεῖζον οὐδὲν πόλει ἀγαθόν, ἢ
γνωρίμους αὐτοὺς αὐτοῖς εἶναι· ὅπου γὰρ μὴ φῶς
ἀλλήλοις ἐστὶν ἀλλήλων ἐν τοῖς τρόποις, ἀλλὰ
σκότος, οὔτ' ἂν τιμῆς τῆς ἀξίας οὔτ' ἀρχῶν οὔτε
δίκης ποτέ τις ἂν τῆς προσηκούσης ὀρθῶς τυγχάνοι. δεῖ δὴ πάντα ἄνδρα ἓν πρὸς ἓν τοῦτο
σπεύδειν ἐν πάσαις πόλεσιν, ὅπως μήτε αὐτὸς
κίβδηλός ποτε φανεῖται ὁτῳοῦν, ἁπλοῦς δὲ καὶ
ἀληθὴς ἀεί, μήτε ἄλλος τοιοῦτος ὢν αὐτὸν
διαπατήσει.

739 Ἡ δὴ τὸ μετὰ τοῦτο φορά, καθάπερ πεττῶν
ἀφ' ἱεροῦ,[1] τῆς τῶν νόμων κατασκευῆς ἀήθης οὖσα
τάχ' ἂν θαυμάσαι τὸν ἀκούοντα τὸ πρῶτον
ποιήσειεν· οὐ μὴν ἀλλ' ἀναλογιζομένῳ καὶ πειρω-
μένῳ φανεῖται δευτέρως ἂν πόλις οἰκεῖσθαι πρὸς
τὸ βέλτιστον. τάχα δ' οὐκ ἄν τις προσδέξαιτο
αὐτὴν διὰ τὸ μὴ σύνηθες νομοθέτῃ μὴ τυραννοῦντι·
τὸ δ' ἐστὶν ὀρθότατα, εἰπεῖν μὲν τὴν ἀρίστην
πολιτείαν καὶ δευτέραν καὶ τρίτην, δοῦναι δὲ
εἰπόντα αἵρεσιν ἑκάστῳ τῷ τῆς συνοικήσεως
Β κυρίῳ. ποιῶμεν δὴ κατὰ τοῦτον τὸν λόγον καὶ

---

[1] The middle line on the draughtsboard: to move a piece
placed on this line was equivalent to "trying one's last chance."

the lawgiver alter in the slightest degree ; to each
section he should assign a god or daemon, or at the
least a hero ; and in the distribution of the land he
should assign first to these divinities choice domains
with all that pertains to them, so that, when
assemblies of each of the sections take place at
the appointed times, they may provide an ample
supply of things requisite, and the people may
fraternize with one another at the sacrifices and gain
knowledge and intimacy, since nothing is of more
benefit to the State than this mutual acquaintance ;
for where men conceal their ways one from another
in darkness rather than light, there no man will
ever rightly gain either his due honour or office, or
the justice that is befitting. Wherefore every man
in every State must above all things endeavour to
show himself always true and sincere towards everyone, and no humbug, and also to allow himself to be
imposed upon by no such person.

The next move in our settling of the laws is one
that might at first hearing cause surprise because
of its unusual character—like the move of a draughts-
player who quits his " sacred line " ;[1] none the
less, it will be clear to him who reasons it out and
uses experience that a State will probably have a
constitution no higher than second in point of
excellence. Probably one might refuse to accept
this, owing to unfamiliarity with lawgivers who are
not also despots :[2] but it is, in fact, the most correct
plan to describe the best polity, and the second
best, and the third, and after describing them to
give the choice to the individual who is charged
with the founding of the settlement. This plan let

[2] Cp. 735 D.

739 τὰ νῦν ἡμεῖς, εἰπόντες ἀρετῇ πρώτην πολιτείαν
καὶ δευτέραν καὶ τρίτην· τὴν δὲ αἵρεσιν Κλεινία
τε ἀποδιδῶμεν τὰ νῦν καὶ εἴ τις ἄλλος [ἂν][1] δή
ποτε ἐθελήσειεν ἐπὶ τὴν τῶν τοιούτων ἐκλογὴν
ἐλθὼν κατὰ τὸν ἑαυτοῦ τρόπον ἀπονείμασθαι τὸ
φίλον αὐτῷ τῆς αὐτοῦ πατρίδος. πρώτη μὲν
τοίνυν πόλις τέ ἐστι καὶ πολιτεία καὶ νόμοι
ἄριστοι, ὅπου τὸ πάλαι λεγόμενον ἂν γίγνηται
C κατὰ πᾶσαν τὴν πόλιν ὅτι μάλιστα· λέγεται δὲ
ὡς ὄντως ἐστὶ κοινὰ τὰ φίλων. τοῦτ' οὖν εἴτε που
νῦν ἐστιν εἴτ' ἔσται ποτέ, κοινὰς μὲν γυναῖκας,
κοινοὺς δὲ εἶναι παῖδας, κοινὰ δὲ χρήματα ξύμπαντα, καὶ πάσῃ μηχανῇ τὸ λεγόμενον ἴδιον
πανταχόθεν ἐκ τοῦ βίου ἄπαν ἐξῄρηται, μεμη-
χάνηται δ' εἰς τὸ δυνατὸν καὶ τὰ φύσει ἴδια κοινὰ
ἁμῇ γέ πῃ γεγονέναι, οἷον ὄμματα καὶ ὦτα καὶ
χεῖρας κοινὰ μὲν ὁρᾶν δοκεῖν καὶ ἀκούειν καὶ
D πράττειν, ἐπαινεῖν τε αὖ καὶ ψέγειν καθ' ἓν ὅτι
μάλιστα ξύμπαντας ἐπὶ τοῖς αὐτοῖς χαίροντας καὶ
λυπουμένους, καὶ κατὰ δύναμιν <τιμᾶν>[2] οἵτινες
νόμοι μίαν ὅτι μάλιστα πόλιν ἀπεργάζονται,
τούτων ὑπερβολῇ πρὸς ἀρετὴν οὐδείς ποτε ὅρον
ἄλλον θέμενος ὀρθότερον οὐδὲ βελτίω θήσεται. ἡ
μὲν δὴ τοιαύτη πόλις, εἴτε που θεοὶ ἢ παῖδες θεῶν
αὐτὴν οἰκοῦσι [πλείους ἑνός],[3] οὕτω διαζῶντες
εὐφραινόμενοι κατοικοῦσι· διὸ δὴ παράδειγμά γε
E πολιτείας οὐκ ἄλλη χρὴ σκοπεῖν, ἀλλ' ἐχομένους
ταύτης τὴν ὅτι μάλιστα τοιαύτην ζητεῖν κατὰ
δύναμιν. ἣν δὲ νῦν ἡμεῖς ἐπικεχειρήκαμεν, εἴη τε

---

[1] [ἂν] bracketed by Naber, Schanz.
[2] <τιμᾶν> I add.
[3] [πλείους ἑνός] bracketed by Gomperz, England.

us now adopt: let us state the polities which rank
first, second, and third in excellence; and the choice
let us hand over to Clinias and to whosoever else
may at any time wish, in proceeding to the selection
of such things, to take over, according to his
own disposition, what he values in his own country.
That State and polity come first, and those laws
are best, where there is observed as carefully as
possible throughout the whole State the old saying [1]
that "friends have all things really in common."   As
to this condition,—whether it anywhere exists now,
or ever will exist,—in which there is community
of wives, children, and all chattels, and all that is
called "private" is everywhere and by every means
rooted out of our life, and so far as possible it is
contrived that even things naturally "private" have
become in a way "communized,"—eyes, for instance,
and ears and hands seem to see, hear, and act in
common,—and that all men are, so far as possible,
unanimous in the praise and blame they bestow,
rejoicing and grieving at the same things, and that
they honour with all their heart those laws which
render the State as unified as possible,—no one will
ever lay down another definition that is truer or better
than these conditions in point of super-excellence.
In such a State,—be it gods or sons of gods that
dwell in it,—they dwell pleasantly, living such a life
as this.   Wherefore one should not look elsewhere
for a model constitution, but hold fast to this one,
and with all one's power seek the constitution that
is as like to it as possible.   That constitution which
we are now engaged upon, if it came into being,

[1] A Pythagorean maxim frequently cited by Plato: cp.
Rep. 424 A, Eurip. *Orest.* 725.

PLATO

739 ἂν γενομένη πως ἀθανασίας ἐγγύτατα καὶ τιμία[1]
δευτέρως· τρίτην δὲ μετὰ ταῦτα, ἐὰν θεὸς ἐθέλῃ,
διαπερανούμεθα. νῦν δ᾽ οὖν ταύτην τίνα λέγομεν
καὶ πῶς γενομένην ἂν τοιαύτην;

Νειμάσθων μὲν δὴ πρῶτον γῆν τε καὶ οἰκίας,
740 καὶ μὴ κοινῇ γεωργούντων, ἐπειδὴ τὸ τοιοῦτον
μεῖζον ἢ κατὰ τὴν νῦν γένεσιν καὶ τροφὴν καὶ
παίδευσιν εἴρηται· νεμέσθων δ᾽ οὖν τοιᾷδε διανοίᾳ
πως, ὡς ἄρα δεῖ τὸν λαχόντα τὴν λῆξιν ταύτην
νομίζειν μὲν κοινὴν αὐτὴν τῆς πόλεως ξυμπάσης,
πατρίδος δὲ οὔσης τῆς χώρας θεραπεύειν αὐτὴν δεῖ
μειζόνως ἢ μητέρα παῖδας, τῷ καὶ δέσποιναν θεὸν
αὐτὴν οὖσαν θνητῶν ὄντων γεγονέναι, ταὐτὰ δ᾽
ἔχειν διανοήματα καὶ περὶ τοὺς ἐγχωρίους θεούς
B τε ἅμα καὶ δαίμονας. ὅπως δ᾽ ἂν ταῦτα εἰς τὸν
ἀεὶ χρόνον οὕτως ἔχοντα ὑπάρχῃ, τάδε προσδια-
νοητέον· ὅσαι εἰσὶ τὰ νῦν ἡμῖν ἑστίαι διανεμη-
θεῖσαι τὸν ἀριθμόν, ταύτας δεῖν ἀεὶ τοσαύτας
εἶναι καὶ μήτε τι πλείους γίγνεσθαι μήτε τί ποτε
ἐλάττους. ὧδ᾽ οὖν ἂν τὸ τοιοῦτον βεβαίως
γίγνοιτο περὶ πᾶσαν πόλιν· ὁ λαχὼν τὸν κλῆρον
καταλειπέτω ἀεὶ ταύτης τῆς οἰκήσεως ἕνα μόνον
κληρονόμον τῶν ἑαυτοῦ παίδων, ὃν ἂν αὐτῷ
μάλιστα ᾖ φίλον, διάδοχον καὶ θεραπευτὴν θεῶν
C καὶ γένους καὶ πόλεως, τῶν τε ζώντων καὶ ὅσους
ἂν ἤδη τέλος εἰς τὸν τότε χρόνον ἔχῃ. τοὺς δὲ
ἄλλους παῖδας, οἷς ἂν πλείους ἑνὸς γίγνωνται,
θηλείας τε ἐκδόσθαι κατὰ νόμον τὸν ἐπιταχθη-
σόμενον, ἄρρενάς τε, οἷς ἂν τῆς γενέσεως ἐλλείπῃ
τῶν πολιτῶν, τούτοις υἱεῖς διανέμειν, κατὰ χάριν

---

[1] τιμία my conj. (also Apelt, independently): ἡ μία MSS.,
edd.

364

would be very near to immortality, and would come second in point of merit. The third we shall investigate hereafter, if God so will; for the present, however, what is this second best polity, and how would it come to be of such a character?

First, let them portion out the land and houses, and not farm in common, since such a course is beyond the capacity of people with the birth, rearing and training we assume. And let the apportionment be made with this intention,—that the man who receives the portion should still regard it as common property of the whole State, and should tend the land, which is his fatherland, more diligently than a mother tends her children, inasmuch as it, being a goddess, is mistress over its mortal population, and should observe the same attitude also towards the local gods and daemons. And in order that these things may remain in this state for ever, these further rules must be observed: the number of hearths, as now appointed by us, must remain unchanged, and must never become either more or less. This will be securely effected, in the case of every State, in the following way: the allotment-holder shall always leave behind him one son, whichever he pleases, as the inheritor of his dwelling, to be his successor in the tendance of the deified ancestors both of family and of State, whether living or already deceased; as to the rest of the children, when a man has more than one, he should marry off the females according to the law that is to be ordained,[1] and the males he should dispose of to such of the citizens as have no male issue, by a friendly arrangement if possible;

---

[1] Cp. 742 C.

740 μὲν μάλιστα· ἐὰν δέ τισιν ἐλλείπωσι χάριτες, ἢ
πλείους ἐπίγονοι γίγνωνται θήλεις ἤ τινες ἄρρενες
ἑκάστων, ἢ καὶ τοὐναντίον ὅταν ἐλάττους ὦσι
D παίδων ἀφορίας γενομένης, πάντων τούτων ἀρχὴν
ἣν ἂν θώμεθα μεγίστην καὶ τιμιωτάτην, αὕτη
σκεψαμένη τί χρὴ χρῆσθαι τοῖς περιγενομένοις
ἢ τοῖς ἐλλείπουσι, ποριζέτω μηχανὴν ὅτι μάλιστα
ὅπως αἱ πεντακισχίλιαι καὶ τετταράκοντα οἰκήσεις
ἀεὶ μόνον ἔσονται. μηχαναὶ δ᾽ εἰσὶ πολλαί· καὶ
γὰρ ἐπισχέσεις γενέσεως οἷς ἂν εὔρους ᾖ γένεσις,
καὶ τοὐναντίον ἐπιμέλειαι καὶ σπουδαὶ πλήθους
γεννημάτων εἰσὶ τιμαῖς τε καὶ ἀτιμίαις καὶ νουθε-
E τήσεσι πρεσβυτῶν περὶ νέους [διὰ λόγων νουθετη-
τικῶν],[1] αἱ πάντως ἀεὶ [2] δύνανται ποιεῖν ὃ λέγομεν.
καὶ δὴ καὶ τό γε τέλος, ἂν πᾶσα ἀπορία περὶ τὴν
ἀνίσωσιν τῶν πεντακισχιλίων καὶ τετταράκοντα
οἴκων γίγνηται, ἐπίχυσις δ᾽ ὑπερβάλλουσα
ἡμῖν πολιτῶν διὰ φιλοφροσύνην τὴν τῶν ξυνοικούντων ἀλλήλοις ξυμβαίνῃ καὶ ἀπορῶμεν, τὸ
παλαιόν που ὑπάρχει μηχάνημα, ὃ πολλάκις
εἴπομεν, ἐκπομπὴ ἀποικιῶν φίλη γιγνομένη παρὰ
φίλων, ὧν ἂν ἐπιτήδειον εἶναι δοκῇ. ἐὰν δ᾽ αὖ
καὶ τοὐναντίον ἐπέλθῃ ποτὲ κῦμα κατακλυσμὸν
741 φέρον νόσων ἢ πολέμων φθορά, ἐλάττους δὲ πολὺ
τοῦ τεταγμένου ἀριθμοῦ δι᾽ ὀρφανίας γένωνται,
ἑκόντας μὲν οὐ δεῖ πολίτας παρεμβάλλειν νόθῃ
παιδείᾳ πεπαιδευμένους, ἀνάγκην δὲ οὐδὲ θεὸς
εἶναι λέγεται δυνατὸς βιάζεσθαι.

---

[1] [διὰ λόγων νουθετητικῶν] bracketed by England.
[2] αἱ πάντως ἀεὶ: ἀπαντῶσαι MSS. (ἅπαντας αἱ Schanz)

[1] i.e. the Law-wardens; cp. 755 B ff.

but where such arrangements prove insufficient, or where the family is too large either in females or in males, or where, on the other hand, it is too small, through the occurrence of sterility,—in all these cases the magistrates, whom we shall appoint as the highest and most distinguished,[1] shall consider how to deal with the excess or deficiency in families, and contrive means as best they can to secure that the 5,040 households shall remain unaltered. There are many contrivances possible : where the fertility is great, there are methods of inhibition, and contrariwise there are methods of encouraging and stimulating the birth-rate, by means of honours and dishonours, and by admonitions addressed by the old to the young, which are capable in all ways of producing the required effect. Moreover, as a final step,—in case we are in absolute desperation about the unequal condition of our 5,040 households, and are faced with a superabundance of citizens, owing to the mutual affection of those who cohabit with one another, which drives us to despair,—there still remains that ancient device which we have often mentioned, namely, the sending forth, in friendly wise from a friendly nation, of colonies consisting of such people as are deemed suitable. On the other hand, should the State ever be attacked by a deluging wave of disease or ruinous wars, and the houses fall much below the appointed number through bereavements, we ought not, of our own free will, to introduce new citizens trained with a bastard training —but " necessity " (as the proverb runs) " not even God himself can compel." [2]

---

[2] A dictum of Simonides; cp. *Protag.* 345 B; *Laws* 818 A ff.

741 Ταῦτ' οὖν δὴ τὸν νῦν λεγόμενον λόγον ἡμῖν φῶμεν παραινεῖν, λέγοντα Ὦ πάντων ἀνδρῶν ἄριστοι, τὴν ὁμοιότητα καὶ ἰσότητα καὶ τὸ ταὐτὸν καὶ ὁμολογούμενον τιμῶντες κατὰ φύσιν μὴ ἀνίετε κατά τε ἀριθ-

B μὸν καὶ πᾶσαν δύναμιν τὴν τῶν καλῶν κἀγαθῶν πραγμάτων· καὶ δὴ καὶ νῦν τὸν ἀριθμὸν μὲν πρῶτον διὰ βίου παντὸς φυλάξατε τὸν εἰρημένον, εἶτα τὸ τῆς οὐσίας ὕψος τε καὶ μέγεθος, ὃ τὸ πρῶτον ἐνείμασθε μέτριον ὄν, μὴ ἀτιμάσητε τῷ τε ὠνεῖσθαι καὶ τῷ πωλεῖν πρὸς ἀλλήλους· οὔτε γὰρ ὁ νείμας κλῆρος [1] ὢν θεὸς ὑμῖν ξύμμαχος, οὔτε ὁ νομοθέτης· νῦν γὰρ δὴ πρῶτον τῷ ἀπειθοῦντι νόμος προστάττει, προειπὼν ἐπὶ τούτοις κληροῦσθαι

C τὸν ἐθέλοντα ἢ μὴ κληροῦσθαι, ὡς πρῶτον μὲν τῆς γῆς ἱερᾶς οὔσης τῶν πάντων θεῶν, εἶτα ἱερέων τε καὶ ἱερειῶν εὐχὰς ποιησομένων ἐπὶ τοῖς πρώτοις θύμασι καὶ δευτέροις καὶ μέχρι τριῶν, τὸν πριάμενον ἢ ἀποδόμενον ὧν ἔλαχεν οἰκοπέδων ἢ γηπέδων τὰ ἐπὶ τούτοις πρέποντα πάσχειν πάθη. γράψαντες δ' ἐν τοῖς ἱεροῖς θήσουσι κυπαριττίνας μνήμας εἰς τὸν ἔπειτα χρόνον καταγεγραμμένας· πρὸς τούτοις δ' ἔτι φυλακτήρια τούτων, ὅπως ἂν

D γίγνηται, καταστήσουσιν ἐν ταύτῃ τῶν ἀρχῶν ἥτις ἂν ὀξύτατον ὁρᾶν δοκῇ, ἵν' αἱ παρὰ ταῦτα ἑκάστοτε παραγωγαὶ γιγνόμεναι μὴ λανθάνωσιν αὐτούς, ἀλλὰ κολάζωσι τὸν ἀπειθοῦντα ἅμα νόμῳ καὶ τῷ θεῷ. ὅσον γὰρ δὴ τὸ νῦν ἐπιταττόμενον ἀγαθὸν ὂν τυγχάνει πάσαις ταῖς πειθομέναις

---

[1] κλῆρος MSS. : κλῆρον MSS. marg., Zur., vulg.

LAWS, BOOK V

Let us then suppose that our present discourse gives the following advice :—My most excellent friends, be not slack to pay honour, as Nature ordains, to similarity and equality and identity and congruity in respect of number and of every influence productive of things fair and good. Above all, now, in the first place, guard throughout your lives the number stated ; in the next place, dishonour not the due measure of the height and magnitude of your substance, as originally apportioned, by buying and selling one to another : otherwise, neither will the apportioning Lot,[1] which is divine, fight on your side, nor will the lawgiver : for now, in the first place, the law lays on the disobedient this injunction :— since it has given warning that whoso wills should take or refuse an allotment on the understanding that, first, the land is sacred to all the gods, and further, that prayers shall be made at the first, second, and third sacrifices by the priests and priestesses,—therefore the man who buys or sells the house-plot or land-plot allotted to him must suffer the penalty attached to this sin. The officials shall inscribe on tablets of cypress-wood written records for future reference, and shall place them in the shrines ; furthermore, they shall place the charge of the execution of these matters in the hands of that magistrate who is deemed to be most keen of vision, in order that all breaches of these rules may be brought to their notice, and they may punish the man who disobeys both the law and the god. How great a blessing the ordinance now described—when the appropriate organisation accompanies it—proves

---

[1] The lot was supposed to record the verdict of God (cp. 690 C, and *Acts* i. 26),—hence its sanctity.

741 πόλεσι τὴν ἑπομένην κατασκευὴν προσλαβόν,
κατὰ τὴν παλαιὰν παροιμίαν οὐδεὶς εἴσεταί ποτε
κακὸς ὢν ἀλλ' ἔμπειρός τε καὶ ἐπιεικὴς ἔθεσι
Ε γενόμενος· χρηματισμὸς γὰρ οὔτ' ἔνεστι σφόδρα
ἐν τῇ τοιαύτῃ κατασκευῇ, ξυνέπεταί τε αὐτῇ μηδὲ
δεῖν μηδ' ἐξεῖναι χρηματίζεσθαι τῶν ἀνελευθέρων
χρηματισμῶν μηδενὶ μηδένα, καθ' ὅσον ἐπ-
ονείδιστος λεγομένη βαναυσία ἦθος ἀποτρέπει
ἐλεύθερον, μηδὲ τὸ παράπαν ἀξιοῦν ἐκ τῶν
τοιούτων ξυλλέγειν χρήματα. πρὸς τούτοις δ'
742 ἔτι νόμος ἔπεται πᾶσι τούτοις, μηδ' ἐξεῖναι χρυσὸν μηδὲ ἄργυρον κεκτῆσθαι μηδένα μηδενὶ
ἰδιώτῃ, νόμισμα δ' ἕνεκα ἀλλαγῆς τῆς καθ'
ἡμέραν, ἣν δημιουργοῖς τε ἀλλάττεσθαι σχεδὸν
ἀναγκαῖον, καὶ πᾶσιν ὁπόσοις [1] χρεία τῶν τοιούτων
μισθοὺς μισθωτοῖς, δούλοις καὶ ἐποίκοις, ἀποτίνειν.
ὧν ἕνεκά φαμεν τὸ νόμισμα κτητέον αὑτοῖς μὲν
ἔντιμον, τοῖς δὲ ἄλλοις ἀνθρώποις ἀδόκιμον.
κοινὸν δ' Ἑλληνικὸν νόμισμα ἕνεκά τε στρατειῶν
καὶ ἀποδημιῶν εἰς τοὺς ἄλλους ἀνθρώπους, οἷον
πρεσβειῶν ἢ καί τινος ἀναγκαίας ἄλλης τῇ πόλει
κηρυκείας, ἐκπέμπειν τινὰ ἂν δέῃ, τούτων χάριν
ἀνάγκη ἑκάστοτε κεκτῆσθαι τῇ πόλει νόμισμα
Β Ἑλληνικόν. ἰδιώτῃ δ' ἂν ἄρα ποτὲ ἀνάγκη τις
γίγνηται ἀποδημεῖν, παρέμενος μὲν τοὺς ἄρχοντας
ἀποδημείτω, νόμισμα δὲ ἂν ποθεν ἔχων ξενικὸν
οἴκαδε ἀφίκηται περιγενόμενον, τῇ πόλει αὐτὸ
καταβαλλέτω πρὸς λόγον ἀπολαμβάνων τὸ ἐπι-

[1] ὁπόσοις Ast: ὁπόσων MSS.

---

[1] The proverb was, perhaps, οὐδεὶς ἄπειρος εἴσεται,—like
experientia docet.

to all the States that obey it—that is a thing which,
as the old proverb[1] says, none that is evil shall
know, but only he that has become experienced and
practised in, virtuous habits.   For in the organisation described there exists no excess of money-
making, and it involves the condition that no
facility should or can be given to anyone to make
money by means of any illiberal trade,—inasmuch
as what is called contemptible vulgarity perverts
a liberal character,—and also that no one should
ever claim to heap up riches from any such source.
Furthermore, upon all this there follows also a law
which forbids any private person to possess any gold
or silver, only coin for purposes of such daily exchange
as it is almost necessary for craftsmen [2] to make use of,
and all who need such things in paying wages to
hirelings, whether slaves or immigrants.   For these
reasons we say that our people should possess coined
money which is legal tender among themselves, but
valueless elsewhere.   As regards the universal
Hellenic coinage,—for the sake of expeditions and
foreign visits, as well as of embassies or any other
missions necessary for the State, if there be need to
send someone abroad,—for such objects as these it is
necessary that the State should always possess Hellenic money.   If a private citizen ever finds himself
obliged to go abroad,[3] he may do so, after first
getting leave from the magistrates ; and should he
come home with any surplus of foreign money, he
shall deposit it with the State, and take for it an

---

[2] They require coined money for their business dealings
with one another : cp. *Rep.* 371 B ff.

[3] Cp. 950 D ff.

742 χωρίον· ἰδιούμενος δ' ἄν τις φαίνηται, δημόσιόν τε
γιγνέσθω καὶ ὁ ξυνειδὼς καὶ μὴ φράζων ἀρᾷ καὶ
ὀνείδει μετὰ τοῦ ἀγαγόντος ἔνοχος ἔστω, καὶ
ζημίᾳ πρὸς τούτοις μὴ ἐλάττονι τοῦ ξενικοῦ
C κομισθέντος νομίσματος. γαμοῦντα δὲ καὶ
ἐκδιδόντα μήτ' οὖν διδόναι μήτε δέχεσθαι
προῖκα τὸ παράπαν μηδ' ἡντινοῦν, μηδὲ νόμισμα
παρακατατίθεσθαι ὅτῳ μή τις πιστεύει, μηδὲ
δανείζειν ἐπὶ τόκῳ, ὡς ἐξὸν μὴ ἀποδιδόναι τὸ
παράπαν τῷ δανεισαμένῳ μήτε τόκον μήτε
κεφάλαιον.

Ταῦτα δ' ὅτι βέλτιστά ἐστι πόλει ἐπιτηδεύματα ἐπιτηδεύειν, ὧδε ἄν τις σκοπῶν ὀρθῶς ἂν
D αὐτὰ διακρίνοι, ἐπαναφέρων εἰς τὴν ἀρχὴν ἀεὶ
καὶ τὴν βούλησιν. ἔστι δὴ τοῦ νοῦν ἔχοντος
πολιτικοῦ βούλησις, φαμέν, οὐχ ἥνπερ ἂν
οἱ πολλοὶ φαῖεν, δεῖν βούλεσθαι τὸν ἀγαθὸν
νομοθέτην ὡς μεγίστην τε εἶναι τὴν πόλιν ᾗ
νοῶν εὖ νομοθετοῖ καὶ ὅτι μάλιστα πλουσίαν,
κεκτημένην δ' αὖ χρυσία καὶ ἀργύρια καὶ κατὰ
γῆν καὶ κατὰ θάλατταν ἄρχουσαν ὅτι πλείστων·
προσθεῖεν δ' ἂν καὶ ὡς ἀρίστην δεῖν βούλεσθαι
τὴν πόλιν εἶναι καὶ ὡς εὐδαιμονεστάτην τόν γε
E ὀρθῶς νομοθετοῦντα. τούτων δὲ τὰ μὲν δυνατά
ἐστι γίγνεσθαι, τὰ δὲ οὐ δυνατά· τὰ μὲν οὖν
δυνατὰ βούλοιτ' ἂν ὁ διακοσμῶν, τὰ δὲ μὴ δυνατὰ
οὔτ' ἂν βούλοιτο ματαίας βουλήσεις οὔτ' ἂν
ἐπιχειροῖ. σχεδὸν μὲν γὰρ εὐδαίμονας ἅμα καὶ
ἀγαθοὺς ἀνάγκη γίγνεσθαι· τοῦτο μὲν οὖν

---

[1] *i.e.* if the citizens are to be happy they must be good.
In what follows it is shown that good men cannot be very

equivalent in home coinage; but should anyone be
found out keeping it for himself, the money shall be
confiscated, and the man who is privy to it and fails
to inform, together with the man who has imported
it, shall be liable to cursing and reproach and, in
addition, to a fine not less than the amount of the
foreign money brought in. In marrying or giving in
marriage, no one shall give or receive any dowry at
all. No one shall deposit money with anyone he
does not trust, nor lend at interest, since it is permissible for the borrower to refuse entirely to pay
back either interest or principal.

That these are the best rules for a State to
observe in practice, one would perceive rightly
if one viewed them in relation to the primary intention. The intention of the judicious statesman is, we say, not at all the intention which
the majority would ascribe to him; they would say
that the good lawgiver should desire that the State,
for which he is benevolently legislating, should be as
large and as rich as possible, possessed of silver and
gold, and bearing rule over as many people as
possible both by land and sea; and they would add
that he should desire the State to be as good and as
happy as possible, if he is a true legislator. Of these
objects some are possible of attainment, some
impossible; such as are possible the organiser of the
State will desire; the impossible he will neither
vainly desire nor attempt. That happiness and
goodness should go together is well-nigh inevitable,[1]
so he will desire the people to be both good and

rich nor very rich men good, therefore also the very rich
cannot be happy.

742 βούλοιτ' ἄν· πλουσίους δ' αὖ σφόδρα καὶ ἀγαθοὺς ἀδύνατον, οὕς γε δὴ πλουσίους οἱ πολλοὶ
καταλέγουσι· λέγουσι δὲ τοὺς κεκτημένους ἐν
ὀλίγοις τῶν ἀνθρώπων πλείστου νομίσματος ἄξια
743 κτήματα, ἃ καὶ κακός τις κεκτῇτ' ἄν. εἰ δ' ἔστι
τοῦτο οὕτως ἔχον, οὐκ ἂν ἔγωγε αὐτοῖς ποτὲ συγ-
χωροίην τὸν πλούσιον εὐδαίμονα τῇ ἀληθείᾳ
γίγνεσθαι μὴ καὶ ἀγαθὸν ὄντα. ἀγαθὸν δὲ ὄντα
διαφερόντως καὶ πλούσιον εἶναι διαφερόντως ἀδύνατον. τί δή; φαίη τις ἂν ἴσως. ὅτι, φαῖμεν ἄν,
ἥ τε ἐκ δικαίου καὶ ἀδίκου κτῆσις πλέον ἢ διπλα-
σία ἐστὶ τῆς ἐκ τοῦ δικαίου μόνον, τά τε ἀναλώ-
ματα μήτε καλῶς μήτε αἰσχρῶς ἐθέλοντα ἀναλίσ-
κεσθαι τῶν καλῶν καὶ εἰς καλὰ ἐθελόντων
δαπανᾶσθαι διπλασίῳ ἐλάττονα. οὔκουν ποτὲ
B ἂν τῶν ἐκ διπλασίων μὲν κτημάτων, ἡμίσεων δὲ
ἀναλωμάτων ὁ τὰ ἐναντία τούτων πράττων γένοιτ'
ἂν πλουσιώτερος. ἔστι δὲ ὁ μὲν ἀγαθὸς τούτων,
ὁ δὲ οὐ κακός, ὅταν ᾖ φειδωλός· <ὅταν δὲ μὴ
φειδωλός,> [1] τότε δή ποτε καὶ πάγκακος· ἀγαθὸς
δέ, ὅπερ εἴρηται τὰ νῦν, οὐδέποτε· ὁ μὲν γὰρ
δικαίως καὶ ἀδίκως λαμβάνων καὶ μήτε δικαίως
μήτε ἀδίκως ἀναλίσκων πλούσιος [ὅταν καὶ
φειδωλὸς ᾖ]. [2] ὁ δὲ πάγκακος ὡς τὰ πολλὰ ὢν
C ἄσωτος μάλα πένης· ὁ δὲ ἀναλίσκων τε εἰς τὰ
καλὰ καὶ κτώμενος ἐκ τῶν δικαίων μόνον οὔτ' ἂν
διαφέρων πλούτῳ ῥᾳδίως ἄν ποτε γένοιτο οὐδ' αὖ

---

[1] ⟨ὅταν δὲ μὴ φειδωλός,⟩ I add, and write δή ποτε for δέ ποτε
of MSS.

[2] [ὅταν . . . ᾖ] bracketed by Susemihl, Schanz.

---

[1] e.g. A (a good man) gains (justly) £300, of which he
spends £100 on necessaries and £100 on noble objects, leaving

happy; but it is impossible for them to be at once both good and excessively rich—rich at least as most men count riches; for they reckon as rich those who possess, in a rare degree, goods worth a vast deal of money, and these even a wicked man might possess. And since this is so, I would never concede to them that the rich man is really happy if he is not also good; while, if a man is superlatively good, it is impossible that he should be also superlatively rich. "Why so?" it may be asked. Because, we would reply, the gain derived from both right and wrong is more than double that from right alone, whereas the expenditure of those who refuse to spend either nobly or ignobly is only one-half the expenditure of those who are noble and like spending on noble objects; consequently, the wealth of men who double their gains and halve their expenditure will never be exceeded by the men whose procedure in both respects is just the opposite.[1] Now of these men, the one is good, and the other not bad, so long as he is niggardly, but utterly bad when he is not niggardly, and (as we have just said) at no time good. For while the one man, since he takes both justly and unjustly and spends neither justly nor unjustly, is rich (and the utterly bad man, being lavish as a rule, is very poor),—the other man, who spends on noble objects, and gains by just means only, is never likely to become either superlatively

him a balance of £100. *B* (a not-good man) gains (justly and unjustly) £600. of which he spends £100 on necessaries, and nothing on noble objects, leaving him a balance of £500. The third type(*C*) is worse than *B* because he not only gains but also spends wrongly. Type *A* shows how the good man is neither very rich nor very poor,—*B*, how the bad man may be very rich,—*C*, how the bad may be very poor.

743 σφόδρα πένης. ὥστε ὁ λόγος ἡμῖν ὀρθός, ὡς οὐκ εἰσὶν οἱ παμπλούσιοι ἀγαθοί· εἰ δὲ μὴ ἀγαθοί, οὐδὲ εὐδαίμονες.

Ἡμῖν δὲ ἡ τῶν νόμων ὑπόθεσις ἐνταῦθα ἔβλεπεν, ὅπως ὡς εὐδαιμονέστατοι ἔσονται καὶ ὅτι μάλιστα ἀλλήλοις φίλοι· εἶεν δὲ οὐκ ἄν ποτε πολῖται φίλοι, ὅπου πολλαὶ μὲν δίκαι ἐν ἀλλήλοις εἶεν, πολλαὶ δὲ ἀδικίαι, ἀλλ᾽ ὅπου ὡς
D ὅτι σμικρόταται καὶ ὀλίγισται. λέγομεν δὴ μήτε χρυσὸν εἶναι δεῖν μήτε ἄργυρον ἐν τῇ πόλει, μήτ᾽ αὖ χρηματισμὸν πολὺν διὰ βαναυσίας καὶ τόκων μηδὲ βοσκημάτων αἰσχρῶν, ἀλλ᾽ ὅσα γεωργία δίδωσι καὶ φέρει, καὶ τούτων ὁπόσα μὴ χρηματιζόμενον ἀναγκάσει ἀμελεῖν ὧν ἕνεκα πέφυκε τὰ χρήματα. ταῦτα δ᾽ ἐστὶ ψυχὴ καὶ σῶμα, ἃ χωρὶς γυμναστικῆς καὶ τῆς ἄλλης παιδείας οὐκ
E ἄν ποτε γένοιτο ἄξια λόγου. διὸ δὴ χρημάτων ἐπιμέλειαν οὐχ ἅπαξ εἰρήκαμεν ὡς χρὴ τελευταῖον τιμᾶν· ὄντων γὰρ τριῶν τῶν ἁπάντων περὶ ἃ πᾶς ἄνθρωπος σπουδάζει, τελευταῖον καὶ τρίτον ἐστὶν ἡ τῶν χρημάτων ὀρθῶς σπουδαζομένη σπουδή, σώματος δὲ πέρι μέση, πρώτη δὲ ἡ τῆς ψυχῆς. καὶ δὴ καὶ νῦν ἣν διεξερχόμεθα πολιτείαν, εἰ μὲν τὰς τιμὰς οὕτω τάττεται, ὀρθῶς νενομοθέτηται· εἰ δέ τις τῶν προσταττομένων αὐτόθι νόμων σωφρο-
744 σύνης ἔμπροσθεν ὑγίειαν ἐν τῇ πόλει φανεῖται ποιῶν τιμίαν ἢ πλοῦτον ὑγιείας καὶ τοῦ σωφρονεῖν, οὐκ ὀρθῶς ἀναφανεῖται τιθέμενος. τοῦτ᾽ οὖν δὴ πολλάκις ἐπισημαίνεσθαι χρὴ τὸν νομοθέτην, τί τε βούλομαι, καί, εἴ μοι ξυμβαίνει τοῦτο ἢ καὶ

---

[1] Cp. 631 C, 697 B, 728 E.

rich or extremely poor. Accordingly, what we
have stated is true,—that the very rich are not
good, and not being good, neither are they
happy.

Now the fundamental purpose of our laws was this,
—that the citizens should be as happy as possible,
and in the highest degree united in mutual friendship. Friendly the citizens will never be where
they have frequent legal actions with one another
and frequent illegal acts, but rather where these are
the fewest and least possible. We say that in the
State there must be neither gold nor silver, nor
must there be much money-making by means of
vulgar trading or usury or the fattening of gelded
beasts, but only such profit as farming offers and
yields, and of this only so much as will not drive a
man by his money-making to neglect the objects for
which money exists : these objects are the soul and
the body, which without gymnastic and the other
branches of education would never become things of
value. Wherefore we have asserted (and that not
once only)[1] that the pursuit of money is to be
honoured last of all : of all the three objects which
concern every man, the concern for money, rightly
directed, comes third and last ; that for the body
comes second ; and that for the soul, first. Accordingly, if it prescribes its honours in this order, the
polity which we are describing has its laws correctly
laid down ; but if any of the laws therein enacted shall
evidently make health of more honour in the State
than temperance, or wealth than health and temperance, it will quite clearly be a wrong enactment.
Thus the lawgiver must ofttimes put this question to
himself—" What is it that I intend ? " and, " Am I

PLATO

744 ἀποτυγχάνω τοῦ σκοποῦ· καὶ οὕτω τάχ᾽ ἂν ἴσως
ἐκ τῆς νομοθεσίας αὐτός τε ἐκβαίνοι καὶ τοὺς
ἄλλους ἀπαλλάττοι, κατ᾽ ἄλλον δὲ τρόπον οὐδ᾽ ἂν
ἕνα ποτέ.

Ὁ δὴ λαχὼν κεκτήσθω, φαμέν, τὸν κλῆρον
B ἐπὶ τούτοις οἷς εἰρήκαμεν. ἦν μὲν δὴ καλὸν καὶ
τἆλλα ἴσα πάντ᾽ ἔχοντα ἕνα ἕκαστον ἐλθεῖν εἰς
τὴν ἀποικίαν· ἐπειδὴ δὲ οὐ δυνατόν, ἀλλ᾽ ὁ μέν
τις πλείω κεκτημένος ἀφίξεται χρήματα, ὁ δ᾽
ἐλάττονα, δεῖ δὴ πολλῶν ἕνεκα τῶν τε κατὰ πόλιν
καιρῶν ἰσότητος ἕνεκα τιμήματα ἄνισα γενέσθαι,
ἵν᾽ ἀρχαί τε καὶ εἰσφοραὶ διανέμωνται κατὰ¹ τὴν
τῆς ἀξίας ἑκάστοις τιμήν, μὴ κατ᾽ ἀρετὴν μόνον
τήν τε προγόνων καὶ τὴν αὑτοῦ, μηδὲ κατὰ σωμά-
C των ἰσχὺς καὶ εὐμορφίας, ἀλλὰ καὶ κατὰ πλούτου
χρῆσιν καὶ πενίας, τὰς τιμάς τε καὶ ἀρχὰς ὡς
ἰσαίτατα τῷ ἀνίσῳ ξυμμέτρῳ δὲ ἀπολαμβάνοντες
μὴ διαφέρωνται. τούτων χάριν τέτταρα μεγέθει
τῆς οὐσίας τιμήματα ποιεῖσθαι χρεών, πρώτους
καὶ δευτέρους καὶ τρίτους καὶ τετάρτους, ἤ τισιν
ἄλλοις προσαγορευομένους ὀνόμασιν, ὅταν τε
μένωσιν ἐν τῷ αὐτῷ τιμήματι καὶ ὅταν πλουσι-
ώτεροι ἐκ πενήτων καὶ ἐκ πλουσίων πένητες
γιγνόμενοι μεταβαίνωσιν εἰς τὸ προσῆκον ἕκαστοι
ἑαυτοῖσι τίμημα.

D   Τόδε δ᾽ ἐπὶ τούτοις αὖ νόμου σχῆμα ἔγωγ᾽
ἂν τιθείην ὡς ἑπόμενον. δεῖ γὰρ ἐν πόλει που,
φαμέν, τῇ τοῦ μεγίστου νοσήματος οὐ μεθεξ-
ούσῃ, ὃ διάστασιν ἢ στάσιν ὀρθότερον ἂν εἴη
κεκλῆσθαι, μήτε πενίαν τὴν χαλεπὴν ἐνεῖναι

¹ διανέμωνται κατὰ: καὶ διανομαὶ MSS. (Ast brackets ἀρχαί
. . . τιμήν)

378

succeeding in this, or am I wide of the mark ? " In this way he might, perhaps, get through the task of legislation himself, and save others the trouble of it ; but in no other way could he ever possibly do so.

The man who has received an allotment shall hold it, as we say, on the terms stated. It would indeed have been a splendid thing if each person, on entering the colony, had had all else equal as well. Since this, however, is impossible, and one man will arrive with more money and another with less, it is necessary for many reasons, and for the sake of equalising chances in public life, that there should be unequal valuations, in order that offices and contributions may be assigned in accordance with the assessed valuation in each case,—being framed not in proportion only to the moral excellence of a man's ancestors or of himself, nor to his bodily strength and comeliness, but in proportion also to his wealth or poverty,—so that by a rule of symmetrical inequality [1] they may receive offices and honours as equally as possible, and may have no quarrelling. For these reasons we must make four classes, graded by size of property, and called first, second, third and fourth (or by some other names), alike when the individuals remain in the same class and when, through a change from poverty to wealth or from wealth to poverty, they pass over each to that class to which he belongs.

The kind of law that I would enact as proper to follow next after the foregoing would be this : It is, as we assert, necessary in a State which is to avoid that greatest of plagues, which is better termed disruption than dissension,[2] that none of its citizens should

[1] i.e. of proportional distribution : cp. 757 A ff. for "political," as distinct from "arithmetical," equality.
[2] Or "class discord."

744 παρά τισι τῶν πολιτῶν μήτ᾽ αὖ πλοῦτον,
ὡς ἀμφοτέρων τικτόντων ταῦτα ἀμφότερα· νῦν
οὖν ὅρον δεῖ τούτων ἑκατέρου τὸν νομοθέτην
φράζειν. ἔστω δὴ πενίας μὲν ὅρος ἡ τοῦ κλήρου
Ε τιμή, ὃν δεῖ μένειν καὶ ὃν ἄρχων οὐδεὶς οὐδενί
ποτε περιόψεται ἐλάττω γιγνόμενον, τῶν τε
ἄλλων κατὰ ταὐτὰ οὐδεὶς ὅστις φιλότιμος ἐπ᾽
ἀρετῇ. μέτρον δὲ αὐτὸν θέμενος ὁ νομοθέτης
διπλάσιον ἐάσει τούτου κτᾶσθαι καὶ τριπλάσιον
καὶ μέχρι τετραπλασίου· πλείονα δ᾽ ἄν τις
κτᾶται τούτων εὑρὼν ἢ δοθέντων ποθὲν ἢ χρη-
ματισάμενος ἤ τινι τύχῃ τοιαύτῃ κτησάμενος
745 ἄλλῃ τὰ περιγιγνόμενα τοῦ μέτρου, τῇ πόλει ἂν
αὐτὰ καὶ τοῖς τὴν πόλιν ἔχουσι θεοῖς ἀπονέμων
εὐδόκιμός τε καὶ ἀζήμιος ἂν εἴη· ἐὰν δέ τις
ἀπειθῇ τούτῳ τῷ νόμῳ, φανεῖ μὲν ὁ βουλόμενος
ἐπὶ τοῖς ἡμίσεσιν, ὁ δὲ ὀφλὼν ἄλλο τοσοῦτον
μέρος ἀποτίσει τῆς αὐτοῦ κτήσεως, τὰ δ᾽ ἡμίσεα
τῶν θεῶν. ἡ δὲ κτῆσις χωρὶς τοῦ κλήρου πάντων
πᾶσα ἐν τῷ φανερῷ γεγράφθω παρὰ φύλαξιν
ἄρχουσιν, οἷς ἂν ὁ νόμος προστάξῃ, ὅπως ἂν αἱ
Β δίκαι περὶ πάντων ὅσα [1] εἰς χρήματα ῥᾴδιαί
τε ὦσι καὶ σφόδρα σαφεῖς.

Τὸ δὴ μετὰ τοῦτο, πρῶτον μὲν τὴν πόλιν
ἱδρῦσθαι δεῖ τῆς χώρας ὅτι μάλιστα ἐν μέσῳ, καὶ
τἆλλα ὅσα πρόσφορα πόλει τῶν ὑπαρχόντων
ἔχοντα τόπον ἐκλεξάμενον, ἃ νοῆσαί τε καὶ εἰπεῖν
οὐδὲν χαλεπόν· μετὰ δὲ ταῦτα μέρη δώδεκα δι-
ελέσθαι, θέμενον Ἑστίας πρῶτον καὶ Διὸς καὶ
Ἀθηνᾶς ἱερόν, ἀκρόπολιν ὀνομάζοντα, κύκλον

---

[1] ὅσα Stephens, Schanz : ὅσαι MSS.

be in a condition of either painful poverty or wealth, since both these conditions produce both these results; consequently the lawgiver must now declare a limit for both these conditions. The limit of poverty shall be the value of the allotment : this must remain fixed, and its diminution in any particular instance no magistrate should overlook, nor any other citizen who aspires to goodness. And having set this as the (inferior) limit, the lawgiver shall allow a man to possess twice this amount, or three times, or four times. Should anyone acquire more than this— whether by discovery or gift or money-making, or through gaining a sum exceeding the due measure by some other such piece of luck,—if he makes the surplus over to the State and the gods who keep the State, he shall be well-esteemed and free from penalty. But if anyone disobeys this law, whoso wishes may get half by laying information, and the man that is convicted shall pay out an equal share of his own property, and the half shall go to the gods. All the property of every man over and above his allotment shall be publicly written out and be in the keeping of the magistrates appointed by law, so that legal rights pertaining to all matters of property may be easy to decide and perfectly clear.

In the next place, the lawgiver must first plant his city as nearly as possible in the centre of the country, choosing a spot which has all the other conveniences also which a city requires, and which it is easy enough to perceive and specify. After this, he must divide off twelve portions of land,—when he has first set apart a sacred glebe for Hestia, Zeus and Athene, to which he shall give the name "acropolis" and circle it round with a ring-wall;

745C περιβάλλοντα, ἀφ' οὗ τὰ δώδεκα μέρη τέμνειν
τήν τε πόλιν αὐτὴν καὶ πᾶσαν τὴν χώραν. ἴσα
δὲ δεῖ γίγνεσθαι τὰ δώδεκα μέρη τῷ τὰ μὲν
ἀγαθῆς γῆς εἶναι σμικρά, τὰ δὲ χείρονος μείζω.
κλήρους δὲ διελεῖν τετταράκοντα καὶ πεντακισ-
χιλίους, τούτων τε αὖ δίχα τεμεῖν ἕκαστον καὶ
ξυγκληρῶσαι δύο τμήματα, τοῦ τ' ἐγγὺς καὶ τοῦ
πόρρω μετέχοντα ἑκάστοτε·[1] τὸ πρὸς τῇ πόλει
μέρος τῷ πρὸς τοῖς ἐσχάτοις [εἷς κλῆρος][2] καὶ τὸ
δεύτερον ἀπὸ πόλεως τῷ ἀπ' ἐσχάτων δευτέρῳ,
D καὶ τἆλλα οὕτω πάντα. μηχανᾶσθαι δὲ καὶ ἐν
τοῖς δίχα τμήμασι τὸ νῦν δὴ λεγόμενον φαυλότη-
τός τε <πέρι>[3] καὶ ἀρετῆς χώρας, ἐπανισουμένους
τῷ πλήθει τε καὶ ὀλιγότητι τῆς διανομῆς. νεῖμαι[4]
δὲ δεῖ καὶ τοὺς ἄνδρας δώδεκα μέρη, τὴν τῆς
ἄλλης οὐσίας <ἀξίαν>[5] εἰς ἴσα ὅτι μάλιστα τὰ
δώδεκα μέρη συνταξάμενον, ἀπογραφῆς πάντων
γενομένης· καὶ δὴ καὶ τὸ μετὰ τοῦτο δώδεκα
θεοῖς δώδεκα κλήρους θέντας ἐπονομάσαι καὶ
καθιερῶσαι τὸ λαχὸν μέρος ἑκάστῳ τῷ θεῷ, καὶ
E φυλὴν αὐτὴν ἐπονομάσαι· τέμνειν δὲ αὖ καὶ τὰ
δώδεκα τῆς πόλεως τμήματα τὸν αὐτὸν τρόπον
ὅνπερ καὶ τὴν ἄλλην χώραν διένεμον· καὶ δύο
νέμεσθαι ἕκαστον οἰκήσεις, τήν τε ἐγγὺς τοῦ
μέσου καὶ τὴν τῶν ἐσχάτων· καὶ τὴν μὲν
κατοίκισιν οὕτω τέλος ἔχειν.

Ἐννοεῖν δὲ ἡμᾶς τὸ τοιόνδ' ἐστὶ χρεὼν ἐκ
παντὸς τρόπου, ὡς τὰ νῦν εἰρημένα πάντα οὐκ
ἄν ποτε εἰς τοιούτους καιροὺς ξυμπέσοι, ὥστε

---

[1] ἑκάστοτε Schanz : ἑκάτερον MSS.
[2] [εἷς κλῆρος] bracketed by Peipers, Schanz.
[3] ⟨πέρι⟩ I add here (Schanz after χώρας).

starting from this he must divide up both the city itself and all the country into the twelve portions. The twelve portions must be equalised by making those consisting of good land small, and those of inferior land larger.   He must mark off 5,040 allotments, and each of these he must cut in two and join two pieces to form each several allotment, so that each contains a near piece and a distant piece,—joining the piece next the city with the piece furthest off, the second nearest with the second furthest, and so on with all the rest.[1]   And in dealing with these separate portions, they must employ the device we mentioned a moment ago, about poor land and good, and secure equality by making the assigned portions of larger or smaller size.   And he must divide the citizens also into twelve parts, making all the twelve parts as equal as possible in respect of the value of the rest of their property, after a census has been made of all.   After this they must also appoint twelve allotments for the twelve gods, and name and consecrate the portion allotted to each god, giving it the name of "phyle." [2]   And they must also divide the twelve sections of the city in the same manner as they divided the rest of the country; and each citizen must take as his share two dwellings, one near the centre of the country the other near the outskirts.   Thus the settlement shall be completed.

But we must by all means notice this,—that all the arrangements now described will never be likely to meet with such favourable conditions that the

------

[1] Cp. 776 A.   [2] i.e. "tribe."

------

[4] νεῖμαι England : νείμασθαι MSS.
[5] ⟨ἀξίαν⟩ I add.

PLATO

746 ξυμβῆναι κατὰ λόγον οὕτω ξύμπαντα γενόμενα
ἄνδρας τε οἳ μὴ δυσχερανοῦσι τὴν τοιαύτην
ξυνοικίαν, ἀλλ' ὑπομενοῦσι χρήματά τε ἔχοντες
τακτὰ καὶ μέτρια διὰ βίου παντὸς καὶ παίδων
γενέσεις ἃς εἰρήκαμεν ἑκάστοις, καὶ χρυσοῦ
στερόμενοι καὶ ἑτέρων ὧν δῆλος ὁ νομοθέτης
προστάξων ἐστὶν ἐκ τούτων τῶν νῦν εἰρημένων,
ἔτι δὲ χώρας τε καὶ ἄστεος, ὡς εἴρηκε, ἐν μέσῳ
τινάς[1] τε καὶ ἐν κύκλῳ οἰκήσεις, πάντῃ σχεδὸν
οἷον ὀνείρατα λέγων ἢ πλάττων καθάπερ ἐκ
B κηροῦ τινὰ πόλιν καὶ πολίτας. ἔχει δὴ τὰ
τοιαῦτα οὐ κακῶς τινὰ τρόπον εἰρημένα, χρὴ δ'
ἐπαναλαμβάνειν πρὸς αὑτὸν τὰ τοιάδε. πάλιν
ἄρα ἡμῖν ὁ νομοθετῶν φράζει τόδε· Ἐν τούτοις
τοῖς λόγοις, ὦ φίλοι, μηδ' αὐτὸν δοκεῖτέ με
λεληθέναι τὸ νῦν λεγόμενον, ὡς ἀληθῆ διεξέρχεταί
τινα τρόπον· ἀλλὰ γὰρ ἐν ἑκάστοις τῶν μελλόντων ἔσεσθαι δικαιότατον οἶμαι τόδε εἶναι, τὸν τὸ
παράδειγμα δεικνύντα, οἷον δεῖ τὸ ἐπιχειρούμενον
γίγνεσθαι, μηδὲν ἀπολείπειν τῶν καλλίστων τε
καὶ ἀληθεστάτων· ᾧ δὲ ἀδύνατόν τι ξυμβαίνει
C τούτων γίγνεσθαι, τοῦτο μὲν αὐτὸ ἐκκλίνειν καὶ
μὴ πράττειν, ὅ τι δὲ τούτου τῶν λοιπῶν ἐγγύτατά
ἐστι καὶ ξυγγενέστατον ἔφυ τῶν προσηκόντων
πράττειν, τοῦτ' αὐτὸ διαμηχανᾶσθαι ὅπως ἂν
γίγνηται· τὸν νομοθέτην δ' ἐᾶσαι τέλος ἐπιθεῖναι
τῇ βουλήσει, γενομένου δὲ τούτου, τότ' ἤδη κοινῇ
μετ' ἐκείνου σκοπεῖν ὅ τί τε ξυμφέρει τῶν εἰρημένων καὶ τί πρόσαντες εἴρηται τῆς νομοθεσίας·
τὸ γὰρ ὁμολογούμενον αὐτὸ αὑτῷ δεῖ που πανταχῇ

---

[1] ἐν μέσῳ τινάς: μεσότητάς MSS., edd.

384

whole programme can be carried out according to plan. This requires that the citizens will raise no objection to such a mode of living together, and will tolerate being restricted for life to fixed and limited amounts of property and to families such as we have stated, and being deprived of gold and of the other things which the lawgiver is clearly obliged by our regulations to forbid, and will submit also to the arrangements he has defined for country and city, with the dwellings set in the centre and round the circumference,—almost as if he were telling nothing but dreams, or moulding, so to say, a city and citizens out of wax. These criticisms are not altogether unfair, and the lawgiver should reconsider the points that follow. So he that is legislating speaks to us again in this wise : " Do not suppose, my friends, that I in these my discourses fail to observe the truth of what is now set out in this criticism. But in dealing with all schemes for the future, the fairest plan, I think, is this—that the person who exhibits the pattern on which the undertaking is to be modelled should omit no detail of perfect beauty and truth ; but where any of them is impossible of realisation, that particular detail he should omit and leave unexecuted, but contrive instead to execute whatever of the remaining details comes nearest to this and is by nature most closely akin to the right procedure ; and he should allow the lawgiver to express his ideal completely ; and when this is done, then and then only should they both consult together as to how far their proposals are expedient and how much of the legislation is impracticable. For the constructor of even the most trivial object, if he is to be

PLATO

746 ἀπεργάζεσθαι καὶ τὸν τοῦ φαυλοτάτου δημιουργὸν
D ἄξιον ἐσόμενον λόγου.

Νῦν δὴ τοῦτ᾽ αὐτὸ προθυμητέον ἰδεῖν μετὰ τὴν
δόξαν τῆς τῶν δώδεκα μερῶν διανομῆς, τὸ τίνα
τρόπον [δῆλον δὴ τὰ δώδεκα μέρη τῶν ἐντὸς
αὐτοῦ πλείστας ἔχοντα διανομὰς] ¹ καὶ τὰ τούτοις
ξυνεπόμενα καὶ ἐκ τούτων γεννώμενα, μέχρι
τῶν τετταράκοντά τε καὶ πεντακισχιλίων· ὅθεν
φρατρίας καὶ δήμους καὶ κώμας, καὶ πρός γε τὰς
πολεμικὰς τάξεις τε καὶ ἀγωγάς, καὶ ἔτι νομίσ-
ματα καὶ μέτρα ξηρά τε καὶ ὑγρὰ καὶ σταθμά·
E πάντα ταῦτα ἔμμετρά τε καὶ ἀλλήλοις σύμφωνα
δεῖ τόν γε νόμον τάττειν. πρὸς δὲ τούτοις οὐδ᾽
ἐκεῖνα φοβητέα, δείσαντα τὴν δόξασαν ἂν
γίγνεσθαι σμικρολογίαν, ἄν τις προστάττῃ πάντα
ὁπόσ᾽ ἂν σκεύη κτῶνται, μηδὲν ἄμετρον αὐτῶν
747 ἐᾶν εἶναι, καὶ κοινῷ λόγῳ νομίσαντα πρὸς πάντα
εἶναι χρησίμους τὰς τῶν ἀριθμῶν διανομὰς καὶ
ποικίλσεις, ὅσα τε αὐτοὶ ἐν ἑαυτοῖς ποικίλλονται
καὶ ὅσα ἐν μήκεσι καὶ ἐν βάθεσι ποικίλματα, καὶ
δὴ καὶ ἐν φθόγγοις καὶ κινήσεσι ταῖς τε κατὰ τὴν
εὐθυπορίαν τῆς ἄνω καὶ κάτω φορᾶς καὶ τῆς
κύκλῳ περιφορᾶς· πρὸς γὰρ ταῦτα πάντα δεῖ
βλέψαντα τόν γε νομοθέτην προστάττειν τοῖς
πολίταις πᾶσιν εἰς δύναμιν τούτων μὴ ἀπολεί-
B πεσθαι τῆς συντάξεως. πρός τε γὰρ οἰκονομίαν
καὶ πρὸς πολιτείαν καὶ πρὸς τὰς τέχνας πάσας
ἓν οὐδὲν οὕτω δύναμιν ἔχει παίδειον μάθημα
μεγάλην, ὡς ἡ περὶ τοὺς ἀριθμοὺς διατριβή· τὸ
δὲ μέγιστον, ὅτι τὸν νυστάζοντα καὶ ἀμαθῆ φύσει
ἐγείρει καὶ εὐμαθῆ καὶ μνήμονα καὶ ἀγχίνουν

---

¹ [δῆλον . . . διανομὰς] I bracket (διελεῖν δεῖ Hermann).

386

of any merit, must make it in all points consistent
with itself."

So now we must endeavour to discern—after we
have decided on our division into twelve parts—in
what fashion the divisions that come next to these
and are the offspring of these, up to the ultimate
figure, 5,040, (determining as they do, the phratries
and demes[1] and villages, as well as the military
companies and platoons, and also the coinage-system,
dry and liquid measures, and weights),—how, I say, all
these numerations are to be fixed by the law so as to
be of the right size and consistent one with another.
Moreover, he should not hesitate, through fear of
what might appear to be peddling detail, to prescribe
that, of all the utensils which the citizens may possess,
none shall be allowed to be of undue size. He must
recognise it as a universal rule that the divisions
and variations of numbers are applicable to all
purposes—both to their own arithmetical variations
and to the geometrical variations of surfaces and
solids, and also to those of sounds, and of motions,
whether in a straight line up and down or circular.[2]
The lawgiver must keep all these in view and
charge all the citizens to hold fast, so far as they
can, to this organised numerical system. For in
relation to economics, to politics and to all the arts,
no single branch of educational science possesses so
great an influence as the study of numbers: its chief
advantage is that it wakes up the man who is by
nature drowsy and slow of wit, and makes him quick

---

[1] "Phratries" and "demes" were sub-divisions of the
"phyle" or tribe.
[2] *i.e.* the laws of arithmetic apply also to plane and solid
geometry, acoustics, and kinetics.

747 ἀπεργάζεται, παρὰ τὴν αὑτοῦ φύσιν ἐπιδιδόντα
θείᾳ τέχνῃ. ταῦτα δὴ πάντα, ἐὰν μὲν ἄλλοις
νόμοις τε καὶ ἐπιτηδεύμασιν ἀφαιρῆταί τις τὴν
ἀνελευθερίαν καὶ φιλοχρηματίαν ἐκ τῶν ψυχῶν
C τῶν μελλόντων αὐτὰ ἱκανῶς τε καὶ ὀνησίμως
κτήσεσθαι, καλὰ τὰ παιδεύματα καὶ προσήκοντα
γίγνοιτ᾽ ἄν· εἰ δὲ μή, τὴν καλουμένην ἄν τις
πανουργίαν ἀντὶ σοφίας ἀπεργασάμενος λάθοι,
καθάπερ Αἰγυπτίους καὶ Φοίνικας καὶ πολλὰ
ἕτερα ἀπειργασμένα γένη νῦν ἔστιν ἰδεῖν ὑπὸ τῆς
τῶν ἄλλων ἐπιτηδευμάτων καὶ κτημάτων ἀνε-
λευθερίας, εἴτε τις νομοθέτης αὐτοῖς φαῦλος ἂν
γενόμενος ἐξειργάσατο τὰ τοιαῦτα, εἴτε χαλεπὴ
τύχη προσπεσοῦσα, εἴτε καὶ φύσις ἄλλη τις
D τοιαύτη. καὶ γάρ, ὦ Μέγιλλέ τε καὶ Κλεινία,
μηδὲ τοῦθ᾽ ἡμᾶς λανθανέτω περὶ τόπων, ὡς
φύσει[1] εἰσὶν ἄλλοι τινὲς διαφέροντες ἄλλων
τόπων πρὸς τὸ γεννᾶν ἀνθρώπους ἀμείνους καὶ
χείρους· οἷς οὐκ ἐναντία νομοθετητέον. οἱ μέν
γέ που, διὰ πνεύματα παντοῖα καὶ δι᾽ εἱλήσεις
ἀλλόκοτοί τ᾽ εἰσὶ καὶ ἐναίσιοι αὐτῶν, οἱ δὲ δι᾽
ὕδατα, οἱ δὲ καὶ δι᾽ αὐτὴν τὴν ἐκ τῆς γῆς
E τροφήν, ἀναδιδοῦσαν οὐ μόνον τοῖς σώμασιν
ἀμείνω καὶ χείρω, ταῖς δὲ ψυχαῖς οὐχ ἧττον
δυναμένην πάντα τὰ τοιαῦτα ἐμποιεῖν, τούτων δ᾽
αὖ πάντων μέγιστον διαφέροιεν ἂν τόποι χώρας,
ἐν οἷς θεία τις ἐπίπνοια καὶ δαιμόνων λήξεις εἶεν,
τοὺς ἀεὶ κατοικιζομένους ἵλεῳ δεχόμενοι καὶ
τοὐναντίον. οὓς[2] ὅ γε νοῦν ἔχων νομοθέτης

---

[1] φύσει: οὐκ MSS. (bracketed by Ast, Schanz)
[2] οὓς Ast: οἷς MSS.

---

[1] Cp. Rep. 436 A.

to learn, mindful and sharp-witted, progressing beyond his natural capacity by art divine. All these subjects of education will prove fair and fitting, provided that you can remove illiberality and avarice, by means of other laws and institutions, from the souls of those who are to acquire them adequately and to profit by them; otherwise you will find that you have unwittingly turned out a "sharper," as we call him, instead of a sage: examples of this we can see to-day in the effect produced on the Egyptians and Phoenicians [1] and many other nations by the illiberal character of their property, and their other institutions,—whether these results are due to their having had a bad lawgiver, or to some adverse fortune that befell them, or else, possibly, to some natural disadvantage. For that, too, is a point, O Megillus and Clinias, which we must not fail to notice,—that some districts are naturally superior to others for the breeding of men of a good or bad type; and we must not conflict with this natural difference in our legislation. Some districts are ill-conditioned or well-conditioned owing to a variety of winds or to sunshine, others owing to their waters, others owing simply to the produce of the soil, which offers produce either good or bad for their bodies, and equally able to effect similar results in their souls as well. Of all these, those districts would be by far the best which have a kind of heavenly breeze, and where the portions of land are under the care of daemons,[2] so that they receive those that come from time to time to settle there either graciously or ungraciously. These districts the judicious lawgiver will examine, so far as examination of such

---

[1] Cp. 745 D *ad fin.*

747 ἐπισκεψάμενος, ὡς ἄνθρωπον οἷόν τ᾽ ἐστὶ σκοπεῖν
τὰ τοιαῦτα, οὕτω πειρῷτ᾽ ἂν τιθέναι τοὺς νόμους.
ὃ δὴ καὶ σοὶ ποιητέον, ὦ Κλεινία· πρῶτον
τρεπτέον ἐπὶ τὰ τοιαῦτα μέλλοντί γε κατοικίζειν
χώραν.

κλ. Ἀλλ᾽, ὦ ξένε Ἀθηναῖε, λέγεις τε παγκάλως
ἐμοί τε οὕτω ποιητέον.

matters is possible for mere man; and he will try to frame his laws accordingly. And you too, Clinias, must adopt the same course; when you are proposing to colonize the country, you must attend to these matters first.

CLIN. Your discourse, Stranger, is most excellent, and I must do as you advise.

751 ΑΘ. Ἀλλὰ μὴν μετά γε πάντα τὰ νῦν εἰρημένα σχεδὸν ἂν ἀρχῶν εἶέν σοι καταστάσεις τῇ πόλει.

ΚΛ. Ἔχει γὰρ οὖν οὕτως.

ΑΘ. Δύο εἴδη ταῦτα περὶ πολιτείας κόσμον γιγνόμενα τυγχάνει, πρῶτον μὲν καταστάσεις ἀρχῶν τε καὶ ἀρξόντων, ὅσας τε αὐτὰς εἶναι δεῖ καὶ τρόπον ὅντινα καθισταμένας· ἔπειτα οὕτω δὴ τοὺς νόμους ταῖς ἀρχαῖς ἑκάσταις ἀποδοτέον, B οὕστινάς τε αὖ καὶ ὅσους καὶ οἵους προσῆκον ἂν ἑκάσταις εἴη. σμικρὸν δὲ ἐπισχόντες πρὸ τῆς αἱρέσεως εἴπωμεν προσήκοντά τινα λόγον περὶ αὐτῆς ῥηθῆναι.

ΚΛ. Τίνα δὴ τοῦτον;

ΑΘ. Τόνδε. παντί που δῆλον τὸ τοιοῦτον, ὅτι μεγάλου τῆς νομοθεσίας ὄντος ἔργου, τῷ[1] πόλιν εὖ παρεσκευασμένην ἀρχὰς ἀνεπιτηδείους ἐπιστῆσαι τοῖς εὖ κειμένοις νόμοις, οὐ μόνον οὐδὲν πλέον εὖ τεθέντων, οὐδ᾽ ὅτι γέλως ἂν πάμπολυς C ξυμβαίνοι, σχεδὸν δὲ βλάβαι καὶ λῶβαι πολὺ μέγισται ταῖς πόλεσι γίγνοιντ᾽ ἂν ἐξ αὐτῶν.

ΚΛ. Πῶς γὰρ οὔ;

ΑΘ. Τοῦτο τοίνυν νοήσωμέν σοι περὶ τῆς νῦν, ὦ φίλε, πολιτείας τε καὶ πόλεως ξυμβαῖνον· ὁρᾷς γὰρ ὅτι πρῶτον μὲν δεῖ τοὺς ὀρθῶς ἰόντας ἐπὶ τὰς τῶν ἀρχῶν δυνάμεις βάσανον ἱκανὴν αὐτούς τε καὶ γένος ἑκάστων ἐκ παίδων μέχρι

---

[1] τῷ Schramm, Schanz: τοῦ MSS.

BOOK VI

ATH. Well then, after all that has now been said, you will next come, I suppose, to the task of appointing magistrates for your State.

CLIN. That is so.

ATH. In this there are two branches of civic organisation involved,—first, the appointment of magistracies and magistrates, with the fixing of the right number required and the proper method of appointment; and next the assignment to each magistracy of such and so many laws as are in each case appropriate.[1] But before we make our selection, let us pause for a moment, and make a statement concerning it of a pertinent kind.

CLIN. What statement is that?

ATH. It is this :—It is a faot clear to everyone that, the work of legislation being a great one, the placing of unfit officers in charge of well-framed laws in a well-equipped State not only robs those laws of all their value and gives rise to widespread ridicule, but is likely also to prove the most fertile source of damage and danger in such States.

CLIN. Undoubtedly.

ATH. Let us then, my friend, mark this result in dealing now with your polity and State. You see that it is necessary, in the first place, that those who rightly undertake official functions should in every case have been fully tested—both themselves and their families—from their earliest years up to the

[1] Cp. 735 A.

751 τῆς αἱρέσεως εἶναι δεδωκότας, ἔπειτα αὖ τοὺς
μέλλοντας αἱρήσεσθαι τεθράφθαι [τε]¹ ἐν ἤθεσι
D νόμων εὖ πεπαιδευμένους πρὸς τὸ δυσχεραίνοντάς
τε καὶ ἀποδεχομένους ὀρθῶς κρίνειν καὶ ἀπο-
κρίνειν δυνατοὺς γίγνεσθαι τοὺς ἀξίους ἑκατέρων.
ταῦτα δὲ οἱ νεωστὶ ξυνεληλυθότες ὄντες τε
ἀλλήλων ἀγνῶτες, ἔτι δ᾽ ἀπαίδευτοι, πῶς ἄν
ποτε δύναιντο ἀμέμπτως τὰς ἀρχὰς αἱρεῖσθαι;

ΚΛ. Σχεδὸν οὐκ ἄν ποτε.

ΑΘ. Ἀλλὰ γὰρ ἀγῶνα προφάσεις <φασὶν>²
οὐ πάνυ δέχεσθαι. καὶ δὴ καὶ σοὶ τοῦτο νῦν
καὶ ἐμοὶ ποιητέον, ἐπείπερ σὺ μὲν δὴ τὴν πόλιν
E ὑπέστης τῷ Κρητῶν ἔθνει προθύμως κατοικιεῖν
δέκατος αὐτός, ὡς φῄς, τὰ νῦν, ἐγὼ δ᾽ αὖ σοὶ
752 ξυλλήψεσθαι κατὰ τὴν παροῦσαν ἡμῖν τὰ νῦν
μυθολογίαν. οὔκουν δή που λέγων γε ἂν μῦθον
ἀκέφαλον ἑκὼν καταλίποιμι· πλανώμενος γὰρ
ἂν ἀπάντῃ τοιοῦτος ὢν ἄμορφος φαίνοιτο.

ΚΛ. Ἄριστ᾽ εἴρηκας, ὦ ξένε.

ΑΘ. Οὐ μόνον γε, ἀλλὰ καὶ δράσω κατὰ
δύναμιν οὕτως.

ΚΛ. Πάνυ μὲν οὖν ποιῶμεν ᾗπερ καὶ λέγομεν.

ΑΘ. Ἔσται ταῦτ᾽, ἂν θεὸς ἐθέλῃ καὶ γήρως
ἐπικρατῶμεν τό γε τοσοῦτον.

B ΚΛ. Ἀλλ᾽ εἰκὸς ἐθέλειν.

ΑΘ. Εἰκὸς γὰρ οὖν. ἑπόμενοι δὲ αὐτῷ λάβωμεν καὶ τόδε.

ΚΛ. Τὸ ποῖον;

---

¹ [τε] bracketed by Stallb., Hermann.
² <φασὶν> added from Schol. on *Crat.* 421 D.

---

¹ Literally, "a contest does not at all admit excuses";
i.e. once engaged in it, you cannot draw back.

time of their selection; and, secondly, that those
who are to be the selectors should have been reared
in law-abiding habits, and be well trained for the
task of rightly rejecting or accepting those candidates
who deserve their approval or disapproval. Yet as
regards this point, can we suppose that men who
have but recently come together, with no knowledge of one another and with no training, could
ever possibly select their officials in a faultless
manner?

CLIN. It is practically impossible.

ATH. Yet, " with the hand on the plough," as they
say, "there is no looking back." [1] And so it must
be now with you and me; for you, as you tell me,[2]
have given your pledge to the Cretan nation that
you, with your nine colleagues, will devote yourself
to the founding of that State; and I, for my part,
have promised to lend you aid in the course of our
present imaginative sketch. And indeed I should
be loth to leave our sketch headless;[3] for it would
look entirely shapeless if it wandered about in that
guise.

CLIN. I heartily approve of what you say,
Stranger.

ATH. And what is more, I shall act as I say to
the best of my power.

CLIN. By all means let us do as we say.

ATH. It shall be done, if God will and if we can
thus far master our old age.

CLIN. Probably God will be willing.

ATH. Probably he will; and with him as leader
let us observe this also—

CLIN. What?

---

[2] 702 B, C.   [3] Cp. *Gorg.* 505 D.

752 ΑΘ. Ὡς ἀνδρείως καὶ παρακεκινδυνευμένως
ἐν τῷ νῦν ἡ πόλις ἡμῖν ἔσται κατῳκισμένη.

ΚΛ. Περὶ τί βλέπων καὶ ποῖ μάλιστα αὐτὸ
εἴρηκας τὰ νῦν;

ΑΘ. Ὡς εὐκόλως καὶ ἀφόβως ἀπείροις ἀνδράσι
νομοθετοῦμεν, ὅπως δέξονταί ποτε τοὺς νῦν τεθέντας νόμους. δῆλον δὲ τό γε τοσοῦτον, ὦ
Κλεινία, παντὶ σχεδὸν καὶ τῷ μὴ πάνυ σοφῷ,
C τὸ μὴ ῥᾳδίως γε αὐτοὺς μηδένας προσδέξεσθαι[1]
κατ᾽ ἀρχάς, εἰ δὲ μείνειάν[2] πως τοσοῦτον χρόνον,
ἕως οἱ γευσάμενοι παῖδες τῶν νόμων καὶ ξυντρα-
φέντες ἱκανῶς ξυνήθεις τε αὐτοῖς γενόμενοι τῶν
ἀρχαιρεσιῶν τῇ πόλει πάσῃ κοινωνήσειαν· γενομένου γε μὴν οὗ λέγομεν, εἴπερ τινὶ τρόπῳ καὶ
μηχανῇ γίγνοιτο ὀρθῶς, πολλὴν ἔγωγε ἀσφά-
λειαν οἶμαι καὶ μετὰ τὸν τότε παρόντα χρόνον
ἂν γενέσθαι τοῦ μεῖναι τὴν παιδαγωγηθεῖσαν
οὕτω πόλιν.

D ΚΛ. Ἔχει γοῦν λόγον.

ΑΘ. Ἴδωμεν τοίνυν πρὸς τοῦτο εἴ πῃ τινα
πόρον ἱκανὸν πορίζοιμεν ἂν κατὰ τάδε. φημὶ
γάρ, ὦ Κλεινία, Κνωσίους χρῆναι τῶν ἄλλων
διαφερόντως Κρητῶν μὴ μόνον ἀφοσιώσασθαι
περὶ τῆς χώρας ἢ νῦν κατοικίζεται, συντόνως δ᾽
ἐπιμεληθῆναι τὰς πρώτας ἀρχὰς εἰς δύναμιν,
ὅπως ἂν στῶσιν ὡς ἀσφαλέστατα καὶ ἄριστα.
τὰς μὲν οὖν ἄλλας καὶ βραχύτερον ἔργον, νομο-
E φύλακας δ᾽ ὑμῖν[3] πρώτους αἱρεῖσθαι ἀναγκαιότατον ἀπάσῃ σπουδῇ.

---

[1] προσδέξεσθαι Stephens : προσδέξασθαι MSS.
[2] μείνειάν Madvig, Schanz : μείναιμέν MSS.

ATH. How bold and adventurous is the fashion in which we shall now have founded this State of ours.

CLIN. What is now specially in your mind, and what makes you say so?

ATH. The fact that we are legislating for in-experienced men without qualms or fears as to how they will accept the laws we have now enacted. Thus much at least is plain, Clinias, to almost every-one—even to the meanest intelligence—that they will not readily accept any of those laws at the start; but if those laws could remain unchanged until those who have imbibed them in infancy, and have been reared up in them and grown fully used to them, have taken part in elections to office in every department of State,—then, when this has been effected (if any means or method can be found to effect it rightly), we have, as I think, a strong security that, after this transitional period of disciplined adolescence, the State will remain firm.

CLIN. It is certainly reasonable to suppose so.

ATH. Let us then consider whether we might succeed in providing an adequate means to this end on the following lines. For I declare, Clinias, that you Cnosians, above all other Cretans, not only ought to deal in no perfunctory manner with the soil which you are now settling, but ought also to take the utmost care that the first officials are appointed in the best and most secure way possible. The selection of the rest of them will be a less serious task; but it is imperatively necessary for you to choose your Law-wardens first with the utmost care.

---

[3] δ' ὑμῖν England : ἀνμιν (or ἂν ἡμῖν) MSS. : δ' ἂν ἡμῖν Zur. : δ' ἡμῖν Hermann.

PLATO

752 ΚΛ. Τίνα οὖν ἐπὶ τούτῳ πόρον καὶ λόγον
ἀνευρίσκομεν;

ΑΘ. Τόνδε. φημί, ὦ παῖδες Κρητῶν, χρῆναι
Κνωσίους διὰ τὸ πρεσβεύειν τῶν πολλῶν πόλεων
κοινῇ μετὰ τῶν ἀφικομένων εἰς τὴν ξυνοίκησιν
ταύτην ἐξ αὑτῶν τε καὶ ἐκείνων αἱρεῖσθαι τριάκοντα μὲν καὶ ἑπτὰ τοὺς πάντας, ἐννέα δὲ καὶ
δέκα ἐκ τῶν ἐποικησόντων,[1] τοὺς δὲ ἄλλους ἐξ
753 αὑτῆς Κνωσοῦ. τούτους δ᾽ οἱ Κνώσιοι τῇ πόλει
σοι δόντων, καὶ αὐτόν σε, πολίτην εἶναι ταύτης
τῆς ἀποικίας καὶ ἕνα τῶν ὀκτωκαίδεκα, πείσαντες
ἢ τινι[2] μετρίᾳ δυνάμει βιασάμενοι.

ΚΛ. Τί δῆτα οὐ καὶ σύ τε καὶ ὁ Μέγιλλος, ὦ
ξένε, ἐκοινωνησάτην ἡμῖν τῆς πολιτείας;

ΑΘ. Μέγα μέν, ὦ Κλεινία, φρονοῦσιν αἱ
Ἀθῆναι, μέγα δὲ καὶ ἡ Σπάρτη, καὶ μακρὰν
ἀποικοῦσιν ἑκάτεραι· σοὶ δὲ κατὰ πάντα ἐμμελῶς ἔχει καὶ τοῖς ἄλλοις οἰκισταῖς κατὰ ταὐτά,
B ὥσπερ τὰ περὶ σοῦ νῦν λεγόμενα. ὡς μὲν οὖν
γένοιτ᾽ ἂν ἐπιεικέστατα ἐκ τῶν ὑπαρχόντων ἡμῖν
τὰ νῦν, εἰρήσθω· προελθόντος δὲ χρόνου καὶ μεινά-
σης τῆς πολιτείας αἵρεσις αὐτῶν ἔστω τοιάδε τις·
πάντες μὲν κοινωνούντων τῆς τῶν ἀρχόντων αἱρέσεως ὁπόσοιπερ ἂν ὅπλα ἱππικὰ ἢ πεζικὰ τιθῶν-
ται καὶ πολέμου κεκοινωνήκωσιν ἐν ταῖς σφετέραις
αὐτῶν τῆς ἡλικίας δυνάμεσι· ποιεῖσθαι δὲ τὴν
αἵρεσιν ἐν ἱερῷ ὅπερ ἂν ἡ πόλις ἡγῆται τιμιώτα-
C τον, φέρειν δ᾽ ἐπὶ τὸν τοῦ θεοῦ βωμὸν ἕκαστον
εἰς πινάκιον γράψαντα τοὔνομα πατρόθεν καὶ
φυλῆς καὶ δήμου ὁπόθεν ἂν δημοτεύηται, παρεγ-

---

[1] ἐποικησόντων Stephens: ἐποικησάντων MSS.

CLIN. What means can we find for this, or what rule?

ATH. This: I assert, O ye sons of Crete, that, since the Cnosians take precedence over most of the Cretan cities, they should combine with those who have come into this community to select thirty-seven persons in all from their own number and the community—nineteen from the latter body, and the rest from Cnosus itself; and those men the Cnosians should make over to your State, and they should make you in person a citizen of this colony and one of the eighteen—using persuasion or, possibly, a reasonable degree of compulsion.

CLIN. Why, pray, have not you also, Stranger, and Megillus lent us a hand in our constitution?

ATH. Athens is haughty, Clinias, and Sparta also is haughty, and both are far distant: but for you this course is in all respects proper, as it is likewise for the rest of the founders of the colony, to whom also our recent remarks about you apply. Let us, then, assume that this would be the most equitable arrangement under the conditions at present existing. Later on, if the constitution still remains, the selection of officials shall take place as follows:—In the selection of officials all men shall take part who carry arms, as horse-soldiers or foot-soldiers, or who have served in war so far as their age and ability allowed. They shall make the selection in that shrine which the State shall deem the most sacred; and each man shall bring to the altar of the god, written on a tablet, the name of his nominee, with his father's name and that of his tribe and of the deme he belongs to, and beside these he shall

---

² ἤ τινι Schanz : ἢ τῇ MSS.

PLATO

753 γράφειν δὲ καὶ τὸ αὑτοῦ κατὰ ταὐτὰ οὕτως ὄνομα. τῷ βουλομένῳ δ' ἐξέστω τῶν πινακίων ὅ τί περ ἂν φαίνηται μὴ κατὰ νοῦν αὑτῷ γεγραμμένον ἀνελόντα εἰς ἀγορὰν θεῖναι μὴ ἔλαττον τριάκοντα ἡμερῶν· τὰ δὲ τῶν πινακίων κριθέντα ἐν πρώτοις μέχρι τριακοσίων δεῖξαι τοὺς ἄρχοντας ἰδεῖν

D πάσῃ τῇ πόλει, τὴν δὲ πόλιν ὡσαύτως ἐκ τούτων φέρειν πάλιν ὃν ἂν ἕκαστος βούληται, τοὺς δὲ τὸ δεύτερον ἐξ αὑτῶν προκριθέντας ἑκατὸν δεῖξαι πάλιν ἅπασι. τὸ δὲ τρίτον φερέτω μὲν ἐκ τῶν ἑκατὸν ὁ βουληθεὶς ὃν ἂν βούληται, διὰ τομίων πορευόμενος· ἑπτὰ δὲ καὶ τριάκοντα, οἷς ἂν πλεῖσται γένωνται ψῆφοι, κρίναντες ἀποφηνάντων ἄρχοντας.

E   Τίνες οὖν, ὦ Κλεινία καὶ Μέγιλλε, πάντα ἡμῖν ταῦτ' ἐν τῇ πόλει καταστήσουσι τῶν ἀρχῶν τε πέρι καὶ δοκιμασιῶν αὐτῶν; ἆρα ἐννοοῦμεν ὡς ταῖς πρῶτον οὕτω καταζευγνυμέναις πόλεσιν ἀνάγκη μὲν εἶναί τινας, οἵτινες δὲ εἶεν ἂν πρὸ πασῶν τῶν ἀρχῶν γεγονότες οὐκ ἔστιν <ἰδεῖν>[1]; δεῖ μὴν ἁμῶς γέ πως, καὶ ταῦτα οὐ φαύλους ἀλλ' ὅτι μάλιστα ἄκρους. ἀρχὴ γὰρ λέγεται μὲν ἥμισυ παντὸς [ἐν ταῖς παροιμίαις][2] ἔργου, καὶ τό γε καλῶς ἄρξασθαι πάντες ἐγκωμιάζομεν ἑκάστοτε· τὸ δ' ἐστί τε, ὡς ἐμοὶ φαίνεται, πλέον ἢ τὸ ἥμισυ, καὶ οὐδεὶς αὐτὸ καλῶς

754 γενόμενον ἐγκεκωμίακεν ἱκανῶς.

---

[1] <ἰδεῖν> I add (H. Richards adds εἰπεῖν).
[2] [ἐν ταῖς παροιμίαις] bracketed by Naber, England.

write also his own name in like manner. Any man who chooses shall be permitted to remove any tablet which seems to him to be improperly written, and to place it in the market-place for not less than thirty days. The officials shall publicly exhibit, for all the State to see, those of the tablets that are adjudged to come first, to the number of 300; and all the citizens shall vote again in like manner, each for whomsoever of these he wishes. Of these, the officials shall again exhibit publicly the names of those who are adjudged first, up to the number of 100. The third time, he that wishes shall vote for whomsoever he wishes out of the hundred, passing between slain victims [1] as he does so: then they shall test the thirty-seven men who have secured most votes, and declare them to be magistrates.

Who, then, are the men, O Clinias and Megillus, who shall establish in our State all these regulations concerning magisterial offices and tests? We perceive (do we not?) that for States that are thus getting into harness for the first time some such persons there must necessarily be; but who they can be, before any officials exist, it is impossible to see. Yet somehow or other they must be there—and men, too, of no mean quality, but of the highest quality possible. For, as the saying goes, "well begun is half done," [2] and every man always commends a good beginning; but it is truly, as I think, something more than the half, and no man has ever yet commended as it deserves a beginning that is well made.

---

[1] An ancient method of solemnly ratifying an agreement: cp. *Genesis* 15. 9 ff.

[2] Literally, "the beginning is the half of every work."

754 ΚΛ. Ὀρθότατα λέγεις.

ΑΘ. Μὴ τοίνυν γιγνώσκοντές γε παρῶμεν αὐτὸ ἄρρητον, μηδὲν διασαφήσαντες ἡμῖν αὐτοῖς τίνα ἔσται τρόπον. ἐγὼ μὲν οὖν οὐδαμῶς εὐπορῶ πλήν γε ἑνὸς εἰπεῖν πρὸς τὸ παρὸν ἀναγκαίου καὶ ξυμφέροντος λόγου.

ΚΛ. Τίνος δή;

ΑΘ. Φημὶ ταύτῃ τῇ πόλει, ἣν οἰκίζειν μέλλομεν, οἷον πατέρα καὶ μητέρα οὐκ εἶναι πλὴν B τὴν κατοικίζουσαν αὐτὴν πόλιν, οὐκ ἀγνοῶν ὅτι πολλαὶ τῶν κατοικισθεισῶν διάφοροι ταῖς κατοικισάσαις πολλάκις ἔνιαι γεγόνασί τε καὶ ἔσονται. νῦν μὴν ἐν τῷ παρόντι, καθάπερ παῖς, εἰ καί ποτε μέλλει διάφορος εἶναι τοῖς γεννήσασιν, ἔν γε τῇ παρούσῃ παιδείας ἀπορίᾳ στέργει τε καὶ στέργεται ὑπὸ τῶν γεννησάντων, καὶ φεύγων ἀεὶ πρὸς τοὺς [οἰκείους][1] ἀναγκαίους μόνους εὑρίσκει ξυμμάχους· ἃ δὴ νῦν φημι Κνωσίοις διὰ τὴν ἐπιμέλειαν πρὸς τὴν νέαν πόλιν καὶ τῇ νέᾳ πρὸς C Κνωσὸν ὑπάρχειν ἑτοίμως γεγονότα. λέγω δὲ καθάπερ εἶπον νῦν δή, δὶς γὰρ τό γε καλὸν ῥηθὲν οὐδὲν βλάπτει, Κνωσίους δεῖν ἐπιμεληθῆναι πάντων τούτων κοινῇ, προσελομένους τῶν εἰς τὴν ἀποικίαν ἀφικομένων τοὺς πρεσβυτάτους τε καὶ ἀρίστους εἰς δύναμιν ἑλομένους μὴ ἔλαττον ἑκατὸν ἀνδρῶν· καὶ αὐτῶν Κνωσίων ἔστωσαν ἑκατὸν ἕτεροι. τούτους δὲ ἐλθόντας φημὶ δεῖν

[1] [οἰκείους] I bracket.

[1] 752 D.

CLIN. Very true.

ATH. Let us not then wittingly leave this first step unmentioned, nor fail to make it quite clear to ourselves how it is to be brought about. I, however, am by no means fertile in resource, save for one statement which, in view of the present situation, it is both necessary and useful to make.

CLIN. What statement is that?

ATH. I assert that the State for whose settlement we are planning has nobody in the way of parents except that State which is founding it, though I am quite aware that many of the colony-States have been, and will be—some of them often—at feud with those which founded them. But now, on the present occasion, just as a child in the present helplessness of childhood—in spite of the likelihood of his being at enmity with his parents at some future date—loves his parents and is loved by them, and always flies for help to his kindred and finds in them, and them alone, his allies,—so now, as I assert, this relationship exists ready-made for the Cnosians towards the young State, owing to their care for it, and for the young State towards the Cnosians. I state once more, as I stated just now,[1]—for there is no harm in duplicating a good statement—that the Cnosians must take a share in caring for all these matters, choosing out not less than 100 men of those who have come into the colony, the oldest and best of them they are able to select; and of the Cnosians themselves let there be another hundred. This joint body [2] must, I say, go to the

---

[2] This body of 200 is to be appointed, as a temporary expedient, to give the State a start by selecting its first necessary officials.

754 εἰς τὴν καινὴν πόλιν συνεπιμεληθῆναι ὅπως αἱ
D τε ἀρχαὶ καταστῶσι κατὰ νόμους καταστᾶσαί
τε δοκιμασθῶσι· γενομένων δὲ τούτων τὴν μὲν
Κνωσὸν τοὺς Κνωσίους οἰκεῖν, τὴν δὲ νέαν πόλιν
αὐτὴν αὑτὴν πειρᾶσθαι σῴζειν τε καὶ εὐτυχεῖν.
οἱ δὲ δὴ γενόμενοι τῶν ἑπτὰ καὶ τριάκοντα νῦν
τε καὶ εἰς τὸν ἔπειτα ξύμπαντα χρόνον ἐπὶ τοῖσδε
ἡμῖν ᾑρήσθωσαν· πρῶτον μὲν φύλακες ἔστωσαν
τῶν νόμων, ἔπειτα τῶν γραμμάτων ὧν ἂν ἕκαστος
ἀπογράψῃ τοῖς ἄρχουσι τὸ πλῆθος τῆς αὑτῶν
E οὐσίας, πλὴν ὁ μὲν μέγιστον τίμημα ἔχων τεττάρων μνῶν, ὁ δὲ τὸ δεύτερον τριῶν, ὁ δὲ τρίτος
δυεῖν μναῖν, μνᾶς δὲ ὁ τέταρτος. ἐὰν δέ τις
ἕτερον φαίνηταί τι παρὰ τὰ γεγραμμένα κεκτημένος, δημόσιον μὲν ἔστω τὸ τοιοῦτον ἅπαν, πρὸς
τούτῳ δὲ δίκην ὑπεχέτω τῷ βουλομένῳ μετιέναι
μὴ καλὴν μηδ' εὐώνυμον, ἀλλ' αἰσχράν, ἐὰν
ἁλίσκηται διὰ τὸ κέρδος τῶν νόμων καταφρονῶν.
αἰσχροκερδείας οὖν αὐτὸν γραψάμενος ὁ βουληθεὶς ἐπεξίτω τῇ δίκῃ ἐν αὐτοῖς τοῖς νομοφύλαξιν·
ἐὰν δ' ὁ φεύγων ὄφλῃ, τῶν κοινῶν κτημάτων μὴ
755 μετεχέτω, διανομὴ δὲ ὅταν τῇ πόλει γίγνηταί τις,
ἄμοιρος ἔστω πλήν γε τοῦ κλήρου, γεγράφθω δὲ
ὠφληκώς, ἕως ἂν ζῇ, ὅπου πᾶς ὁ βουλόμενος
αὐτὰ ἀναγνώσεται. μὴ πλέον δὲ εἴκοσιν ἐτῶν
νομοφύλαξ ἀρχέτω, φερέσθω δ' εἰς τὴν ἀρχὴν
μὴ ἔλαττον ἢ πεντήκοντα γεγονὼς ἐτῶν· ἑξηκον-
τούτης δὲ ἐνεχθεὶς δέκα μόνον ἀρχέτω ἔτη, καὶ
κατὰ τοῦτον τὸν λόγον, ὅπως, ἄν τις πλέον

---

[1] See above, 752 E.

new State and arrange in common that the magistrates be appointed according to the laws and be tested after appointment. When this has been done, then the Cnosians must dwell in Cnosus, and the young State must endeavour by its own efforts to secure for itself safety and success. As to the men who belong to the thirty and seven,[1] both now and for all future time, let us select them for the following purposes: First, they shall act as Wardens of the laws, and secondly as Keepers of the registers in which every man writes out for the officials the amount of his property, omitting four minae if he be of the highest property-class, three if he be of the second class, two if he be of the third, and one if he be of the fourth class. And should anyone be proved to possess anything else beyond what is registered, all such surplus shall be confiscated; and in addition he shall be liable to be brought to trial by anyone who wishes to prosecute —a trial neither noble nor fair of name, if he be convicted of despising law because of lucre. So he that wishes shall charge him with profiteering, and prosecute him by law before the Law-wardens themselves; and if the defendant be convicted, he shall take no share of the public goods, and when-ever the State makes a distribution, he shall go portionless, save for his allotment, and he shall be registered as a convicted criminal, where anyone who chooses may read his sentence, as long as he lives. A Law-warden shall hold office for no more than twenty years, and he shall be voted into office when he is not under fifty years of age. If he is elected at the age of sixty, he shall hold office for ten years only; and by the same rule, the more he exceeds the minimum age, the shorter shall be his term of office;

755B ὑπερβὰς ἑβδομήκοντα ζῇ, μηκέτι ἐν τούτοις τοῖς
ἄρχουσι τὴν τηλικαύτην ἀρχὴν ὡς ἄρξων διανοηθήτω.

Τὰ μὲν οὖν περὶ τῶν νομοφυλάκων ταῦτα
εἰρήσθω προστάγματα τρία, προϊόντων δὲ εἰς
τοὔμπροσθε τῶν νόμων ἕκαστος προστάξει τούτοις τοῖς ἀνδράσιν ὧντινων αὐτοὺς δεῖ πρὸς τοῖς
νῦν εἰρημένοις προσεπιμελεῖσθαι· νῦν δ' ἐξῆς
ἄλλων ἀρχῶν αἱρέσεως πέρι λέγοιμεν ἄν. δεῖ
γὰρ δὴ τὰ μετὰ ταῦτα στρατηγοὺς αἱρεῖσθαι,
C καὶ τούτοις εἰς τὸν πόλεμον οἷόν τινας ὑπηρεσίας
ἱππάρχους καὶ φυλάρχους καὶ τῶν πεζῶν φυλῶν
κοσμητὰς τῶν τάξεων, οἷς πρέπον ἂν εἴη τοῦτ'
αὐτὸ τοὔνομα μάλιστα, οἷον καὶ οἱ πολλοὶ ταξιάρχους αὐτοὺς ἐπονομάζουσι. τούτων δὴ στρατηγοὺς μὲν ἐξ αὐτῆς τῆς πόλεως ταύτης οἱ νομοφύλακες προβαλλέσθων, αἱρείσθων δ' ἐκ τῶν προβληθέντων πάντες οἱ τοῦ πολέμου κοινωνοὶ γενό-
μενοί τε ἐν ταῖς ἡλικίαις καὶ γιγνόμενοι ἑκάστοτε.
ἐὰν δέ τις ἄρα δοκῇ τινι τῶν μὴ προβεβλημένων
D ἀμείνων εἶναι τῶν προβληθέντων τινός, ἐπονο-
μάσας ἀνθ' ὅτου ὅντινα προβάλλεται, τοῦτ' αὐτὸ
ὀμνὺς ἀντιπροβαλλέσθω τὸν ἕτερον· ὁπότερος δ'
ἂν δόξῃ διαχειροτονούμενος, εἰς τὴν αἵρεσιν
ἐγκρινέσθω. τρεῖς δέ, οἷς ἂν ἡ πλείστη χειροτονία γίγνηται, τούτους εἶναι στρατηγούς τε καὶ
ἐπιμελητὰς τῶν κατὰ πόλεμον, δοκιμασθέντων
καθάπερ οἱ νομοφύλακες. ταξιάρχους δὲ αὐτοῖσι
προβάλλεσθαι μὲν τοὺς αἱρεθέντας στρατηγούς

so that if he lives beyond the age of seventy, he must no longer fancy that he can remain among these officials holding an office of such high importance.

So, for the Law-wardens, let us state that these three duties are imposed on them, and as we proceed with the laws, each fresh law will impose upon these men whatever additional duties they ought to be charged with beyond those now stated. And now we may go on to describe the selection of the other officials. Commanders must be selected next, and as subordinates to them, for purposes of war, hipparchs, phylarchs, and officers to marshal the ranks of the foot-phylae,—to whom the name of "taxiarchs," [1] which is in fact the very name which most men give to them, would be specially appropriate. Of these, commanders shall be nominated by the Law-wardens from among the members of our State only; and from those nominated the selection shall be made by all who either are serving or have served in war, according to their several ages. And if anyone deems that someone of the men not nominated is better than one of those nominated, he shall state the name of his nominee and of the man whom he is to replace, and, taking the oath about the matter, he shall propose his substitute; and whichever of the two is decided on by vote shall be included in the list for selection. And the three men, who have been appointed by the majority of votes to serve as commanders and controllers of military affairs, shall be tested as were the Law-wardens. The selected commanders shall nominate for themselves taxiarchs, twelve for each

[1] *i.e.* "rank-leaders."

PLATO

755E δώδεκα ἑκάστῃ φυλῇ [ταξίαρχον]·[1] τὴν δ' ἀντι-
προβολὴν εἶναι, καθάπερ τῶν στρατηγῶν ἐγίγνετο, τὴν αὐτὴν καὶ περὶ τῶν ταξιαρχῶν καὶ τὴν
ἐπιχειροτονίαν καὶ τὴν κρίσιν. τὸν δὲ ξύλλογον
τοῦτον ἐν τῷ παρόντι, πρὶν πρυτάνεις τε καὶ
βουλὴν ᾑρῆσθαι, τοὺς νομοφύλακας συλλέξαντας
εἰς χωρίον ὡς ἱερώτατόν τε καὶ ἱκανώτατον
καθίσαι χωρὶς μὲν τοὺς ὁπλίτας, χωρὶς δὲ τοὺς
ἱππέας, τρίτον δ' ἐφεξῆς τούτοις πᾶν ὅσον
ἐμπολέμιον· χειροτονούντων δὲ στρατηγοὺς μὲν
[καὶ ἱππάρχους][2] πάντες, ταξιάρχους δὲ οἱ τὴν
756 ἀσπίδα τιθέμενοι· φυλάρχους δὲ αὐτοὶ αὑτοῖς[3]
πᾶν τὸ ἱππικὸν αἱρείσθω· ψιλῶν δὲ ἢ τοξοτῶν ἤ
τινος ἄλλου τῶν ἐμπολεμίων ἡγεμόνας οἱ στρα-
τηγοὶ ἑαυτοῖς καθιστάντων. ἱππάρχων δὴ κατά-
στασις ἂν ἡμῖν ἔτι λοιπὴ γίγνοιτο. τούτους οὖν
προβαλλέσθων μὲν οἵπερ καὶ τοὺς στρατηγοὺς
προὐβάλλοντο, τὴν δὲ αἵρεσιν καὶ τὴν ἀντιπρο-
βολὴν τούτων τὴν αὐτὴν γίγνεσθαι καθάπερ ἡ
τῶν στρατηγῶν ἐγίγνετο, χειροτονείτω δὲ τὸ
B ἱππικὸν αὐτοὺς ἐναντίον ὁρώντων τῶν πεζῶν, δύο
δὲ οἷς ἂν πλείστη χειροτονία γίγνηται, τούτους
ἡγεμόνας εἶναι πάντων τῶν ἱππευόντων. τὰς δὲ
ἀμφισβητήσεις τῶν χειροτονιῶν μέχρι δυοῖν εἶναι·
τὸ δὲ τρίτον ἐὰν ἀμφισβητῇ τις, διαψηφίζεσθαι
τούτους οἷσπερ τῆς χειροτονίας μέτρον ἑκάστοις
ἕκαστον ἦν.

Βουλὴν δὲ εἶναι μὲν τριάκοντα δωδεκάδας· ἑξήκοντα δὲ καὶ τριακόσιοι γίγνοιντο ἂν πρέποντες

---

[1] [ταξίαρχον] bracketed by F. H. Dale.
[2] [καὶ ἱππάρχους] bracketed by Stallb., Schanz.

tribe; and here, in the case of the taxiarchs, just as in the case of the commanders, there shall be a right of counter-nomination, and a similar procedure of voting and testing. For the present—before that prytaneis[1] and a Boulé have been elected—this assembly shall be convened by the Law-wardens, and they shall seat it in the holiest and roomiest place available, the hoplites on one side, the horse-soldiers on another, and in the third place, next to these, all who belong to the military forces. All shall vote for the commanders, all who carry shields for the taxiarchs; all the cavalry shall elect for themselves phylarchs; the commanders shall appoint for themselves captains of skirmishers, archers, or any other branch of service. The appointment of hipparchs we have still remaining. They shall be nominated by the same persons who nominated the commanders, and the mode of selection and counter-nomination shall be the same in their case as in that of the commanders: the cavalry shall vote for them in full sight of the infantry, and the two who secure most votes shall be captains of all the cavalrymen. No more than two challenges of votes shall be allowed: if anyone makes a third challenge, it shall be decided by those who had charge of the count on the occasion in question.

The Boulé (or "Council") shall consist of thirty dozen—as the number 360 is well-adapted for the

---

[1] *i.e.* members of a "prytany," or twelfth part of the Boulé (or Council): for the functions of these bodies, see 758 B ff.

---

[3] αὐτοὶ αὑτοῖς: αὖ τούτοις MSS.: αὑτοῖς Ast.

756C ταῖς διανομαῖς· μέρη δὲ διανείμαντας τέτταρα
[κατὰ ἐνενήκοντα τὸν ἀριθμὸν] [1] τούτων, ἐξ ἑκάστου τῶν τιμημάτων φέρειν ἐνενήκοντα βουλευτάς·
πρῶτον μὲν ἐκ τῶν μεγίστων τιμημάτων ἅπαντας
φέρειν ἐξ ἀνάγκης, ἢ ζημιοῦσθαι τὸν μὴ πειθόμενον τῇ δοξάσῃ ζημίᾳ· ἐπειδὰν δ' ἐνεχθῶσι, τούτους μὲν κατασημήνασθαι, τῇ δὲ ὑστεραίᾳ φέρειν
ἐκ τῶν δευτέρων τιμημάτων κατὰ ταὐτὰ καθάπερ
τῇ πρόσθεν, τρίτῃ δ' ἐκ τῶν τρίτων τιμημάτων
φέρειν μὲν τὸν βουλόμενον, ἐπάναγκες δὲ εἶναι
D τοῖς τῶν τριῶν τιμημάτων, τὸ δὲ τέταρτόν τε καὶ
σμικρότατον ἐλεύθερον ἀφεῖσθαι τῆς ζημίας ὃς
ἂν αὐτῶν μὴ βούληται φέρειν. τετάρτῃ δὲ φέρειν
μὲν ἐκ τοῦ τετάρτου καὶ σμικροτάτου τιμήματος
ἅπαντας, ἀζήμιον δ' εἶναι τὸν ἐκ τοῦ τετάρτου
καὶ τρίτου τιμήματος, ἐὰν ἐνεγκεῖν μὴ βούληται·
τὸν δ' ἐκ τοῦ δευτέρου καὶ πρώτου μὴ φέροντα
ζημιοῦσθαι, τὸν μὲν ἐκ τοῦ δευτέρου τριπλασίᾳ
E τῆς πρώτης ζημίας, τὸν δ' ἐκ τοῦ πρώτου τετρα-
πλασίᾳ. πέμπτῃ δὲ ἡμέρᾳ τὰ κατασημανθέντα
ὀνόματα ἐξενεγκεῖν μὲν τοὺς ἄρχοντας ἰδεῖν πᾶσι
τοῖς πολίταις, φέρειν δ' ἐκ τούτων αὖ πάντα
ἄνδρα ἢ ζημιοῦσθαι τῇ πρώτῃ ζημίᾳ. ὀγδοήκοντα
δὲ καὶ ἑκατὸν ἐκλέξαντας ἀφ' ἑκάστων τῶν τιμημάτων, τοὺς ἡμίσεις τούτων ἀποκληρώσαντας
δοκιμάσαι, τούτους δ' εἶναι τὸν ἐνιαυτὸν βου-
λευτάς.

Ἡ μὲν αἵρεσις οὕτω γιγνομένη μέσον ἂν ἔχοι
μοναρχικῆς καὶ δημοκρατικῆς πολιτείας, ἧς ἀεὶ
δεῖ μεσεύειν τὴν πολιτείαν· δοῦλοι γὰρ ἂν καὶ

---

[1] [κατὰ . . . ἀριθμὸν] bracketed by England.

sub-divisions : they shall be divided into four groups ; and 90 councillors shall be voted for from each of the property-classes.[1] First, for councillors from the highest property-class all the citizens shall be compelled to vote, and whoever disobeys shall be fined with the fine decreed. When these have been voted for, their names shall be recorded. On the next day those from the second class shall be voted for, the procedure being similar to that on the first day. On the third day, for councillors from the third class anyone who chooses shall vote ; and the voting shall be compulsory for members of the first three classes, but those of the fourth and lowest class shall be let off the fine, in case any of them do not wish to vote. On the fourth day, for those from the fourth and lowest class all shall vote ; and if any member of the third or fourth class does not wish to vote, he shall be let off the fine ; but any member of the first or second class who fails to vote shall be fined—three times the amount of the first fine in the case of a member of the second class, and four times in the case of one of the first class. On the fifth day the officials shall publish the names recorded for all the citizens to see ; and for these every man shall vote, or else be fined with the first fine ; and when they have selected 180 from each of the classes, they shall choose out by lot one-half of this number, and test them ; and these shall be the Councillors for the year.

The selection of officials that is thus made will form a mean between a monarchic constitution and a democratic ; and midway between these our constitution should always stand. For slaves will never

---

[1] Cp. Ar. *Pol.* 1266ª14 ff.

PLATO

757 δεσπόται οὐκ ἄν ποτε γένοιντο φίλοι, οὐδὲ ἐν
ἴσαις τιμαῖς διαγορευόμενοι φαῦλοι καὶ σπουδαῖοι.
τοῖς γὰρ ἀνίσοις τὰ ἴσα ἄνισα γίγνοιτ᾽ ἄν, εἰ μὴ
τυγχάνοι τοῦ μέτρου. διὰ γὰρ ἀμφότερα ταῦτα
στάσεων αἱ πολιτεῖαι πληροῦνται. παλαιὸς γὰρ
λόγος ἀληθὴς ὤν, ὡς ἰσότης φιλότητα ἀπεργάζεται, μάλα μὲν ὀρθῶς εἴρηται καὶ ἐμμελῶς· ἥτις
δ᾽ ἐστί ποτε ἰσότης ἡ τοῦτο αὐτὸ δυναμένη, διὰ
τὸ μὴ σφόδρα σαφὴς εἶναι σφόδρα ἡμᾶς διατα-
B ράττει. δυοῖν γὰρ ἰσοτήτοιν οὔσαιν, ὁμωνύμοιν
μέν, ἔργῳ δὲ εἰς πολλὰ σχεδὸν ἐναντίαιν, τὴν μὲν
ἑτέραν εἰς τὰς τιμὰς πᾶσα πόλις ἱκανὴ παρ-
αγαγεῖν καὶ πᾶς νομοθέτης, τὴν μέτρῳ ἴσην καὶ
σταθμῷ καὶ ἀριθμῷ, κλήρῳ ἀπευθύνων εἰς τὰς
διανομὰς αὐτήν· τὴν δὲ ἀληθεστάτην καὶ ἀρίστην
ἰσότητα οὐκέτι ῥᾴδιον παντὶ ἰδεῖν. Διὸς γὰρ δὴ
κρίσις ἐστί, καὶ τοῖς ἀνθρώποις ἀεὶ σμικρὰ μὲν
ἐπαρκεῖ, πᾶν δὲ ὅσον ἂν ἐπαρκέσῃ πόλεσιν ἢ καὶ
C ἰδιώταις, πάντ᾽ ἀγαθὰ ἀπεργάζεται· τῷ μὲν γὰρ
μείζονι πλείω, τῷ δ᾽ ἐλάττονι σμικρότερα νέμει,
μέτρια διδοῦσα πρὸς τὴν αὐτῶν φύσιν ἑκατέρῳ,
καὶ δὴ καὶ τιμὰς μείζοσι μὲν πρὸς ἀρετὴν ἀεὶ
μείζους, ἥττους [1] δὲ τοὐναντίον ἔχουσιν ἀρετῆς
τε καὶ παιδείας, τὸ πρέπον ἑκατέροις ἀπονέμει
κατὰ λόγον. ἔστι γὰρ δή που καὶ τὸ πολιτικὸν
ἡμῖν ἀεὶ τοῦτ᾽ αὐτὸ τὸ δίκαιον· οὗ καὶ νῦν ἡμᾶς
ὀρεγομένους δεῖ καὶ πρὸς ταύτην τὴν ἰσότητα, ᾧ

---

[1] ἥττους : τοῖς MSS., edd. (Stephens and Schanz mark a
lacuna after παιδείας)

---

[1] Cp. *Gorg.* 508 A, B ; Ar. *Pol.* 1301[b] 29 ff. ; *Eth. N.* 1131[b] 27,
1158[b] 30 ff. The " arithmetical" equality which merely
counts heads and treats all alike is here contrasted with

be friends with masters, nor bad men with good, even
when they occupy equal positions—for when equality
is given to unequal things, the resultant will be unequal, unless due measure is applied; and it is
because of these two conditions that political organisa-
tions are filled with feuds. There is an old and
true saying that "equality produces amity," which is
right well and fitly spoken; but what the equality is
which is capable of doing this is a very troublesome
question, since it is very far from being clear. For
there are two kinds of equality [1] which, though identical in name, are often almost opposites in their practical
results. The one of these any State or lawgiver
is competent to apply in the assignment of honours,
—namely, the equality determined by measure,
weight and number,—by simply employing the lot to
give even results in the distributions; but the truest
and best form of equality is not an easy thing for everyone to discern. It is the judgment of Zeus, and
men it never assists save in small measure, but
in so far as it does assist either States or individuals,
it produces all things good; for it dispenses more to
the greater and less to the smaller, giving due
measure to each according to nature; and with regard to honours also, by granting the greater to
those that are greater in goodness, and the less to
those of the opposite character in respect of goodness
and education, it assigns in proportion what is fitting
to each. Indeed, it is precisely this which constitutes
for us "political justice," which is the object we
must strive for, Clinias; this equality is what we

that truer "proportional" equality which takes account of
human inequality, and on which "distributive justice" (as
Aristotle terms it) is based: cp. also 744 C.

757 Κλεινία, ἀποβλέποντας τὴν νῦν φυομένην κατοι-
D κίζειν πόλιν· ἄλλην τε ἄν ποτέ τις οἰκίζῃ, πρὸς
ταὐτὸ τοῦτο σκοπούμενον χρεὼν νομοθετεῖν, ἀλλ'
οὐ πρὸς ὀλίγους τυράννους ἢ πρὸς ἕνα ἢ καὶ
κράτος δήμου τι, πρὸς δὲ τὸ δίκαιον ἀεί· τοῦτο
δ' ἐστὶ τὸ νῦν δὴ λεχθέν, τὸ κατὰ φύσιν ἴσον
ἀνίσοις ἑκάστοτε δοθέν. ἀναγκαῖόν γε μὴν καὶ
τούτοις παρωνυμίοισί ποτε προσχρήσασθαι πόλιν
ἅπασαν, εἰ μέλλει στάσεων ἑαυτῇ μὴ προσκοι-
νωνήσειν κατά τι μέρος· τὸ γὰρ ἐπιεικὲς καὶ
E ξύγγνωμον τοῦ τελέου καὶ ἀκριβοῦς παρὰ δίκην
τὴν ὀρθήν ἐστι παρατεθραυμένον, ὅταν γίγνηται·
διὸ τῷ τοῦ κλήρου ἴσῳ ἀνάγκη προσχρήσασθαι
δυσκολίας τῶν πολλῶν ἕνεκα, θεὸν καὶ ἀγαθὴν
τύχην καὶ τότε ἐν εὐχαῖς ἐπικαλουμένους ἀπορ-
θοῦν αὐτοῖς[1] τὸν κλῆρον πρὸς τὸ δικαιότατον.
οὕτω δὴ χρηστέον ἀναγκαίως μὲν τοῖν ἰσοτήτοιν
758 ἀμφοῖν, ὡς δ' ὅτι μάλιστα ἐπ' ὀλιγίστοις τῇ
ἑτέρᾳ, τῇ τῆς τύχης δεομένῃ.

Ταῦτα οὕτω διὰ ταῦτα, ὦ φίλοι, ἀναγκαῖον
τὴν μέλλουσαν σώζεσθαι δρᾶν πόλιν. ἐπειδὴ
δὲ ναῦς τε ἐν θαλάττῃ πλέουσα φυλακῆς ἡμέρας
δεῖται καὶ νυκτὸς ἀεί, πόλις τε ὡσαύτως ἐν
κλύδωνι τῶν ἄλλων πόλεων διαγομένη καὶ παντο-
δαπαῖσιν ἐπιβουλαῖς οἰκεῖ κινδυνεύουσα ἁλίσ-
κεσθαι, δεῖ δὴ δι' ἡμέρας τε εἰς νύκτα καὶ ἐκ
νυκτὸς συνάπτειν πρὸς ἡμέραν ἄρχοντας ἄρχουσι,
B φρουροῦντάς τε φρουροῦσι διαδεχομένους ἀεὶ καὶ
παραδιδόντας μηδέποτε λήγειν. πλῆθος δὲ οὐ
δυνατὸν ὀξέως οὐδέποτε οὐδὲν τούτων πράττειν,
ἀναγκαῖον δὲ τοὺς μὲν πολλοὺς τῶν βουλευτῶν

---

[1] αὐτοῖς H. Richards : αὐτοὺς MSS.

must aim at, now that we are settling the State that is being planted. And whoever founds a State elsewhere at any time must make this same object the aim of his legislation,—not the advantage of a few tyrants, or of one, or of some form of democracy, but justice always; and this consists in what we have just stated, namely, the natural equality given on each occasion to things unequal. None the less, it is necessary for every State at times to employ even this equality in a modified degree, if it is to avoid involving itself in intestine discord, in one section or another,—for the reasonable and considerate, wherever employed, is an infringement of the perfect and exact, as being contrary to strict justice; for the same reason it is necessary to make use also of the equality of the lot, on account of the discontent of the masses, and in doing so to pray, calling upon God and Good Luck to guide for them the lot aright towards the highest justice. Thus it is that necessity compels us to employ both forms of equality; but that form, which needs good luck, we should employ as seldom as possible.

The State which means to survive must necessarily act thus, my friends, for the reasons we have stated. For just as a ship when sailing on the sea requires continual watchfulness both by night and day, so likewise a State, when it lives amidst the surge of surrounding States and is in danger of being entrapped by all sorts of plots, requires to have officers linked up with officers from day to night and from night to day, and guardians succeeding guardians, and being succeeded in turn, without a break. But since a crowd of men is incapable of ever performing any of these duties smartly, the bulk of the Councillors

758 ἐπὶ τὸ πλεῖστον τοῦ χρόνου ἐᾶν ἐπὶ τοῖς αὑτῶν
ἰδίοισι μένοντας εὐθημονεῖσθαι τὰ κατὰ τὰς
αὑτῶν οἰκήσεις, τὸ δὲ δωδέκατον μέρος αὑτῶν ἐπὶ
δώδεκα μῆνας νείμαντας ἐν ἐφ' ἑνὶ παρέχειν
αὑτοὺς φύλακας, ἰόντι τέ τινι ποθεν ἄλλοθεν εἴτε
C καὶ ἐξ αὐτῆς τῆς πόλεως ἑτοίμως ἐπιτυχεῖν, ἄν
τε ἀγγέλλειν βούληταί τις ἐάν τ' αὖ πυνθάνεσθαί
τι τῶν ὧν προσήκει πόλει πρὸς πόλεις ἄλλας
ἀποκρίνεσθαί τε καὶ ἐρωτήσασαν ἑτέρας ἀπο-
δέξασθαι τὰς ἀποκρίσεις, καὶ δὴ καὶ τῶν κατὰ
πόλιν ἑκάστοτε νεωτερισμῶν ἕνεκα παντοδαπῶν
εἰωθότων ἀεὶ γίγνεσθαι, ὅπως ἂν μάλιστα μὲν μὴ
D γίγνωνται, γενομένων δὲ ὅτι τάχιστα αἰσθομένης
τῆς πόλεως ἰαθῇ τὸ γενόμενον· διὸ ξυλλόγων τε
ἀεὶ δεῖ τοῦτο εἶναι τὸ προκαθήμενον τῆς πόλεως
κύριον καὶ διαλύσεων τῶν τε κατὰ νόμους τῶν τε
ἐξαίφνης προσπιπτουσῶν τῇ πόλει. ταῦτα μὲν
οὖν πάντα τὸ δωδέκατον ἂν μέρος τῆς βουλῆς εἴη
τὸ διακοσμοῦν, τὰ ἕνδεκα ἀναπαυόμενον τοῦ
ἐνιαυτοῦ μέρη· κοινῇ δὲ μετὰ τῶν ἄλλων ἀρχῶν
δεῖ τὰς φυλακὰς ταύτας φυλάττειν κατὰ πόλιν
τοῦτο τὸ μόριον τῆς βουλῆς ἀεί.

Καὶ τὰ μὲν κατὰ πόλιν οὕτως ἔχοντα μετρίως
E ἂν εἴη διατεταγμένα· τῆς δὲ ἄλλης χώρας πάσης
τίς ἐπιμέλεια καὶ τίς τάξις; ἆρ' οὐχ ἡνίκα πᾶσα
μὲν ἡ πόλις, σύμπασα δὲ ἡ χώρα κατὰ δώδεκα
μέρη διανενέμηται, τῆς πόλεως αὐτῆς ὁδῶν καὶ
οἰκήσεων καὶ οἰκοδομιῶν καὶ λιμένων καὶ ἀγορᾶς
καὶ κρηνῶν καὶ δὴ καὶ τεμενῶν καὶ ἱερῶν καὶ
πάντων τῶν τοιούτων ἐπιμελητὰς δεῖ τινας
ἀποδεδειγμένους εἶναι;

must necessarily be left to stay most of their time at
their private business, to attend to their domestic
affairs; and we must assign a twelfth part of them
to each of the twelve months, to furnish guards in
rotation, so as promptly to meet any person coming
either from somewhere abroad or from their own
State, in case he desires to give information or to
make enquiries about some matter of international
importance; and so as to make replies, and, when
the State has asked questions, to receive the replies;
and above all, in view of the manifold innovations
that are wont to occur constantly in States, to prevent if possible their occurrence, and in case they do
occur, to ensure that the State may perceive and
remedy the occurrence as quickly as possible. For
these reasons, this presidential section of the State
must always have the control of the summoning and
dissolving of assemblies, both the regular legal assemblies and those of an emergency character. Thus a
twelfth part of the Council will be the body that
manages all these matters, and each such part shall
rest in turn for eleven-twelfths of the year: in common with the rest of the officials, this twelfth section
of the Council must keep its watch in the State over
these matters continually.

This disposition of affairs in the city will prove a
reasonable arrangement. But what control are we
to have, and what system, for all the rest of the
country? Now that all the city and the whole
country have each been divided up into twelve parts,
must not supervisors be appointed for the roads of
the city itself, the dwellings, buildings, harbours,
market, springs, and for the sacred glebes also and
the temples, and all such things?

758 ΚΛ. Πῶς γὰρ οὔ ;

759 ΑΘ. Λέγωμεν δὴ τοῖς μὲν ἱεροῖς νεωκόρους τε
καὶ ἱερέας καὶ ἱερείας δεῖν γίγνεσθαι· ὁδῶν δὲ καὶ
οἰκοδομιῶν καὶ κόσμου τοῦ περὶ τὰ τοιαῦτα
ἀνθρώπων τε, ἵνα μὴ ἀδικῶσι, καὶ τῶν ἄλλων
θηρίων ἐν αὐτῷ τε τῷ τῆς πόλεως περιβόλῳ καὶ
προαστείῳ, ὅπως ἂν τὰ προσήκοντα πόλεσι
γίγνηται, ἑλέσθαι δεῖ τρία μὲν ἀρχόντων εἴδη,
περὶ μὲν τὸ νῦν δὴ λεχθὲν ἀστυνόμους ἐπονο-
μάζοντα, τὸ δὲ περὶ ἀγορᾶς κόσμον ἀγορανόμους,
ἱερῶν δὲ ἱερέας, οἷς μέν εἰσι πάτριαι ἱερωσύναι
B καὶ αἷς, μὴ κινεῖν· εἰ δέ, οἷον τὸ πρῶτον κατοι-
κιζομένοις εἰκὸς γίγνεσθαι περὶ τὰ τοιαῦτα, ἢ
μηδενὶ ἢ τισιν ὀλίγοις [οἷς] ἤδη [1] καθεστήκοι,
καταστατέον ἱερέας τε καὶ ἱερείας νεωκόρους
γίγνεσθαι τοῖς θεοῖς. τούτων δὴ πάντων τὰ μὲν
αἱρετὰ χρή, τὰ δὲ κληρωτὰ ἐν ταῖς καταστάσεσι
γίγνεσθαι, μιγνύντας πρὸς φιλίαν ἀλλήλοις
δῆμον καὶ μὴ δῆμον ἐν ἑκάστῃ χώρᾳ καὶ πόλει,
ὅπως ἂν μάλιστα ὁμονόων [2] εἴη. τὰ μὲν οὖν τῶν
C ἱερέων [3] τῷ θεῷ ἐπιτρέποντα αὐτῷ τὸ κεχαρισμένον
γίγνεσθαι, κληροῦν οὕτω τῇ θείᾳ τύχῃ ἀποδιδόντα, δοκιμάζειν δὲ τὸν ἀεὶ λαγχάνοντα πρῶτον
μὲν ὁλόκληρον καὶ γνήσιον, ἔπειτα ὡς ὅτι μάλιστα
ἐκ καθαρευουσῶν οἰκήσεων, φόνου δὲ ἁγνὸν καὶ
πάντων τῶν περὶ τὰ τοιαῦτα εἰς τὰ θεῖα ἁμαρ-
τανομένων αὐτὸν καὶ πατέρα καὶ μητέρα κατὰ
ταὐτὰ βεβιωκότας. ἐκ Δελφῶν δὲ χρὴ νόμους

---

[1] [οἷς] ἤδη: οἷς μὴ MSS. : ὀλιγίστοις Stephens.
[2] ὁμονόων England : ὁμονοῶν MSS.
[3] ἱερέων Stobaeus : ἱερῶν MSS.

CLIN. Certainly.

ATH. Let us state, then, that for the temples there must be temple-keepers and priests and priestesses; and for roads and buildings and the due ordering thereof, and for men, and beasts too, to prevent their doing wrong, and to secure that the order proper to States is observed both within the city bounds and in the suburbs, we must select three kinds of officers: those who deal with the matters just mentioned we shall call "city-stewards," and those dealing with the ordering of the market, "market-stewards." Priests of temples, or priestesses, who hold hereditary priesthoods should not be disturbed; but if,—as is likely to be the case in such matters with a people who are being organised for the first time,—few or none have them already established, then we must establish priests and priestesses to be temple-keepers for the gods. In establishing all these offices, we must make the appointments partly by election and partly by lot,[1] mingling democratic with non-democratic methods, to secure mutual friendliness, in every rural and urban district, so that all may be as unanimous as possible.[2] As to the priests, we shall entrust it to the god himself to ensure his own good pleasure, by committing their appointment to the divine chance of the lot; but each person who gains the lot we shall test, first, as to whether he is sound and true-born, and secondly, as to whether he comes from houses that are as pure as possible, being himself clean from murder and all such offences against religion, and of parents that have lived by the same rule. They ought to bring

[1] Cp. Ar. *Pol.* 1300ª 19 ff.
[2] Cp. 738 D ff., 771 E f.

759 περὶ τὰ θεῖα πάντα κομισαμένους καὶ κατα-
στήσαντας ἐπ' αὐτοῖς ἐξηγητὰς τούτοις χρῆσθαι.
D κατ' ἐνιαυτὸν δὲ εἶναι καὶ μὴ μακρότερον τὴν
ἱερωσύνην ἑκάστην, ἔτη δὲ μὴ ἔλαττον ἑξήκοντα
ἡμῖν εἴη γεγονὼς ὁ μέλλων καθ' ἱεροὺς νόμους
περὶ τὰ θεῖα ἱκανῶς ἁγιστεύσειν· ταῦτα δὲ καὶ
περὶ τῶν ἱερειῶν ἔστω τὰ νόμιμα. τοὺς δὲ
ἐξηγητὰς τρὶς φερέτωσαν μὲν αἱ τέτταρες φυλαὶ
τέτταρας ἕκαστον ἐξ αὐτῶν, τρεῖς δὲ οἷς ἂν
πλείστη γένηται ψῆφος δοκιμάσαντας ἐννέα
πέμπειν εἰς Δελφοὺς ἀνελεῖν ἐξ ἑκάστης τριάδος
E ἕνα· τὴν δὲ δοκιμασίαν αὐτῶν καὶ τοῦ χρόνου
τὴν ἡλικίαν εἶναι καθάπερ τῶν ἱερέων. οὗτοι
δὲ ἔστων ἐξηγηταὶ διὰ βίου· τὸν δέ γε λιπόντα
προαιρείσθωσαν αἱ τέτταρες φυλαί, ὅθεν ἂν
ἐκλίπῃ. ταμίας δὲ δὴ τῶν τε ἱερῶν χρημάτων
ἑκάστοις τοῖς ἱεροῖς καὶ τεμενῶν καὶ καρπῶν
760 τούτων καὶ μισθώσεων κυρίους αἱρεῖσθαι μὲν ἐκ
τῶν μεγίστων τιμημάτων τρεῖς εἰς τὰ μέγιστα
ἱερά, δύο δ' εἰς τὰ σμικρότερα, πρὸς δὲ τὰ
ἐμμελέστατα ἕνα· τὴν δὲ αἵρεσιν τούτων καὶ τὴν
δοκιμασίαν γίγνεσθαι καθάπερ ἡ τῶν στρατηγῶν
ἐγίγνετο. καὶ τὰ μὲν αὖ περὶ τὰ ἱερὰ ταῦτα
γιγνέσθω.

Ἀφρούρητον δὲ δὴ μηδὲν εἰς δύναμιν ἔστω.
πόλεως μὲν οὖν αἱ φρουραὶ πέρι ταύτῃ γιγνέ-
σθωσαν, στρατηγῶν ἐπιμελουμένων καὶ ταξιάρχων
καὶ ἱππάρχων καὶ φυλάρχων καὶ πρυτάνεων καὶ
B δὴ καὶ ἀστυνόμων καὶ ἀγορανόμων, ὁπόταν

---

[1] i.e. official exponents of sacred law ; cp. 775 A, 828 B.
[2] The 12 tribes are divided into 3 groups of 4 each : each
group appoints 3, making 9 in all : the other 3 required

420

from Delphi laws about all matters of religion, and appoint interpreters [1] thereof, and make use of those laws. Each priestly office should last for one year and no longer; and the person who is to officiate in sacred matters efficiently according to the laws of religion should be not less than sixty years old: and the same rules shall hold good also for priestesses. For the interpreters the tribes shall vote four at a time, by three votings, for four men, one from each tribe; [2] and when the three men for whom most votes are cast have been tested, they shall send the other nine to Delphi for the oracle to select one from each triad; and the rules as to their age and testing shall be the same as for the priests. These men shall hold office for life as interpreters; and when one falls out, the four tribes [3] shall elect a substitute from the tribe he belonged to. As treasurers to control the sacred funds in each of the temples, and the sacred glebes, with their produce and their rents, we must choose from the highest property-classes three men for the largest temples, two for the smaller, and one for the least extensive; and the method of selecting and testing these shall be the same as that adopted in the case of the commanders. Such shall be the regulations concerning matters of religion.

Nothing, so far as possible, shall be left unguarded. As regards the city, the task of guarding shall be in charge of the commanders, taxiarchs, hipparchs, phylarchs and prytaneis, and also of the city-stewards and market-stewards, wherever we

to make up the full number (12) are selected by the Oracle from the 9 candidates next on the list.

[3] *i.e.* the tribal group by which he was elected.

760 αἱρεθέντες ἡμῖν καταστῶσί τινες ἱκανῶς· τὴν δὲ
ἄλλην χώραν φυλάττειν πᾶσαν κατὰ τάδε.
δώδεκα μὲν ἡμῖν ἡ χώρα πᾶσα εἰς δύναμιν ἴσα
μόρια νενέμηται, φυλὴ δὲ μία τῷ μορίῳ ἑκάστῳ
ἐπικληρωθεῖσα [κατ᾽ ἐνιαυτὸν][1] παρεχέτω πέντε
οἷον ἀγρονόμους τε καὶ φρουράρχους,[2] τούτοις δ᾽
ἔστω καταλέξασθαι τῆς αὑτῶν φυλῆς ἑκάστῳ
C δώδεκα [τῶν πέντε][3] ἐκ τῶν νέων, μὴ ἔλαττον ἢ
πέντε καὶ εἴκοσιν ἔτη γεγονότας, μὴ πλεῖον δὲ ἢ
τριάκοντα. τούτοις δὲ διακληρωθήτω τὰ μόρια
τῆς χώρας κατὰ μῆνα ἕκαστα ἑκάστοις, ὅπως ἂν
πάσης τῆς χώρας ἔμπειροί τε καὶ ἐπιστήμονες
γίγνωνται πάντες. δύο δ᾽ ἔτη τὴν ἀρχὴν καὶ τὴν
φρουρὰν γίγνεσθαι φρουροῖς τε καὶ ἄρχουσιν.
ὅπως δ᾽ ἂν τὸ πρῶτον λάχωσι τὰ μέρη, [τοὺς τῆς
χώρας τόπους][4] μεταλλάττοντας ἀεὶ τὸν ἑξῆς
τόπον ἑκάστου μηνὸς ἡγεῖσθαι τοὺς φρουράρχους
D ἐπὶ δεξιὰ κύκλῳ· τὸ δ᾽ ἐπὶ δεξιὰ γιγνέσθω τὸ
πρὸς ἕω. περιελθόντος δὲ τοῦ ἐνιαυτοῦ τῷ
δευτέρῳ ἔτει, ἵνα ὡς πλεῖστοι τῶν φρουρῶν μὴ
μόνον ἔμπειροι τῆς χώρας γίγνωνται κατὰ μίαν
ὥραν τοῦ ἐνιαυτοῦ, πρὸς τῇ χώρᾳ δὲ ἅμα καὶ τῆς
ὥρας ἑκάστης περὶ ἕκαστον τὸν τόπον τὸ γιγνόμενον ὡς πλεῖστοι καταμάθωσιν, οἱ τότε ἡγούμενοι πάλιν ἀφηγείσθωσαν εἰς τὸν εὐώνυμον ἀεὶ
E μεταβάλλοντες τόπον, ἕως ἂν τὸ δεύτερον δι-
εξέλθωσιν ἔτος. τῷ τρίτῳ δὲ ἄλλους ἀγρονόμους
αἱρεῖσθαι καὶ φρουράρχους [τοὺς πέντε τῶν
δώδεκα ἐπιμελητάς].[5]

Ἐν δὲ δὴ ταῖς διατριβαῖς τῷ τόπῳ ἑκάστῳ τὴν

---

[1] [κατ᾽ ἐνιαυτὸν] bracketed by England.
[2] φρουράρχους Euseb., Herm. : φυλάρχους MSS.

have such officials properly selected and appointed.
All the rest of the country must be guarded in
the following manner: we have marked out the
whole country as nearly as possible into twelve
equal portions: to each portion one tribe shall be
assigned by lot, and it shall provide five men to
act as land-stewards and phrourarchs ("watch-cap-
tains"); it shall be the duty of each of the Five to
select twelve young men from his own tribe of an
age neither under 25 nor over 30. To these groups
of twelve the twelve portions of the country shall
be assigned, one to each in rotation for a month
at a time, so that all of them may gain experience
and knowledge of all parts of the country. The
period of office and of service for guards and officers
shall be two years. From the portion in which
they are stationed first by the lot they shall pass
on month by month to the next district, under the
leadership of the phrourarchs, in a direction from
left to right,—and that will be from west to east.
When the first year is completed, in order that
as many as possible of the guards may not only
become familiar with the country in one season of
the year, but may also learn about what occurs in
each several district at different seasons, their
leaders shall lead them back again in the reverse
direction, constantly changing their district, until
they have completed their second year of service.
For the third year they must elect other land-
stewards and phrourarchs.

During their periods of residence in each district

---

³ [τῶν πέντε] bracketed by F. H. Dale.
⁴ [τοὺς . . . τόπους] bracketed by England.
⁵ [τοὺς . . . ἐπιμελητάς] bracketed by Schanz.

760 ἐπιμέλειαν εἶναι τοιάνδε τινά· πρῶτον μὲν ὅπως
εὐερκὴς ἡ χώρα πρὸς τοὺς πολεμίους ὅτι μάλιστα
ἔσται, ταφρεύοντάς τε ὅσα ἂν τούτου δέῃ καὶ
ἀποσκάπτοντας καὶ ἐνοικοδομήμασιν[1] εἰς δύναμιν εἴργοντας τοὺς ἐπιχειροῦντας ὁτιοῦν τὴν
761 χώραν καὶ τὰ κτήματα κακουργεῖν, χρωμένους
δ᾽ ὑποζυγίοις καὶ τοῖς οἰκέταις τοῖς ἐν τῷ τόπῳ
ἑκάστῳ πρὸς ταῦτα, δι᾽ ἐκείνων ποιοῦντας, ἐκείνοις ἐπιστατοῦντας, τῶν οἰκείων ἔργων αὐτῶν
ἀργίας ὅτι μάλιστα ἐκλεγομένους. δύσβατα δὲ
δὴ πάντα ποιεῖν τοῖς ἐχθροῖς, τοῖς δὲ φίλοις
ὅτι μάλιστα εὔβατα ἀνθρώποις τε καὶ ὑποζυγίοις καὶ βοσκήμασιν, ὁδῶν τε ἐπιμελουμένους,
ὅπως ὡς ἡμερώταται ἕκασται γίγνωνται, καὶ τῶν
ἐκ Διὸς ὑδάτων, ἵνα τὴν χώραν μὴ κακουργῇ,
μᾶλλον δ᾽ ὠφελῇ ῥέοντα ἐκ τῶν ὑψηλῶν εἰς
B τὰς ἐν τοῖς ὄρεσι νάπας ὅσαι κοῖλαι, τὰς ἐκροὰς
αὐτῶν εἴργοντας οἰκοδομήμασί τε καὶ ταφρεύ-
μασιν, ὅπως ἂν τὰ παρὰ τοῦ Διὸς ὕδατα κατα-
δεχόμεναι καὶ πίνουσαι, τοῖς ὑποκάτωθεν ἀγροῖς
τε καὶ τόποις πᾶσι νάματα καὶ κρήνας ποιοῦ-
σαι, καὶ τοὺς αὐχμηροτάτους τόπους πολυύδρους
τε καὶ εὐύδρους ἀπεργάζωνται· τά τε πηγαῖα
ὕδατα, ἐάν τέ τις ποταμὸς ἐάν τε καὶ κρήνη
ᾖ, κοσμοῦντες φυτεύμασί τε καὶ οἰκοδομήμασιν
C εὐπρεπέστερα καὶ συνάγοντες μεταλλείαις νάματα πάντα ἄφθονα ποιῶσιν ὑδρείας τε καθ᾽
ἑκάστας τὰς ὥρας, εἴ τί που ἄλσος ἢ τέμενος
περὶ ταῦτα ἀνειμένον [ᾖ],[2] τὰ ῥεύματα ἀφιέντες
εἰς αὐτὰ τὰ τῶν θεῶν ἱερὰ κοσμῶσι. πανταχῇ

---

[1] ἐνοικοδομήμασιν Schneider: ἐν οἰκοδομήμασιν MSS.
[2] [ᾖ] bracketed by Schanz.

their duties shall be as follows: first, in order to
ensure that the country shall be fenced as well as
possible against enemies, they shall make channels
wherever needed, and dig moats and build cross-
walls, so as to keep out to the best of their power
those who attempt in any way to damage the
country and its wealth; and for these purposes
they shall make use of the beasts of burden and
the servants in each district, employing the former
and supervising the latter, and choosing always,
so far as possible, the times when these people
are free from their own business. In all respects
they must make movement as difficult as possible
for enemies, but for friends—whether men, mules
or cattle—as easy as possible, by attending to
the roads, that they all may become as level as
possible, and to the rain-waters, that they may
benefit instead of injuring the country, as they
flow down from the heights into all the hollow
valleys in the mountains: they shall dam the out-
flows of their flooded dales by means of walls and
channels, so that by storing up or absorbing the
rains from heaven, and by forming pools or springs in
all the low-lying fields and districts, they may
cause even the driest spots to be abundantly
supplied with good water. As to spring-waters,
be they streams or fountains, they shall beautify
and embellish them by means of plantations and
buildings, and by connecting the pools by hewn
tunnels they shall make them all abundant, and
by using water-pipes they shall beautify at all
seasons of the year any sacred glebe or grove that
may be close at hand, by directing the streams
right into the temples of the gods. And every-

PLATO

761 δὲ ἐν τοῖς τοιούτοις γυμνάσια χρὴ κατασκευάζειν
τοὺς νέους αὐτοῖς τε καὶ τοῖς γέρουσι γεροντικὰ
λουτρὰ [θερμὰ]¹ παρέχοντας, ὕλην παρατιθέντας
D αὔην [καὶ ξηρὰν]² ἄφθονον, ἐπ᾽ ὀνήσει καμνόντων τε νόσοις καὶ πόνοις τετρυμένα γεωργικοῖς
σώματα δεχομένους εὐμενῶς ἰατροῦ δέξιν μὴ
πάνυ σοφοῦ βελτίονα συχνῷ.

Ταῦτα μὲν οὖν καὶ τὰ τοιαῦτα πάντα κόσμος τε
καὶ ὠφέλεια τοῖς τόποις γίγνοιτ᾽ ἂν μετὰ παιδιᾶς
οὐδαμῇ ἀχαρίτου· σπουδὴ δὲ περὶ ταῦτα ἥδε ἔστω.
τοὺς ἑξήκοντα ἑκάστους τὸν αὐτῶν τόπον φυλάττειν μὴ μόνον πολεμίων ἕνεκα ἀλλὰ καὶ τῶν φίλων
φασκόντων εἶναι. γειτόνων δὲ καὶ τῶν ἄλλων
E πολιτῶν ἢν ἄλλος ἄλλον ἀδικῇ, δοῦλος ἢ ἐλεύθερος, δικάζοντας τῷ ἀδικεῖσθαι φάσκοντι, τὰ μὲν
σμικρὰ αὐτοὺς τοὺς πέντε ἄρχοντας, τὰ δὲ μείζονα
μετὰ τῶν δώδεκα [τοὺς ἑπτακαίδεκα]³ δικάζειν
μέχρι τριῶν μνῶν, ὅσα ἂν ἕτερος ἑτέρῳ ἐπικαλῇ.
δικαστὴν δὲ καὶ ἄρχοντα ἀνυπεύθυνον οὐδένα
δικάζειν καὶ ἄρχειν δεῖ πλὴν τῶν τὸ τέλος ἐπιτι-
θέντων οἷον βασιλέων. καὶ δὴ καὶ τοὺς ἀγρονόμους τούτους, ἐὰν ὑβρίζωσί τι περὶ τοὺς ὧν
762 ἐπιμελοῦνται, προστάξεις τε προστάττοντες
ἀνίσους καὶ ἐπιχειροῦντες λαμβάνειν τε καὶ
φέρειν τῶν ἐν ταῖς γεωργίαις μὴ πείσαντες, καὶ
ἐὰν δέχωνταί τι κολακείας ἕνεκα διδόντων ἢ [καὶ
δίκας]⁴ ἀδίκως διανέμωσι, ταῖς μὲν θωπείαις
ὑπείκοντες ὀνείδη φερέσθωσαν ἐν πάσῃ τῇ πόλει,
τῶν δὲ ἄλλων ἀδικημάτων ὅ τι ἂν ἀδικῶσι τοὺς

---

¹ [θερμὰ] bracketed by Naber, England.
² [καὶ ξηρὰν] I bracket.
³ [τοὺς ἑπτακαίδεκα] bracketed by Hug, Schanz.

where in such spots the young men should erect
gymnasia both for themselves and for the old men
—providing warm baths for the old: they should
keep there a plentiful supply of dry wood, and
give a kindly welcome and a helping hand to sick
folk and to those whose bodies are worn with the
toils of husbandry—a welcome far better than a
doctor who is none too skilful.

They shall carry on these, and all similar operations,
in the country districts, by way of ornament as well as
use, and to furnish recreation also of no ungraceful
kind. The serious duties in this department shall be
as follows:—The Sixty must guard each their own district, not only because of enemies, but in view also
of those who profess to be friends. And if one either
of the foreign neighbours or of the citizens injures
another citizen, be the culprit a slave or a freeman,
the judges for the complainant shall be the Five
officers themselves in petty cases, and the Five each
with their twelve subordinates in more serious cases,
where the damages claimed are up to three minae.
No judge or official should hold office without being
subject to an audit, excepting only those who, like
kings, form a court of final appeal. So too with
regard to these land-stewards: if they do any
violence to those whom they supervise, by imposing
unfair charges, or by trying to plunder some of their
farm-stores without their consent, or if they take a
gift intended as a bribe, or distribute goods unjustly
—for yielding to seduction they shall be branded
with disgrace throughout the whole State; and in
respect of all other wrongs they have committed

---

⁴ [καὶ δίκας] bracketed by England.

762 ἐν τῷ τόπῳ, τῶν μέχρι μνᾶς ἐν τοῖς κωμήταις καὶ
γείτοσιν ὑπεχέτωσαν ἑκόντες δίκας, τῶν δὲ μειζόνων ἑκάστοτε ἀδικημάτων ἢ καὶ τῶν ἐλαττόνων,
B ἐὰν μὴ 'θέλωσιν ὑπέχειν πιστεύοντες τῷ μεθί-
στασθαι κατὰ μῆνας εἰς ἕτερον ἀεὶ τόπον φεύγον-
τες ἀποφευξεῖσθαι, τούτων πέρι λαγχάνειν μὲν
ἐν ταῖς κοιναῖς δίκας τὸν ἀδικούμενον, ἐὰν δ' ἕλῃ,
τὴν διπλασίαν πραττέσθω τὸν ὑποφεύγοντα καὶ
μὴ ἐθελήσαντα ὑποσχεῖν ἑκόντα τιμωρίαν.

Διαιτάσθων δὲ οἵ τε ἄρχοντες οἵ τε ἀγρονόμοι
τὰ δύο ἔτη τοιόνδε τινὰ τρόπον. πρῶτον μὲν δὴ
C καθ' ἑκάστους τοὺς τόπους εἶναι ξυσσίτια, ἐν οἷς
κοινῇ τὴν δίαιταν ποιητέον ἅπασιν· ὁ δὲ ἀπο-
συσσιτήσας κἂν ἡντιναοῦν ἡμέραν ἢ νύκτα ἀποκοι-
μηθεὶς μὴ τῶν ἀρχόντων ταξάντων ἢ πάσης τινὸς
ἀνάγκης ἐπιπεσούσης, ἐὰν ἀποφήνωσιν αὐτὸν οἱ
πέντε καὶ γράψαντες θῶσιν ἐν ἀγορᾷ καταλελυ-
κότα τὴν φρουράν, ὀνείδη τε ἐχέτω τὴν πολιτείαν
ὡς προδιδοὺς τὸ ἑαυτοῦ μέρος, κολαζέσθω τε
πληγαῖς ὑπὸ τοῦ συντυγχάνοντος καὶ ἐθέλοντος
D κολάζειν ἀτιμωρήτως. τῶν δὲ ἀρχόντων αὐτῶν
ἐάν τίς τι δρᾷ τοιοῦτον αὐτός, ἐπιμελεῖσθαι μὲν
τοῦ τοιούτου πάντας τοὺς ἑξήκοντα χρεών, ὁ δὲ
αἰσθόμενός τε καὶ πυθόμενος μὴ ἐπεξιὼν ἐν τοῖς
αὐτοῖς ἐνεχέσθω νόμοις καὶ πλείονι τῶν νέων
ζημιούσθω· περὶ τὰς τῶν νέων ἀρχὰς ἠτιμώσθω [1]
πάσας. τούτων δὲ οἱ νομοφύλακες ἐπίσκοποι
ἀκριβεῖς ἔστωσαν, ὅπως ἢ μὴ γίγνηται τὴν ἀρχὴν
ἢ γιγνόμενα τῆς ἀξίας δίκης τυγχάνῃ.

---

[1] ἠτιμώσθω Schanz : ἠτιμάσθω MSS.

against people in the district, up to the value of one mina, they shall voluntarily submit to trial before the villagers and neighbours; and should they on any occasion, in respect of either a greater or lesser wrong, refuse thus to submit,—trusting that by their moving on every month to a new district they will escape trial,—in such cases the injured party must institute proceedings at the public courts, and if he win his suit, he shall exact the double penalty from the defendant who has absconded and refused to submit voluntarily to trial.

The mode of life of the officers and land-stewards during their two years of service shall be of the following kind. First, in each of the districts there shall be common meals, at which all shall mess together. If a man absents himself by day, or by sleeping away at night, without orders from the officers or some urgent cause, and if the Five inform against him and post his name up in the market-place as guilty of deserting his watch, then he shall suffer degradation for being a traitor to his public duty, and whoever meets him and desires to punish him may give him a beating with impunity. And if any one of the officers themselves commits any such act, it will be proper for all the Sixty to keep an eye on him; and if any of them notices or hears of such an act, but fails to prosecute, he shall be held guilty under the same laws, and shall be punished more severely than the young men; he shall be entirely disqualified from holding posts of command over the young men. Over these matters the Law-wardens shall exercise most careful supervision, to prevent if possible their occurrence, and, where they do occur, to ensure that they meet with the punishment they deserve.

762E Δεῖ δὴ πάντ᾽ ἄνδρα διανοεῖσθαι περὶ ἁπάντων
ἀνθρώπων ὡς ὁ μὴ δουλεύσας οὐδ᾽ ἂν δεσπότης
γένοιτο ἄξιος ἐπαίνου, καὶ καλλωπίζεσθαι χρὴ τῷ
καλῶς δουλεῦσαι μᾶλλον ἢ τῷ καλῶς ἄρξαι, πρῶτον μὲν τοῖς νόμοις, ὡς ταύτην τοῖς θεοῖς οὖσαν
δουλείαν, ἔπειτ᾽ ἀεὶ τοῖς πρεσβυτέροις τε καὶ ἐντί-
μως βεβιωκόσι τοὺς νέους.   μετὰ δὲ ταῦτα τῆς καθ᾽
ἡμέραν διαίτης δεῖ τῆς ταπεινῆς καὶ ἀπύρου [1]
γεγευμένον εἶναι τὰ δύο ἔτη ταῦτα τὸν τῶν
ἀγρονόμων γεγονότα. ἐπειδὰν γὰρ δὴ κατα-
763 λεγῶσιν οἱ δώδεκα, ξυνελθόντες μετὰ τῶν πέντε
βουλευέσθωσαν ὡς οἷόνπερ οἰκέται οὐχ ἕξουσιν
αὑτοῖς ἄλλους οἰκέτας τε καὶ δούλους, οὐδ᾽ ἐκ τῶν
ἄλλων γεωργῶν τε καὶ κωμητῶν τοῖς ἐκείνων ἐπὶ
τὰ ἴδια χρήσονται ὑπηρετήματα διακόνοις, ἀλλὰ
μόνον ὅσα εἰς τὰ δημόσια· τὰ δ᾽ ἄλλα αὐτοὶ δι᾽
αὑτῶν διανοηθήτωσαν ὡς βιωσόμενοι διακονοῦν-
τές τε καὶ διακονούμενοι ἑαυτοῖς, πρὸς δὲ τούτοις
πᾶσαν τὴν χώραν διεξερευνώμενοι θέρους καὶ
B χειμῶνος σὺν τοῖς ὅπλοις φυλακῆς τε καὶ
γνωρίσεως ἕνεκα πάντων ἀεὶ τῶν τόπων. κινδυνεύει γὰρ οὐδενὸς ἔλαττον μάθημα εἶναι δι᾽ ἀκρι-
βείας ἐπίστασθαι πάντας τὴν αὑτῶν χώραν· οὗ
δὴ χάριν κυνηγέσια καὶ τὴν ἄλλην θήραν οὐχ
ἧττον ἐπιτηδεύειν δεῖ τὸν ἡβῶντα ἢ τῆς ἄλλης
ἡδονῆς ἅμα καὶ ὠφελείας τῆς περὶ τὰ τοιαῦτα
γιγνομένης πᾶσι. τούτους οὖν αὐτούς τε καὶ τὸ
ἐπιτήδευμα εἴτε τις κρυπτοὺς εἴτε ἀγρονόμους
εἴθ᾽ ὅ τι καλῶν χαίρει τοῦτο προσαγορεύων,

---

[1] ἀπύρου Apelt, England : ἀπόρου MSS.

Now it is needful that every man should hold the view, regarding men in general, that the man who has not been a servant will never become a praiseworthy master, and that the right way to gain honour is by serving honourably rather than by ruling honourably—doing service first to the laws, since this is service to the gods, and, secondly, the young always serving the elder folk and those who have lived honourable lives. In the next place, he who is made a land-steward must have partaken of the daily rations, which are coarse and uncooked, during the two years of service. For whenever the Twelve have been chosen, being assembled together with the Five, they shall resolve that, acting like servants, they will keep no servants or slaves to wait on themselves, nor will they employ any attendants belonging to the other farmers or villagers for their own private needs, but only for public requirements; and in all other respects they shall determine to live a self-supporting life, acting as their own ministers and masters, and thoroughly exploring, moreover, the whole country both by summer and winter, under arms, for the purpose both of fencing and of learning each several district. For that all should have an accurate knowledge of their own country is a branch of learning that is probably second to none: so the young men ought to practise running with hounds and all other forms of hunting, as much for this reason as for the general enjoyment and benefit derived from such sports. With regard, then, to this branch of service—both the men themselves and their duties, whether we choose to call them secret-service men or land-stewards or by any other name—every single man who means to

763C προθύμως πᾶς ἀνὴρ εἰς δύναμιν ἐπιτηδευέτω, ὅσοι μέλλουσι τὴν αὐτῶν πόλιν ἱκανῶς σώζειν.

Τὸ δὲ μετὰ τοῦτο ἀρχόντων αἱρέσεως ἀγορανόμων πέρι καὶ ἀστυνόμων ἦν ἡμῖν ἑπόμενον. ἕποιντο δ' ἂν ἀγρονόμοις ἀστυνόμοι τρεῖς ἑξήκοντα οὖσι, τριχῇ δώδεκα μέρη τῆς πόλεως διαλαβόντες, μιμούμενοι ἐκείνους, τῶν τε ὁδῶν ἐπιμελούμενοι τῶν κατὰ τὸ ἄστυ καὶ τῶν ἐκ τῆς χώρας λεωφόρων εἰς τὴν πόλιν ἀεὶ τεταμένων καὶ τῶν οἰκοδο-
D μιῶν, ἵνα κατὰ νόμους γίγνωνται πᾶσαι, καὶ δὴ καὶ τῶν ὑδάτων, ὁπόσ' ἂν αὐτοῖς πέμπωσι καὶ παραδιδῶσιν οἱ φρουροῦντες τεθεραπευμένα, ὅπως εἰς τὰς κρήνας ἱκανὰ καὶ καθαρὰ πορευόμενα κοσμῇ τε ἅμα καὶ ὠφελῇ τὴν πόλιν. δεῖ δὴ καὶ τούτους δυνατούς τε εἶναι καὶ σχολάζοντας τῶν κοινῶν ἐπιμελεῖσθαι· διὸ προβαλλέσθω μὲν πᾶς ἀνὴρ ἐκ τῶν μεγίστων τιμημάτων ἀστυνόμον ὃν ἂν βούληται, διαχειροτονηθέντων δὲ καὶ ἀφικομένων
E εἰς ἓξ οἷς ἂν πλεῖσται γίγνωνται, τοὺς τρεῖς ἀποκληρωσάντων οἷς τούτων ἐπιμελές· δοκιμασθέντες δὲ ἀρχόντων κατὰ τοὺς τεθέντας αὐτοῖς νόμους.

Ἀγορανόμους δ' ἑξῆς τούτοις αἱρεῖσθαι μὲν ἐκ τῶν δευτέρων καὶ πρώτων τιμημάτων πέντε, τὰ δ' ἄλλα αὐτῶν γίγνεσθαι τὴν αἵρεσιν καθάπερ ἡ τῶν ἀστυνόμων, δέκα ἐκ τῶν ἄλλων χειροτονηθέντων [1] τοὺς πέντε ἀποκληρῶσαι, καὶ δοκιμασθέντας αὐτοὺς ἄρχοντας ἀποφῆναι. χειροτονείτω δὲ πᾶς πάντα· ὁ

---

[1] χειροτονηθέντων : χειροτονηθέντας MSS. (cp. England, who brackets δέκα . . . ἀποφῆναι)

guard his own State efficiently shall do his duty zealously to the best of his power.

The next step in our choice of officials is to appoint market-stewards and city-stewards. After the land-stewards (sixty in number) will come the three city-stewards, who shall divide the twelve sections of the city into three parts, and shall copy the land stewards in having charge of the streets of the city and of the various roads that run into the city from the country, and of the buildings, to see that all these conform to the requirements of the law; and they shall also have charge of all the water-supplies conveyed and passed on to them by the guards in good condition, to ensure that they shall be both pure and plentiful as they pour into the cisterns, and may thus both beautify and benefit the city. Thus it is needful that these men also should have both the ability and the leisure to attend to public affairs. Therefore for the office of city-steward every citizen shall nominate whatever person he chooses from the highest property-class; and when these have been voted on, and they have arrived at the six men for whom most votes have been cast, then those whose duty it is shall select the three by lot; and after passing the scrutiny, these men shall execute the office according to the laws ordained for them.

Next to these they must elect five market-stewards from the second and first property-classes: in all other respects the mode of their election shall be similar to that of the city-stewards; from the ten candidates chosen by voting they shall select the five by lot, and after scrutiny declare them appointed. All shall vote for every

764 δὲ μὴ 'θέλων, ἐὰν εἰσαγγελθῇ πρὸς τοὺς ἄρχοντας,
ζημιούσθω πεντήκοντα δραχμαῖς πρὸς τῷ κακὸς
εἶναι δοκεῖν. ἴτω δ' εἰς ἐκκλησίαν καὶ τὸν κοινὸν
ξύλλογον ὁ βουλόμενος, ἐπάναγκες δ' ἔστω τῷ
τῶν δευτέρων καὶ πρώτων τιμημάτων, δέκα δραχμαῖς ζημιουμένῳ ἐὰν μὴ παρὼν ἐξετάζηται τοῖς
ξυλλόγοις. τρίτῳ δὲ τιμήματι καὶ τετάρτῳ μὴ
ἐπάναγκες, ἀλλὰ ἀζήμιος ἀφείσθω, ἐὰν μή τι
παραγγείλωσιν οἱ ἄρχοντες πᾶσιν ἔκ τινος ἀνάγ-
B κης ξυνιέναι. τοὺς δὲ δὴ ἀγορανόμους τὸν περὶ
τὴν ἀγορὰν κόσμον διαταχθέντα ὑπὸ νόμων
φυλάττειν καὶ ἱερῶν καὶ κρηνῶν ἐπιμελεῖσθαι
τῶν κατ' ἀγοράν, ὅπως μηδὲν ἀδικῇ μηδείς, τὸν
ἀδικοῦντα δὲ κολάζειν, πληγαῖς μὲν καὶ δεσμοῖς
δοῦλον καὶ ξένον, ἐὰν δ' ἐπιχώριος ὤν τις περὶ τὰ
τοιαῦτα ἀκοσμῇ, μέχρι μὲν ἑκατὸν δραχμῶν
νομίσματος αὐτοὺς εἶναι κυρίους διαδικάζοντας,
μέχρι δὲ διπλασίου τούτου κοινῇ μετὰ ἀστυνόμων
C ζημιοῦν δικάζοντας τῷ ἀδικοῦντι. τὰ αὐτὰ δὲ
καὶ ἀστυνόμοις ἔστω ζημιώματά τε καὶ κολάσεις
ἐν τῇ ἑαυτῶν ἀρχῇ, μέχρι μὲν μνᾶς αὐτοὺς ζη-
μιοῦντας, τὴν διπλασίαν δὲ μετὰ ἀγορανόμων.

Μουσικῆς δὲ τὸ μετὰ τοῦτο καὶ γυμναστικῆς
ἄρχοντας καθίστασθαι πρέπον ἂν εἴη, διττοὺς
ἑκατέρων, τοὺς μὲν παιδείας αὐτῶν ἕνεκα, τοὺς δὲ
ἀγωνιστικῆς. παιδείας μὲν βούλεται λέγειν ὁ νόμος
γυμνασίων καὶ διδασκαλείων ἐπιμελητὰς κόσμου
D καὶ παιδεύσεως ἅμα καὶ τῆς περὶ ταῦτα ἐπιμελείας
τῶν φοιτήσεών τε πέρι καὶ οἰκήσεων ἀρρένων καὶ

434

official : any man who refuses to do so, if reported to the officials, shall be fined fifty drachmae, besides being declared to be a bad citizen. Whoso wishes shall attend the Ecclesia and the public assembly ; and for members of the second and first property-classes attendance shall be compulsory, anyone who is found to be absent from the assemblies being fined ten drachmae ; but for a member of the third or fourth class it shall not be compulsory, and he shall escape without a fine, unless the officials for some urgent reason charge everyone to attend. The market-stewards must see to it that the market is conducted as appointed by law : they must supervise the temples and fountains in the market, to see that no one does any damage ; in case anyone does damage, if he be a slave or a stranger, they shall punish him with stripes and bonds, while if a native is guilty of such misconduct, they shall have power to inflict a fine up to a hundred drachmae of their own motion, and to fine a wrongdoer up to twice that amount, when acting in conjunction with the city-stewards. Similarly, the city-stewards shall have power of fining and punishing in their own sphere, fining up to a mina of their own motion, and up to twice that sum in conjunction with the market-stewards.

It will be proper next to appoint officials for music and gymnastics,—two grades for each department, the one for education, the other for managing competitions. By education-officers the law means supervisors of gymnasia and schools, both in respect of their discipline and teaching and of the control of the attendances and accommodation both for girls and boys. By competition-officers it means umpires

764 θηλειῶν κορῶν, ἀγωνίας δὲ ἔν τε τοῖς γυμνικοῖς καὶ
περὶ τὴν μουσικὴν ἀθλοθέτας ἀθληταῖς, διττοὺς
αὖ τούτους [περὶ μουσικὴν μὲν ἑτέρους, περὶ
ἀγωνίαν δ' ἄλλους].[1] ἀγωνιστικῆς μὲν οὖν ἀνθρώπων τε καὶ ἵππων τοὺς αὐτούς, μουσικῆς δὲ
ἑτέρους μὲν τοὺς περὶ μονῳδίαν τε καὶ μιμητικήν,
E οἷον ῥαψῳδῶν καὶ κιθαρῳδῶν καὶ αὐλητῶν καὶ
πάντων τῶν τοιούτων ἀθλοθέτας αἱρετοὺς[2] πρέπον
ἂν εἴη γίγνεσθαι, τῶν δὲ περὶ χορῳδίαν ἄλλους.
πρῶτον δὴ περὶ τὴν τῶν χορῶν παιδιὰν παίδων τε
καὶ ἀρρένων[3] καὶ θηλειῶν κορῶν ἐν ὀρχήσεσι καὶ
τῇ τάξει τῇ ἁπάσῃ γιγνομένῃ[4] μουσικῇ τοὺς
ἄρχοντας αἱρεῖσθαί που χρεών· ἱκανὸς δὲ εἷς
ἄρχων αὐτοῖς, μὴ ἔλαττον τετταράκοντα γεγονὼς
765 ἐτῶν. ἱκανὸς δὲ καὶ περὶ μονῳδίαν εἷς, μὴ ἔλαττον ἢ τριάκοντα γεγονὼς ἐτῶν, εἰσαγωγεύς τε εἶναι
καὶ τοῖς ἀμιλλωμένοις τὴν διάκρισιν ἱκανῶς ἀπο-
διδούς. τὸν δὴ χορῶν ἄρχοντα καὶ διαθετῆρα
αἱρεῖσθαι χρὴ τοιόνδε τινὰ τρόπον. ὅσοι μὲν
φιλοφρόνως ἐσχήκασι περὶ τὰ τοιαῦτα, εἰς τὸν
ξύλλογον ἴτωσαν, ἐπιζήμιοι ἐὰν μὴ ἴωσι· τούτου
δὲ οἱ νομοφύλακες κριταί· τοῖς δ' ἄλλοις, ἐὰν μὴ
βούλωνται, μηδὲν ἐπάναγκες ἔστω. καὶ τὴν
προβολὴν δὴ τὸν αἱρούμενον ἐκ τῶν ἐμπείρων
B ποιητέον, ἔν τε τῇ δοκιμασίᾳ κατηγόρημα ἐν τοῦτ'
ἔστω καὶ ἀπηγόρημα, τῶν μὲν ὡς ἄπειρος ὁ λαχών,
τῶν δ' ὡς ἔμπειρος· ὃς δ' ἂν εἷς ἐκ προχειροτονηθέντων δέκα λάχῃ δοκιμασθεὶς τὸν ἐνιαυτὸν τῶν
χορῶν ἀρχέτω κατὰ νόμον. κατὰ ταὐτὰ δὲ τούτοις

---

[1] [περὶ . . . ἄλλους] bracketed by England.
[2] αἱρετοὺς : ἑτέρους MSS., edd. (bracketed by Stallb.)
[3] ἀρρένων : ἀνδρῶν MSS., edd.

for the competitors both in gymnastic and in music, these also being of two grades. For competitions there should be the same umpires both for men and for horses; but in the case of music it will be proper to have separate umpires for solos and for mimetic performances,—I mean, for instance, one set chosen for rhapsodists, harpers, flute-players, and all such musicians, and another set for choral performers. We ought to choose first the officials for the playful exercise of choirs of children and lads and girls in dances and all other regular methods of music; and for these one officer suffices, and he must be not under forty years of age. And for solo performances one umpire, of not less than thirty years, is sufficient, to act as introducer [1] and to pass an adequate judgment upon the competitors. The officer and manager of the choirs they must appoint in some such way as the following. All those who are devoted to these subjects shall attend the assembly, and if they refuse to attend they shall be liable to a fine—a matter which the Law-wardens shall decide: any others who are unwilling to attend shall be subject to no compulsion. Every elector must make his nomination from the list of those who are experts: in the scrutiny, affirmation and negation shall be confined to one point only—on the one side, that the candidate is expert, on the other side, that he is not expert; and whichever of the ten who come first on votes is elected after the scrutiny shall be the officer for the year in charge of the choirs according to law. In the same way as these they

---

[1] *i.e.* to take entries and assign places to the competitors.

⁴ γιγνομένην England : γιγνομένῃ MSS.

765 καὶ ταύτῃ ὁ λαχὼν τὸν ἐνιαυτὸν ἐκεῖνον τῶν ἀφικομένων εἰς κρίσιν μονῳδιῶν τε καὶ συναυλιῶν ἀρχέτω,
C [εἰς τοὺς κριτὰς ἀποδιδοὺς ὁ λαχὼν τὴν κρίσιν].[1]
μετὰ δὲ ταῦτα χρεὼν ἀγωνίας ἀθλοθέτας αἱρεῖσθαι τῆς περὶ τὰ γυμνάσια ἵππων τε καὶ ἀνθρώπων
ἐκ τῶν τρίτων τε καὶ ἔτι τῶν δευτέρων τιμημάτων.
εἰς δὲ τὴν αἵρεσιν ἔστω μὲν ἐπάναγκες τοῖς τρισὶ
πορεύεσθαι τιμήμασι, τὸ σμικρότατον δὲ ἀζήμιον
ἀφείσθω. τρεῖς δ᾽ ἔστωσαν οἱ λαχόντες, τῶν
προχειροτονηθέντων μὲν εἴκοσι, λαχόντων δὲ ἐκ
τῶν εἴκοσι τριῶν, οὓς ἂν καὶ ψῆφος ἡ τῶν δοκι-
D μαζόντων δοκιμάσῃ. ἐὰν δέ τις ἀποδοκιμασθῇ
καθ᾽ ἡντιναοῦν ἀρχῆς λῆξιν καὶ κρίσιν, ἄλλους
ἀνθαιρεῖσθαι κατὰ ταὐτὰ καὶ τὴν δοκιμασίαν
ὡσαύτως αὐτῶν πέρι ποιεῖσθαι.

Λοιπὸς δὲ ἄρχων περὶ τὰ προειρημένα ἡμῖν
ὁ τῆς παιδείας ἐπιμελητὴς πάσης θηλειῶν τε
καὶ ἀρρένων. εἷς μὲν δὴ καὶ ὁ τούτων ἄρξων
ἔστω κατὰ νόμους, ἐτῶν μὲν γεγονὼς μὴ ἔλαττον ἢ πεντήκοντα, παίδων δὲ γνησίων πατήρ,
μάλιστα μὲν υἱέων καὶ θυγατέρων, εἰ δὲ μή,
E θάτερα· διανοηθήτω δὲ αὐτός τε ὁ προκριθεὶς
καὶ ὁ προκρίνων ὡς οὖσαν ταύτην τὴν ἀρχὴν
τῶν ἐν τῇ πόλει ἀκροτάτων ἀρχῶν πολὺ μεγίστην.
παντὸς γὰρ δὴ φυτοῦ ἡ πρώτη βλάστη καλῶς
ὁρμηθεῖσα πρὸς ἀρετὴν τῆς αὑτοῦ φύσεως κυριω-
τάτη τέλος ἐπιθεῖναι τὸ πρόσφορον, τῶν τε ἄλλων
φυτῶν καὶ τῶν ζῴων ἡμέρων καὶ ἀγρίων [καὶ
766 ἀνθρώπων].[2] ἄνθρωπος δέ, ὥς φαμεν, ἥμερον,
ὅμως μὴν παιδείας μὲν ὀρθῆς τυχὸν καὶ φύσεως

---

[1] [εἰς . . . κρίσιν] bracketed by Wagner, Schanz.
[2] [καὶ ἀνθρώπων] bracketed by England.

shall appoint the officer elected to preside for the
year over those who enter for competitions in solos
and joint performances on the flute. Next it is
proper to choose umpires for the athletic contests
of horses and men from among the third and the
second property-classes: this election it shall be
compulsory for the first three classes to attend, but
the lowest class shall be exempt from fines for non-
attendance. Three shall be appointed: twenty
having been first selected by show of hand, three
out of the twenty shall be chosen by lot; and they
shall be subject also to the approval of the scrutineers.
Should any candidate be disqualified in any voting
or testing for office, they shall elect a substitute, and
carry out the scrutiny by the same method as in the
case of the original candidate.

In the department we have been dealing with,
we have still to appoint an officer who shall
preside over the whole range of education of
both boys and girls. For this purpose there
shall be one officer legally appointed: he shall
not be under fifty years of age, and shall be the
father of legitimate children of either sex, or
preferably of both sexes. Both the candidate that
is put first, and the elector who puts him first, must
be convinced that of the highest offices of State
this is by far the most important. For in the case
of every creature—plant or animal, tame [1] and wild
alike—it is the first shoot, if it sprouts out well, that
is most effective in bringing to its proper development the essential excellence of the creature in
question. Man, as we affirm, is a tame creature:
none the less, while he is wont to become an animal

---

[1] *i.e.* "domesticated" animals, and "garden" plants.

766 εὐτυχοῦς θειότατον ἡμερώτατόν τε ζῷον γίγνεσθαι
φιλεῖ, μὴ ἱκανῶς δὲ ἢ μὴ καλῶς τραφὲν ἀγριώτα-
τον ὁπόσα φύει γῆ. ὧν ἕνεκα οὐ δεύτερον οὐδὲ
πάρεργον δεῖ τὴν παίδων τροφὴν τὸν νομοθέτην
ἐᾶν γίγνεσθαι, πρῶτον δὲ ἄρξασθαι, χρεὼν τὸν
μέλλοντα αὐτῶν ἐπιμελήσεσθαι καλῶς αἱρεθῆναι,
τῶν ἐν τῇ πόλει ὃς ἂν ἄριστος εἰς πάντα ᾖ, τοῦτον
B κατὰ δύναμιν ὅτι μάλιστα αὐτοῖς καθιστάντα
προστάττειν¹ ἐπιμελητήν. αἱ πᾶσαι τοίνυν
ἀρχαὶ πλὴν βουλῆς καὶ πρυτάνεων εἰς τὸ τοῦ
Ἀπόλλωνος ἱερὸν ἐλθοῦσαι φερόντων ψῆφον
κρύβδην, τῶν νομοφυλάκων ὅντιν᾽ ἂν ἕκαστος
ἡγῆται κάλλιστ᾽ ἂν τῶν περὶ παιδείαν ἄρξαι
γενομένων· ᾧ δ᾽ ἂν πλεῖσται ψῆφοι ξυμβῶσι,
δοκιμασθεὶς ὑπὸ τῶν ἄλλων ἀρχόντων τῶν ἑλο-
μένων, πλὴν νομοφυλάκων, ἀρχέτω ἔτη πέντε,
ἕκτῳ δὲ κατὰ ταὐτὰ ἄλλον ἐπὶ ταύτην τὴν ἀρχὴν
C αἱρεῖσθαι.

Ἐὰν δέ τις δημοσίαν ἀρχὴν ἄρχων ἀποθάνῃ πρὶν
ἐξήκειν αὐτῷ τὴν ἀρχὴν πλεῖον ἢ τριάκοντα ἐπι-
δεομένην ἡμερῶν, τὸν αὐτὸν τρόπον ἐπὶ τὴν ἀρχὴν
ἄλλον καθιστάναι οἷς ἦν τοῦτο προσηκόντως μέλον.
καὶ ἐὰν ὀρφανῶν ἐπίτροπος τελευτήσῃ τις, οἱ
προσήκοντες καὶ ἐπιδημοῦντες πρὸς πατρὸς καὶ
μητρὸς μέχρι ἀνεψιῶν παίδων ἄλλον καθιστάντων
ἐντὸς δέκα ἡμερῶν, ἢ ζημιούσθων ἕκαστος δραχμῇ
D τῆς ἡμέρας, μέχριπερ ἂν τοῖς παισὶ καταστήσωσι
τὸν ἐπίτροπον.

Πᾶσα δὲ δήπου πόλις ἄπολις ἂν γίγνοιτο ἐν
ᾗ δικαστήρια μὴ καθεστῶτα εἴη κατὰ τρόπον·
ἄφωνος δ᾽ αὖ δικαστὴς ἡμῖν καὶ μὴ πλείω τῶν

most godlike and tame when he happens to possess
a happy nature combined with right education, if his
training be deficient or bad, he turns out the wildest
of all earth's creatures. Wherefore the lawgiver
must not permit them to treat the education
of children as a matter of secondary or casual
importance ; but, inasmuch as the presiding official
must be well selected, he must begin first by
charging them to appoint as president, to the best of
their power, that one of the citizens who is in every
way the most excellent. Therefore all the officials—
excepting the Council and the prytaneis—shall go to
the temple of Apollo, and shall each cast his vote for
whichever one of the Law-wardens he deems likely
best to control educational affairs. He who gains
most votes, after passing a scrutiny held by the
selecting officials, other than the Law-wardens, shall
hold office for five years : in the sixth year they
shall elect another man for this office in a similar
manner.

If anyone holding a public office dies more than
thirty days before his office terminates, those whose
proper duty it is must appoint a substitute in the same
manner. If a guardian of orphans dies, the relations,
who are residents, on both the father's and mother's
side, as far as cousin's children, shall appoint a
substitute within ten days, failing which they shall
each be fined one drachma *per diem* until they have
appointed the guardian for the children.

A State, indeed, would be no State if it had no
law-courts properly established ; but a judge who was
dumb and who said as little as litigants at a pre-

---

¹ προστάττειν MSS. : προστάτην καὶ Zur., vulg.

766 ἀντιδίκων ἐν ταῖς ἀνακρίσεσι φθεγγόμενος, καθάπερ ἐν ταῖς διαίταις, οὐκ ἄν ποτε ἱκανὸς
γένοιτο περὶ τὴν τῶν δικαίων κρίσιν· ὧν ἕνεκα
οὔτε πολλοὺς ὄντας ῥᾴδιον εὖ δικάζειν οὔτε
ὀλίγους φαύλους. σαφὲς δὲ ἀεὶ τὸ ἀμφισβητού-
Ε μενον χρεὼν γίγνεσθαι παρ᾽ ἑκατέρων, ὁ δὲ χρόνος
ἅμα καὶ τὸ βραδὺ τό τε πολλάκις ἀνακρίνειν
πρὸς τὸ φανερὰν γίγνεσθαι τὴν ἀμφισβήτησιν
ξύμφορον· ὧν ἕνεκα πρῶτον μὲν εἰς γείτονας
ἰέναι χρὴ τοὺς ἐπικαλοῦντας ἀλλήλοις καὶ τοὺς
φίλους τε καὶ ξυνειδότας ὅτι μάλιστα τὰς
767 ἀμφισβητουμένας πράξεις· ἐὰν δ᾽ ἄρα μὴ ἐν
τούτοις τις ἱκανὴν κρίσιν λαμβάνῃ, πρὸς ἄλλο
δικαστήριον ἴτω· τὸ δὲ τρίτον, ἂν τὰ δύο
δικαστήρια μὴ δύνηται διαλλάξαι, τέλος ἐπι-
θέτω τῇ δίκῃ.

Τρόπον δή τινα καὶ τῶν δικαστηρίων αἱ
καταστάσεις ἀρχόντων εἰσὶν αἱρέσεις· πάντα
μὲν γὰρ ἄρχοντα ἀναγκαῖον καὶ δικαστὴν
εἶναί τινων, δικαστὴς δὲ οὐκ ἄρχων καί τινα
τρόπον ἄρχων οὐ πάνυ φαῦλος γίγνεται τὴν τόθ᾽
ἡμέραν ᾗπερ ἂν κρίνων τὴν δίκην ἀποτελῇ.
Β θέντες δὴ καὶ τοὺς δικαστὰς ὡς ἄρχοντας λέγωμεν
τίνες ἂν εἶεν πρέποντες καὶ τίνων ἄρα δικασταὶ
καὶ πόσοι ἐφ᾽ ἕκαστον.

Ἀναγκαιότατον[1] μὲν τοίνυν ἔστω δικαστήριον ὅπερ ἂν αὐτοὶ ἑαυτοῖς ἀποφήνωσιν ἕκαστοι,
κοινῇ τινὰς ἑλόμενοι· δύο δὴ τῶν λοιπῶν ἔστω
κριτήρια, τὸ μὲν ὅταν τίς τινα ἰδιώτην ἰδιώτης,
ἐπαιτιώμενος ἀδικεῖν αὐτόν, ἄγων εἰς δίκην
βούληται διακριθῆναι, τὸ δ᾽ ὁπόταν τὸ δημόσιον

[1] ἀναγκαιότατον: κυριώτατον MSS. (τὸ πρῶτον Susemihl)

liminary inquiry,[1] as do arbitrators,[2] would never prove efficient in deciding questions of justice; consequently it is not easy for a large or for a small body of men to judge well, if they are of poor ability. The matter in dispute on either side must always be made clear, and for elucidating the point at issue, lapse of time, deliberation and frequent questionings are of advantage. Therefore those who challenge each other must go first to the neighbours and friends who know most about the actions in dispute : if a man fails to get an adequate decision from them, he shall repair to another court; and if these two courts are unable to settle the matter, the third court shall put an end to the case.

In a sense we may say that the establishment of law-courts coincides with the election of officials ; for every official must be also a judge of certain matters, while a judge, even if not an official, may be said to be an official of no little importance on the day when he concludes a suit by pronouncing his judgment. Assuming then that the judges are officials, let us declare who will make suitable judges, and of what matters, and how many shall deal with each case.

The most elementary form of court is that which the two parties arrange for themselves, choosing judges by mutual agreement ; of the rest, there shall be two forms of trial,—the one when a private person accuses a private person of injuring him and desires to gain a verdict by bringing him to trial, and the other when a person believes that the

---

[1] *i.e.* an inquiry into the grounds of a proposed action at law, to decide whether or not it should be brought into court.

[2] *i.e.* persons appointed to settle points in dispute, so as to avoid a legal trial in the regular courts.

767 ὑπό τινος τῶν πολιτῶν ἡγῆταί τις ἀδικεῖσθαι
C καὶ βουληθῇ τῷ κοινῷ βοηθεῖν. λεκτέον δ᾽
ὁποῖοί τ᾽ εἰσὶ καὶ τίνες οἱ κριταί. πρῶτον δὴ
δικαστήριον ἡμῖν γιγνέσθω κοινὸν ἅπασι τοῖς
τὸ τρίτον ἀμφισβητοῦσιν ἰδιώταις πρὸς ἀλλήλους, γενόμενον τῇδέ πῃ. πάσας δὴ τὰς ἀρχάς,
ὁπόσαι τε κατ᾽ ἐνιαυτὸν καὶ ὁπόσαι πλείω χρόνον
ἄρχουσιν, ἐπειδὰν μέλλῃ νέος ἐνιαυτὸς μετὰ
θερινὰς τροπὰς τῷ ἐπιόντι μηνὶ γίγνεσθαι, ταύτης τῆς ἡμέρας τῇ πρόσθεν πάντας χρὴ τοὺς
ἄρχοντας συνελθεῖν εἰς ἓν ἱερὸν καὶ τὸν θεὸν
D ὀμόσαντας οἷον ἀπάρξασθαι πάσης ἀρχῆς ἕνα
δικαστήν, ὃς ἂν ἐν ἀρχῇ ἑκάστῃ ἄριστός τε εἶναι
δόξῃ καὶ ἄριστ᾽ ἂν καὶ ὁσιώτατα τὰς δίκας τοῖς
πολίταις αὐτῷ τὸν ἐπιόντα ἐνιαυτὸν φαίνηται
διακρίνειν. τούτων δὲ αἱρεθέντων γίγνεσθαι μὲν
δοκιμασίαν ἐν τοῖς ἑλομένοις αὐτοῖς· ἐὰν δὲ ἀποδοκιμασθῇ τις, ἕτερον ἀνθαιρεῖσθαι κατὰ ταὐτά.
τοὺς δὲ δοκιμασθέντας δικάζειν μὲν τοῖς τἆλλα
δικαστήρια φυγοῦσι, τὴν δὲ ψῆφον φανερὰν
E φέρειν. ἐπηκόους δ᾽ εἶναι καὶ θεατὰς τούτων τῶν
δικῶν ἐξ ἀνάγκης μὲν βουλευτὰς καὶ τοὺς ἄλλους
ἄρχοντας τοὺς ἑλομένους αὐτούς, τῶν δὲ ἄλλων τὸν
βουλόμενον. ἐὰν δέ τις ἐπαιτιᾶταί τινα ἑκόντα
ἀδίκως κρῖναι τὴν δίκην, εἰς τοὺς νομοφύλακας
ἰὼν κατηγορείτω· ὁ δὲ ὀφλὼν τὴν τοιαύτην δίκην
ὑπεχέτω μὲν τοῦ βλάβους τῷ βλαφθέντι τὸ
διπλάσιον [1] τίνειν, ἐὰν δὲ μείζονος ἄξιος εἶναι
δόξῃ ζημίας, προστιμᾶν τοὺς κρίναντας τὴν δίκην

---

[1] διπλάσιον Ritter, England : ἥμισυ MSS.

State is being injured by one of the citizens and
desires to succour the common weal. Who and
what sort the judges are must now be explained.
First, we must have a court common to all private
persons who are having their third [1] dispute with
one another. It shall be formed in this way. On
the day preceding the commencement of a new year
of office—which commences with the month next after
the summer solstice—all the officials, whether holding office for one year only or longer, shall assemble
in the same temple and, after adjuring the god, they
shall dedicate, so to say, one judge from each body
of officials, namely, that member of each body whom
they deem the best man and the most likely to decide
the suits for his fellow-citizens during the ensuing year
in the best and holiest way. These being chosen,
they shall undergo a scrutiny before those who have
chosen them; and should any be disqualified, they
shall choose a substitute in like manner. Those
who pass the scrutiny shall act as judges for those
who have escaped the other courts, and they shall
cast their votes openly. The Councillors, and all the
other officials, who have elected them, shall be
obliged to attend these trials, both to hear and to
see ; and anyone else that wishes may attend. Anyone who accuses a judge of deliberately giving an
unjust judgment shall go to the Law-wardens and
lay his charge before them : a judge that is convicted
on such a charge shall submit to pay double the
amount of the damage done to the injured party ;
and if he be held to deserve a greater penalty, the
judges of the case shall estimate what additional

---

[1] Apparently, this refers to the third court (of appeal)
mentioned above, 767 A 2 ff.

767 ὅ τι χρὴ πρὸς τούτῳ παθεῖν αὐτὸν ἢ ἀποτίνειν
τῷ κοινῷ καὶ τῷ τὴν δίκην δικασαμένῳ. περὶ
δὲ τῶν δημοσίων ἐγκλημάτων ἀναγκαῖον πρῶτον
768 μὲν τῷ πλήθει μεταδιδόναι τῆς κρίσεως· οἱ γὰρ
ἀδικούμενοι πάντες εἰσίν, ὁπόταν τις τὴν πόλιν
ἀδικῇ, καὶ χαλεπῶς ἂν ἐν δίκῃ φέροιεν ἄμοιροι
γιγνόμενοι τῶν τοιούτων διακρίσεων, ἀλλ᾽ ἀρχήν
τε εἶναι χρὴ τῆς τοιαύτης δίκης καὶ τελευτὴν
εἰς τὸν δῆμον ἀποδιδομένην, τὴν δὲ βάσανον ἐν
ταῖς μεγίσταις ἀρχαῖς τρισίν, ἃς ἂν ὅ τε φεύγων
καὶ ὁ διώκων ξυνομολογῆτον· ἐὰν δὲ μὴ δύνησθον
κοινωνῆσαι τῆς ὁμολογίας αὐτοί, τὴν βουλὴν
B ἐπικρίνειν αὐτῶν τὴν αἵρεσιν ἑκατέρου. δεῖ δὲ
δὴ καὶ τῶν ἰδίων δικῶν κοινωνεῖν κατὰ δύναμιν
ἅπαντας· ὁ γὰρ ἀκοινώνητος ὢν ἐξουσίας τοῦ
συνδικάζειν ἡγεῖται τὸ παράπαν τῆς πόλεως οὐ
μέτοχος εἶναι. διὰ ταῦτ᾽ οὖν δὴ καὶ κατὰ φυλὰς
ἀναγκαῖον δικαστήριά τε γίγνεσθαι καὶ κλήρῳ
δικαστὰς ἐκ τοῦ παραχρῆμα ἀδιαφθόρους ταῖς
δεήσεσι δικάζειν· τὸ δὲ τέλος κρίνειν πάντων τῶν
τοιούτων ἐκεῖνο τὸ δικαστήριον ὅ φαμεν εἴς γε
ἀνθρωπίνην δύναμιν ὡς οἷόν τε ἀδιαφθορώτατα
C παρεσκευάσθαι τοῖς μὴ δυναμένοις μήτε ἐν τοῖς
γείτοσι μήτε ἐν τοῖς φυλετικοῖς δικαστηρίοις
ἀπαλλάττεσθαι.

Νῦν δὴ περὶ μὲν δικαστήρια ἡμῖν, ἃ δή φαμεν
οὔθ᾽ ὡς ἀρχὰς οὔθ᾽ ὡς μὴ ῥᾴδιον εἰπόντα ἀναμφισβητήτως εἰρηκέναι, περὶ μὲν ταῦτα οἷον
περιγραφή τις ἔξωθεν περιγεγραμμένη τὰ μὲν

---

[1] The whole of this account (766 E–768 C) of courts and
judges is confused and confusing. It would seem that 2

punishment must be inflicted, or what payment made to the State and to the person who took proceedings. In the matter of offences against the State it is necessary, first of all, that a share in the trial should be given to the populace, for when a wrong is done to the State, it is the whole of the people that are wronged, and they would justly be vexed if they had no share in such trials; so, while it is right that both the beginning and the ending of such a suit should be assigned to the people, the examination shall take place before three of the highest officials mutually agreed upon by both defendant and plaintiff: should they be unable by themselves to reach an agreement, the Council must revise the choice of each of them. In private suits also, so far as possible, all the citizens must have a share; for the man that has no share in helping to judge imagines that he has no part or lot in the State at all. Therefore there must also be courts for each tribe, and judges appointed by lot and to meet the sudden occasion must judge the cases, unbiassed by appeals; but the final verdict in all such cases must rest with that court which we declare to be organised in the most incorruptible way that is humanly possible, specially for the benefit of those who have failed to obtain a settlement of their case either before the neighbours or in the tribal courts.[1]

Thus as concerns the law-courts—which, as we say, cannot easily be called either " offices " or " non-offices " without ambiguity—this outline sketch serves to describe them in part, though there is a

classes of suits are indicated, public and private, and 3 kinds of courts, viz. (1) local courts (composed of neighbours), (2) tribal courts, (3) courts of appeal.

447

768 εἴρηκε, τὰ δ' ἀπολείπει σχεδόν· πρὸς γὰρ τέλει
νομοθεσίας ἡ δικῶν ἀκριβὴς [νόμων]¹ θέσις ἅμα
καὶ διαίρεσις ὀρθότατα γίγνοιτ' ἂν μακρῷ. ταύ-
D ταις μὲν οὖν εἰρήσθω πρὸς τῷ τέλει περιμένειν
ἡμᾶς, αἱ δὲ περὶ τὰς ἄλλας ἀρχὰς καταστάσεις
σχεδὸν τὴν πλείστην εἰλήφασι νομοθεσίαν. τὸ
δὲ ὅλον καὶ ἀκριβὲς περὶ ἑνός τε καὶ πάντων τῶν
κατὰ πόλιν καὶ πολιτικὴν πᾶσαν διοίκησιν² οὐκ
ἔστι γενέσθαι σαφές, πρὶν ἂν ἡ διέξοδος ἀπ'
ἀρχῆς τά τε δεύτερα καὶ τὰ μέσα καὶ πάντα
μέρη τὰ ἑαυτῆς ἀπολαβοῦσα πρὸς τέλος ἀφίκηται.
E νῦν μὴν ἐν τῷ παρόντι μέχρι τῆς τῶν ἀρχόντων
αἱρέσεως γενομένης τελευτὴ μὲν τῶν ἔμπροσθεν
αὕτη γίγνοιτ' ἂν ἱκανή, νόμων δὲ θέσεως ἀρχὴ
καὶ ἀναβολῶν ἅμα καὶ ὄκνων οὐδὲν ἔτι δεομένη.

ΚΛ. Πάντως μοι κατὰ νοῦν, ὦ ξένε, τὰ ἔμπροσθεν εἰρηκώς, τὴν ἀρχὴν νῦν τελευτῇ προσάψας
περὶ τῶν τε εἰρημένων καὶ τῶν μελλόντων
ῥηθήσεσθαι, ταῦτα ἔτι μᾶλλον ἐκείνων εἴρηκας
φιλίως.

769 ΑΘ. Καλῶς τοίνυν ἂν ἡμῖν ἡ πρεσβυτῶν
ἔμφρων παιδιὰ μέχρι δεῦρ' εἴη τὰ νῦν διαπε-
παισμένη.

ΚΛ. Καλὴν τὴν σπουδὴν ἔοικας δηλοῦν τῶν
ἀνδρῶν.

ΑΘ. Εἰκός γε. τόδε δ' ἐννοήσωμεν, εἰ σοὶ
δοκεῖ καθάπερ ἐμοί.

ΚΛ. Τὸ ποῖον δή; καὶ περὶ τίνων;

ΑΘ. Οἶσθ' ὅτι καθάπερ ζωγράφων οὐδὲν πέρας
ἔχειν ἡ πραγματεία δοκεῖ περὶ ἑκάστων τῶν

---

¹ [νόμων] bracketed by Bekker.
² διοίκησιν Ast, Schanz: διοικήσεων MSS.

good deal it omits; for detailed legislation and definition concerning suits would most properly be placed at the conclusion of the legislative code.[1] So let these matters be directed to wait for us at the conclusion; and I should say that the other official posts have had most of the legislation they require for their establishment. But a full and precise account concerning each and all of the State departments and the whole of the civic organisation it is impossible to give clearly until our review has embraced every section of its subject, from the first to the very last, in proper order. So now, at the point where we stand—when our exposition has reached so far as to include the election of the officials—we may find a fit place to terminate our previous subject, and to commence the subject of legislation, which no longer needs any postponements or delays.

CLIN. The previous subject, Stranger, you have treated to our entire satisfaction; but we welcome still more heartily the way you have linked up your past statements with your future statements—the end with the beginning.

ATH. It seems, then, that up to now our ancients' game of reason [2] has been finely played.

CLIN. You are showing, I think, how fine is the serious work of our citizens.

ATH. Very probably: but let us see whether you agree with me about another point.

CLIN. What is it, and whom does it concern?

ATH. You know how, for instance, the painter's art in depicting each several subject seems never to

---

[1] Cp. 853 A ff., 956 B ff.
[2] *i.e.* the "game" of legislation, cp. 685 A, 712 B.

769B ζώων, ἀλλ' ἢ τοῦ χραίνειν ἢ ἀποχραίνειν, ἢ ὅ τι
δή ποτε καλοῦσι τὸ τοιοῦτον οἱ ζωγράφων παῖδες,
οὐκ ἄν ποτε δοκεῖ παύσασθαι κοσμοῦσα, ὥστε
ἐπίδοσιν μηκέτ' ἔχειν εἰς τὸ καλλίω τε καὶ φανε-
ρώτερα γίγνεσθαι τὰ γεγραμμένα.

ΚΛ. Σχεδὸν ἐννοῶ ἀκούων καὶ αὐτὸς ταῦτα ἃ
λέγεις, ἐπεὶ ἐντριβής γε οὐδαμῶς γέγονα τῇ
τοιαύτῃ τέχνῃ.

ΑΘ. Καὶ οὐδέν γε ἐβλάβης. χρησώμεθά γε
μὴν τῷ νῦν παρατυχόντι περὶ αὐτῆς ἡμῖν λόγῳ
C τὸ τοιόνδε, ὡς εἴ ποτέ τις ἐπινοήσειε γράψαι τε
ὡς κάλλιστον ζῷον καὶ τοῦτ' αὖ μηδέποτε ἐπὶ τὸ
φαυλότερον ἀλλ' ἐπὶ τὸ βέλτιον ἴσχειν τοῦ ἐπι-
όντος ἀεὶ χρόνου, ξυννοεῖς ὅτι θνητὸς ὤν, εἰ μή
τινα καταλείψει διάδοχον ὃς [1] ἐπανορθοῦν τε, ἐάν
τι σφάλληται τὸ ζῷον ὑπὸ χρόνων, καὶ τὸ
παραλειφθὲν ὑπὸ τῆς ἀσθενείας τῆς ἑαυτοῦ πρὸς
τὴν τέχνην οἷός τε εἰς τὸ πρόσθεν ἔσται φαιδρύ-
νων ποιεῖν ἐπιδιδόναι, σμικρόν τινα χρόνον αὐτῷ
πόνος παραμενεῖ πάμπολυς;

ΚΛ. Ἀληθῆ.

D ΑΘ. Τί οὖν; ἆρ' οὐ τοιοῦτον δοκεῖ σοι τὸ τοῦ
νομοθέτου βούλημα εἶναι; πρῶτον μὲν γράψαι
τοὺς νόμους πρὸς τὴν ἀκρίβειαν κατὰ δύναμιν
ἱκανῶς· ἔπειτα προϊόντος τοῦ χρόνου καὶ τῶν
δοξάντων ἔργῳ πειρώμενον ἆρ' οἴει τινὰ οὕτως
ἄφρονα γεγονέναι νομοθέτην, ὥστ' ἀγνοεῖν ὅτι
πάμπολλα ἀνάγκη παραλείπεσθαι τοιαῦτα, ἃ
δεῖ τινὰ ξυνεπόμενον ἐπανορθοῦν, ἵνα μηδαμῇ
χείρων, βελτίων δὲ ἡ πολιτεία καὶ ὁ κόσμος
E ἀεὶ γίγνηται περὶ τὴν ᾠκισμένην αὐτῷ πόλιν;

[1] ὃς Hermann, Schanz: τοῦ MSS.

get to an end, and in its embellishing it seems as if it would never stop laying on colours or taking them off—or whatever the professional painters term the process—and reach a point where the picture admits of no further improvement in respect of beauty and lucidity.

CLIN. I, too, remember hearing something of the fact you mention, although I am by no means practised in that kind of art.

ATH. You are none the worse for that. We may still use this fact, which it has occurred to us to mention, to illustrate the following point. Suppose that a man should propose to paint an object of extreme beauty, and that this should never grow worse, but always better, as time went on, do you not see that, since the painter is mortal, unless he leaves a successor who is able to repair the picture if it suffers through time, and also in the future to improve it by touching up any deficiency left by his own imperfect craftsmanship, his interminable toil will have results of but short duration?

CLIN. True.

ATH. Well then, do you not think that the purpose of the lawgiver is similar? He purposes, first, to write down the laws, so far as he can, with complete precision; next, when in the course of time he puts his decrees to the test of practice, you cannot suppose that any lawgiver will be so foolish as not to perceive that very many things must necessarily be left over, which it will be the duty of some successor to make right, in order that the constitution and the system of the State he has organised may always grow better, and never in any way worse.[1]

[1] Cp. *Polit.* 298 A ff.

769 κλ. Εἰκός, πῶς γὰρ οὔ; βούλεσθαι πάντα ὁντινοῦν τὸ τοιοῦτον.

αθ. Οὐκοῦν εἴ τίς τινα μηχανὴν ἔχοι πρὸς τοῦτο, ἔργῳ καὶ λόγοις τίνα τρόπον διδάξειεν ἂν ἕτερον εἴτε μείζονα εἴτε ἐλάττω περὶ τοῦτ᾽ ἔχειν ἔννοιαν, ὅπως χρὴ φυλάττειν καὶ ἐπανορθοῦν νόμους, οὐκ ἄν ποτε λέγων ἀπείποι τὸ τοιοῦτον πρὶν ἐπὶ τέλος ἐλθεῖν;

770 κλ. Πῶς γὰρ οὔ;

αθ. Οὐκοῦν ἐν τῷ νῦν παρόντι ποιητέον ἐμοὶ καὶ σφῷν τοῦτο;

κλ. Τὸ ποῖον δὴ λέγεις;

αθ. Ἐπειδὴ νομοθετεῖν μὲν μέλλομεν, ᾕρηνται δὲ ἡμῖν νομοφύλακες, ἡμεῖς δ᾽ ἐν δυσμαῖς τοῦ βίου, οἱ δ᾽ ὡς πρὸς ἡμᾶς νέοι, ἅμα μέν, ὥς φαμεν, δεῖ νομοθετεῖν ἡμᾶς, ἅμα δὲ πειρᾶσθαι ποιεῖν καὶ τούτους αὐτοὺς νομοθέτας τε καὶ νομοφύλακας εἰς τὸ δυνατόν.

B κλ. Τί μήν; εἴπερ οἷοί τέ γ᾽ ἐσμὲν ἱκανῶς.

αθ. Ἀλλ᾽ οὖν πειρατέα γε καὶ προθυμητέα.

κλ. Πῶς γὰρ οὔ;

αθ. Λέγωμεν δὴ πρὸς αὐτούς· Ὦ φίλοι σωτῆρες νόμων, ἡμεῖς περὶ ἑκάστων ὧν τίθεμεν τοὺς νόμους πάμπολλα παραλείψομεν· ἀνάγκη γάρ· οὐ μὴν ἀλλ᾽ ὅσα γε μὴ σμικρὰ καὶ τὸ ὅλον εἰς δύναμιν οὐκ ἀνήσομεν ἀπεριήγητον καθάπερ τινὶ περιγραφῇ· τοῦτο δὲ δεήσει συμπληροῦν ὑμᾶς τὸ περιηγηθέν. ὅποι δὲ βλέποντες δράσετε
C τὸ τοιοῦτον, ἀκούειν χρή. Μέγιλλος μὲν γὰρ καὶ ἐγὼ καὶ Κλεινίας εἰρήκαμέν τε αὐτὰ ἀλλήλοις οὐκ ὀλιγάκις ὁμολογοῦμέν τε λέγεσθαι καλῶς·

CLIN. This, of course, is what everyone naturally desires.

ATH. Suppose then that a man knew of a device indicating the way in which he could teach another man by deed and word to understand in a greater or less degree how he should conserve or amend laws, surely he would never cease declaring it until he had accomplished his purpose.

CLIN. He certainly would not.

ATH. Must not we three act thus on the present occasion?

CLIN. What is it you mean?

ATH. We are about to make laws, and Law-wardens have been appointed by us; therefore, since we are in the evening of life, while those compared to us are youthful, we should not only legislate, as we say, ourselves, but also make legislators, as well as Law-wardens, of these very same men, so far as we can.

CLIN. We should,—if, that is to say, we are capable of so doing.

ATH. At any rate we must try, and try hard.

CLIN. By all means.

ATH. Let us address them thus :—" Beloved Keepers of the Laws, in many departments of our legislation we shall leave out a vast number of matters (for we needs must do so); yet, notwithstanding, all important matters, as well as the general description, we shall include, so far as we can, in our outline sketch. Your help will be required to fill in this outline ; and you must listen to what I say about the aim you should have before you in doing so. Megillus, Clinias and I have often stated to one another that aim, and we agree that it is rightly stated ; so

PLATO

770 ὑμᾶς δὲ ἡμῖν βουλόμεθα ξυγγνώμονάς τε ἅμα
καὶ μαθητὰς γίγνεσθαι, βλέποντας πρὸς ταῦτα
εἰς ἅπερ ἡμεῖς ξυνεχωρήσαμεν ἀλλήλοις τὸν
νομοφύλακά τε καὶ νομοθέτην δεῖν βλέπειν. ἦν
δὲ ἡ συγχώρησις ἓν ἔχουσα κεφάλαιον, ὅπως ποτὲ
D ἀνὴρ ἀγαθὸς γίγνοιτ᾽ ἂν τὴν ἀνθρώπῳ προσήκουσαν ἀρετὴν τῆς ψυχῆς ἔχων ἔκ τινος ἐπιτηδεύματος ἤ τινος ἤθους ἢ ποιᾶς σιτήσεως[1] ἢ ἐπιθυμίας ἢ δόξης ἢ μαθημάτων ποτέ τινων, εἴτε
ἄρρην τις τῶν ξυνοικούντων οὖσα ἢ φύσις εἴτε
θήλεια, νέων ἢ γερόντων, ὅπως εἰς ταὐτὸν τοῦτο
ὃ λέγομεν τεταμένη σπουδὴ πᾶσα ἔσται διὰ
παντὸς τοῦ βίου, τῶν δ᾽ ἄλλων ὁπόσα ἐμπόδια
τούτοις μηδὲν προτιμῶν φανεῖται μηδ᾽ ὁστισοῦν,
E τελευτῶν δὲ καὶ πόλεως, ἐὰν[2] ἀνάστατον ⟨ἂν⟩
ἀνάγκη φαίνηται γίγνεσθαι πρὶν ἐθέλειν δούλειον
ὑπομεῖναν[3] ζυγὸν ἄρχεσθαι ὑπὸ χειρόνων, ἢ
λείπειν φυγῇ τὴν πόλιν, ὡς πάντα τὰ τοιαῦτ᾽ ἄρ᾽
ἔσθ᾽ ὑπομενετέον πάσχοντας πρὶν ἀλλάξασθαι
πολιτείαν ἢ χείρους ἀνθρώπους πέφυκε ποιεῖν.
ταῦτα ἡμεῖς τε ἔμπροσθεν ξυνωμολογησάμεθα,
καὶ νῦν ὑμεῖς ἡμῶν εἰς ταῦτα ἑκάτερα βλέποντες
ἐπάνιτε[4] καὶ ψέγετε τοὺς νόμους, ὅσοι μὴ ταῦτα
771 δυνατοί, τοὺς δὲ δυνατοὺς ἀσπάζεσθέ τε καὶ
φιλοφρόνως δεχόμενοι ζῆτε ἐν αὐτοῖς· τὰ δ᾽ ἄλλα
ἐπιτηδεύματα καὶ πρὸς ἄλλα τείνοντα τῶν ἀγαθῶν λεγομένων χαίρειν χρὴ προσαγορεύειν.

Ἀρχὴ δὲ ἔστω τῶν μετὰ ταῦτα ἡμῖν νόμων ἥδε

---

[1] σιτήσεως : κτήσεως MSS., edd. (ποτ᾽ ἀσκήσεως Apelt).
[2] ἐὰν : ἐὰν MSS. Also I add ⟨ἂν⟩.
[3] ὑπομεῖναν Stallb. : ὑπομείνασα MSS.

454

we desire you to be in immediate unison with us, as
our disciples, and to aim at those objects at which, as
we three have agreed, the lawgiver and Law-warden
ought to aim. The sum and substance of our agreement was simply this : that whatsoever be the way
in which a member of our community—be he of the
male or female sex, young or old,—may become a
good citizen, possessed of the excellence of soul which
belongs to man, whether derived from some pursuit
or disposition, or from some form of diet, or from
desire or opinion or mental study,—to the attainment
of this end all his efforts throughout the whole of his
life shall be directed ; and not a single person shall
show himself preferring any object which impedes
this aim ; in fine, even as regards the State, he must
allow it to be revolutionised, if it seems necessary,
rather than voluntarily submit to the yoke of slavery
under the rule of the worse, or else he must himself
quit the State as an exile : all such sufferings men
must endure rather than change to a polity which
naturally makes men worse. This is what we
previously agreed upon [1] : so do you now keep both
these objects of ours in view as you revise the laws,
and censure all the laws which are unable to effect
them, but welcome all such as are able to do so, and,
adopting them wholeheartedly, rule your lives by
them. All other practices, which tend towards
' goods ' (so-called), other than these, you must bid
farewell to."

For a beginning of the laws which are to follow,

[1] 688 E, 742 E.

---

[4] ἐπάνιτε Apelt, England : ἐπαινεῖτε MSS. (Schanz brackets
ἐπαινεῖτε καί).

PLATO

771 τις, ἀφ' ἱερῶν ἠργμένη. τὸν ἀριθμὸν γὰρ δὴ δεῖ
πρῶτον ἀναλαβεῖν ἡμᾶς τὸν τῶν πεντακισχιλίων
καὶ τετταράκοντα, ὅσας εἶχέ τε καὶ ἔχει τομὰς
B προσφόρους ὅ τε ὅλος ἅμα καὶ ὁ κατὰ φυλάς, ὃ δὴ
τοῦ παντὸς ἔθεμεν δωδεκατημόριον, ἐν καὶ εἴκοσιν
εἰκοσάκις ὀρθότατα φύν. ἔχει δὲ διανομὰς δώδεκα
μὲν ὁ πᾶς ἀριθμὸς ἡμῖν, δώδεκα δὲ καὶ ὁ τῆς
φυλῆς. ἑκάστην δὴ τὴν μοῖραν διανοεῖσθαὶ χρεὼν
ὡς οὖσαν ἱερὸν θεοῦ δῶρον, ἑπομένην τοῖς μησὶ καὶ
τῇ τοῦ παντὸς περιόδῳ. διὸ καὶ πᾶσαν πόλιν
ἄγει μὲν τὸ ξύμφυτον ἱεροῦν αὐτάς, ἄλλοι δὲ
ἄλλων ἴσως ὀρθότερον ἐνείμαντό τε καὶ εὐτυχέστε-
C ρον ἐθείωσαν τὴν διανομήν. ἡμεῖς δὲ οὖν νῦν φαμὲν
ὀρθότατα προῃρῆσθαι τὸν τῶν πεντακισχιλίων
καὶ τετταράκοντα ἀριθμόν, ὃς πάσας τὰς διανομὰς
ἔχει μέχρι τῶν δώδεκα ἀπὸ μιᾶς ἀρξάμενος πλὴν
ἑνδεκάδος· αὕτη δ' ἔχει σμικρότατον ἴαμα· ἐπὶ
θάτερα γὰρ ὑγιὴς γίγνεται δυοῖν ἑστίαιν ἀπο-
νεμηθείσαιν. ὡς δ' ἐστὶ ταῦτα ἀληθῶς ὄντα,
κατὰ σχολὴν οὐκ ἂν πολὺς ἐπιδείξειε μῦθος.
πιστεύσαντες δὴ τὰ νῦν τῇ παρούσῃ φήμῃ καὶ
D λόγῳ νείμωμέν τε ταύτῃ,[1] καὶ ἑκάστῃ μοίρᾳ θεὸν
ἢ θεῶν παῖδα ἐπιφημίσαντες, βωμούς τε καὶ τὰ
τούτοις προσήκοντα ἀποδόντες, θυσιῶν πέρι
ξυνόδους ἐπ' αὐτοῖς ποιώμεθα δύο τοῦ μηνός,
δώδεκα μὲν τῇ τῆς φυλῆς διανομῇ, δώδεκα δὲ αὐτῷ
τῷ τῆς πόλεως διαμερισμῷ, θεῶν μὲν δὴ πρῶτον
χάριτος ἕνεκα καὶ τῶν περὶ θεούς, δεύτερον δὲ

---

[1] ταύτῃ : ταύτην MSS. : αὐτὴν Ast.

---

[1] Cp. 737 E ff.

we must commence with things sacred. First, we must consider anew[1] the number 5,040, and the number of convenient subdivisions which we found it to contain both as a whole and when divided up into tribes : the tribal number is, as we said, a twelfth part of the whole number, being in its nature precisely 20×21. Our whole number has twelve subdivisions, and the tribal number also has twelve ; and each such portion must be regarded as a sacred gift of God, conformed to the months and to the revolution of the universe. Wherefore also every State is guided by native instinct to hold them sacred, although some men possibly have made their divisions more correctly than others, or have consecrated them more happily. We, in any case, affirm now that we are perfectly correct in first selecting the number 5,040, which admits of division by all the numbers from 1 to 12, excepting only 11—and this omission is very easily remedied, since the mere subtraction of two hearths from the total restores an integral number as quotient :[2] that this is really true we could show, at our leisure, by a fairly short explanation. For the present, then, we shall trust to the oracular statement just delivered, and we shall employ these subdivisions, and give to each portion the name of a God, or of a child of Gods, and bestow on it altars and all that belongs thereto ; and at these we shall appoint two assemblies every month for sacrifice—of which twelve (yearly) shall be for the whole tribal division, and twelve for its urban section only ; the object of these shall be, first, to offer thanksgiving to the gods and to do them service, and secondly, as we should

[2] $5,040 = (11 \times 458) + 2.$

771 ἡμῶν αὐτῶν οἰκειότητός τε πέρι καὶ γνωρίσεως
ἀλλήλων, ὡς φαῖμεν ἄν, καὶ ὁμιλίας ἕνεκα πάσης.
E πρὸς γὰρ δὴ τὴν τῶν γάμων κοινωνίαν καὶ ξύμ-
μιξιν ἀναγκαίως ἔχει τὴν ἄγνοιαν ἐξαιρεῖν παρ᾽
ὧν τέ τις ἄγεται καὶ ἃ καὶ οἷς ἐκδίδωσι, περὶ
παντὸς ποιούμενον ὅτι μάλιστα τὸ μὴ σφάλλεσθαι μηδαμῶς ἐν τοῖς τοιούτοις κατὰ τὸ δυνατόν.
τῆς οὖν τοιαύτης σπουδῆς ἕνεκα χρὴ καὶ τὰς
παιδιὰς ποιεῖσθαι χορεύοντάς τε καὶ χορευούσας
772 κόρους καὶ κόρας, καὶ ἅμα δὴ θεωροῦντάς τε καὶ
θεωρουμένους μετὰ λόγου τε καὶ ἡλικίας τινὸς
ἐχούσης εἰκυίας προφάσεις, γυμνοὺς καὶ γυμνὰς
μέχριπερ αἰδοῦς σώφρονος ἑκάστων. τούτων δ᾽
ἐπιμελητὰς πάντων καὶ κοσμητὰς τοὺς τῶν χορῶν
ἄρχοντας γίγνεσθαι, καὶ νομοθέτας μετὰ τῶν
νομοφυλάκων, ὅσων [1] ἂν ἡμεῖς ἐκλείπωμεν τάτ-
τοντας.

Ἀναγκαῖον δέ, ὅπερ εἴπομεν, περὶ τὰ τοιαῦτα
πάντα ὅσα σμικρὰ καὶ πολλὰ νομοθέτην μὲν
B ἐκλείπειν, τοὺς δ᾽ ἐμπείρους ἀεὶ κατ᾽ ἐνιαυτὸν
γιγνομένους αὐτῶν ἀπὸ τῆς χρείας μανθάνοντας
τάττεσθαι καὶ ἐπανορθουμένους κινεῖν κατ᾽ ἐνιαυ-
τόν, ἕως ἂν ὅρος ἱκανὸς δόξῃ τῶν τοιούτων νομίμων καὶ ἐπιτηδευμάτων γεγονέναι. χρόνος μὲν
οὖν μέτριος ἅμα καὶ ἱκανὸς γίγνοιτ᾽ ἂν τῆς ἐμπειρίας δεκαέτηρος θυσιῶν τε καὶ χορειῶν, ἐπὶ πάντα
καὶ ἕκαστα ταχθείς, ζῶντος μὲν τοῦ τάξαντος
C νομοθέτου κοινῇ, τέλος δὲ σχόντος αὐτὰς ἑκάστας τὰς ἀρχὰς εἰς τοὺς νομοφύλακας εἰσφερούσας
τὸ παραλειπόμενον τῆς αὐτῶν ἀρχῆς ἐπαν-

[1] ὅσων Aldus: ὅσον MSS.

assert, to promote fellowship amongst ourselves and
mutual acquaintance and association of every
sort. For, in view of the fellowship and intercourse
of marriage, it is necessary to eliminate ignorance,
both on the part of the husband concerning the
woman he marries and the family she comes from,
and on the part of the father concerning the man
to whom he gives his daughter; for it is all-
important in such matters to avoid, if possible, any
mistake. To achieve this serious purpose, sportive
dances should be arranged for boys and girls; and
at these they should both view and be viewed, in
a reasonable way and on occasions that offer a suitable pretext, with bodies unclad, save so far as sober
modesty prescribes. Of all such matters the officers
of the choirs shall be the supervisors and controllers,
and also, in conjunction with the Law-wardens, the
lawgivers of all that we leave unprescribed.[1]

It is, as we said, necessary that in regard to all
matters involving a host of petty details the lawgiver should leave omissions, and that rules and
amendments should be made from year to year
by those who have constant experience of them
from year to year and are taught by practice, until
it be decided that a satisfactory code has been
made out to regulate all such proceedings. A fair
and sufficient period to assign for such experimental
work would be ten years, both for sacrifices and for
dances in all their several details; each body of
officials, acting in conjunction with the original lawgiver, if he be still alive, or by themselves, if he be
dead, shall report to the Law-wardens whatever is
omitted in their own department, and shall make

[1] Cp. 764 E f.

772 ὀρθοῦσθαι, μέχριπερ ἂν τέλος ἔχειν ἕκαστον
δόξῃ τοῦ καλῶς ἐξειργάσθαι· τότε δὲ ἀκίνητα
θεμένους ἤδη χρῆσθαι μετὰ τῶν ἄλλων νόμων,
οὓς ἔταξε κατ᾽ ἀρχὰς ὁ θεὶς αὐτοῖς νομοθέτης. ὧν
πέρι κινεῖν μὲν ἑκόντας μηδέποτε μηδέν· εἰ δέ τις
D ἀνάγκη δόξειέ ποτε καταλαβεῖν, πάσας μὲν τὰς
ἀρχὰς χρὴ ξυμβούλους, πάντα δὲ τὸν δῆμον καὶ
πάσας θεῶν μαντείας ἐπελθόντας, ἐὰν συμφωνῶσι
πάντες, οὕτω κινεῖν, ἄλλως δὲ μηδέποτε μηδαμῶς,
ἀλλὰ τὸν κωλύοντα ἀεὶ κατὰ νόμον κρατεῖν.

Ὁπόθεν [1] τις οὖν καὶ ὁπηνίκα τῶν πέντε καὶ
εἴκοσι γεγονότων ἔτη σκοπῶν καὶ σκοπούμενος ὑπ᾽
ἄλλων κατὰ νοῦν ἑαυτῷ καὶ πρέποντα εἰς παίδωι
κοινωνίαν καὶ γένεσιν ἐξευρηκέναι πιστεύει
<γάμον>,[2] γαμείτω μὲν πᾶς ἐντὸς τῶν πέντε καὶ
E τριάκοντα ἐτῶν· τὸ δὲ πρέπον καὶ τὸ ἅρμοττον
ὡς χρὴ ζητεῖν, πρῶτον ἐπακουσάτω· δεῖ γάρ, ὥς
φησι Κλεινίας, ἔμπροσθεν τοῦ νόμου προοίμιον
οἰκεῖον ἑκάστῳ προτιθέναι.

ΚΛ. Κάλλιστα, ὦ ξένε, διεμνημόνευσας, ἔλαβές
τε τοῦ λόγου καιρὸν καὶ μάλ᾽ ἐμοὶ δοκοῦντ᾽ εἶναι
σύμμετρον.

ΑΘ. Εὖ λέγεις. Ὦ παῖ, τοίνυν φῶμεν ἀγαθῶν
773 πατέρων φύντι, τοὺς παρὰ τοῖς ἔμφροσιν εὐδόξους
γάμους χρὴ γαμεῖν, οἵ σοι παραινοῖεν ἂν μὴ
φεύγειν τὸν τῶν πενήτων μηδὲ τὸν τῶν πλουσίων
διώκειν διαφερόντως γάμον, ἀλλ᾽ ἐὰν τἆλλα ἰσάζῃ,
τὸν ὑποδεέστερον ἀεὶ τιμῶντα εἰς τὴν κοινωνίαν
ξυνιέναι. τῇ τε γὰρ πόλει ξύμφορον ἂν εἴη ταύτῃ

---

[1] ὁπόθεν Aldus, England : ὁπότε MSS.
[2] ⟨γάμον⟩ I add.

it good, until each detail seems to have reached its proper completion: this done, they shall decree them as fixed rules, and employ them as well as the rest of the laws originally decreed by the law-giver. In these they must never make any change voluntarily; but if it should ever be thought that a necessity for change has arisen, all the people must be consulted, as well as all the officials, and they must seek advice from all the divine oracles; and if there is a general consent by all, then they may make a change, but under no other conditions at any time; and the objector to change shall always prevail according to law.

When any man of twenty-five[1] years of age, viewing and being viewed by others, believes that he has found in any quarter a mate to his liking and suitable for the joint procreation of children, he shall marry, in every case before he is thirty-five; but first let him hearken to the direction as to how he should seek what is proper and fitting, for, as Clinias maintains, one ought to introduce each law by a prelude suitable thereto.[2]

CLIN. A very proper reminder, Stranger,—and you have chosen, in my opinion, a most opportune point in your discourse for making it.

ATH. You are right. So let us say to the son of noble sires: My child, you must make a marriage that will commend itself to men of sense, who would counsel you neither to shun connexion with a poor family, nor to pursue ardently connexion with a rich one, but, other things being equal, to prefer always an alliance with a family of moderate means. Such a course will benefit both the State

[1] But cp. 721 B. [2] Cp. 720 E.

773 ταῖς τε ξυνιούσαις ἑστίαις· τὸ γὰρ ὁμαλὸν καὶ
ξύμμετρον ἀκράτου μυρίον διαφέρει πρὸς ἀρετήν.
κοσμίων τε πατέρων χρὴ προθυμεῖσθαι γίγνεσθαι
B κηδεστὴν τὸν αὑτῷ ξυνειδότα ἰταμώτερον ἅμα καὶ
θᾶττον τοῦ δέοντος πρὸς πάσας τὰς πράξεις φερό-
μενον· τὸν δ' ἐναντίως πεφυκότα ἐπὶ τἀναντία χρὴ
κηδεύματα πορεύεσθαι. καὶ κατὰ παντὸς εἷς
ἔστω μῦθος γάμου· τὸν γὰρ τῇ πόλει δεῖ συμφέ-
ροντα μνηστεύειν γάμον ἕκαστον, οὐ τὸν ἥδιστον
αὑτῷ. φέρεται δέ πως πᾶς ἀεὶ κατὰ φύσιν πρὸς
τὸν ὁμοιότατον αὑτῷ, ὅθεν ἀνώμαλος ἡ πόλις ὅλη
C γίγνεται χρήμασί τε καὶ τρόπων ἤθεσιν· ἐξ ὧν ἃ
μὴ βουλόμεθα ξυμβαίνειν ἡμῖν καὶ μάλιστα
ξυμβαίνει ταῖς πλείσταις πόλεσι. ταῦτα δὴ διὰ
λόγου μὲν νόμῳ προστάττειν, μὴ γαμεῖν πλούσιον
πλουσίου μηδὲ πολλὰ δυνάμενον πράττειν ἄλλου
τοιούτου, θάττους δὲ ἤθεσι πρὸς βραδυτέρους καὶ
βραδυτέρους πρὸς θάττους ἀναγκάζειν τῇ τῶν
γάμων κοινωνίᾳ πορεύεσθαι, πρὸς τῷ γελοῖα εἶναι
θυμὸν ἂν ἐγείραι πολλοῖς· οὐ γὰρ ῥᾴδιον ἐννοεῖν
D ὅτι πόλιν εἶναι δεῖ δίκην κρατῆρος κεκραμένην, οὗ
μαινόμενος μὲν οἶνος ἐγκεχυμένος ζεῖ, κολαζόμενος
δὲ ὑπὸ νήφοντος ἑτέρου θεοῦ καλὴν κοινωνίαν
λαβὼν ἀγαθὸν πῶμα καὶ μέτριον ἀπεργάζεται.
τοῦτ' οὖν γιγνόμενον ἐν τῇ τῶν παίδων μίξει
διορᾶν, ὡς ἔπος εἰπεῖν, δυνατὸς οὐδείς. τούτων
δὴ χάριν ἐὰν μὲν νόμῳ τὰ τοιαῦτα ἀναγκαῖον,

---

[1] Cp. *Polit.* 310 C ff.

and the united families,[1] since in respect of
excellence what is evenly balanced and symmetrical
is infinitely superior to what is untempered. The
man who knows he is und ly hasty and violent in
all his actions should win a bride sprung from steady
parents ; while the man that is of a contrary nature
should proceed to mate himself with one of the
opposite kind. Regarding marriage as a whole
there shall be one general rule : each man must
seek to form such a marriage as shall benefit the
State, rather than such as best pleases himself.
There is a natural tendency for everyone to make
for the mate that most resembles himself, whence
it results that the whole State becomes ill-balanced
both in wealth and in moral habits ; and because
of this, the consequences we least desire are those
that generally befall most States. To make express
enactments about these matters by law—that, for
instance, a rich man must not marry into a rich
family, nor a man of wide power with a powerful
family, or that man of hasty tempers must be
obliged to seek alliances with those of slower
tempers, and the slow with the hasty—this, besides
being ridiculous, would cause widespread resentment ; for people do not find it easy to perceive
that a State should be like a bowl of mixed wine,
where the wine when first poured in foams madly,
but as soon as it is chastened by the sober deity of
water, it forms a fair alliance, and produces a potion
that is good and moderate. That this is precisely
what happens in the blending of children is a thing
which hardly anyone is capable of perceiving ; therefrom in the legal code we must omit such rules, and
merely try by the spell of words to persuade each

773E ἐπάδοντα δὲ πείθειν πειρᾶσθαι τὴν τῶν παίδων
ὁμαλότητα αὐτῶν αὑτοῖς τῆς τῶν γάμων ἰσότητος
ἀπλήστου χρημάτων οὔσης περὶ πλείονος ἕκαστον
ποιεῖσθαι, καὶ δι' ὀνείδους ἀποτρέπειν τὸν περὶ τὰ
χρήματα ἐν τοῖς γάμοις ἐσπουδακότα, ἀλλὰ μὴ
γραπτῷ νόμῳ βιαζόμενον.

Περὶ γάμων δὴ ταῦτ' ἔστω παραμύθια λεγόμενα, καὶ δὴ καὶ τὰ ἔμπροσθε τούτων ῥηθέντα,
ὡς χρὴ τῆς ἀειγενοῦς φύσεως ἀντέχεσθαι τῷ
παῖδας παίδων καταλείποντα ἀεὶ τῷ θεῷ ὑπη-
774 ρέτας ἀνθ' αὑτοῦ παραδιδόναι. πάντα οὖν ταῦτα
καὶ ἔτι πλείω τις ἂν εἴποι περὶ γάμων, ὡς
χρὴ γαμεῖν, προοιμιαζόμενος ὀρθῶς. ἂν δ' ἄρα
τις μὴ πείθηται ἑκών, ἀλλότριον δὲ αὑτὸν καὶ
ἀκοινώνητον ἐν τῇ πόλει ἔχῃ καὶ ἄγαμος ὢν γένηται πεντεκαιτριακοντούτης, ζημιούσθω κατ' ἐνιαυτὸν ἕκαστον, ὁ μέγιστον μὲν τίμημα κεκτημένος
ἑκατὸν δραχμαῖς, ὁ δὲ τὸ δεύτερον ἑβδομήκοντα,
τρίτον δὲ ἑξήκοντα, ὁ δὲ τὸ τέταρτον τριάκοντα·
B τοῦτο δ' ἔστω τῆς Ἥρας ἱερόν. ὁ δὲ μὴ ἐκτίνων
κατ' ἐνιαυτὸν δεκαπλάσιον ὀφειλέτω. πραττέσθω
δὲ ὁ ταμίας τῆς θεοῦ, μὴ ἐκπράξας δὲ αὐτὸς
ὀφειλέτω καὶ ἐν ταῖς εὐθύναις τοῦ τοιούτου λόγον
ὑπεχέτω πᾶς. εἰς μὲν οὖν χρήματα ὁ μὴ 'θέλων
γαμεῖν ταῦτα ζημιούσθω, τιμῆς δὲ παρὰ τῶν
νεωτέρων ἄτιμος πάσης ἔστω, καὶ μηδεὶς ὑπ-
ακουέτω μηδὲν αὐτῷ ἑκὼν τῶν νέων· ἐὰν δὲ κολάζειν
τινὰ ἐπιχειρῇ, πᾶς τῷ ἀδικουμένῳ βοηθείτω καὶ
C ἀμυνέτω, μὴ βοηθῶν δὲ ὁ παραγενόμενος δειλός

¹ 721 B ff. By reproduction man secures a continuous share in the life of the divine Universe; cp. 903 C.

one to value the equality of his children more
highly than the equality of a marriage with inordi-
nate wealth, and by means of reproaches to divert
from his object him who has set his heart on marrying for money, although we may not compel him by
a written law.

Concerning marriage these shall be the exhortations given, in addition to those previously given,[1]
declaring how it is a duty to lay hold on the ever-
living reality by providing servants for God in our
own stead; and this we do by leaving behind us
children's children. All this and more one might say
in a proper prelude concerning marriage and the
duty of marrying. Should any man, however, refuse
to obey willingly, and keep himself aloof and un-
partnered in the State, and reach the age of thirty-
five unmarried, an annual fine shall be imposed upon
him, of a hundred drachmae if he be of the highest
property-class, if of the second, seventy, if of the
third, sixty, if of the fourth, thirty. This fine shall
be consecrated to Hera.[2] He that fails to pay the
fine in full every year shall owe ten times the
amount of it, and the treasurer of the goddess shall
exact this sum, or, failing to exact it, he shall owe
it himself, and in the audit he shall in every case
be liable to account for such a sum. This shall be
the money-fine in which the man who refuses to
marry shall be mulcted, and as to honour, he shall
receive none from the younger men, and no young
man shall of his own free-will pay any regard to
him: if he attempt to punish any person, everyone
shall come to the assistance of the person maltreated
and defend him, and whoever is present and fails

[2] As goddess of marriage.

774 τε ἅμα καὶ κακὸς ὑπὸ τοῦ νόμου πολίτης εἶναι
λεγέσθω.

Περὶ δὲ προικὸς εἴρηται μὲν καὶ πρότερον,
εἰρήσθω δὲ πάλιν, ὡς ἴσα ἀντὶ ἴσων ἐστὶ τὸ [1] μήτε
λαμβάνειν τι μήτ' ἐκδιδόναι τι, [2] ⟨οὐδ' εἰκὸς ἀγάμους
ὄντας⟩ διὰ χρημάτων ἀπορίαν γηράσκειν τοὺς πένη-
τας—τὰ γὰρ ἀναγκαῖα ὑπάρχοντά ἐστι πᾶσι—των ἐν
ταύτῃ τῇ πόλει, ὕβρις δὲ ἧττον γυναιξὶ καὶ δουλεία
ταπεινὴ καὶ ἀνελεύθερος διὰ χρήματα τοῖς γήμασι
D γίγνοιτ' ἄν. καὶ ὁ μὲν πειθόμενος ἐν τῶν καλῶν δρῴη
τοῦτ' ἄν· ὁ δὲ μὴ πειθόμενος ἢ διδοὺς ἢ λαμβάνων
πλέον ἢ πεντήκοντα ἄξια δραχμῶν ἐσθῆτος χάριν, ὁ δὲ
μνᾶς, ὁ δὲ τριῶν ἡμμναίων, ὁ δὲ δυεῖν μναῖν ὁ τὸ μέγιστον τίμημα κεκτημένος, ὀφειλέτω μὲν τῷ δημοσίῳ
τοσοῦτον ἕτερον, τὸ δὲ δοθὲν ἢ ληφθὲν ἱερὸν ἔστω τῆς
Ἥρας τε καὶ τοῦ Διός, πραττόντων δὲ οἱ ταμίαι
E τούτοιν τοῖν θεοῖν, καθάπερ ἐρρήθη τῶν μὴ
γαμούντων πέρι τοὺς ταμίας ἐκπράττειν ἑκάστοτε
τοὺς τῆς Ἥρας ἢ παρ' αὐτῶν ἑκάστους τὴν ζημίαν
ἐκτίνειν.

Ἐγγύην δὲ εἶναι κυρίαν πατρὸς μὲν πρῶτον,
δευτέραν πάππου, τρίτην δὲ ἀδελφῶν ὁμοπα-
τρίων· ἐὰν δὲ μηδὲ εἷς ᾖ τούτων, τὴν πρὸς
μητρὸς μετὰ τοῦτο εἶναι κυρίαν ὡσαύτως· ἐὰν δ'
ἄρα τύχῃ τις ἀήθης συμβαίνῃ, τοὺς ἐγγύτατα
γένους ἀεὶ κυρίους εἶναι μετὰ τῶν ἐπιτρόπων. ὅσα

[1] τὸ MSS. τῷ Aldus, Zur.
[2] λαμβάνειν τι μήτε ἐκδιδόναι (τι) Cornarius : λαμβανοντι . . .
ἐκδιδόντι MSS. ⟨οὐδ' . . . ὄντας⟩ I add, exempli gratia, to
fill up the lacuna assumed by Schneider and Schanz : (MSS.
Marg. and Stallb. read διδάσκειν for γηράσκειν, Apelt. γεραίρειν).

[1] 742 C.
[2] i.e. for the bride's "trousseau," given by her father to

thus to give assistance shall be declared by law to be both a cowardly and a bad citizen.

Concerning dowries it has been stated before,[1] and it shall be stated again, that an equal exchange consists in neither giving nor receiving any gift; nor is it likely that the poor amongst the citizens in this state should remain till old age unmarried for lack of means—for all have the necessaries of life provided for them—; and the result of this rule will be less insolence on the part of the wives and less humiliation and servility on the part of the husband because of money. Whoso obeys this rule will be acting nobly; but he that disobeys—by giving or receiving for raiment [2] a sum of over fifty drachmae, or over one mina, or over one and a half minae, or (if a member of the highest property-class) over two minae,—shall owe to the public treasury a sum equal thereto, and the sum given or received shall be consecrated to Hera and Zeus, and the treasurers of these deities shall exact it,—just as it was the rule,[3] in cases of refusal to marry, that the treasurers of Hera should exact the fine in each instance, or else pay it out of their own pockets.

The right of betrothal belongs in the first place to the father, next to the grandfather, thirdly to the full brothers; failing any of these, it rightly belongs next to relatives on the mother's side in like order; in case of any unwonted misfortune, the right shall belong to the nearest of kin in each case, acting in conjunction with the guardians.[4] Concerning the

the bridegroom. Fifty drachmae is the maximum value allowed for the lowest class, a mina for the next lowest, and so on upwards.

[3] Cp. 774 B.

[4] For these " guardians " (of orphans) see 926 E ff

775 δὲ προτέλεια γάμων ἤ τις ἄλλη περὶ τὰ τοιαῦτα
775 ἱερουργία μελλόντων ἢ γιγνομένων ἢ γεγονότων
προσήκουσά ἐστι τελεῖσθαι, τοὺς ἐξηγητὰς ἐρω-
τῶντα χρὴ καὶ πειθόμενον ἐκείνοις ἕκαστον ἡγεῖσθαι πάντα ἑαυτῷ μετρίως γίγνεσθαι.

Περὶ δὲ τῶν ἑστιάσεων, φίλους μὲν χρὴ καὶ
φίλας μὴ πλείους πέντε ἑκατέρων συγκαλεῖν, συγ-
γενῶν δὲ καὶ οἰκείων ὡσαύτως τοσούτους ἄλλους
ἑκατέρων· ἀνάλωμα δὲ μὴ γίγνεσθαι πλέον ἢ κατὰ
τὴν οὐσίαν μηδενί, τῷ μὲν εἰς χρήματα μεγίστῳ
B μνᾶν, τῷ δ' ἥμισυ τοῦ τοσούτου, τῷ δ' ἐφεξῆς οὕτω,
καθάπερ ὑποβέβηκεν ἑκάστῳ τὸ τίμημα. καὶ τὸν
μὲν πειθόμενον τῷ νόμῳ ἐπαινεῖν χρὴ πάντας, τὸν
δὲ ἀπειθοῦντα κολαζόντων οἱ νομοφύλακες ὡς
ἀπειρόκαλόν τε ὄντα καὶ ἀπαίδευτον τῶν περὶ τὰς
νυμφικὰς Μούσας νόμων. πίνειν δὲ εἰς μέθην
οὔτε ἄλλοθί που πρέπει, πλὴν ἐν ταῖς τοῦ τὸν
οἶνον δόντος θεοῦ ἑορταῖς, οὐδ' ἀσφαλές, οὔτ' οὖν
δὴ περὶ γάμους ἐσπουδακότα, ἐν οἷς ἔμφρονα
μάλιστα εἶναι πρέπει νύμφην καὶ νυμφίον μετα-
C βολὴν οὐ σμικρὰν βίου μεταλλάττοντας, ἅμα δὲ
καὶ τὸ γεννώμενον ὅπως ὅτι μάλιστα ἐξ ἐμφρόνων
ἀεὶ γίγνηται· σχεδὸν γὰρ ἄδηλον ὁποία νὺξ ἢ φῶς
αὐτὸ γεννήσει μετὰ θεοῦ. καὶ πρὸς τούτοις δεῖ
μὴ τῶν σωμάτων διακεχυμένων ὑπὸ μέθης γίγνεσθαι τὴν παιδουργίαν, ἀλλ' εὐπαγὲς ἀπλανὲς
ἡσυχαῖόν τε ἐν μήτρᾳ[1] ξυνίστασθαι τὸ φυόμε-
νον· ὁ δὲ διῳνωμένος αὐτός τε φέρεται πάντη
καὶ φέρει, λυττῶν κατά τε σῶμα καὶ ψυχήν.

---

[1] μήτρᾳ Cornarius, England : μοίρᾳ MSS.

[1] Cp. 700 B, 722 D.

preliminary marriage-sacrifice and all other sacred ceremonies proper to be performed before, during, or after marriage, each man shall enquire of the Interpreters, and believe that, in obeying their directions, he will have done all things duly.

Concerning marriage-feasts,—both parties should invite their male and female friends, not more than five on each side, and an equal number of the kinsfolk and connexions of both houses: in no case must the expense exceed what the person's means permit—one mina for the richest class, half that amount for the second, and so on in proportion, according as the valuation grows less. He that obeys the law should be praised by all; but him that disobeys the Law-wardens shall punish as a man of poor taste and ill-trained in the "nomes"[1] of the nuptial Muses. Drinking to excess is a practice that is nowhere seemly[2]—save only at the feasts of the God, the Giver of wine,—nor yet safe; and certainly it is not so for those who take marriage seriously; for at such a time above all it behoves both bride and bridegroom to be sober, seeing that the change in their life is a great one, and in order to ensure, so far as possible, in every case that the child that is begotten may be sprung from the loins of sober parents: for what shall be, with God's help, the night or day of its begetting is quite uncertain. Moreover, it is not right that procreation should be the work of bodies dissolved by excess of wine, but rather that the embryo should be compacted firmly, steadily and quietly in the womb. But the man that is steeped in wine moves and is moved himself in every way, writhing both in body and soul; con-

[1] p. 674 A f.

775D σπείρειν οὖν παράφορος ἅμα καὶ κακὸς ὁ μεθύων,
ὥστ᾿ ἀνώμαλα καὶ ἄπιστα καὶ οὐδὲν εὐθύπορον
ἦθος οὐδὲ σῶμα ἐκ τῶν εἰκότων γεννῴη ποτ᾿ ἄν.
διὸ μᾶλλον μὲν ὅλον τὸν ἐνιαυτὸν καὶ βίον χρή,
μάλιστα δὲ ὁπόσον ἂν γεννᾷ χρόνον, εὐλαβεῖσθαι
καὶ μὴ πράττειν μήτε ὅσα νοσώδη ἑκόντα εἶναι
μήτε ὅσα ὕβρεως ἢ ἀδικίας ἐχόμενα· εἰς γὰρ τὰς
τῶν γεννωμένων ψυχὰς καὶ σώματα ἀναγκαῖον
Ε ἐξομοργνύμενον ἐκτυποῦσθαι καὶ τίκτειν πάντη
φαυλότερα· διαφερόντως δὲ ἐκείνην τὴν ἡμέραν
καὶ νύκτα ἀπέχεσθαι τῶν περὶ τὰ τοιαῦτα·
ἀρχὴ γὰρ ὡς [1] θεὸς ἐν ἀνθρώποις ἱδρυμένη σώζει
πάντα, τιμῆς ἐὰν τῆς προσηκούσης αὐτῇ παρ᾿
ἑκάστου τῶν χρωμένων λαγχάνῃ.

Νομίσαντα δ᾿ εἶναι χρὴ τὸν γαμοῦντα ταῖν
776 οἰκίαιν ταῖν ἐν τῷ κλήρῳ τὴν ἑτέραν οἷον νεοττῶν
ἐγγέννησιν καὶ τροφήν, χωρισθέντα ἀπὸ πατρὸς
καὶ μητρὸς τὸν γάμον ἐκεῖ ποιεῖσθαι καὶ τὴν
οἴκησιν καὶ τὴν τροφὴν αὑτοῦ καὶ τῶν τέκνων.
ἐν γὰρ ταῖς φιλίαις ἐὰν μὲν πόθος ἐνῇ τις, κολλᾷ
καὶ συνδεῖ πάντα ἤθη· κατακορὴς δὲ ξυνουσία
καὶ οὐκ ἴσχουσα τὸν διὰ χρόνου πόθον ἀπορρεῖν
ἀλλήλων ποιεῖ ὑπερβολαῖς πλησμονῆς. ὧν δὴ
χάριν μητρὶ καὶ πατρὶ καὶ τοῖς τῆς γυναικὸς
Β οἰκείοις παρέντας χρὴ τὰς αὑτῶν οἰκήσεις, οἷον
εἰς ἀποικίαν ἀφικομένους αὐτούς, ἐπισκοποῦντάς
τε ἅμα καὶ ἐπισκοπουμένους οἰκεῖν, γεννῶντάς τε
καὶ ἐκτρέφοντας παῖδας, καθάπερ λαμπάδα τὸν

---

[1] ὡς Ast : καὶ MSS. (Schanz brackets καὶ θεὸς).

---

[1] For the importance of ἀρχή (here personified) cp. 753 E,
765 E : possibly ἀρχὴ σώζει πάντα was a proverb.

sequently, when drunk, a man is clumsy and bad at
sowing seed, and is thus likely to beget unstable
and untrusty offspring, crooked in form and character.
Wherefore he must be very careful throughout all
the year and the whole of his life—and most
especially during the time he is begetting—to
commit no act that involves either bodily ailment
or violence and injustice; for these he will inevitably stamp on the souls and bodies of the offspring, and will generate them in every way
inferior. From acts of such a kind he must especially abstain on the day and night of his marriage;
for the Beginning that sits enshrined as a goddess [1]
among mortals is the Saviour of all, provided
that she receives the honour due to her from
each one who approaches her.

The man who marries must part from his father
and mother, and take one of the two houses [2]
in his allotment, to be, as it were, the nest
and home of his chicks, and make therein his
marriage and the dwelling and home of himself and his children. For in friendships the
presence of some degree of longing seems to
cement various dispositions and bind them together; but unabated proximity, since it lacks
the longing due to an interval, causes friends to
fall away from one another owing to an excessive
surfeit of each other's company. Therefore the
married pair must leave their own houses to their
parents and the bride's relations, and act themselves
as if they had gone off to a colony, visiting and
being visited in their home, begetting and rearing
children, and so handing on life, like a torch,[3] from

[1] Cp. 745 C, D.   [3] Cp. *Rep.* 328 A.

776 βίον παραδιδόντας ἄλλοις ἐξ ἄλλων, θεραπεύ-
οντας ἀεὶ θεοὺς κατὰ νόμους.

Κτήματα δὲ τὸ μετὰ τοῦτο ποῖα ἄν τις κεκτημένος ἐμμελεστάτην οὐσίαν κεκτῆτο ; τὰ μὲν οὖν
πολλὰ οὔτε νοῆσαι χαλεπὸν οὔτε κτήσασθαι, τὰ
δὲ δὴ τῶν οἰκετῶν χαλεπὰ πάντη. τὸ δ᾽ αἴτιον,
οὐκ ὀρθῶς πως καί τινα τρόπον ὀρθῶς περὶ αὐτῶν
C λέγομεν· ἐναντία γὰρ ταῖς χρείαις καὶ κατὰ τὰς
χρείας αὖ ποιούμεθα περὶ δούλων καὶ τὰ λεγόμενα.

ΜΕ. Πῶς δ᾽ αὖ τοῦτο λέγομεν ; οὐ γάρ πω
μανθάνομεν, ὦ ξένε, ὅ τι τὰ νῦν φράζεις.

ΑΘ. Καὶ μάλα γε, ὦ Μέγιλλε, εἰκότως· σχεδὸν
γὰρ πάντων τῶν Ἑλλήνων ἡ Λακεδαιμονίων
εἱλωτεία πλείστην ἀπορίαν παράσχοιτ᾽ ἂν καὶ
ἔριν τοῖς μὲν ὡς εὖ, τοῖς δ᾽ ὡς οὐκ εὖ γεγονυῖά
ἐστιν· ἐλάττω δὲ ἥ τε Ἡρακλεωτῶν δουλεία τῆς
D τῶν Μαριανδυνῶν καταδουλώσεως ἔριν ἂν ἔχοι,
τὸ Θετταλῶν τ᾽ αὖ πενεστικὸν ἔθνος. εἰς ἃ καὶ
πάντα τὰ τοιαῦτα βλέψαντας ἡμᾶς τί χρὴ ποιεῖν
περὶ κτήσεως οἰκετῶν ; ὃ δὴ παριὼν τῷ λόγῳ
ἔτυχον εἰπών, καὶ σύ με εἰκότως τί ποτε φράζοιμι
ἠρώτησας, τόδ᾽ ἐστίν· ἴσμεν ὅτι που πάντες
εἴποιμεν ἂν ὡς χρὴ δούλους ὡς εὐμενεστάτους
ἐκτῆσθαι καὶ ἀρίστους· πολλοὶ γὰρ ἀδελφῶν ἤδη
δοῦλοι καὶ υἱέων τισὶ κρείττους πρὸς ἀρετὴν
πᾶσαν γενόμενοι σεσώκασι δεσπότας καὶ κτή-

---

[1] These ancient inhabitants of N.E. Bithynia were conquered by the people of Heraclea Pontica and made tributary
vassals.

one generation to another, and ever worshipping the gods as the laws direct.

Next, as regards possessions, what should a man possess to form a reasonable amount of substance? As to most chattels, it is easy enough both to see what they should be and to acquire them; but servants present all kinds of difficulties. The reason is that our language about them is partly right and partly wrong; for the language we use both contradicts and agrees with our practical experience of them.

MEG. What mean we by this? We are still in the dark, Stranger, as to what you refer to.

ATH. That is quite natural, Megillus. For probably the most vexed problem in all Hellas is the problem of the Helot-system of the Lacedaemonians, which some maintain to be good, others bad; a less violent dispute rages round the subjection of the Mariandyni [1] to the slave-system of the Heracleotes, and that of the class of Penestae to the Thessalians.[2] In view of these and similar instances, what ought we to do about this question of owning servants? [3] The point I happened to mention in the course of my argument,—and about which you naturally asked me what I referred to,— was this. We know, of course, that we would all agree that one ought to own slaves that are as docile and good as possible; for in the past many slaves have proved themselves better in every form of excellence than brothers or sons, and have saved

[2] Cp. Ar. *Pol.* 1269ᵃ 36. "Penestae" (= serfs) were the old Aeolian inhabitants of Thessaly, subdued by the Heraclid invaders.

[3] Cp. Ar. *Pol.* 1259ᵇ 22 ff.

776Ε ματα τάς τε οἰκήσεις αὐτῶν ὅλας. ταῦτα γὰρ
ἴσμεν που περὶ δούλων λεγόμενα.

ΜΕ. Τί μήν;

ΑΘ. Οὐκοῦν καὶ τοὐναντίον ὡς ὑγιὲς οὐδὲν
ψυχῆς δούλης οὐδὲ πιστεύειν οὐδέποτ' οὐδὲν τῷ
γένει δεῖ τὸν νοῦν κεκτημένον; ὁ δὲ σοφώτατος
ἡμῖν τῶν ποιητῶν καὶ ἀπεφήνατο, ὑπὲρ τοῦ
777 Διὸς ἀγορεύων, ὡς

ἥμισυ γάρ τε νόου, φησίν, ἀπαμείρεται εὐρύοπα
Ζεὺς
ἀνδρῶν οὓς ἂν δὴ κατὰ δούλιον ἦμαρ ἕλησι.

ταῦτα δὴ διαλαβόντες ἕκαστοι τοῖς διανοήμασιν
οἱ μὲν πιστεύουσί τε οὐδὲν γένει οἰκετῶν, κατὰ
δὲ θηρίων φύσιν κέντροις καὶ μάστιξιν οὐ τρὶς
μόνον, ἀλλὰ πολλάκις, ἀπεργάζονται δούλας τὰς
ψυχὰς τῶν οἰκετῶν· οἱ δ' αὖ τἀναντία τούτων
δρῶσι πάντα.

ΜΕ. Τί μήν;

Β ΚΛ. Τί οὖν δὴ χρὴ ποιεῖν τούτων, ὦ ξένε,
διαφερομένων οὕτω περὶ τῆς ἡμετέρας αὖ χώρας
ἡμᾶς, τῆς τε κτήσεως ἅμα καὶ κολάσεως τῶν
δούλων πέρι;

ΑΘ. Τί δ', ὦ Κλεινία; δῆλον ὡς ἐπειδὴ δύσ-
κολόν ἐστι τὸ θρέμμα ἄνθρωπος καὶ πρὸς τὴν
ἀναγκαίαν διόρισιν, τὸ δοῦλόν τε ἔργῳ διορί-
ζεσθαι καὶ ἐλεύθερον καὶ δεσπότην, οὐδαμῶς
εὔχρηστον ἐθέλει εἶναί τε καὶ γίγνεσθαι.

ΚΛ. Φαίνεται.

ΑΘ. Χαλεπὸν δὴ τὸ κτῆμα· ἔργῳ γὰρ πολλά-
C κις ἐπιδέδεικται περὶ τὰς Μεσσηνίων συχνὰς
εἰωθυίας ἀποστάσεις γίγνεσθαι, καὶ περί γε τὰς

their masters and their goods and their whole houses. Surely we know that this language is used about slaves?

MEG. Certainly.

ATH. And is not the opposite kind of language also used,—that the soul of a slave has no soundness in it, and that a sensible man should never trust that class at all? And our wisest poet, too, in speaking of Zeus, declared[1] that—

"Of half their wits far-thundering Zeus bereaves
Those men on whom the day of bondage falls."

Thus each party adopts a different attitude of mind: the one places no trust at all in the servant-class, but, treating them like brute beasts, with goads and whips they make the servants' souls not merely thrice but fifty times enslaved; whereas the other party act in precisely the opposite way.

MEG. Just so.

CLIN. Since this difference of opinion exists, Stranger, what ought we to do about our own country, in regard to the owning of slaves and their punishment?

ATH. Well now, Clinias, since man is an intractable creature, it is plain that he is not at all likely to be or become easy to deal with in respect of the necessary distinction between slave and free-born master in actual experience.

CLIN. That is evident.

ATH. The slave is no easy chattel. For actual experience shows how many evils result from slavery,—as in the frequent revolts in Messenia, and in the States where there are many servants

[1] *Odyss.* xvii. 322 f.

PLATO

777 τῶν ἐκ μιᾶς φωνῆς πολλοὺς οἰκέτας κτωμένων
πόλεις, ὅσα κακὰ ξυμβαίνει, καὶ ἔτι τὰ τῶν
λεγομένων περιδίνων τῶν περὶ τὴν Ἰταλίαν γιγνομένων παντοδαπὰ [κλοπῶν]¹ ἔργα τε καὶ
παθήματα. πρὸς ἅ τις ἂν πάντα² βλέψας δια-
πορήσειε τί χρὴ δρᾶν περὶ ἁπάντων τῶν τοιούτων. δύο δὴ λείπεσθον μόνω μηχανά, μήτε
D πατριώτας ἀλλήλων εἶναι τοὺς μέλλοντας ῥᾷον
δουλεύσειν ἀσυμφώνους τε εἰς δύναμιν ὅτι μάλιστα, τρέφειν δ' αὐτοὺς ὀρθῶς μὴ μόνον ἐκείνων
ἕνεκα, πλέον δὲ αὐτῶν προτιμῶντας. ἡ δὲ τροφὴ
τῶν τοιούτων μήτε τινὰ ὕβριν ὑβρίζειν εἰς τοὺς
οἰκέτας, ἧττον δέ, εἰ δυνατόν, ἀδικεῖν ἢ τοὺς ἐξ
ἴσου. διάδηλος γὰρ ὁ φύσει καὶ μὴ πλαστῶς
σέβων τὴν δίκην, μισῶν δὲ ὄντως τὸ ἄδικον, ἐν
τούτοις τῶν ἀνθρώπων ἐν οἷς αὐτῷ ῥᾴδιον ἀδικεῖν·
ὁ περὶ τὰ τῶν δούλων οὖν ἤθη καὶ πράξεις γιγνό-
E μενός τις ἀμίαντος τοῦ τε ἀνοσίου πέρι καὶ
ἀδίκου σπείρειν εἰς ἀρετῆς ἔκφυσιν ἱκανώτατος
ἂν εἴη· ταὐτὸν δ' ἔστ' εἰπεῖν τοῦτο ὀρθῶς ἅμα
λέγοντα ἐπί τε δεσπότῃ καὶ τυράννῳ καὶ πᾶσαν
δυναστείαν δυναστεύοντι πρὸς ἀσθενέστερον ἑαυτοῦ. κολάζειν γε μὴν ἐν δίκῃ δούλους δεῖ, καὶ
μὴ νουθετοῦντας ὡς ἐλευθέρους θρύπτεσθαι
ποιεῖν· τὴν δὲ οἰκέτου πρόσρησιν χρὴ σχεδὸν
ἐπίταξιν πᾶσαν γίγνεσθαι, μὴ προσπαίζοντας
778 μηδαμῇ μηδαμῶς οἰκέταις, μήτ' οὖν θηλείαις
μήτε ἄρρεσιν· ἃ δὴ πρὸς δούλους φιλοῦσι πολλοὶ σφόδρα ἀνοήτως θρύπτοντες χαλεπώτερον

¹ [κλοπῶν] bracketed by Naber, Schanz (κλωπῶν Burges).
² ἂν πάντα Stobaeus, Burnet : ἅπαντα MSS.

476

kept who speak the same tongue, not to speak of
the crimes of all sorts committed by the "Corsairs," [1]
as they are called, who haunt the coasts of Italy,
and the reprisals therefor. In view of all these
facts, it is really a puzzle to know how to deal with
all such matters. Two means only are left for us
to try—the one is, not to allow the slaves, if they
are to tolerate slavery quietly, to be all of the same
nation, but, so far as possible, to have them of
different races,—and the other is to accord them
proper treatment, and that not only for their sakes,
but still more for the sake of ourselves. Proper
treatment of servants consists in using no violence
towards them, and in hurting them even less, if
possible, than our own equals. For it is his way
of dealing with men whom it is easy for him to
wrong that shows most clearly whether a man is
genuine or hypocritical in his reverence for justice
and hatred of injustice. He, therefore, that in dealing with slaves proves himself, in his character and
action, undefiled by what is unholy or unjust will
best be able to sow a crop of goodness,—and this we
may say, and justly say, of every master, or king,
and of everyone who possesses any kind of absolute
power over a person weaker than himself. We
ought to punish slaves justly, and not to make
them conceited by merely admonishing them as we
would free men. An address to a servant should
be mostly a simple command : there should be no
jesting with servants, either male or female, for by
a course of excessively foolish indulgence in their
treatment of their slaves, masters often make life

---

[1] The peculiar term περίδινοι (" circling round ") seems to
have been applied especially to these sea-rovers of the
Tarentine coast.

778 ἀπεργάζεσθαι τὸν βίον ἐκείνοις τε ἄρχεσθαι καὶ
ἑαυτοῖς ἄρχειν.

ΚΛ. Ὀρθῶς λέγεις.

ΑΘ. Οὐκοῦν ὅτε τις οἰκέταις κατεσκευασμένος
εἰς δύναμιν εἴη πλήθει καὶ ἐπιτηδειότητι πρὸς
ἑκάστας τὰς τῶν ἔργων παραβοηθείας, τὸ δὴ
μετὰ τοῦτο οἰκήσεις χρὴ διαγράφειν τῷ λόγῳ;

ΚΛ. Πάνυ μὲν οὖν.

B ΑΘ. Καὶ ξυμπάσης γε ὡς ἔπος εἰπεῖν ἔοικε
τῆς οἰκοδομικῆς πέρι τήν γε δὴ νέαν καὶ ἀοίκητον
ἐν τῷ πρόσθεν πόλιν ἐπιμελητέον εἶναι, τίνα
τρόπον ἕκαστα ἕξει τούτων περί τε ἱερὰ καὶ
τείχη. γάμων δ' ἦν ἔμπροσθεν ταῦτα, ὦ Κλεινία·
νῦν δ' ἐπείπερ λόγῳ γίγνεται, καὶ μάλ' ἐγχωρεῖ
ταύτῃ γίγνεσθαι τὰ νῦν· ἔργῳ μὴν ὅταν γίγνηται,
ταῦτ' ἔμπροσθεν τῶν γάμων, ἐὰν θεὸς ἐθέλῃ,
C ποιήσαντες ἐκεῖνα ἤδη τότε ἐπὶ πᾶσι τοῖς τοιούτοις ἀποτελοῦμεν. νῦν δὲ μόνον ὅσον τινὰ τύπον
αὐτῶν δι' ὀλίγων ἐπεξέλθωμεν.

ΚΛ. Πάνυ μὲν οὖν.

ΑΘ. Τὰ μὲν τοίνυν ἱερὰ πᾶσαν πέριξ τήν τε
ἀγορὰν χρὴ κατασκευάζειν, καὶ τὴν πόλιν ὅλην
ἐν κύκλῳ πρὸς τοῖς ὑψηλοῖς τῶν τόπων, εὐερκείας
τε καὶ καθαρότητος χάριν· πρὸς δὲ αὐτοῖς οἰκήσεις τε ἀρχόντων καὶ δικαστήρια,[1] ἐν οἷς
τὰς δίκας ὡς ἱερωτάτοις οὖσι λήψονταί τε καὶ
D δώσουσι, τὰ μὲν ὡς ὁσίων πέρι, τὰ δὲ καὶ τοιούτων θεῶν ἱδρύματα· καὶ ἐν τούτοις [δικαστήρια,
ἐν οἷς][2] αἵ τε τῶν φόνων πρέπουσαι δίκαι
γίγνοιντ' ἂν καὶ ὅσα θανάτων ἄξια ἀδικήματα.

---

[1] δικαστήρια Burges: δικαστηρίων MSS.
[2] [δικαστήρια, ἐν οἷς] bracketed by England.

harder both for themselves, as rulers, and for their slaves, as subject to rule.

CLIN. That is true.

ATH. Suppose, then, that we are now, to the best of our power, provided with servants sufficient in number and quality to assist in every kind of task, should we not, in the next place, describe our dwellings?

CLIN. Most certainly.

ATH. It would seem that our city, being new and houseless hitherto, must provide for practically the whole of its house-building, arranging all the details of its architecture, including temples and walls. These things are really, Clinias, prior to marriage; but since our construction is now a verbal one, this is a very suitable place to deal with them; when we come to the actual construction of the State, we shall, God willing, make the houses precede marriage, and crown all our architectural work with our marriage-laws. For the present we shall confine ourselves to a brief outline of our building regulations.

CLIN. Certainly.

ATH. The temples we must erect all round the market-place, and in a circle round the whole city, on the highest spots, for the sake of ease in fencing them and of cleanliness: beside the temples we will set the houses of the officials and the law-courts, in which, as being most holy places, they will give and receive judgments,—partly because therein they deal with holy matters, and partly because they are the seats of holy gods; and in these will fittingly be held trials for murder and for all crimes worthy of

479

778 περὶ δὲ τειχῶν, ὦ Μέγιλλε, ἔγωγ᾽ ἂν τῇ Σπάρτῃ
ξυμφεροίμην τὸ καθεύδειν ἐᾶν ἐν τῇ γῇ κατα-
κείμενα τὰ τείχη καὶ μὴ ἐπανιστάναι, τῶνδε
εἵνεκα. καλῶς μὲν καὶ ὁ ποιητικὸς ὑπὲρ αὐτῶν
λόγος ὑμνεῖται, τὸ χαλκᾶ καὶ σιδηρᾶ δεῖν εἶναι
E τὰ τείχη μᾶλλον ἢ γήϊνα· τὸ δ᾽ ἡμέτερον ἔτι
πρὸς τούτοις γέλωτ᾽ ἂν δικαίως πάμπολυν ὄφλοι,
τὸ κατ᾽ ἐνιαυτὸν μὲν ἐκπέμπειν εἰς τὴν χώραν
τοὺς νέους, τὰ μὲν σκάψοντας, τὰ δὲ ταφρεύσον-
τας, τὰ δὲ καὶ διά τινων οἰκοδομήσεων εἴρξοντας
τοὺς πολεμίους, ὡς δὴ τῶν ὅρων τῆς χώρας οὐκ
ἐάσοντας ἐπιβαίνειν, τεῖχος δὲ περιβαλοίμεθα,
ὃ πρῶτον μὲν πρὸς ὑγίειαν ταῖς πόλεσιν οὐδαμῶς
συμφέρει, πρὸς δέ τινα μαλθακὴν ἕξιν ταῖς ψυχαῖς
τῶν ἐνοικούντων εἴωθε ποιεῖν, προκαλούμενον εἰς
αὐτὸ καταφεύγοντας μὴ ἀμύνεσθαι τοὺς πολε-
779 μίους, μηδὲ τῷ φρουρεῖν ἀεί τινας ἐν αὐτῇ νύκτωρ
καὶ μεθ᾽ ἡμέραν, τούτῳ τῆς σωτηρίας τυγχά-
νειν, τείχεσι δὲ καὶ πύλαις διανοεῖσθαι φρα-
χθέντας τε καὶ καθεύδοντας σωτηρίας ὄντως ἕξειν
μηχανάς, ὡς ἐπὶ τὸ μὴ πονεῖν γεγονότας, ἀγνο-
οῦντας δ᾽ αὖ τὴν ῥαστώνην, ὡς ὄντως ἐστὶν ἐκ
τῶν πόνων· ἐκ ῥαστώνης δέ γε, οἶμαι, τῆς αἰσχρᾶς
οἱ πόνοι καὶ ῥαθυμίας πεφύκασι γίγνεσθαι πάλιν·
ἀλλ᾽ εἰ δὴ τεῖχός γέ τι χρεὼν ἀνθρώποις εἶναι,
B τὰς οἰκοδομίας χρὴ τὰς τῶν ἰδίων οἰκήσεων οὕτως
ἐξ ἀρχῆς βάλλεσθαι, ὅπως ἂν ᾖ πᾶσα ἡ πόλις
ἓν τεῖχος, ὁμαλότητί τε καὶ ὁμοιότησιν εἰς τὰς
ὁδοὺς πασῶν τῶν οἰκήσεων ἐχουσῶν εὐέρκειαν·

---

[1] Unknown. Cp. Arist. Pol. 1330ᵇ 32 ff., and the saying of
Lycurgus (quoted by Plutarch, Lycurg. xix.) οὐκ ἂν εἴη
ἀτείχιστος πόλις ἅτις ἀνδράσι οὐ πλίνθοις ἐστεφάνωται. "Earth"
480

death. As to walls, Megillus, I would agree with
your Sparta in letting the walls lie sleeping in the
ground, and not wake them up, and that for the
following reasons. It is a fine saying of the poet,[1]
and often repeated, that walls should be made of
bronze and iron rather than of earth. But our plan,
in addition to this, would deserve to raise roars of
laughter,—I mean the plan of sending young men
into the country every year to dig and trench and
build, so as to keep the enemy out[2] and prevent
their ever setting foot on the borders of the land—
if we were also to build a wall round; for, in the
first place, a wall is by no means an advantage to
a city as regards health, and, moreover, it usually
causes a soft habit of soul in the inhabitants, by
inviting them to seek refuge within it instead of
repelling the enemy; instead of securing their
safety by keeping watch night and day, it tempts
them to believe that their safety is ensured if they
are fenced in with walls and gates and go to sleep,
like men born to shirk toil, little knowing that ease
is really the fruit of toil, whereas a new crop of toils
is the inevitable outcome, as I think, of dishonour-
able ease and sloth. But if men really must have a
wall, then the building of the private houses must
be arranged from the start in such a way that the
whole city may form a single wall; all the houses
must have good walls, built regularly and in a similar
style, facing the roads,[3] so that the whole city will

(like πλίνθοι) here means really "stone," the soil of Greece
being rocky.

 [2] Cp. 760 E.

 [3] These "roads" (or streets) would divide the city into
blocks, surrounded by continuous walls formed by the outer
circle of houses, all of the same size and shape.

481

779 ἰδεῖν τε οὐκ ἀηδὲς μιᾶς οἰκίας σχῆμα ἐχούσης
αὐτῆς, εἴς τε τὴν τῆς φυλακῆς ῥαστώνην ὅλῳ
καὶ παντὶ πρὸς σωτηρίαν γίγνοιτ᾽ ἂν διάφορος.
τούτων δέ ὡς¹ ἂν μένῃ² τὰ κατ᾽ ἀρχὰς οἰκο-
δομηθέντα, μέλειν μὲν μάλιστα τοῖς ἐνοικοῦσι
C πρέπον ἂν εἴη, τοὺς δὲ ἀστυνόμους ἐπιμελεῖσθαι
καὶ προσαναγκάζοντας τὸν ὀλιγωροῦντα ζημι-
οῦντας, καὶ πάντων δὴ τῶν κατὰ τὸ ἄστυ κα-
θαρότητός τ᾽ ἐπιμελεῖσθαι, καὶ ὅπως ἰδιώτης
μηδεὶς μηδὲν τῶν τῆς πόλεως μήτε οἰκοδομήμασι
μήτε οὖν ὀρύγμασιν ἐπιλήψεται. καὶ δὴ καὶ
ὑδάτων τῶν ἐκ Διὸς εὐροίας τούτους ἐπιμελεῖσθαι
χρεών, καὶ ὅσα ἐντὸς πόλεως ἢ ὁπόσα ἔξω πρέπον
ἂν οἰκεῖν εἴη. ταῦτα δὲ πάντα ξυνιδόντες ταῖς
D χρείαις οἱ νομοφύλακες ἐπινομοθετούντων καὶ
τῶν ἄλλων ὁπόσα ἂν ὁ νόμος ἐκλείπῃ δι᾽ ἀπορίαν.
ὅτε δὲ ταῦτά τε καὶ τὰ περὶ ἀγορὰν οἰκοδομήματα
καὶ τὰ περὶ τὰ γυμνάσια καὶ πάντα ὅσα διδασ-
καλεῖα κατεσκευασμένα περιμένει τοὺς φοιτητὰς
καὶ θεατὰς θέατρα, πορευώμεθα ἐπὶ τὰ μετὰ τοὺς
γάμους, τῆς νομοθεσίας ἑξῆς ἐχόμενοι.

ΚΛ. Πάνυ μὲν οὖν.

ΑΘ. Γάμοι μὲν τοίνυν ἡμῖν ἔστωσαν γεγονότες,
ὦ Κλεινία· δίαιτα δὲ πρὸ παιδογονίας οὐκ ἐλάτ-
E των ἐνιαυσίας γίγνοιτ᾽ ἂν τὸ μετὰ τοῦτο, ἣν δὴ
τίνα τρόπον χρὴ ζῆν νυμφίον καὶ νύμφην ἐν
πόλει διαφερούσῃ τῶν πολλῶν ἐσομένῃ, τὸ δὴ
τῶν νῦν εἰρημένων ἐχόμενον εἰπεῖν, οὐ πάντων
εὐκολώτατον, ἀλλὰ ὄντων οὐκ ὀλίγων τῶν ἔμπροσθεν τοιούτων τοῦτο ἔτι ἐκείνων τῶν πολλῶν
δυσχερέστερον ἀποδέχεσθαι τῷ πλήθει. τό γε

¹ ὡς Burnet : ἕως MSS.

have the form of a single house, which will render its appearance not unpleasing, besides being far and away the best plan for ensuring safety and ease for defence. To see that the original buildings remain will fittingly be the special charge of the inmates; and the city-stewards should supervise them, and compel by fines those who are negligent, and also watch over the cleanliness of everything in the city, and prevent any private person from encroaching on State property either by buildings or diggings. These officers must also keep a watch over the proper flowing of the rain-water, and over all other matters, whether within or without the city, that it is right for them to manage. All such details—and all else that the lawgiver is unable to deal with and omits—the Law-wardens shall regulate by supplementary decrees, taking account of the practical requirements. And now that these buildings and those of the market-place, and the gymnasia, and all the schools have been erected and await their inmates, and the theatres their spectators, let us proceed to the subject which comes next after marriage, taking our legislation in order.

CLIN. By all means.

ATH. Let us regard the marriage ceremony as now completed, Clinias; next will come the period before child-birth, which will extend to a full year: how the bride and bridegroom ought to pass this time in a State that will be unlike most other States,—that is to be our next theme, and it is not the easiest of things to explain; we have uttered not a few hard sayings before, but none of them all will the mass find harder to accept than this.

---

² μένῃ Schneider: μὲν ῇ MSS.

779 μὴν δοκοῦν ὀρθὸν καὶ ἀληθὲς εἶναι πάντως
ῥητέον, ὦ Κλεινία.

ΚΛ. Πάνυ μὲν οὖν.

ΑΘ. Ὅστις δὴ διανοεῖται πόλεσιν ἀποφαίνε-
780 σθαι νόμους, πῆ τὰ δημόσια καὶ κοινὰ αὐτοὺς
χρὴ ζῆν πράττοντας, τῶν δὲ ἰδίων ὅσον ἀνάγκη
μηδὲ οἴεται δεῖν, ἐξουσίαν δὲ ἑκάστοις εἶναι τὴν
ἡμέραν ζῆν ὅπως ἂν ἐθέλῃ, καὶ μὴ πάντα διὰ
τάξεως δεῖν γίγνεσθαι, προέμενος δὲ τὰ ἴδια ἀνομοθέτητα ἡγεῖται τά γε κοινὰ καὶ δημόσια ἐθελήσειν
αὐτοὺς ζῆν διὰ νόμων, οὐκ ὀρθῶς διανοεῖται.
τίνος δὴ χάριν ταῦτα εἴρηται ; τοῦδε, ὅτι φήσομεν
δεῖν ἡμῖν τοὺς νυμφίους μηδὲν διαφερόντως μηδὲ
ἧττον ἐν ξυσσιτίοις τὴν δίαιταν ποιεῖσθαι τοῦ
B πρὸ τῶν γάμων χρόνου γενομένου. καὶ τοῦτο
μὲν δὴ θαυμαστὸν ὂν ὅτε κατ' ἀρχὰς πρῶτον
ἐγένετο ἐν τοῖς παρ' ὑμῖν τόποις, πολέμου τινὸς
αὐτό, ὥς γ' εἰκός, νομοθετήσαντος ἤ τινος ἑτέρου
τὴν αὐτὴν δύναμιν ἔχοντος πράγματος ἐν ὀλιγαν-
θρωπίαις ὑπὸ πολλῆς ἀπορίας ἐχομένοις· γευ-
σαμένοις δὲ καὶ ἀναγκασθεῖσι χρήσασθαι τοῖς
ξυσσιτίοις ἔδοξε μέγα δὴ φέρειν[1] εἰς σωτηρίαν
C τὸ νόμιμον, καὶ κατέστη δὴ τρόπῳ τινὶ τοιούτῳ
τὸ ἐπιτήδευμα ὑμῖν τὸ τῶν ξυσσιτίων.

ΚΛ. Ἔοικε γοῦν.

ΑΘ. Ὃ δὴ ἔλεγον, ὅτι θαυμαστὸν ὂν τοῦτό
ποτε καὶ φοβερὸν ἐπιτάξαι τισὶ νῦν οὐχ ὁμοίως

---

[1] δὴ φέρειν: διαφέρειν MSS. (φέρειν ci. Schanz)

---

[1] Cp. 821 A ; Epist. 7. 330 A.

All the same, what we believe to be right and true must by all means be stated,[1] Clinias.

CLIN. Certainly.

ATH. Whoever proposes to publish laws for States, regulating the conduct of the citizens in State affairs and public matters, and deems that there is no need to make laws for their private conduct, even in necessary matters, but that everyone should be allowed to spend his day just as he pleases, instead of its being compulsory for everything, public and private, to be done by a regular rule, and supposes that, if he leaves private conduct unregulated by law, the citizens will still consent to regulate their public and civil life by law,—this man is wrong in his proposal. For what reason have I said this? For this reason,—because we shall assert that the married people must take their meals at the public messes neither more nor less than they did during the time preceding marriage. When the customs of the public mess first arose in your countries—probably dictated by a war or by some event of equal potency, when you were short of men and in dire straits,—it seemed an astonishing institution; but after you had had experience of these public messes and had been obliged to adopt them, the custom seemed to contribute admirably towards security; and in some such way as that the public mess came to be one of your established institutions.[2]

CLIN. That is likely enough.

ATH. So, though this was once, as I said, an astonishing and alarming institution to impose on people, a man who tried to impose it as a law nowa-

[2] Cp. Ar. *Pol.* 1272ᵃ 2 ff.

780 τῷ προστάττοντι δυσχερὲς ἂν εἴη νομοθετεῖν αὐτό.
τὸ δ' ἑξῆς τούτῳ, πεφυκός τε ὀρθῶς ἂν γίγνεσθαι
γιγνόμενον, νῦν τε οὐδαμῇ γιγνόμενον, ὀλίγου [τε]¹
ποιοῦν τὸν νομοθέτην, τὸ τῶν παιζόντων, εἰς
πῦρ ξαίνειν καὶ μυρία ἕτερα τοιαῦτα ἀνήνυτα
D πονοῦντα² δρᾶν, οὐ ῥᾴδιον οὔτ' εἰπεῖν οὔτ' εἰπόντα
ἀποτελεῖν.

ΚΛ. Τί δὴ τοῦτο, ὦ ξένε, ἐπιχειρῶν λέγειν
ἔοικας σφόδρα ἀποκνεῖν ;

ΑΘ. Ἀκούοιτ' ἄν, ἵνα μὴ πολλὴ διατριβὴ
γίγνηται περὶ τοῦτ' αὐτὸ μάτην. πᾶν μὲν γὰρ ὅ
τί περ ἂν τάξεως καὶ νόμου μετέχον ἐν πόλει
γίγνηται πάντα ἀγαθὰ ἀπεργάζεται, τῶν δὲ
ἀτάκτων ἢ τῶν κακῶς ταχθέντων λύει τὰ πολλὰ
τῶν εὖ τεταγμένων ἄλλα ἕτερα. ὃ δὴ καὶ νῦν
ἐφέστηκε περὶ³ τὸ λεγόμενον. ὑμῖν γάρ, ὦ
E Κλεινία καὶ Μέγιλλε, τὰ μὲν περὶ τοὺς ἄνδρας
ξυσσίτια καλῶς ἅμα καὶ ὅπερ εἶπον θαυμαστῶς
καθέστηκεν ἐκ θείας τινὸς ἀνάγκης, τὸ δὲ περὶ
τὰς γυναῖκας οὐδαμῶς ὀρθῶς ἀνομοθέτητον
781 μεθεῖται καὶ οὐκ εἰς τὸ φῶς ἦκται τὸ τῆς ξυσσι-
τίας αὐτῶν ἐπιτήδευμα, ἀλλ' ὃ καὶ ἄλλως γένος
ἡμῶν τῶν ἀνθρώπων λαθραιότερον μᾶλλον
καὶ ἐπικλοπώτερον ἔφυ, τὸ θῆλυ, διὰ τὸ
ἀσθενές, οὐκ ὀρθῶς τοῦτο εἴξαντος τοῦ νομοθέτου
δύστακτον ὂν ἀφείθη. διὰ δὲ τούτου μεθειμένου
πολλὰ ὑμῖν παρέρρει, πολὺ ἄμεινον ἂν ἔχοντα
εἰ νόμων ἔτυχεν ἢ τὰ νῦν· οὐ γὰρ ἥμισυ μόνον
ἐστίν, ὡς δόξειεν ἄν, τὸ περὶ τὰς γυναῖκας ἀκοσ-

___

¹ [τε] bracketed by Badham, England.
² πονοῦντα Ast, Schanz : ποιοῦντα MSS.
³ ὃ . . . περὶ : οὗ . . . πέρι MSS., edd. (πεῖρα Badham).

days would not find it an equally difficult task. But the practice which follows on this institution, and which, if carried out, would be really successful,—although at present it nowhere is carried out, and so causes the lawgiver (if he tries) to be practically carding his wool (as the proverb has it) into the fire, and labouring in vain at an endless tale of toils,—this practice it is neither easy to state nor, when stated, to carry into effect.

CLIN. Why do you show so much hesitation, Stranger, in mentioning this?

ATH. Listen now, so that we may not spend much time on the matter to no purpose. Everything that takes place in the State, if it participates in order and law, confers all kinds of blessings; but most things that are either without order or badly-ordered counteract the effects of the well-ordered. And it is into this plight that the practice we are discussing has fallen. In your case, Clinias and Megillus, public meals for men are, as I said, rightly and admirably established by a divine necessity, but for women this institution is left, quite wrongly, unprescribed by law, nor are public meals for them brought to the light of day; instead of this, the female sex, that very section of humanity which, owing to its frailty, is in other respects most secretive and intriguing, is abandoned to its disorderly condition through the perverse compliance of the lawgiver. Owing to your neglect of that sex, you have had an influx of many consequences which would have been much better than they now are if they had been under legal control. For it is not merely, as one might suppose, a matter affecting one-half of our whole task—this matter of neglecting

781Β μήτως περιορώμενον, ὅσῳ δὲ ἡ θήλεια ἡμῖν φύσις
ἐστὶ πρὸς ἀρετὴν χείρων τῆς τῶν ἀρρένων,
τοσούτῳ διαφέρει πρὸς τὸ πλέον ἢ ἥμισυ[1] εἶναι.
τοῦτ' οὖν ἐπαναλαβεῖν καὶ ἐπανορθώσασθαι καὶ
πάντα συντάξασθαι κοινῇ γυναιξί τε καὶ ἀνδράσιν ἐπιτηδεύματα βέλτιον πρὸς πόλεως εὐδαιμονίαν. νῦν δὲ οὕτως ἧκται τὸ τῶν ἀνθρώπων
γένος οὐδαμῶς εἰς τοῦτο εὐτυχῶς, ὥστε οὐδὲ
μνησθῆναι περὶ αὐτοῦ ἐν ἄλλοις γ' ἐστὶ τόποις
C καὶ πόλεσι νοῦν ἔχοντος, ὅπου μηδὲ ξυσσίτια
ὑπάρχει τὸ παράπαν δεδογμένα κατὰ πόλιν εἶναι.
πόθεν δή τίς γε ἔργῳ μὴ καταγελάστως ἐπιχειρήσει γυναῖκας προσβιάζεσθαι τὴν σίτων καὶ
ποτῶν ἀνάλωσιν φανερὰν θεωρεῖσθαι; τούτου
γὰρ οὐκ ἔστιν ὅ τι χαλεπώτερον ἂν ὑπομείνειε
τοῦτο τὸ γένος· εἰθισμένον γὰρ δεδυκὸς καὶ σκο-
τεινὸν ζῆν, ἀγόμενον δ' εἰς φῶς βίᾳ πᾶσαν
ἀντίτασιν ἀντιτεῖνον, πολὺ κρατήσει τοῦ νομο-
D θέτου· τοῦτ' οὖν ἄλλοθι μέν, ἥπερ εἶπον, οὐδ' ἂν
τὸν λόγον ὑπομείνειε τὸν ὀρθὸν ῥηθέντα ἄνευ
πάσης βοῆς, ἐνθάδε δὲ ἴσως ἄν. εἰ δὴ δοκεῖ
λόγου γ' ἕνεκα μὴ ἀτυχῆ τὸν περὶ πάσης τῆς
πολιτείας γενέσθαι λόγον, ἐθέλω λέγειν ὡς ἀγαθόν ἐστι καὶ πρέπον, εἰ καὶ σφῷν ξυνδοκεῖ ἀκούειν·
εἰ δὲ μή, ἐᾶν.

ΚΛ. Ἀλλ', ὦ ξένε, θαυμαστῶς τό γε ἀκοῦσαι
νῷν πάντως που ξυνδοκεῖ.

ΑΘ. Ἀκούωμεν δή. θαυμάσητε δὲ μηδὲν ἐὰν
ὑμῖν ἄνωθέν ποθεν ἐπιχειρεῖν δόξω· σχολῆς γὰρ
E ἀπολαύομεν καὶ οὐδὲν ἡμᾶς ἐστι τὸ κατεπεῖγον τὸ
μὴ πάντη πάντως σκοπεῖν τὰ περὶ τοὺς νόμους.

---

[1] ἥμισυ : διπλάσιον MSS., edd. (cp. 767 E).

to regulate women,—but in as far as females are inferior in goodness to males, just in so far it affects more than the half. It is better, then, for the welfare of the State to revise and reform this institution, and to regulate all the institutions for both men and women in common. At present, however, the human race is so far from having reached this happy position, that a man of discretion must actually avoid all mention of the practice in districts and States where even the existence of public meals is absolutely without any formal recognition. How then shall one attempt, without being laughed at, actually to compel women to take food and drink publicly and exposed to the view of all? The female sex would more readily endure anything rather than this: accustomed as they are to live a retired and private life, women will use every means to resist being led out into the light, and they will prove much too strong for the lawgiver. So that elsewhere, as I said, women would not so much as listen to the mention of the right rule without shrieks of indignation; but in our State perhaps they will. So if we agree that our discourse about the polity as a whole must not—so far as theory goes—prove abortive, I am willing to explain how this institution is good and fitting, if you are equally desirous to listen, but otherwise to leave it alone.

CLIN. Nay, Stranger, we are both inexpressibly desirous to listen.

ATH. Let us listen, then. And do not be surprised if you find me taking the subject up again from an early point. For we are now enjoying leisure, and there is no pressing reason to hinder us from considering laws from all possible points of view.

781 ΚΛ. Ὀρθῶς εἴρηκας.

ΑΘ. Πάλιν τοίνυν ἐπὶ τὰ πρῶτα ἐπαναχω-
ρήσωμεν λεχθέντα. εὖ γὰρ δὴ τό γε τοσοῦτον
χρὴ πάντ᾽ ἄνδρα ξυννοεῖν, ὡς ἡ τῶν ἀνθρώπων
γένεσις ἢ τὸ παράπαν ἀρχὴν οὐδεμίαν εἴληχεν
782 οὐδ᾽ ἕξει ποτέ γε τελευτήν, ἀλλ᾽ ἦν τε ἀεὶ καὶ
ἔσται πάντως, ἢ μῆκός τι [τῆς ἀρχῆς][1] ἀφ᾽ οὗ
γέγονεν ἀμήχανον [ἂν χρόνον][2] ὅσον γεγονὸς ἂν
εἴη.

ΚΛ. Τί μήν;

ΑΘ. Τί οὖν; πόλεων συστάσεις καὶ φθορὰς
καὶ ἐπιτηδεύματα παντοῖα τάξεώς τε καὶ ἀταξίας
καὶ βρώσεως[3] (καὶ πωμάτων τε ἅμα καὶ βρωμάτων)
ἐπιθυμήματα παντοδαπὰ πάντως καὶ περὶ πᾶσαν
τὴν γῆν ἆρ᾽ οὐκ οἰόμεθα γεγονέναι, καὶ στροφὰς
ὡρῶν παντοίας, ἐν αἷς τὰ ζῷα μεταβάλλειν αὑτῶι
Β παμπληθεῖς μεταβολὰς εἰκός;

ΚΛ. Πῶς γὰρ οὔ;

ΑΘ. Τί οὖν; πιστεύομεν ἀμπέλους τε φανῆναί
πού ποτε πρότερον οὐκ οὔσας; ὡσαύτως δὲ καὶ
ἐλάας καὶ τὰ Δήμητρός τε καὶ Κόρης δῶρα;
Τριπτόλεμόν τέ τινα τῶν τοιούτων γενέσθαι
διάκονον; ἐν ᾧ δὲ μηδὲ ταῦτα ἦν πω[4] χρόνῳ,
μῶν οὐκ οἰόμεθα τὰ ζῷα, καθάπερ νῦν, ἐπὶ τὴν
ἀλλήλων ἐδωδὴν τρέπεσθαι;

ΚΛ. Τί μήν;

---

[1] [τῆς ἀρχῆς] bracketed by Ast.
[2] [ἂν χρόνον] I bracket (χρόνου Ast).

CLIN. Very true.

ATH. Let us, then, revert again to our first statements.[1] Thus much at least every man ought to understand,—that either the human race never had a beginning at all, and will never have an end, but always was and always will be, or else it must have been in existence an incalculable length of time from the date when it first began.

CLIN. Undoubtedly.

ATH. Well then, do we not suppose that all the world over and in all sorts of ways there have been risings and fallings of States, and institutions of every variety of order and disorder, and appetites for food—both meats and drinks—of every kind, and all sorts of variations in the seasons, during which it is probable that the animals underwent innumerable changes?

CLIN. Certainly.

ATH. Are we to believe, then, that vines, not previously existing, appeared at a certain stage; and olives, likewise, and the gifts of Demeter and Korê?[2] And that some Triptolemus was the minister of such fruits? And during the period that these fruits were as yet non-existent, must we not suppose that the animals turned, as they do now, to feeding on one another.

CLIN. Of course.

[1] 676 A ff.

[2] Or Persephone, daughter of the Earth-mother, Demeter. Triptolemus was a mythical hero of Eleusis, worshipped as the inventor and patron of agriculture.

---

[3] Ast and Schanz bracket καὶ βρώσεως: I mark the next six words as parenthetic (στρωμάτων for βρωμάτων Apelt).

[4] πω England: τῷ MSS.

782C ΑΘ. Τὸ δὲ μὴν θύειν ἀνθρώπους ἀλλήλους ἔτι
καὶ νῦν παραμένον ὁρῶμεν πολλοῖς· καὶ τοὐναντίον ἀκούομεν ἐν ἄλλοις, ὅτε οὐδὲ βοὸς ἐτόλμων
μὲν[1] γεύεσθαι θύματά τε οὐκ ἦν τοῖς θεοῖσι ζῷα,
πέλανοι δὲ καὶ μέλιτι καρποὶ δεδευμένοι καὶ
τοιαῦτα ἄλλα ἁγνὰ θύματα, σαρκῶν δ᾽ ἀπείχοντο
ὡς οὐχ ὅσιον ὂν ἐσθίειν οὐδὲ τοὺς τῶν θεῶν βωμοὺς
αἵματι μιαίνειν, ἀλλὰ Ὀρφικοί τινες λεγόμενοι
βίοι ἐγίγνοντο ἡμῶν τοῖς τότε, ἀψύχων μὲν
D ἐχόμενοι πάντων, ἐμψύχων δὲ τοὐναντίον πάντων
ἀπεχόμενοι.

ΚΛ. Καὶ σφόδρα λεγόμενα ἅ γ᾽ εἴρηκας, καὶ
πιστεύεσθαι πιθανά.

ΑΘ. Πρὸς οὖν δὴ τί ταῦτα, εἴποι τις ἄν, ὑμῖν
πάντ᾽ ἐρρήθη τὰ νῦν;

ΚΛ. Ὀρθῶς ὑπέλαβες, ὦ ξένε.

ΑΘ. Καὶ τοίνυν, ἐὰν δύνωμαι, τὰ τούτοις ἑξῆς,
ὦ Κλεινία, πειράσομαι φράζειν.

ΚΛ. Λέγοις ἄν.

ΑΘ. Ὁρῶ πάντα τοῖς ἀνθρώποις ἐκ τριττῆς
χρείας καὶ ἐπιθυμίας ἠρτημένα, δι᾽ ὧν ἀρετή τε
E αὐτοῖς ἀγομένοις ὀρθῶς καὶ τοὐναντίον ἀποβαίνει
κακῶς ἀχθεῖσι. ταῦτα δ᾽ ἐστὶν ἐδωδὴ μὲν καὶ
πόσις εὐθὺς γενομένοις, ἣν πέρι ἅπασαν πᾶν ζῷον
ἔμφυτον ἔρωτα ἔχον, μεστὸν οἴστρου τ᾽ ἐστὶ καὶ
ἀνηκουστίας τοῦ λέγοντος ἄλλο τι δεῖν πράττειν
πλὴν τὰς ἡδονὰς καὶ ἐπιθυμίας τὰς περὶ ἅπαντα
ταῦτα ἀποπληροῦντας[2] λύπης τῆς ἁπάσης ἄρδην[3]
783 σφᾶς ἀπαλλάττειν· τρίτη δὲ ἡμῖν καὶ μεγίστη

---

[1] ἐτόλμων μὲν Schanz : ἐτολμῶμεν MSS.
[2] ἀποπληροῦντας : ἀποπληροῦντα MSS., edd.

ATH. The custom of men sacrificing one another is, in fact, one that survives even now among many peoples; whereas amongst others we hear of how the opposite custom existed, when they were forbidden so much as to eat an ox, and their offerings to the gods consisted, not of animals, but of cakes of meal and grain steeped in honey, and other such bloodless sacrifices, and from flesh they abstained as though it were unholy to eat it or to stain with blood the altars of the gods; instead of that, those of us men who then existed lived what is called an "Orphic life," keeping wholly to inanimate food and, contrariwise, abstaining wholly from things animate.

CLIN. Certainly what you say is widely reported and easy to credit.

ATH. Someone might ask us—" For what purpose have you now said all this?"

CLIN. A correct surmise, Stranger.

ATH. So I will try, if I can, Clinias, to explain the subject which comes next in order.

CLIN. Say on.

ATH. I observe that with men all things depend on a threefold need and desire, wherein if they proceed rightly, the result is goodness, if badly, the opposite. Of these desires they possess those for food and drink as soon as they are born; and about the whole sphere of food every creature has an instinctive lust, and is full of craving, and quite deaf to any suggestion that they ought to do anything else than satisfy their tastes and desires for all such objects, and thus rid themselves entirely of all pain. Thirdly comes our greatest need and keenest

---

[3] ἄρδην: ἀεὶ δεῖν MSS. (Ast brackets δεῖν)

783 χρεία καὶ ἔρως ὀξύτατος ὕστατος μὲν ὁρμᾶται,
διαπυρωτάτους δὲ τοὺς ἀνθρώπους μανίαις ἀπεργάζεται πάντως, ὁ περὶ τὴν τοῦ γένους σπορὰν
ὕβρει πλείστῃ καόμενος. ἃ δὴ δεῖ τρία νοσήματα
τρέποντας[1] εἰς τὸ βέλτιστον παρὰ τὸ λεγόμενον
ἥδιστον τρισὶ μὲν τοῖς μεγίστοις πειρᾶσθαι
κατέχειν, φόβῳ καὶ νόμῳ καὶ τῷ ἀληθεῖ λόγῳ,
προσχρωμένους μέντοι Μούσαις τε καὶ ἀγωνίοισι
θεοῖς σβεννύναι τὴν αὔξην τε καὶ ἐπιρροήν.

B   Παίδων δὲ δὴ γένεσιν μετὰ τοὺς γάμους θῶμεν,
καὶ μετὰ γένεσιν τροφὴν καὶ παιδείαν. καὶ τάχ᾽
ἂν οὕτω προϊόντων τῶν λόγων ὅ τε νόμος ἡμῖν
ἕκαστος περαίνοιτο εἰς τοὔμπροσθεν, ⟨καὶ⟩[2] ἐπὶ
ξυσσίτια ἡνίκ᾽ ἂν ἀφικώμεθα, τὰς τοιαύτας
κοινωνίας εἴτε ἄρα γυναικῶν εἴτε ἀνδρῶν δεῖ
μόνων γίγνεσθαι, προσμίξαντες αὐτοῖς ἐγγύθεν
ἴσως μᾶλλον κατοψόμεθα, τά τε ἐπίπροσθεν
αὐτῶν, ἔτι νῦν ὄντα ἀνομοθέτητα, τάξαντες αὐτὰ
C ἐπίπροσθεν ποιησόμεθα, καὶ ὅπερ ἐρρήθη νῦν δή,
κατοψόμεθά τε αὐτὰ ἀκριβέστερον μᾶλλόν τε
τοὺς προσήκοντας αὐτοῖς καὶ πρέποντας νόμους
ἂν θεῖμεν.

ΚΛ. Ὀρθότατα λέγεις.

ΑΘ. Φυλάξωμεν τοίνυν τῇ μνήμῃ τὰ νῦν δὴ
λεχθέντα· ἴσως γὰρ χρείαν ποτ᾽ αὐτῶν πάντων
ἕξομεν.

ΚΛ. Τὰ ποῖα δὴ διακελεύει;

ΑΘ. Ἃ τοῖς τρισὶ διωριζόμεθα ῥήμασι· βρῶσιν
μὲν ἐλέγομέν που, καὶ δεύτερον πόσιν, καὶ ἀφρο-
D δισίων δέ τινα διαπτόησιν τρίτον.

---

[1] τρέποντας Stephens : τρέποντα MSS.
[2] ⟨καὶ⟩ I add, and read ἡνίκ᾽ ἂν ἀφικώμεθα for ἡνίκα ἀφικόμεθα of MSS. (Zur. and Ald. add εἰς after ἀφικόμεθα).

lust, which, though the latest to emerge, influences the soul of men with most raging frenzy—the lust for the sowing of offspring that burns with utmost violence. These three morbid states[1] we must direct towards what is most good, instead of what is (nominally) most pleasant, trying to check them by means of the three greatest forces—fear, law, and true reasoning,—reinforced by the Muses and the Gods of Games, so as to quench thereby their increase and inflow.

So let us place the subject of the production of children next after that of marriage, and after their production, their nurture and education. If our discourse proceeds on these lines, possibly each of our laws will attain completion, and when we come to the public meals, by approaching these at close quarters we shall probably discern more clearly whether such associations ought to be for men only, or for women as well ; and thus we shall not only prescribe the preliminaries that are still without legal regulation, and place them as fences before the common meals, but also, as I said just now, we shall discuss more exactly the character of the common meals, and thus be more likely to prescribe for them laws that are suitable and fitting.

CLIN. You are perfectly right.

ATH. Let us, then, bear in mind the things we mentioned a moment ago ; for probably we shall need them all presently.

CLIN. What are the things you bid us remember ?

ATH. Those we distinguished by the three terms we used : we spoke, you recollect, of eating, secondly of drinking, and thirdly of sexual excitement.

[1] The soul is in a "diseased" state when wholly dominated by any irrational desire or passion.

PLATO

783   κλ.   Πάντως, ὦ ξένε, μεμνησόμεθά που ὧν τὰ
νῦν διακελεύει.

αθ.   Καλῶς. ἔλθωμεν δ᾽ ἐπὶ τὰ νυμφικά,
διδάξοντές τε αὐτοὺς πῶς χρὴ καὶ τίνα τρόπον
τοὺς παῖδας ποιεῖσθαι, καὶ ἐὰν ἄρα μὴ πείθωμεν,
ἀπειλήσοντές τισι νόμοις.

κλ.   Πῶς ;

αθ.   Νύμφην χρὴ διανοεῖσθαι καὶ νυμφίον ὡς
ὅτι καλλίστους καὶ ἀρίστους εἰς δύναμιν ἀποδει-
E ξομένους παῖδας τῇ πόλει.   πάντες δ᾽ ἄνθρωποι
κοινωνοὶ πάσης πράξεως, ἡνίκα μὲν ἂν προσέχω-
σιν αὑτοῖς τε καὶ τῇ πράξει τὸν νοῦν, πάντα καλὰ
καὶ ἀγαθὰ ἀπεργάζονται, μὴ προσέχοντες δὲ ἢ μὴ
ἔχοντες νοῦν τἀναντία.   προσεχέτω δὴ καὶ ὁ
νυμφίος τῇ τε νύμφῃ καὶ τῇ παιδοποιίᾳ τὸν νοῦν,
κατὰ ταὐτὰ δὲ καὶ ἡ νύμφη, τοῦτον τὸν χρόνον
διαφερόντως ὃν ἂν μήπω παῖδες αὐτοῖς ὦσι γεγο-
784 νότες.   ἐπίσκοποι δ᾽ ἔστωσαν τούτων ἃς εἱλόμεθα
γυναῖκες, πλείους εἴτ᾽ ἐλάττους, τοῖς ἄρχουσιν
ὁπόσας ἂν δοκῇ προστάττειν τε καὶ ὁπόταν, πρὸς
τὸ τῆς Εἰλειθυίας ἱερὸν ἑκάστης ἡμέρας ξυλλε-
γόμεναι μέχρι τρίτου μέρους [ὥρας],[1] οἳ δὴ συλλε-
χθεῖσαι διαγγελλόντων ἀλλήλαις εἴ τίς τινα ὁρᾷ
πρὸς ἄλλ᾽ ἄττα βλέποντα ἄνδρα ἢ καὶ γυναῖκα
τῶν παιδοποιουμένων ἢ πρὸς τὰ τεταγμένα ὑπὸ
τῶν ἐν τοῖς γάμοις θυσιῶν τε καὶ ἱερῶν γενομένων.
B ἡ δὲ παιδοποιία καὶ φυλακὴ τῶν παιδοποιουμένων
δεκέτις ἔστω, μὴ πλείω δὲ χρόνον, ὅταν εὔροια ᾖ
τῆς γενέσεως.   ἂν δὲ ἄγονοί τινες εἰς τοῦτον
γίγνωνται τὸν χρόνον, μετὰ τῶν οἰκείων καὶ

---

[1] [ὥρας] I bracket.

[1] Goddess of childbirth.

CLIN. We shall certainly remember the things you now bid us, Stranger.

ATH. Very good. Let us now come to the nuptials, so as to instruct them how and in what manner they ought to produce children, and, if we fail to persuade them, to threaten them by certain laws.

CLIN. How?

ATH. The bride and bridegroom must set their minds to produce for the State children of the greatest possible goodness and beauty. All people that are partners in any action produce results that are fair and good whensoever they apply their minds to themselves and the action, but the opposite results when either they have no minds or fail to apply them. The bridegroom, therefore, shall apply his mind both to the bride and to the work of procreation, and the bride shall do likewise, especially during the period when they have no children yet born. In charge of them there shall be the women-inspectors whom we have chosen,—more or fewer of them, according to the number and times of their appointments, decided by the officials; and they shall meet every day at the temple of Eileithyia,[1] for, at the most, a third part [of the day];[2] and at their meetings they shall report to one another any case they may have noticed where any man or woman of the procreative age is devoting his attention to other things instead of to the rules ordained at the marriage sacrifices and ceremonies. The period of procreation and supervision shall be ten years and no longer, whenever there is an abundant issue of offspring; but in case any are without issue to the end of this period, they shall take counsel in common to

[2] *I.e.*, presumably, for as much as 8 hours when necessary.

784 ἀρχουσῶν γυναικῶν διαζεύγνυσθαι κοινῇ βουλευο-
μένους εἰς τὰ πρόσφορα ἑκατέροις. ἐὰν δ' ἀμφι-
σβήτησίς τις γίγνηται περὶ τῶν ἑκατέροις πρεπόν-
των καὶ προσφόρων, δέκα τῶν νομοφυλάκων ἑλο-
C μένους, οἷς ἂν ἐπιτρέψωσιν οἷδ' ἢ [1] τάξωσι, τούτοις
ἐμμένειν. εἰσιοῦσαι δ' εἰς τὰς οἰκίας τῶν νέων αἱ
γυναῖκες, τὰ μὲν νουθετοῦσαι, τὰ δὲ καὶ ἀπει-
λοῦσαι παυόντων αὐτοὺς τῆς ἁμαρτίας καὶ ἀμα-
θίας· ἐὰν δ' ἀδυνατῶσι, πρὸς τοὺς νομοφύλακας
ἰοῦσαι φραζόντων, οἱ δ' εἰργόντων. ἂν δὲ καὶ
ἐκεῖνοί πως ἀδυνατήσωσι, πρὸς τὸ δημόσιον ἀποφηνάντων, ἀναγράψαντές τε καὶ ὀμόσαντες ἦ μὴν
ἀδυνατεῖν τὸν καὶ τὸν βελτίω ποιεῖν· ὁ δὲ
D ἀναγραφεὶς ἄτιμος ἔστω, μὴ ἑλὼν ἐν δικαστηρίῳ
τοὺς ἐγγράψαντας, τῶνδε· μήτε γὰρ εἰς γάμους
ἴτω μήτε εἰς τὰς τῶν παίδων ἐπιτελειώσεις, ἂν δὲ
ἴῃ, πληγαῖς ὁ βουληθεὶς ἀθῷος αὐτὸν κολαζέτω.
τὰ αὐτὰ δὲ καὶ περὶ γυναικὸς ἔστω νόμιμα· τῶν
ἐξόδων γὰρ τῶν γυναικείων καὶ τιμῶν καὶ τῶν εἰς
τοὺς γάμους καὶ γενέθλια [2] τῶν παίδων φοιτήσεων
μὴ μετεχέτω, ἐὰν ἀκοσμοῦσα ὡσαύτως ἀναγραφῇ
καὶ μὴ ἕλῃ τὴν δίκην.

E Ὅταν δὲ δὴ παῖδας γεννήσωνται κατὰ νόμους,
ἐὰν ἀλλοτρίᾳ τις περὶ τὰ τοιαῦτα κοινωνῇ γυναικὶ
ἢ γυνὴ ἀνδρί, ἐὰν μὲν παιδοποιουμένοις ἔτι, τὰ
αὐτὰ ἐπιζήμια αὐτοῖς ἔστω καθάπερ τοῖς ἔτι
γεννωμένοις εἴρηται· μετὰ δὲ ταῦτα ὁ μὲν σωφρο-
νῶν καὶ σωφρονοῦσα εἰς τὰ τοιαῦτα ἔστω πάντα
εὐδόκιμος, ὁ δὲ τοὐναντίον ἐναντίως τιμάσθω,

[1] οἷδ' ἢ Ritter: οἷδε MSS.: οἱ δὲ καὶ Zur., vulg.
[2] γενέθλια Burnet: γενέσια MSS.

498

decide what terms are advantageous for both parties, in conjunction with their kindred and the women-officials, and be divorced. If any dispute arises as to what is fitting and advantageous for each party, they shall choose ten of the Law-wardens, and abide by the regulations they shall permit or impose. The women-inspectors shall enter the houses of the young people, and, partly by threats, partly by admonition, stop them from their sin and folly : if they cannot do so, they shall go and report the case to the Law-wardens, and they shall prevent them. If they also prove unable, they shall inform the State Council, posting up a sworn statement that they are "verily unable to reform So-and-so." The man that is thus posted up,—if he fails to defeat those who have thus posted him in the law-courts,—shall suffer the following disqualifications : he shall not attend any marriage or children's birthday feasts, and if he does so, anyone who wishes may with impunity punish him with blows. The same law shall hold good for the women : the offender shall have no part in women's excursions, honours, or invitations to weddings or birthday feasts, if she has been similarly posted up as disorderly and has lost her suit.

And when they shall have finished producing children according to the laws, if the man have sexual intercourse with a strange woman, or the woman with a man, while the latter are still within the procreative age-limit, they shall be liable to the same penalty as was stated for those still producing children. Thereafter the man and woman that are sober-minded in these matters shall be well-reputed in every way ; but the opposite kind of esteem, or rather disesteem, shall be shown to persons of the

785 μᾶλλον δὲ ἀτιμαζέσθω. καὶ μετριαζόντων μὲν
περὶ τὰ τοιαῦτα τῶν πλειόνων ἀνομοθέτητα σιγῇ
κείσθω, ἀκοσμούντων δὲ νομοθετηθέντα ταύτῃ
πραττέσθω κατὰ τοὺς τότε τεθέντας νόμους.

Βίου μὲν ἀρχὴ τοῦ παντὸς ἑκάστοις ὁ πρῶτος
ἐνιαυτός· ὃν γεγράφθαι χρεὼν ἐν ἱεροῖσι πατρῴοις
ζωῆς ἀρχὴν κόρῳ καὶ κόρῃ· παραγεγράφθαι [1] δ᾽ ἐν
τοίχῳ λελευκωμένῳ ἐν πάσῃ φρατρίᾳ τὸν ἀριθμὸν
τῶν ἀρχόντων τῶν ἐπὶ τοῖς ἔτεσιν ἀριθμουμένων.
τῆς δὲ φρατρίας ἀεὶ τοὺς ζῶντας μὲν γεγράφθαι
B πλησίον, τοὺς δ᾽ ὑπεκχωροῦντας τοῦ βίου ἐξαλεί-
φειν. γάμου δὲ ὅρον εἶναι κόρῃ μὲν ἀπὸ ἑκκαί-
δεκα ἐτῶν εἰς εἴκοσι, τὸν μακρότατον χρόνον
ἀφωρισμένον, κόρῳ δὲ ἀπὸ τριάκοντα μέχρι τῶν
πέντε καὶ τριάκοντα. εἰς δὲ ἀρχὰς γυναικὶ μὲν
τετταράκοντα, ἀνδρὶ δὲ τριάκοντα ἔτη· πρὸς πόλεμον δὲ ἀνδρὶ μὲν εἴκοσι μέχρι τῶν ἑξήκοντα ἐτῶν·
γυναικὶ δέ, ἢν ἂν δοκῇ χρείαν δεῖν χρῆσθαι πρὸς
τὰ πολεμικά, ἐπειδὰν παῖδας γεννήσῃ, τὸ δυνατὸν
καὶ πρέπον ἑκάσταις προστάττειν μέχρι τῶν
πεντήκοντα ἐτῶν.

[1] παραγεγράφθαι Orelli, Schanz : παραγεγράφθω MSS.

opposite character. Sexual conduct shall lie un-mentioned or unprescribed by law when the majority show due propriety therein; but if they are dis-orderly, then what is thus prescribed shall be executed according to the laws then enacted.

For everyone the first year is the beginning of the whole life: it ought to be inscribed as life's beginning for both boy and girl in their ancestral shrines: beside it, on a whited wall in every phratry, there should be written up the number of the archons who give its number to the year; and the names of the living members of the phratry shall be written always close together, and those of the deceased shall be erased. The limit of the marriage-age shall be from sixteen to twenty years—the longest time allowed—for a girl, and for a boy from thirty to thirty-five. The limit for official posts shall be forty for a woman and thirty for a man. For military services the limit shall be from twenty years up to sixty for a man; for women they shall ordain what is possible and fitting in each case, after they have finished bearing children, and up to the age of fifty, in whatever kind of military work it may be thought right to employ their services.

Printed in Great Britain by
Richard Clay (The Chaucer Press), Ltd.,
Bungay, Suffolk

THE LOEB CLASSICAL LIBRARY

Latin Authors

AMMIANUS MARECLLINUS. Translated by J. C. Rolfe. 3 Vols.

APULEIUS: THE GOLDEN ASS (METAMORPHOSES). W. Adlington (1566). Revised by S. Gaselee.

ST. AUGUSTINE: CITY OF GOD. 7 Vols. Vol. I. G. E. McCracken. Vol. II. W. M. Green. Vol. IV. P. Levine. Vol. V. E. M. Sanford and W. M. Green. Vol. VI. W. C. Greene.

ST. AUGUSTINE, CONFESSIONS OF. W. Watts (1631). 2 Vols.

ST. AUGUSTINE, SELECT LETTERS. J. H. Baxter.

AUSONIUS. H. G. Evelyn White. 2 Vols.

BEDE. J. E. King. 2 Vols.

BOETHIUS: TRACTS and DE CONSOLATIONE PHILOSOPHIAE. Rev. H. F. Stewart and E. K. Rand.

CAESAR: ALEXANDRIAN, AFRICAN and SPANISH WARS. A. G. Way.

CAESAR: CIVIL WARS. A. G. Peskett.

CAESAR: GALLIC WAR. H. J. Edwards.

CATO: DE RE RUSTICA; VARRO: DE RE RUSTICA. H. B. Ash and W. D. Hooper.

CATULLUS. F. W. Cornish; TIBULLUS. J. B. Postgate; PERVIGILIUM VENERIS. J. W. Mackail.

CELSUS: DE MEDICINA. W. G. Spencer. 3 Vols.

CICERO: BRUTUS, and ORATOR. G. L. Hendrickson and H. M. Hubbell.

[CICERO]: AD HERENNIUM. H. Caplan.

CICERO: DE ORATORE, etc. 2 Vols. Vol. I. DE ORATORE, Books I. and II. E. W. Sutton and H. Rackham. Vol. II. DE ORATORE, Book III. De Fato; Paradoxa Stoicorum; De Partitione Oratoria. H. Rackham.

CICERO: DE FINIBUS. H. Rackham.

CICERO: DE INVENTIONE, etc. H. M. Hubbell.

CICERO: DE NATURA DEORUM and ACADEMICA. H. Rackham.

CICERO: DE OFFICIIS. Walter Miller.

CICERO: DE REPUBLICA and DE LEGIBUS; SOMNIUM SCIPIONIS. Clinton W. Keyes.

OVID: FASTI. Sir James G. Frazer.

OVID: HEROIDES and AMORES. Grant Showerman.

OVID: METAMORPHOSES. F. J. Miller. 2 Vols.

OVID: TRISTIA and EX PONTO. A. L. Wheeler.

PERSIUS. Cf. JUVENAL.

PETRONIUS. M. Heseltine; SENECA; APOCOLOCYNTOSIS. W. H. D. Rouse.

PHAEDRUS AND BABRIUS (Greek). B. E. Perry.

PLAUTUS. Paul Nixon. 5 Vols.

PLINY: LETTERS. Melmoth's Translation revised by W. M. L. Hutchinson. 2 Vols.

PLINY: NATURAL HISTORY.
10 Vols. Vols. I.–V. and IX. H. Rackham. Vols. VI.–VIII. W. H. S. Jones. Vol. X. D. E. Eichholz.

PROPERTIUS. H. E. Butler.

PRUDENTIUS. H. J. Thomson. 2 Vols.

QUINTILIAN. H. E. Butler. 4 Vols.

REMAINS OF OLD LATIN. E. H. Warmington. 4 Vols. Vol. I. (ENNIUS AND CAECILIUS.) Vol. II. (LIVIUS, NAEVIUS, PACUVIUS, ACCIUS.) Vol. III. (LUCILIUS and LAWS OF XII TABLES.) Vol. IV. (ARCHAIC INSCRIPTIONS.)

SALLUST. J. C. Rolfe.

SCRIPTORES HISTORIAE AUGUSTAE. D. Magie. 3 Vols.

SENECA: APOCOLOCYNTOSIS. Cf. PETRONIUS.

SENECA: EPISTULAE MORALES. R. M. Gummere. 3 Vols.

SENECA: MORAL ESSAYS. J. W. Basore. 3 Vols.

SENECA: TRAGEDIES. F. J. Miller. 2 Vols.

SIDONIUS: POEMS and LETTERS. W. B. ANDERSON. 2 Vols.

SILIUS ITALICUS. J. D. Duff. 2 Vols.

STATIUS. J. H. Mozley. 2 Vols.

SUETONIUS. J. C. Rolfe. 2 Vols.

TACITUS: DIALOGUES. Sir Wm. Peterson. AGRICOLA and GERMANIA. Maurice Hutton.

TACITUS: HISTORIES AND ANNALS. C. H. Moore and J. Jackson. 4 Vols.

TERENCE. John Sargeaunt. 2 Vols.

TERTULLIAN: APOLOGIA and DE SPECTACULIS. T. R. Glover. MINUCIUS FELIX. G. H. Rendall.

VALERIUS FLACCUS. J. H. Mozley.

VARRO: DE LINGUA LATINA. R. G. Kent. 2 Vols.

VELLEIUS PATERCULUS and RES GESTAE DIVI AUGUSTI. F. W. Shipley.

VIRGIL. H. R. Fairclough. 2 Vols.

VITRUVIUS: DE ARCHITECTURA. F. Granger. 2 Vols.

Greek Authors

ACHILLES TATIUS. S. Gaselee.

AELIAN: ON THE NATURE OF ANIMALS. A. F. Scholfield. 3 Vols.

AENEAS TACTICUS, ASCLEPIODOTUS and ONASANDER. The Illinois Greek Club.

AESCHINES. C. D. Adams.

AESCHYLUS. H. Weir Smyth. 2 Vols.

ALCIPHRON, AELIAN, PHILOSTRATUS: LETTERS. A. R. Benner and F. H. Fobes.

ANDOCIDES, ANTIPHON, Cf. MINOR ATTIC ORATORS.

APOLLODORUS. Sir James G. Frazer. 2 Vols.

APOLLONIUS RHODIUS. R. C. Seaton.

THE APOSTOLIC FATHERS. Kirsopp Lake. 2 Vols.

APPIAN: ROMAN HISTORY. Horace White. 4 Vols.

ARATUS. Cf. CALLIMACHUS.

ARISTOPHANES. Benjamin Bickley Rogers. 3 Vols. Verse trans.

ARISTOTLE: ART OF RHETORIC. J. H. Freese.

ARISTOTLE: ATHENIAN CONSTITUTION, EUDEMIAN ETHICS, VICES AND VIRTUES. H. Rackham.

ARISTOTLE: GENERATION OF ANIMALS. A. L. Peck.

ARISTOTLE: HISTORIA ANIMALIUM. A. L. Peck. Vol. I.

ARISTOTLE: METAPHYSICS. H. Tredennick. 2 Vols.

ARISTOTLE: METEOROLOGICA. H. D. P. Lee.

ARISTOTLE: MINOR WORKS. W. S. Hett. On Colours, On Things Heard, On Physiognomies, On Plants, On Marvellous Things Heard, Mechanical Problems, On Indivisible Lines, On Situations and Names of Winds, On Melissus, Xenophanes, and Gorgias.

ARISTOTLE: NICOMACHEAN ETHICS. H. Rackham.

ARISTOTLE: OECONOMICA and MAGNA MORALIA. G. C. Armstrong; (with Metaphysics, Vol. II.).

ARISTOTLE: ON THE HEAVENS. W. K. C. Guthrie.

ARISTOTLE: ON THE SOUL. PARVA NATURALIA. ON BREATH. W. S. Hett.

ARISTOTLE: CATEGORIES, ON INTERPRETATION, PRIOR ANALYTICS. H. P. Cooke and H. Tredennick.

ARISTOTLE: POSTERIOR ANALYTICS, TOPICS. H. Tredennick and E. S. Forster.

ARISTOTLE: ON SOPHISTICAL REFUTATIONS.
On Coming to be and Passing Away, On the Cosmos. E. S. Forster and D. J. Furley.

ARISTOTLE: PARTS OF ANIMALS. A. L. Peck; MOTION AND PROGRESSION OF ANIMALS. E. S. Forster.

ARISTOTLE: PHYSICS. Rev. P. Wicksteed and F. M. Cornford. 2 Vols.

ARISTOTLE: POETICS and LONGINUS. W. Hamilton Fyfe; DEMETRIUS ON STYLE. W. Rhys Roberts.

ARISTOTLE: POLITICS. H. Rackham.

ARISTOTLE: PROBLEMS. W. S. Hett. 2 Vols.

ARISTOTLE: RHETORICA AD ALEXANDRUM (with PROBLEMS. Vol. II.) H. Rackham.

ARRIAN: HISTORY OF ALEXANDER and INDICA. Rev. E. Iliffe Robson. 2 Vols.

ATHENAEUS: DEIPNOSOPHISTAE. C. B. GULICK. 7 Vols.

BABRIUS AND PHAEDRUS (Latin). B. E. Perry.

ST. BASIL: LETTERS. R. J. Deferrari. 4 Vols.

CALLIMACHUS: FRAGMENTS. C. A. Trypanis.

CALLIMACHUS, Hymns and Epigrams, and LYCOPHRON. A. W. Mair; ARATUS. G. R. MAIR.

CLEMENT of ALEXANDRIA. Rev. G. W. Butterworth.

COLLUTHUS. Cf. OPPIAN.

DAPHNIS AND CHLOE. Thornley's Translation revised by J. M. Edmonds; and PARTHENIUS. S. Gaselee.

DEMOSTHENES I.: OLYNTHIACS, PHILIPPICS and MINOR ORATIONS. I.–XVII. AND XX. J. H. Vince.

DEMOSTHENES II.: DE CORONA and DE FALSA LEGATIONE. C. A. Vince and J. H. Vince.

DEMOSTHENES III.: MEIDIAS, ANDROTION, ARISTOCRATES, TIMOCRATES and ARISTOGEITON, I. AND II. J. H. Vince.

DEMOSTHENES IV.–VI.: PRIVATE ORATIONS and IN NEAERAM. A. T. Murray.

DEMOSTHENES VII.: FUNERAL SPEECH, EROTIC ESSAY, EXORDIA and LETTERS. N. W. and N. J. DeWitt.

DIO CASSIUS: ROMAN HISTORY. E. Cary. 9 Vols.

DIO CHRYSOSTOM. J. W. Cohoon and H. Lamar Crosby. 5 Vols.

DIODORUS SICULUS. 12 Vols. Vols. I.–VI. C. H. Oldfather. Vol. VII. C. L. Sherman. Vol. VIII. C. B. Welles. Vols. IX. and X. R. M. Geer. Vols. XI.–XII. F. Walton, General Index, R. M. Geer.

DIOGENES LAERTIUS. R. D. Hicks. 2 Vols.

DIONYSIUS OF HALICARNASSUS: ROMAN ANTIQUITIES. Spelman's translation revised by E. Cary. 7 Vols.

EPICTETUS. W. A. Oldfather. 2 Vols.

EURIPIDES. A. S. Way. 4 Vols. Verse trans.

EUSEBIUS: ECCLESIASTICAL HISTORY. Kirsopp Lake and J. E. L. Oulton. 2 Vols.

GALEN: ON THE NATURAL FACULTIES. A. J. Brock.

THE GREEK ANTHOLOGY. W. R. Paton. 5 Vols.

GREEK ELEGY AND IAMBUS with the ANACREONTEA. J. M. Edmonds. 2 Vols.

THE GREEK BUCOLIC POETS (THEOCRITUS, BION, MOSCHUS).
J. M. Edmonds.

GREEK MATHEMATICAL WORKS. Ivor Thomas. 2 Vols.

HERODES. Cf. THEOPHRASTUS: CHARACTERS.

HERODOTUS. A. D. Godley. 4 Vols.

HESIOD AND THE HOMERIC HYMNS. H. G. Evelyn White.

HIPPOCRATES and the FRAGMENTS OF HERACLEITUS. W. H. S.
Jones and E. T. Withington. 4 Vols.

HOMER: ILIAD. A. T. Murray. 2 Vols.

HOMER: ODYSSEY. A. T. Murray. 2 Vols.

ISAEUS. E. W. Forster.

ISOCRATES. George Norlin and LaRue Van Hook. 3 Vols.

ST. JOHN DAMASCENE: BARLAAM AND IOASAPH. Rev. G. R.
Woodward, Harold Mattingly and D. M. Lang.

JOSEPHUS. 9 Vols. Vols. I.–IV.; H. Thackeray. Vol. V.;
H. Thackeray and R. Marcus. Vols. VI.–VII.; R. Marcus.
Vol. VIII.; R. Marcus and Allen Wikgren. Vol. IX. L. H.
Feldman.

JULIAN. Wilmer Cave Wright. 3 Vols.

LUCIAN. 8 Vols. Vols. I.–V. A. M. Harmon. Vol. VI. K.
Kilburn. Vols. VII.–VIII. M. D. Macleod.

LYCOPHRON. Cf. CALLIMACHUS.

LYRA GRAECA. J. M. Edmonds. 3 Vols.

LYSIAS. W. R. M. Lamb.

MANETHO. W. G. Waddell: PTOLEMY: TETRABIBLOS. F. E.
Robbins.

MARCUS AURELIUS. C. R. Haines.

MENANDER. F. G. Allinson.

MINOR ATTIC ORATORS (ANTIPHON, ANDOCIDES, LYCURGUS,
DEMADES, DINARCHUS, HYPERIDES). K. J. Maidment and
J. O. Burtt. 2 Vols.

NONNOS: DIONYSIACA. W. H. D. Rouse. 3 Vols.

OPPIAN, COLLUTHUS, TRYPHIODORUS. A. W. Mair.

PAPYRI. NON-LITERARY SELECTIONS. A. S. Hunt and C. C.
Edgar. 2 Vols. LITERARY SELECTIONS (Poetry). D. L. Page.

PARTHENIUS. Cf. DAPHNIS and CHLOE.

PAUSANIAS: DESCRIPTION OF GREECE. W. H. S. Jones. 4
Vols. and Companion Vol. arranged by R. E. Wycherley.

PHILO. 10 Vols. Vols. I.–V.; F. H. Colson and Rev. G. H.
Whitaker. Vols. VI.–IX.; F. H. Colson. Vol. X. F. H.
Colson and the Rev. J. W. Earp.

PHILO: two supplementary Vols. (*Translation only.*) Ralph
Marcus.

PHILOSTRATUS: THE LIFE OF APOLLONIUS OF TYANA. F. C.
Conybeare. 2 Vols.

6

PHILOSTRATUS: IMAGINES; CALLISTRATUS: DESCRIPTIONS. A. Fairbanks.

PHILOSTRATUS and EUNAPIUS: LIVES OF THE SOPHISTS. Wilmer Cave Wright.

PINDAR. Sir J. E. Sandys.

PLATO: CHARMIDES, ALCIBIADES, HIPPARCHUS, THE LOVERS, THEAGES, MINOS and EPINOMIS. W. R. M. Lamb.

PLATO: CRATYLUS, PARMENIDES, GREATER HIPPIAS, LESSER HIPPIAS. H. N. Fowler.

PLATO: EUTHYPHRO, APOLOGY, CRITO, PHAEDO, PHAEDRUS. H. N. Fowler.

PLATO: LACHES, PROTAGORAS, MENO, EUTHYDEMUS. W. R. M. Lamb.

PLATO: LAWS. Rev. R. G. Bury. 2 Vols.

PLATO: LYSIS, SYMPOSIUM, GORGIAS. W. R. M. Lamb.

PLATO: REPUBLIC. Paul Shorey. 2 Vols.

PLATO: STATESMAN, PHILEBUS. H. N. Fowler; ION. W. R. M. Lamb.

PLATO: THEAETETUS and SOPHIST. H. N. Fowler.

PLATO: TIMAEUS, CRITIAS, CLITOPHO, MENEXENUS, EPISTULAE. Rev. R. G. Bury.

PLOTINUS: A. H. Armstrong. Vols. I.–III.

PLUTARCH: MORALIA. 15 Vols. Vols. I.–V. F. C. Babbitt. Vol. VI. W. C. Helmbold. Vols. VII. and XIV. P. H. De Lacy and B. Einarson. Vol. IX. E. L. Minar, Jr., F. H. Sandbach, W. C. Helmbold. Vol. X. H. N. Fowler. Vol. XI. L. Pearson and F. H. Sandbach. Vol. XII. H. Cherniss and W. C. Helmbold.

PLUTARCH: THE PARALLEL LIVES. B. Perrin. 11 Vols.

POLYBIUS. W. R. Paton. 6 Vols.

PROCOPIUS: HISTORY OF THE WARS. H. B. Dewing. 7 Vols.

PTOLEMY: TETRABIBLOS. Cf. MANETHO.

QUINTUS SMYRNAEUS. A. S. Way. Verse trans.

SEXTUS EMPIRICUS. Rev. R. G. Bury. 4 Vols.

SOPHOCLES. F. Storr. 2 Vols. Verse trans.

STRABO: GEOGRAPHY. Horace L. Jones. 8 Vols.

THEOPHRASTUS: CHARACTERS. J. M. Edmonds. HERODES, etc. A. D. Knox.

THEOPHRASTUS: ENQUIRY INTO PLANTS. Sir Arthur Hort, Bart. 2 Vols.

THUCYDIDES. C. F. Smith. 4 Vols.

TRYPHIODORUS. Cf. OPPIAN.

XENOPHON: CYROPAEDIA. Walter Miller. 2 Vols.

XENOPHON: HELLENICA, ANABASIS, APOLOGY, and SYMPOSIUM. C. L. Brownson and O. J. Todd. 3 Vols.

XENOPHON: MEMORABILIA and OECONOMICUS. E. C. Marchant.

XENOPHON: SCRIPTA MINORA. E. C. Marchant and G. W. Bowersock.

DESCRIPTIVE PROSPECTUS ON APPLICATION

London   WILLIAM HEINEMANN LTD
Cambridge, Mass.   HARVARD UNIVERSITY PRESS